WE WHO WRESTLE
WITH GOD

WE WHO WRESTLE WITH GOD

—— ⅄ ——

Perceptions of
the Divine

DR. JORDAN B. PETERSON

PORTFOLIO | PENGUIN

Portfolio / Penguin
An imprint of Penguin Random House LLC
penguinrandomhouse.com

Most Portfolio books are available at a discount when purchased in quantity for sales promotions or corporate use. Special editions, which include personalized covers, excerpts, and corporate imprints, can be created when purchased in large quantities. For more information, please call (212) 572-2232 or email specialmarkets@penguinrandomhouse.com. Your local bookstore can also assist with discounted bulk purchases using the Penguin Random House corporate Business-to-Business program. For assistance in locating a participating retailer, email B2B@penguinrandomhouse.com.

ISBN 9780593542538 (hardcover)
ISBN 9780593542545 (ebook)
ISBN 9780593854013 (international edition)

Printed in the United States of America
1st Printing

Book design by Chris Welch

To my recently deceased mother,
Beverley Ann Peterson,
who, like all of us, wrestled with God
(she more happily than not).

CONTENTS

Frontispiece: Carrion Comfort ✦ *xi*

Foreshadowing: The Still, Small Voice ✦ *xv*

1.

IN THE BEGINNING *1*

1.1. God as creative spirit ✦ *1*

1.2. The spirit of man in the highest place ✦ *7*

1.3. The real and its representation ✦ *11*

1.4. Eve from Adam ✦ *22*

1.5. In God's image ✦ *27*

2.

ADAM, EVE, PRIDE,
SELF-CONSCIOUSNESS, AND THE FALL   *39*

2.1. The image of God in the eternal garden ♦ *39*

2.2. Pride versus the sacred moral order ♦ *43*

2.3. The incompleteness of Adam and the arrival of Eve ♦ *51*

2.4. The eternal sins of Eve and Adam ♦ *54*

2.5. The eternal serpent ♦ *59*

2.6. Naked suffering as the fruit of sin ♦ *64*

2.7. Loss of Paradise and the flaming sword ♦ *75*

3.

CAIN, ABEL, AND SACRIFICE   *89*

3.1. The identity of sacrifice and work ♦ *89*

3.2. The hostile brothers of good and evil ♦ *98*

3.3. The sacred patterning of the political ♦ *104*

3.4. The good shepherd as archetypal leader ♦ *107*

3.5. The sacrifice pleasing to God ♦ *113*

3.6. Creatively possessed by the spirit of resentment ♦ *117*

3.7. Humility and faith versus pride, despair, and vengeful anger ♦ *130*

3.8. Fratricide, then worse ♦ *141*

4.

NOAH: GOD AS THE CALL TO PREPARE   *157*

4.1. Giants in the land ♦ *157*

4.2. Sin and the return of chaos ♦ *159*

4.3. Salvation by the wise and the reestablishment of the world ◆ *166*

4.4. The faithless son doomed to enslavement ◆ *183*

5.

THE TOWER OF BABEL: GOD VERSUS TYRANNY AND PRIDE *191*

5.1. Lucifer and the engineers ◆ *191*

5.2. Pride and the fall, reprise: Descent into hell itself ◆ *210*

5.3. Inability to understand one another ◆ *217*

5.4. God—or else ◆ *227*

6.

ABRAHAM: GOD AS SPIRITED CALL TO ADVENTURE *241*

6.1. Go forth ◆ *241*

6.2. The devil at the crossroads ◆ *262*

6.3. Life as sacrificial secession ◆ *267*

6.4. Sex and parasitism ◆ *271*

6.5. Sacrifice and transformation of identity: Abram, Sarai, and Jacob ◆ *280*

6.6. With the angels into the abyss ◆ *293*

6.7. The pinnacle of sacrifice ◆ *308*

7.

MOSES I: GOD AS DREADFUL
SPIRIT OF FREEDOM *317*

7.1. The Jews as unwelcome sojourners and slaves ♦ *317*

7.2. The fiery tree as revelation of being and becoming ♦ *322*

7.3. Return to the tyrannical kingdom ♦ *336*

7.4. Back to the land of doubling down ♦ *344*

7.5. The inevitable interregnum of chaos and the guiding spirit ♦ *357*

7.6. The subsidiary state as alternative to tyranny and slavery ♦ *374*

7.7. The Commandments as explicit revelation of custom ♦ *384*

8.

MOSES II: HEDONISM AND
INFANTILE TEMPTATION *403*

8.1. Materialism and orgiastic celebration ♦ *403*

8.2. Desperate reestablishment of the covenant ♦ *409*

9.

JONAH AND THE ETERNAL ABYSS *465*

9.1. Jonah repents of his virtue ♦ *488*

CONCLUSION *495*

Notes ♦ *507*

CARRION COMFORT

Not, I will not, carrion comfort, Despair, not feast on thee;
Not untwist—slack they may be—these last strands of man
In me ór, most weary, cry *I can no more*. I can;
Can something, hope, wish day come, not choose not to be.
But ah, but O thou terrible, why wouldst thou rude on me
Thy wring-world right foot rock? lay a lionlimb against me? scan
With darksome devouring eyes my bruisèd bones? and fan,
O in turns of tempest, me heaped there; me frantic to avoid thee and flee?

Why? That my chaff might fly; my grain lie, sheer and clear.
Nay in all that toil, that coil, since (seems) I kissed the rod,
Hand rather, my heart lo! lapped strength, stole joy, would laugh, chéer.
Cheer whom though? The hero whose heaven-handling flung me, fóot tród
Me? or me that fought him? O which one? is it each one? That night, that year
Of now done darkness I wretch lay wrestling with (my God!) my God.[1]

Earlier drafts of the final line:

Of darkness done, that I wretch wrestled, I wrung with God.
Now done I know that I wretch wrestled, I wrung with, God.
Done now, I know that I wretch wrestled, I wrung with God.
Of darkness, now done with, I wretch in wrestle wrung.

—*Gerald Manley Hopkins (1885)*

The history of supreme beings whose structure is celestial is of the utmost importance for an understanding of the religious history of humanity as a whole. We cannot even consider writing that history here, in a few pages. But we must at least refer to a fact that to us seems primary. Celestially structured supreme beings tend to disappear from the practice of religion, from cult; they depart from among men, withdraw to the sky, and become remote, inactive gods (*dei otiosi*). In short, it may be said of these gods that, after creating the cosmos, life, and man, they feel a sort of fatigue, as if the immense enterprise of the Creation had exhausted their resources. So they withdraw to the sky . . . .[2]

—*Mircea Eliade*, The Sacred and the Profane (1959)

FORESHADOWING:
THE STILL, SMALL VOICE

We begin our journey, our wrestling with God, with a singular story. It is one that presents a remarkably weighty idea, in the dramatic form typical of the biblical narratives—an idea that can help us understand why we should explore these increasingly forsaken ancient stories. It is the story of the prophet Elijah, also known as Elias, and it offers one of the most fundamental characterizations or definitions of God. The prophet in question lived in the time of King Ahab and his wife Jezebel, in the ninth century BC. Though his story is a brief one, Elijah is notable among the prophets for two reasons: his strange departure from earth, and his much later appearance alongside Moses and Jesus of Nazareth at the pinnacle of Mount Tabor during the Transfiguration, when Jesus revealed his divine identity to his disciples (Matthew 17:1-9; Mark 9:2-8, and Luke 9:28-37). That term, *transfiguration*, was employed by the Latin translators of the original Greek text, who referred to that event with the word *metamorphoō*, with its connotations of the qualitative transformation of caterpillar into butterfly. Human beings grow and develop as they mature—assuming they mature—in a manner nearly as radical as that of the winged insect. As the apostle Paul notes in 1

Corinthians 11–13: "When I was a child, I spake as a child, I understood as a child, I thought as a child: but when I became a man, I put away childish things." It is thus far from irrelevant that the Greek word *psyche* (ψυχή)—the root from which the term *psychology* is derived; the signifier for the human spirit or soul—literally means butterfly.

Profound as that linkage is between soul and butterfly, it is not the only reason for the comparison. Butterflies are also capable of astonishing feats of navigation. This is something at least near-miraculous, given their fragility and hypothetically limited intelligence. In this navigational capacity—and, perhaps, in their brevity of life and restrictions—they are similar to human beings, who have traveled from their African point of origin to every corner of the planet, no matter how distant and inhospitable. The gossamer-winged insects are also beautiful, exceptionally symmetrical, and remarkable in their capability to perceive in relationship to that beauty and symmetry, and select mates accordingly. They can detect deviations from both characteristics with stunning accuracy. This reveals a high capacity for judgment, in relationship to the ideal: another ability that the perfectly crafted insect shares with the human psyche. Why is all this relevant to our account of the prophet Elijah and to the understanding of life? Because his manner of death, and his later appearance in the company of the transfigured Christ, are both representative, or symbolic, of the psyche's capacity for qualitative and revolutionary transmutation.

We are informed in Kings 2:2 that Elijah is taken up bodily into heaven while still alive, a privilege that the Old Testament awards only to him and the prophet Enoch (Genesis 5:24). It is of course part and parcel of Christian tradition that Jesus ascends into heaven, in a similar manner, after his resurrection (Luke 24:50–53; Acts 1:9–11). Much of Christendom also accepts the doctrine of the Assumption of Mary, the taking up of her body and soul into heaven after her death, but that is the extent of such phenomena. Ascension or assumption to the divine realm marks the presence of someone very notable indeed. At the time of Elijah's assumption, he is in the company of Elisha, his disciple and successor. They are traveling from Gilgal to Bethel, both places of deep biblical import. Gilgal is, for example, the place where the Israelites set up a memorial to God to commemorate safe passage over the River Jordan to the promised land (Joshua 4:19–24). Bethel, for its part, means "house of God." It first appears in Genesis 28:10–22 as the place where Jacob dreams of an upward-reaching ladder to heaven with angels—intermediaries between the divine and man—descending and ascending upon it. In this dream, God reaffirms to Jacob the covenant He had made with Abraham and Isaac, promising him numerous offspring, land, and divine protection. Any story that features its heroes moving from a place of momentous occurrence to another of equivalent or even greater consequence is an account of the idea of "significant journey" itself—a description of a path of life being realized in the optimally adventurous and meaningful manner. It is in keeping with this that Elijah's last and greatest adventure occurs at or near Bethel, the site of the vision of Jacob's Ladder. Elisha is with him:

> And it came to pass, when they were gone over, that Elijah said unto Elisha, Ask what I shall do for thee, before I be taken away from thee. And Elisha said, I pray thee, let a double portion of thy spirit be upon me.
>
> And he said, Thou hast asked a hard thing: nevertheless, if thou see me when I am taken from thee, it shall be so unto thee; but if not, it shall not be so.
>
> And it came to pass, as they still went on, and talked, that, behold, there appeared a chariot of fire, and horses of fire, and parted them both asunder; and Elijah went up by a whirlwind into heaven.
>
> And Elisha saw it, and he cried, My father, my father, the chariot of Israel, and the horsemen thereof. And he saw him no more: and he took hold of his own clothes, and rent them in two pieces.
>
> *2 Kings 2:9–12*

Here, Elijah is delivered into the Kingdom of God, in the same manner that the great seeker after beauty and navigator of the insect world takes wing into the heavens after its metamorphosis. This rise into the realm of the divine on the part of the prophet sets the stage for his later reappearance with Jesus on the pinnacle of Mount Tabor:

> And after six days Jesus taketh Peter, James, and John his brother, and bringeth them up into a high mountain apart,
>
> And was transfigured before them: and his face did shine as the sun, and his raiment was white as the light.
>
> And, behold, there appeared unto them Moses and Elias talking with him.
>
> Then answered Peter, and said unto Jesus, Lord, it is good for us to be here: if thou wilt, let us make here three tabernacles; one for thee, and one for Moses, and one for Elias.
>
> While he yet spake, behold, a bright cloud overshadowed them: and behold a voice out of the cloud, which said, This is my beloved Son, in whom I am well pleased; hear ye him.
>
> And when the disciples heard it, they fell on their face, and were sore afraid.
>
> *Matthew 17:1–6*

A similarly awe-inducing transformation occurs in the accounts of Moses: "And it came to pass, when Moses came down from Mount Sinai with the two tables of testimony in Moses' hand, when he came down from the mount, that Moses wist not that the skin of his face shone while he talked with him. And when Aaron and all the children of Israel saw Moses, behold, the skin of his face shone; and they were afraid to come nigh him" (Exodus 34:29–30). This shining is the co-occurrence of the ultimate up, so to speak, with what is normally merely human—an indication of the descent of the divine to the profane, or the ascent of the profane or wordly upward.

It therefore makes perfect sense, symbolically speaking, that such revolutions in character or transmutations of psyche occur on mountaintops. The summit of the holy mountain is the mythical place where heaven and earth touch, where the merely material meets the transcendent and divine. Further, life is well portrayed as a series of uphill journeys. For pessimists, that is the dread fate of Sisyphus, doomed to roll a rock up a mountain to the peak only to have it roll back down, so the process must be endlessly repeated. A more optimistic interpreter of life might see instead the opportunities for personal transformation. When we have climbed a new mountain and reached the pinnacle—that is, attained our aim—we have brought something successfully to an end, fulfilled a proximal vision, and become more than we were. When we have reached the top, at least of our present climb, we can also see everything laid out in front of us, including the next challenge—the next possibility for play, maturation, and growth; the next calling for transformational sacrifice. The continually ascending progress represented by a series of uphill climbs, each with its peak experience, is a variant of the path of ascension represented by Jacob's Ladder, the spiraling rise into the heavens toward the Kingdom of God, with God Himself beckoning at the high point—on the apex of the highest conceivable mount.

There is much more to the story of Elijah than his assumption into God's kingdom and his final transformation. The great prophet lived in the time of the divided kingdom of Israel and Judah. At that point, the people of Israel labored under the rule of King Ahab, who turned them to the worship of gods other than Yahweh, the traditional deity of Abraham, Isaac, and the chosen people. This perversion of aim occurred as a direct consequence of Ahab's marriage to Jezebel, a wealthy, privileged princess of Phoenicia—one who brought her false gods in tow in the aftermath of her wedding. Baal, her god of choice, was a Phoenician/Canaanite deity of nature, responsible for fertility, rain, thunder, lightning, and dew. Ahab's new wife, who was nothing if not direct, killed most of the prophets of Yahweh during her attempts to establish Baal's primacy. It is said that Jezebel's husband, fully under her sway, "did more to provoke the Lord God of Israel to anger than all the kings of Israel that were before him" (1 Kings 16:33). Elijah warns the king against his weakness and idolatry, telling him that the consequences of his misguided rule will be years of drought so severe that even the dew will cease to appear.

As Baal was the god deemed directly responsible for the life-giving rain, Elijah's predicted drought clearly undermined the authority of the god and his priests, as well as the people's trust in Ahab, their king, and Jezebel. The literary motif of the "parched kingdom" employed in this narrative fragment is a stably meaningful symbolic trope. This was evidenced, for example, in the Disney animated masterpiece *The Lion King*. When Scar, the evil brother of the rightful king, deposes Mufasa, true King of Pride Rock, he banishes his son, Simba, to the periphery of the kingdom. Consequently, the rain ceases to fall and the animals the lions hunt and depend on vanish. When Simba retakes the throne, the rain returns. The fairy tale *The Water of Life* by the Brothers Grimm elaborates on this theme, presenting it as the adventure of a younger brother charged with bringing the water that revitalizes to his dying father. Something similar is indicated in the Book of Exodus, with its contrast between the stonelike rigidity of the intransigent pharaoh and the dynamic mastery of water characteristic of Moses. When the wrong principle is established as supreme—when a false king is set upon the throne or an impious ethos prevails—the people quickly find themselves deprived of the very water of life. More deeply, however, a kingdom oriented around the wrong pole—that worships the wrong gods, so to speak—suffers psychologically or spiritually.

After declaring the drought and retiring to the desert, where he is initially fed by ravens and drinks from a brook, the prophet's own stores dry up. God directs Elijah forthwith to a widow in the town of Zarephath. He finds her by a well and asks for water and bread. She responds, "As the Lord thy God liveth, I have not a cake, but an handful of meal in a barrel, and a little oil in a cruise: and behold, I am gathering two sticks, that I may go in and dress it for me and my son, that we may eat it, and die" (1 Kings 17:12). Elijah reassures her, saying that God will not allow privation into her house: "For thus saith the Lord God of Israel, The barrel of meal shall not waste, neither shall the cruse of oil fail, until the day that the Lord sendeth rain upon the earth" (1 Kings 17:14). It may seem strange that an emissary of God finds it necessary to turn to an impoverished widow for sustenance. But the biblical accounts are subtle and sophisticated. Here, the story of Elijah stresses first, the importance even of the lowly (the widow, in this instance); second, the necessity of moral orientation even under conditions of privation (the widow's willingness to provide hospitality, an obligation that will resurface in our investigations); and third, the absolute dependence of abundance upon proper moral orientation on the part of all, regardless of their status.

The undue and manipulative influence the wife of the weak king brings to bear on her feckless and faithless husband threatens the integrity of the state itself. In part, she represents the oft-dangerous attraction of the strange ideas and customs that can invade and permeate a society under the guise of the creative, sophisticated, and new. Before the objection arises—"The authors of the biblical stories were inexcusably prejudiced, even xenophobic"—it is right to consider Old Testament figures such as Moses's father-in-law, Jethro, who figures so importantly in the Book of Exodus (see, particularly, 18:17–23); Rahab, a courageous and faithful prostitute from Jericho (Joshua 2); and Naaman (2 Kings 5), whose humility and faith allowed for his healing at the hands of Elisha. These are all individuals who, despite, or even because of, their foreignness, perceive with an untrammeled eye and conduct them-selves morally, and they therefore play a corrective role when the Israelites corrupt themselves. Sometimes the new parasitizes and poisons, and some-times it restores and renews. Wisdom is, not least, the ability to discriminate help from hindrance in such cases.

The poor but good woman who has lost her husband is subtly presented as desirable opposite to the arrogant and dangerous queen Jezebel. Why? For most of human history, widowhood was a dire state of affairs, particularly when the women so afflicted had dependent children. In the biblical corpus, the figure of the widow is therefore often used to represent vulnerability, powerlessness, and existence on the social and economic fringe. Her misera-ble state of affairs might well be regarded as an ever-present form of cosmic injustice. It is for this reason as well as for the moral edification of his people, that the spirit of God calls on the Israelites to redress this inequity—to forgo the temptations of narrow self-centeredness and greed and to leave something for the dispossessed:

> And when ye reap the harvest of your land, thou shalt not wholly reap the corners of thy field, neither shalt thou gather the gleanings of thy harvest.

And thou shalt not glean thy vineyard, neither shalt thou gather every grape of thy vineyard; thou shalt leave them for the poor and stranger: I am the Lord your God.

Leviticus 19:9–10

This principle is elaborated in the Book of Deuteronomy, along with an additional point: at some stage in life, each and every individual will depend on others; therefore, a properly structured psyche and society are arranged so that this inevitable dependence meets with necessary care and concern. There is no sense in establishing a society that fails to care for the people who compose it at every stage of their development, from vulnerable to able, productive and generous.

When thou gatherest the grapes of thy vineyard, thou shalt not glean it afterward: it shall be for the stranger, for the fatherless, and for the widow.

And thou shalt remember that thou wast a bondman in the land of Egypt: therefore I command thee to do this thing.

Deuteronomy 24:21–22

The widow who is generous despite her poverty embodies the pattern of reciprocal sacrificial conduct and mutual aid that characterizes a mature, reliable individual and a peaceful and productive state alike. She stands in the starkest contrast to the privileged queen whose self-absorption threatens the psyche and community.

As the story of Elijah continues, the idea that the psychological and social hierarchy of values must organize itself under the appropriate ruler—or, more abstractly, the proper principle—is driven further home. The prophet leaves Zarephath and sets up what might be regarded in colloquial terms as the showdown at Mount Carmel. He convinces the head of Ahab's palace, Obadiah, to gather all the prophets of Baal, as well as the people of Israel, at the mountain's foot. Two sacrificial altars are prepared: one for Baal, under the control of his prophets; the other for Yahweh, under the dominion of

Elijah. Each god is called on to ignite the altar fire that will consume the sacrifice. Baal's prophets pray for hours to no avail. Elijah soaks his altar with water three times (just to drive his point home), and then requests Yahweh's intercession. A fire immediately descends from heaven and immolates the sacrifice and even the altar itself. Yahweh's supremacy is thus established. The prophets of Baal are executed, and an "abundance of rain" (1 Kings 18:41) immediately returns. There can be no wealth in the absence of a true moral order. Under the guidance of the appropriate animating spirit, privation can be made a distant memory.

None too happy, Jezebel directs her wrath at Elijah. The hapless prophet therefore flees deep into the barren wilderness. He takes shelter in a cave, where God speaks to him (1 Kings 19). The receipt of revelation in a solitary place is a common storytelling trope. Internal voices and imaginative experience become more likely under conditions of isolation, when external verbal communication is minimized, and in darkness and silence, where external sensory stimuli are dramatically reduced. This increases the likelihood of revelatory experience—for better or worse. At a deeper level, this may be because the neurological systems of the right hemisphere, which (at least in right-handed people) are more associated with unconscious and implicit thought and action, can take control of verbal and imagistic experience when they are not drowned out or otherwise suppressed by the more normal conditions of social interaction and sensory input.[1]

Elijah expresses great frustration and hopelessness, believing that his attempts to remain faithful have resulted in nothing but disaster: "And he said, I have been very jealous for the Lord God of hosts: for the children of Israel have forsaken thy covenant, thrown down thine altars, and slain thy prophets with the sword; and I, even I only, am left; and they seek my life, to take it away" (1 Kings 19:10). God says to him, "Go forth, and stand upon the mount before the Lord. And, behold, the Lord passed by, and a great and strong wind rent the mountains, and brake in pieces the rocks before the Lord; but the Lord was not in the wind: and after the wind an earthquake; but the Lord was not in the earthquake: And after the earthquake a fire; but the Lord was not in the fire: and after the fire a still small voice" (1 Kings 19:11–12). There are many famous phrases in the Bible, and "a still small voice" is certainly one of them. It is at this moment that Elijah—and through him, mankind—comes to understand that God is not in the wind, no matter its ferocity, nor in the earthquake, regardless of its magnitude, but is something within; the voice of conscience itself; the internal guide to what is right and wrong; that autonomous spirit that resides in each soul and shames us before ourselves, draws attention to our shortcomings and sins, and generates the impulse to repent, apologize, and atone.

This is a discovery of unparalleled magnitude: the possibility of establishing a relationship with God by attending to conscience. God grants man and woman free will, even though He wants the allegiance of His created creatures and also wishes to guide them. How can He best manage to reconcile these competing desires? Not by command, force, or fear but by the provision of a voice, an image, or even a feeling that can nudge and suggest or shame and humiliate quietly and softly (even though it is capable of magnifying its intensity when necessary). This identifying of conscience with God is made increasingly explicit within at least certain streams of Christian thinking. The nineteenth-century British theologian Cardinal Newman, for example, insisted on exactly that in much of his writing:

> The Divine Law, then, is the rule of ethical truth, the standard of right and wrong, a sovereign, irreversible, absolute authority in the presence of men and Angels. "The eternal law," says St. Augustine, "is the Divine Reason or Will of God, commanding the observance, forbidding the disturbance, of the natural order of things." "The natural law," says St. Thomas, "is an impression of the Divine Light in us, a participation of the eternal law in the rational creature." This law, as apprehended in the minds of individual men, is called "conscience"; and though it may suffer refraction in passing into the intellectual medium of each, it is not therefore so affected as to lose its character of being the Divine Law, but still has, as such, the prerogative of commanding obedience.[2]

This can well be considered a more powerful and justified argument than the now much more frequently used "argument from design"—the insistence that the complexity of nature necessarily indicates an active creator. In 1 and 2 Kings lays the revelatory groundwork for a much more psychological and relational definition of the Supreme Deity, detaching God from the pagan theater of the natural world (awe-inspiring as nature might indeed be) and placing Him, wonderfully and terribly, inside us all. It is Elijah's realization that sets the stage for the account of Jonah, as well—for the mysterious tale of the prophet who first rejects and then obeys the call of the still small voice, and whose exploits constitute the story that closes this volume. The fundamental and revolutionary importance of Elijah's contribution is signified by the miracle of his bodily assumption into heaven. This event, prefiguring Jonah's deliverance from the belly of the whale, as well as Christ's resurrection, indicates Elijah's unparalleled success as a prophet. The biblical texts and their characterization of God simply cannot be understood in the absence of appreciation for Elijah's unparalleled significance as a prophet and for the vital importance of his transformative and revolutionary realization. After encountering the story of Elijah, we perceive the nature of being—ours and that of the divine—differently, more clearly, and more directly and personally. Our eyes are opened and we can hear in a new way.

Why the story as the foundation even for the act of perception itself? Alternatively, for the transformation of the act of perception itself? Because the world has to be filtered through the mechanism of story to become comprehensible or even apprehensible; because the world is simply too complicated to attend to and to navigate within the absence of aim and character (which are defining features of story itself). An infinite plethora of facts present themselves, continually, for our consideration: one fact per phenomenon, perhaps, and more—a fact not only for every phenomenon but for all their possible combinations. That is simply too many facts. The same problem obtains with regard to outcomes: every action, every possible cause, produces an exponential branching of effects—far too many to contemplate, consider, and take into account. This is an intractable problem; something that philosopher Daniel C. Dennett famously characterized as "a new, deep episte-mological problem."[3] There are a near-infinite number of ways to categorize—hence, to perceive—a finite number of objects. We do not and cannot attend with equal devotion to everything occurring always and everywhere around us. Instead, with every glance, we prioritize the facts. In doing so, we attend to very little and ignore much. We do so in keeping with our aim. We do so to gain what we need and want—but what is that? It might be the foolishness of our momentary whim, when we are or have remained infantile, or childish, and oriented toward the immediate gratification of our desires. It might be our desire to obtain the power that makes such gratification possible despite the presence or even objections of the others we are forced to contend with as we navigate forward. It might instead be mature establishment of the ties that bind and give true meaning to our lives—the ties of marriage, family, friendship, trade, and state. Perhaps, as well, it is the harmonious and pro-ductive integration of present and future in the autonomous individual that makes up true maturity and responsible conduct, both cooperative and com-petitive.

We weigh the facts we encounter in accordance with our values. We ele-vate some pathways forward, things in the world, and people to a higher place than others, consigning everything deemed lesser to the netherworld of impediment, obstacle, enemy, or foe, or to the invisible domain of irrele-vance. Thus we order, simplify, and reduce the world, prior even to encoun-tering it. This prioritizing is not merely a passive process. It is, instead, an active giving up, offering, or sacrifice. We are not the submissive receivers of simply self-evident truths. Every perception is an effort as much as it is a sensation. Every perception requires the movement of eyes, the inquiry of fingers, or the direction of hearing. Everything we experience is irreducibly dependent upon motivation and action instead of reflexively sensory—with sensation therefore never occurring simply prior to action. Whatever occu-pies our attention—whatever we are conscious of, however briefly—is thus something elevated for the moment to the highest place, celebrated and wor-shipped, whether we know it or not. We must specify what is most valuable, currently, and not anything and everything else, even to see. Those elements of momentary, even pinpoint, attention are in turn themselves organized more or less coherently (depending on the degree of our integrity) into a pyramidal structure of worth. That structure, moreover, is either one with something at the top—our ultimate aim—or is the house divided against itself that cannot stand (Mark 3:25). We see the world through a hierarchy of value. This is the map we use to guide our navigation through the unknown territory in which we would otherwise be lost. *We perceive, therefore, in accordance with our aim.* That is a remarkable and insufficiently heralded realization, implying as it does nothing less than that both our misery and our joy depend on our values.

We elevate what we most highly regard to the utmost place of supremacy or sovereignty. We aim at the upward target we deem central, however momentarily. We bring our consciousness itself to bear on what we define as worthy of the expenditure of our attention and the efforts of our action. We begin our continual journey forward by positing a good—a good that is at least better than our point of departure. This is an act of faith as well as one of sacrifice: *faith*, because the good could be elsewhere; *sacrifice*, because in the pursuit of any particular good we determine to forgo all others. All of our perceptions are allies—"spiritual partners"—of our first and determining decision. Our aim delineates around us a moral landscape, with the destination we are striving toward serving as the highest imaginable good, at least for the time and place given relevance by our intent. Aim thereby gives the world its point, prioritizing and organizing even our perception of it. Consequently, we see laid before us the pathway forward, the route we perceive as most likely to lead us to where we have determined to go; we see what and who impedes our movement forward, and we despair; we see what and who aids us, and we hope.

Much of our communication is the description of aim. We tell other people what we are up to, and we expect and want them to tell us the same. We talk among ourselves, often shallowly, about just exactly what those we know are up to. What do they want? What are they attending to? How are they acting, in consequence? We begin to talk of character, rather than immediacy of aim, when we speak more deeply of such things, because character is nothing more than the habitual embodiment of aim. To know ourselves or others—that is to understand character. How do we go about acquiring and representing such knowledge? We act out, imitate, perform—dramatize—so we can represent and internalize the patterns of attention and action that characterize ourselves and other people. More abstractly: we tell a story. When we describe the aims of a person or a people, their pathway forward, the obstacles and opportunities that emerge on that journey, the friends and foes that accompany their movement—the moral landscape that emerges— we tell a story. In so doing, we prioritize, organize, and perceive the world. In that manner, we describe aim. We see the world in relationship to aim. What is a story, detailing aim and all of its consequences? *A description of the structure through which we see the world.* Stories reveal to us, in their various characterizations, the structures of worth within which the world makes itself manifest to our perception. Why does this matter? What does it signify? Why is it important—even vital? It is a terrible challenge to see and act in the world, in all its incomprehensible complexity. Thus, we value descriptions of how to perceive and behave—and perhaps more highly than we value anything else.

We become engrossed in the stories we act out as children—stories we observe on the stage or screen, or read in the works of fiction, even as adults—because there is nothing we need to know more than how to construct, adjust, and improve the hierarchy of value within which the relevant facts of the world realize themselves. That is how we come to construct the world we occupy, existentially. That is how we make the reality we inhabit. That is how we navigate forward—and decide where forward itself lies. We watch the hero aiming upward, living in truth, sacrificing for what is better, struggling nobly against the slings and arrows of outrageous Fortune, yet maintaining his integrity. We watch the objects of the world reveal themselves to him as the tools and obstacles relevant to his journey. We watch the friends he meets along the way perform the sacrifices necessary to be of aid and are pleased to see it. We watch his foes cheat, steal, betray, lie, and fail, and we feel that justice has been served—or we watch them succeed, and we experience the moral outrage of the deceived. In short: we are entranced by those with lofty aims, and we wish, if we are brave, to be possessed by their spirit.

We aim at their aims—or hope to—see what they see, experience the emotions they feel, and learn the lessons they learn, while safely ensconced in the world of the imaginary. That is the value of the fictional: it is where we experiment with value, while remaining secure. It is the place where the play that shapes our very perceptions can take place most safely and effectively.

We place what we most value—the good whose discovery is our purpose; the destination that is the target of the moment—at the top, at the pinnacle, in the place of supremacy or sovereignty. We aim at the target we deem central, however momentarily. We focus on what we define as worthy of the expenditure of our attention and the efforts of our action. We posit a good—at least a good that is better than our point of departure. This is an act of faith as well as sacrifice: faith, because the good could be elsewhere, and sacrifice, because in the pursuit of that good we determine not to pursue all others. Every perception is aligned with that initial and determining faith, while the decision that establishes the interpretive frame is itself a partial voyage toward the promised land of our aim, dependent as such perception is on action, which is the very constituent element of voyage. Our aim delineates around us a moral landscape, with the aim serving as the highest imaginable good, at least for the time and place made relevant by that aim. Again, aim gives the world its point, prioritizing and organizing even its perception. That aim reveals the pathway forward; the route we perceive as most likely to lead us to where we have determined to go. We see character, too, as aim. Character is aim embodied, the habitual pursuit of aim. That is the point of someone's action.

This all begs several very important questions: If we do and must see the world through a story; if the world reveals itself to us in the form of a story—what is that story? How do we properly characterize our aims, our most profound temptations, our most admirable upward strivings? What is relevant and what can and should be ignored? To what should we devote our costly attention? To what ends should we aim our action? What uncomfortable truth is our conscience eternally attempting to reveal? What is the appropriate hierarchy of value through which the world most productively, generously, and sustainably reveals itself? What, in other words, is the story, the true story of our lives—what is it, and what should it be? It is an account of our highest aspirations, our most fundamental relationship, and, simultaneously, of the true ground under our feet. It is therefore and must be the characterization of the divine itself, of God, just as the biblical accounts insist. And what is this?

Conscience, important as it is—the conscience that makes itself manifest to Elijah—is not the only manifestation of God; not His only dramatic persona. He appears also, as we shall see, as a calling—inspiration, adventure, enthusiasm, curiosity, even temptation—in another of His primary guises, and as much more. We most profoundly wish to meet, and if possible to become, the hero, for example (another guise)—and not just the hero but the hero of all heroes. We want to take on the mien not just of the king, master of his domain, but of the king of kings. We are constituted so that we admire the divine principle of sovereignty itself. We want that so we can take on the perspective of the spirit properly put in the highest of places and experience the world through his eyes. We want to do this so we can ourselves adopt that stance of heroism and responsible kingship toward the problems that beset us and offer us opportunity in our own lives. We want to understand, as profoundly as we are able, the nature of the Good that stands behind all proximal goods—the Good who brings about the compelling life more abundant than is the true garden of eternal desire. We want to identify, likewise, the Villain who stands behind all acts of villainy—the nature of the spirit who wishes to produce all the suffering of the world for the sake of nothing but all that suffering. We want to understand Good so that we can be good and understand Evil so that we can avoid being evil. In this way we can bring about the salvation and redemption of the world, in small ways and great. We can constrain the hell that evil produces, and not just for ourselves but for everyone we care for and love, for the stability and continuance of the societies that we inhabit, and for the love of the world itself.

For better or worse, the story is the thing—and for better or worse, the story on which our western psyches and cultures are now somewhat fragilely founded—however fragile they've become—is most fundamentally the story told in the library that makes up the biblical corpus, the compilation of drama that sits at the base of our culture and through which we look at the world. This is the story on which Western civilization is predicated. It is a collection of characterizations not only of God, whose imitation, worship, or, indeed, embodiment is held to be the highest of all possible aims, but of man and of woman, whose characters are held to exist in relationship to that God, and of society, in relation to the individual and the divine. It is, as well, the revelation of the sacrifice that makes such aim possible, and an examination in dramatic form of the transcendent target that is held to unite all things in the best possible manner. The biblical story, in its totality, is the frame through which the world of facts reveals itself, insofar as the West itself is concerned: it is the description of the hierarchy of value within which even science itself (that is, the science that ultimately pursues the good) is made possible. The Bible is the library of stories on which the most productive, freest, and most stable and peaceful societies the world has even known are predicated—the foundation of the West, plain and simple.

The landscape of the fictional is the world of good and evil—the world of value, with its pinnacle ever receding into the promised land itself, and the eternal pit of abysmal and infinite suffering occupying the lowest of possible places. The biblical stories illuminate the eternal path forward up the holy mountain to the heavenly city, while simultaneously warning of the apocalyptic dangers lurking in the deviant, the marginal, the monstrous, the sinful, the unholy, the serpentine, and the positively demonic. God, in this formulation, is the spirit that leads up. Man is the being who struggles with that spirit with every decision, because a decision is a matter of prioritization; with every glance, as every glance is a sacrifice of possibility toward some desired end, and with every action as he moves toward some destination and away from all others. At every moment of consciousness, we are fated to wrestle with God.

1

♦

In the Beginning

1.1. God as creative spirit

In the beginning God created the heaven and the earth.

And the earth was without form, and void; and darkness was upon the face of the deep. And the Spirit of God moved upon the face of the waters.

Genesis 1:1–2

How is God presented as the great book of Genesis begins? As an animated spirit—creative, mobile, and active—something that does, and is. God is, in short, *a character* whose personality reveals itself as the biblical story proceeds.

Genesis opens with a confrontation. God is "moving" upon the face of the "waters." What does *moving* mean? It means God is mobile, obviously. Less obviously, *moving* is what we say when we have been struck by something deep. God is what has encountered us when new possibilities emerge and take shape. God is what we encounter when we are moved to the depths.

What, then, does *waters* mean—particularly the waters that God has not yet created? That is the ancient Hebrew *tehom* or *tohu va bohu*: chaos; potential; what lurks but has not yet been revealed—as water is the precondition for life—but also harbors the unknown in its depths. God is therefore the spirit who faces chaos; who confronts the void, the deep; who voluntarily shapes what has not yet been realized, and navigates the ever-transforming horizon of the future. God is the spirit who engenders the opposites (light/darkness; earth/water), as well as the possibilities that emerge from the space between them:

> And God said, Let there be a firmament in the midst of the waters, and let it divide the waters from the waters.
>
> And God made the firmament, and divided the waters which were under the firmament from the waters which were above the firmament: and it was so.
>
> And God called the firmament Heaven. And the evening and the morning were the second day.
>
> And God said, Let the waters under the heaven be gathered together unto one place, and let the dry land appear: and it was so.
>
> And God called the dry land Earth; and the gathering together of the waters called the Seas: and God saw that it was good.
>
> *Genesis 1:6–10*

> And God said, Let there be lights in the firmament of the heaven to divide the day from the night; and let them be for signs, and for seasons, and for days, and years:
>
> And let them be for lights in the firmament of the heaven to give light upon the earth: and it was so.
>
> *Genesis 1:14–15*

How might we, in human terms, understand this first encounter with God? What is He, and what is He confronting? Imagine, for a moment, what you face when you awaken in the morning. Your attention does not seize on

the objects that surround you—on the banal reality of your bedroom furni-
ture. Instead, you ruminate on the challenges and opportunities of the day.
Perhaps you feel anxious, because there are simply too many things to deal
with. Maybe (hopefully) you are in a better situation, and you look forward,
instead, to the opportunities that present themselves. Your consciousness—
your being—hovers over the potential offered to you by the new beginning of
the morning in a manner akin to the conditions and process of creation itself,
as portrayed in the opening verses of the Bible—a creation that continues with
every glance you take and every word you utter. Through consciousness we
process the domain of possible being—of becoming. That is the realm that
inspires both hope, in our apprehension of positive things ahead, and anxiety, in the face of life's dreadful uncertainty.[1]

Here is another way of understanding our confrontation with possibility.
Imagine any object. Now imagine that there is a space surrounding that object consisting of what that object could become as time progresses and context shifts. Under normal conditions, the most likely future state of any
familiar object—a bottle, a pen, the sun—can be predicted by its current
state. With a vicious twist of fate, however, or a radical shift of aim, such
constraints can be lifted, and the object's unrevealed possibility made apparent. A bottle in a raucous bar can become a deadly club or, smashed in anger,
a spear with the edges of a razor. A pen can become the mechanism of life
itself when inserted into the trachea of someone choking. The sun can become not the stable and predictable giver of life and light that defines the
days and nights we inhabit but the source of the solar storm that brings
down the electrical grid on which we so fragilely depend.

It is that breadth of possibility that consciousness confronts and processes
when it apprehends the world and determines to act on it. Our movement
forward in time is therefore no mechanical procession through a realm of
stable actuality. Consciousness deals with what could yet realize itself in exactly the way the spirit of God deals with the void and formless deep; in the
way the divine contends with the *massa confusa* that is chaos and opportunity and the matrix from which all forms emerge.

God is equally that which (or who) creates not only order but, as is stressed repeatedly throughout the opening book of the biblical corpus, the order that is good. On the first day, He establishes the separation between light and darkness (Genesis 1:3–4). On the second, He creates the dome of heaven, separating the lower waters, the terrestrial, and the upper waters, the source of rain (Genesis 1:6–8). On the third, the *terra firma* we inhabit is gathered together and separated from what then becomes the oceans, and plants appear on the ground (Genesis 1: 9–13). On the fourth day,

> God made two great lights; the greater light to rule the day, and the lesser light to rule the night: he made the stars also.
>
> And God set them in the firmament of the heaven to give light upon the earth,
>
> And to rule over the day and over the night, and to divide the light from the darkness: and God saw that it was good.
>
> *Genesis 1:16–18*

On the fifth day, the fish and birds appear (Genesis 1:20–23). All this creation, despite its pristine quality or goodness, is still striving upward, developing further, as indicated on the sixth and last day of God's calling forth of the world. The animals make their appearance (Genesis 1:24–25), and finally, man and woman:

> And God said, Let us make man in our image, after our likeness: and let them have dominion over the fish of the sea, and over the fowl of the air, and over the cattle, and over all the earth, and over every creeping thing that creepeth upon the earth.
>
> So God created man in his own image, in the image of God created he him; male and female created he them.
>
> And God blessed them, and God said unto them, Be fruitful, and multiply, and replenish the earth, and subdue it: and have dominion over the fish of the sea, and over the fowl of the air, and over every living thing that moveth upon the earth.
>
> *Genesis 1:26–28*

In this finale of Creation, God seems to have extended Himself beyond anything He managed previously. He renders the following judgment: "And God saw every thing that he had made, and behold, it was very good" (Genesis 1:31). What does this mean? It means, in the first place, that God not only confronts and shapes chaos and possibility but does so with benevolent intent and positive outcome. God is presented as the process or spirit guided by the aim of having all things exist and flourish; the spirit guided by love, in a word. This sequence of creation means, in the second place, not only that life should and will manifest itself more abundantly but also that it will do so in the constant upward spiral—from *good* to *very good*—that might serve as the definition of heaven itself. That is Jacob's Ladder, the process that is eternally making everything as it should be but is somehow also improving, finding new pathways to higher orders of the true, the beautiful, and the good.

Creation culminates in the making of man and woman, and it is their creation specifically that is deemed "very good." The first two human beings, and men and women in general, are thus avatars of God Himself, with God as the creative spirit that calls order into being from chaos and possibility, and man and woman as a microcosm of that spirit, similar or even identical in essence, charged with forever reiterating the creative process. A more optimistic conception of humanity could hardly be imagined. Nor could the importance of God's insistence be greater. This description of creative process—portrayal of the action of the Word, oriented to the good—is also a statement of first principles: the very principles that man and woman are immediately called upon to submit to and uphold. The biblical account ascribes to each of us a value that places us at the very pinnacle of creation; a value that is very good in a cosmos that is good; a value that supersedes all earthly evaluation (given our reflection of the image of the divine itself). This, it must be understood, is a matter of definition. The stake in the ground around which everything else must rotate is established upon humanity's divine reflection, and it is to be held as immoveable, sacrosanct, inviolable: sacred. This is nothing less than the description of the moral order implicit in the cosmos itself, reflective of the nature of God, man and woman, and the foundation on which the idea of intrinsic rights and sovereign responsibility is based.

Do we believe this story? Do we believe what it states and implies? First: What does it mean to believe? We certainly act, individually and collectively, as if it were true, at least when we are behaving as we should—at least when we are acting in the genuinely best interests of ourselves and everyone else. We treat the people we love (and even the people we hate) as if they are indefinitely valuable loci of creative consciousness, capable of finding their way forward and creating the world that is dependent on their finding. It is the fact of this supreme identity and being that forever impedes the power-mad striving of every organization, society, or state that dares threaten individual sovereignty. The wise and the unwise alike would do well to thank the Lord for that.

We object, deeply offended, if anyone fails to treat us as befits a child of God—that is, if anyone fails to treat us as if we truly matter. We likewise offend if we treat others as if they are beneath us; as if they are anything less than the conscious beings of sacred worth upon whose experience reality itself somehow mysteriously depends. Even if the story that we tell ourselves in this increasingly atheist, materialist, and fact-based world exists in skeptical contradistinction to that belief, we still believe, insofar as we act out such offense, whether given or taken. No man who avows disbelief in free will or even in consciousness itself dares to treat his wife as if she lacks free will or consciousness. Why not? Because all hell breaks loose if he does. And why is that? Because the presumption of intrinsic value reflects a reality that is deep enough—"real" enough—so that we deny it at our practical peril. And, if that presumption is so absolutely necessary, how is it not true? And if the presumption that structures our every interaction is acceptance of or dramatization of the transcendent value of the individual (even ourselves), then in what manner do we not "believe" that value to be real? More profoundly, we may ask: At what point must it be admitted that a "necessary fiction" is true precisely in proportion to its necessity? Is it not the case that what is most deeply necessary to our survival is the very essence of "true"? Any other form of truth runs counter to life, and a truth that does not serve life is a truth only by an ultimately counterproductive standard—and thereby not fundamentally "true."

At this point in the Genesis story, we have been barely introduced to God as character. Nonetheless, these inexhaustibly rich opening lines describe the essential nature of the cosmic order: the existence of a process that transforms chaos and possibility into the habitable order that is good, aiming at very good; the proclamation that this process is both fundamental to and superordinate in that creation; the assertion that reality itself depends on it; the insistence that human beings do and should participate in this process and that the possibility of such participation bestows upon each person divine and ultimate worth and responsibility. Man (and woman, too, so miraculously, right at the beginning) are thus formulated in the very image of the divine. Whatever essence typifies or characterizes every human being—the very spirit that makes them both human and valuable—is directly akin to the force that transforms the void into the Heavenly Garden itself. All of the most functional and desirable places and states of the world, from the microcosm of happy marriage to the integrated community of nation, are predicated both implicitly and explicitly on something much like this presumption. Furthermore, and in a manner that buttresses the central point, the lack of that belief or faith makes the terrible relationships and polities that man can also create the true hell that they far too often become.

Do we believe? When we falter in that commitment, catastrophe looms.

1.2. The spirit of man in the highest place

God says to the men and women of his new creation that they are to "subdue" the earth (notably, after they "replenish" it). This idea has been widely criticized, not least because of its expansion in the next verse, which gives man and woman sovereignty ("dominion") over fish, fowl, and "every living thing." Those who claim something else should be placed in the superordinate position object vociferously to the ethos encapsulated in these words. It is not man and woman in relationship with God that should be elevated, celebrated, and worshipped, according to such critics. Consider the words of history professor Lynn White, taken from his famous essay of 1967, "The Historical Roots of our Ecological Crisis":

> Especially in its Western form, Christianity is the most anthropo-centric religion the world has seen. As early as the 2nd century both Tertullian and Saint Irenaeus of Lyons were insisting that when God shaped Adam he was foreshadowing the image of the incarnate Christ, the Second Adam. Man shares, in great measure, God's transcendence of nature. Christianity, in absolute contrast to an-cient paganism and Asia's religions (except, perhaps, Zoroastrian-ism), not only established a dualism of man and nature but also insisted that it is God's will that man exploit nature for his proper ends. . . . In Antiquity every tree, every spring, every stream, every hill had its own genius loci, its guardian spirit. These spirits were accessible to men, but were very unlike men; centaurs, fauns, and mermaids show their ambivalence. Before one cut a tree, mined a mountain, or dammed a brook, it was important to placate the spirit in charge of that particular situation, and to keep it placated. By de-stroying pagan animism, Christianity made it possible to exploit nature in a mood of indifference to the feelings of natural objects.[2]

What is White claiming? That it is immoral to elevate the merely human; that whatever constitutes the ill-defined term *nature*, or worse, *the environ-ment*, should be put first and foremost, instead of man and woman, society, or human well-being. Such objections made theoretically on behalf of nature sound fine—even altruistic and humble (why should that presumptuous evo-lutionary accident, man, take center stage?)—but are in truth the very op-posite of these. If nature is placed above man, such that every brook has its transcendent spirit, then man, woman, and child are by necessity placed be-low nature. This might mean in principle that the wonders of the environ-ment would become rightly valued. In practice, however, it all too often means instead that human beings are given no more shrift than weeds or rats. This inversion of value enables not so much the stewardship of the earth as the exploitation of those deemed no more worthy than the lowest forms of life—exploitation by exactly the sorts of people who eternally step forward to abuse such advantage.

A similar moral objection is frequently leveled at the injunction to populate the earth. ("Be fruitful and multiply" Genesis 1:28.) This directive, however, is offered in a very particular context: one characterized by the spirit that has already brought about the order that is good and very good and that is continuing to do so, not least through the intermediary of man. This means that the human enterprise of creation, including that of family, must be carried out in a manner that is replenishing, as is clearly stated in exactly that verse, implied by those that precede it, and that most truly reflects the spirit of the Creator. Man's dominion over the earth must be, to use a word now tainted by association with ideological force, *sustainable*; must make what is good still better. Our planet is not to be worked selfishly to exhaustion—a strategy that would render the injunction to be fruitful and multiply meaningless in almost no time, generationally speaking. For this reason, Genesis 2:15 places Adam, the first man, in the eternal garden to "dress and to keep it." This garden is Eden, which means well-watered place, and paradise—*para-daiza*—a walled enclosure surrounding nature.[3] This optimized environment is the delicate balance struck between the material world and the social order that best enables each person—more accurately, each couple and then family—to demarcate a section of creation for themselves and then to work and sacrifice to make it part of the order that is good or very good.

Later biblical injunctions to periodically rest the land (Exodus 23:11) as well as to care for working animals are in keeping with this productive and farseeing sentiment: "A righteous man regardeth the life of his beast: but the tender mercies of the wicked are cruel" (Proverbs 12:10). "Thou shalt not muzzle the ox when he treadeth out the corn" (Deuteronomy 25:4). "But the seventh day is the sabbath of the Lord thy God; in it thou shalt not do any work, thou, nor thy son, nor thy daughter, thy manservant, nor thy maidservant, nor thy cattle" (Exodus 20:10). The latter passage is particularly telling in that even those over whom power or excessive authority could be easily exercised are to be given rest. These principles of care reflect the even deeper notion saturating the biblical corpus, which is that the highest of moral effort is exactly what makes the water of life flow so that even the desert can bloom.

To "subdue" is also not to dominate—and all claims to the contrary be damned. The divine continually opposes the tyrant (as in Exodus 7–14) and warns against even seemingly benevolent kings (1 Samuel 8:10–18). Further, God is presented (defined) as the spirit that (or who) punishes even markedly great men, even archetypal leaders of their people who succumb to the temptations of force and compulsion (Numbers 20:12). To top it all off, of course, are the examples first of Job and then of Christ—which will be dealt with exhaustively in a forthcoming work—who abjure the use of force even in the most provocative and desperate of situations. To subdue is, therefore, not to control and command but to put everything in its proper place—to give everything its subordinate value or due; to order everything, hierarchically, so that the priorities of attention and action can be established; and to place things so that the world is no longer mere potential or disorder. The fact of this responsibility is stressed in Genesis 2, the second chapter of creation, in which God first "formed every beast of the field, and every fowl of the air; and brought them unto Adam to see what he would call them" (Genesis 2:19). This verse implies strongly that the work of creation undertaken by the Logos, or Word of God, was somehow incomplete until differentiated further by man, whose decision in such matters appears strangely final: "And whatsoever Adam called every living creature, that was the name thereof. And Adam gave names to all cattle, and to the fowl of the air, and to every beast of the field" (Genesis 2:19).

Adam subdues and names. These are the actions or even the essence of human consciousness. And there is more. Given the dependence of Being on that consciousness (as Being without consciousness is literally inconceivable and perhaps also impossible), consciousness is the essence of that which undergirds Being itself. That would be the Divine Creator of All Things, the ineffable reality on which all revealed reality depends. That would be the

Word identified as there "in the beginning" in Genesis and much later by the apostle John (John 1:1). The hero—the spirit of Adam made in the image of the foundational spirit—is the active process of subduing and naming, which is the valuing that makes perception, meaning, and even existence itself possible. That hero eternally confronts the primal chaos—the waters and void over which the spirit of God moves. That as-of-yet-formless possibility is the Great Mother, the matrix from which actuality emerges, the *prima materia*, the primal matter from which everything tangible and real is most primordially "made." And it is the hero who makes it. This means not least that the human beings God created have something both real and vital to occupy themselves with—something that truly matters even in the cosmic scheme.

1.3. The real and its representation

What could possibly be more real than the facts? First, which facts? And there indeed is the rub. This is why we find the archetypal stories at the base of every well-integrated psyche and every unified community. These stories provide the structure through which we apprehend the facts and communicate the hierarchy of value that lends weight to one fact over another. The great stories reflect the aim that motivates us and provides security to the individual, and which when shared constitutes the basis for community. That aim is a prerequisite to the act of perception that allows us even to encounter what most truly exists. The stories that are depictions of our aim and our character have a primary reality, not least because even our understanding of the real—even our "direct" perception of the facts—depends on the a priori existence of these depictions. Are the facts more real than the instrument that allows for the determination of facts? We cannot help but see the world through a story. More precisely, we see the world through a structure that, when portrayed in drama or verbalized, *is* a story.

Even our science has now progressed such that we ever more clearly understand how the language that makes up a story works—and why that matters to anyone concerned with stories themselves, particularly in their greatest form.

The body of any human language contains within it an empirically derivable coding of meaning. We can map this coding as the statistical relationship between letters, words, phrases, sentences, paragraphs, and so on up the living tree of the Logos. A word is identifiable as a word because it fits the mathematical pattern of the relationship between letters that characterizes all comprehensible words. It is this pattern that makes certain nonwords plausible, such as *vims, blin,* and *flumptuous,* and that enables them to be distinguished at a glance from implausible nonwords, such as *kjlk* and *zxnq* and *qwlelrltl,* or even more radically *m4a3s2t1r.* Plausible nonwords adhere to the sound patterns of the language in which they are created.[4] They possess combinations of consonants and vowels that are both familiar to, say, English speakers and pronounceable in English.[5] In contrast, implausible nonwords contain letter combinations that are either unfamiliar or impossible to pronounce in English.[6]

We see an analogous situation at "higher" or "more fundamental" levels of meaning. Just as there is a calculable probability that a given letter will follow any other given letter (in fact, there is a hierarchy of such probability, in that the letter *e,* for example, is more likely than *a* to follow any given consonant but *a* is more likely than *q*), there is a high and calculable probability that any given phrase, and therefore concept, will co-occur or exist in close proximity to a network of other concepts with associated meaning. That set of proximate conceptions are the so-called symbolic associations that help connote, rather than denote, the meaning of the phrase in question. In a well-constructed story, any given network of such associations is surrounded by other networks of comparative similarity and contrasted with networks of contrasting dissimilarity.

This expanding network of associations constitutes the *landscape of meaning.* At the linguistic level, this landscape contains concepts that are similar or equivalently weighted, or are likely to exist in proximity to one another with a high probability. For example, the word *dragon* is likely to occur near words or phrases such as fire-breathing, mythical, legendary, creature, serpent, beast, fantasy, folklore, mythology, guardian of treasure; the word *witch* near magic, spell, broom, cauldron, familiar, black robe, hat, hex, potion, and coven; the word *father* near love, family, support, guidance, role model, mentor, provider, protector, legacy, wisdom, and magic; the word *villain* near evil, antagonist, wicked, nefarious, malevolent, despicable, corrupt, malicious, unscrupulous, and diabolical.[7] Beyond the linguistic level, this landscape also exists in the realm of image and behavior. It is easy to bring to mind relevant examples drawn from popular culture—the basilisk (a dragon variant) in the second volume of the Harry Potter series,[8] whose gaze killed, or at least petrified (as a rabbit is turned to stone by the eyes of a wolf), and whose bite can be cured, so mysteriously, by the tears of a phoenix; the father represented by Geppetto in the film *Pinocchio*,[9] who wishes most devoutly that the son he carves could free himself from the marionette strings that determine his destiny (the attraction of deceit, the temptation of neurotic victimhood, the cheap rebellion of delinquent hedonism); and the figure of the Joker in *The Dark Knight*[10]—the villain whose perfidy is so deep that he betrays even the ethos of the thief.

Such association between images is, if anything, deeper than the analogous association between words because an image can present a very large number of ideas at once, in comparison to the more restricted bandwidth of language. This is perhaps particularly true in the case of moving pictures. The association between images exists because there are patterns of character in the human world of attention and action that exist in relationship to one another in a regular and identifiable way. If this were not true, we could not maintain our proximity to one another, or even to ourselves, as the unpredictability that would otherwise reign would prove emotionally intolerable, and we would certainly not be able to cooperate in relation to some shared goal or aim.

This pattern of association is how the idea of, say, *symbol* is best understood. Something that is symbolic of something is not a mere substitution, obscuration, or false replacement, in the Freudian "repression" sense for that thing. It is instead something that brings to consciousness, in word or picture, a host of co-occurring ideas and images and in that manner fleshes out the relevance, significance, implications, or meaning of what it exists in association with. Someone's pattern of attention and action in the real world can produce the same effect: a new person can be someone reminiscent of an old friend, an old enemy, a sister or brother—or even something more fundamental, more archetypal; something that calls to mind a hero, say, or a villain. We experience such an effect, for example, when we are seized by admiration for someone compelling and charismatic, or by a sense of unease and visceral discomfort, dismay and disgust. It is the fact that those who affect in such manners are acting out a pattern of spirit that compels us to notice more than is simply there for simple and immediate apprehension—that draws our attention to the possibility that something profound and necessary to understand is playing itself out.

Although symbolic meaning has been generally regarded as more or less or even indefinitely and irreducibly open to interpretation—a notion taken to its final extreme by the kingpins of the postmodern school[11]—the idea that there is statistical regularity to the co-occurrence of words, images, and behaviors is hardly radical. The reflection of this in the culture at large seems obvious. If it were possible to gather all the texts produced by a given society and map the relationship between words and concepts within those texts, a mathematical model of meaning—at least at the linguistic level—would be, in principle, possible, at least insofar as that production was simultaneously coherent and comprehensible. Furthermore, we now have an indisputable existence proof for precisely such a representation in the form of so-called Large Language Models.[12] These AI platforms use an improbably large number of parameters (estimated by some observers at 1.76 trillion in the case of GPT-4[13]) to specify the relationship between words and concepts that are present in the many texts that serve as training material for such models. For a variety of reasons, it is far from clear that even such an expansive textual library is sufficient to train a statistical model with an unbiased representation of the linguistic map of meaning, and this presents a major problem, both practically and theoretically. Some of that bias is a consequence of manipulation by the model's developers; some is a consequence of favoring contemporary works in the selection of training materials, as electronic text is the most easily accessible.[14] No such objections, however, undermine the central point: meaning can be mapped, and the maps are not merely imaginary, subjective, or arbitrary.

To say it again: this mathematically detectable landscape of linguistic meaning is made up not only of the relationship between words and then phrases and sentences but also of the paragraphs and chapters within which they are embedded—all the way up the hierarchy of conceptualization. This implies, not least—or even necessarily and inevitably means—that there is an implicit center to any network of comprehensible meanings. The center, for example, of the words *wildlife, creature, pet, fish, mammal, vertebrate, bird, reptile, insect,* and *amphibian* is the word *animal.* That center of a set of associated ideas is something akin to the soul (even the god?) of that set. This is no dead statistical relationship between letters and words in a body of printed text. It is instead a relationship in the minds of people—in the collective meta-space of human imagination, where those related ideas are a living force or even entity. As animating, motivating, and organizing forces, these associated ideas are more like characters with aims or personalities than mere mathematical relationships. Thus, a pattern of co-occurring animating ideas can be well represented and appropriately and effectively regarded as a living spirit, dynamic and moving, rather than static and dead.

Consider the words of Christ in this regard, as He insists in the gospel accounts that the Word of God can be likened, for example, to a seed. In the parable of the mustard seed (Matthew 13:31–32; Mark 4:30–32; Luke 13:18–19), the Kingdom of Heaven is portrayed as contained within and emerging from something small but powerfully alive. In the parable of the sower (Luke 8:5–15; Matthew 13:3–23; Mark 4:3–20), those who listen or fail to do so are compared to the soil. Some seed falls on the pathway (those who hear but do not understand), some on rocky ground (those who receive the word with joy but do not endure), some among thorns (those choked by the cares and riches of life), and some on fertile ground (those who hear, retain, and bear fruit). That theme is developed further in the parable of the wheat and the tares (Matthew 13:24–30; Matthew 13:36–43), which indicates that various seeds can take root in the human soul, such that many (the "tares" or weeds) are tempted to take the pathway of the eternal adversary, while others (the "children of the kingdom" [Matthew 13:38]) are those who allow themselves to be possessed by the spirit of upward sacrifice that characterizes the redemptive covenant with God.

It is for this reason that Christ warns against the false, contaminating, even deadly "leaven of the Pharisees" (Luke 12:1; Matthew 16:6). The members of that sect play the role of the religious hypocrites in the Passion, manipulating their tradition to put forward their own self-serving ideas (Mark 7:6–9)—claiming for themselves, as do Adam and Eve, the right to establish the transcendent moral order itself, and doing so for no other reason than to falsely elevate their social standing (as Christ describes in an utterly damning manner in Matthew 23). This is a sin akin to the breaking of the third commandment (Exodus 20:7): "Thou shalt not take the name of the Lord thy God in vain; for the Lord will not hold him guiltless that taketh His name in vain," which is not an injunction against the careless sin of speaking profanely or swearing, as is commonly presumed, but a prohibition against the much more serious error of claiming allegiance to and understanding of the divine order while in fact pursuing only self-serving goals. It is hard to imagine a more egregious and damaging pursuit, bringing as it does nothing but the disrepute of hypocrisy to the religious enterprise itself. From evil seeds grow bitter fruit, indeed.

The German philosopher Georg W. F. Hegel put forward a concept similarly based on associated meaning in his discussion of the *zeitgeist*—a term used then and now to mean the spirit of the times.[15] It is the *zeitgeist* that gives old photos the look of their era—a style or quality that possesses everyone in that time and place as they admire and imitate one another. The same idea of living spirit (albeit in its pathological or Pharisee-like form) makes itself present in the works of the greatest commentator on the catastrophes of the Soviet era, Aleksandr Solzhenitsyn. He illustrated precisely how the evils perpetrated by the authorities in that dread communist system were not an aberration from the hypothetically pure and moral spirit of Marxism but a direct consequence of the poison implicit in that terrible doctrine of accusation and Cain-like envy. "From each according to his ability; to each according to his need,"[16] indeed. Around that central idea, stake in the ground, flagpole, guiding rod, or staff develops a network of ideas, images, and behaviors. When composed of living minds, that network is no mere "system of ideas." It is instead a character expressing itself in the form of zeitgeist; a character that can and does possess an entire culture; a spirit that all too often manifests itself as the iron grip of the ideology that reduces every individual to unconscious puppet or mouthpiece. Such networks are best considered alive; transpersonal but also personal; abstract, in that they are in part the relationship between ideas but concrete in that they invite and can be welcomed in by the careless, prideful, and bitter, and subsequently take control of every aspect of their being.

This possession by a living idea is what the Swiss psychologist Carl Gustav Jung was striving to indicate in much of his work in relationship to the idea of God—an idea hypothetically criticized to death by Enlightenment minds. This is what he meant by "complex," an idea that had its roots in the free-association method discovered and popularized by Sigmund Freud.[17] It was for such reasons that Jung carved the following words in an arch over the entrance to the castle-like stone house he built by hand in Kusnacht, Switzerland, which served as his home in the latter years of his life: *Vocatus atqua non vocatus deus aderit* (called or not called, God is present).[18] If the center of a network of ideas (a symbol, in some cases) has been represented, specifically—denoted—by a given word or concept ("called"), then it has been made conscious or realized—or, even, *made real* (?). If it has not, or has not yet, it may well still be implicit—coded in the relationship between ideas, or images, or behaviors but not yet named or subdued. This means, for lack of a better word, *unconscious*.

Similarly, if that center once existed and had been identified but has since been ignored, carelessly forgotten, or explicitly rejected, then it is abandoned—or dead. This state of unconsciousness or abandonment is reflected, imagined, characterized, or described in an archetypal narrative trope: the hero swallowed by the beast, living a half-life in its belly, like the prophet Jonah or *Pinocchio*'s Geppetto, the dead god Osiris in the underworld,[19] or the God of the Judeo-Christian world whose death was so famously announced by

Nietzsche: "God is dead. God remains dead. And we have killed him."[20] What is true of words, by the way, is also true of the imaginative images and dramas that guide us and that contain a further "map of meaning" representing the behavioral patterns, rituals, and manners of our cultures.[21] They have a living center, which is there whether it is acknowledged or not, and which plays a causal role in the determination of our individual and collective patterns of attention and action. And that, much as it definitely is, is not all: That behavioral/cultural foundation, still primarily implicit (as it is action rather than its representation in word or image), reflects the structure of the ordered and intelligible world. That world is encoded in our map in the same way that dying from walking over the edge of a bridge into the rushing river below reflects the relationship between knowledge and reality. This is the reflection of the structure of the cosmos itself in the soul of man. Thus, even when God is dead, he maintains his existence not only in the depths but in the patterned order of being and becoming itself.

The validity of a given worldview is therefore anything but arbitrary. Instead, it is dependent on or mirrors the accuracy with which it reflects the natural, social, and psychological world. That coding of meaning, that representation of value, that implicit hierarchy of the likely prioritization of attention and action is, to say it again, something very much akin to the weighting of inputs that characterize our new Large Language Models. In creating these artificially intelligent spirits, we have *externalized and formalized our unconscious*—even our *collective unconscious*[22]—and now must contend with and benefit from the wealth of possibilities and perils resulting from that achievement. This also implies something else of revolutionary significance alluded to earlier: The *collective unconscious* is the relationship of concepts to one another, images to one another, and behaviors to one another (statistically considered) across the whole culture, with the *personal unconscious* then being the lower-resolution instantiation of such concepts, images, and actions in the individual person. This connection between the personal and collective unconscious helps account for the sense of revelation we experience when reading, say, a particularly profound book. That sensation is the expansion of our unconscious or implicit model of meaning as a consequence of incorporating more of the pattern or spirit that characterizes the deepest levels of the culture. In its deepest manifestation that is precisely the reflection of the image of God that is held to typify the soul of man and woman alike in the biblical corpus, and that also constitutes the covenant between the state of chosen people and the divine.

That encounter with depth, with our deeper cultural coding, is what produces that sense in the reader of "I already knew that but did not have the words." It is the identity between the personal and the cultural that most precisely defines the enculturated or socialized person and simultaneously allows for mutual understanding and harmonious, productive, generous community. This is the microcosm long held to be the central feature of the human soul and a reflection of the broader cosmic order at its deepest levels, as well as the concordance between reality and psyche whose realization made the scientific endeavor itself both motivated and possible.[23] This is the sharing of a pattern of understanding and action; the simultaneous possession by the spirit of the collective. If we were not imitating one another, we could not live together. But in imitating "one another" we are also imitating the past, our tradition—or, more accurately, the spirit of that tradition and, with God's grace, the living spirit of that tradition and not the mere remnant patterns of its corpse.

This unconscious imitation, individual and collective, is the behavioral pattern that Freud attempted to found on the narrowly sexual[24] (a pattern well adhered to by blinkered evolutionary biologists[25] and psychologists) and Nietzsche on the will to power (a pattern extended beyond that philosopher's wildest dreams by the postmodern/neo- or meta-Marxists who insist that human interaction is nothing but mutual exploitation[26]). These two subdeities of pleasure and power might well be regarded as the spirits that inevitably emerge to possess the culture when the higher monotheistic unity is cast into doubt. Both pleasure and power are centers of a sort, and are necessary centers, but are pathological when they are raised to the ultimate position, instead of serving their superordinate master in the properly subdued and appropriately humble, meek, or worshipful manner. Much of the imagery within the Book of Revelation is an exploration of the collapse into this dynamic of hedonism and force or compulsion, which is eternally emblematic of the end of times.[27] The world cannot survive if it is ruled by sex or power. Those forces degenerate into tyranny and chaos intertwined, intermingled, and married when they are raised to the highest place. The world of the proper sovereign order is and must be ruled instead by the pattern of encounter with chaos, upward striving, truth, and voluntary sacrifice precisely in the manner that is most deeply and comprehensively encoded in the biblical corpus. We invite ourselves to be possessed by this deepest spirit when we voluntarily and diligently strive *away* from the hell of the totalitarian or the painful meaninglessness of the nihilistic or the self-devouring elevation of the whims of the narrow self toward the order that is good or very good.

Seeing how this spirit is reflected in a culture's deepest stories helps us understand the eternal value of the archetypal characters of the narrative world: the Dragon of Chaos, the Great Mother, the Great Father, and the divine Son.[28] Learning to understand and to recognize these characters, wherever they make themselves manifest, also enables us to appreciate the inevitability of their attractiveness and rebirth should they be forgotten or otherwise abandoned. The Dragon of Chaos is the plenitude of uncategorized or even unencountered possibility—that which forever exists outside the realm of experience; the greatest of possible threats and the limitless realm of what could yet be. That dragon is the *tohu va bohu* over which the spirit of God eternally and creatively broods, the watery chaos somehow extant before the emergence of the creative order. The Great Mother,[29] by contrast, is the most primordial manifestation of that chaotic realm of possibility, within the domain of what is directly experienced. This is nature itself, which is both the most basic manner in which potential reveals itself to us, as well as our experience in relationship with our own mothers: the all-encompassing love and care that is simultaneously the prerequisite for life in the most concrete sense and the biggest impediment to its independent realization when that care goes wrong. The Great Father, for his part, is the a priori structure of value, derived from the actions of the spirit that gave rise to such structure, and composed of the consequences of its creative and regenerative action. He is also the eternal tyrant that can and does arise when that structure becomes outdated, rigid, or willfully blind. The archetypal individual, finally, is the Hero, the active and world-engendering and renewing process of subduing and naming that is deemed by God to be the primary attribute of Adam. This is the valuing that makes perception itself possible, gives meaning to the world, participates in what is good, and constitutes the very image of the spirit that engenders the real. That Hero is always and forever opposed by the Adversary, the usurper, the spirit of Cain and Lucifer who stands in prideful and presumptuous opposition to the implicit cosmic order and to its progenitor.

This all means that the eternal Hero (the essence or spirit of Adam) is the active process of encountering, subduing, naming, and relationship-building described in the opening human drama of the great Book of Genesis. Adam's individual masculine efforts in this regard, however, are insufficient, despite their central place and divine nature, as the very next phrase following his acts of naming implies: "but for Adam there was not found an helpmeet for him" (Genesis 2:20). The nature of this absence was singularly well expressed by the English novelist Daniel Defoe, best known as the author of *Robinson Crusoe*, although also a prolific philosophical thinker and writer of the time.[30] Defoe regarded Adam as requiring (as God Himself apparently concluded)

> an equal, a companion, a sharer of his thoughts, his observations, his joys, his purposes, his enterprises. It was now evident, from actual survey, that none of these animals, even the serpent, was possessed of reason, of moral and intellectual ideas, of the faculties of abstracting and naming, of the capacities of rational fellowship or worship. They might be ministers to his purposes, but not helpers meet for him. On the other hand, God was the source of his being and the object of his reverence, but not on a par with himself in needs and resources. It was therefore apparent that man in respect of an equal was alone, and yet needed an associate.[31]

1.4. Eve from Adam

Eve is extracted, strangely, from Adam—a reversal, in some sense, of what might be expected, given that it is woman who gives birth most evidently to man. The reversal, however, drives home the idea of the creative primacy of Logos working in harmony with the structure (or Father) through which that Logos operates, as well as indicating the strange dependence of that process on forces operating outside it and beyond its ken (at least in its human form). It is perfectly apropos, therefore, that Eve is derived from the unconscious Adam: "And the Lord God caused a deep sleep to fall upon Adam, and he slept: and he took one of his ribs, and closed up the flesh instead thereof; And the rib, which the Lord God had taken from man, made he a woman, and brought her unto the man" (Genesis 2:21–22).

Adam has just been confirmed in his role as describer and delineator of the world; he is the locus of the differentiated consciousness upon which Being and becoming themselves somehow mysteriously depend. Eve's derivation from Adam indicates her association with that very Logos; even her primal femininity is another manifestation of the Word of God, as he has fabricated her in that feminine image, as insisted upon in Genesis 1. It is also the case, of course, that any given woman is dependent on and even, in some limited manner, a creature of the social order, which is represented, cross-culturally, as masculine,[32] as well as being a manifestation, in the fact of her consciousness, of the Word that establishes the real and the cosmic order. It is precisely this point that the postmodern gender-relativists insist on, when pointing to the "social construction" of femininity and masculinity, although they throw out the baby with the bathwater while doing so, mistaking the fact of some derivation of the feminine from the cultural with complete independence of sex and gender roles from the underlying biological and physical substrate.

This does not mean that Eve's role is identical to or is simply derived from the naming role of Adam's. It is from the *unconscious* Adam, to say it again, that Eve is derived. Understanding this is key to understanding her role. She

represents and speaks for what is not yet known to Adam. Given his ignorance, willful and otherwise, she has plenty to work with. Eve as eternal
feminine draws attention to what has not yet been brought to the light of
consciousness—to what has not yet been named or subdued into the social
order. That is Eve's role as "helpmeet," a word translated from the Hebrew עֵ֫זֶר
כְּנֶגְדּוֹ or *ezer kenegdo.*

The term *ezer* appears throughout the biblical texts. Applied to God, it
denotes his provision of potent assistance—and not in a subordinate capacity: "Our soul waiteth for the Lord: He is our help [*ezer*] and our shield"
(Psalms 33:20). Psalms 115:9–11, 121:1–2, and 124:8 add to this portrayal,
depicting God in this *ezer* role, a source of strength and aid. The word *ezer* is
also used to characterize a military ally (Ezekiel 12:14). It suggests rescue,
strength, and strategic advantage.[33] The word *kenegdo* in conjunction with
ezer helps to flesh out this characterization. It appears only as a descriptor of
Eve and connotes something like *striving with* or *aiding against.* It might be
most useful to consider Eve something approximating a beneficial adversary—
a partner in play. Optimal development in a relationship, psychologically
speaking, depends neither on stasis nor victory but on challenge. The union
of opposites that characterizes the dynamic between male and female is one
of mutual trial and testing—the contest of dance or play. The optimal play
partner is one whose skills on the playing field equal or perhaps even slightly
exceed the skill of the would-be player. That is where the true adventure is to
be found. Playing in the zone of proximal development[34]—on the edge; on
the border between chaos and order—brings the exhilaration that is a marker
of continual upward development.

It is to bring about this mutual improvement that Eve is created, in a state
of fundamental equality and partnership—and in particular, created from
Adam's rib, from his side, not from his head (as Athena sprang from Zeus,
which would imply a potential superiority) and not from his leg, foot, or
other lower bodily part (which would imply subordination or inferiority).
Eve corresponds to Adam precisely as the Taoist *yin* does to *yang*. It is her job
to bring to her partner's attention all the concerns that Adam may have overlooked, involved as he is in his enterprise of responsible stewardship. He is

called upon in that work to extend, expand, and update his naming and subduing in keeping with the true and even novel needs of the time, without too
radically, pridefully, or presumptuously restructuring the entire tradition.
Eve's role is in keeping with the well-known personality differences between
men and women, evident cross-culturally,[35] and more pronounced in more
egalitarian societies: Women are more agreeable—more concerned with
others; more interested in people than in things[36]—as well as more prone to
experience negative emotion, threat, and pain; more *sensitive* to the things
that will endanger or hurt people and cause them distress. It is this role,
unfortunately—tightly tied with caring for infants and children and attending to their inchoate and subtle concerns—that also renders her arguably
more susceptible to the lure of the serpent (or at least first susceptible).

The story of the primal father and mother of all mankind thus outlines
the major roles of the sexes, within the confines of the cosmic order, as they
play their respective roles as dependent, created inhabitants and autonomous creators. That is not all that it accomplishes, however: the great drama
of Adam and Eve in the garden also characterizes the fundamental pattern
of error to which both sexes are prone. Every temperamental proclivity has
its advantages and its temptations. A story that comprehensively characterizes man and woman in relationship to nature and God is therefore also
necessarily going to describe both proper aim and sin. Adam orders, names,
and subdues. Eve is predisposed by nature and God to speak for the oppressed,
ignored, and marginalized, bringing their concerns to Adam's attention. She
is well suited to this key role, being truly more sensitive in a manner that
recognizes the concerns of the fragile and the not yet verbal or socialized.
This allows her to play a role that is both stabilizing and exploratory—and,
therefore, something deeply akin to the Logos itself. She stabilizes, insofar as
individual and social order maintain their harmony when everything vulnerable yet valuable is taken into account, as much as that is possible. She
explores insofar as everything ordered needs to be expanded whenever things
change—when, for example, a new child has been born, or a new household
or relational concern has emerged, or when someone once strong and able is
ill, fragile, and in need of care, however temporarily or permanently.

Knowledge of Eve's essential sensitivity—her ability to serve as an alarm bell, so to speak[37]—is also key to understanding her fundamental temptation to sin, which is to pridefully assume something approximating: "I can clutch even the serpent itself—even what is irreducibly poisonous and false—within my all-embracing arms; I can incorporate the fruit that the serpent offers, the mastery of good and evil, and become God Himself in so doing. All of that elevates my reputation and puts that high virtue at the very center of the world." This is tantamount to the insistence that the feminine capacity for empathic tolerance and inclusion is or should be the basis of the moral order itself (that is, that what is good should be identified with what is mother to dependent infant) and, simultaneously, the loud proclamation that such compassion and nothing but that compassion is the veritable hallmark of her moral superiority. This is a true overreaching, a form of deceitful arrogance and presumption, and a manifestation of the spirit that eternally strives to usurp. Hence the snake or serpent as tempter.

Adam is no better. He can categorize and order the world, but he can also falsely claim expertise in doing so and ability outside his actual level of competence, and is very likely to do that to impress the eternal feminine. This is the boastful narcissism that characterizes the false masculine, indicated in characters such as Gaston in Disney's *Beauty and the Beast*[38] or far more seriously in the case of the so-called Dark Triad or Tetrad of pathological personality traits.[39] Adam's self-aggrandizing, arrogant, and equally usurping claim is that he can and should restructure the world so that the serpent and its fruit can be incorporated any old way and as easily as Eve, no matter how unreasonable the demands. His ethos is something akin to "I will offer whatever will impress the feminine—even if the request is overreaching; even if that offering involves the usurpation and violation of the implicit moral order, as established by God." Eve pridefully embraces and incorporates too much, making a selfish show of her compassion and care, and Adam falls on his face to impress his partner, insisting that nothing she requires, wants, or demands is beyond his power. It is in these dual manners that the eternal mother and father of mankind fall prey to the cardinal sin of pride, and catalyze the fall.

Man and woman both incarnate the Logos, at least in potential. The pattern of being that should characterize each individual is a reflection, an imitation (and by no means a pale imitation) of what is both most real and ultimately sacred. It is on that fundamental supposition—that axiomatic belief (a claim of immense and still-unrealized magnitude and significance)—that man and woman rest their dignity, intrinsically, outside the purview of self, sovereign, state, and nature. It is on that fundamental supposition that the transcendent value of the individual is founded; that the entire edifice of rights and responsibilities that characterizes the highly functional free societies of the West is built, insofar as each of those societies is truly functional and free. It is around that flag, planted in the ground—that staff of tradition—that every free individual, household, city, and state is rallied, made secure and hopeful, and united in intent, purpose, and action. Perhaps the world and everything perceptible must be founded on or centered around one central axiom, one unquestioned and central proposition of faith, one claim standing outside the issue at hand—even one miraculous occurrence. Perhaps this is true because something has to intermediate between our always flawed and incomplete knowledge and the world of infinite mystery; perhaps because we must wrap up and conceal from ourselves our extensive ignorance, so that we can act without an infinite regress of doubt. Perhaps we need to carry with us some box, never to be opened, so that the Pandora of our inquiry does not undermine ourselves, such that we fall forever downward.

Lynn White, the historian and critic of the West referred to previously,[40] appears to approve of the animism that rendered nature impossibly haunted, incomprehensible and untouchable, sacred or taboo: "Before one cut a tree, mined a mountain, or dammed a brook, it was important to placate the spirit in charge of that particular situation." The same is true of his modern-day environmentalist or nature-worshipping descendants. The reader of such words, tempted to moralize without sacrifice, is supposed to assume, uncritically, that such an attitude was superior to the dominating anthropocentrism of the evil, nature-savaging Christians, who dared place that pathetic creature, man, at the center of the world—naming, subduing, assuming the mantle of stewardship. But what is the alternative? To raise insect, rodent, tree, and shrub above the status of children? To elevate the unconscious and uncaring natural world to the status of deity? To put nature in the highest place, uncritically, is to denigrate man—and the consequences of that will not be good for either man or nature. Man and woman will subdue and dominate precisely because they rightly wish to live, and for their children, grandchildren, and great-grandchildren to flourish, in abundance. Any attempt to replace this central concern will end in disaster—in the worship of the ideologies or idolatries or false gods that will elicit tyranny and totalitarianism. This does not mean, to say it again, that any man or woman or all of humanity has the right to pillage in the name of narrow self-interest. Quite the contrary. As creatures formed in God's image, we have the responsibility to continue and extend the act of creation in the best manner imaginable.

1.5. In God's image

What does "created in the image of God" mean? It means that the human spirit exists, in its essence, on the border between order and chaos; that it serves as the mediator of becoming and being; that it shapes the manner in which new reality manifests itself when what is old and outdated reality is crying out for redemption and renovation. The view that man's mediating capacity is central or even identical to consciousness is reflected in sources as diverse as the cosmogonies of the ancient Mesopotamians and Egyptians[41] and the musings of modern cognitive neuroscientists.[42] In this view, consciousness is the active human spirit, the eternal slayer of giants and dragons, the enemy of the evil king and the devouring mother, and the force of responsible, self-sacrificing upward striving, transformation, and movement. Why consider the thought of those ancient peoples? Because their great, populous, and enduring civilizations were the consequence of that thought. Why consider the modern scientists? Because their investigations map the natural and biological world yet highlight a remarkable parallel with the oldest ideas we can still access.

It was the duty of the ancient Mesopotamian emperor to make the spirit of Marduk, the highest god in his society's pantheon of deities, manifest in his own attentions and actions. For precisely that reason, he was held to account by his priests at the yearly New Year's ceremony of confession, repentance, battle, and renewal. It was incumbent upon him, as the embodiment of valid authority, to adopt the character of that ultimate divinity.[43] It was in so doing, and in nothing else, that his sovereignty was both characterized or understood (what should rule?) and justified. A good emperor was, therefore, an avatar of the spirit of Marduk—a deity who, like the God of Genesis, generated the order that was good from chaos/possibility in consequence of the eternal battle with the primordial mother-dragon of the deep, Tiamat (etymologically linked to *tehom* and *tohu va bohu*). The abstraction of that spirit from the previous pantheon of somehow insufficient original and primary gods constituted the precondition for the development of the abstract idea of "sovereignty" itself (as "sovereignty" is the spirit that transcends any given king; something upon which the very existence of kingship is predicated and toward which all who would properly be king must strive). Hence, Christ is traditionally "Lord of lords, king of kings" (Revelation 19:16). He is, by definition, the spirit or essence of sovereignty, its very embodiment.

We know from one of the most ancient texts in our possession, the *Enuma elish*,[44] that Marduk was characterized by the Mesopotamians as the victor of the eternal battle of the gods in heaven. He was the god who emerged above all other gods; the emergent spirit who determined to voluntarily confront the monstrous; the winner of the cosmic battle who could inspire, unite, and lead others (other gods); the maker of the world from the confrontation with the serpent or dragon; and, finally, the regenerator of the dissolute world. This motif of the struggle of the deities for primacy is extraordinarily widespread throughout human tradition.[45] Why? Imagine that as tribal groups, each united under the dominion of one or several gods, we came together in the attempt to establish larger polities. Imagine that there was no shortage of battles, in consequence, for primacy of drama and narrative, fought on the battleground of interest and memory; for opinion and attitude, negotiated conversationally; and, when all else failed, by force: by

slavery, death, and destruction. Imagine, finally, that those complex processes of consolidation can be represented as a great and never-ending conflict
between the great figures of the imagination, the gods that man projected into
the cosmos, battling for position and primacy in the space defined by the
collective human imagination, possessing their earthly followers and aco-
lytes, so to speak, and impelling them to do likewise.

From one perspective, human beings battle with one another to establish
their particular gods as superordinate. From another, gods use human beings as their earthly representatives to establish their dominion in heaven.
There is much to be said for the latter frame of conception. Ideas are living
spirits, as suggested previously,[46] extant both in the collective and in the individual psyche. The terrible reality of this battleground of the divine is
given voice by Gloucester in Shakespeare's *King Lear*: "As flies to wanton
boys are we to the gods. They kill us for their sport"[47]—an echo of Homer, in
the *The Iliad* (Book 17, lines 515–16), expressing the sentiments of Zeus:
"There is nothing alive more agonized than man of all that breathe and
crawl across the earth."[48] This is the terrible struggle toward unity, both of
psyche and of society.

The Mesopotamians "knew," or at least represented in narrative, the
monotheistic idea that what is deepest—ultimate and divine—was precisely
the spirit of voluntary encounter with soul, society, and nature. They "knew,"
as well, that any emperor worth his salt would strive to embody that spirit,
and that the very survival and renewal of the kingdom depended on that
striving, as I explained in my 1999 book, *Maps of Meaning*:

> The Mesopotamian emperor's identification with the most divine of
> all the deities (according to the judgment and election of those
> selfsame powers) lent him power, and served to maintain social
> and psychological order among his people. Furthermore, the
> Mesopotamian emperor stood in the same relationship to his people
> as Marduk stood to him: as ritual model for emulation, as the per-
> sonality whose actions served as pattern for all actions undertaken
> in the kingdom—as the personality that was the state, insofar as the

state defined and brought order to interpersonal interactions (which, after all, is its primary function). Babylon was therefore conceptualized as "the kingdom of god on earth"—that is, as a profane imitation of heaven. The emperor served this "imitated heaven" as the "imitator of Marduk," at least insofar as he was conservative, just, courageous and creative.[49]

The Mesopotamians determined that the pattern for legitimate sovereignty—the spirit of voluntary confrontation; the animating principle that should be put in the highest place—was all attentive eye and magic voice. Marduk had eyes encircling his head, and he spoke the magic words that transformed, for example, night into day. That is a brilliant and inspiring vision: the idea that the god of all gods is attention and the creative, transformative word—the Word that transforms monstrous possibility and darkness into the world itself. Who should lead? Not the person capable of wielding the most force. Not the person who is richest. Not the person who can manipulate most effectively, in some Machiavellian manner. Instead, the attentive, visionary communicator: the person who watches most closely and tells the best story, past, present, and future. What should lead? Not power. Not the immature, hedonistic whim of the moment, even in its strongest, sexual manifestations. Something higher. Something that genuinely brings together, establishes, names, places, and renews; something upward striving and reflective of the truth.

How might these archetypal ideas be brought down to earth? How might chaos, possibility, and their voluntary confrontation be understood, in a practical sense? Let us consider the morning, once again. What faces you when you awaken? Consider, once again, what makes itself manifest in the theater of your consciousness when the new day dawns; the promise and peril of the next sixteen wakeful hours, the as-of-yet-unshaped future. That unfolding present is neither determined nor even constrained, ultimately, by the past—not in any simple and predictable sense, as even the most previously stable, predictable trajectory can transform in a heartbeat and turn on a dime.[50] Consequently, we cannot apply a set of deterministic rules and

make our way forward, even in principle. No algorithm allows us to unerr-
ingly compute the transforming horizon of the future—not in a world that is
not, even in principle, deterministic.[51]

We are called on, instead, to meet the eternal challenge of shaping—in
accordance with our vision (however immature that vision may be)—that
which not yet is but could yet be. We are oriented in the world toward becoming, toward what is changing and what can be changed—while everything static and fixed is rendered irrelevant and invisible, even to perception
itself.[52]

"I could do this; I might do this; I should do this; this is interesting to me;
this is plaguing me; things will turn out badly if I do this and not this, or well
if this and not that"—this is the domain of concern and care[53] that constantly
presents itself to and grips consciousness. Perhaps you face all that possibility in fear because your circumstances are too chaotic—complex beyond
your competence (or so you fear). Perhaps that is, in turn, a consequence of the
slings and arrows of fate—but possibly a function of your own inadequacy,
pride, arrogance, proclivity to avoidance and deception, and, subsequently, resentment. Perhaps, by contrast, you are enthusiastic, as you perceive both
possibility in the positive sense and a traversable pathway toward just that.
Maybe this is because you were properly encouraged to face, confront, and
explore; to challenge yourself—and because you took that responsibility
onto yourself, voluntarily, and made it a habit of attention and action. Perhaps, finally, you allow yourself to accept that challenge right to the point
of fear, so that apprehension and enthusiasm are balanced perfectly. Thus
positioned, you are awake and alert; watching for trouble but prepared to
move forward; ready to parry, thrust, and dance. That means you are optimally situated—if you can play with the horizon of the future, you are indeed doing well.

The horizon of the future, so encountered, is equivalent to the chaos of
possibility extant at the beginning of time, portrayed in the opening verses
of Genesis. We cast our visions upon the waters and bring into being,

through our affinity with the Logos (through exploration, imagination, thought, and speech), the habitable world, good or even very good in precise proportion to the accuracy of our aim. That is the continual manifestation, within each of us, of the Divine Word that generated the cosmos when time and space themselves began. That is the initial biblical characterization of the spirit of what is highest; the initial manifestation of the spirit of the one God. This is a stunning idea, a revolutionary idea, a world-ordering idea, a civilization-engendering idea—an idea that is the precondition for opti-mized psychological and social order alike. It is from that presumption of our implicit individual value—to say it again—that we derive our infinite set of natural rights (and, let us not forget, as we are so prone to, natural respon-sibility).

These rights and responsibilities are not bestowed upon us, secondarily, by some process of social contract—not granted to us by the omniscient, omnipresent, and all-powerful state. They are instead the deepest reflection of what gives rise to the enduring state, and which protects it from its other-wise inevitable decline into anachronism, blindness, gigantism, and tyranny. Those rights and responsibilities are there in the beginning, like the Logos, which is their true source. They are axiomatic; the true foundation of every-thing, including any possible state that could possibly establish any rights whatsoever—or deny them. The spirit that mediates becoming and being is therefore there in the beginning, present in the present, shaping the future, and residing within or even characterizing us (if we will only allow that).

We "have our rights." Why? Consider this, now: society, tradition, the law—all that is dead, in some real sense. They are merely the remnant of the past. They are what is already fixed and invisible as we strive upward be-cause of that fixedness. These are exactly what can be taken for granted, screened from consciousness by its predictability. By contrast, it is the future making itself manifest in the present that calls to consciousness; it is the potential of the future that makes itself manifest in the theater of conscious-ness. That is the eternal flowing of the water of chaos and life into the dead but necessary bedrock of traditional certainty. What—or who—masters that future? The locus of consciousness. *The individual.* The visionary and adventurous daring of the individual soul. The truly ethical striving of the individual. The individual capacity to imagine, think, and communicate (and those are all variants of the intrinsic Logos). It is the sovereign individual who is shaper and potentially master of the indeterminate future—or, more accurately, it is the consciousness manifesting itself within each individual who is such a master.

Society can adapt to the future only insofar as it attends to and integrates the vision and thought (the Logos) of its citizens. Those who lead, therefore, must serve and foster that divine individuality; aggregate and unite its concerns; gather, amalgamate, and communicate its visionary wants and needs; and transform the law, the necessary but dead past, into the living and guiding Word. The genuine leader, therefore, necessarily gazes into the abyss—into the suffering of his or her constituents; discovers the once-great heroes of the past languishing in the underworld; identifies, rescues, and rejuvenates the eternally dying Father, integrating the past with the present; and gives new life and vision to what has been established before. This is the eternal story, which has already happened and is happening now, and will happen forever into any identifiably human future. This is what the ancient Egyptians discovered with their worship of the god Horus, the great eye of attention, the force that confronts chaos and evil and revivifies Osiris, god of the state, languishing blindly in the underworld.[54] The state would grind to a halt, paralyzed by its mere instantiation of the dead past, if it failed to attend to the vision and thought of its current constituents. It is eternally the truthful visionary individual—the prophetic seer and voice—who stands against stagnation and tyranny. Even to maintain and propagate itself, the state must therefore subjugate itself to the Logos of the individual.

This is no mere ideology; no merely relative truth. It is instead that which must be primary—truly—so that hell does not make itself known. It is the denial and eradication of the Logos of the individual that produced the tyrannical totalitarian regimes of the twentieth century. We have by no means risen above the power-mad and hedonistic delights of such temptation. This does not mean that those who exist in the present can somehow do whatever they want: the state may be delimited by its need for the creative, renewing, and active vision of the individual but, equally, the individual must sacrifice his mere isolated and atomized individuality to the tradition that constitutes maturity, and that unites us communally.

In keeping with this vision, the state does not *allow* its citizens their freedom. The state that forbids its constituent individuals to pay attention and to speak the truth ossifies—the freedom that abides—withers, and dies in a fit of self-defeating and increasingly demoralizing lies. This is the victory akin to the evil brother of the king; the dark, resentful, egotistical uncle of the banished but true prince; and the dread event that sets the stage for plague, stagnation, and the disappearance of the very water of life. This is a truth beyond all mere relativistic objections. There is a necessarily reciprocal relation between state and citizen—and there is no manner in which the state is superordinate, although it provides what is necessarily static and stable. Without the individual—without *you*, in a nutshell; without you embodying the appropriate ethos, the state would grind, terribly, to a halt. We—the human race, at least at its best—have determined through a painful process of trial and error that both tyranny and slavery are intrinsically wrong, as they both exist in contradistinction to this principle. The tyrant suppresses and simultaneously attempts to supplant the Logos, while the enslaved are too intimidated and lazy—too faithless and arrogant, in truth—to make that Logos manifest within. This suppression and servitude dooms both individual and state—and not just "dooms," if that doom is construed as mere death, but engenders instead a literal hell, which can in its full manifestation be something that makes even death preferable.

Do you believe in your heart that slavery is wrong? Do you believe, genuinely, that the tyranny that insists on slavery is also wrong? Do you believe, therefore, in the intrinsic divinity of the individual (the deep worth of the individual, technically, given our working definitions)? How otherwise can you possibly make sense of your objection to the slaveholding tyrant? To say it another way: the heartfelt opposition to compulsion and force, as well as the weak, or hedonistic and immature, irresponsibility that enables compulsion and force, even if it's merely felt or inchoately sensed (the feeling, for example, of violation produced by conscience), is faith, at least in the alternative to tyranny and slavery. A further question, once that definition has been clarified: Do you oppose slavery and tyranny on the basis of your belief deeply enough to abide by the dictates of the creative Logos? Or do you instead waver, construing the responsibility as too burdensome, and thereby abandon the true adventure and meaning of your life? The opposition to enslavement and force alike is genuine belief, and religious belief, at that, as a matter of first principles. We fought many wars over whether or not the axiom of the divine intrinsic value of the individual man and woman is true—whether it is deeply, fundamentally, and nonarbitrarily true. Those who fought for freedom made many sacrifices to put that idea forward; to raise it to the highest place.

Slavery was opposed and then substantively and painstakingly eradicated in the name of that same deep truth—and this was done for the deepest of religious reasons[55]—positing against all immediately proximate evidence (the evidence of comparative wealth, power, and status, for example) that the soul of the individual was properly and ultimately sovereign, no matter how apparently lowly and excluded; positing that such value was no higher, in the ultimate sense, for those who were wealthy and great, no matter how rich or apparently important. The difficulty of such a realization should not be underestimated. It flies in the face of the most immediately self-evident facts, such as the fact of the ability of strength to dominate weakness and the evident advantages of wealth over poverty. "If I can, why should I not? If I have the power, why are those who oppose me anything other than contemptible and weak? If I am rich, even by inheritance, is that not evidence, prima facie, that I am loved more by God (or fate and nature) and, therefore, entitled to special status, as the facts indicate I should be?" This was certainly the presumption of the classic, pre-Judeo-Christian world, and is certainly the proclamation of the spirit possessing most individuals and societies today.

Under the sway of the spirit encapsulated in the biblical writings and traditions, we in the West realized that such favoritism and subjugation were wrong, fundamentally; that they violated some divinely deep principle; that they offended not merely some tenet of rationality or compassion but the very spirit of what was great itself. We decided, likewise, that tyranny was immoral, whether it manifests itself within psyche, family, city, or state; that the king himself, regardless of his power, must bow to what is truly sovereign; and, more importantly, that there is some "celestial reality" that is forever and truly superordinate to any earthly or secular ruler or even to an explicit principle or law. It would be very careless and dangerous of us to forget that the impetus to do so—to eradicate slavery and tyranny; to subordinate authority to the transcendentally sovereign—was clearly (and I am speaking historically as well as psychologically) a consequence of the ethos established in nascent but potent form at the beginning of the Genesis account.[56]

Do we "believe" that we are made, man and woman alike, in the very image of God? And, if so, what does it mean to believe? And if not, what do we believe instead—or do we merely believe in nothing and suffer the terrible anxiety-provoking, hope-devouring, and socially destabilizing consequences of that? With the belief in "God above" in place, what do our marriages, families, friendships, and societies look like—and how do they appear when something else is substituted instead as goal or foundation? Is it not the case that tyranny or slavery will rule—and immediately—at all of those levels (and, equally, at the level of the intrapersonal, psychological, or spiritual) if this cornerstone is rejected? And that tyranny and slavery are also inevitably allied with the domination of hedonistic whim and the short-term, immature, and narrowly self-centered gratification of desire that does not and cannot make for either a sustainable self-realization or a productive, generous, and harmonious polity.

And what does acceptance of this proposition of divine intrinsic value mean if it is fully realized?

2

◆

Adam, Eve, Pride, Self-Consciousness, and the Fall

2.1. The image of God in the eternal garden

In Genesis 1, a series of narrative propositions emerge: that existence is the consequence of an eternal, transcendent spirit acting upon potential itself; that the habitable order that is good emerges from the workings of that spirit; that man and woman are made in the likeness of that spirit; and that this spirit is what has proper and eternal dominion over creation. Genesis 1 insists that man and woman are veritable images of God. Such an image is not God, precisely, but a low-resolution sampling of the original; something of the same nature, in many ways, on a lesser, more restricted scale; something that is *kenotic*,[1] emptied, in relationship to the original; something that is an *icon* or even *avatar*[2] of the original. These presumptions are echoed very soon thereafter in Genesis 2, a chapter that offers a more deeply embodied, primal portrayal: "And the Lord God formed man of the dust of the ground, and breathed into his nostrils the breath of life; and man became a living soul" (Genesis 2:7).

Is the idea of man as an image of God not utterly preposterous? How could flawed man, even the lowliest man or woman, possess a direct relationship to the divine? Man, with his propensity for decrepitude, suffering, and death; his self-evident insignificance contrasted with nature and the cosmos; the brevity of his life—why attribute value to something so fleeting in its existence and contemptible in its inadequacy? But, in the absence of that divine proposition, where would we be? How could the common man otherwise be credited with any a priori status whatsoever—particularly in relation to those fully capable of enacting the principle of might that would otherwise definitely make right, and often threatens to, regardless? How could we possibly manage without the tradition of inalienable rights and intrinsic individual responsibility that is the logical consequence of that axiomatic proclamation of our sacred worth? That insistence is a notion both unlikely and significant beyond measure. It is perhaps the greatest idea ever revealed—and, as the central idea of the biblical corpus, it is the very foundation of the Judeo-Christian tradition. This is an axiom, a proclamation—something that must be established as a cornerstone before any society whatsoever can appear; something that must be accepted "in faith" as a necessary rule before the game can even begin.

Much of the faith that is truly religious is of the same form: it is not the insistence that something superstitious or impossible was true but the proclamation and definition of what constitutes, comprises, or characterizes the real and that should therefore be attended to most diligently and acted on. This is irreducibly a decision, not least because we can never know enough ahead of time to be certain, and must move forward with assumption in the face of our ignorance. Marriage offers a helpful analogy: a marriage cannot commence without faith in its permanence. Is the evidence for its permanence there prior to the commitment? No. Furthermore, the evidence that would be necessary cannot be gathered in any manner without the a priori commitment—the vow to play that particular game and none other. All the crucial decisions of life are made on principle, not in consequence of sufficient evidence. That does not mean that we should move forward stupidly and blindly. Whenever we face the truly unknown, however, we are obliged to move forward with faith. The alternative is grim indeed.

In Genesis 2, God's transformation of chaos and nothingness into habitable being is particularized. God creates the first truly human place of habitation:

> And the Lord God planted a garden eastward in Eden; and there he put the man whom he had formed.
>
> And out of the ground made the Lord God to grow every tree that is pleasant to the sight, and good for food; the tree of life also in the midst of the garden, and the tree of knowledge of good and evil.
>
> And a river went out of Eden to water the garden; and from thence it was parted, and became into four heads.
>
> *Genesis 2:8–10*

This garden is the optimal human environment, represented in imaginative abstraction. It is the archetypal dwelling place where culture or order (the walls) and nature or chaos (the plants, trees, birds, and animals) coexist in proper balance. It is both origin and eternal perfect destination: the "walled garden" (for that is what the word *paradise—pairi daiza*—means[3]), the well-watered place (for that is what the word *Eden* means[4]). It is the reestablishment of that optimal place that is the implicit goal of every homeowner who envisions a backyard garden; his or her own fenced-in variant of the original Eden. (And even if the fence is manifest only in the abstract, as ownership, the enclosure is still walled by the boundaries of social convention.)

Men and women work or sacrifice naturally toward establishing an environment that eternally circumscribes nature within culture; one that protects and shelters while also enabling and providing opportunity. We dream of our own private green and natural space and, failing that, at least an apartment close to a park. We want it hemmed in—separated; bordered. We want to know exactly what we are responsible for and have a right to in relation to the expectation and property of others. We then strive to make it beautiful, peaceful, and secure, and are intrinsically oriented toward that perfection. That orientation is a spirit; a process or pattern that inhabits us, piques our interest, directs our attention, and motivates our action. What do we want to happen there, in our gardens, if and when we get it right? We may well be incapable of tending the whole world, but we can manage our own small private natural spaces, and that is far from nothing.

How might we envision such a place? What are we doing with that small section of land if we summon the right spirit? When a new building was established in traditional India:[5]

> [B]efore a single stone is laid, "the astrologer shows what spot in the foundation is exactly above the head of the snake that supports the world. The mason fashions a little wooden peg from the wood of the Khadira tree, and with a coconut drives the peg into the ground at this particular spot, in such a way as to peg the head of the snake securely down. . . . If this snake should ever shake its head really violently, it would shake the world to pieces."[6] A foundation stone is placed above the peg. The cornerstone is thus situated exactly at the "center of the world." But the act of foundation at the same time repeats the cosmogonic act, for to "secure" the snake's head, to drive the peg into it, is to imitate the primordial gesture of Soma (Rig Veda II, 12, 1) or of Indra when the latter "smote the Serpent in his lair" (Rig Veda, VI, 17, 9), when his thunderbolt "cut off his head" (Rig Veda I, 52, 10).[7]

This pegging down of the shifting snake that underlies everything, no matter how invisibly, is the planting of the rod of custom or flagstaff in the center, to stabilize and orient ourselves and the community. It is the dynamic between guiding staff and serpent that Moses has mastered and displays for the Pharaoh, the Egyptians, and the Israelites. It is even the spear that St. George and St. Michael drive through the heart of the dragon, to defeat chaos and evil. We want and need our walled garden to be delimited; we want it to be ours, so that we can benefit, in the long run, from our short-term sacrifices of time, effort, and money in pursuit of our dream: hence the walls. We invite nature to express herself within the confines of those constraints in a manner that is attractive and interesting. We work toward that goal—that vision of the promised land. In that work, we find peace and happiness. We can sit out there with our family and our friends in a hospitable manner, dining at the celestial table, so to speak. There is a spirit that inhabits us while we do that, if it is done properly. It is the same Word that gives rise to garden and cosmos. The proper environment of the men and women made in the image of God is the place optimally balanced between culture and nature—between order and chaos. That is also the place, as we have seen, of optimized consciousness.

This Edenic environment has been traditionally represented (and is so described in the text) as a territory divided by rivers into four parts: "And a river went out of Eden to water the garden; and from thence it was parted, and became into four heads" (Genesis 2:10). Such a division and arrangement forms a geometric structure known as a mandala,[8] which is a cross superimposed on a circle and often (but not necessarily) surrounded by a square. A mandala is a representation of optimized order, as such: the psychological or conceptual equivalent of paradise.[9] This fourfold division, stemming from a center, is the place man always stands in the world, with the cardinal directions (north, south, east, and west) stretching out from there. It has the same cruciform structure as a cathedral, which is an architectural image of the idea of a divine or heavenly center as well as a concrete instantiation of Eden. The garden theme permeates cathedral design, duplicating the primeval forest in stone with branching, treelike arches and illumination flooding in through its stained-glass windows, just as the sunlight in a grove filters through leaves and branches.

2.2. Pride versus the sacred moral order

In Genesis 2, God establishes the walled garden and grants man dominion over it: "And the Lord God commanded the man, saying, Of every tree of the garden thou mayest freely eat" (Genesis 2:15). In this manner, God provides man and woman with almost complete freedom to explore, incorporate, and

otherwise use everything the world provides, with two important excep-
tions: First is the command to exercise dominion in a manner that replenishes the earth and puts everything in its proper place (Genesis 1:28) and,
likewise, to dress the garden and keep it (Genesis 2:15).[10] Second, they are to
avoid ingesting the fruit of one of the central trees in the garden: "But of the
tree of the knowledge of good and evil, thou shalt not eat of it: for in the day
that thou eatest thereof thou shalt surely die" (Genesis 2:17).

Life in the properly managed Edenic garden is something extant in a state
of dynamic play—order challenged, updated, and extended by chaos; man
dynamically juxtaposed against, competing, and cooperating with woman;
man and woman operating according to God's will (realizing themselves as
images of God), continually extending and further perfecting that which is
already good or very good. Paradise thus has the same nature as a great piece
of music—say, the third movement of Bach's *Third Brandenburg Concerto*—
a composition unparalleled both in its ability to balance the predictable and
expected against the unpredictable and novel, and to simultaneously bring
forth out of something already beautiful and perfect something ever more
beautiful and still more perfect. This is a mode of being, of ever-improving
harmony, exemplified by music, the "condition" toward which "all art constantly aspires."[11] This is the good that can become very good.

But humanity is also called upon while attending and acting to leave the
very moral foundations of the world in place, unchallenged—or even untouched, entirely, in the rejection of the forbidden fruit. Something is therefore deemed to remain necessarily forever beyond human judgment, with
regard to the nature of good and evil; something is to be set immovably at
the base, or elevated, permanently, to the highest place; something is to be
regarded as transcendentally untouchable or ineffable. Is this not precisely
the set of moral principles already established and insisted upon? The fact of
the eternal interplay between order and chaos, God and *tehom*; the presumption that the order realized by the Word is good and that human beings
are very good; the idea that man and woman are made in the image of God?
These axioms are not to be made part of the domain of human knowledge or
replaced by some hypothetically useful or convenient earthly dogma. They

are, instead, to remain sacred; to forever serve and be regarded and treated as the very preconditions for that knowledge.

Genesis 2 therefore extends the characterization of God, presenting him as the spirit that warns against overreach—against the cardinal sin of pride. What might *overreach* mean? Paradise, or Eden, is eternally a garden, with two primordial fruit-bearing trees at its center: "And out of the ground made the Lord God to grow every tree that is pleasant to the sight, and good for food; the tree of life also in the midst of the garden, and the tree of knowledge of good and evil" (Genesis 2:9). These two trees bear some deep and mysterious relationship to each other. The tree of life bears the fruit whose incorporation brings life, even eternal life. The tree of the knowledge of good and evil is its opposite; it is the tree that harbors the eternal serpent and bears the fruit whose incorporation brings death.

What does this mean? *That which is necessarily and inevitably axiomatic— that upon which everything else depends—is to be touched at great peril.* That which is axiomatic and foundational provides protection against the chaos that shatters; against the entropy that swirls, dissolves, consumes hope, and drowns. Something has to be held as sacred—in this case, the very foundation upon which good and evil themselves are predicated. This is the stake driven through the head of the underground serpent whose movement would otherwise shake the world to pieces. It is a (the?) great sin of pride to question that which on everything necessarily depends. *Do not touch what must necessarily remain sacred.* Otherwise, the center cannot hold, and things fall apart. Something has to be the unmovable object—the sacred staff, the unshakeable pillar, and even, perhaps, the tree for the serpent. Something has to be that around which everything else arranges itself. That is God Himself, ineffable though He may be. The closer to God the presumption, the more care must be taken in its approach, let alone its rejection or revolutionary overthrow. Extraordinary claims require extraordinary evidence—something said in many forms by many people.[12]

The attempt to make the moral enterprise a matter of human judgment rather than to leave in place a necessary minimum of assumptions is to make the prideful move that transforms the rock upon which the house would otherwise stand into the sand that shifts, moves, and devours when the storm comes. It is in keeping with this that Christ—the very incarnation of the Word that established such principles—much later insists:

> Therefore whosoever heareth these sayings of mine, and doeth them, I will liken him unto a wise man, which built his house upon a rock:
>
> And the rain descended, and the floods came, and the winds blew, and beat upon that house; and it fell not: for it was founded upon a rock.
>
> And every one that heareth these sayings of mine, and doeth them not, shall be likened unto a foolish man, which built his house upon the sand:
>
> And the rain descended, and the floods came, and the winds blew, and beat upon that house; and it fell: and great was the fall of it.
>
> *Matthew 7:24–27*

The finite and known is surrounded by the infinite and unknown. The former cannot subsume the latter; if it tries, overextending itself, it risks perishing. It is necessary, even crucial, to understand: the periphery, the margin, is not merely a singular antithesis to the one at the center, nor its opposite, as is commonly presumed. The opposite of the one is not the other but the many, and then the innumerable, and then the monstrous, and then inconceivable, and then the utter chaos that is worse than death. The opposite of the one is multiplicity itself—the very multiplicity whose revolutionary triumph might well deprioritize the center, however temporarily it manages such a thing. Nonetheless, that "victory" will wreak havoc among whatever peripheral or experimental phenomena that had managed to find a place in the margin of tolerance that necessarily surrounds any ideal.

This is true not least because the peripheral or experimental has a more fragile grip on identity than the center and can therefore be destabilized with greater ease. The semifunctional or avant-garde operates therefore nearer those who walk the straight and narrow path than among the extreme outliers of the frontier, regardless of their opinion about such matters. The extreme outliers are monsters who would devour and destroy everything, including the avant-garde (and perhaps and likely the latter first). To put it another way: The fringe can exist around the center with some care taken on both sides. It can exist in a fragile but perhaps mutually beneficial truce (given the advantages of both stability and variation). If the fringe clamors to be centered, however, in consequence of falling prey to the resentment and bitterness that is almost inevitably part of life in the shadow of the ideal, then the fringe of the fringe will begin to make its appearance. When the ideal, that terrible but necessary judge, weakens—and maybe in a manner that is welcome to the excluded, even the oppressed—then the predatory and parasitical dragons of the truly chaotic come storming back. What then? The now falsely elevated, previously marginal, and now hypothetically centered are the first heads on the chopping block.

It is also the case that centering the margin would eliminate whatever hedonic utility the marginal in fact possesses. It is the fact of the transgression, and the novelty that accompanies such deviant action, that raises the fetish, whatever its nature, to the status of aphrodisiac. Novelty itself is a form of incentive reward. Thus, participation in novel acts (which are by definition marginal, although they can be positive in an exploratory way as well as rebellious in a merely transgressive way) heightens pleasure. This is as true for aesthetic pleasures ranging from the gustatory to the artistic as it is on the sexual front. Thus, the movement of the marginal to the position of norm or ideal undermines even the pathologically immature exacerbation of pleasure that is the goal of so many marginal practices—and threatens even the more genuine and valid pleasure that is to be experienced as a consequence of participation in the true and even redemptive avant-garde. This is another disadvantage, particularly to the creative, of all attempts to permanently subvert the normal or ideal order. If everyone is or has to wear a dog mask, for example, no one can have any disobedient fun in one.

Because the marginal is multiplicity, the marginalized cannot be celebrated, as celebrated means raised to the place of primacy, and a plethora cannot be made the focus of singular attention. By definition. By the very fact of the difference between the one and the many. The man who bites off more than he can chew, or the society that does the same, therefore risks choking, risks death, or worse, in the attempt to incorporate the inedible. The knowledge of man cannot, in the final analysis, maintain its integrity in the face of everything that is as of yet and possibly even forever unknown. What stops the infinite regress of doubt in the face of genuine ultimate ignorance? To ask why, why, why, why, why—forever.

When I was teaching at the University of Toronto, I often demonstrated this to my seminar students, choosing one of them to harass—asking him or her, "Why did you do the readings for this class?" ("Because I wanted to be prepared for the discussion.") "Why did it matter to you if you were thus prepared?" ("Because I wanted to do well in the class.") "Why did you care to do well?" ("Because I wanted to pass the course.") "Why does it matter to you if you pass the course?" ("Because I want to get my degree.") "Why do you care to get your degree?" ("I want to be competitive in the job market after I graduate.") "Why does such success make any difference to you?" It was at this point, climbing Jacob's Ladder or descending into the underworld, that the going often began to get difficult for the person so questioned. "If I do not have a good job, I will be miserable and have no money." "Why does it matter to anyone, including you, if you are suffering and broke?" At the end of Tolstoy's *Confessions*, detailing not least his descent into an intensely suicidal nihilism and consequent emergence, the great Russian author describes a dream (condensed and rearranged for the purposes of the present illustration):

> I see that I am lying in bed. Feeling neither good nor bad, I am lying on my back. But I begin to wonder whether it is a good thing for me to be lying there; and it seems to me that there is something wrong with my legs; whether they are too short or uneven, I do not know, but there is something awkward about them. Only now do I ask myself what had not yet occurred to me: where am I and what am I lying on? I begin to look around, and the first place I look is down

toward where my body is dangling, in the direction where I feel I must soon fall. I look below, and I cannot believe my eyes. I am resting on a height such as I could never have imagined, a height altogether unlike that of the highest tower or mountain. Looking about my bed, I see that I am lying on some cords woven together and attached to the sides of the bed. My heels are resting on one of the cords and my lower legs on another in an uncomfortable way. Somehow I know that these cords can be shifted. My heart stops, and I am overcome with horror. It is horrible to look down there. I feel that if I look down, I will immediately slip from the last cord and perish. I do not look, yet not looking is worse, for now I am thinking about what will happen to me as soon as the last cord breaks. I feel that I am losing the last ounce of my strength from sheer terror and that my back is slowly sinking lower and lower. Another instant and I shall break away.

Above me there is also an abyss. I gaze into this abyss of sky and try to forget about the one below, and I actually do forget. The infinity below repels and horrifies me; the infinity above attracts me and gives me strength. Thus I am hanging over the abyss suspended by the last of the cords that have not yet slipped out from under me. I know I am hanging there, but I am only looking upward, and my terror passes. As it happens in a dream, a voice is saying, "Mark this, this is it!" I gaze deeper and deeper into the infinity above me, and I seem to grow calm.[13]

There is no necessary place or point where the questioning ends. It can all too easily become the infinite regress that quells motivation and petrifies or paralyzes. No students attending in a class—indeed, no people participating in any activity whatsoever—do so without assuming something; do so except on the basis of a faith, however implicit that faith might be. The buck has to stop somewhere. Otherwise, they would be mired in doubt, indecisive, stuck at a crossroads, falling apart, headed every which or no way at all, instead of focusing on the task at hand. This state of confusion is all too likely. When individuals and societies lose faith in their goals, at any level of the "heavenly hierarchy," they question and then subvert their identity or purpose, and end up lost in the desert: anxious, depressed, and devoid of hope; bitter and cynical; untethered and nihilistic; hedonistic and power-mad. Paralytic inaction and fragmented confusion are the default state. This happens when the integrity or even the existence of the topmost level becomes questionable—and perhaps most devastatingly, even if the full consequences of this collapse take decades or longer to manifest. Thus, a certain faith in cosmos, garden, and self constitutes a necessary foundation for forward movement; an inescapable foundation, even, because the alternative is the infinite regress of doubt and the descent into the abyss.

None of this is to say that deep questioning is never called for: in the face of repeated failure, the presumptions guiding our movement must be challenged, step-by-step; deeper, incrementally, if modest correction fails. But the baby should not be thrown out with the bathwater every time an obstacle appears. This is particularly true when the baby in question is the divine infant. What is the rule, instead? Minimal correction necessary to keep the ship on course, or to reestablish a new destination. How can we find what we have faith in, even if we do not know, explicitly, that such faith is there? By noting where our questioning stops, whether the questions are asked by another person or realized themselves, personally, in the form of doubt. If the blocks of our foundation have not been made explicit—made conscious objects of apprehension or statable, imaginable, or at least imitable principles—they are still there implicitly, insofar as the journey uphill is continuing. A religious tradition is the revelation and communication of the necessarily axiomatic, at least in dramatic and narrative form. These stories that unite keep everyone moving in the same direction, looking at the same world, experiencing the same emotions; there is little difference between that and productive peace. Is it true that the more these stories are understood, as well as told, the more union appears, both psychologically and communally? It is a good thing to imitate, act out, and imagine, but if conscious understanding is also on board, then one additional source of disunion has been not only eliminated but transformed into something that can now serve as an active participant rather than as a mere critical observer.

The axioms of traditional morality are stakes in the ground, rods of tradition—but every rod of tradition has its accompanying serpent, the living spirit that originally established the tradition and that constantly renews it.

2.3. The incompleteness of Adam and the arrival of Eve

Adam's role as naming spirit has just been established when the story takes an odd segue: "And Adam gave names to all cattle, and to the fowl of the air, and to every beast of the field; but for Adam there was not found an help meet for him" (Genesis 2:20). It is not Eve who is directly assigned the task of naming. She is instead a necessary partner to that conceptualizing process, speaking or standing (optimally, in a beneficial or even playful manner) for that which has not yet been included in the domain of conceptualization or within the process of generating the habitable order that is good or very good. Why? Well, she is, after all, the archetypal mother of mankind, as well as mate and partner to Adam. Perhaps that outsider status is the eternal situation of the child—with his or her individual and particularized peculiarities and idiosyncrasies as well as notable and unique special talents. Any new child, for example—or any change in the circumstances or personality of any child—must be incorporated into the currently extant functional order, Adam's domain, which must in consequence broaden or transform to meet the new set of wants and needs. The cry of the child—more generally, the vulnerable or excluded—is the paramount concern of the eternal mother.

There are a variety of potential reasons for the marked and consistent sex differences discussed earlier.[14] Some of these differences arise in women at the time of sexual maturation, and for reasons related to precisely that. The difference in the experience of negative emotion and, therefore, self-consciousness emerges in adolescence.[15] This is perhaps because the size and strength differences between men and women—particularly in the upper-body power so key to victory in physical combat[16]—also appear at that time, making additional anxiety-mediated caution in relationship to men necessary and wise. Further, it is at puberty when the potential cataclysm of unwanted pregnancy first threatens. But the fundamental driving force behind the differentiation of women from men in personality and interest is likely the need for heightened responsivity to threat and for close relationships that aid in care for dependent others. It is postadolescent women who are most reliably and consistently called on to care for vulnerable infants, for example. There is no reason to assume, a priori, that the emotional responses of women have evolved only for their immediate personal benefit (rather than to aid in both survival and reproductive success, considered over the longer term). It makes more sense to consider the heightened anxiety and self-consciousness of women a negotiated solution to the joint problems of the mother-infant dyad. The depth of such proclivity for self-sacrifice should not be underestimated. It reaches into the very bones themselves. Women can detect while breastfeeding the lack of sufficient calcium in the bodies of their infants, for example, and will even decalcify their own skeletons, spilling the resultant excess into their breast milk to redress the lack in their children.[17]

It is no coincidence, perhaps, that the sacred image of woman is not so much woman as it is woman and infant. What is a woman, alone? A target of short-term sexual gratification, made so by the venality of men oriented toward such a pursuit, although enticed into such things by the possession of her own hedonism? A pawn in the patriarchal order, just as a man might be, although without the full panoply of benefits that social status per se confers upon men?[18] There is no reason whatsoever to assume that the fundamental unit of psychological integration or social order is the atomized and subjectively defined individual. This goes for men, too, who are unlikely to be men and much more likely to be immature hedonists or manipulative power players until they become masters of the responsibility that appears with woman and child. The classic liberal emphasis on the individual works only when the individual, so defined, is already enmeshed however unconsciously in a transcendental ethos or story that makes his or her individuality one of voluntarily self-sacrificial responsibility rather than a manifestation of might or whim.

Women's heightened self-consciousness spills over into the domain of men because men are required to adapt themselves to women and their concerns. The female proclivity for increased experience of negative emotion and heightened sensitivity to interpersonal interaction and conflict means that they are also more likely to highlight, by inference and direct action, the perennial inadequacy of men. This is why the scales fall from Adam's eyes when he eats the fruit offered to him by Eve: he becomes self-conscious, aware of his own nakedness (something he then forever blames on the woman, or on God Himself, for creating her). The male need to be attractive to women means that men will bend over backward to provide[19]—or, in the case of pathological men, appear to provide[20]—whatsoever is desired by a potential mate. Women are much more likely than men to reject others, sexually and with regard to relationship. They are much more likely to refuse a given sexual overture, when so-called short-term mating opportunities arise.[21] They also precipitate divorce in some seventy percent of cases.[22] Further, women are more prone to engage in indirect, relational aggression and gossip (with the end goal of socially ostracizing a potential rival).[23] This proclivity arguably increases the self-consciousness of men: Women, with their higher capacity for decoding nonverbal behavior, are also more sensitive to displays of female physical attractiveness and "mate poaching" behavior, such as flirting, and are likely to punish that harshly, even among their friends. "Heaven has no rage like love to hatred turned, nor hell a fury like a woman scorned."[24]

What does this all suggest? Women aggregate the concerns of those they are specialized, in some deep sense, to attend to and care for. They then bring these concerns to the attention of their male partners, specialized, in turn, for outward striving, confronting the natural enemies of hearth and kin, competing and cooperating for hierarchical positioning and garnering the benefits thereof in the broader social world. In that manner, women benefit from the additional resources that men can bring to bear on the problems of dependent care, even as they struggle under the necessity of providing that care. Men, in turn, benefit from an expansion of their self-consciousness, and then consciousness, under the pressure of women's heightened sensitivity, while bearing the brunt of the harsh evaluation and rejection that is part and parcel of that gift.[25]

2.4. The eternal sins of Eve and Adam

Now the serpent was more subtil than any beast of the field which the Lord God had made. And he said unto the woman, Yea, hath God said, Ye shall not eat of every tree of the garden?

And the woman said unto the serpent, We may eat of the fruit of the trees of the garden:

But of the fruit of the tree which is in the midst of the garden, God hath said, Ye shall not eat of it, neither shall ye touch it, lest ye die.

And the serpent said unto the woman, Ye shall not surely die:

For God doth know that in the day ye eat thereof, then your eyes shall be opened, and ye shall be as gods, knowing good and evil.

And when the woman saw that the tree was good for food, and that it was pleasant to the eyes, and a tree to be desired to make one wise, she took of the fruit thereof, and did eat, and gave also unto her husband with her; and he did eat.

And the eyes of them both were opened, and they knew that they were naked; and they sewed fig leaves together, and made themselves aprons.

Genesis 3:1–7

Imagine that your life is progressing well. You dwell in an orderly, beautiful garden, optimally balanced between structure and possibility. But you have neither incorporated nor conquered all things. You have established a conceptual structure, but a fringe remains: that which or indeed those who do not fit the ordered pattern and are marginalized. Should the order be restructured so that all those who do not fit can now be included? This is not simply managed. A veritable multitude of forms lurk on the margin. No multiplicity can be made the center of a unity, and there is no perception, much less stability or hope, in the absence of a unity. All? All is too much. Inclusion of the margin means entropy overwhelms order—and if the margin is not sufficient to overwhelm, the margin of the margin will most definitely suffice. Every fringe has its more extreme fringe.

The act of categorization is a determination of order—the order that is necessary but also forever incomplete (and sometimes direly so). Therefore, something or someone must stand for that which has not yet been brought or incorporated into the structure of order. The union of the capacity to categorize and order with the necessity of attending to that which is still outside and lost constitutes the complete human spirit, most accurately reflecting the spirit of God. Genesis emphasizes this unity: "Therefore shall a man leave his father and his mother, and shall cleave unto his wife: and they shall be one flesh" (Genesis 2:24). C. G. Jung notes further:

> [M]an's imagination has been preoccupied with this idea over and over again on the high and even the highest levels of culture, as we can see from the late Greek and syncretic philosophy of Gnosticism. The hermaphroditic rebus had an important part to play in the natural philosophy of the Middle Ages. And in our own day we hear of Christ's androgyny in Catholic mysticism.[26]

This unity of masculine and feminine will be seen in the heroic Christ who exists in implicit form (say, as the unborn Savior of the World) within Mary; or the maternal, implicit within Christ, manifest as the love that redeems the world. The feminine (Mary) is thus the mandorla that encapsulates both God the Father and the crucified Son. This union is the order, superimposed on a background of chaos and possibility, giving rise to the redemptive self-sacrificing Word itself—the Word that is in turn the divine individual who, fully and completely, accepts his fate in the world; his destiny. The consequence of this union—at least initially, when it is operating in the proper spirit—is ultimate protection against the catastrophe of self-consciousness (represented as "nakedness"): "And they were both naked, the man and his wife, and were not ashamed" (Genesis 2:25). That self-consciousness is precisely what emerges in the aftermath of prideful overreach.

Eve falls prey to temptation and consorts with the serpent. That serpent is both what is marginal, even monstrous (as the snake is a truly and genuinely poisonous agent), and the eternal temptation of pride—the pride that wishes to usurp or take the place of God. We can imagine the serpent's approach, whispering, "Embrace me, and take to yourself the prerogative of the divine, mastery over the moral order itself—definition of good and evil itself." Eve's sin and, therefore, the eternal temptation or flaw of the feminine? "My compassion is so all-encompassing that it can convert and incorporate even that which is deadly poison; my compassion is so total that it can transform such poison into veritable nourishment—and the nourishment of the enlightened, at that." This sudden awareness of something that is deeply unconscious produces a spasm of self-consciousness. Eve discovers the dread depth of her presumption; Adam follows, as he allows himself to be tempted by his new partner—and, in doing so, by her new partner, who is both the poisonous serpent and, at a higher level of abstraction, the eternal adversary himself (as the most poisonous of possible snakes). Both the mother and father of mankind are tempted to assimilate something that cannot and must not be consumed, albeit for different reasons, specific to each sex—and everything falls apart. The enlightenment longed for and motivating this sin certainly descends, as Genesis immediately relates—although not in the manner expected, and not in a manner that anyone truly awake and properly humble would wish for.

The serpent is "subtil," camouflaged, lurking; masquerading as something that it is not; indistinguishable from the undergrowth or foliage; blending in almost perfectly with what has already been taken for granted; tempting the unwary to assume that it is something it is not:[27] "It looks so harmless! What could possibly go wrong?" This is the parasite's or predator's pretense of irrelevance. "Could the gates not open for them, too?" That is a fine question, when it is motivated by a compassion that is truly discerning, judicious, and discriminating, but something utterly inappropriate when it is asked for no other reason than to falsely and deceptively elevate the perceived moral status of the questioner. Eve's sin: hearkening to the blandishments of the eternally serpentine.[28] Adam's sin? Hearkening endlessly to the voice of Eve. Sins of pride, in both cases: in Eve's, the narcissism of compassion: "I am the mother who can encompass all." Adam's sin: "I can retool and rename order itself, indefinitely—all to impress Eve." Both presume too much—albeit for different reasons (reasons that nonetheless find their union in that prideful sin).

The temptation that eternally confronts the woman, therefore, is the idea that maternal benevolence can be pridefully extended to the entire world, to even the most poisonous of snakes, and the associated temptation to make much of that, on the social front—to use her compassion, however ill-placed and false, to claim unearned moral virtue and ability, to draw undeserved attention to herself from individual men of interest or within her broader social community. Maternal compassion is the spirit of the feminine, bestowed on the individual woman. It is not something to take pride in, as it is not, as such, an individual accomplishment. It is instead something that can be invited in to possess and that must be regarded in humility as a gift from God—a talent bestowed, rather than a flag of virtue to be presumptuously and self-servingly paraded. The parallel temptation confronting the man is to hearken to this false voice of inclusive and indiscriminate familiarity and kinship, and to claim for his own self-serving and self-aggrandizing purposes the capacity to expand beyond its limits the domain over which he has established a certain degree of mastery.

There is a corresponding and equally deadly sin of Adam—the fundamental temptation or flaw of the masculine, the proclamation to Eve: "I can incorporate, master, name and subdue, and put into proper order anything that you bring before me, no matter how overreaching, preposterous, or even outright deadly the presumption that it be included." All to impress Eve, as men do so often to impress women. One terrible reality of this destructive dance is how closely it resembles the deepest moral striving and ability, when genuine (we should strive to further our domain of care, and to extend our responsibility), and the worst of all possible sins, the eternal fall, when it is not (when we falsely lay claim to what we have managed and mastered). God help us all, truly, in the face of our prideful compassion and false confidence. How much of the suffering of the world is a consequence of presumptuous overreach; of the desire to usurp, and to claim for ourselves something that we cannot manage, do not deserve, and should serve instead of strive to so falsely master? How much suffering enters the world with the fall of man into presumption and pride? There is something to this insistence that is ignored at our peril.   *Believe in God or Belong to God*

The concerns Eve brings to Adam force him to restructure his personality and, more broadly, the social order he has established and is responsible for both maintaining and updating. Every man is, of course, a work in progress, and the social order is always incomplete, not least as a consequence of its exclusionary and often too-arbitrary nature. But that does not mean that all men can perforce be rejected until some perfect specimen emerges, or that order can be dispensed with altogether, or that it can be infinitely, immediately, and on demand expanded. Further, the inadequacy of man does not imply the superiority of women, and the presumption of that superiority, on moral grounds, inevitably leads to devastating consequences. Of course, the reverse is equally true.

Imagine that something is not known to a given man, or that he is not taking appropriate care in some regard—particularly when he should have known or cared, given his age, knowledge, competence, or status. Some might perceive in this lack a lurking immaturity or other shameful inadequacy. Now, imagine that lack is suddenly highlighted, in direct consequence of female dissatisfaction and rejection, emotional or sexual. Then consider the anger, bitterness, and even desire for revenge—against her, world, himself, and God—that might emerge. As Adam said to God, unforgivably: "The woman whom thou gavest to me, she gave me of the tree, and I did eat" (Genesis 3:12). The first man could have taken another tack: he could have rejected his new partner's request, remained obedient to the divine, and forgone the fall entirely, instead of pridefully accepting Eve's challenge. Even in the aftermath of his error, he could have refused to cast the blame on his mate and the divine force that produced her, accepted responsibility for his insufficiency, and atoned. But no; worse, he doubled down on his pride, extending it even to self-righteously and self-pityingly claiming moral superiority over God. Thus, everything that transpired, and that continues to do so.

To eat is to consume, incorporate, assimilate, develop, grow. Not everything can be eaten, however—only what is meet, so to speak; only everything in proper proportion—and certainly not what is poison, no matter how tempting and attractive. The serpent is anomaly itself; the infinite forever lurking within the finite; that which does not fit. It is the dragon whose treasure eternally tempts. It is also, however, that which cannot be incorporated. The fruit of the immortal serpent is that which cannot be made edible. But the temptation to bite off more than can be chewed nonetheless perpetually beckons. My S, n

2.5. The eternal serpent

Why do we associate the serpent in the garden with Satan himself? There is no direct indication of such a relationship in the text itself, so we have to look more broadly for an answer—to nature, to tradition, and to context. The serpent is the proximal predator or adversary—that which is poison and which devours, concretely, here and now, as in the case of an actual viper, crocodile, shark, or python. Satan, by contrast—and extension—is the adversary, *as such*. The bite of a poisonous snake is certainly to be feared. Children have to be protected against such an eventuality, and it is a heroic task to confront a poisonous reptile and to provide such shelter. Imagine this task, writ large: Satan is the psychological or abstract equivalent of the concretely predatory and venomous; the worst of all conceivable snakes; the eternal meta-snake. His dwelling place is not the undergrowth of the garden of the natural world but the nether reaches of the human soul. His defeat occurs as a consequence not of hunting and killing, as when a nest of vipers is put to the flame, but of true moral striving, which is the most fundamental

pattern of the activities characterizing, for example, the serpent-slaying saints
George and Patrick, and the archangel Michael, at the end or culmination of
time (Revelation 12:7–9):

> And there was war in heaven: Michael and his angels fought against
> the dragon; and the dragon fought and his angels,
>
> And prevailed not; neither was their place found any more in
> heaven.
>
> And the great dragon was cast out, that old serpent, called the
> Devil, and Satan, which deceiveth the whole world: he was cast out
> into the earth, and his angels were cast out with him.

Satan as the essence of the predatory, parasitical, and reptilian is the spirit
of murderous resentment, the prince of lies and darkness—the adversary of
being, the shameless accuser, the essence of malevolence. He is as well the
King of Pride—the pride that sets itself up over God and claims that the
transcendent can be dispensed with, in favor of his rule. This characterization is stressed in the opening stanzas of John Milton's *Paradise Lost*, which
give the following account of the great deceiver:

> Th' infernal Serpent; he it was, whose guile
> Stird up with Envy and Revenge, deceiv'd
> The Mother of Mankind, what time his Pride
> Had cast him out from Heav'n, with all his Host
> Of Rebel Angels, by whose aid aspiring
> To set himself in Glory above his Peers,
> He trusted to have equal'd the most High,
> If he oppos'd; and with ambitious aim
> Against the Throne and Monarchy of God
> Rais'd impious War in Heav'n and Battel proud
> With vain attempt.[29]

It is specifically the pride of Satan, according to Milton, that entices forward the corresponding sentiment—and wish to rule—in Eve (and then in

Adam). To know good and evil is not merely to possess the knowledge of what is moral, as both Adam and Eve already know the rules: "And the Lord God commanded him, You may eat freely from every tree of the garden, but you must not eat from the tree of the knowledge of good and evil; for in the day that you eat of it, you will surely die" (Genesis 2:16–17). The "knowledge" indicated refers to the complete mastery that would allow for what is good and evil to be fashioned, altered, and defined by human design. This is precisely what the spirit of satanic pride offers Eve, even implying as he does so that the only reason for the original prohibition was something akin to God's envy or jealousy: "For God doth know that in the day ye eat thereof, then your eyes shall be opened, and ye shall be as gods, knowing good and evil" (Genesis 3:5). This is the taking to self not merely the ability to re-value all values, in the sense meant and recommended by Nietzsche,[30] but the ability to create values—to serve as the veritable source of value itself: the capability of God Himself.

This capability is simply not within the purview of man. The eternal values are given, as the bedrock of the identity that confers upon man and woman the essence of humanity itself. To be human is to share not only physical but metaphysical form—the very identity of value that is, for example, a precondition for any communication that does not degenerate into an infinite regress of questioning. Thus, we might ask someone, "Why are you angry?" but are not required to inquire, "What do you mean, 'angry'?" as the fact of our shared structure of bedrock values means that we all know, as humans, what being angry means. The same can be said not only of our basic emotional, or motivational states, but also of the manner in which those potentially competing states come to organize themselves into higher-order unities, both psychological and social. There is a domain of allowable variation, and experimentation is allowed and even encouraged on the fringe. But there is also an immutable center. This is the self-evident fact that gives the concept of "shared humanity," or even "human being," both its reality and its comprehensibility.

This means, by necessity, that any man or woman who steps outside the domain of the eternal human values has essentially ceased to be human and has therefore not so much transcended the human as destroyed it. What such stepping outside almost inevitably means in practice, as well, is not the grand and heroic transvaluation upward envisioned by Nietzsche. It is instead the degeneration and fragmentation of a uniting morality into hedonistic whim or the false incorporation or suppression of all such slavish impulse under the rubric of power. This is the elevation of narrow self-will to the highest conceivable place, in the guise of ultimate freedom. ("I can abide by whatever values I choose"—something that almost immediately deteriorates into "I can do whatever I want" or, more accurately, "Whatever impulse grips me rules.") This is simultaneously the presumption of subjective omniscience, omnipresence, and omnipotence. ("I have the capacity to determine the very definition of right and wrong, valuable and contemptible, good and evil.") It might be objected: Is this capacity not desirable? The appropriate response to that question is simple: Do you live, successfully, as of now, in Paradise? If not, does that mean that the cosmic order itself is of questionable validity, or that your perspective is dreadfully flawed? Better pray that it is the latter, rather than the former, because there is no hope if it is the former. Better look toward your own inadequacy and attempt to rectify it before calling God out for His insufficiency.

Milton's Satan is the prideful spirit who forever aims his ambition to reign "though in Hell"—a fate deemed better than to "serve in Heav'n."[31] Pride of this nature is allied symbolically, traditionally, and in the literary realm with the arrogance of intellect, the Luciferian spirit that regards its own knowledge, paradoxically, as both sufficiently sovereign and capable of limitless expansion. Faust, the protagonist of Goethe's great play by that name, is an exemplar of that prideful overreaching, driven as he is by an overweening desire for knowledge, understanding, and experience transcending all necessary and desirable human limits. Like Eve, and then Adam, Faust wants to possess more than is rightly allotted to the earthly sphere. Mephistopheles himself explains this to God:

> Forsooth! He serves you after strange devices:
> No earthly meat or drink the fool suffices:

The Beatitudes is the new 10 commandments. They are my rock. I do not presume to be omniscie[nt] It is the One. The opposite of one is not the other, but the ma[...]

His spirit's ferment far aspireth;
Half conscious of his frenzied, crazed unrest,
The fairest stars from Heaven he requireth,
From Earth the highest raptures and the best,
And all the Near and Far that he desireth
Fails to subdue the tumult of his breast.[32]

Such motivation begs the question: Is it knowledge or power that Faust more truly seeks, with all that intellectual inquiry only serving as a disguise? He certainly thinks highly enough of himself to justify the most cynical speculation concerning his aim:

I'm cleverer, true, than those fops of teachers,
Doctors and Magisters, Scribes and Preachers;
Neither scruples nor doubts come now to smite me,
Nor Hell nor Devil can longer affright me.[33]

It is by no means for nothing that the cloak of choice for Mephistopheles is that of a "Traveling Scholar."[34]

To return to Eve: If the current order does not serve that which is most vulnerable (and to do so is the moral injunction of femininity itself, in some real sense), then it is insufficient by definition. This does not at all mean, however, that everything outside, abandoned or marginal, is properly construed as vulnerable and deserving, or that everything should be appreciated and served, with no discrimination or judgment whatsoever, and all at once—or that the affectation of all-encompassing compassion is laudatory. The mere act of noting vulnerability, genuine or otherwise, by no means constitutes all that is good. The claim that it does is the essence of feminine pride, and it goes eternally before the fall. Good is much more complex and difficult than the compassion that is an instinct, or a divine gift—no matter how profound that compassion might be. This means that it is in the admirable nature of the feminine to call the attention of the masculine to that which is vulnerable and not being properly served—but that call can be amplified counterproductively by the temptations of narcissistic pride, to say it again: the spirit of God is that which warns us against acting incautiously in relation to the eternal serpent in the garden; that which advises us to beware of the temptation to take on, in the wrong attitude, more than we can rightfully bear.

2.6. Naked suffering as the fruit of sin

There is a Christian conceit that suffering itself is a consequence of the sin of Eve and Adam.[35] This is an idea directly derived from the punishment meted out by God in the aftermath of original sin to snake, man, and woman (or earned rightfully by reptile and human alike). The prideful serpent is doomed to crawl in the dust that is simultaneously death, the presumptuous woman to suffer and serve man in that suffering, and the arrogant and careless man to toil in sorrow against the pricks and die:

> And the Lord God said unto the serpent, Because thou hast done this, thou art cursed above all cattle, and above every beast of the field; upon thy belly shalt thou go, and dust shalt thou eat all the days of thy life:
>
> And I will put enmity between thee and the woman, and between thy seed and her seed; it shall bruise thy head, and thou shalt bruise his heel.
>
> Unto the woman he said, I will greatly multiply thy sorrow and thy conception; in sorrow thou shalt bring forth children; and thy desire shall be to thy husband, and he shall rule over thee.
>
> And unto Adam he said, Because thou hast hearkened unto the voice of thy wife, and hast eaten of the tree, of which I commanded thee, saying, Thou shalt not eat of it: cursed is the ground for thy sake; in sorrow shalt thou eat of it all the days of thy life;
>
> Thorns also and thistles shall it bring forth to thee; and thou shalt eat the herb of the field;

In the sweat of thy face shalt thou eat bread, till thou return unto
the ground; for out of it wast thou taken: for dust thou art, and unto
dust shalt thou return. (Genesis 3:14–19)

Consider, for a moment, the conditions of your own life. If you have not
encountered the spirit who punishes you for overweening pride, you are either fortunate beyond belief or self-deceptive to the point of delusion. It is
rightly said that "pride goeth before destruction, and an haughty spirit before a fall" (Proverbs 16:18). If you presume to be much more than you are—
if you presume a caring (Eve) or a competence (Adam) beyond that which is
properly yours—then you have taken upon yourself more than you can
rightfully manage, even though you may not immediately realize it. The
complexity of the world, which you have carelessly invited in, will overwhelm you, and you will suffer, dreadfully. If you take on, in your vanity,
more than you can master, you will pay the price and fail, and experience
anxiety, grief, shame, and pain. It is therefore an open question whether suffering itself is a consequence of the structure of existence (of our subjugation
to disease, insanity, social rejection, malevolence, and death), or whether it is
equally or more (or even completely) a consequence of the foolish self-conceit
that tempts us to claim, narcissistically, more than is warranted.

Imagine that we confronted that which is anomalous—that which is outside and rejected—in the proper proportion; that we took on only those tasks
for which we were truly suited. Imagine that on the feminine side we insisted
on our capacity only for the benevolent care we could competently provide,
and without resentment. Imagine that on the masculine side we admitted
to the insufficiency of our conceptions, without insisting too self-servingly
or tyrannically on their comprehensiveness or completeness, or agreeing too
thoughtlessly to adjust them merely to impress. To what degree could we
then face the challenges of the world, serious though they might be, in the
spirit that could genuinely rise to meet and master them? To what degree
could that be managed, say, in the spirit of serious play, rather than adopted
as a too-demanding, too-burdensome, and consequently suffering-ridden
venture? We desire above all, and appropriately, to find something to strive

for and against. We search for an optimized challenge, not infantile dependency; for adventure, confrontation, and combat. We hope to find dragons of precisely the size we can slay—the size matched to or even slightly exceeding our levels of confidence and ability.[36] That is the zone of proximal development,[37] the place we play most effectively[38]—the place we are most or at least optimally conscious. Could we not potentially dispense with much of the suffering in life—even contend most effectively against death itself—if we wholeheartedly and without reservation brought all the resources we have to bear on our problems? How much do we suffer because suffering is inevitable, given the limits of our mortal frames, and how much because we presume too much in our pride?

On the compassionate side—Eve's side: we smother our children with the wonders of our excessive care so that we can benefit narcissistically and undeservedly from the praise given us by those who too-carelessly observe our not-at-all-selfless sacrifice. On the side of conceptualization and order— Adam's side: we can benefit narcissistically by falsely inflating our value to others. This means that we can put ourselves forward (and this is a typically masculine temptation) as productive and generous, when we are in fact neither. This is precisely the ploy of the so-called Dark Tetrad personalities[39]— the narcissists, manipulators, psychopaths, and sadists, who manifest the very worst of masculine pride. (The feminine equivalent has been somewhat understudied—probably because it is less likely to express itself in serious physical violence or theft.[40]) Why does the latter of these four pathological traits—sadism, or delight in the pain of others—co-occur with the former three (and, no doubt, with the female equivalent[41])? The proclivity to instrumentally use others for the sake of ill-gotten gains certainly allies itself with the willingness to employ force and compulsion. That, in turn, can and does transform itself into an overweening contempt for others. (How else to justify the gains?) And after that? Into the belief or rationalization that whatever is contemptible is deserving of torture—even the belief that such torture is required on moral grounds? "Maybe the weak have a lesson to learn. Maybe I'm just the one to teach them." Maybe some of that rationale is, as well, the desire for revenge on the targets of torture for being the pushovers who enabled the great sin of instrumental use and exploitation in the first place. Does the tyrant necessarily come to hate the slaves whose acquiescence—justifiable or not; forced or not—perverted his soul?

Here is a fundamental question of religious faith: Do you believe that there is a spirit that both warns against and opposes pride? If, in the course of examining your own life, you conclude that you have never fallen because of pride, or never been taken to task because of your tendency toward over-reach, you are saintlike in the extreme, willfully blind in a manner that will lead you inevitably toward the pit, or an outright liar, and doomed for that. Those are the options, as pride eternally goes before a fall. What dread spirit is it that brings about the fall? And in what manner are you subordinate to that, regardless of what you believe or claim to believe, at the propositional level? It is after Eve hearkens to the voice of the serpent, insisting that she can incorporate what is in its essence poisonous—and after Adam, that primal fool, allows himself to claim similar power or immunity—that the fall itself occurs. The scales fall from the eyes of both God's wayward children. They can now see, as if they were gods, much of what they were not yet capable of consciously comprehending. They have taken unto themselves the burden of unearned wisdom. They now know, but do not know how to live with the knowledge. It is at that point that suffering, in principle, enters the world: knowledge of good and evil; awareness of death, or even death itself; the expulsion from Paradise; the requirement to sacrifice and work. The unhappy couple have discovered their primal nakedness:

> And when the woman saw that the tree was good for food, and that it was pleasant to the eyes, and a tree to be desired to make one wise, she took of the fruit thereof, and did eat, and gave also unto her husband with her; and he did eat.
>
> And the eyes of both of them were opened, and they knew that they were naked; so they sewed together fig leaves and made coverings for themselves.
>
> *Genesis 3:6–7*

I have long read the enhancement of vision (the falling scales) as the loss of childhood innocence and the beginning of true self-consciousness: that man and woman alike became aware at some point in the distant past of the temporal limits of human existence; of the fact that suffering, death, and malevolence were part and parcel of life.[42] Read in this manner, self-consciousness and knowledge of nakedness are the same thing. Imagine yourself unclothed, onstage, in front of thousands of people. This is no different than the display for all to see of your too-human fragility, imperfection, and vulnerability; your inability to speak the divine words that could fill you with confidence, despite that vulnerability; the impossibility of presenting your sorry self without shame.

The fact of the emergence of sophisticated self-realization with maturity implies that some of the fall is a mere consequence of growth. People abandon their childish naivete—not without pain—as they come to confront the bedrock realities of life: the harshness of the natural world; the tyranny of the social world; the sinful impulsive and hedonistic proclivities of the tempted individual. It is by no means obvious, in addition, that our descent into the cynicism that is so often the replacement for childhood trust and wonder is not an improvement, in some dark and necessary manner. Here is a paradoxical juxtaposition: the fall from childhood naivete is a prerequisite to maturity—but, again, pride goes before a fall, and often in a manner that makes that fall from a far greater and more dangerous height than it strictly needed to be. So a fall seems in some sense necessary but is definitely increased in its severity by unnecessary presumption and the desire to usurp. How to reconcile these warring opposites? I suspect that the entire biblical narrative is in some sense precisely that attempt: How do we progress forward, eternally, with hope intact and a minimum of catastrophe?

To become self-conscious is to know nakedness, limitation, and mortality; to regard this emergent self as something bounded off from everything without; to feel alienated from intimate partner or other family member, from the broader culture, from nature, from the cosmos, and from God: to feel particularized. To become self-conscious is also to suffer from that emergent separateness, in part because everything not-self (and that is a lot)

can now be perceived as both limitation and threat, arrayed in some fundamental sense against the now-isolated individual. With self-consciousness
comes scheming: instrumental action and a self-interest precisely as narrow
as the new and restricted conceptualization of the self. To view the self as
"apart" is also to be motivated to serve the now-isolated self, and only that.
Why should I not be solely concerned with my own skin, precious and vulnerable as it is? Three considerations are relevant to fleshing out that question
(so to speak). The first is that the experience of self-consciousness is, technically, indistinguishable from suffering. The second is that focus on the now
narrowly and separately perceived self motivates selfish, instrumental, and
manipulative behavior. The third is that the emergence of self-consciousness
directly interferes with practical performance and behavior.

The discovery of the relationship between self-consciousness and suffering was made inadvertently by the psychologists who analyzed the terms
formally employed to describe human personality. Personality famously has
five dimensions: extraversion, neuroticism, agreeableness, conscientiousness,
and openness to experience.[43] The second dimension, neuroticism, which has
also been termed "negative emotionality,"[44] is the axis most useful when considering the psychological significance of inadvertently opened eyes and the
consequent awareness of self. Individuals high in neuroticism are more prone
to anxiety and pain and its variants and correlates (guilt, shame, disappointment, frustration, anger, disgust, and others). The researchers who derived
one of the first and most influential principal personality models and mea-
surement instruments (the so-called NEO-PI-R questionnaire) also discovered
that self-conscious experience was so tightly allied with neurotic suffering
that the former was best conceptualized as an integral subcomponent of the
latter.[45]

The relationship between explicit self-consideration and anxiety, depression, pain, and so on has been studied in some detail. The social psychologist
Mark Richard Leary and his colleagues found, for example, that those experiencing high levels of self-consciousness were also more likely to engage in
strategies of "impression management:"[46] that is, to scheme and plot to best
ensure that they were being "perceived" in social situations in a manner they

desire. Such strategies coincide frequently with the deception of self and others—accompanied by all the associated pitfalls of the lie. There is little difference between self-directed focus and suffering. That is an important realization in itself, but there is still more. It is equally true that there is a dangerous temptation associated with self-conscious suffering—the temptation to manipulate so that the painful state of subjective awareness and evaluation is ameliorated. This happens when "I must manipulate others such that they think well of me" replaces "I must place myself in continual sacrificial service to my future self and to others."

The person who becomes suddenly self-conscious finds him- or herself trapped in the unpleasant experience of the moment. Continual existence in such a state appears virtually indistinguishable from trait anxiety[47] and proclivity to depression (even psychosis),[48] as well as oft-painful and counterproductive social maladjustment.[49] The consequence? Temptation to form an alliance with the snake, so to speak; temptation to manipulate, twist, and bend the fabric of reality so that negative emotion can be reduced by whatever deception is deemed necessary; willingness to falsify speech, action, self-perception, and the perception of others such that undeserved benefits might flow forward. Self-consciousness also interferes with performance, more objectively measured—even expert performance—as well as increasing negative and decreasing positive emotion. The emergence of self-consciousness increases the "cognitive load" of people speaking publicly, distracting them from the task at hand.[50] Likewise, experts who "choke under pressure" often do so because they substitute for the neurological systems that now mediate their well-practiced and automatized performance the not-at-all-specialized general alarm system that produces self-reflective negative emotion.[51] Their attention is therefore fractured, and task-specific focus is disrupted. This is perhaps part of why trait neuroticism is negatively associated with academic and career performance.[52]

What is the alternative? To attempt to not think about the self that does nothing but immediately and perversely focus attention right back on that self? Or the switching of concern from the narrow present and current whim to the community and the future? Instead of acting "self-consciously," in the service of the narrowly conceived, narcissistic, and immediate self, it is possible to act with the good of, say, your wife or husband utmost in mind—or the good of your other family members, broader society, nation, nature, or even God. It would be possible to act, similarly, with the personal but higher self in mind: the self extended beyond the emotional or motivational state of the moment; the self that operates optimally across the many contexts that make up the totality of experience. That more-extended self is inevitably wiser and more social than the self here and now, as it must take into account long temporal spans and diverse places and situations.

The next narrative segment in Genesis drives this point home. Shortly after Adam's vision is so terribly transformed, God comes to him in the Garden and invites him for a walk (something the two had apparently done together previously, as a matter of unquestioned habit). Adam demurs, hiding behind a conveniently placed bush. Further, he attributes his emergent cravenness to the now-realized fact of his nakedness: "And the Lord God called unto Adam, and said unto him, Where art thou? And he said, I heard thy voice in the garden, and I was afraid, because I was naked; and I hid myself" (Genesis 3:11). Immediately after follows the moment[53] when he compounds that sin by blaming Eve and then the God who had created her:

> And he said, Who told thee that thou wast naked? Hast thou eaten of the tree, whereof I commanded thee that thou shouldest not eat?
>
> And the man said, The woman whom thou gavest to be with me, she gave me of the tree, and I did eat.
>
> And the Lord God said unto the woman, What is this that thou hast done? And the woman said, The serpent beguiled me [tricked me (New Revised Standard Version); deceived me (Douay-Rheims Bible); caused me to forget (Literal Standard Version)], and I did eat.
>
> *Genesis 3:11–13*

Adam's attitude—his self-aggrandizing complaint to God; his total abdication of responsibility for his (eternal) fall? "Remember that woman you made for me, that *ezer kenegdo*?"[54] In her pride and willingness to usurp, she hearkened to the voice of the spirit of the poisonous and inedible, and tempted me to claim the ability to incorporate even that. Now, in consequence of my overreaching, I cannot stop seeing myself for the sorry creature that I am, and I am so ashamed that I can no longer walk unselfconsciously with the true spirit of the Divine in the garden. How dare she exist! How dare you make her and offer her to me!" Here, too, lurks pride, in the guise both of self-presumed right to judge woman and God, and in outright refusal to admit to insufficiency, error, or sin. Instead of taking the path that could lead to atonement and even the return of Paradise, Adam instead casts aspersions on his necessary and much-desired partner, who was the greatest and final gift of God—and then compounds his already ungrateful and resentful and profound error by calling God himself to account.

All this is the universal story of humankind in its sorrier states, the primordial and archetypal tale of the endless war between the sexes. The woman blames the man for the strictures and shortcomings of the social order—for its inability to fully encompass all that cries out for inclusion. The man blames the woman for revealing to him his own shortcomings—and, worse, manifests a great resentment toward the structure of being itself: "How could God have possibly made a world so terrible that it contained these terrifying, judgmental women?" The biblical corpus has been and is constantly criticized for its hypothetical "patriarchal bias"—something so hypothetically self-evident that it does not even need to be documented.[55] Suffice it to say in brief but profound rejoinder that Adam does not come off well at all in this most fundamental and determinative of exchanges.

How much of our suffering emerges because we are not humble enough to learn? Because we insist tyrannically that what we already know is sufficient and absolute? Because we demand recognition for a reputation (for abiding by a code of moral conduct) that we have failed to earn? Because we shrink away in cowardice from the great expanse of the unknown and mysterious? Because we have insufficient faith in the goodness of Being and man? Is all that not necessarily on us? Is that responsibility not self-evidently the ultimate truth? If we were sufficiently enlightened—if we made full use of all that has been provided to us, to say it again—would suffering vanish? Would it be at least replaced by the great, voluntarily undertaken adventure of life? This may seem too optimistic a conclusion. Perhaps, however, it is only too optimistic, in the naive sense, if the difficulty of such enlightenment has not been taken properly into account. In the Christian world, such enlightenment is technically indistinguishable from the invitation to take up the cross and tread the path of Jesus (Matthew 16:24), which is of course the most demanding of all paths, journeys, and attitudes: that resounding, dauntingly courageous, and apparently impossible-to-emulate "yes" to everything, regardless of suffering.

Once God discovers that naked self-consciousness has emerged in the world, the cataclysm of the fall begins. He now makes himself manifest as the spirit that sets the soul of woman in opposition to the eternal serpent (Genesis 3:15); that indicates the subjugation of Eve, however unhappily and unjustifiably, to pain in pregnancy and childbirth and desire for a man that will in his and her sin rule over her (Genesis 3:16); that indicates the now-cursed state of the ground and the consequent necessity of toil, hard labor, work, and death (Genesis 3:17–19); that sets the skins of sacrificed animals protectively between man and woman and now-hostile nature (Genesis 3:21); and that decrees the now-inevitable departure of his human creations from Paradise itself (Genesis 3:23).

Why pain in pregnancy and childbirth? There are evolutionary trade-offs between cortical expansion—associated with a commensurate increase in the size of infant skull—and width of female pelvic opening.[56] Any narrower, and babies would have to be born even more undeveloped, fetal, dependent, and vulnerable than they already are, to a degree essentially unparalleled in the mammalian world. Any wider and women would have trouble running. The human birth channel is so tight that babies have developed compressible skulls to deal with the passage. None of this makes for comfort in childbearing. Why emergent authority, under Adam? It is not a consequence of any evident essential intrinsic male superiority, say, in general cognitive ability[57] or conscientiousness[58] (the best two predictors of general competence[59]). It is instead and most simply and obviously because the increased dependency that pregnant and nursing women inevitably manifest, caring so intensely and primarily as they do for their infants (as well as dependent others), puts them at a comparative disadvantage in competing for social position and "dominance" with men.[60] It is also the case that women, worldwide, look for men of a higher social status than they themselves possess.[61] Without that distance, there is little likelihood of romantic or erotic attraction. With that distance, there is the risk of subordination.

Why the cursed state of the ground? Is it not because increased self-consciousness and the knowledge of the uncertain future that accompanies it motivate us to toil in the present—to delay gratification; to work—to stave off privation and suffering in the future?[62] The concepts of *work* and *sacrifice* are essentially identical. Work is the sacrifice of the immediate delights of the present to the future and to the community. The fact that work becomes necessary after expulsion from Paradise means that the question of what form of work best suffices or fails—what form of sacrifice best pleases or most displeases God—immediately becomes the paramount question. Man is destined to work: What then is the great work; the form of sacrifice most pleasing to what is highest? This is the central concern of the entire biblical corpus and all its literary derivatives; something truly indistinguishable from the issue of the meaning or significance of life, or even Being itself—or even the nature of the Creator Himself in relationship to man.

Why clothing in the skins of animals? Is it not because that terrible self-knowing nakedness now needs protection, which can be obtained at the expense of other living things? And is it not the case that such intermediation is the very essence or definition of culture, as well as its prime purpose, standing as it does between man and woman and nature, and that the sacrifice such protection requires means that the "patriarchy" is by necessity soaked with blood? This means that the most primordial clothing provided by God to naked and alienated man is emblematic of the entire morally ambivalent, flawed but still heroic cultural ("patriarchal") enterprise of man, undertaken by man to provide his naked carcass and soul with the protection necessary when he is no longer walking with the Divine. What is the story? Man is eternally protected from the ravages of a now-hostile nature by the intermediation of society—with the best protection offered by a society predicated on the voluntary offerings of God (this despite man's expulsion from His offered Paradise). Why, finally, the expulsion from Paradise? Because self-consciousness—an inevitable consequence of overweening pride—is indistinguishable from suffering and alienation from the divine.

2.7. Loss of Paradise and the flaming sword

After all this, the capstone to the chapter: the spirit of God is also that which sets the cherubim and their accompanying sword of flame, that turns every which way, on the road or pathway to paradise (Genesis 3:24). Adam and Eve—and their descendants—cannot return to the Garden of Eden, unless they can withstand the trial of those blades of fire. This prohibition seems in some real sense to be a self-evident condition of reality: There can be nothing allowed in heaven that is not heavenly; nothing in Paradise that is not truly paradisal. Everything unworthy must therefore be cut or burned away. Is there any difference, conceptually, between those flaming blades and the fires of hell? Might it not be the case that the damned are damned insofar as they have established a terrifying distance between themselves and God—a distance that makes the magnitude of the sacrifice and reconfiguration necessary to reconcile their evil with God something daunting to the point of holy terror? Might it not be the case that those suffering in that manner are doing so because they have invited the darkness in, and collaborated with it, such that they cannot easily forgive themselves? That would make the reality of hell precisely equivalent to eternal or cosmic justice—the necessary consequence of the eventual or even hypothetical state where nothing is hidden and everything made manifest: "For nothing is secret that will not be revealed, nor anything hidden that will not be known and come to light" (Luke 8:17).

The errors of our pride and presumption burden us with what would have to be sacrificed or cut away. If we were to endeavor once again to walk with God, how much would we each have to shed, so that only what was truly worthy of perfect existence remained? How much is our much-vaunted

selfhood merely layer upon layer of protective pretense, deception, or rationalization for avoidance and rejection of responsibility? How much is detritus and deadwood? And doesn't there exist a very deep rationale—even one
offering a casual account—for the barring of the way to the tree of life to
those who are still steeped in sin? If the cost of achieving life eternal is the
perfection of the father referred to by Christ (Matthew 5:48), then the barring of the way to the tree of life to still-fallen man and woman is something
both inevitable and right. What is still sinful cannot attain the heavenly
reward. Paradise would simply not be Paradise if it contained anything
unworthy.

What else might the fact of the cherubim and the flaming sword of judgment mean? That the capacity for human judgment and evaluation—essential
to human subduing and naming; part of the manifestation of the image of
the Word or Logos in human form—is also and by necessity that which ex-
cludes and forbids. This is part of what compassion, or even mercy itself in
its immediate form, might well find objectionable. Nonetheless, what is painful in the short term—easily confused with what is merely cruel—may well be
salutary and for the best in the medium- to long-term, or all things considered. Thought itself can be productively considered in this light. The process
of problem formulation, creative inspiration, and critical evaluation appears
very much akin in its central structure to the attempt to communicate with
the gods, or with God Himself, through the process known as prayer. As the
millennia progressed, much that was originally religious became, first, semantic and, second, secular. Is it not likely that the same happened in the
case of thought?

Consider the stages of the search for understanding, with the first being
the admission that progress is lacking on some important front. This is humility as precondition for revelation. A scientist, for example, endeavoring
to expand his domain of knowledge (and by implication, the body of human
knowledge) must contemplate the limitations of his current presuppositions;
must get on his knees, however abstractly, and open up his admittedly too-
ignorant and insufficient self to the possibility of learning something new.
The thinker must, in other words, ask himself, or something within himself,

a question. It is at this juncture that the scientific endeavor encounters the transcendent: What precisely is this "self" that is being questioned—as opposed, say, to the "self" that is questioning? If the answer is nascent within, in some manner, why did the ignorance driving the exploratory process reign initially? Why does the question have to be posed to begin with? To pose the question slightly differently: What aspect of "self" is answering, as opposed to the self that is questioning?

Very little attention has been paid by scientists to the emergence of the "research hypothesis" that drives the entire endeavor. The same might be said about the mysterious emergence of the problems that confront philosophers and thinkers in the humanities, although the issue is most salient on the scientific side, given the empirical insistence that everything is given by the self-evident facts. Those writing scientific papers invariably do so as if the question they are trying to answer, and the tentative formulation of solution they are putting forward as their hypothesis, came to them in some algorithmic manner as the next logical or even deterministic step in the incremental progress within their field of study. This presumption is so deep, so implicit, that scientists are called on to write the introductions and even the conclusions of their research papers as if that was the process by which their investigations proceeded, and the manner in which their initial question presented itself.

Even if all that was true, and it is not, the "next step" into the unknown is never mapped in its entirety. If it were, it would not be a step into the unknown but knowledge already garnered and mastered. Further, if the question is not "trivial"—a criticism commonly levied at someone taking a too-obvious next step in a too-algorithmic manner—then it has to be a leap into the beyond, which is what makes it "daring" or, when successful, a "breakthrough." A research question that does not address a sufficiently hard problem—one that is, in consequence, truly unanswered—will attract no interest or attention from researchers or readers of the scientific literature, just as a research hypothesis too obvious will attract no funding and will disappear, uncited, if by some chance it is ever published. The same obscure fate awaits a question so opaque or a hypothesis so original that it beggars the comprehension of even those on the advanced edge of the discipline. The question put forth must therefore be compelling—the hypothesis sufficiently original—within some difficult to define but communally established bounds. This means that the question must exist on the border between order and chaos; it must contain an admixture of the truly unknown. This is true for all communication whatsoever that manages to be worthwhile and instructive. It is also the case that the greater the (still plausible and understandable) leap forward, the more credit is instantly due the investigator or communicator, and the more revolutionary and laudable the research. The degree to which the inquiry is optimal in challenge appears to be indexed by its capacity to elicit interest on the part of investigator, peer, and audience alike. The cutting edge is by definition the most fascinating place.

The identity of exploratory thought, even its most stringent, scientific manifestation, with humble openness to (religious) revelation is not the only place of parallel between prayer and secularized thought. Consider how the process actually unfolds, in either case. First, there is admission of insufficiency. This differs little from confession or humility ("There is something vital that I do not know"), contrition ("I am less than I could be if I knew"), or even the religious virtue of meekness or lowliness (see Psalms 37:11 and Matthew 5:5). Before individuals think, they must have something to think about. They must be beset by a problem that is intriguing or distressing; a problem that calls, or that appeals to conscience. They must believe, further, that the problem is worth addressing, that addressing it is possible, and that addressing it would be good (assuming as we are going to for the sake of argument that they are aiming up). Finally, they must as well be characterized by faith in the creative revelatory process; faith in its existence and its benevolence. Such faith is something like the belief that if you have a question (and one, say, that is genuine or real rather than false), that "thinking up an answer" is both possible and worthwhile or valuable, at least in principle.

Supplication follows: the prayer or request for revelation that is the opening up of the psyche to insight and sacrificial restructuring. The scientist (the philosopher, the humanist, the sinner) gets down on his knees, in all humility, and admits to himself, his field, and God the utter depths of his ignorance. This is not an overstatement with regard to the degree of commitment of the genuine empiricist: any scientist worth his salt is pursuing something akin to a lifelong devotion to his question of interest. In the absence of such heartfelt dedication, there is simply not enough motivational force available to a more casual researcher to do his necessarily painstaking work properly. After this admission, the searcher opens himself up to insight[63]— something that appears indistinguishable, conceptually and ontologically, from revelation. The very words used to describe the revelatory experience indicate exactly the autonomy and externality of its origin: a "truly inspired thought," a "stroke of brilliance"—"it came to me that," "I realized that," "I saw things in a new light," "I was moved" (or "something moved within me"), "my perspective shifted," "the ground shifted," "the gates opened up"—all such language indicates in some sense the deliverance of knowledge. But from where? And how? And why? All this is left undisclosed when someone says "something came to me"—whether it is question or tentative answer or hypothesis—and it is all simply taken as a given, say, in a scientific research report.

There is yet more overlap on the creative side between the hypothetically scientific and religious practice. There is the lengthy apprenticeship of the thinker, a practice derived not from the rationalist or empiricist tradition but from the practice of monasticism, which was in turn a manifestation of the desire to unify aim upward. This is the training of scientists to doubt even their own presumptions and to search diligently for the truth. This is escape from the tyranny of oft-unexamined ideology and the enslavement to usurper and cliché that intellectual subjugation constitutes. This is willingness on the part of the thinker, scientific and otherwise, to sacrifice his previous conceptualizations, in consequence of his pursuit of the truth, no matter how valued or fundamental those were. This is tantamount, as well, to accepting the necessity of "death and rebirth" as a precondition for scientific progress; acceptance of the idea that some preconditions and commitments will have to be sacrificed and new ones welcomed in replacement. There is little difference between such acceptance and "subordination of the self" to "divine will."

This self-sacrificial and humble service is the offering most pleasing to God, so to speak: the wholehearted, a priori commitment to the truth, which is to be followed no matter where it leads, like the Holy Spirit itself—"The wind bloweth where it listeth, and thou hearest the sound thereof, but canst not tell whence it cometh, and whither it goeth: so is every one that is born of the Spirit" (John 3:8). This is all a lot, but there is yet more to the parallels between religious practice and genuine thought. The thinker—the scientist—opening himself up to the emergence of a hypothesis is preparing himself, as has been intimated, for the receipt (but from where?) of corrective information. He is striving to become the fertile and welcoming ground on which the new seeds of the revelation vouchsafed to him find their purchase. This makes him nothing less than the Bride of Christ, in the symbolic language. This might be a bitter pill to swallow for those who presume that the scientific and the religious are somehow diametrically opposed.

The seeking scientist, explorer, and thinker is also called upon to evaluate the newly revealed notions, making their appearance in the theater of his imagination, as in "Beloved, believe not every spirit, but try the spirits whether they are of God: because many false prophets are gone out into the world" (1 John 4:1). This is the subjugation of the received insight or revelation to critical thinking. Why is this necessary? Why would the God who reveals lead astray or deceive? This is the wrong way of considering the problem. It is not so much the source of revelation that should be evaluated as potentially false but the motivations of the seeker, and the nature of the spirit that subsequently responds. It is only God Himself who speaks when called upon when the question has been posed or prayer offered in the perfect manner. If the reasons for investigation and the request for revelation are self-serving, resentful, deceitful, and arrogant, then the spirit that comprises the essence of those impulses is what will answer.

Separating the answers of the former from the falsehoods of the latter requires a painful discernment and discrimination—the willingness to separate chaff from wheat and sheep from goats. That is subjugation to the terrible flaming sword that stands at the gates of Paradise. That, in turn, requires what is best understood as soul-searching—an evaluation of all the potentially counterproductive motivations that may have corrupted the insight: "Do I believe this only because it requires the least effort? Because it conveniently furthers my career? Because it exists in contradistinction to the theories of those I am competing with?" Such assessment also calls into question the purpose or aim actually served by the new idea: "Do I believe this because it is an idea that is in keeping with my commitment to serve the truth, in relationship to the ethical goal toward which I am genuinely aiming? Or, once again, does it only do something for me, when what is me is construed in the narrowest of senses?" Such soul-searching is, invariably, an intense self-criticism: "Did I properly call upon what is highest to aid me in my exploratory venture, or did I falter, and allow myself to become possessed by concerns other than those allied with the upward striving, redemptive path of the truth? If not, what spirit did I then call upon—and, as a result, what spirit answered—when I sent forward my query?" It is also the case, of course—and finally—that the scientist or thinker is impelled to evangelize the results of their quest. He does so by speaking and by writing, attempting to spread the doctrine of the newly revealed truth.

We could make this understanding of emergence even clearer by returning to our developing understanding that perceptions are *navigating functions*. What we see is dependent on where we are determined to head, as what makes itself manifest to us even in the realm of fact are pathways forward and impediments[64] to that progress (with everything else relegated to the realm of irrelevance and invisibility). This is equally true of what we think. Thought enables us to navigate in abstraction before embarking on our real-world adventures. What makes itself manifest to us when we question and receive a corresponding revelation are therefore the abstract equivalents of orienting, directional perceptions. We admit to our insufficiencies, in relation to our goals and priorities, and ask ourselves the questions which, if answered properly, would move us closer to our desired destinations. Lurking behind all such admissions and questionings, implicitly if not explicitly, is our sense of final destination and our ultimate priority.

This is the spirit that occupies the peak of the mountaintop, or the ever-receding pinnacle of Jacob's Ladder. That is the god we worship, however

unconsciously, the spirit that guides our perceptions and shapes our emotions (as thoughts can and do make us feel), and, most terrifying, the source
that answers when we knock, ask, and seek (Matthew 7:7–8). Thus, if we are
aiming, however insentiently, at something other than what is highest, something other than what is highest will produce the revelations that we are
seeking. Imagine it this way: every choice of destination has its reason, its
motivation. The pathways to destinations aimed at by motivations that are
resentful, immature, self-serving, bitter, and vengeful (murderous, genocidal,
deicidal) will be demarcated by spirits with those natures. If you pray (think)
toward improper ends, then you will be answered by demonic voices.

   Carl Jung noted our generalized proclivity to "succumb in the most un-
critical way to the slightest possibility of finding some kind of answer or
certainty."[65] Jung was describing a form of willful blindness. Later psychologists rediscovered this tendency as "the availability heuristic": the proclivity
of a perceiver or thinker to judge the credibility of a claim by how quickly
and easily it sprang to mind.[66] With the psyche so susceptible to revelation
and so disinclined to question what emerges, post-intuition critical evaluation is of crucial importance. We must be willing to let counterproductive
ideas die. That is the sacrifice that most truly is critical thought itself. That
sacrifice means that our ideas can perish, so that we do not act them out and
perish. Critical thought—the death, however painful, of our ideas, however
cherished—is a substitutionary sacrifice, the eradication of a part instead of
the whole. As Christ insists, "And if thy right eye offend thee, pluck it out,
and cast it from thee: for it is profitable for thee that one of thy members
should perish, and not that thy whole body should be cast into hell. And if
thy right hand offend thee, cut it off, and cast it from thee: for it is profitable
for thee that one of thy members should perish, and not that thy whole body
should be cast into hell" (Matthew 5:29–30).

   The process of thought is akin to the Logos also because it is dialogical. The Russian linguist Lev Vygotsky believed that the ability to think
semantically was the replication of dialogue within the mind of a single individual:[67] that, for all intents and purposes, thought constituted the abstract, internalized argument between different avatars. A single mind can

house many personalities. This is a truth particularly evident in our dream states, when different personalities literally appear on the imaginative scene, complete with capability of independent action and discourse. The same thing is true of the human ability to imagine fictional characters—or, more directly, the possible actions, attitudes, and reactions of other living people, in abstract contemplation. The ability to hold internal dialogue, even between intensely competing "personalities," so to speak, is apparently an ability that can be honed and taught. Socrates may have fostered precisely that ability first and foremost among known human beings, formalizing, clarifying, and transmitting the technologies of thought, giving rise to philosophy as such; literally teaching people to think on their own (or at least to think far more efficiently), rather than to rely unquestioningly on revelation or interpersonal argumentation. He accomplished at least this much in the course of his famous dialogues.[68]

Every idea that is alive (and that is every idea that announces itself as truly worthy of consideration) expresses itself not as a mere description but as a personality with an aim, a viewpoint, a world gathered around it, and a full panoply of emotional responses and associated ideas. Dialogue is the battle between the personality of various ideas. The internal dialogue that is thought is the war between competing personalities, in the theater of the imagination, and the death of the losers (complete with the pain that such death by necessity entails). This process of warring idea-personality within is no different than the war of the gods in heaven, played out on the broader, communal scale: it is merely ("merely") that war playing itself out locally, in the psyche of the thinker, and then in the imaginations of those affected by his thought. It is in this manner that the Logos of the individual—the process of his consciousness—establishes and revitalizes the cosmic order.

The need for trial by fire is further exemplified by way of analogy in the key alchemical idea *in sterquiliniis invenitur*: literally, "in filth it will be found"; alternatively, "that which you most need to find will be found where you least want to look."[69] The greatest challenge to what is and what should be, by consensus and tradition, is always to be found in what is least familiar and most frightening. Residing as it does at our weakest psychological point, it is also very likely contaminated with willful blindness: we are likely to leave unfamiliar that which is most daunting. This is why treasure and the maidens that are truly the greatest treasure are by universal agreement guarded by dragons, and also why it is sacrifice that pleases God, as the encounter with something truly new in the attempt to rise requires the abandonment of all that currently blocks movement forward. This often necessitates the sacrifice of that which is most loved. It is much easier to understand the terrible demands so often put forward by God in this light: everything must be offered to that which is highest for perfection to make itself manifest "in Earth, as it is in heaven" (Matthew 6:10). Progress in thinking—in science itself—is dependent on willingness to confront chaos while under the dominion of the spirit that aims upward, toward the order that is good or very good.

Apprehension of the anxiety, pain, hopelessness, and confusion associated with that sacrifice—the death of our previous preconceptions—is the reason for opposition to the freedom of religion, conscience, association, and thought that is the hallmark of tyranny. The tyrant rejects humility, insisting that all that needs to be known is already known. He abandons his relationship with the spirit that reveals and redeems, doubles down when his presumptions are shown to be inadequate (Exodus 7–10), falls under the sway of his evil brother (the tempter and usurper, the lord of power and of deception), and refuses the constant little deaths upon which the maintenance of life most truly depends. In doing so, or in avoiding so doing, he dooms himself and his society to the cataclysm that will eventually destroy everything. *The death of a guiding idea produces disorientation on the way to enlightenment.*

It is apprehension of the reality and inevitability of that desert state—that intermediary grief, hopelessness, and confusion—that makes us approach enlightenment or its messengers with trepidation, resistance, or outright hostility. Would the surgery necessary to remove all that is not properly aligned or meet within us not risk killing the patient—or, at least, leave him or her begging for death? We so often reject penitence, even when accused, with reason, by those who love us (and who we know love us). We reject the necessity of transformation, sticking blindly and stubbornly to our guns. We remain slaves to our own narrow, self-serving whims because we refuse to acknowledge even a hint of our own self-produced inadequacy. Who among us could therefore survive the kind of winnowing that would allow only what was best within us to stand? Thus, we avoid the healing death of the fire that is simultaneously God and the redeeming Word. As the Gospel of Thomas has it, "Whoever is near me is near the fire, and whoever is far from me is far from the (Father's) kingdom" (saying 82).[70]

The cherubim and God's purgatorial weapon, the whirling, flaming sword, guarding the gate to the paradisal garden (Genesis 3:24), are dramatic expressions of that complex of ideas. The essential moral of the entire biblical corpus is therefore foreshadowed in these opening stories, which unfold and reveal their implicit secrets across the millennia, as great revelations are wont to do: "Another parable put he forth unto them, saying, The kingdom of heaven is like a grain of mustard seed, which a man took, and sowed in his field: Which indeed is the least of all seeds: but when it is grown, it is the greatest among herbs, and becometh a tree, so that the birds of the air come and lodge in the branches thereof" (Matthew 13:31–32). And what is the true nature of that cutting and burning that destroys but also plants, prunes, and redeems? How hostile is nature, itself, intrinsically, with its offering of mortal vulnerability? How much suffering is intrinsic to life itself—and to be laid, therefore, at the feet of God; blamed upon God? And how much is instead a consequence of presumption and pride, of failure to hit the mark, of sin itself—and to be laid, therefore, not so much at the feet of mankind but taken on as our own irresponsible personal shortcoming? Is that not the crux of the matter; the true cross?

A stitch in time saves nine—or so goes the maxim. The Dutch build their dikes to withstand the worst storm in ten thousand years.[71] The US Army Corps of Engineers built the earthworks in New Orleans to weather (perhaps) the worst storm in less than a century.[72] Then came the hurricane. Was that an act of God, to use the insurer's term, or the consequence of willful blindness? Whenever the catastrophe of nature, state, or individual is visited upon any of us, the terrible questions immediately arise: Had we been better, would we have escaped unscathed? Had we made the proper sacrifices, would the dread spirit of the punishing God have passed over us? These are in truth open questions. What answers emerge from the biblical corpus, piecemeal, step-by-step? *It is all on you*—with God as Guide. That is an unbearable burden, although a noble burden; certainly a challenge; possibly the ultimate challenge; possibly the secret to life and of the return to Paradise itself.

3

◆

Cain, Abel, and Sacrifice

3.1. The identity of sacrifice and work

With the entry of toil into the world, after the fall of Adam and Eve, the question of sacrifice emerges, and by necessity, given the close relationship or even identity between the former and the latter. The necessity for work has already been indicated, in consequence of the presumption of the mother and father of mankind, sorely tempted by the blandishments of the serpent. Man and woman, unwilling to walk with God, are fated to labor, and often bitterly. Why? At least in part for philosophical, spiritual, or religious reasons, as those who reject the upward-spiraling path of the Logos must instead grapple counterproductively and bitterly with intransigent fate. If your aim were true, would the pathway forward be overgrown with "thorns and thistles" (Genesis 3:18)? Would you be constantly inclined to "kick against the pricks" (Acts 9:5)? Or would the golden road reveal itself as a series of doors that would open if you only knocked on them, or as a quest that would enable the asker to receive, and the seeker to find (Matthew 7:7–8)? Would all that could all too easily be effortful drudgery then become childlike play?

Key to understanding the story of Cain and Abel, the first true human beings (as they are born in the way of all men, while their parents, Adam and Eve, were made directly by God), is recognition that it is a story about work, an essentially unique human activity. Bees make honey, and beavers make dams, but neither is equivalent to the many diverse forms of work that engage human beings. Very little, if any, of the latter is reducible to the comparatively simple patterns of instinct that drive other creatures. The story of the first two human beings, the hostile brothers, presents the two fundamentally opposed patterns of sacrifice or offering that characterize the human psyche. Where does work, per se, enter the story? Cain and Abel both have their occupations. The former is a tiller of the ground, while the latter is a shepherd, a keeper of flocks. More subtle, however, is the presentation of the relationship between work and sacrifice—a relationship that is properly and deeply understood as a shared identity. With this identity clear, the emphasis in the biblical texts on sacrifice as characterizing the relationship between man and God (and vice versa) becomes comprehensible and of immediate practical import, as well as identifiable as perhaps the most profound and necessary of all truths.

First, to render this claim of identity comprehensible, a question: What is work? If I am doing what needs to be done, instead of what I want to do for the sake of present gratification, I am *working*. "Needs to be done" in what sense—and compared to what? Work is the subjugation of whim or, more precisely, it's integration with other needs and desires into something of a higher and more complete order. Work is, to state it differently, the delay of gratification, and a sacrifice made in the service of others. It is an investment to best ensure the beneficence of the future, whose price must be paid in the present; an investment, as well, in the good will of the others on whose behalf something valuable (time, energy, attention) has been given up now. That means that when I am working I am replacing what I wish I could be doing right now—replacing what would otherwise seize my immediate attention and desire—with some demand of transcendent yet still brute necessity, all things considered; with something more calculated and longer term. This giving up or offering often is and can well be considered in any case as a contractual, communal, or covenantal obligation, implicit or explicit—one designed to meet the needs and wants of others (my family, my friends, my colleagues or partners, as well—and this is more difficult to understand, but crucial—as my future self).

There is perhaps no pattern of action more difficult to enact than voluntary subjugation of the present to the other and the future, given the conflict of that pursuit with the powerful appetitive, motivational, and emotional forces that strive to possess us and demand immediate gratification. Human beings are the only creatures that have ever come to understand how to subjugate now to later, routinely—as part of our mode of being—and are certainly the only creatures who determined how to ritualize, imaginatively understand, and then semantically represent that pattern of subjugation, work, and sacrifice. We had to learn all that (to sacrifice; to represent the pattern of sacrifice) the hard way, of course. We had to learn to work. Is there any purpose more profound for the great brains that characterize our species and require such lengthy socialization to develop than to transcend the instinctual and direct it toward the concerns of others and the future? Perhaps: What developed along with that process of maturation was the ability to act out what we had learned about work—about sacrifice—so that we could understand it more deeply, dramatically, and explicitly (as well as doing the work). Doing so enabled us to transmit that understanding in the form of stories, to ourselves, each other, and our children.

We formulated dramatic stories about our sacrificial efforts and then attempted to analyze the stories, to make the representations they had already distilled through abstraction ever more explicit, comprehensible, and memorable. At the same time, we learned how to make psychological sacrifices, instead or in addition to the concrete offerings made on altars and in temples: to identify outdated or otherwise counterproductive ideas; to let them burn away, no matter how much we once or still loved them, so that something new could rise. As we have seen: there is little or no difference between such psychological sacrifice and what we now consider, rather bloodlessly, "critical thinking." The difficulty of all this should not be underestimated: it was a hard slog out of the immediacy of animal being into the realm where the future and the community mattered, even in the moment. Coming to understand what we had done and what it meant was another stunning accomplishment: What exactly are we and should we be working for? Sacrificing to? These questions still plague us all in the form of meaning: What is the meaning of our effortful striving? Of our lives and the work that defines our lives?

What, then, do we do when we work? We sacrifice the impulsive pleasures of the moment to the broader necessity of extended and social life. There is more, however: we also sacrifice, simultaneously, the multiplicity of things we could be attending to or doing (those are the same things) to a unity of present purpose. The philosopher of science, Karl Popper, said something wise that bears directly on this issue: "Our knowledge can only be finite, while our ignorance must necessarily be infinite."[1] We must work toward some small subset of goals, with every action organized under their rubrics. We must reduce that subset even further, even to unity, in order to "get our priorities straight." Otherwise, our efforts work at cross-purposes. This amplifies their difficulties, increases our confusion, breeds conflict, and destroys hope.[2] It is for such reasons that the Gospel states, "And if a kingdom be divided against itself, that kingdom cannot stand. And if a house be divided against itself, that house cannot stand" (Mark 3:24–25). The complexity of work and sacrifice does not end there. We must also arrange our aims so that we can proceed in a manner that not only benefits our particular plans but also makes us ever more able to formulate and pursue other plans—and with other people. A delicate balancing act, indeed; a difficult challenge, to establish such sweeping harmony; many plates to spin and balls to juggle while standing on the ultimate tightrope.

If you serve a multiplicity, instead of a unity, you are confused, anxious, aimless, and hopeless.[3] But if you serve a unity, what unity do—and should—you serve? The most comprehensive unity would unite psychologically ("spiritually," speaking theologically); would make of the tremendous hierarchical complexity of our neural architecture something singular, at the pinnacle of order or process.[4] It would furthermore and simultaneously place that singular integrated individuality into congruence with the social world and the surrounding natural order; into harmony with the communal and natural Logos. When people aim at the same targets, celebrate the same festivals—worship the same gods—they are united. This is as true psychologically as it is socially. United people typically perceive the same objects, conceptualize the same ideas, agree on friend and foe, and feel the same emotions. As individuals, they are not subject to an internal war of fractious spirits, competing for possession; as members of a true society, they are not riven apart by competing gods and striving, consequently, in different directions. The diverse and disparate elements of their nervous systems are aiming in the same direction, in synchrony—within that nervous system, and between the nervous systems of different but united people. If all that is within a person has united in service to the same transcendent unity, he or she will be pulled apart with doubt and spiral into misery and hopelessness. If two people serve the same unity, they can work together, sacrifice together, navigate treacherous and difficult terrain together; can cooperate and compete together, and can do so voluntarily, productively, and peacefully. People aiming at the same unified target are psychologically integrated embodiments of the same spirit. This union of the individual and the collective is indistinguishable from fully socialized maturation.

Imagine an audience within a stadium, theater, or church, attending a particularly significant game, watching an intense drama, or listening intently to a gripping speech. Everyone is focused and silent, eyes on the ball, or the star, or the singer, although reserving the right to burst spontaneously—as if they were one—into appreciative applause. They are all celebrating the same goal, following the same plot, attending to the same point, and deriving the same moral from the speech. These are all variations on the same theme. Consider the case of a compelling and unifying speech. When expertly delivered, a public address is a monologue, but with a communal or social quality. One person is onstage, speaking, to be sure, but that speaking person is also attending and listening to the people he is addressing, and intently, if he is truly expert. He is continually and actively assessing the audience, person by person, to best ensure that each word is timed, properly; landing, perfectly; aimed, precisely; making itself manifest in keeping with the expectations, desires, apprehensions, and hopes of the listeners. This is true even of the game, of the play, or the singer and musician, although the transformations brought about by participation in those events are more subtle and implicit, even though they may sometimes be deeper.

The unity that compels attention and unites action in such circumstances is participation in a process—the *dialogos* (*dia-logos*)—that requires of the speaker and the listener alike that old preconceptions be sacrificed and re-placed by something new, more comprehensive, and elegant. As P. K. Feyera-bend, the Austrian philosopher of science, so famously noted: "Scientists try to eliminate their false theories, they try to let them die in their stead. The believer—whether animal or man—perishes with his false beliefs."[5] This is an indication of the import of voluntary sacrifice, in game, literature, art, and in the scientific process itself: it is a veritable substitution for death. Any occur-rence of genuine depth and quality has a sacrificial element. A multiplicity has unified, in a stadium or theater, in a state of voluntary celebration and so given up its diversity, in service of the higher purpose. The same thing also occurs, and more explicitly, in a house of worship. That voluntary celebration; that worship—they are the same thing. This becomes particularly evident, per-haps, in the case of a musical performance, where the same melody, rhythm, and universally known and loved words grip both attention and compulsion to action (the latter being the tendency to dance) and unites. Toward what does music aim? Toward an ever-elaborating, upward-spiraling pattern of harmony. Toward a state where something already compelling and harmonious and great is replaced by something still better. Up Jacob's eternal ladder to heaven.

All in all, however, as you sit with eyes and ears attuned to the football field, the stage, the lectern, integrating yourself, you do so in concord with everyone else there. That is something that holds particularly true when the joint is jumping, so to speak. That is the collective and near-total (under op-timal conditions) seizure of attention and action by the ongoing perfor-mance, the spectacle—and the fact of the latter word, and its concordance with the name of a device to enhance or even allow for vision, is revealing. There is something deep about such seizure; something beyond the moment, even though it immerses you in that moment; something you will pay (that is, sacrifice) for; something religious, by definition, insofar as "the religious" and "that which is deep" are the same thing. The religious is what most profoundly seizes attention and compels action. The religious is the calling of the depths. It is capture by the shine in the darkness of the pearl of great price. It is the apprehension of such treasure that grips the members of the most fortunate and enthusiastic audiences—those who are most effectively entertained (which means, etymologically speaking, held mutually, intertwined, engaged, delighted, and receiving hospitality[6]).

Imagine, with all this in mind, gazing upward into a star-laden sky on the darkest and clearest of nights, far from the city lights, with the infinite expanse of heaven laid in front of you. Consider the apprehension of awe thereby produced. That is the heights, calling to you, in a manner that is deeply embodied, even instinctual—or, more accurately, calling to the best in you. You may feel small or insignificant in comparison, but only because you confront something greater, and there is in that very act of encountering what is greater the realization *that greater itself exists*, and that it can and should be strived toward. This the paradoxical consequence, it might be said, of falling to your knees: it is simultaneously an act of humility and a revelation of what could yet be, even "within." It is very difficult to unpack such experience, to make its nature explicit, in no small part because it is the experience of the finite apprehending the infinite. That primary experience of awe in the face of the cosmos itself is, perhaps, the fundament of the religious enterprise—and the inexhaustible fundament: you could describe the nature of that encounter forever and never be finished with it.

We are always seized by awe when we find ourselves in the grip of something; when our attention is focused, whether voluntarily or involuntarily, or in the strange situation where both are the case simultaneously: when we cannot help but notice but then decide, of our own accord, to investigate. It is in this manner, in part, that our destiny reveals itself—where we find our calling. This is exactly what happens to Moses in his famous encounter with the burning bush:

Now Moses kept the flock of Jethro his father in law, the priest of
Midian: and he led the flock to the backside of the desert, and came
to the mountain of God, even to Horeb.

And the angel of the Lord appeared unto him in a flame of fire
out of the midst of a bush: and he looked, and, behold, the bush
burned with fire, and the bush was not consumed.

And Moses said, I will now turn aside, and see this great sight,
why the bush is not burnt.

And when the Lord saw that he turned aside to see, God called
unto him out of the midst of the bush, and said, Moses, Moses. And
he said, Here am I.

And he said, Draw not nigh hither: put off thy shoes from off thy
feet, for the place whereon thou standest is holy ground.

Moreover he said, I am the God of thy father, the God of Abraham, the God of Isaac, and the God of Jacob. And Moses hid his
face; for he was afraid to look upon God.

Exodus 3:1–6

We are always compelled by variants of the burning bush; by the encounter with something that is both enduring in its being and furiously becoming, simultaneously. There is nowhere this happens more evidently than in
the case of life itself, defined by its fire from within. Consider, for example,
van Gogh's paintings of sunflowers or irises,[7] or the blooms apprehended in
verse by Aldous Huxley, glowing intensely to him, in his mescaline-heightened
state.[8] Something is always glimmering at the periphery, trying to make itself known—and what is greatest does so when we are most truly endeavoring to aim up. We can respond, or turn away, from the clarion call of
opportunity; of adventure. If we reject the calling, however, the doorway disappears. If we make such turning away a practice (make of such rejection the
sad spirit of our life), opportunity and adventure as such disappear, leaving
behind the normality our refusal has rendered dull and pointless, stripped of
its magic, disenchanted and hopeless. This is one pattern of egregious sin;
one of the fundamental ways we divorce ourselves from the workings of

what is truly redeeming within us—and outside of us. If, by contrast, we respond, opportunity deepens and multiplies, until what is most profound and most truly inexhaustible makes itself manifest. This is precisely the pathway trodden by the greatest of scientists, mystics, saints, and artists. This is how God speaks from the depths of the true encounter with what flickers, flames, and lives.

It is crucial to note that Moses's encounter is dialogical: God, or God's angel, reveals himself, but Moses has to "turn aside" (that is, go out of his way, deviate from his preconceived task to voluntarily attend) before the revelation makes itself complete. It is the same for all of us: our attention is gripped by phenomena that we find spontaneously interesting or by problems that bug us (shades of *Pinocchio*'s Jiminy Cricket[9]). If we take seriously what compels us or bothers us—that is, if we peer deeply enough into the abyss that lurks behind them—we will see and hear what we can tolerate of the spirit of God making itself present to us. What does this mean? *If you pay enough attention to anything, everything will be revealed.* In this manner, Michelangelo's great statue of David is a burning bush—the revelation of a great opportunity. The problem of the evil of Auschwitz is a burning bush—the revelation of a terrible problem, with an equally dramatic and valuable solution. The Holy Spirit itself is the compelling dialectic of calling and conscience.[10] The snitch encountered by the boy wizard Harry Potter in J. K. Rowling's multivolume drama[11] is a symbol of the former, making its appearance to the seeker, and a manifestation of the spirit Mercurius, or Hermes, the winged messenger of the gods,[12] an emissary of the dreamworld of the unconscious—a psychopomp who flits on the border between the human and the divine. The cricket plays the role of the latter, the conscience, for the marionette Pinocchio, who is aiming to become a real boy, impeded though he might be by the temptations of pride and arrogance, deceit and hedonism. The attention-getting chirp of the cricket is what bugs us—what sets off the cognitive equivalent of the primordial parasite-and-predator detection systems we refer to when we say "something is really bugging me" or "it really got under my skin" (shades of the plagues of flies and locusts that later bedevil the intransigent and tyrannical [resentful, murderous, genocidal] Pharaoh of the Exodus account). It is by no means coincidence that the diminutive companion of the puppet/boy striving to realize himself shares initials with the Savior of the Christian tradition.[13]

God is the ultimate up in the upward aim. The work that truly redeems; the work that is truly pleasing to God—that is the complete sacrifice of all for what is truly highest. It is that work that God calls upon Cain and Abel and us all to undertake: we undertake that work in the twin manners characterizing the adversarial brothers.

3.2. The hostile brothers of good and evil

We have discussed what unites us; the drama or story that unifies our perceptions. Let us now consider what divides us; more specifically, what does so most deeply. The conflicts that divide us both within and without can be most profitably conceptualized as battles between the stories that inhabit or possess us, at our voluntary invitation, and through which we view the world. If two or more people are locked in conflict, it is because the ways they specify their attention differ—and, sometimes, at a profound level. That is not the mere consequence of differing opinions, say, about the putatively same set of facts. It is something much more fundamental, because the facts—or, more accurately, the set of facts that reveal themselves to you—are a function of the story you have overlaid on the source from which you are deriving information. A story is a description of the structure through which the world is prioritized; and the conflicts that divide us, a matter of differing aim or will.

Knowing this, you might ask, "What stories most fundamentally clash?" To put it differently: "What is the most basic of oppositions? Or, what spirits or characters are most antagonistic to one another?" It is in the story of Cain and Abel that we find the first focused characterization of this conflict, war, or internal division. Remember, once again, that Cain and Abel are also the first two real human beings—as Adam and Eve are made directly by God, and in the garden before the fall, rather than being born in the profane world of history. It is very telling, therefore, that the two brothers exist in absolute conflict—a terrible dramatization of human destiny. As the Soviet dissident Alexander Solzhenitsyn so famously put it:

> The line separating good and evil passes not through states, nor between classes, nor between political parties either—but right through every human heart—and through all human hearts. This line shifts. Inside us, it oscillates with the years. And even within hearts overwhelmed by evil, one small bridgehead of good is retained.[14]

Some of that essential fraternal conflict is social; familial, in its most basic social manifestation, and then more broadly a consequence of comparatively abstract social structuring. Both levels of strife are held to simultaneously characterize the primordial brothers:

> And Adam knew Eve his wife, and she conceived, and bare Cain, and said, I have gotten a man from the Lord.
> And she again bare his brother Abel. And Abel was a keeper of sheep, but Cain was a tiller of the ground.
>
> *Genesis 4:1*

It is a miracle how much information can be compacted into so little space. To truly understand even these few lines, we must consider the frequent reality of sibling rivalry and, in a broader social context, the conflict of interest that constantly emerges between, for example, farmer and rancher. With regard to the former: intrafamilial sibling rivalry is common—perhaps to the point of normative.[15] This can all too easily become something pathologically extreme. Siblings who encounter chronic, intense levels of this rivalry are at risk "for a range of negative outcomes, including anxiety, depression, low self-esteem, and interpersonal difficulties"[16] as well as "reduced academic and social achievement."[17] Such intrafamilial conflict may, in addition, elevate the incidence rate and severity of borderline personality disorder[18] (particularly among females), narcissism,[19] and psychopathy[20] (although direction of causality in such cases is not precisely clear, and the process is most likely bidirectional).

This propensity for sibling rivalry is, in turn, a reflection of the comparatively helpless and dependent state of the newborn human infant.[21] Because human beings are born earlier than mammals (even primates) of comparable body mass or size,[22] we experience a uniquely extended period of postnatal, preadult dependency.[23] Human infants and children require a tremendous investment of attention, and conflicts for that scarce resource, within a family, are therefore very likely to emerge. This potential for conflict is likely to be exacerbated if the siblings in question are born in quick succession, as their periods of maximal dependence then overlap. The recommended waiting time is two to three years,[24] although there are no doubt other disadvantages associated with such spacing. The probability of conflict is particularly high when siblings are of the same sex—and, therefore, fighting for more similarly available resources.

It is implied at minimum by omission in the text of the Cain and Abel narrative that such close spacing occurs in the case of the brothers in question, as nothing happens (at least nothing worthy of note) in the time separating the birth of one from the other. If a new baby arrives when an older sibling is one or two years of age, the older child is almost immediately no longer the baby, and certainly not the primary baby. The mother therefore must sacrifice some of the attention she had been giving to the older child and turn it to the newborn, while the previous baby has to accept not being the baby anymore. He or she may be enticed with care into accepting the benefits of an expanded maturity but can also become jealous of the interloper—and in a very angry and profound manner. Such familial conflicts do not necessarily attenuate or disappear as maturity progress, and can remain intense throughout adulthood.

There is an analogous divergence of interest in the story with regard to the comparative position of farmer (Cain) and rancher (Abel). This is sibling rivalry echoed at a more distant social level. Those who differentially occupy these positions are likely to run into disputes over property rights, access to grazing land, and (in the modern world) pesticide or other chemical use.

Such conflicts occur in traditional and modern societies alike.[25] The Cain and Abel story presents these more distal social struggles as variants of the pattern established in an arguably more basic sense by brothers, battling most fundamentally and primally—even while still in the womb, as in the (later) case of Esau and Jacob: "He took his brother by the heel in the womb, and by his strength he had power with God" (Hosea 12:3); variants include "in his vigor he wrestled with God" (Berean Standard Bible). Jacob is born, explicitly, on the heel of his brother (Genesis 25:26). His very name, arguably derived from the Hebrew *âqêb*, means "one who seeks to trip up or supplant," who is "as if from the first, desirous to pull his brother back, and get in front of him. . . . The character of the man was thus prefigured at birth . . . over-reaching, or outwitting, by cunning and strategy."[26] Two brothers are destined to war; two dramatic personages war within our breasts; two spirits divide us, within our communities; the upward and downward aims eternally compete for the possession of the soul of man.

This motif of deadly opposition is perhaps foremost among the archetypal tropes characterizing popular fiction and other forms of dramatic entertainment (certainly in the action and adventure genre, although opposition between paired brothers or their equivalent also features in romance—consider, for example, Disney's *Beauty and the Beast*[27]). J. K. Rowling's juvenile wizard Harry Potter is opposed, as a boy and young man, to Draco Malfoy (although even more fundamentally, in his ultimate super-wizard guise, to Voldemort, He Who Must Not Be Named). The danger posed by the former is (as we shall see) not least a consequence of the interpenetration of the latter, as a consequence of the deepest ongoing battle. This partial possession also characterizes Potter himself, who serves unwittingly as a "horcrux" for his archenemy, carrying unwittingly within him a piece of the dark one's soul.[28] That theme of shadow-within-hero is very well developed in the *Batman* film series, particularly in *The Dark Knight*,[29] in which the Joker, Batman's archnemesis, tempts Batman continually to adopt his own dark and anarchically destructive attitude, not least to successfully overcome the Joker himself.

The same trope manifests itself in the opposition between DC Comics' characters Superman and Lex Luthor, Marvel's Thor and Loki, and the characters of Frodo and Gollum in Tolkien's *Lord of the Rings* trilogy.[30] The protagonist of heroic humility embodied in the hobbit is contrasted, as well, with the arrogance and pride of the overweening Sauron, master of the One Ring of—what else could it be?—Power, in a manner very much akin to the portrayal of the relationship between Potter and Voldemort. This is an indication of the patterning of one of the hostile brothers—the one with downward aim—on the archetype of Lucifer, or Satan, the spirit that most truly or deeply stands behind all proximal or personal manifestations of the archvillain.

It is no coincidence, therefore, that the primary antagonist of such stories is frequently both intellectually arrogant and a worshipper of technology. Consider, in this light, the age-old juxtaposition of Lucifer with the intellect (the Miltonian Lucifer is the light-bringer, God's highest angel gone most wrong, the prideful intellect;[31] Goethe's Mephistopheles is the temptation posed to the arch-intellectual Faust[32]). This relationship is reflected in popular culture in the character of the[33] villain Scar in *The Lion King*, the enemy both of tradition (Mufasa) and the young, reborn, and rightful king (Simba); of Felonious Gru, of *Despicable Me*[34] fame; of Jafar in *Aladdin*;[35] of Syndrome in *The Incredibles*;[36] and of Tolkien's aforementioned Sauron, creator of the One Ring, breeder of the monstrous orc and architect of *Barad-dûr*, Babellike tower of the all-seeing dark eye. The intellectually arrogant and presumptuous also have a pronounced tendency to turn to technological solutions, solely, to redress the apparent inequities of being. This is not to say that the enterprise of building is intrinsically evil. In its proper place, it is good, or even very good, but the presumptuous builders take false pride in the productions of their imagination and attempt to attribute to themselves the talent that makes such enterprise possible. We will return to that theme when we analyze the relationship between the descendants of Cain and the erection of the Tower of Babel.

The possibility for essential conflict is constant—a reflection of our biology, at its deepest level, and of our hyper-sociality, social dependence, and striving for relative position. This is why the very brief narrative of Cain and

Abel immediately makes sense when we read it, even if we cannot explicitly say why. Conflict has a pattern, eternally emerging in families among siblings and in more distant but still analogous rivals. The motif of the hostile brothers represents in both character and plot the endless battle between opposed modes of sacrifice, forms of work, ways of sacrificing in relationship to the unity of the future, and visions of what that unity might be. The very deepest of storytellers do not necessarily split the hostile brothers into separate characters, to be clear: they tend to portray the interplay of opposed modes of sacrifice within the soul of each individual, protagonist and antagonist alike.

It is also clearly the case and for the same reason that the most realistic and believable of heroes are by no means perfect people (and so are interpenetrated, to some interesting and necessary degree, by the spirit of Cain), while the most compelling villains are clearly those in whom some good still dwells. The Mafia or other organized-criminal characters dramatized so successfully by American filmmakers provide very good examples of the latter (consider, for example, Tony Soprano in *The Sopranos*[37], or Walter White or, even more so, Jesse Pinkman in *Breaking Bad*[38]). This is something also obviously true of many of Dostoevsky's characters, the prime example perhaps being *Crime and Punishment*'s Raskolnikov,[39] the complex family members portrayed in *The Brothers Karamazov*,[40] and the various abstract idol worshippers of *The Possessed* (or *The Demons*).[41] The most dramatic representations of such conflict constitute the very soul of great literature.

The story of Cain and Abel is an attempt by the collective human imagination to distill, transmit, and remember the essentials of good and bad into a single narrative. How did we come to undertake this effort? One answer would be "divine inspiration," and that is a good answer, at a very high-order level of analysis. Another (in truth, a variant of the first answer) is that people have been telling each other stories forever—acting them out, perhaps, even before that—and that some of the stories were more pointed, interesting, and memorable than others. Particular instances of what is good and bad drew attention and were remembered. These were then distilled into something approximating their central tendency or essence. The greatest

stories, told by the best storytellers, gripped people's attention in an unforgettable manner and burned themselves into imagination and concept, collective and personal. This might be regarded as a collaboration between the
image and word (the Logos) that gripped attention and the image and word
(the Logos) that compelled memory. This collaboration continued for tens
and perhaps hundreds of thousands of years. Stories thus told and remembered became better and better and, simultaneously, deeper and deeper. And
no one wrote them or invented them, precisely; or, more accurately, perhaps,
everyone did: and that is the action, so to speak, of Jung's collective unconscious.[42]

3.3. The sacred patterning of the political

Much of the divide that bedevils the world is a consequence of the opposition of the two attitudes that are so definitively portrayed in the original
biblical story of the hostile brothers. The story of Cain and Abel therefore
has a significance that extends directly into the political, as well (or, more
accurately, constitutes the political, insofar as the sacred has collapsed into
it). It constitutes the pattern for the victim/victimizer narrative that plays
such a key role in the ideologies of resentment that so truly characterize our
time, although not uniquely, as the drama thus portrayed is eternal. The
story is a meta-truth—a frame within which the facts of the world are held to
reveal themselves; a structure that defines all the truths those who dally with
ideological possession are capable of seeing and of acting on. What is the
game? Believers in such stories—devotees of such theories—first note, and
with gleeful dismay, the obvious disparities that exist in the world (a feat no
different than observing the qualitative differences between things that most
truly make up the world).

   Then who resentfully dwell upon the fact of such distinctions (those of
sex, race, class, ethnicity, "gender," attractiveness—even age, weight, height)
and point an accusing finger at those who unequally benefit from their positioning at the desirable end of the resultant distribution. Finally, they

presume—in the most self-serving imaginable manner—that all such inequality, which is an inevitable consequence of difference itself, is something due instead to compulsion, force, and oppression. This hypothesis is particularly pernicious in that the accusation that it constitutes always contains a kernel of truth. No society is so pure that the inevitably differentiated rewards that it offers are awarded purely on the basis of merit, however that is defined: power and even corrupted power (as the two go so often hand in hand) always play at least some role. Some of those who are rich are narcissists and manipulative psychopaths, even in the highly functional and generally honest and productive societies of the West. Some of those who have social status have it because of dynasty and nepotism (which are the classic pathways to relative success in societies that do not rely on more abstracted and objective measurements of merit).[43] The fact that corrupted routes to success do exist and are utilized by some corrupt individuals does not in any way indicate that all such routes are corrupted or, worse, that all those who are successful are also corrupt. When a society assumes the latter (or when the latter has become true), then all hell is likely to break loose.

It might be finally noted that division into group categories of oppression and attribution of the resultant inequality to nothing but power does not yet exhaust the fame. The simplification that such a conceptual scheme constitutes means that all responsibility to think further is lifted: all social arrangements are made between oppressor and oppressed, whether of the couple, family, business, town, state, country, or religion. This is also very convenient, but no more so than is the conjoined opportunity for instant and undeserved moral virtue. Once the world is divided, such that those unfairly on top have been segregated conceptually from those unfairly suffering on the bottom, the pathway to messianic status is magically revealed: moral effort becomes nothing but allyship with the victims, however hypothetical, merely emotional, purely conceptual, or self-serving—even psychopathic—that allyship might be.

The resentful, then murderous, then genocidal Jacobins who first planned the French Revolution and then took it over completely were the spiritual descendants of Cain. Karl Marx is Cain to the core, construing society as nothing but a battleground of power; assuming that any qualitative judgment regarding the value of comparative sacrifice is a game rigged by the victors. He failed completely (and purposefully) to separate wheat from chaff in the totalizing condemnation of the "bourgeoisie," regarding them in consequence of their success as only parasites, predators, and thieves, and gave no credit whatsoever for the wealth and stable societal structure they produced as a result of their conscientious, diligent, honest, and productive labor. The modern meta-Marxists, the postmodern power players, have, as it were, metastasized Marx—but, more deeply, the spirit of Cain—extending the diagnosis of corrupted power to every possible categorization by group that can be applied to man and woman.

All success, according to such accounts, takes place in a landscape of misery, characterized by intrinsically scarce and limited resources. All the games that people might play and find comparative success or failure within are games of force and compulsion, all equal in their intrinsic value (or lack thereof). They are not games at all, but battlegrounds of tyrant and slave, with the roles distributed involuntarily and in a purely deterministic or socially constructed manner. All the successful contenders in such pathological contests win because they hoard and deprive, and all those who fail—and on any dimension whatsoever—do so unfairly, through no fault of their own. In keeping with such presumptions, there is held to be no true effort, no conscientious striving or effort—a conclusion obviously much to the benefit of the truly psychopathic, predatory, parasitical, and worse. Such hypotheses are much to the benefit of those who wish only to use power and force to obtain their essentially hedonistic and narrowly self-centered goals; worse yet, much to the benefit of those who justify their striving after power with the claim that all games are, in the final analysis, battles of power, and that anyone who claims the contrary is merely revealing the depth of their capacity to selfishly manipulate. It is with such rationales that the stage is set for the dominion of hell, which is the eternal stage-play of those who jockey for nothing but comparative status—and for the rise to predominance within the confines of that terrible drama of the worst of all possible devils. This is a consequence of the imitation of Cain—and the fate of the Canaanites, the children of Cain, who are constantly defeated in the biblical tales by those who live by the Logos and pledge their devotion truly to God.

3.4. The good shepherd as archetypal leader

"And Abel was a keeper of sheep" (Genesis 4:2). Why a keeper of sheep? In the Old Testament, the image of the shepherd appears constantly, in a literal sense and as a metaphor for spiritual leadership: "The Lord is my shepherd; I shall not want. He maketh me to lie down in green pastures: he leadeth me beside the still waters" (Psalms 23:1–2). Isaiah echoes such sentiments, in relationship to the character of God: "He shall feed his flock like a shepherd: he shall gather the lambs with his arm, and carry them in his bosom, and shall gently lead those that are with young" (Isaiah 40:11), insisting as well that lost humanity can be understood most profoundly through the metaphor of straying sheep (a trope referred back to in the New Testament): "All we like sheep have gone astray; we have turned every one to his own way; and the Lord hath laid on him the iniquity of us all" (Isaiah 53:6). Ezekiel (34:2–3) upbraids the shepherds of Israel for attending to their own narrow needs before considering the people, "Son of man, prophesy against the shepherds of Israel, prophesy, and say unto them, Thus saith the Lord God unto the shepherds; Woe be to the shepherds of Israel that do feed themselves! Should not the shepherds feed the flocks? Ye eat the fat, and ye clothe you with the wool, ye kill them that are fed: but ye feed not the flock." When the patriarch Jacob/Israel delivers his blessing upon Joseph, to take a further example, he does so as follows:

> Then he blessed Joseph and said, "May the God before whom my fathers Abraham and Isaac walked faithfully, the God who has been my shepherd all my life to this day, the Angel who has delivered me from all harm—may he bless these boys." (Genesis 48:16, New International Version)

Shepherds in biblical times faced a stunningly difficult environment—one requiring endurance, skill, and courage. Shepherds had to protect their flocks from predators, including wolves and lions, navigate treacherous terrain to locate food and water, and endure extremes of heat and cold. The young David is precisely such a hero/shepherd. He faces the giant Philistine warrior—the archetypal prepared enemy—with nothing but a slingshot, a skill with which he has developed while caring for his flock. God selected David for precisely such virtues:

> He also chose David His servant, And took him from the sheepfolds;
>
> From following the ewes great with young he brought him to feed Jacob his people, and Israel his inheritance.
>
> So he fed them [alternative: "shepherded them," New King James Version] according to the integrity of his heart; and guided them by the skillfulness of his hands.
>
> *Psalms 78:70–72*

Thus, the shepherd is an image of the mightiest hero, albeit in ordinary guise, armed with little but courage and faith, successfully confronting the worst in nature and man while devoting his service to the least and most vulnerable. These are precisely the crucial yet paradoxical masculine virtues captured by Michelangelo's statue of David, with its great hands and stance of strength, grace, and ready alertness. That statue is simultaneously ideal and reproach, target and judge, and contains within it the terror of the beauty that eternally does the same thing, and that frightens and intimidates people into a careless second-rate taste and aesthetic ethos. Kitsch does not discriminate or judge, appealing cheaply to sentiment and the hypocritical moral virtue of the reflexively compassionate. Hence, for example, the sentimental attractiveness of the ceramic plates adorned with kittens famously favored by J. K. Rowlings's Dolores Umbridge, underworld queen of the do-gooding authoritarians.[44]

To be a shepherd is also to lead and to guide—and to do that in a caring manner, despite the ability to stave off predators. That means that the classic shepherd is in some real sense the ideal man, the eminently and persistently desirable combination of someone monstrous enough to confront and master the beasts that lurk in the night yet productive, kind, and generous enough to provide and share. Such men are the true target of both women's innermost desire[45] and of the proclivity of men to admire their fellows, even though both can be fooled in their admiration by narcissistic, psychopathic, manipulative, and even sadistic pretenders.[46] This admirable dual proclivity has to come from the heart, as well, and cannot be purchased or faked, unlike its false, manipulative, and instrumental counterpart. It is for such reasons that Christ says of Himself:

> I am the good shepherd: the good shepherd giveth his life for the sheep.
> But he that is an hireling, and not the shepherd, whose own the sheep are not, seeth the wolf coming, and leaveth the sheep, and fleeth: and the wolf catcheth them, and scattereth the sheep.
> The hireling fleeth, because he is an hireling, and careth not for the sheep.
>
> *John 10:11–13*

When properly integrated, the traits that might also predispose someone to callousness, uncaring, and even psychopathy can constitute the very basis for an implacable courage and strength.[47] Women dispense with most men in their choice of partner because finding someone who optimally walks the line is very difficult—not least because it is genuinely difficult in fact to walk it. The eternal quandary of women? "If I find the right man, he will keep away the monsters, but if I get one who is too monstrous himself, then I am in trouble (even though he might be perversely sexy): He will be a monster to me, as well as to others, and that is not a good plan. I need to find someone who is half-monster and half-kind." It is for this reason that the "civilizable monster" is, arguably, the prime character in both the romantic and pornographic fiction preferred by women.[48]

Best of luck locating—or being—him.

When we sacrifice, we bargain with the future. We give up something now in the faith that our offering will be returned, and with interest. The future is the unrealized horizon of possibility, the chaos that was obtained at the beginning of time, the potential that still confronts our Logos in the here and now—the very realm of trouble and opportunity or dragon and treasure that eternally confronts us. When we sacrifice—when we work—we establish what is in effect a contractual relationship with that possibility and, simultaneously, with the community, our future "higher" or "deeper" self, and becoming itself. We are, in effect, making a deal: *I will give up something now. As a result, I will receive something—and something better—in the future.* It might be argued that this deal is made not with God but with the social world, even "the patriarchy."

In such a case, what is construed in religious terms as the covenant becomes something more like the classic social contract: I work for others, and store up reputation and favor. That is repaid to me in the future. Alternatively, I invest in or work my property, the "right" to which is bestowed upon me by social agreement, as is the right to benefit from my investment. This assumption of mere social contract is an ill-advised and false move, however, both conceptually and ontologically. Societies only remain their viability, and at every level of complexity from couple to state, when they are predicated on an underlying ethos that is not itself mere agreement, although such agreement is necessary. Something deeper is required; some reflection of a deeper reality—one that is the precondition for the genuine establishment and maintenance of the necessary agreements of the social world; one that is predicated, for example, on respect for both God and the soul and, therefore, for the individual.

All games are not equally playable. Failure to recognize this stark fact is a (the?) fundamental flaw of the moral relativist and idiot, ideology-possessed revolutionary alike (and the presumptions of the former tend to be those of the latter, and vice versa). If society loses all respect for the integrity of the person and degenerates into a consequent nihilism, or hedonism, or striving for dominance, then the "social contract" will immediately become unsustainable—in a word, moot. This happens all the time, in moments of revolution or ideological possession, and the results are inevitably dire. If society is not structured such that the primary relationships within it are both voluntary and responsible—that is, sacrificial, and in the upward manner—then the arrangements made between people will not truly be agreements. They will instead be outright lies—that is, contracts that no one involved with has any intention of fulfilling—attempts to gain the upper hand for the delights of even fleeting status or permanent power, or impulsive, narrowly self-focused and temporary manifestations of immature whim. No contracts of that nature will hold, particularly not in times of trouble. People will not cooperate, upward, under such conditions. Neither will they compete, productively, according to the rules, nor honor the deals they have made, which are not deals at all but their Luciferian parodies. What was the infamous old Soviet joke?—and it's a good one: "We pretend to work, and they pretend to pay us." If the social order is not Logos-predicated, in other words, it will not be the order that is good, and certainly not the order that is very good. It might very well be hell, instead; hell at least in its earthly form—and is even in that form something that will be experienced as well-nigh eternal.

This relationship to what is highest, simultaneously personal, and contractual is what is meant in the deepest sense by *covenant*. God refers to this covenant when He tells Cain, as we shall see, that he would be accepted if he only did what was right (Genesis 4:7). There is a very deep connection between this idea of contract or covenant and the idea that man should exist in relationship with what is to be properly placed at the pinnacle or serve as proper foundation. How is this to be understood? Consider this: our personalities are our means of adaptation to the world in the broadest sense—to the psychological, social, and natural worlds, considered as a unity. We regard what is most central to us, as conscious beings, as our personality. We know and treat ourselves and one another as personalities. We identify with our personalities—and personalities exist, by definition, in relationship. We are organized, at the supreme level of our being, as personalities. Personality, to put it another way, is our chosen mode of adaptation, of being in the world, our essence, our spirit.

We face the world as personalities. We have evolved, even speaking scientifically, as personalities. Personalities cannot exist, except in relationship. Thus, it is by no means unreasonable, and may in fact be reasonably regarded as necessary, to deem our sacrificial covenant with the future, our potential selves, with others, and with the pattern of the cosmic order as a *relationship*. Why? To say it again: *because we inevitably exist, as human beings, in relationship.* This consideration, however, begs another fundamental question: Relationship with what—or who? The answer, at minimum: with the future, toward whose improvement we eternally work; to whose betterment we sacrifice. With those around us: parents, children, wives and husbands, friends, coworkers; fellow citizens and souls. With the order of the natural world, balanced with that of the community. More deeply, with the spirit of the Creator itself, as it makes itself manifest across situation and time. And ask yourself this, from your no doubt still dubious atheist, materialist, and Darwinian stance: Why would we be organized at the highest level of identity as a sacrificing or working personality—with all the attendant assumption of relationship that would justify such organization—if doing so were anything other than a functional means of adaptation to what is most deeply real?

And that is not all. There is also escaping from the necessity of the hypothesis of personality and even necessarily sacrificial personality in relationship to any manifestation of the inevitable patterning of attention and action. This is even true if we are impulsive and immature; if we are governed, for example, by hedonistic whim: such a whim is nothing but a short-term covenant ("If I pursue this immediate desire, in this particular way, I may obtain what I want"). The hedonist merely sacrifices to the short-term sequential gods of his whim, instead of to some higher-order or deeper psychological and social unity. Why sacrifice? At least because he allows himself to be pulled one way, here and now, rather than any of the many other ways that might clamor to do such pulling; also because he offers up the integrated, responsible, and adventurous future self he might have been, had he forgone his immaturity, to the pleasures of the moment. Shades of Peter Pan and the Lost Boys; shades of Pinocchio and the slavish delinquents of Pleasure Island.

The hedonist, possessed by his desire, may even identify with that god, in the moment or even quasi-permanently (*quasi* because there will be no real commitment, as that would require precisely the sacrifice that is being rejected). He may presume ownership or, more truly, sovereignty over his current whim ("I am what it is that wants, within me"); claim sexual proclivity or other desire, for example, as the very hallmark of personal being and becoming. This makes every hedonist a polytheist, willing to invite in and to celebrate or worship (that is, to place at the pinnacle or make foundational) the diverse range of spirits corresponding to his or her momentary impulses and drives. All claims to the contrary, however: someone possessed by lust, anger, hunger, or envy is not the master of that ancient motivation or hierarchy of motivation but its slave. The orgiastic and materialistic worshippers of the golden calf are hardly masters of their own fate.

3.5. The sacrifice pleasing to God

Once an understanding or conceptualization of the necessity of sacrifice or work and of their identity is established, new questions immediately and inevitably arise in the imagination of the seeker of the truth: What work *works best*? What *sacrifices*, to use the symbolic representation, will be most enthusiastically accepted by self, fellow man, and natural world—will most please God? Understood in this manner, the question of proper offering is properly conceived as ultimate in its difficulty, no different than asking, "What is the purpose or meaning of life?" Cain and Abel, standing at the very dawn of profane history, face that abysmal or heavenly mystery, directly, in the immediate aftermath of their parents' fall and expulsion and the subsequent entry of obstacle and toil into the world. The interaction between the diametrically opposed and hostile brothers establishes the pattern of the great drama of temptation that forever characterizes our familial and social relationships and the course of our own hearts. One spirit—one pattern of fraternal and religious attention and action—exists in absolute opposition to the other. One brother habitually offers to the world and God what is apparently required to maintain the optimal relationship with the earthly and the highest. The other cannot or refuses to do so, fails, shakes his fist at God in rage, and then kills the first, his very ideal.

Abel's offerings are acceptable to God. Cain's are not: "And the Lord had respect unto Abel and to his offering: But unto Cain and to his offering he had not respect" (Genesis 4:4–5). But what does Abel do, in comparison and contrast with his unhappy brother? He works honestly and hard, sacrificing most diligently and completely, offering what is both firstborn and of the highest quality. What is "firstborn" is the intent of an offering, a piece of work, a job. It sets the tone, establishes the pattern, and constitutes the aim. What is of highest quality is first, without blemish—thus the perfect offering— and then that which provides the most value (represented in the image-laden and symbolic language of the story as the richest of all possible sources of food). The divine requirement for quality in necessary and acceptable sacrifice is a theme returned to and developed thoroughly in many of the following biblical texts. The Book of Leviticus, part of the accounts of the exploits and adventures of Moses and the Chosen People, provides a further elaboration—a step forward in codification or explicit representation:

> Ye shall offer at your own will a male without blemish, of the beeves, of the sheep, or of the goats.
>
> But whatsoever hath a blemish, that shall ye not offer: for it shall not be acceptable for you.
>
> And whosoever offereth a sacrifice of peace offerings unto the Lord to accomplish his vow, or a freewill offering in beeves or sheep, it shall be perfect to be accepted; there shall be no blemish therein.
>
> Blind, or broken, or maimed, or having a wen, or scurvy, or scabbed, ye shall not offer these unto the Lord, nor make an offering by fire of them upon the altar unto the Lord.
>
> Either a bullock or a lamb that hath any thing superfluous or lacking in his parts, that mayest thou offer for a freewill offering; but for a vow it shall not be accepted.

Ye shall not offer unto the Lord that which is bruised, or crushed, or broken, or cut; neither shall ye make any offering thereof in your land.

Neither from a stranger's hand shall ye offer the bread of your God of any of these; because their corruption is in them, and blemishes be in them: they shall not be accepted for you.

Leviticus 22:19–25

Harmony with the cosmic order can't be established by foisting off on the divine something that is damaged and useless for current purpose, and therefore all-too-conveniently and hypocritically offered as an indication of aim, purpose, and intent. This is a variant of the vain using of God's name, which becomes something strictly forbidden in commandments handed down to Moses in the Exodus text. Everything possible must be directed upward to the highest possible aim, for the unselfconscious walking with God that characterizes Abel's mode of being to become possible. The idea that such offering must be of the highest quality is already implicitly axiomatic at the time when the Cain and Abel story emerges, although the story represents that understanding, and furthers it. Only God knows, so to speak, how much intense striving for clear conceptualization proceeded that stunningly clear, distilled, and unforgettable formulation.

Cain also offers not the heavenly fruit, or the highest aspirations of the spirit, but "the fruit of the ground" (Genesis 4:4). Abel, by contrast, offers not only the perfect firstborn but the "fat thereof" (also Genesis 4:4), the most fruitful or richest part, representing the peak, best, or finest of something. The cooking and burning of animal fat during sacrifices was also held to release an aroma that God experienced according to various descriptions (Leviticus 3:16) as "sweet savour" (King James Version), "refreshing" (Literal Standard Version), "pleasing" (New International Version), and, perhaps most interesting, given the serious advantages of not irritating the very agent of divine justice, "soothing" (Amplified Bible): "And the priest shall burn them upon the altar: it is the food of the offering made by fire for a sweet savour: all the fat is the Lord's." The best part is by necessity God's. This is a matter of definition, as much as practical sense and theological, spiritual, or psychological realization. Of course what is most likely to work is the whole-hearted offering of what is best. Of course what is best should be devoted to the highest imaginable purpose. Anything else is not aiming at success; at life more abundant; at reestablishment of the Garden of Eden. Anything else is aiming at failure; the dull misery of mediocrity or the unbearable suffering of the abysmal itself.

Abel is a shepherd—and we have already indicated why.[49] He offers the lambs he raises to God; offers, in good faith, the best cuts, butchered from the most perfect animals, abiding by the doctrine later delineated in Leviticus and elsewhere. Cain makes sacrifices too. He is a farmer. He offers the plants he grows to God.

> And Abel was a keeper of sheep, but Cain was a tiller of the ground:
>> And in process of time it came to pass, that Cain brought of the fruit of the ground an offering unto the Lord.
>> And Abel, he also brought of the firstlings of his flock and of the fat thereof. And the Lord had respect unto Abel and to his offering.
>
> *Genesis 4:2–4*

Alternative translations for "the firstlings of his flock and of the fat thereof," varying the theme of highest quality: *the best portions of the first-born lambs from his flock* (New International Version); *the [finest] firstborn of his flock and the fat portions* (Amplified Bible); *the firstborn lamb from his sheep and . . . the Lord the best parts of it* (Contemporary English Version); and *some choice parts of the firstborn animals from his flock* (God's Word Translation). Let us reiterate: among the people who wrote these lines the firstborn of an animal or, indeed, a human being, had special status—was implicitly or even explicitly consecrated to God[50]—so that the choicest cut from a firstborn lamb was indeed the best of the best.

Cain, however, does not do so well in his offerings. To say the least.

3.6. Creatively possessed by the spirit of resentment

God's respect for Abel's offerings is not echoed in the case of his brother. Why? Cain appears to be keeping something in reserve, holding something back, failing to put his best foot forward. His offerings are first damned by faint praise: Abel's offerings are defined explicitly in the text as of the highest quality, while little is said about what Cain brings to the table. Further, and more definitively, Cain is directly upbraided by God for his half-hearted and deceitful efforts: "If thou doest well, shalt thou not be accepted? and if thou doest not well, sin lieth at the door" (Genesis 4:7). Alternative translations include:

"If you do what is right, will you not be accepted? But if you do not do what is right, sin is crouching at your door; it desires to have you, but you must rule over it" (New International Version)

"If you do well, will you not be accepted? And if you do not do well, sin is crouching at the door. Its desire is contrary to you, but you must rule over it" (English Standard Version)

"If you do well, won't you be accepted? But if you don't do well, sin is lying outside your door, ready to attack. It wants to control you, but you must master it" (God's Word Translation)

"If you had done the right thing, you would be smiling; but because you have done evil, sin is crouching at your door. It wants to rule you, but you must overcome it" (Good News Translation).

This idea of encroaching sin makes itself manifest again, in varied form and much later in the biblical texts, in 1 Peter 5:8: "Be sober, be vigilant; because your adversary the devil, as a roaring lion, walketh about, seeking whom he may devour."[51] It is useful to outline Cain's situation to understand what is meant by the fact of this devil at the door. Abel's wayward brother is unhappy—of fallen countenance—in the aftermath of his failure. He takes it up with God. God informs him that he would be successful if only he did well—that is, make the exceptional offering that life truly demands. God then explains Cain's predicament in a more sophisticated and also much more cutting, burning, and damning manner. It is not exactly that failure, per se, has produced the misery of the would-be-successful plaintiff. The divine indicates that it is instead his *response to failure*. Instead of noting his error, rectifying his ways, and improving the quality of his sacrifices—instead of confessing, repenting, and atoning, it might be said—Cain instead opens the door to something that both justifies and amplifies his rebellion and resentment.

A very deep causal analysis is transpiring in a few short lines in relationship to the existence and effect and voluntary, invitational relationship with the sin that lies or crouches at the door. This can be profitably explored in two manners: first, in the tradition of biblical exegesis itself; second, in explicating the parallel between this story and certain obscure variations of the story of the Egyptian redeemer-god Horus's battle with Seth. Seth was the Egyptian version of Satan, the eternal destroyer of tradition and of the vision that redeems and resurrects.[52] Note first the consequence of Cain's failure to do well; of his rejection of the opportunity to go all in, or to fully commit; of his failure to offer his best. God smiles, so to speak, upon Abel and his sacrifice: "But unto Cain and his offering he had not respect" (Genesis 4:5). Cain's response? "And Cain was very wroth, and his countenance fell" (Genesis 4:5). Other translations amplify the nature of this response: Cain is angry and downcast (New International Version); dejected (New Living Translation); indignant, annoyed, and hostile (Amplified Bible); furious and despondent (Holman Christian Standard Bible); sorrowful (Brenton Septuagint Translation); unable to hide his feelings (Contemporary English Version) and prone to scowl (Good News Translation); and upset and depressed (International Standard Version). The Scottish preacher and writer Alexander Maclaren (1910), well known at the time and after for his biblical expositions, had the following to say about this passage:

Strange as the words sound, if I mistake not, they convey some very solemn lessons, and if well considered, become pregnant with meaning. The key to the whole interpretation of them is to remember that they describe what happens after, and because of, wrong-doing. They are all suspended on *If thou doest not well.* Then, in that case, for the first thing—*sin lieth at the door.* Now the word translated here *lieth* is employed only to express the crouching of an animal, and frequently of a wild animal. The picture, then, is of the wrong-doer's sin lying at his door there like a crouching tiger ready to spring, and if it springs, fatal. "If thou doest not well, a wild beast crouches at thy door."

Then there follow, with a singular swift transition of the metaphor, other words still harder to interpret, and which have been, as a matter of fact, interpreted in very diverse fashions. "And unto thee shall be its desire, and thou shalt rule over it." Where did we hear these words before? They were spoken to Eve, in the declaration of her punishment. They contain the blessing that was embedded in the curse. "Thy desire shall be to thy husband, and he shall rule over thee." The longing of the pure womanly heart to the husband of her love, and the authority of the husband over the loving wife—the source of the deepest joy and purity of earth, is transferred, by a singularly bold metaphor, to this other relationship, and, in horrible parody of the wedded union and love, we have the picture of the sin, that was thought of as crouching at the sinner's door like a wild beast, now, as it were, wedded to him. He is mated to it now, and it has a kind of tigerish, murderous desire after him, while he on his part is to subdue and control it.[53]

There is a very interesting parallel between this story and an account in the ancient Egyptian texts detailing the relationship of the primary gods and goddess of that state,[54] who were Osiris, Seth, Isis, and Horus.[55] Horus and Seth are contending gods, whose battle is very much reminiscent of the opposition between Abel and Cain, respectively. The former is the Egyptian god of careful attention and renewal; the latter the eternal plotter and power-mad social climber.[56] Horus returns from a youth and adolescence spent in exile to confront Seth, who is his evil uncle, after the latter has overthrown his father and usurped the throne (much like King Arthur or Simba in Disney's *The Lion King*). They battle terribly for dominance or, in the case of the hero, authority. Some variants have Horus losing an eye in the confrontation with Seth. This is an indication of the danger posed by the fact of a transcendent and ultimate malevolence to consciousness itself. Others (for example, *The Contendings of Horus*[57]) stress that a sexual relationship is forced upon Horus by Seth (successfully, in part, or unsuccessfully, depending on the text), akin to that which apparently transpires between Cain and sin. While the two wrestle, Seth attempts to sexually abuse Horus. In some versions, Seth's seed enters the body of Horus and makes him ill. This is very much reminiscent of the idea of the horcrux developed by author J. K. Rowling[58]—the intrusion of something living, something seedlike, into the soul itself. In other versions (including the *Contendings* text itself), Horus thwarts Seth by catching the seed in his hands, whereupon his mother, Isis, reverses the game, offering Horus's seed to Seth, in secret, and defeating him, in consequence. The meaning of this should be made clear: the corrupting influence of Seth is his seminal idea, while the redeeming influence of Horus is his. The former can terribly threaten the latter, but the latter can triumph as well—and continually—over the former.

The sexual metaphor is apt, as well as frightening, because the voluntary union of Cain with sin has a creative element. We understand this, at some implicit level, not least because our curses when we curse dreadful fate reflect such understanding or mirror that complex of meaning. We describe ourselves as being f**ked with, when manipulated or deceived; as being f**ked over, when something has not gone our way; of things being all f**ked up, when they are not laying themselves out as we would like (and most likely because our sacrifices have been truly second-rate). There is a real bitterness in such complaints, when they are not made in a humorous manner; a bitterness that is both the claiming of the much-vaunted and I-can-do-no-wrong status of victim, and an accusation that something is flawed at the fundament of the cosmic or even divine order.

God takes it upon himself to indicate and insist that Cain's misery is not caused in some simple deterministic manner by the fact of his second-rate work or sacrifice (even though his failure itself is caused by exactly that). There is failure, certainly, but that is held to be something separate from the emotional response to the failure; something separate even from the understanding of its causal consequences. God implies that Cain could react to and interpret his downfall in a manner that differs from the manner he has chosen and is more appropriate, acceptable, and productive. He could, for example, become contrite, and strive to improve—even to be grateful for the lesson that failure has brought him. He could engage in the radical acceptance of fault and the consequent painful retooling of personality. He could subject himself voluntarily to the terrible swift sword and let the deadwood be cut and burned away. Instead, Cain invites in the devil himself. Worse: It is also not merely that Cain allows himself to be possessed, such that he is deprived of his will or that he blindly follows like a hapless puppet, controlled in a simply deterministic manner. Quite the contrary: as a creature with inviolable free will, he enters instead into a voluntary and blackly creative relationship with the temptation crouching in predatory form at his doorstep. He willingly enables it to have its way with him. Then he broods over what has been so terribly born. No one moves to murder from mere resentment without a lengthy period of oh-so-delightfully obsessive dwelling and fantasizing.[59]

The perverse relationship Cain develops with sin enables that dread spirit to bloom in all its particulars: enables the more abstract beckoning spirit of evil to manifest itself concretely in the specific time and place of the present; enables the antihuman adversarial spirit to incarnate. The sinner therefore consorts, freely and voluntarily—*malitia praecogitata* (malice aforethought[60])—with what might be described as the general spirit of mayhem. By doing so, he takes within himself the leaven of malice and makes it his own. This makes manifest in the world his particularized, embodied, creative destiny of mayhem, justified by his own resentments, jealousies, disappointments, frustrations, rages, and victimizations (often real, as suffering and injustice is often real). Every school shooter, for example, has his now-stereotyped manifesto—his false prophecy; his well-developed and long-brooded-upon rationale. The fact that such missives are frequently understandable and even capable of eliciting some recognition and sympathy for what is human, all-too human, does not make the associated and well-rationalized crime any less reprehensible. Everyone has sufficient reason for evil.

It is this undeniable fact of intermediary collaborative process that makes a mockery of any simpleminded attempts to draw a causal pathway between the tragic circumstances of a given person's life and their consequent descent into evil. This is another variant of brute empiricism and idiot determinism: "hurt people become bad" is not a well-developed causal theory. The hypothesis that bad people use the inevitable hurts they have suffered in their lives—many of which they arguably brought upon themselves—to justify their evil is equally plausible, and there is no reason not to assume, at minimum, that it is a little from column A and a little from column B. And, a few words might well be said in favor of arguments for the fundamental role for the pathway from manipulative victimhood rather than pain to evil. First, it is obviously the case that someone motivated to do harm will claim every possible self-justification for doing so, and that doing so is an inextricable part or even the main feature of the evil they are aiming at. Second, although the temptation toward, say, resentment might loom large—particularly when a person has been betrayed as well as damaged—the pact with sin simply does not have to be made, let alone encouraged, cultivated, and nurtured.

Someone victimized, however unfairly, could well and should conclude from their experience not that such hurt should be paid forward, or extended in its application even to God Himself, but that such acts are wrong, and to reject their furtherance instead of identifying with and mimicking the perpetrator (transmitting childhood abuse down the generations, for example). If this were not true, every family would rapidly become a horror show, as all abuse would be conserved and transmitted and therefore inevitably spread until everyone was contaminated and perpetrating. Most people offered the example of the bully or worse will choose not to duplicate but to reject it, such that its damaging effect is ameliorated across time, rather than exaggerated and expanded. The human race would be in a sorry state indeed and in no time if this was not the case. Thus the more accurate model is not "evil comes from pain" (inequality, betrayal, oppression, even tragedy) but "hurt people recover, forgive, and move on."[61]

Work as sacrifice in the Cain and Abel narrative is the attempt to act out the essence of work, to understand its central tendency, to portray or conceptualize the nature of the efforts of man. This occurs first in dramatic representation—literal acting out; the equivalent of the pretend play that is so formative among children. Then it is represented in dramatic imagination; afterward, if possible, it is explicitly formulated as story and description. We are still in the latter stage, despite the intermediating centuries, with regard to our full understanding of sacrifice, as the process of coming to full, explicit consciousness is a difficult one, with an unknown extent or upper limit. The great Swiss genetic epistemologist and developmental psychologist Jean Piaget noted that children are prone to imitate themselves: that they will note actions they have taken that produce a desired or interestingly unexpected outcome, "become conscious" of those actions (that is, notice that and how they undertook them), and then copy or mimic themselves, re-presenting the action in reenactment.[62] This is partially the formulation of skill, ability, or habit (if sufficiently repeated) and partially a bridge to understanding, as opposed to simply doing.

Early childhood games, such as peekaboo, emerge when an infant and an adult perform such acts of ritualization together, synchronizing their efforts, establishing a game-rule-like regularity in iterated action and reaction. Constancy and predictability of fair exchange with optimally interesting variation: the genesis of trade. We trade every time we imitate one another; each time we open our mouths to speak. We offer each other the fruits of our exploratory and conscientious effort and derive immense nourishment in return. This is not just a metaphor: it is one thing to offer someone food, but something else completely to teach them how to provision themselves. Christ is, for example, the miraculous provider of water (John 4:13–14), loaves, and fishes (Matthew 14:15–21) because He embodies or stands for or represents or is the ethos of complete voluntary self-sacrifice upon which productive activity and trade itself rests. This might be understood as the full manifestation of the offerings of Abel that, in comparison with Cain's, earned the respect of God (Genesis 4:4). This is a viewpoint that takes into account the reliance of provision even of so-called "natural resources" on an individual and socially-instantiated ethos that makes the very use, even the discovery, of such resources possible, productive, and sustainable.

The self-mimicry described by Piaget can well be considered the basis of ritual. Imagine, however, that in the case of the imitation that most truly characterizes human play something somewhat more complex is occurring; something much more sophisticated than the mere mimicry or exact duplication of a single action; something more akin to the mimicry of a set of related actions. In this case, that set of related actions would be various ways and means of giving something up in the present to best ensure, or at least to place a bet on, the future and its potential returns. The consequence of such mimicry is, most concretely, the drama of the sacrificial altar. More abstractly or psychologically it is the drama of bargaining with possibility; the drama of negotiating with the future, or the future self—the drama of establishing a contractual covenant with the very spirit of being. The full manifestation of this drama would be the personality predicated upon the offering that is the most comprehensive possible or even conceivable. That would be the incarnation of the personality that lights or illuminates the world (Matthew 5:14–15); the very Word made flesh (John 1:14).

The imagery used to define the method of communication with the divine in the ancient story at hand is very concrete and archaic, according to the conventions of modern sensibility, and relies on a series of implicit metaphorical conventions or presumptions. Up is good compared with down. Down is demoralized, hunched, slumped. Down is downcast, with fallen countenance. Down is dirt, dust, contamination, and multiplicity. Up is progress compared with descent; compared with failure. Heaven is good (and progress). Heaven is up, and the unity of all integrated upward aim. The ultimate up is skyward; thus, heaven is skyward. God is the ultimate good. The ultimate good, God, therefore must reside in heaven. Smoke rises up.

Smoke is essence, gist, or spirit. The entity residing in or characterizing the ultimate up can detect the quality of a sacrifice in the upward rising smoke. Finally, the offering that aims up most successfully is the complete and perfect investment that best pleases God. Because of the concreteness of this archaic content and imagery, it is easy for modern people (and quite the existential relief) to overlook the very brief story's deep sophistication in problem statement, revelation, deliberation, and conclusion. Once the reasons for or logic of the referents is made clear, however, that casual overlooking is no longer possible. It is following such realization that the real trouble—the real adventure—can begin.

Why might heaven be up? Because the sky is beyond us, and therefore representative of what is eternally beyond. Because up is the proper aim, as opposed, metaphorically, to down; because we "look up" to people we admire, thus constituting their character as our eventual aim; because if we look down we can see only what we are standing on and not where we are going; because to "look down" on is to be contemptuous of; because contemplation of the heavens to which we might raise our eyes inspires awe and the desire to imitate; because we can come to be what we imitate most devoutly; and because we can in truth navigate by the position of the heavenly bodies. As linguist and philosopher George Lakoff notes:

> *Up is good* is an image-schema that is based on the universal human experience of being upright, vertical, and oriented toward the sky. The metaphorical entailments of the image-schema are highly systematized and can be observed in a wide variety of domains. It is a pervasive, deep-seated, and highly conventionalized metaphor in our language and thought.[63]

We can understand from this why the metaphor of up versus down springs to mind, is available for use, makes sense, and can be communicated—and, as well, how that understandable and communicable sense depends on embodiment. An upright man is motivated, optimistic, gazing forward, and moving, in stark contrast with someone defeated, slumped, and looking at the ground. *Up* is positive emotion and approach; *down* is collapsed and avoidant. The meaning of "up" is therefore not a mere reflection of its relationship to other words but a reference to a shared category of experience, whose nature is in turn dependent on the shared psychophysiological structures—the embodiment or incarnation—that gives all human experience its particular quality, and that makes it broadly and understandably similar and communicable.

Why does God reside in heaven? Because the awe that enters and inspires us when we gaze upward at the sun or moon or the starry realm of the night sky puts us in touch, at an instinctual level, with the spirit that "descended"— "the same also that ascended up far above all heavens, that he might fill all things" (Ephesians 4:10).[64] Why is the God who occupies the highest upward place concerned about the quality of sacrifice? *Why*, exactly, is something far from clear; a question whose answer inevitably shades into the ineffable. It is at least in part because all things worth doing either have no relationship with one another, or conflict in their realization, or both reflect and are united, in some mysterious manner, with the transcendent good itself—as those are the only three options. If irrelevant to one another, uniting them within the confines of a single personality or society becomes a difficult endeavor—one that is only exaggerated, to the point of impossibility, if instead they exist in a difference that is irreconcilable. To what end, then—if any—do and should all things strive? Toward the ultimate up, perhaps? Toward the final good, however that might be described? This appears as the hypothesis or insistence of the monotheism of the biblical stories, and is the alternative, by definition, to dissociation or paradoxical opposition. That is certainly the idea implicit, say, in the imagery of Jacob's Ladder, which presents a never-ending spiraling hierarchy of up, toward a heaven that is already good, but is still and endlessly getting better:

> And Jacob went out from Beersheba, and went toward Haran.
> And he lighted upon a certain place, and tarried there all night, because the sun was set; and he took of the stones of that place, and put them for his pillows, and lay down in that place to sleep.

And he dreamed, and behold a ladder set up on the earth, and the top of it reached to heaven: and behold the angels of God ascending and descending on it.

And, behold, the Lord stood above it, and said, I am the Lord God of Abraham thy father, and the God of Isaac.

Genesis 28:10–13

Consider, too—or remember—that any directed attention or action is a unity, however temporary, of many diverse spirits and materials. Even to move my hand to grip a glass to bring it to my mouth requires both sacrifice and singularity of purpose. The former is the prioritization of the demands of thirst over every other current motivating spirit. The latter is the domination of the pattern of attention and action that serves the purposes of the movement in question over all other potential actions. Such a unity is necessarily integrated into a higher unity, or the action is shallow, even pointless. Although there is some immediate pleasure in the consequences of my action, in the refreshment of the drink, I quench my thirst most fundamentally to serve my other purposes. These tend to be arranged upward, and hierarchically, insofar as what I am doing most broadly has a point and a purpose. There is no reason to assign an arbitrary ceiling to the fact of that upward striving: to posit that unity exists, say, at the level of the local action, but not at any higher point or, indeed, at the highest of all conceivable points. This is expressed symbolically—in an image-laden, dramatic, and literary manner— in the idea of a ladder, pole, or tree bridging the gap between Earth and Heaven. This is one of the most ancient ideas of mankind, stretching back to Paleolithic times and the shamanic rituals employing the imagery of the cosmic tree. As the great Romanian historian of religion Mircea Eliade notes:

[W]e find the symbolism of the liana or vine stretching from earth to heaven in the Iranian, Slav, and Finno-Ugrian areas, and the symbolism of the cosmic tree (which is also a liana) in the Iranian, Indo-European, and Altaic areas, as well as in America and among the Oceanic peoples.[65]

[T]he tree is often considered to be the ladder that connects the three levels of the cosmos: the underworld, the earth, and the sky.[66]

The symbolism of the Cosmic Tree and the World Pillar, the Tree of Life and the Ladder of the Gods, is one of the most widespread and deeply rooted in human culture. It is not an exaggeration to say that no other symbol touches the core of the sacred so universally, and none is capable of conveying to any mind, regardless of its cultural background, the same meaning and force.[67]

The spirit of being and becoming strives upward, toward a continual unfolding of forms. Man is made in the image of that spirit and is called on to sacrifice without reservation in the pursuit of its manifestation. The integrity of the psyche and the stability and productivity of the community are in fact predicated on the willingness to do so. This is by no means some arbitrary supposition. It is instead the deepest possible reflection of the cosmic order, founded on the principle of voluntary offering upward. This is the order that cannot be pridefully rejected by woman or man without the direst of consequences; the order, by definition, that the Luciferian spirit opposes and attempts to usurp—by definition.

Some sacrifices work (are accepted), while others clearly do not and are rejected. This is one of the inalienable facts of life. It is the reason both for much celebrating and rejoicing and for an endless abysmal bitterness. If this is the fundamental fact, then the fundamental question of being—the fundamental moral, rather than factual question—might well be, "What or how should you offer, or sacrifice, to God, to solve the problem of what is acceptable to God—the problem of what is likely to be successful, in the highest of possible senses?" The answer proffered by the ancient authors? The best you have—or heaven help you: or, even more starkly, "If you bring forth what is within you, what you bring forth will save you. If you do not bring forth what is within you, what you do not bring forth will destroy you."[68] It is in establishing this relationship between talent, opportunity, and responsibility that God ensures the maintenance of the eternal balance of justice. This is the meaning of the analogous warning, "For unto whomsoever much is given, of him shall be much required" (Luke 12:48). The level of sacrifice demanded by the divine is proportionate to the degree of privilege awarded however apparently arbitrarily to the fortunate or withheld from the lowly.

Cain's great and archetypal sin is therefore best understood as his holding back, his hiding of his God-given light "under a bushel," his putting it in "a secret place" (Luke 11:33), his failing to offer his best. This is not good, as far as God is concerned—not acceptable to God—but it is also neither acceptable to nor good for Cain—or, as it turns out, for Abel, for God, for the descendants of Cain, or for the whole human race, insofar as those who compose it are tempted by the same spirit that beckoned at the murderous brother's door. Cain burns angrily not only because he has withheld his best, and angered the divine, but because he thereby forgoes what is best in his life, in so doing. The sacrificial ritual—a burnt offering, in this case—is the attempt to signal evidence about quality of offering and, at a deeper level, intent, up the hierarchy of value (the cosmic tree, so to speak) to the highest possible "heavenly" place. This enables establishment of the proper relationship with what is highest. Cain's failure to do this properly means that he deprives himself of what could be the true romantic adventure of his life; the adventure that might justify that very life, and provide it with the significance that is the most effective antidote to nihilistic bitterness and resentful rebellion. It is by no means only the lack of the external, social trappings of success (which are not forthcoming because of his lack of true effort) that embitters Abel's hostile brother. It is the absence of meaning in his life attendant upon his arrogant, deceitful, and slothful withholding.

What, then, is the moral of the story? What is its point, or aim? The insistence that life more abundant requires a complete and total commitment, with every glance, with every word, with every action. We are called upon, in the face of life's overwhelming difficulties and opportunities, to offer no less than absolutely everything we have—everything, conceptualized more appropriately, that we have been given and should be grateful for (rather than, say, "proud of"). Cain and Abel play out this pattern in the concrete manner of material offering. Later in the biblical accounts and in the depths of the increasingly sophisticated and self-reflective soul the essence of a sacrifice becomes its intent, rather than its concrete reality; becomes the psychological offering or aim, rather than the material thing given up—but the seeds for this more sophisticated understanding are already sown in the story of Cain and Abel. Aim up, and offer all that you have.

3.7. Humility and faith versus pride, despair, and vengeful anger

What does it mean, to *do well* or to *not do well*; to *succeed* or to *fail*? The people who formulated and retold the biblical stories in the attempt to answer those perennial existential questions were just as intelligent and wise as we are today—perhaps more so, given the extreme difficulty of their existence and the moral demands that difficulty placed upon them. They were trying to understand something, to prioritize their attention in accordance with that understanding, and to aim properly, in consequence. They were trying to determine how to comport themselves so that they could bargain—formulate a contract, agreement, or covenant—with the central spirit of Being itself, and to do so victoriously. They were, as well, trying to formulate a picture of the deviant path, away from victory and toward failure, for the purposes of contrast, so that consort with the spirit that tempts along that path could be avoided. Everyone always has and always will need and want to understand how to manage exactly that: to select and traverse the right path forward and to avoid the worst detours and pitfalls. That is precisely the guidance provided by calling and conscience, which are the primary twin messengers of God.

This can be most prosaically and reductively understood as the attempt to balance the requirements (the needs and wants) of the present, which appear as immediate desire, with the more abstracted but also vital reality of the future. This means "do not do anything today, in the grip of your impulse, that will compromise tomorrow (or next week, month, or year)." Alternatively— although there is in fact no difference between the two: "do not compromise your social relations (given how badly you are outnumbered) by prioritizing the necessities of the moment." Such reductionism leads to an incomplete and oversimplified understanding of such "balance," however. The covenant is not merely the bargain between present and future and individual and community but a contract ensuring a relationship between individual and community and *the spirit of individual and community*. That spirit has so far in the story been conceptualized as the process that establishes order in its contending with possibility; the heavenly father that, or who, establishes the moral order, forbids its alteration, and punishes deviation from the straight and narrow path; the proper target of sacrifice and the judge of its quality. This is not merely the order itself—God, the Father, it might be said— although it is also that. It is as well the pattern of active confrontation with the unknown that even the Father depends upon, and in some sense is. These are not calls to a childish superstition. They are instead definitions (characterizations) of the spirit of the ultimate up. They are definitions of God. They are attempts to establish the axiom of ultimate unity as the foundation of the real—as what eternally keeps dread, pain, and death at bay, gives meaning and purpose, and inspires hope.

Abel's sacrifices are met with praise, while Cain's are not. Cain gets nowhere in his life not because God or the world is arbitrary but because his sacrifices are insufficient. This is an insistence that echoes the divine prohibition against consuming the fruit of the tree of the knowledge of good and evil; the insistence that there is an implicit moral order—the suffusing of the whole of the being and becoming with the creative spirit that is its Originator and Continuer. It is not up to man or woman to usurp the right to create that moral order, or to attempt to circumvent its strictures pridefully, or in a Machiavellian or otherwise manipulative and false manner. Instead, we are built, so to speak, to honor and reflect that order—to adapt to it, to interpret signs of failure not as insufficiency on the part of the cosmos and its creator, but as evidence of personal insufficiency, to strive such that only what is best is offered and, if that is not good enough, to search for something better yet.

Cain rejects all that—all of that personal responsibility—attempting instead to shape the entire world in the image of his inadequacy. When this fails, as it must, he invites the spirit of bitterness to dwell within him, instead of setting his house in order. In doing so, he rejects even the advice of God, who when he calls upon him states in no uncertain terms (quite the contrary) that his wayward son would yet be accepted, if he did well, and that his bitterness and resentment is a consequence of his voluntary dalliance with sin. Rather than changing, therefore, as God suggests—a very early manifestation of the idea of an inner voice of conscience—Cain kills his brother and, in doing so, turns against being and becoming itself; deeper yet, against God Himself, as the creator of that being. Instead of making his bed, gratefully, Cain becomes murderous, and more: deicidal. He kills Abel, of course, but he does so, in the final analysis, to obtain vengeance against God. This is the true description of the deepest possible bitterness and hatred. The bitter man with fallen countenance does so in the same spirit that possesses Adam when he so resentfully charges woman and God with the responsibility for his own fall and consequent cowardly hiding; in the same spirit that Job's wife calls upon her suffering husband to adopt when he is brought low by the machinations of Satan, and loses everything: wealth, health, dignity, and companionship. "Curse God, and die," she says (Job 2:9)—and even compassionately, perhaps, observing as she does her husband's utter and apparently undeserved misery.

The Abel whose success burns so deeply is, after all, God's favored son. His murder is therefore the ultimate revenge against that hypothetically unfairly favoring Father. It does not take a particularly perspicacious reader to see in that murder not only of the innocent but the positively good the precursor to the fate of Christ. Cain is tempted by the spirit of sin itself—just as his parents were, in the Garden of Eden, although in somewhat variant form. He embraces that tempter with open arms, and then works diligently with that dread essence to create a vengeance as terrible as he could imagine. In this light, it is worthwhile to consider this stark fact: There is no shortage of modern atheists who, despite their disbelief, remain perfectly willing, like Cain—and unlike Abel and Job—to shake their fist at God.[69] They may claim to be doing so on behalf of the victims of the world, themselves included. They may even believe that this is the case, even though someone truly perspicacious and discerning would be very skeptical about the validity of such an attribution. There nonetheless lurks a terrible unconscious darkness in such a claim. The great Russian novelist Fyodor Dostoevsky's murderous Raskolnikov, protagonist of *Crime and Punishment*, that stellar masterpiece, certainly imagines himself as heroic savior to the oppressed and poor, as well as daring transgressor of even the most fundamental norms and ideals of the world.

It does not take much introspection—particularly in relation to bitterness— to understand Cain. There is not a man or woman alive who has not been racked at some point with envy, resentful at failure, wishing harm to the comparatively successful (the terribly ideal). It is very difficult not to curse God, so to speak, when everything is falling apart around you, particularly when the justice of that disintegration appears questionable, as it so often does. Cain fails. Then he renders himself self-righteously cynical and bitter enough to take up the issue with God Himself. This is, to put it mildly, a preposterous thing to do, a true sin of arrogance, resentment, and deceit. God—whatever or whoever He might be—is by definition beyond the scope of human judgment, as He reminds Job much later in the biblical corpus:

Canst thou draw out leviathan with an hook? or his tongue with a cord which thou lettest down?

Canst thou put an hook into his nose? or bore his jaw through with a thorn?

Will he make many supplications unto thee? will he speak soft words unto thee?

Will he make a covenant with thee? wilt thou take him for a servant for ever?

Wilt thou play with him as with a bird? or wilt thou bind him for thy maidens?

Shall the companions make a banquet of him? shall they part him among the merchants?

Canst thou fill his skin with barbed irons? or his head with fish spears?

Lay thine hand upon him, remember the battle, do no more.

Behold, the hope of him is in vain: shall not one be cast down even at the sight of him?

None is so fierce that dare stir him up: who then is able to stand before me?

Job 41:1–10

He beholdeth all high things: he is a king over all the children of pride.

Job 41:34

God is He who eternally defeats even the monstrous Leviathan itself, confronting and overcoming chaos, underworld, and the possibility signified, not least, by the terrible dragon, source of the greatest treasures of the world. He cannot therefore be trifled with, *no matter the justification.*

Man is simply in no position to question the fundamental order of reality—not at its deepest levels. To do so is rebellion, and not of the heroic sort, no matter how it is dressed up or justified. To do so is the sin of pride; the insistence that the forbidden fruit is edible and that its incorporation bestows wisdom; the very pride that not only goes before but is the very essence of the fall. Failure to abide by or mimic the moral order of the creative spirit of being and becoming as if it were good is no different than failure to adapt to the deepest reality—or, more accurately, stubborn, bitter, and prideful refusal to do so, which is the most egregious, deepest, and counterproductive form of failure. That is most truly a failure of the faith on which life itself, let alone life more abundant, eternally and necessarily depends. It is therefore the deepest of moral requirements to hold life and God to be good—no matter what. No matter what. This is a terrible truth. There are no circumstances under which failure to do so can be redefined as success, even when (as in the latter case both of the long-suffering Job and of Christ Himself) the decision even to discontinue living or to lash out in homicidal or even genocidal anger could be understandable to the compassionate and all-too-human onlooker. It is much better even under conditions of extreme and apparently unjust suffering to reaffirm our commitment to life more abundant and to undergo the changes necessary to bear our terrible cross. This is a terrible truth, given what human beings are inevitably called on to bear. The ultimate promise of the covenant, however, is that the spirit of God, reflected in such radical acceptance, abides with us in our suffering and confrontation with evil. And what can withstand the man who has God truly on his side?

Unlike Cain, Job has the sense to hold his tongue in the face of God's reminder of his ineffable mystery and omniscient, omnipresent, and omnipotent sovereignty. The latter realizes, properly and pragmatically (given that stubbornness and bitterness do nothing but make suffering worse), that he is in no position as a mortal creature to render judgment about the propriety not only of Being but of the very creator or precondition of that Being. In his misery, Job therefore responds to God contritely, in a manner opposite to that of Cain:

I know that thou canst do every thing, and that no thought can be withholden from thee.

Who is he that hideth counsel without knowledge? therefore have I uttered that I understood not; things too wonderful for me, which I knew not.

Hear, I beseech thee, and I will speak: I will demand of thee, and declare thou unto me.

I have heard of thee by the hearing of the ear: but now mine eye seeth thee.

Wherefore I abhor myself, and repent in dust and ashes.

Job 42:2-6

Even though the nature of Job's sins, such as they might be, are not evident to him—even though he may even well be in some fundamental sense innocent—he does not fall prey to the temptation of pride. Instead, he searches his conscience for his own flaws and repents as completely as is possible. C. G. Jung famously and controversially suggested that this decision put Job in a position of moral superiority to God Himself,[70] as YHWH put Job to the ultimate test, visiting upon him tragedy after tragedy, at the instigation of none other than Satan, his most wayward and incomprehensible son, and that it was this imbalance in moral order that instigated the Passion.[71] There is, after all, no indication in the text that Job, unlike Cain, has done anything to deserve his terrible fate—quite the contrary, as Job's goodness is testified to by God Himself (Job 8).

God nonetheless puts his faithful son, so to speak, to a severe test, handing him over to Satan to torture, wagering with the devil that Job will not lose faith. This is a decision that at least seems profoundly unfair, to say the least. How, then, is this terrible story to be understood, existentially, if not theologically? First: It is clearly the case that the innocent suffer, and often worse than the guilty, who are at least relieved in the deepest sense by the fact of their punishment, as Dostoevsky was at pains to establish in the case of Raskolnikov, once again, in *Crime and Punishment*. The fact of this undeserved suffering is one of the existential truths that makes life itself appear if not utterly unbearable then at least unjustifiable. Its reality is so profound that it is a central theme of Christ's incarnation. Second: It is the case, at least arguably, that the God within can be called on to defend against the God without (so to speak) against the vagaries of fate.

All the horrors of life—destruction of family, disease, disfigurement, and unwarranted social accusation and judgment—come raining down on Job, who refuses despite it all to lose faith and to succumb to (dally with, more accurately) bitterness, resentment, and nihilism. He rejects the route of Cain, maintaining his faith in himself, life, and God, and is rewarded, in the final analysis, with the provision of something more complete and of higher quality than all that he has lost. Finally, perhaps: Job has faith in himself, and in God, but God also has faith in Job, and in man, in general. He is the fatherly Spirit who insists that we can triumph against adversity, no matter how profound the challenge. He is therefore the spirit of encouragement that makes itself manifest in the advice of our fathers and our more courageous mothers when they say, "Go out, into the world, with all its challenges and opportunities, and prevail; learn to handle the serpents, instead of hiding or fleeing from them." Why would God throw Job, or any of us, into the ring, even with the devil himself? Because He is confident in our victory. Who, then, is God? The spirit within us that is eternally confident in our victory. This is another indication of what is to be properly and necessarily put in the highest place—another characterization of the ultimate unity; another definition of God.

We are certain to experience encounters of sufficient magnitude and apparent injustice in the course of our lives to make bitterness and cynicism appear little more than the necessary and boon companions of the desire for justice. Who among us has not or will not be tempted to scream in frustration, rage, and despair at the sky; to curse fate itself for the dreadful burden that existence has placed on us; to not only lose faith but to view that very loss as nothing short of a moral inevitability, even a requirement (reacting as we are to the all-too-obvious evidence, the terrible facts at hand)? But none of that is helpful. All such bitter albeit apparently justified and requisite faithlessness does is transform what might otherwise be mere tragedy ("mere") into something much more like hell. When we are called upon to suffer injustice and tragedy, is our suffering not inevitably multiplied manifold by acquiescence to the blandishments of anger, envy, resentment, and vengefulness? The serpent that lurks forever in the garden is thus best confronted in a spirit antithetical to that of resentment and arrogant, wounded pride, no matter how much poison it is exuding or has delivered. Is that not the best pathway forward in times of true trouble? Hence the emphasis on humility as a virtue in the Old Testament and the New. To wit: "The fear of the Lord is the instruction of wisdom; and before honor is humility" (Proverbs 15:33); "And whosoever shall exalt himself shall be abased; and he that shall humble himself shall be exalted" (Matthew 23:12).

Heedless of all this, rejecting all this, Cain enters into a creative union with the spirit of sin and renders himself murderously vengeful. He does so, instead of changing—instead of undergoing a transformative metanoia; instead of confessing, repenting, and determining to do better, even when called out by God Himself. This rejection is the very sin against the Holy Spirit that Christ defines as unforgivable (Matthew 3:28–30). Job takes a different tack. He remains faithful—retains his belief in the essential goodness of both himself and, therefore, man, as well as God—even though his circumstances are such that he is pushed beyond any reasonable human limit. In consequence of his enduring upward aim and faithful conviction, all that he has lost (all that has been so unjustly taken from him) is restored—and more:

> So the Lord blessed the latter end of Job more than his beginning:
> for he had fourteen thousand sheep, and six thousand camels, and a
> thousand yoke of oxen, and a thousand she asses.
>
> He had also seven sons and three daughters.
>
> And he called the name of the first, Jemima; and the name of the
> second, Kezia; and the name of the third, Kerenhappuch.
>
> And in all the land were no women found so fair as the daughters
> of Job: and their father gave them inheritance among their brethren.
>
> After this lived Job an hundred and forty years, and saw his sons,
> and his sons' sons, even four generations.
>
> So Job died, being old and full of days.
>
> *Job 42:12–17*

It might well be objected: the ends do not justify the means. The fact that God raises Job to heights beyond what he had previously attained does not mean that it is somehow magically acceptable for the Absolute to have killed his children, destroyed his possessions, compromised his health, and undermined his reputation: not at least if we are applying human standards of evaluation. But the spirit of being and becoming itself is and must forever remain in some important sense beyond such standards, not least because we are faced with the task of reconciling ourselves to the vagaries of existence, no matter how extreme the demand. Why? At least because the alternative—paralyzing subjugation to terror, catastrophic loss of all hope, possession by rage, vengeful obsession, and descent into madness—is worse, inconceivably worse. The insistence of Job is that the properly faithful human being retains his upward aim and devotion—no matter what. Those are dread words indeed. But it is that insistence that enables Job to regain his feet and to prevail once again—even to do better after the cataclysm. Given the inevitability of failure and catastrophe—and even the apparent injustice of fate—what could possibly be better and even more believable news?

It may be hard for someone in the position of the merely human to forgive God, so to speak, for his or her terrible trials and tribulations, deserved and undeserved alike. That is not the point being made in the story of Cain and Abel, nor in the Book of Job. What is put forward instead is a proposition: when terrible things happen—tragic things, unjust things—faith, humility, and courage, despite all (to say it again), nonetheless constitute the best strategy, the best pathway forward. That path might not even be all that good— might even appear as the soul of misery itself, particularly in the short term—but it could still well be better than the infinitely terrible potential alternative. We all need desperately to know how to make the best of a bad deal. Breaking faith with the spirit of being and becoming itself is not an advisable strategy. Quite the contrary.

Cain convinces himself of something like the following: "Here I am, breaking myself in half in my efforts; trying to do my best, yet nothing is going my way. And there goes Abel, waltzing so blithely and easily through life—granted everything, loved by everyone, smiled upon by God. How can that possibly be fair? Is all that not only unjust but also emblematic of some deep and fundamental flaw in existence itself?" Thinking that way—daring to think that way—the soon-murderous brother calls out God: "What are You up to? What kind of world did You make, where my labor is futile, my sacrifices unrecognized, my alienation total—all the while Abel is dancing away with all those who love him, in an endlessly welcoming and productive field of spring, women, and flowers." And God immediately makes a bad situation worse for his wayward son, responding, as conscience, in the most unwelcome terms imaginable—once again: "If thou doest well, shalt thou not be accepted? and if thou doest not well, sin lieth at the door. And unto thee *shall be* his desire, and thou shalt rule over him" (Genesis 4:7). The emphasis on desire is telling, as is the imagery of the doorstep, combined with the necessity of an invitation to enter, submission to the will of God (as an alternative), and the insistence that mastery of such temptation is both necessary and possible.

God says to Cain, in effect, "Sin crouched at your door, like a sexually aroused predator—and you invited it in, knowing full well it was sin, and let it have its way with you." God lets Cain know, in no uncertain terms, that the fault lies in the human domain—and it is God Himself speaking, rather than something or someone easily disavowed, a fact which of course heightens the devastation. The Lord says, in effect: "The flaw here is not with me. It is with you. You have allowed something terrible to enter into your soul, and engaged in unholy intercourse with it. Worse: you did it of your own free will, and you know it, and you could have done otherwise—and you know it." How is this to be understood? Imagine that you are bitter, cynical, nihilistic, and faithless, because you do not believe that you are getting what you had bargained for. Perhaps you have your reasons. On what do you begin to dwell? On what do you begin to brood? What do you invite in, to take hold of you? Those are all variants on the sexual metaphor: How are you then tempted to enter into a creative partnership with evil? To put it, once again, in the bluntest colloquially Anglo-Saxon manner possible: How f**ked up are you willing to allow yourself to become?

Cain wishes most devoutly for God to take responsibility for the pain and disappointment attendant on human existence. God upbraids him in a manner precisely opposite to what he most longs to hear. Cain's request is therefore not only rejected: God turns the tables on him. This makes Cain even more unhappy and vengeful. It is one terrible thing to have your sacrifices rejected, and to fail. A whole new level of existential misery emerges, however, when you are informed in some incontrovertible manner by exactly what or who you are accusing that your own conduct is fully and completely to blame for your failure and misery; that you have made everything much worse than it had to be by your refusal to do even what you know to be right. This is a very damning judgment, and it could not happen to Cain at a worse time. This is what typically occurs in the case of the most damning of judgments.

3.8. Fratricide, then worse

After a colloquy of this sort—after God Himself has let it be known that the hell now occupied by Cain was brought about by the latter's own personal shortcoming, wrongdoing, and vengefulness—a sensible person would disappear, meditate, and repent, regardless of the fact that coming back from such an abysmal place would be something both difficult and unlikely. Instead, and somewhat predictably, given the dark side of human nature, Cain doubles down on his presumption and pride, rises up in his thoroughly self-justified anger, and kills Abel: "And Cain talked with Abel his brother: and it came to pass, when they were in the field, that Cain rose up against Abel his brother, and slew him" (Genesis 4:8). He does so, furthermore, after lying to his good and much-admired brother in the most manipulative and ironic possible manner—after inviting him to cooperate in the very work or sacrifice over which their paths diverged and their differences arose, according to other translations of the verse ("One day Cain suggested to his brother, 'Let's go out into the fields'" [New Living Translation]). Worse, Cain does so after discussing the recent conversation with God, which implies betrayal subsequent to sharing something deeply private and painful and, therefore, establishing a bond of trust ("And Cain told Abel his brother" [New American Standard Bible, 1977]; "Cain talked with Abel his brother [about what God had said]" [Amplified Bible]). It is difficult to conceive of a strategy more false and manipulative.

Cain destroys God's favorite, God's ideal, to attain vengeance on that favored ideal and, simultaneously, on God. In doing so, however, the murderous brother also destroys his own ideal, because it is Abel that Cain most desires to be. It was Cain's lack of what Abel has, and is, that served as the deepest source of his torment. When he slays his brother, therefore, Cain demolishes all that is holding him together; everything that protects him from despair; all that offers him guidance and hope when lost; everything that enables him to progress forward, upward, to the eternal promised land. There is a moral order. Beware of unintended consequences when it is violated. The

murderous brother commits, in a very real sense, the unforgivable sin, sever-
ing any chance of further relationship with God. From some dark lands
there is no hope of returning:

> For if we sin willfully after that we have received the knowledge of
> the truth, there remaineth no more sacrifice for sins,
>
> But a certain fearful looking for of judgment and fiery indigna-
> tion, which shall devour the adversaries.
>
> He that despised Moses' law died without mercy under two or
> three witnesses:
>
> Of how much sorer punishment, suppose ye, shall he be thought
> worthy, who hath trodden under foot the Son of God, and hath
> counted the blood of the covenant, wherewith he was sanctified, an
> unholy thing, and hath done despite unto the Spirit of grace?
>
> *Hebrews 10:26–29*

Insofar as Abel is a precursor to, foreshadowing of, or "type"[72] of Christ,
and Cain the same in relationship to Satan, the parallel between Cain's sin
and the sin against the Holy Spirit (Matthew 12:31–32) is apt. In consequence, God tells Cain:

> So now you are cursed from the earth, which has opened its mouth
> to receive your brother's blood from your hand.
>
> When thou tillest the ground, it shall not henceforth yield unto
> thee her strength; a fugitive and a vagabond shalt thou be in the
> earth.
>
> *Genesis 4:11–12*

Nothing the now-damned brother works toward will ever come about. He
will wander and hide forever. Such is the fate of the individual who murders
his own highest aspirations—the ultimate form, perhaps, of hiding the light
under the proverbial bushel (Matthew 5:15). Cain understands he is lost,
with the same certainty he knew he was at fault, following his last dialogue

with God. He cries out, in consequence, from the depths of the abyss: "[M]y punishment is greater than I can bear. Behold, thou hast driven me out this day from the face of the earth; and from thy face shall I be hid; and I shall be a fugitive and a vagabond in the earth; and it shall come to pass, that every one that findeth me shall slay me" (Genesis 4:14–15). This is once again reminiscent of Dostoevsky's Raskolnikov, who in the aftermath of his dreadful—and hypothetically successful and justified—crime finds himself so alienated from everything he had so unconsciously taken for granted that punishment comes as nothing less than a relief.

Who can live after destroying his ideal? After destroying that ideal in a deeply premeditated act of spite? Who can live after destroying his ideal, knowing full well that the fault for doing lies unquestionably at his own feet? Who can live after finally destroying all connection to the transcendent and absolute? And why is Cain a vagabond in the land of Nod (which means "land of the wanderer")? Because all those who pattern themselves after Cain become alienated from everyone: they deceive, and cheat, and offer what is second-best. The people around them catch on, in short order, and determine to have no further relationship. In consequence, the bitter and the voluntarily second-rate have to seek out new territories to despoil, new hosts to parasitize, new innocents to corrupt. Colloquially, as well, to visit the land of Nod is to go to sleep (thanks to the poet Robert Louis Stevenson[73]). This is to be, or to remain, or to become (however willfully) unconscious, just as Cain is unconscious—just as those who hide their lights are unconscious—in his unwillingness to awaken to the reality of his true nature and his obligation to God.

And this is only the beginning of the ensuing, spiraling, multiplying hell. Cain's children and their children walk in their father's dread footsteps, and worse. Cain's fifth-generation descendant, Lamech, kills one man for wounding him (Genesis 4:23), prophesying proudly that anyone who dares kill him in return will be avenged not the mere seven times that would be experienced by anyone daring to kill Cain (Genesis 4:15) but by seventy-seven times (Genesis 4:24). As noted in the Cambridge Bible for Schools and Colleges[74]:

The first note of warfare is sounded in this fierce exultation in a deed which has exceeded the limits of self-defense and passed into the region of the blood-feud. The possession of new weapons and the lust of revenge are here recorded as the typical elements of the war spirit. "Although, technically, the law of Vengeance was satisfied by a 'life for a life,' yet in practice the avenging of blood was often carried to the utmost length of ruthless ferocity. For one life many were taken, the murderer and his kinsfolk together."[75]

The story worsens even more after that—proving, once again, that hell is most truly a bottomless abyss; proving that no matter how bad things get, there is some damned thing that might yet be done to worsen what is already a terrible situation. The descendants of Cain, carrying the spirit of his sin, degenerate into an accelerating murderousness—a tendency that culminates, perhaps, in the doings of Tubal-Cain, the "instructor of every artificer in brass and iron" (Genesis 4:22), and, along with his brothers, Jabal and Jubal, the first makers of weapons of war.

Together, they "taught men to form weapons of brass, and iron, and taught them the use of armor, and introduced war into the world. And when they had made these things, they made war upon each other, and the multitude of weapons went, at once, to try their inventions."[76]

This is an outline of the causal pathway not only to the corruption of the soul but to the degeneration of the state itself, as well as the technology upon which the state hypothetically depends and certainly utilizes. First, the individual fails to make the proper sacrifices. Second, he lies about it in a self-serving manner. Third, he nurses his bitterness, alienating himself from the Divine, purposefully, working himself over time into a self-righteous fit, collaborating with the spirit of sin. Then he destroys his own ideal to obliterate the terrible judge and to wreak vengeance upon the spirit of the cosmic order. Then his descendants disseminate that pattern of destructiveness throughout all of society, until every last man and woman is irredeemably corrupt—and all of that stemming from the original failure to work in earnest and gratefully—and do so while turning to the inappropriate worship of technological prowess. Then absolutely everything collapses in catastrophe. It is no coincidence whatsoever that the cataclysmic twinned stories of the flood and the collapse of the tower of the faithless, presumptuous, and authoritarian state follows on the heels of the terrible tale of the hostile brothers. The unerring eye for an edit that managed exactly this sequencing is a profound, even miraculous indication of the genius of the collective unconscious or divine hand that penned and assembled the text.

God attempts to forestall this spiraling descent into the abyss. He marks Cain, to forestall the emergence of the pattern of continual and expanding revenge and mutual destruction. Why does He do so? The meaning of this marking is elaborated on in H. D. M. Spence-Jones's late nineteenth-century *Pulpit Commentaries* about the Bible:

1. To show that "Vengeance is mine; I will repay, saith the Lord."

2. To prove the riches of the Divine clemency to sinful men.

3. To serve as a warning against the crime of murder. To this probably there is a reference in the concluding clause: ["]And the Lord set a mark upon— gave a sign to (LXX.)—Cain, lest any finding him should kill him.["] Commentators are divided as to whether this was a visible sign to repress avengers (the Rabbis, Luther, Calvin, Piscator, &c.), or an inward assurance to Cain himself that he should not be destroyed (Aben Ezra, Dathe, Rosenmüller, Gesemus, Tuch, Kalisch, Delitzsch).[77]

"Dearly beloved, avenge not yourselves, but rather give place unto wrath: for it is written, Vengeance is mine; I will repay, saith the Lord" (Romans 12:19). Why is this written? Why is this transfer of responsibility for revenge— even, perhaps, for justice—necessary? Because a civilized society must place a delay between the revelation of a crime and identification of a perpetrator and the reaction to that crime—first, to remove from the victim or the victim's family the terrible burden of vengeance, and second, to protect society from the consequences of vengeance-seeking. The longing for justice requires that the guilty do not go unpunished ("The voice of thy brother's blood crieth unto me from the ground" [Genesis 4:10]), but it is very difficult to distinguish that longing from the wish for revenge, which can be a devouring force, both psychologically and socially. It certainly could be argued that the former—that longing for justice—is in fact a later-developing and more sophisticated or equilibrated expression of the impetus toward revenge, and one that requires precisely a delay in responding and the intermediation of an external and comparatively dispassionate agent so that everything relevant can be taken into account before the necessary sentencing.

Cain's sin thus can be seen to initiate the accelerating tit-for-tat pattern of response that culminates first in blood feud, which can easily span generations, and that may well constitute the pattern for the more or less continuous warfare potentially characterizing the norm in our ancestral past.[78] Why did it take us so many hundreds of thousands of years to progress toward complex cooperation and productive peace, despite attaining our current genetic identity that long ago in the past?[79] Was it at least in part because we mired ourselves in pointless cycles of self-reinforcing revenge?[80] That is not all, of course: it is difficult for the force that enables and justifies theft from the productive to be replaced by a truly productive social contract or covenant, but failure to do so was no doubt a major contributing factor to the impoverishment and brutalization of human existence and remains so today. A distrustful society will never be an abundant and peaceful society. The ever-present threat of honor killing is a major deterrent to trust, even though the tilt in that direction might be regarded as a moral improvement over the stance characterized by mere take-it-on-the-chin-and-cower weakness. Furthermore, and in consequence, the impulse toward such "honor" is deep and a priori—there, in the beginning; there, as a matter of immature but powerful instinct (although not abject cowardice, to say it again), and not something easily subdued or, better, transcended.

If you or someone close to you is hurt by someone else—particularly if there is an element of malevolence or of unforgivable willful blindness and carelessness about the transgression—the pull for retaliation appears most temptingly in the guise of moral necessity: "If I was a good, honorable, courageous person—a proper defendant of my family and territory—I would be

duty bound to take steps to wreak havoc on the perpetrator of this atrocity"
(and there is certainly plenty to be said in support of that proposition). But
that is a road dangerous to embark on. First, at a psychological level, that
impulse to vengeance rapidly becomes something indistinguishable from
pride. The fathers who kill their own daughters when they are raped, for example, do so for no other reason than pride: their pride, in fact ("honor"), is
precisely what is besmirched by the transgression.[81] That is not desire for
justice—or, even for revenge. It is overweening presumption, and something
capable of destabilizing everything—and willing to.

Civilized societies, with their monopoly on power, take to themselves the
scale and sword of justice. In so doing, they lift the moral burden off the
targets of criminality and malevolence, allowing them to return to their
lives, free of the demands of just punishment, protecting society simultaneously from the perversely respectable danger of the honor code:

> During the time men live without a common power to keep them all
> in awe, they are in that condition which is called war; and such a
> war as is of every man against every man. . . . In such condition,
> there is no place for Industry; because the fruit thereof is uncertain;
> and consequently no Culture of the Earth; no Navigation, nor use of
> the commodities that may be imported by Sea; no commodious
> Building; no Instruments of moving, and removing such things as
> require much force; no Knowledge of the face of the Earth; no ac-
> count of Time; no Arts; no Letters; no Society; and which is worst of
> all, continuall feare, and danger of violent death; And the life of
> man, solitary, poore, nasty, brutish, and short.[82]

In a civilized state (one that allows for sophisticated socialization and
psychological integration; one that allows for productive, generous, and stable peace), the state—more deeply, the law—becomes the intermediary between perpetrator and victim. It is doing so, it might well be said, as an
emissary of the divine, insofar as the divine will can be realized in this profane
world. The mark of Cain is therefore—in keeping with this—the protection of

God, the spirit of the law, as well it might be said, extended to the perpetrator, to protect not only perpetrator but also the victim, in the deepest possible sense, and the stability of society itself. This is why the right to vengeance is rightfully reserved for the transcendent spirit of unity.

After God puts His mark on Cain, the latter departs: "And Cain went out from the presence of the Lord, and dwelt in the land of Nod, on the east of Eden" (Genesis 4:16). More specifically, however, he lives at such distance from God's grace that his place of habitation is indistinguishable from hell. This is how Milton describes the situation of Lucifer himself, after his fall from grace:

> At once as far as Angels kenn he views
> The dismal Situation waste and wilde,
> A Dungeon horrible, on all sides round
> As one great Furnace flam'd, yet from those flames
> No light, but rather darkness visible
> Serv'd onely to discover sights of woe,
> Regions of sorrow, doleful shades, where peace
> And rest can never dwell, hope never comes
> That comes to all; but torture without end
> Still urges, and a fiery Deluge, fed
> With ever-burning Sulphur unconsum'd:
> Such place Eternal Justice had prepar'd
> For those rebellious, here thir prison ordained
> In utter darkness, and thir portion set
> As far remov'd from God and light of Heav'n
> As from the Center thrice to th' utmost Pole.[83]

A section from *The Pulpit Commentary* is dead relevant here:

And Cain went out from the presence of the Lord. Not simply ended his interview and prepared to emigrate from the abode of his youth (Kalisch); but, more especially, withdrew from the neighborhood of the cherubim (v/de on ver. 14). And dwelt in the land of Nod. The

geographical situation of Nod (Knobel, China?) cannot be determined further than that it was on the east of Eden, and its name,
Nod, or wandering (cf. vers. 12, 14; Psalms 56:8), was clearly derived
from Cain's fugitive and vagabond life (vide Michaelis, 'Suppl,' p. 1612;
and cf. Furst, 'Lex.,' sub voce), "which showeth, as Josephus well
conjectureth, that Cain was not amended by his punishment, but
waxed worse and worse, giving himself to rapine, robbery, oppression, deceit" (Willet).[84]

Out of "the presence of the Lord" is the same terrible distance that Milton
describes as "from the Center thrice to th' utmost pole"; the same terrible
distance indicated by the geography of Dante's *Inferno*, with the ultimate
occupant of the deepest possible pit Satan himself. That is a reflection of the
moral claim that evil is a consequence of remoteness from God, rather than
something in and of itself. C. G. Jung objected to this characterization, to
some degree, indicating that such a notion of evil risks underestimating its
autonomous nature, capability to possess, and the threat that it posed.[85] He
thus adopted a more dualistic view, which has as its advantage the call to
seriousness that the hypothesis of an active and motivated spirit of evil constitutes. The alternative and more classically Christian view (this is not to
cast aspersions on Jung, whose concentration on the centrality of evil was
particularly apropos after the events of World War II) is also of great utility:
the notion that God is a center around which all good revolves, the very
trunk of the great trees of life and moral knowledge, and that hell increases
in severity in proportion to the extremes of marginal existence, distant from
that center.

This lifestyle of vagabond—of alienated nomad, far from the societal
norm or ideal—is precisely that adopted by the pitiless and oft-sadistic career criminals known to moderns as psychopaths,[86] that small minority,
even among the criminals, as well as those who commit the most frequent
and often worst crimes.[87] "Not fit for decent society"—that is not outdated
Victorian moralizing but wisdom: those who refuse to make the proper sacrifices and who attack their very brothers in resentful vengeance (particularly

when they are deservedly successful) are also those doomed to wander, as their brethren in turn discover their propensity for deceit, betrayal, and vengeance, sever all ties with them, and force them on the path to find new and still-naive victims. This motif of hellish distance is echoed in the Commentary insistence that Cain "withdrew from the neighborhood of the cherubim." The cherubim, as we have seen,[88] are the winged forms who guard the east gate to the Garden of Eden along with the flaming sword that turns every which way. These cherubim are angels of judgment, from whose discerning eye nothing less than heavenly is allowed to slip. They are the monsters perched at the very edge of categories themselves, where judgment is most called for and most difficult. They are the judges of edge cases.

Clarifying this point requires a return to discussion of the fact of and relationship between the margin and the center.[89] Every element of order—that is, every perception and conception; every form of organization, psychological and social—has an ideal at its center (and indeed has a center, more generally speaking), surrounded by a margin. That margin is not its opposite, to say it again, as a simple thesis/antithesis conceptualization might have it. It is instead the infinitely graduated plurality of difference or opposition that surrounds anything identifiable. It is instead the world and all its complexity juxtaposed against the specific, comprehensible, familiar, particular, and useful. The margin is thus "less than ideal" by definition, according to the presumptions of definition that allow for anything central to exist. Its existence is inevitable, as plurality has its place, in contrast to unity, and it is also a place of necessary freedom and experimentation. Nonetheless, it contains "monstrous forms." It can in that manner be a form of hell, not least as distance from the ideal, or God, whose judgment becomes ever more extreme and threatening in precise proportion to the degree of deviation. The increasingly unrepentant sinner can therefore apprehend little more than the burgeoning anger of God. The fact of that inability can also, so perversely, justify continuation of, or further, sin. That is a true self-devouring spiral downward toward the abyss.

Cain lies, and habitually. That path of lies leads him down the road to fratricide, the destruction of his own ideal, and estrangement from himself, man, and God—from center to lonely, vagabond margin. Someone who lies clearly steps away from the Good, the truthful and upward-oriented Logos who makes the cosmos that is good. More prosaically, perhaps: Someone who lies steps away from his own judgment. This occurs first in the edge cases, where careful discrimination is most difficult, where the lie is therefore most easily engaged in and rationalized. It can all too easily become the habit in all cases, however, as the hierarchy of value through which the world must be viewed becomes pathologized. With practice, the lie becomes not so much the deviation from the proper and truthful mode of being but the lens through which the world itself is increasingly viewed. The liar therefore comes to inhabit a story where everything is improperly ordered; given the wrong due. This warps the world, so it becomes a place of alienation from self, community, and God; so that it becomes a field that brings forth nothing but thorns; so that the divine itself becomes little more than the most terrible of judgments. Those who lie come to value the wrong things—and to do this consciously, at least at the moment of each lie.

Alternatively, and more poetically: those who come to lie also engage in the worship of false idols (something akin to Cain's openness to possession by and collusion with the Luciferian spirit). This misattribution of value—something that becomes automatized when practiced; becomes habit; becomes character itself—means that the world is now subdued in a false order, named with the wrong names, such that nothing ends up in its proper place, and that things of less value are given priority over those greater. How could it be otherwise, in the case of the lie, which is by definition the falsification of the real? Of course judgment becomes profoundly impaired when everything has been valued improperly, particularly when that has become a habit so deeply ingrained through practice that it becomes true of perception itself. As Father Zossima insists, in Dostoevsky's *The Brothers Karamazov*:

> Above all, don't lie to yourself. The man who lies to himself and listens to his own lie comes to such a pass that he cannot distinguish the truth within him, or around him, and so loses all respect for himself and for others. And having no respect he ceases to love, and

in order to occupy and distract himself without love he gives way to passions and coarse pleasures, and sinks to bestiality in his vices, all from continual lying to other men and to himself. The man who lies to himself can be more easily offended than anyone. You know it is sometimes very pleasant to take offence, isn't it? A man may know that nobody has insulted him, but that he has invented the insult for himself, has lied and exaggerated to make it picturesque, has caught at a word and made a mountain out of a molehill—he knows that himself, yet he will be the first to take offence, and will revel in his resentment till he feels great pleasure in it, and so pass to genuine vindictiveness.[90]

This is truly a descent into Dante's abyss, the pathway to an ever-deepening and expanding hell. When a man is living by a false story—valuing, celebrating, naming, and subduing everything improperly—nothing can possibly work out for him. Worse, as alluded to previously,[91] all his adventures become false, as well, because the goals he pursues are illusory, based as they are on the deception of self and other.

The opportunities that beckon are not real; the obstacles that emerge in the pursuit are only figments of the imagination. When the world is subdued in improper order, no plans can possibly work. Lies render the presumptions that would otherwise support functional plans unreliable and invalid. This means that the liar is doomed to continual failure—that his increasingly false sacrifices will be increasingly and forever brutally rejected. This is exactly what happens, for example, to the pharaoh in the great story of Exodus, who doubles down on his tyrannical insistence, as the ever more terrible plagues mount (Exodus 7–13). When the sacrifice that is false and insufficient reigns, anxiety mounts, as does hopelessness. How can the future appear bright when nothing turns out the way it is supposed to or, even if the desired but false end is attained, no true satisfaction makes itself manifest? How can any relationship be maintained when deception—worse, self-deception—rules? The liar is hopeless, lacks direction, and is destined for conflict not only with all the others who cannot understand or outright refuse to share his lies but with whatever remains of his true self; his true conscience; his true calling. Impair your judgment, until you have no judgment at all. Then die, and painfully, because you refused (and continually) to sacrifice your presumption; your false ideas—even when you knew with certainty that they were false.

We have now dealt with the full narrative of the hostile brothers, although not entirely with its extended consequences. Cain's sin not only leads to the chaos of the flood, as the effects of resentful bitterness cascade from the personal to the social, but to the authoritarian catastrophe of the Tower of Babel, as those who turn from God and the path of proper sacrifice must turn to alternative means to unify and ensure successful adaptation. Cain's descendants are also the builders, the engineers, the makers of cities, musical instruments, tools, and implements of war (Genesis 4:17–23). This is not to say that building or engineering is something wrong in itself; only that the fundamental problem of ethical conduct is not amenable to a technological solution. There are no "better tools" in the hands of misguided strivers. Better tools when the aim is wrong merely means more rapid movement down the wrong road, or toward the wrong *up*.

If proper conduct is rejected as the basis for the necessary covenant with being and becoming—as in the case of Cain and his descendants—then technical mastery beckons as an attractive substitute. It also has as its attraction appeal to the Luciferian pride that inevitably accompanies the desire and willingness to reject the absolute and transcendent. It is a given, in some real sense, that the mastery of tools has lifted much of the burden from human life—but it is also true that any given technology can be employed for evil purposes as much as good (and that the law of unintended consequences also lurks eternally as a complicating problem). Technological development, in the service of what god? This is the eternal conundrum that finds its expression in the popular and recurring trope of runaway technology: *Ex Machina* (2014), *The World's End* (2013), *The Matrix* (1999), *The Truman Show* (1998), *Jurassic Park* (1993), *RoboCop* (1987), *The Terminator* (1984), *Blade Runner* (1982), *The Black Hole* (1979), *The Stepford Wives* (1975), *Westworld* (1973), *The Andromeda Strain* (1971), *2001: A Space* Odyssey (1968),

The Time Machine (1960), *The Fly* (1958), *The War of the Worlds* (1953), *The Man in the White Suit* (1951), *The Day the Earth Stood Still* (1951), *The Invisible Man* (1933), *The Island of Lost Souls* (1932), *Frankenstein* (1931), and *Metropolis* (1926).

This list, although comprehensive, is by no means exhaustive—but it does indicate with its breadth the degree to which the combined problem of pride, resentment, and the worship of the technological both preoccupies the imagination and poses a serious threat to humanity itself. The answer provided by the earliest stories in Genesis and then echoed through the biblical corpus? No solution outside the proper universal and uniting ethos can quell anxiety, provide hope, and equilibrate social discord no matter how conceptually and technically sophisticated. In fact, in the absence of such an ethos, technology threatens, rather than benefits: technology becomes the handmaiden of power, or the means of escape from responsibility and the true moral order. The turning away from God and the failure to sacrifice properly corrupts and degenerates and, simultaneously, motivates the efforts of the prideful intellect to build structures that obviate the need for God and the burdensome moral striving that relationship with Him requires.

Where must the story of the descendants of Adam and Eve therefore and inevitably proceed to from here? Downward, inevitably, to the utter chaos of the flood; upward, alternatively, to the domain of totalitarian order, and the skyscraper reaching all too triumphantly heavenward, nonetheless doomed to collapse. Those are the two pathways we encounter next. What is the alternative? The far more difficult, sophisticated, and complex path of the welcome and ultimate sacrifice, ultimately pleasing to God, laid out in the entire remaining corpus of the biblical narrative.

4

—— ◆ ——

Noah: God as the Call
to Prepare

4.1. Giants in the land

After Abel dies and Cain departs for the vagabond land of Nod, Adam and Eve find themselves blessed with another son. That son is Seth, whom tradition regards both as a replacement for Abel and the ancestor of all who conduct themselves and sacrifice properly: "And Adam again had relations with his wife, and she gave birth to a son and named him Seth, saying, 'God has granted me another seed in place of Abel, since Cain killed him'" (Genesis 4:25). Various commentators have concluded the following in their centuries of study: "Seth was called appointed because he was appointed by God to be the father of the righteous and to replace Abel, whom Cain had killed;"[1] "It is well known that Jesus was of the line of David, who was the descendant of Seth;"[2] "This means, as well, that the messianic line was established through Seth and not through Cain."[3] Among other things, these conclusions indicate that the pattern of attention and value established and typified by Abel did not die with him—and, more generally, cannot die—and that the same pattern in some manner was not only immediately reestablished but characterizes both King David and Christ Himself. This idea is echoed in the highly evocative and image-laden manner typical of the biblical corpus—particularly of the very oldest stories—in a phrase that otherwise appears mysterious and opaque: "There were giants in the earth in those days; and also after that, when the sons of God came in unto the daughters of men, and they bare children to them, the same became mighty men which were of old, men of renown" (Genesis 6:4).

These lines have spawned speculation far beyond the ordinary sort. The Nephilim, these giants, have been considered honorable robbers, "lawless gallants," mighty men, "unique in size"—even fallen angels.[4] The simplest explanation, anthropologically and psychologically, is that what is remembered across time is not so much the specific empirical details of a given life, no matter how notable, but the abstracted pattern of what is notable in general about life. Thus, in collective memory, the exploits (even the essence) of the ancestor become a purified amalgam of all that grips attention and compels mimicry (in the heroic or antiheroic sense—as a villain is as good a lesson as a leading man). The efforts of the ancient Romans to deify their emperors is a well-known manifestation of this same tendency. The same process is undertaken today among authors of fiction, who abstract out from the many characters in their imaginations a central pattern or spirit of character that is maximally compelling and memorable.

When a person departs and is, say, eulogized, the most memorable of their exploits are brought to mind and communicated. In a culture dependent on the oral transmission of information, multigenerationally, an ancestor's most memorable qualities are going to become conflated in collective memory, especially after all those who actually remember a given person shuffle off this mortal coil. The stories, however, can live on, but in compressed and purified form, with the attendant characters living as active entities in imagination. The pattern of the ancestral heroes inevitably emerges and tilts with time toward virtual or actual deification. As Mircea Eliade points out: "The passage from ancestor worship to theism occurs when the ancestor is divinized, that is, when he is transformed into a god. This transformation is made possible by the discovery of the sacred, or rather, by the identification of a particular manifestation of the sacred with the ancestor."[5] He says, similarly, elsewhere: "Ancestor worship is one of the factors that favours the development of monotheism. In the course of time, the ancestors are more and more identified with the god, and finally the god completely replaces the ancestors."[6]

Thus, history becomes fictionalized, although "fiction" is best regarded in such a context as the creation of abstracted meta-truths, rather than the antithesis of "fact" and, therefore, of truth itself. The life of an ordinary man, which cannot even in principle be remembered in its totality, is thus reduced to the best (or worst) of his exploits—to the gist or heart of the matter—and joins in spirit with the similar exploits of his peers and forefathers, to become the veritable giants of the past. With time, therefore, kings become what is sovereign itself, or its antithesis; become the King of Kings, or the force that eternally opposes that supreme kingship. Noah is one such giant, one such quasi-deified ancestral hero, a descendant of Seth, the second Abel; a son of the fallen angels who walked the earth in those days; a man favored by God, like the prelapsarian Adam—a model for admiration and emulation, made even more memorable by the stark contrast between his attitude and behavior and that of his contemporaneous peers.

4.2. Sin and the return of chaos

At the point in the unfolding biblical narrative when Noah enters the story, the wickedness of Cain's descendants has come to dominate the entirety of human endeavor. This is a particularly negative example of the gigantism that comes to characterize the exploits of those in the past. In consequence of this widespread emergence and utter dominance of the tendency toward evil, God determines to destroy what He has created: "And God saw that the wickedness of man was great in the earth, and that every imagination of the thoughts of his heart was only evil continually" (Genesis 6:5). This means a variant retelling of the story both of the fall of man and the murder of Abel: another account of the inevitable fall and then destruction of those who reject the fundamental moral order, those who are insufficient in their sacrifices, those who turn toward bitter vengeance and the exploitation of self and others—those who turn against God.

This is no spiteful action on God's part, to be clear. It is instead the starkest of warning to those tempted to deviate: the road to the Promised Land is straight, narrow, and hard (Matthew 7:14), while the road downward to perdition is broad and immediately inviting. It is not that God is vengeful; quite the contrary. It is instead that His insistence on an inviolable moral order, superordinate to the merely human, is correct, and that this order is so real that transgressions against it have real consequences. This reflects the reality of the human condition: life is a game whose price of entry is death, and worse. Human existence is the most serious of businesses. Thus, the wages of sin are real and consequential. In our pride and rebellion, we thus can and do make, like Milton's Lucifer, a hell of heaven, striving to bring even out of what is good something miserable and terrible.

> So stretched out huge in length the Arch-fiend lay,
> Chained on the burning lake; nor ever thence
> Had risen, or heaved his head, but that the will
> And high permission of all-ruling Heaven
> Left him at large to his own dark designs,
> That with reiterated crimes he might
> Heap on himself damnation, while he sought
> Evil to others.[7]

Cain's descendants fall into sin, and the cosmic order degenerates until there is no option but that of complete collapse. This might seem harsh—is, indubitably, harsh—but it is clearly the case that civilizations can fail, utterly, and be subsumed so completely by chaos that even their memory vanishes. This truth is captured in the biblical text of the story of Noah—and is a motif that is in fact very widespread, because of its fundamental truth. In the Mesopotamian creation myth, for example (the *Enuma elish*), the creator-goddess/ dragon Tiamat similarly regrets her decision to act generatively. Her wayward first children (gods, in this account, rather than men, as in the story of

Noah) heedlessly slay Apsu, Tiamat's male consort—order itself—and attempt to make a home in or on his corpse. This act of extreme carelessness enrages Nature, the mother of all things—the very Tiamat who then threatens them all with destruction. This is another example first of turning against, or showing contempt for, both tradition and the Holy Father, on the part of the inhabitants of the created world, and second of the inevitable consequences of doing so.

This narrative trope indicates in part that cultures who concentrate too much on what passes for present wisdom ("we can dispense with the superstitious foolishness of the past") will lose the vertical traditional orientation that protects them against mere fads of consensus. There is a cumulative wisdom in mankind, but it is not a mere consequence of the incessant noise and clamor of the present day. It is instead something that has been gathered across an immense span of time, in many situations, and as a consequence of the observations and reminiscences of many cultures. Its rejection in favor of the whim-possessed idiocy even of the collective present is all too often a precursor to the crimson flood, particularly when those whims are as they are wont to be hedonistic, power-mad, revolutionary, and political.

The trope of destruction of the sinful by the gods also indicates that those who abandon and betray the spirit that makes for life more abundant because they are wallowing undeservedly in the wealth of material comfort left for them by the great and forward strivers of the past doom themselves however immaturely and unwittingly to the incursion of chaos and eventual destruction. It is patricide or regicide—the most extreme possible act of overweening pride, willful blindness, and careless blasphemy. The fact of this disdainful murder enrages Tiamat, the chaos/mother of all things. She determines to wipe her wayward progeny from the face of the earth, engendering a host of terrible soldiers to aid her in her battle, placing a deity known as Kingu, a veritable Satan, at their head:

> bearing monster serpents
> Sharp of tooth and not sparing the fang.
> With poison instead of blood she filled their bodies.

Ferocious dragons she clothed with terror,

She crowned them with fear-inspiring glory and made them like gods,

So that he who would look upon them should perish from terror.[8]

The god Marduk, who rises to rule all the Mesopotamian gods, is precisely he who confronts the monstrous chaos of potential in a manner directly analogous to that of the Hebrew Yahweh, who overthrows Leviathan and Behemoth (Job 40–41) at the beginning of time. Most generally (archetypally) speaking: That superordinate deity battles either the giant representative of the current state or society (a now-false God the Father), or chaos itself, most often in the guise of a terrible feminine force with serpentine features (the Great Mother).[9] What is meant by the motif of the careless slaying of Apsu, avatar of order, in contrast to the chaos of Tiamat? *Those who carelessly destroy the living spirit of the past invite the return of chaos itself.* Nietzsche warned of exactly this when he announced the death of God, prophesying that nihilism and resentment would rise up terribly in the aftermath of this dreadful murder:

> God is dead. God remains dead. And we have killed him. How shall we comfort ourselves, the murderers of all murderers? What was holiest and mightiest of all that the world has yet owned has bled to death under our knives: who will wipe this blood off us? What water is there for us to clean ourselves? What festivals of atonement, what sacred games shall we have to invent? Is not the greatness of this deed too great for us?[10]

The intuition of such backlash lingers in our souls. The apocalyptic dread that seizes us in our apprehension that nature herself will rebel, for example, against our technological presumption is a modern re-presentation of precisely this theme. *We deaden the past at our great peril.* The spirit of our ancestors created the infrastructure that supports us, technically; developed the skills that we mimic in our productive endeavors; established the mores, rituals, habits, and presumptions that unite us psychologically and socially, and provided us with direction. We can reduce that, irresponsibly, to a spirit-less corpse and attempt, in a parasitical manner, to live off or unconsciously within what has been gathered or garnered in consequence. This is a losing game, however, as what is being devoured in that unearned manner is not being simultaneously replenished or restocked. Once the storehouse has been discovered, it can be looted and exhausted; once the brand has been established, it can be raped. Nonetheless, once the carefully accumulated wealth of the past has been depleted, all hell is certain to break loose. This is an eternal truth. Modern stories put forward the same motif. In Disney's *The Lion King*,[11] the kingdom of Pride Rock is reduced to waste following the arrogant and careless murder of the proper ruler, Mufasa. The agent of his destruction is his brother, Scar, as close an analog to Cain as could be con-jured in the modern imagination (with a bit of Milton's Lucifer thrown in, just to drive the point home). The rightful king is killed by the resentful brother. The once-lush kingdom is reduced to a desert. Everyone is enslaved. Starvation threatens. There is no difference between that and the return of chaos.

We subvert the spirit of proper order at our peril. When we do so, or threaten to do so, harbingers of doom emerge and announce themselves to the profound, wise, and attentive—as in the case of Noah. Nietzsche was very much alert to such danger, noting that we would be threatened in the upcoming centuries both by the spirit of resentment and by nihilism. Ni-etzsche warned not least of the emergence of the spirit of resentment among those he pilloried as deeply poisonous spiders:

> For that man be delivered from revenge, that is for me the bridge to the highest hope, and a rainbow after long storms. The tarantulas, of course, would have it otherwise. "What justice means to us is pre-cisely that the world befilled with the storms of our revenge"—thus they speak to each other. "We shall wreak vengeance and abuse on all whose equals we are not"—thus do the tarantulahearts vow. "And 'will to equality' shall henceforth be the name for virtue; and against all that has power we want to raise our clamor!"[12]

Their "justice," however, is always what is most harmful to the higher men. They want to crucify those who devise their own virtue! They hate the lonely ones among them who are always devising their own virtue—they hate the present ones. They always speak against the present ones and call them "heretics" and "lawbreakers"— and yet they are the complaisant ones. They always talk in terms of "equal rights" and "equal obligation": The rights of the herd! They want to be herded together with safety in numbers, with regard to everything that flatters or gives rise to fear! They are a herd: Their "good conscience" is indeed a bad conscience, an incapacity for standing alone. They always know what is most tender and harmless—like a toothless old woman; they call that "goodness," and they themselves are "the good men." The offence of the herdsmen against the higher men is always the same—they force them to become herdsmen themselves. For the most part, they themselves do not believe in their ideal of the herd, and they inwardly despise it; but still they want it! That is what I call "the revolt of the herdsmen"![13]

Dostoevsky made the essentially identical case, at precisely the same time, not least in his novel *The Possessed,* alternatively translated as *The Devils.*

The possession of the modern mind by what Nietzsche characterized as *ressentiment* is most profitably and deeply understood as a modern variant of the eternal spirit of Cain: "Ressentiment itself, if it needs a concept and a word, indicates a certain powerlessness and impotence of the will: one feels something to be injurious but is nevertheless incapable of preventing it; one is too weak to take revenge or wage war, or one despairs of doing so. Hence one has recourse to any means of hurting, with the help of which one can strike indirectly, that is, by means of injury to something that does not belong to him, to something that is loved and respected by the person who is to be injured."[14] As Walter Kaufmann, the great late twentieth-century translator and interpreter of Nietzsche, explains further: "In Nietzsche's view, ressentiment is a disease of the weak, who envy and hate the strong and the successful and who seek to bring them down by attacking their values and ideals. Ressentiment arises from a sense of powerlessness and frustration, and it is often expressed as a desire for revenge or a desire to tear down those who are perceived as being more powerful or successful."[15]

Dostoevsky, in *The Devils*, describes the process whereby the Russian soul fell under "that legion of isms that came to Russia from the West: idealism, rationalism, empiricism, materialism, utilitarianism, positivism, socialism, anarchism, nihilism, and, underlying them all, atheism."[16] The great Russian novelist and essayist carefully details the danger he saw looming over Russia and the rest of the world in a manner that both uncannily parallels Nietzsche and prefigures the horrors of the so-called Gulag archipelago, whose machinations were laid bare by Aleksandr Solzhenitsyn a century later.[17] I drove this point home in my foreword to the fiftieth-anniversary commemorative edition of the latter masterwork:

> Members of the bourgeoisie? Beyond all redemption! They had to go, as a matter of course! What of their wives? Children? Even—their grandchildren? Off with their heads, too! All were incorrigibly corrupted by their class identity, and their destruction therefore ethically necessitated. How convenient, that the darkest and direst of all possible motivations could be granted the highest of moral standings! That was a true marriage of hell and of heaven. What values, what philosophical presumptions, truly dominated, under such circumstances? Was it desire for brotherhood, dignity, and freedom from want? Not in the least—not given the outcome. It was instead and obviously the murderous rage of hundreds of thousands of biblical Cains, each looking to torture, destroy and sacrifice their own private Abels. There is simply no other manner of accounting for the corpses.[18]

The same spirit that inspired Nietzsche and Dostoevsky made itself known to Noah, when he found himself, despite himself, possessed by the intuition that a calamity of apocalyptic magnitude was pending. Why? Because the spirit of Cain had come to rule the world.

4.3. Salvation by the wise and the reestablishment of the world

The most ancient of prophets is described in the following terms: "Noah was a just man and perfect in his generations, and Noah walked with God" (Genesis 6:9). Noah, who "found favor in the eyes of the Lord" (Genesis 6:8), is thus characterized as a man as good as could be expected, given the limitations of his time and place (hence "in his generations"). This is as good as it gets, except in the most exceptional of human cases, as we are all to some degree creatures of the specific environment we find ourselves thrown into. To "walk with God" is to inhabit that Edenic space characterized by the absence of the self-consciousness that is simultaneously presumptuous and neurotic (as Adam before becoming aware of his nakedness could do the same). A man aiming at what is highest and concentrating on the truth, instead of focusing on and promoting his own self-centered interest, lacks self-consciousness because what he is attending to is *not about him*—at least not as an isolated being, trapped in the carnal now. He is doing something other than following the instinctual and immediate dictates of his impulsive and narcissistic self-interest. That latter tactic ensures only the emergence of involuntary self-reflection and painful self-consciousness, as we have seen[19]: "Am I making the impact I want and need so desperately to make? Am I impressing those whom I am parading myself in front of? Am I winning this argument? Am I emerging as the victor in this contest of status? Am I successfully insisting on my publicly displayed moral virtue?" The alternative is to "walk (unselfconsciously) with God."

Imagine being onstage—a daunting proposition for everyone. You are delivering a talk, concentrating on the take-home message, giving a lecture—or participating in some equally clichéd enterprise. In consequence, you are worrying: "Is my message coming across? Do I sound like I know what I am talking about? Will the audience find me interesting and impressive? What are people thinking of me?" This is all instrumental, self-serving reasoning, and suffering self-consciousness will necessarily and inevitably ensue. You will feel nervous and unsure in precise proportion to the degree that the event is inappropriately about you—about your "performance." What is the alternative to such strategizing? Onstage (and elsewhere, for that matter), it is simple: *strive to address the issue under consideration as honestly and clearly as possible.* Then the event is no longer about you, so there is no reason for self-consciousness. It becomes instead and properly so about the search for truth in relation to the question at hand. That question, too, must be an honest one; one you truly regard as of crucial import. Why otherwise waste your time and the time of those in the audience? The same logic can and should be applied to every situation in life. Why should it be? There is no superior approach. How could there be an approach equal to confronting what is actually there?

If the presentation is about illuminating the topic of utmost current interest and bringing clarity to the matter, instead of devoted to you and your concerns, the reasons for self-consciousness vanish, not least because that self is no longer in the picture. What could be there instead, guiding your conduct, is the spirit of honest explanation and the attempt to reveal and generate the order that is good (Genesis 1). What could be there is the attempt to clarify and explicate, in the service of what is highest, and for no other reason. This means to speak in a manner that abides by the truth and to say what calls out and plagues conscience or calls to be said—not for the sake of reputation but because the stark reality of the situation can best be expressed in that manner. This means to publicly wayfind (and is that not the task of the genuine leader?); to sacrifice the merely instrumental and narrowly self-serving and to replace it with what is truly higher, while maintaining faith that truthful revelation will produce the order that is good or even very good, regardless of all "evidence" to the contrary. That is the mysterious secret to genuine confidence on stage and, more generally, in life. "All the world's a stage, And all the men and women merely players; They have their exits and their entrances, And one man in his time plays many parts."[20]

Everything else is the shallow and ultimately pointless, deceptive, manipulative, impulsive, and self-defeating mimicry of the narcissist.

The immediate consequence of failure to lie may well be suffering or, equally, failure to gain an advantage that is not, in fact, deserved. Indeed, avoidance of short-term pain and inappropriate movement forward are the two greatest reasons to lie. Do lies work in this regard? Sometimes, and for a time; otherwise, the motivation to deceive would not exist. That "evidence" is no final proof, however, of the superiority of the lie to the truth. The twin issues of time frame and cross-situational validity inevitably raise their hydra-like heads. Over the medium to long term, with regard to the stability and sustainability of psyche and community alike, nothing suffices but the truth, "all things considered," as they must optimally be. Faith in the truth that establishes, regenerates, and redeems is voluntary acceptance or recognition of that fact, allied with the decision to live in keeping with that conclusion. The realization of that necessity is what is portrayed as the descent of the baptismal dove that serves as the initiation to the Kingdom of Heaven (Matthew 3:16–17), or as receipt of the Paraclete or Comforter or guide that Christ promises to leave with his disciples after His departure (John 14:26). That faith in the truth is the alliance between man and the word that creates at the beginning of time and for eternity the veritable reflection of the image of God in which man and woman are made (as outlined in Genesis 1).

In the story of Noah and the flood, the entire weight of the world's renewal comes to rest on the shoulders of one man, one properly behaving descendant of Seth, Abel's fraternal substitute or replacement—one truly good man. This is a matter of no small psychological import, because this is always the situation, existentially speaking. As Solzhenitsyn points out: "And this, I submit, is the most important thing in life: to live and to create out of one's own truth, or one's own chaos, as the case may be, even if it is only a single word or a single vision. For we are each of us inevitably heroes of our own lives, and if we are not, then we have missed the whole point of our existence."[21] This is a truth constantly echoed in the biblical corpus. Each prophet (Moses, Elijah, and Jeremiah perhaps foremost among them) is, typically, a lone voice "crying in the wilderness" (Mark 1:1–4). Likewise, when God determines to destroy the cities of Sodom and Gomorrah—dwelling places lost, like the whole world of Noah's peers, in wickedness and sin—Abraham gets Him to agree to spare the force of His destruction if, first, fifty, but eventually, as a consequence of continual bargaining, only ten righteous men can be discovered in those places of habitation.

What is the idea being put forth here? That truth is such a potent force that even the tyranny of the overwhelming majority cannot prevail against it. And how could it prevail, unless reality itself did not exist, and everything was reducible to human presumption and whim? A whole polity set against the spirit of being and becoming itself is still wrong—and wrong in a manner that the consensus multiplies and deepens, rather than alleviates. There is no more wrong than when everyone agrees to be wrong. That is the very definition of a totalitarian state, which are not so much top-down tyrannies as collective agreements to abide by nothing but the lie.[22] A society that retains enough of the proper covenant so that a few or even one still dare speak freely within its confines can be protected from utter cataclysm by that faith and courage. This is part of the reason why protection of free speech is not so much a right, and certainly not one granted benevolently by the state, but the pillar upon which a stable and yet dynamically adaptive society is predicated and founded. The "right" is there only so that the responsibility can be shouldered—the responsibility to speak in a manner that reflects the spirit of the cosmic order. This is the properly ordered "free" speech that establishes, renews, and redeems—both individual and state. The state can never therefore find itself in a position where it can rightfully dispense with or deny the right to free speech, as it depended on that right for its very establishment and still relies on it for criticism, correction, and resurrection.

This is yet another terrible truth, indicating as it does that the salvation of the world itself depends in some impossible and mysterious fashion on the determination of each sovereign individual, touched by the spirit of divine worth, to dwell within the garden of the truth and to allow the voice and the will of the God he walks with in that garden to guide his attention, action, and utterance. As Dostoevsky has it in *The Brothers Karamazov*, "every one of us is undoubtedly responsible for all men—and everything on earth, not merely through the general sinfulness of creation, but each one personally for all mankind and every individual man."[23] He continues this train of thought later in the novel: "There is only one means of salvation, then take yourself and make yourself responsible for all men's sins, that is the truth, you know, friends, for as soon as you sincerely make yourself responsible for everything and for all men, you will see at once that it is really so, and that you are to blame for everyone and for all things."[24] What could this utterly preposterous but nonetheless stellar or profound and fundamental claim possibly mean? It sounds on first encounter like nothing so much as a kind of manic insanity.

Is it not clearly the case, however, that each of us serves as an example to ourselves as much as to others and that we can do some good in this regard, making the world a less evil place than it might otherwise be? And is it not true that we do not and cannot know the upper limit to this influence? If you were a better person—even, perhaps, the best person you could possibly be; the person who has pulled out all the stops in his adventurous sojourning forward—how much better would everyone else be, in direct consequence? And if such an effect is truly possible, is it not equally true in some mysterious manner that the sins of the world are the result of your own inadequacy, your own failure to bear sufficient responsibility? And is this also not a logical and necessary corollary of your making in the image of God and your supposedly self-evident[25] status as a center of the cosmos itself? And is this not the very reason that in our free Western societies the individual is set apart even from the social and the consensual as a figure of infinite implicit worth? And if the integrity of psyche and community depend on that setting apart, how can it be judged as other than true? Your failure to bring everything you can to bear on the matters at hand leaves a hole in the structure of being itself. That might well be the true impediment to the establishment of the Kingdom of God on Earth. Woe truly and inevitably be to him by whom this sin mars the world.

It is exactly such responsibility that is accepted by Noah. He encounters God in a manner that differs from that of Adam and Eve, who experience

Him as creative force and maker of boundaries, or of Cain and Abel, who encounter Him as ideal and judge. God's manifestation to the first prophet is, however, still a reflection of the same underlying unity—hence *monotheism*: it is the same singular spirit making itself manifest, however varied in its characterization—or so is the insistence of the text, which juxtaposes and sequences its various stories precisely to make that point. God is for the captain-designate of the ark the intuition of the wise that the storm is gathering; the realization that the time has come to batten down the hatches and to make the house shipshape. Modern people are obsessed with the idea of "believing in" God, as if that decision is one of positing, or refusing to posit, some material existence or absence thereof or some mere description, like the description of an object. God exists, according to the implicit dictates of such a formulation in the same manner that a table exists—or in the manner that an imaginary table truly does not exist. This conceptualization of belief typifies, in the modern world, both so-called believers, or people of faith, and agnostics and atheists alike. Such is the depth of our current state of ignorance. To believe is much more truly and usefully to commit to; to sacrifice everything to; to be voluntarily possessed by. True belief is therefore the ultimate relationship, not the mere description of some state of affairs.

Imagine Noah's situation, whatever the metaphysics of God's ultimate reality might be. Consider the choices that confront him, the nature of the possibility that shines forth for him. He can either assume the accuracy of his intuition, assume that he is wrong in his suspicions, or waver in a confused manner between those two presumptions. Those choices constitute his entire range of options. This is a state of affairs that has little to do, once again, with the existence of God, as material fact. It might be objected: there are additional choices that such an analysis does not take into consideration. Noah could, for example, turn his attention to an endless potential variety of other concerns. Turning away, however, is not a true alternative choice. It is instead the most serpentine and Machiavellian form of avoidance of conscience—a form of missing the proper mark by hypocritical substitution. This is lying by omission, rather than commission—the all-too-easily-rationalizable lie of avoidance, the most subtle form of deception, self- and otherwise. Hiding from necessity, even by doing some other hypothetically right thing, does not make the necessity any less real. It just obscures the way forward, confuses, kills hope, and divides. Noah therefore has what are in essence two choices: to prepare, or to ignore by one means or another the concerns that now plague and preoccupy him; to attend to his true duty, or to ignore the prime dictate of the "still small voice," which we will explore when it speaks, most famously, to Elijah, as in Kings 19:12.

Noah's "faith," therefore, is not the explicit statement of his belief in an imaginary being, as the follower or formulator of creeds might have it, but his identity with a certain spirit of conceptualization, apprehension, and forward movement. Does God exist for Noah? Does Noah *believe*? Here is the situation, properly construed: God is for Noah by definition what guides him, what seizes him, as he makes his way forward, *no matter what he decides to do*. All his choices must therefore be properly construed as decisions and acts of faith, because he does not and cannot truly know what is coming. Why conceptualize this, specifically, as faith in "God"? Because Noah must elevate something to the highest place (something that therefore is functionally equivalent to "God") so that every other choice has been sacrificed and forgone, that which now guides established as fundamental or superordinate, and movement forward made possible. The fact that this uniting spirit is "God" would remain true even if Noah explicitly disavowed any so-called "religious" belief. Belief in something beyond what is known is a prerequisite for attention and action on behalf of any creature who, like man, is and must remain fundamentally ignorant. This is true for every man and woman who has ever existed, exists now, and will ever exist. Noah's "belief" in God is therefore not the formulaic recitation of an explicit proclamation of belief, although it could be also that, but his willingness to act when called on by the deepest inclinations of his soul. What you allow to move you: that is your belief in God or in some second-rate substitute. This is a matter of definition— not least within the story we are considering. The same applies in general to all the stories currently under consideration.

Noah is a wise man, seized by the intuition of an impending flood. He determines to move forward in accordance with that revelation, regardless of difficulty or opposition. It is God—and, once again, by definition—who is the ultimate source, foundation, or aim of that conviction. *That is the very point of the text.* The story of Noah, like all the ancient stories we will consider, is thus not an argument for the existence of God, rendered against the doubt of believer and unbeliever alike, but a description of what is to be held properly in the very highest of places, so that the continuation of man, society, and world may be ensured. How does Noah justify his belief? How, more precisely, does he find the courage of his convictions? It is not for nothing that he is described as wise. A wise man is someone who has consistently paid attention, informed himself and others as a consequence, told himself and others the truth, insofar as he was capable, and acted in accordance with that truth.

A wise man has been continually aiming up and abiding by the truth. His hierarchy of value is therefore uncorrupted by lies, and his vision consequentially untrammeled. His capacity to receive a beneficial and accurate revelation was thereby honed, practiced, developed, and perfected, as was his ability to differentiate between a true or deep revelation, let us say, and the mere temptations of momentary hedonic whim. That might be regarded as the capacity of the wise for sagacious deliberation. Noah has practiced orienting his eyes heavenward; practiced identifying the way-markers that led uphill. He has learned how to place himself in a position to receive the revelation that is reliable, and to then follow its dictates. He has removed the beam from his eye, opened his ears to hear, knocked on the door, so that it will open, and sought, so that he could find. Noah has refused to tell himself the lies that tempt with the pleasures of short-term gratification and avoidance of ultimate responsibility. Thus, he can see what is right in front of his eyes, and can and will note, before anyone else, the gathering clouds. He therefore has faith in himself and what is highest, and can and will act accordingly. This is his relationship, his covenant with God. By definition. This means that he has the same relationship to himself, and to the cosmic order, as someone might have with another person they admire greatly, and whose advice they would rely on in times of trouble. Such people are those whom observation and reputation have deemed sagacious, careful, capable of delay of gratification, other-oriented in the proper manner, and mature.

Questions of faith: When you believe the storm is approaching, do you batten down the hatches and prepare, or not? Do you hearken to your intuition, or not? Do you trust yourself, or not? And if you do not, is it not because you have become untrustworthy to yourself in the same way that another person might have revealed himself as untrustworthy to you? If you do not trust yourself, is it not because (as in the case of that unreliable other) you have continually lied to yourself and obscured your own vision? Have you not thereby undermined the ground on which you could have otherwise stood? Is the ability to accurately intuit and to react appropriately wisdom, or not? Perhaps you have conducted yourself in a manner that enables you to rely on your deepest intuitions: then you are following the spirit of that intuition. You are acting out that spirit or inviting it to possess you. You are celebrating or even worshipping that spirit, sacrificing to that spirit (as everything else is rendered secondary or even nonexistent), manifesting faith in that spirit, *believing* in that spirit. If you reject the call, or the demand, of conscience when it reveals itself, say, as a warning to prepare—or even if you offer a half-hearted "yes"—then you are instead denying that spirit and manifesting faith in something else. There is simply no non-faith-predicated path forward.

> And God saw that the wickedness of man was great in the earth, and that every imagination of the thoughts of his heart was only evil continually.
>
> And it repented the Lord that he had made man on the earth, and it grieved him at his heart.
>
> And the Lord said, I will destroy man whom I have created from the face of the earth; both man, and beast, and the creeping thing, and the fowls of the air; for it repenteth me that I have made them.
>
> But Noah found grace in the eyes of the Lord
>
> *Genesis 6:1–8*

The degeneration spoken of in these verses, a result of the sin of Cain and its spread, is something that can and does realize itself everywhere when it emerges; something that occurs at the micro and macro level simultaneously; something that makes up the motivation for every personal glance and expression and the aim of every executive, legislative, and judicial decision. This is the multiheaded hydra of the degenerate patriarchal state, or the rise of the terrible dragon-mother of chaos that is the inevitable alternative to individual integrity, sustainable, voluntary social structure, harmony with the cosmic order, and fealty to God. The proclivity to sin or the "wickedness of man" is the true root cause of the chaos that envelops us in our personal lives first when we let things fall apart around us in our personal lives—and then on the familial, community, state, or global stage when the web of lies so generated becomes sufficiently broad. It is not often that any of us experience a truly apocalyptic occurrence, although it is not precisely rare: in the twentieth century alone, there were two world wars, the utter and still-unresolved catastrophe of fascism and communism, mass-scale economic upheaval and dislocation, the dawn of the atomic and computer ages, and the sexual revolution. But even within the smaller confines of our personal lives, things continually and apocalyptically disintegrate and revert to a chaos of confusion and possibility. A once-thriving business becomes corrupt as its founders turn away from the attention and diligent practice necessary to maintain its operations. A marriage collapses for the same reasons. Unmaintained friendships likewise wane or even reverse. All the best-laid plans of mice and men can and do go astray—partly because everything tends toward entropic decay, of its own accord, and partly because we can speed that process by aiming badly or not at all, as Mircea Eliade so brilliantly and trenchantly observes:

> The majority of the flood myths seem in some sense to form part
> of the cosmic rhythm: the old world, peopled by a fallen humanity,
> is submerged under the waters, and some time later a new world
> emerges from the aquatic "chaos." In a large number of variants, the
> flood is the result of the sins (or ritual faults) of human beings:

sometimes it results simply from the wish of a divine being to put an end to mankind ... the chief causes lie at once in the sins of men and the decrepitude of the world.[26]

This pattern of degeneration inevitably makes itself manifest at every level of order, from psyche to nation—even at the level of the hypothetical "environment" or the natural world, and for the same fundamental reason.

Noah therefore faces, albeit on the largest possible scale (as befits a giant of old), what everyone faces all the time in relationship to their own personal plans and schemes, well or poorly conceived and formulated as they may be. How does he manage? He builds the ark, of course, to carry him, his family, and the natural world itself through the catastrophe. Nonetheless, the solution that Noah offers is not, in the final analysis, technological. The first great prophet and postlapsarian savior has the character that enables him to muster the forces and resources necessary to build the ark, to convince his family of the necessity to do so, and to navigate the secure container he has built through the subsequent terrible storms. This means that his integrity is first and foremost, and his technical ability something subdued in the appropriate manner and in the appropriate place in the "heavenly hierarchy" below that. We all do what Noah is called upon to do, with varying degrees of commitment and success, throughout our lives. Noah's character, and ours, is proximally his humility, wisdom, goodness and productive generosity, and sheltering and encouraging nature, but more distally the indwelling of the protective and all-seeing spirit of God. By definition. And it was as true then as it is true now that such character is at the deepest level of reality the true reflection of the image of God. It is for such reasons that all truly admirable people are, first, admirable, and similar in the fact of their admirability: they all embody something deep, necessary, creative, active, wise, truthful, and loving. This means, in the symbolic language, that they most truly reflect the image of their creator.

Why the *prima facie* absurd insistence that Noah is responsible not only for the survival of his family and the human race but for all the animals that inhabit the antediluvian world? Recall for a moment the fact that Adam is called on to serve as steward of the Garden of Eden.[27] This is a description of an inevitability. The cognitive, psychological, or spiritual advantage that human beings have over all other creatures makes it eternally the case that the very existence of other creatures is increasingly dependent on the quality of our moral choices. If we do not shepherd even the wilderness—the environment whose proper stewardship now so thoroughly obsesses us—then its vast resources, whose presence had little or nothing to do with us, become rapidly depleted. We have already eliminated a vast array of animals of approximately our size, who either competed with us for scarce resources, preyed foolishly and ultimately counterproductively upon us, or served too temptingly as a source of food.

This has occurred on continent-wide scales and in the oceans, and is by no means a phenomenon limited to the last few hundred years, or something that is merely and modernly a consequence of the tremendous recent expansion of our technological prowess. Human beings made their presence known in the Western hemisphere a maximum of twenty thousand years ago.[28] Within a few millennia, the once-plentiful major mammals, occupying approximately the human niche (mastodons and mammoths, saber-toothed cats, giant ground sloths, the armadillo-like glyptodonts, American lions, and dire wolves) had all disappeared.[29] The same thing happened to a variety of marsupials in Australia, although even more distantly in the past, as humans arrived there some fifty thousand years ago,[30] and even longer ago to both giant tortoises[31] and birds (particularly on islands).[32] These brute and sobering facts make a mockery of the idiotic Rousseauian noble-savage presumption that less technologically advanced or even specifically non-European people lived in some sort of unchanging and pristine harmony with an equally unchanging and primeval nature.

Spears and clubs, particularly when wielded by a cooperative hunting group, are a sufficiently radical advance in technology so that even fierce and adept predators stand little long-term chance against human foes. The situation obtaining on the high seas is if anything more dire: up to 90 percent of the population of large predatory fish populations in the North Atlantic, including cod, tuna, and swordfish, had already been depleted by the end of the 1800s due to overfishing and other human activities. Since then, ninety percent of remaining stocks have disappeared.[33] The point? *Without ultimately upward-aiming men there are even no animals.* The necessity for the appropriate (properly subdued) moral concern about nonhuman creatures is therefore highlighted not only in the original command of God to Adam to cultivate, work, tend, watch over, take care of, dress and keep the garden (Genesis 2:25, various translations) but in the similar injunctions interspersed throughout the Old Testament. Beasts of burden, like human beings, are thus to be granted a Sabbath (Exodus 20:10); the aforementioned oxen who "treadeth out the corn" are not to be muzzled while doing so, so they can benefit to some degree by their own labor, eating while working (Deuteronomy 25:4–5; 1 Corinthians 9:9); and the righteous man is deemed one who "regardeth the life of his beast." In stark contrast, "the tender mercies of the wicked are cruel" (Proverbs 12:10).

Human beings are therefore responsible, for better or worse, not only for their own individual integrity and the proper governance of the social world but for the animals, domestic and wild alike, with whom they share the planet. This does not mean in any manner that animals have rights, as the existence of "right" is dependent on the capacity to reciprocate, but it certainly does mean that we are traditionally held to a high ethical standard in our relationship with other creatures, and that their very survival depends, as noted, on the wisdom even of our personal choices. The resurgence of dietary restrictions predicated on hypothetically moral grounds—the practice of vegetarianism foremost among them—is a consequence at least in part of that deep ethical necessity, misplaced and crippled though it certainly is as a solution to the ultimate problem of proper moral conduct, or even of proper stewardship. Although it is true that "not that which goeth into the mouth defileth a man; but that which cometh out of the mouth, this defileth a man" (Matthew 15:11), it is still and truly the case that the sacrifice of something living to ensure our continued survival is an act that should be consecrated to the highest possible purpose. Otherwise conscience comes to call, as it apparently has for an growing number of increasingly guilt-ridden consumers and second-rate sacrificers.[34] It is clearly time in the modern world to confess our sins, repent, aim truly upward, tell the truth, and make the requisite difficult offerings. Instead, we insist on praying in public and using the name of God in vain, attributing to ourselves divine motivation when brandishing publicly our cards and gestures of protest and mouthing our hackneyed self-aggrandizing vegan and more generally ideological slogans and clichés of envy and resentment. "Teaching for doctrines the commandments of men" (Matthew 15:9) is hypocrisy, indeed—therefore:

> And when thou prayest, thou shalt not be as the hypocrites are: for they love to pray standing in the synagogues and in the corners of the streets, that they may be seen of men. Verily I say unto you, They have their reward.
>
> But thou, when thou prayest, enter into thy closet, and when thou hast shut thy door, pray to thy Father which is in secret; and thy Father which seeth in secret shall reward thee openly.
>
> But when ye pray, use not vain repetitions, as the heathen do: for they think that they shall be heard for their much speaking.
>
> Be not ye therefore like unto them: for your Father knoweth what things ye have need of, before ye ask him.

There is no difference between the modern professional protestors, brandishing his or her moral virtue like a club, and the Pharisees who conspired to crucify Christ. That is all part of the eternal story.

God, unhappy with the sinful state of the world, displeased by the blind and willful turning away of His should-be sons, commands Noah, the man wise in his generations, to build a giant boat and to place within it "thou, and thy sons, and thy wife, and thy sons' wives with thee."

> And of every living thing of all flesh, two of every sort shalt thou bring into the ark, to keep them alive with thee; they shall be male and female.

> Of fowls after their kind, and of cattle after their kind, of every creeping thing of the earth after his kind, two of every sort shall come unto thee, to keep them alive.
>
> *Genesis 6:29–31*

For forty days and forty nights the deluge comes, pouring rain and rising waters, and everything upon the surface of the earth is washed away:

> And the waters prevailed exceedingly upon the earth; and all the high hills, that were under the whole heaven, were covered.
>
> Fifteen cubits upward did the waters prevail; and the mountains were covered.
>
> And all flesh died that moved upon the earth, both of fowl, and of cattle, and of beast, and of every creeping thing that creepeth upon the earth, and every man.
>
> *Genesis 7:20–22*

Thus Noah, the wise man who hearkens to the cautionary voice of God, builds the ark that eternally guides himself, his family, his community, and even the natural order itself through the storms.

The promised and prophesied storms last the prototypical forty days and nights, but the waters remain high for four times that length of time. Finally, however, the divine anger is quenched, the mountaintops reappear, and the new covenant is established. In the aftermath of this reemergence of the world from the watery chaos, God repeats to Noah the injunction given to Adam (Genesis 1:28): "be fruitful, and multiply upon the earth" (Genesis 8:17; Genesis 9:1). In response, Noah initiates the habitation of this new cosmos with an approved sacrifice (Genesis 8:20), repeating the proper actions of Abel and forswearing the temptations of Cain. This means that the first prophet reconsecrates the world to God, establishing the upward aim as paramount, in contrast to the disorientation, confusion, self-serving hedonism, and mad power-striving that characterized the descendants of the fratricidal, arrogant, and resentful brother. As a result, God swears to forgo such total vengeance in the future: "And the Lord smelled a sweet savour; and the Lord said in his heart, I will not again curse the ground any more for man's sake; for the imagination of man's heart is evil from his youth; neither will I again smite any more every thing living, as I have done. While the earth remaineth, seedtime and harvest, and cold and heat, and summer and winter, and day and night shall not cease" (Genesis 8:21–22). In this manner, and now, and in the future: *the honest sacrifice of the wise and good man is what forever forestalls the apocalypse.* This is equally true at the personal and social levels; equally true in matters both micro- and macrocosmic in scope.

God also takes this occasion to remind human beings of their immense responsibility as stewards of this new and renewed garden, in parallel with the abundance simultaneously offered: "And the fear of you and the dread of you shall be upon every beast of the earth, and upon every fowl of the air, upon all that moveth upon the earth, and upon all the fishes of the sea; into your hand are they delivered. Every moving thing that liveth shall be meat for you; even as the green herb have I given you all things" (Genesis 9:2–3). The very essence of life itself, however, is to be reserved for God and not transgressed upon: "But flesh with the life thereof, which is the blood thereof, shall ye not eat" (Genesis 9:4). This appears to mean something like maintenance of proper respect for the gift or even existence of life; the soul of life itself: "while man is permitted to have the body for his food, as being the mere vessel which contains this life, the gift itself must go back to God, and the blood as its symbol be treated with reverence."[35] This appears to be a repetition of the injunction not to transgress against or to go too far—a forbidding reminiscent of and analogous to the prohibition against devouring the fruit of the tree of the knowledge of good and evil; a reminder that there is something that should remain sacred even in the midst of all attempts to satiate.

This limitation is driven home by accompanying limitations: killing for food (assuming the proper sacrificial attitude) is morally permitted, but the killing that is careless or murderous is to be distinguished and forbidden. The New Living Translation puts it this way: "And I will require the blood of anyone who takes another person's life. If a wild animal kills a person, it must die. And anyone who murders a fellow human must die. If anyone takes a human life, that person's life will also be taken by human hands. For God made human beings in his own image" (Genesis 9:5–6). Arguably, this also establishes the preconditions for just war: only the conflicts that are truly motivated by the attempt to maintain the self-sacrificial covenant with the divine are justified. Separating this from the doctrine of "ends justify the means" is no easy matter, but the fact of this difficulty should not come as a surprise. There is virtually nothing that presents a greater challenge than getting the moral house in order, particularly in the case of armed group conflict. The nature of the new covenant is also further clarified:

> Then God spoke to Noah and to his sons with him, saying
>
> And I, behold, I establish my covenant with you, and with your seed after you;
>
> And with every living creature that is with you, of the fowl, of the cattle, and of every beast of the earth with you; from all that go out of the ark, to every beast of the earth.
>
> And I will establish my covenant with you; neither shall all flesh be cut off any more by the waters of a flood; neither shall there any more be a flood to destroy the earth.
>
> *Genesis 9:8–11*

At the end of all this, God, feeling well pleased with Noah and his sacrifice, famously hangs the rainbow in the sky. This is the perennial symbol that the storms have cleared and a sign of the permanence of this new agreement:

> And God said, This is the token of the covenant which I make between me and you and every living creature that is with you, for perpetual generations:
>
> I do set my bow in the cloud, and it shall be for a token of a covenant between me and the earth.

And it shall come to pass, when I bring a cloud over the earth,
that the bow shall be seen in the cloud:

And I will remember my covenant, which is between me and you
and every living creature of all flesh; and the waters shall no more
become a flood to destroy all flesh.

Genesis 9:12–15

The rainbow is the full spectrum implicit in the transcendent and heavenly unity of the white light of the sun. It represents the ideally subdued community, which is the integration of the diversity of those who compose it into the singular harmony of present, balanced with future, and the individual, balanced with society. Also, it is simultaneously the interplay of the heavenly—that very sunlight that is offered from above—with the water that is also chaos, the *tohu va bohu* or *tehom*, and the source of the potential from which the world emerges. It is the balance between order, or the principle of order—the possibility of illumination or enlightenment itself—with the natural world, signifying the seamless integration of the divine will with material world. The rainbow is in all these manners a complex and highly appropriate symbol of the newly renewed covenant.

4.4. The faithless son doomed to enslavement

The story of Noah now takes a surprising turn. After departing from the ark, Noah and his sons and daughters immediately get to work (reflected and echoed in the fact of Noah's sacrifices). Noah, who is "a man of the soil" (Genesis 9:20), plants a vineyard, brews some wine, and somewhat carelessly over-imbibes—although, to be sure, he has just been through an awful lot. He ends up splayed out, naked, inside the private confines of his tent, in the aftermath of this too-intense celebration. One of his sons, Ham, takes the opportunity to treat his father with some contempt in his moment of vulnerability and weakness. He passes by Noah's tent, with its flap open, and observes his unclothed state. That is already a breach, not least of privacy, but Ham immediately compounds his error. He takes a jealous and arrogant delight in the revelation of his great father's all-too-human imperfection, as evidenced in the gossiping and narcissistic reputation-savaging that he attempts to embark on with his brothers: "And Ham, the father of Canaan, saw the nakedness of his father and told his two brethren without" (Genesis 9:22). What Ham saw is described with the Hebrew word הָרָעַ:

> Signifying to make naked, from a kindred root to which (סתר) comes the term expressive of the nakedness of Adam and Eve after eating the forbidden fruit (Genesis 3:7). The sin of Ham—"not a trifling and unintentional transgression" (Von Bohlen)—obviously lay not in seeing what perhaps he may have come upon unexpectedly, but (1) in wickedly rejoicing in what he saw, which, considering who he was that was overcome with wine, "the minister of salvation to men, and the chief restorer of the world," the relation in which he stood to Ham—that of father—the advanced age to which he had now come, and the comparatively mature years of Ham himself, who was "already more than a hundred years old," should have filled him with sincere sorrow; *sed nunquam vino victum pattern filius risisset, nisi prius ejecisset animo illam reverentiam et opinionem, quae in liberis de parentibus ex mandato Dei existere debet.* [But a son would never have laughed at a father conquered by wine unless he had first expelled from his mind that reverence and respect that, according to God's command, children ought to have for their parents.] (Luther)[36]; and (2) in reporting it, doubtless with a malicious purpose, to his brethren ["and told his two brethren without"], possibly inviting them to come and look upon their father's shame.[37]

It is for such reasons that Ham is regarded by tradition as the progeniture of the Canaanites—the descendants of Cain, to say it again, characterized in the biblical corpus as the eternally idolatrous and morally corrupt people, and the people over whom and over whose territory God therefore grants the Israelites dominion. This narrative subplot and characterization drives home a very harsh lesson: children (descendants, physical and spiritual) of those who lack all respect for their parents will be ruled over both inevitably and justly by the offspring of those who properly honor and revere their mothers and fathers, ancestors, and traditions. It is easy enough for conceptually addled moderns to confuse this warning with something like "arbitrary prejudice against the Canaanites," with such prejudice also construed in the modern sense. This says nothing, or very little, about the ancient Israelites, however, and much instead about the ideological addling of the modern mind.[38]

The idea that contempt for tradition, parental and otherwise, will be met with severe punishment hearkens back, once again,[39] to the *Enuma elish*, the story of the original Mesopotamian gods, against whom the great female dragon of chaos Tiamat marshals her terrible forces. It is those first children— the fractious spirits, it might be said, of first-order instinct itself—who carelessly and arrogantly slay Apsu, the spirit of habitable order—and who then attempt to live both ungratefully and unproductively on the resultant corpse. This regicide, this parasitic inversion of social structure, this contempt for ancestral sacrifice, results in the visitation of a dreadful punishment on the wayward progeny of Tiamat. All the horrors of existence array themselves against them in the form of every imaginable demon and monster. This is certainly the metaphoric equivalent of a flood. To look with contempt on the nakedness or vulnerability of your father is simultaneously to tempt out of the abyss the eternal dragon of chaos and the vengeful wrath of God. Ingratitude veers perilously close in this manner to the cardinal and overweening sin of Luciferian pride.

Ham's brothers righteously and wisely refuse to join in the mockery, choosing instead to extend an appropriate respect to the tradition that has just shepherded them through the cataclysm, and to do so even in a moment when the vulnerability and proclivity for error of the bearer of that tradition has revealed itself in the starkest and most basic manner possible: "Then Shem and Japheth took a garment, laid it on both their shoulders, and walked backward and covered the nakedness of their father. Their faces were turned backward, and they did not see their father's nakedness" (Genesis 9:23). It is a great error to judge someone (worse, to hold them in contempt) solely on their behavior at their weakest moments. Every single person dead or alive judged in that manner would end up damned. Further, all gratitude for the gifts bequeathed upon us by those who lived in the past would vanish. That necessary gratitude—necessary to keep the productive spirit of the past alive—would be carelessly replaced, instead, by a thoroughly undeserved and narcissistic attitude of comparative virtue: "we in the modern world are above all that." Thus proclaim the desecrators of statues and monuments[40] and, increasingly, great works of art.[41]

That careless dismissal and arrogant presumptuousness is tantamount, to say it again, to the killing of Apsu undertaken by the careless elder gods of the long-vanished Mesopotamian world. The hell that broke loose then, according to the ancient mythological account, threatens no less now, in the immediate aftermath of Ham's betrayal. The fact that Ham reacts one way to the evidence of his father's imperfection, and Shem and Japheth another, has long-term and determinative significance:

> And Noah awoke from his wine, and knew what his younger son had done unto him. And he said, Cursed be Canaan; a servant of servants shall he be unto his brethren. And he said, Blessed be the Lord God of Shem; and Canaan shall be his servant. God shall enlarge Japheth, and he shall dwell in the tents of Shem; and Canaan shall be his servant. (Genesis 9:24–26)

It is impossible for anyone who holds his tradition in contempt, and arrogates to himself an unearned comparative moral version of it, to simultaneously embody that tradition, let alone its best. To the degree that such embodiment is necessary, in relationship to present or future success (and it is necessary, to the degree that tradition has genuinely brought forward the proper spirit and practice of comprehensive adaptation), failure to make it manifest will produce comparative failure. Thus, the spiritual heirs of

Noah's faithless son, Ham, who was characterized by careless contempt for the perceived weakness of his father, will always and inevitably end up in second place—or worse, as the veritable servants of, or even enslaved by, those who hold the proper attitude, not least concerning proper filial respect. It is not as if Shem and Japheth are naive, either, in their attitude and actions toward their father: they accept the fact that he has a fallen aspect, but make their respect known, regardless. This is something approximating their capacity to appropriately separate wheat from chaff, as in Matthew 3:12— something akin to establishing a wise and responsible filial relationship to the spirit of the Father and the past. Everything past does not have to be brought forward; some appreciation for the faults of the paternal can be developed in the course of the maturation of the son—but a fundamental attitude of reverence must be maintained. This is something for us all to relearn in these days of hypocritical and prideful apology for the sins of the past, both real and imaginary: "Honor thy father and thy mother: that thy days may be long upon the land which the Lord thy God giveth thee" (Exodus 20:12).

Noah lives long, in exactly that manner—and, implicitly, for that reason— although such a destiny also properly befits a "man of renown": "And Noah lived after the flood three hundred and fifty years. And all the days of Noah were nine hundred and fifty years: and he died" (Genesis 9:28–29). His example, like that of Abraham, the next great prophet, establishes the pattern of proper being for those who abide by the spirit of God, manifested not least through the father, wise in his generations. This is the pattern characteristic of the descendants of Shem (such as Abraham) and of Japheth, the true heirs of Seth and the proper spirit of sacrifice, reverence, and worship, who spread across the lands: "By these were the isles of the Gentiles divided in their lands; every one after his tongue, after their families, in their nations" (Genesis 10:5). Variant alternate translations insist upon the maritime prowess of these descendants, for example, stressing in this manner their adaptability; their tendency to disseminate effectively: "Their descendants became the seafaring peoples that spread out to various lands, each identified by its own language, clan, and national identity" (New International Version); "From these, [the people of] the coastlands of the nations were separated and spread into their lands, every one according to his own language, according to their constituent groups (families), and into their nations" (Amplified Bible), while the children of Ham are held to be those "who occupy the second place."[42] This is all to drive home the point that the pattern of success that characterizes the faithful, upward-aiming, and courageous children of Seth must be predicated on respect both for tradition in its human form and for the spirit, or Word, whose manifestation has eternally given rise to that tradition.

5

◆

The Tower of Babel:
God versus Tyranny and Pride

5.1. Lucifer and the engineers

The Bible's first builders of cities, fabricators of musical instruments, and weapons of war—the individuals who pursue technological solutions—are, significantly, the children of Cain. We read this directly in the text, and it is true thematically, insofar as the pursuit of technology engaged in by these builders constitutes both a substitute for proper ethical striving and a form of worship of the intellect. They are the engineers, builders, and inhabitants of the eternal Babylon, the city of the prideful and presumptuous.

Some of the largest buildings first built by people when establishing the first cities took the architectural form of the ziggurat, a stepped pyramid. Ziggurats were common in the ancient Near East,[1] but also appeared elsewhere, most notably in Central America.[2] A ziggurat reaches to the sky, step-by-step, in a fashion clearly reminiscent of a hierarchy. In fact, ziggurat-like, or pyramidal, forms are often employed in the modern world by graphic designers who wish to display a relationship of hierarchical dependency.[3] Ziggurats had their practical functions, serving as places of sacrifice or other sacred rituals, often associated with the temple complexes central to ancient cities and housing various economic and administrative operations. However, they were primarily monuments to the grandeur or grandiosity of a given ruler or, in a more generous interpretation, his society. The higher the ziggurat, the grander the potentate—and, by inference—the more intimidating the polity.

The Egyptians devoted tremendous resources to the construction of their pyramids, similar in design and purpose to the ziggurats, in the similar attempt to elevate the status of their pharaohs to near-godly levels. To the degree that the pyramidal form was a paean to the idea of divine hierarchy—with the gold cap representing the attending eye that sits atop any properly arranged hierarchical symbolic form—their soaring creations were perhaps justified, in a deeper and non-egoistic sense. Considered in that light, the pyramids are an early architectural expression of striving toward God, seen again millennia later in the great cathedrals of the late Middle Ages and later Renaissance. Eliade comments on architecture as bridge to the heavens:

> As for the assimilation of temples to cosmic mountains and their function as links between earth and heaven, the names given to Babylonian sanctuaries themselves bear witness: they are called "Mountain of the House," "House of the Mountain of all Lands," "Mountain of Storms," "Link between Heaven and Earth," and the like. The ziggurat was literally a cosmic mountain; the seven stories represented the seven planetary heavens; by ascending them, the priest reached the summit of the universe. . . . But it was also in Babylon that the connection between earth and the lower regions was made, for the city had been built on *bab apsi*, "the Gate of Apsu," *apsu* being the name for the waters of chaos before Creation. The same tradition is found among the Hebrews; the rock of the Temple in Jerusalem reached deep into the *tehom*, the Hebrew equivalent of *apsu*.[4]

To the degree that the efforts of a whole society were devoted instead toward the celebration of the ego of a given ruler or people, however, the construction of a ziggurat or pyramid could devolve pathologically into the worship of a false god—putting in the place of the functional and truly integrating divine ideal something proximate, self-serving, arrogant, power-mad, and prideful.

A specific Babylonian construction—a massive, stepped tower dedicated to the god Marduk—is often cited as the source of the idea for the Tower of Babel in the Bible, as Edward Lipiński, the Polish-Belgian biblical scholar, explains: "The story of the Tower of Babel was perhaps inspired by the Etemenanki of Babylon, which was described by Herodotus and by Berossus, as well as by the Tower of Borsippa, the temple-tower of the god Nabu."[5] Etemenanki was constructed in the sixth century BCE by King Nebuchadnezzar II,[6] a ruler who sought to rebuild the city of Babylon as a symbol of his power and authority. Insofar as this ziggurat was built to glorify Marduk, triumphantly emergent king of the gods, symbol of vision and the magic words of the truth (as was apparently its purpose[7]), it illustrated something approximating a monotheistic hierarchy. Insofar as its construction redounded to the glory of Nebuchadnezzar II, it was an expression of narcissistic presumption.

The Tower of Babel story may also have been influenced by a corpus of Near Eastern myths featuring failed attempts to approach, breach, or storm the heavens, and appears "strikingly similar" to the Mesopotamian myth of Enmerkar and the Lord of Aratta, which tells of a tower that is confounded by the gods.[8] This tale, found in the Sumerian epic poem *Enmerkar and the Lord of Aratta*, dating back to the twenty-third century BCE, features a king who sought to establish his dominion over other cities and nations. He did so by building a towering structure that would reach the heavens, believing that this tower would serve as a symbol of his power and authority, and would enable him to communicate with the gods. The Lord of Aratta, a neighboring city, had his people build a higher edifice, believing that this would bring him even closer than king Enmerkar to the gods. The gods themselves, angered by the pride and arrogance of the two kings, confounded their language and scattered them across the earth, preventing them from completing their towers.[9]

It also appears that the account of the Tower of Babel was influenced by the political and religious rivalries between different Mesopotamian city-states. The prominent Dutch scholar Karel van der Toorn suggests that "the story may reflect a polemic against Babylon and its ambitions in the southern Mesopotamian plain."[10] The ancient Hebrews might certainly have had political reasons to choose the metaphor of Babylon as emblematic of the overweening pride of power-based empires, just as the city of Rome was chosen for such a role by the early Christians.[11] This does not change the fact that the story of the tower of Babel most fundamentally attempts to explore the nature and dangers of something deeper than the spirit of a single authoritarian culture—rather than being a critique of Babylon or any other empire. The narrative is not political—or if it is, it is so only in the service of a higher or deeper meaning. The same can be said of many of the biblical narratives that mention specific societies or even specific people: they are to be regarded as types or patterns, with what is specific and identifiable used only to characterize a deeper truth.

How is that aim realized in the story at hand? The answer can be profitably approached from multiple vantage points. First, the terms *Babel* and *Babylon* are clearly related in terms of etymology and geography, derived as they arguably are from the Akkadian word *Babili(m)*, which means "gate of the god."[12] The name Babel, on the other hand, is related to the word Babylon [*Babili(m)*], but might have been additionally derived from or influenced by the Hebrew root *balal* (בָּלַל), meaning "to confuse" or "to mix up." The connection between the terms *Babili(m)* and *Babel* is apparently a result of linguistic adaptation, or borrowing, over time. The Hebrew word *Babel* likely reflects the Semitic pronunciation of the Akkadian term *Babili(m)*. The biblical narrative connects the city of Babylon with the tower of Babel, suggesting that Babylon was built on the same site where the tower was attempted to be built. The attempt to build the tower was a sign of human arrogance and rebellion against God. God punished the builders—as in the case of *Enmerkar and the Lord of Aratta*—by making it impossible for them to understand one another and destroying the unity of their society. It can be seen from this etymology that "Babel" represents many things: empire and the presumptions of empire; arrogance in tandem with technological might; the confusion that prevails when the aims of psyche and society have gone astray.

Although the first builders of cities are the descendants of Cain, tradition has it that the city of Babylon, specifically, is founded by Nimrod, who does so in an act of God-defying hubris.[13] Nimrod is a direct descendant of Noah's son Ham, who reveled in the site of his father's nakedness and whose descendants were consequently cursed with failure and slavery (Genesis 9: 20–27). Babylon is, therefore, not only the city of arrogant empire but also the prototypical dwelling place of the son who lacks respect for his father and who therefore places himself in a position of unearned moral superiority. Nimrod is described in the biblical text in terms reminiscent or indicative of those who seek power for power's sake, as "the first on earth to be a mighty man" (Genesis 10:8 English Standard Version), "the first powerful man on earth" (Holman Christian Standard Bible), or "the world's first great conqueror" (Good News Translation). Thus, the idea of overweening pride, might, and the lust for conquest is linked through the metaphor of his ancestry to the city-building/technological enterprise, and more precisely to the founding of the city Babylon.

The story of the Tower of Babel is in its essence another retelling of the ever-present temptations and dangers of hubris—a warning against humanity's marked proclivity to arrogance and misguided ambition. It cautions against the temptations of the Luciferian intellect: the desire, manifest not least in Eve, Adam, and Cain, to exceed the proper human place, define good and evil themselves, and attain the heights—and by means other than identification with God and subordination to the intrinsic, preestablished and eternal moral order. In building a tower that "reaches to the heavens," the engineers and technicians of Babel, or Babylon, and their associated rulers and states aimed to make a name not for God but for themselves. In their pride, they claimed divinity and overstepped the bounds that kept them properly ensconced within the true cosmic and metaphysical order. This all reflects the eternal alliance of the tyrannical spirit with the impetus toward intellectual and technical self-aggrandizement. The misguided and fatally presumptuous builders of the catastrophically unstable tower sought to obtain power over their environment—psychological, social, natural, and metaphysical—and to master it completely for narrowly self-centered reasons.

It is instructive in this regard to understand that Cain, who invited the Luciferian spirit to dwell within him, is also explicitly described in the biblical text as the first to build a city (Genesis 4:17), in addition to being the forerunner of those who made various technological artifacts, including tents (Jabal), musical instruments (Jubal), and metal tools and weapons (Tubal-Cain) (Genesis 4:21–22). It is thus that the engineers, in general, and the builders of the Tower of Babel, more specifically, are portrayed as Cain's spiritual descendants, taking pride in their creations and their mastery of the physical world, ignoring the spiritual hierarchy and the divinely ordained limitations. This disregard for the higher divine order inevitably produces a consequential disarray and chaos, as seen in the confusion of languages produced when the Tower of Babel collapses.[14] The meaning of the story extends beyond its traditional and reductive understanding as a primitive theory about the origin of diverse tongues.[15] The arrogant belief in the power of technology and, more deeply, the presumption that the technical intellect can and should rule even over divinity corrupts the entirety of psyche and state so completely that words themselves in such a state lose their meaning—a meaning that only exists if it is shared; that only exists in relationship to a universal point of reference.

This disintegration emerges as even the implicit unity that lends them intelligibility is destroyed by the cascading consequences of the demolition of the proper order of understanding. This is exactly what is happening in our society now—a society increasingly unable to agree on the meaning of the most fundamental referents—the words *man* and *woman* foremost among them.[16] Misdirection of aim destroys the purpose that brings people together in peaceful and productive competition and cooperation, and makes it impossible for each to understand what the other is doing. Words rely for their utility on their nesting within a framework of shared meaning. They must remain tools employed for the same task; chess pieces in the same game (as the philosopher Ludwig Wittgenstein so pertinently noted[17]). This does not mean that the eternally lurking potential catastrophe of the Tower of Babel *is an indication of the pathology of intellect and its striving, per se.* It is not an idiot invitation to a thoughtlessly and reactionary Ludditism. In its unadulterated and properly humble form, the intelligence that leads to technical mastery can and should be a stellar reflection of the Logos, a faculty well and appropriately regarded as the greatest gift bestowed by the Creator upon man.

The presumptuous totalitarian catastrophe is instead the terrible consequences that inevitably emerge when the spirit of that intellect goes most direly and dreadfully wrong. This is why Lucifer—even Satan himself—was traditionally regarded, not least by Milton, as the highest but also most wayward angel in God's heavenly hierarchy ("brighter once amidst the host Of Angels, than that starr the Starrs among").[18] That spirit of enlightenment is the most valuable imaginable or possible faculty when it stays in its proper place—the true bringer of light—but the worst of all possible masters, when it attempts to reign supreme. The development of civilization, intellect, and technology—progress, in a word—is therefore not to be regarded as inherently sinful or evil. It becomes so only when it is held to be the supreme path forward—or worse, when the offering of that pathway is made in a manner that falsely elevates the perceived status of those making the offer. This is the attempt by the engineer or builder to be worshipped as the engine of creative progression itself, in the attempt to impress and dominate and, when such attempts fail, to seek the revenge of the unjustly spurned (echoes of Cain). This is no different than the attempt to usurp the throne of God himself, and is also a retelling of the central sin of man, as in the fall of Adam. There is no greater imaginable sin of pride.

There is still more to this pattern of aberrant Babylonian conception and aim, although it is subtle, dreamlike, encapsulated only in poetic form, and prone to elude easy notice or understanding. To comprehend it fully, the more extended descriptions of Babylon and its inhabitants, male and female alike, must be considered. The abuse of technological power, as documented in the story of the Tower of Babel, might well and appropriately be regarded as a masculine proclivity. There is, however, a feminine counterpart. This is inevitable, as when things fall apart on the side of the male, there is bound to be a corresponding deterioration, or perversion, on the side of the female, joined together as the two sexes are ineluctably are in their development, attitudes, patterns of attention, and actions. How could the city placing the worst possible spirit in the highest place—elevating the veritable and mysterious "abomination of desolation" (Daniel 9:27, Daniel 11:31; Daniel 12:11; Matthew 24:15)—also therefore fail to be inhabited by the degenerates of the female world? How could it not open itself up to possession by the very spirit of that degeneration?

The key to understanding the nature of the feminine descent into chaos in the biblical text is to be found in identification of the common, uniting and context-establishing theme of habitation in Babylon—the degenerate city that also happens to be the habitation of the matriarch of all whores: "And the woman was arrayed in purple and scarlet color, and decked with gold and precious stones and pearls, having a golden cup in her hand full of abominations and filthiness of her fornication: And upon her forehead was a name written, Mystery, Babylon The Great, The Mother Of Harlots And Abominations Of The Earth" (Revelation 17:4–5). It is all the people who inhabit the great but false edifice who become unable to communicate, after all—men, and women with them. What happens when the patriarchal degenerates, and loses its unity; when it cheapens itself, and becomes sinful? The matriarchal loses its higher purposes, as well, fracturing and regressing, making itself subject to the twin forces of power and hedonism that inevitably rise up when the God who. properly reigns above dies, however temporarily.

The Whore of Babylon is the spirit that makes herself present—even worshipped—when women employ the power of sexual seductiveness as a tool of manipulation and advance and for the purposes of immediate hedonistic self-gratification. This—the degeneration of femininity into commoditized sex—is an inevitable consequence of moral failure on the masculine side, even though it is not something only to be laid at the feet of men. The proclivity for this to occur is an analog to the temptations of the Luciferian intellect. The immense sexual attractiveness of healthy, beautiful women is a gift or talent that, like intelligence, can go terribly wrong. This is much more likely to occur, of course, when the male community has abandoned its responsibility, not least to abide by the sacred dictates of monogamy—to substitute for that casual pleasure and worship of the power that makes such pleasure at least temporarily more available (albeit only to a few, however unsustainably and unreliably, in the final analysis, even to them). This is not to understate the complicity of women: the temptation to flaunt and profit by what is attractive regardless of consequences, future and social, is a clear and prominent hallmark of female manipulativeness and immaturity. The Dark Triad or Tetrad traits described previously in relation to men[19] predict also, for example, feminine proclivity to trade sex for desired resources (money, most directly) or to avoid the productive and generative responsibility of marriage and motherhood.[20]

Considering the antithetical relationship, symbolically speaking, between the image of the Whore of Babylon and the traditional ideal of feminine nature aids in the further understanding of the degeneration of the state of pathological aim. That traditional ideal is, of course, the Virgin and the Child. A society that worships the former and forgoes the latter understands femininity only in terms of the undeniable raw sexual power of women (as the labor that women can provide, insofar as they can substitute, however well or poorly, for men, makes them not exactly women, but honorary men). A society that venerates the virgin, by contrast, elevates the status of women who voluntarily forgo manipulative and self-serving deployment of the power of their sexual attractiveness. One that extends this celebration to the sacred duo of woman and child (a truly mature attitude) orients itself to the long term, aiming at the stable communal relationships that best suit children and also most effectively and maturely satisfy the deepest needs of men and women, all things considered.

What does "all things considered" mean, in such a context? It means in a manner that best ensures psychological integration and stability, in consequence of the continual dialogue and dance that characterizes a committed marriage. It means in a manner that most thoroughly guarantees and stabilizes a productive, peaceful, and hospitable society, with committed couples serving that society as basic and necessary foundation. In all alternative arrangements, men and women drift—fall apart at the seams, and terribly. The understanding of femininity as relational (understanding of woman as inseparable in some fundamental sense from infant—and, therefore, from husband) is a crucial element of a functional society. There is every reason to think that in the absence of such conceptualization the psyches of both man and woman also fail to develop or disintegrate. Does this mean that "single woman" is a category of the undesirable? No more and no less than "single man."

Consider the following comments, made by English clergyman and noted biblical scholar Charles John Ellicott (1819–1905):

> Jeremiah (Jeremiah 51:7) called Babylon a "golden cup in the hand of the Lord." The cup had made all the earth drunken; the cup of intoxication, splendid and attractive, was full of an evil power, which robbed men's senses and degraded them. The great city of the world ever holds out such a glittering cup, which "Most do taste through fond intemperate desire. Soon as the potion works, their human countenance, Th' express resemblance of the gods, is changed Into some brutish form."[21]

The "brutish form" referred to is the true identity lurking behind the mask of shallow sexual attractiveness monetized in the present world so often, and in so many diverse forms—all produced, distributed, and purchased by the technological sons of Cain. The full domain of such sin and the all-encompassing span of its nature is revealed within the relevant texts, as well, in other complex manners. First is the association between Babylon and harlotry, *per se*, which we have already alluded to: The denigration and exploitation of women (by others and by themselves), particularly on the sexual front, is linked in the biblical corpus and then more explicitly by commentators with the rise of the prideful and technocratic spirit of Babel.

This may well be something necessary to reflect upon in a time when tech-nology has allied itself with prostitution in a manner so widespread and per-vasive that it is a kind of perverse miracle. Some twenty-five percent of total web traffic involves the dissemination of pornographic material.[22] This is certainly the technologically-mediated subjugation of the feminine to the hedonistic and narrowly economic and, more deeply, the alliance of the prostitute (or her virtual equivalents) with the terrible spirit of arrogant irre-sponsibility characterizing the builders of the eternal Babylon. It was the possibility of broad access to pornographic material that was even one of the driving factors for both the development and widespread instantaneous and enthusiastic adoption of the world wide web.[23]

As Sigmund Freud so necessarily insisted: never underestimate the role sexual motivation plays in the determination of human behavior, no matter how apparently complex.[24] It is relevant in this regard and certainly not by chance that it is precisely the engineers who are trying so desperately to lit-erally build women—the very women who will not come to them volun-tarily, in reality, because of their oft-parodied and essentially too-narrow undesirability, magnified in repulsiveness by their appalling and resentful intellectual pride. It is also the engineers who have built the systems that bring the modern whores of Babylon and their delectable but untouchable succubus delights to the sticky laptops of the basement-dwelling techno-incels. Ellicott later comments in another relevant passage on Revelation 18:24:

> It is not by seductiveness only that her guilt is measured: her hands are defiled with blood: the blood of prophets, who had witnessed against her: of saints, whose holy lives were a protest against her sins, and so hateful to her. . . . Babylon, the world city, is founded on those principles, the logical outcome of which is violence, blood-shed, and hostility to the highest right: those who die by her hands, few or many, are the evidence that the whole tendency of her power is against holiness and truth.[25]

There are echoes here, too, of Christ's damning accusation against those who elevate themselves, parading false virtue, while simultaneously transgressing against precisely the spirit they claim to embody:

> Woe unto you, scribes and Pharisees, hypocrites! because ye build the tombs of the prophets, and garnish the sepulchers of the righteous,
>
> And say, If we had been in the days of our fathers, we would not have been partakers with them in the blood of the prophets.
>
> Wherefore ye be witnesses unto yourselves, that ye are the children of them which killed the prophets.
>
> Fill ye up then the measure of your fathers [alternatively: "go ahead and finish what your ancestors started." (New International Version)]
>
> *Matthew 23:29–32*

The sinners upbraided by Christ are those who have willingly broken the mysterious third commandment. ("Thou shalt not take the name of the Lord thy God in vain; for the Lord will not hold him guiltless that taketh his name in vain" [Exodus 20:7].) As discussed earlier,[26] this commandment forbids the claiming of divine virtue or service to God when the pursuit in question is purely that of self-interest; forbids the subversion of what is highest to what is manipulatively cunning and instrumental. Just as the Pharisees transgress against the spirit of God they have sworn to uphold, thereby "killing" that spirit—or, metaphorically, the prophets who bore its message—the ultimate harlot's actions violate the principles of the central uniting spirit so profoundly that the proper metaphor is one of drunken murderousness.

This is a warning about the danger of the subjugation of sexuality to narrow economic "self-interest" and hedonic pleasure—and, more broadly, another caution (more to the engineers or other prideful intellects): do not engage in the (so-often-disdainful) display of your intellect to attract the source of sexual pleasure, particularly of the short-term variety. Hint: it will

seldom work, anyway. Why else would men be driven to the sex bots designed to "replace women"[27]—the very real women, who tend in their hyper-
gamous choosiness to be utterly devastating to men's pride? Who manage in
that way to be the very agents of the acute self-consciousness that necessarily
characterizes the most wayward, misaligned, and fallen of men? The rejec-
tion-predicated bitterness so engendered can and does drive men to murderousness and far worse. The Tower of Babel is a structure that contains
many chambers, each showcasing men and women in their worst light: precisely the light that shines forth so darkly, in direct consequence of false
worship.

What is the full meaning of this complex web of associations? First, that
the technological/industrial enterprise itself can be driven by a false pride in
mechanical mastery; second, that such pride is likely to ally itself with the
spirit of domination, conquest, and power; third, that the subjugation of the
feminine to (or the outright alliance of the corrupt feminine with) that ally is
inevitable—and that such subjugation or willing participation also presents
a profound psychological and social danger; fourth, and even more deeply,
that the whole Tower of Babel enterprise is associated with the kind of Luciferian pride that goes before the most profound and devastating of falls. It is
for this reason that there are hints in the biblical corpus of the rebellion of
Lucifer, a spirit characterized in the Book of Job not only as an angel but as a
veritable "son of God,"[28] and of a great and subsequent battle in heaven. This
is the great theme lurking behind the temptation of Adam and Eve and, subsequently, of Cain; of the hardening of the heart of the Pharaoh and the
proclivity of the slavish Israelites to lose faith and rebel; of the torment of
Job; and of the offering of the blandishments of the devil himself in the wilderness to the wandering and starving Christ:

How art thou fallen from heaven, O Lucifer, son of the morning!
how art thou cut down to the ground, which didst weaken the nations!

For thou hast said in thine heart, I will ascend into heaven, I will
exalt my throne above the stars of God:

> I will sit also upon the mount of the congregation, in the sides of
> the north: I will ascend above the heights of the clouds; I will be like
> the most High.
>
> *Isaiah 14:12–14*

The fall of the spirit of prideful intellectual/technical presumption produces devastating psychological consequences—consequences that spill inevitably over into the social, the universal, and the eternal. Much has been
made of these hints of schism in the divine realm. The great English poet
John Milton made the elaboration of such ideas the main project of his life,
taking pains to portray Lucifer as the highest angel in God's heavenly kingdom gone, as we have seen,[29] most terribly wrong, and the author of the hell
he himself inhabits, along with his deluded followers, in consequence of his
rebellion.[30] It is for such purposes that Milton details the relationship between or even identity of the spirit of Lucifer and the bringer of the deadly
knowledge that doomed Eve and Adam in the Garden of Eden, associating
that spirit as well with the prideful desire to supplant God:

> He trusted to have equal'd the most High,
> If he oppos'd; and with ambitious aim
> Against the Throne and Monarchy of God
> Rais'd impious War in Heav'n and Battel proud
> With vain attempt.[31]

The consequence? The generation of hell as eternal dwelling place for Lucifer and his followers, defined as distance from what is unifying and transcendent; defined as the place of permanent terror, hopelessness, confusion,
conflict, and misery. How can anyone read this great poem and not think of
the arrogant aerial spirit that made itself so starkly manifest in the ideological catastrophes of the twentieth century?

> Him the Almighty Power
> Hurld headlong flaming from th' Ethereal Skie
> With hideous ruine and combustion down

To bottomless perdition, there to dwell
In Adamantine Chains and penal Fire,
Who durst defie th' Omnipotent to Arms.

Nine times the Space that measures Day and Night
To mortal men, he with his horrid crew
Lay vanquisht, rowling in the fiery Gulfe
Confounded though immortal: But his doom
Reserv'd him to more wrath; for now the thought
Both of lost happiness and lasting pain
Torments him; round he throws his baleful eyes
That witness'd huge affliction and dismay
Mixt with obdurate pride and stedfast hate:

At once as far as Angels kenn he views
The dismal Situation waste and wilde,
A Dungeon horrible, on all sides round
As one great Furnace flam'd, yet from those flames
No light, but rather darkness visible
Serv'd onely to discover sights of woe,

Regions of sorrow, doleful shades, where peace
And rest can never dwell, hope never comes
That comes to all; but torture without end
Still urges, and a fiery Deluge, fed
With ever-burning Sulphur unconsum'd:
Such place Eternal Justice had prepar'd
For those rebellious, here thir prison ordained
In utter darkness, and thir portion set
As far remov'd from God and light of Heav'n
As from the Center thrice to th' utmost Pole.[32]

Lucifer means "light-bringer" in Latin—shades of the Promethean deliverer of fire. The intellectual Luciferian thus delivers or at least promises a

perverse form of enlightenment—a form that is a parody, in fact, of genuine or true enlightenment. Milton elaborates on the psychological consequences of the Luciferian attitude:

Farewel happy Fields
Where Joy for ever dwells: Hail horrours, hail
Infernal world, and thou profoundest Hell
Receive thy new Possessor: One who brings
A mind not to be chang;d by Place or Time.
The mind is its own place, and in it self
Can make a Heav'n of Hell, a Hell of Heav'n.[33]

The poet describes, as well, the motivation such a psychological state inevitably produces, in relationship to social behavior and the broader world:

To do ought good never will be our task,
But ever to do ill our sole delight,
As being the contrary to his high will
Whom we resist. If then his Providence
Out of our evil seek to bring forth good,
Our labor must be to pervert that end,
And out of good still to find means of evil.[34]

Just as the resentful, fratricidal impulse of Cain expands to include and then doom the whole world, the Luciferian impulse, manifest in the city of Babylon, dooms itself and all those who welcomed it to damnation and destruction:

And he cried mightily with a strong voice, saying, Babylon the great is fallen, is fallen, and is become the habitation of devils, and the hold of every foul spirit, and a cage of every unclean and hateful bird.

For all nations have drunk of the wine of the wrath of her fornication, and the kings of the earth have committed fornication with her, and the merchants of the earth are waxed rich through the abundance of her delicacies.

Revelation 18:2–3

The knowledge contained in our dramas indicates, at least, our implicit or provisional understanding of this spirit of wounded and arrogant intellect. It is therefore truly a matter of question how much our inability to fully and explicitly understand it is a consequence of willful blindness instead of mere ignorance. The nature of this spirit of the damned is, after all, characterized exceptionally widely across literature and popular entertainment. The great German author Johann Wolfgang von Goethe's *Faust* perhaps provides the most famous early modern example (*Faust* [1808]; *Faust II* [1832]). Mary Shelley's *Frankenstein: the Modern Prometheus* (1818), featuring Victor Frankenstein as the avatar of the Luciferian intellect, made its appearance at about the same time. Aldous Huxley's *Brave New World* (1932), which came more than a hundred years later—and which still feels very modern—also weaves in themes of the corrupt feminine (in that sexual attitudes in Huxley's future dystopia are so lax that objection to casual promiscuity has become socially unacceptable). George Orwell's classic *1984* (1949) is perhaps the most famous twentieth-century literary example of the dystopian Luciferian/Babylonian nightmare.

Consider in the same vein the many dystopian movies of the past century: *Metropolis* (1927), *Blade Runner* (1982), *RoboCop* (1987), *Minority Report* (2002), *Ex Machina* (2015), and most explicitly and famously in *The Terminator* series, which includes *The Terminator* (1984), *Terminator 2: Judgment Day* (1991), *Terminator 3: Rise of the Machines* (2003), *Terminator Salvation* (2009), *Terminator Genisys* (2015), *Terminator: Dark Fate* (2019). Remarkably enough, it is in some part demand for realistic portrayal of such apocalyptic Luciferian scenarios and parodies that drive the market for increased computational power. The laptops that we commonly use to perform relatively mundane tasks, such as word processing, spreadsheet manipulation, online video management, and internet search, do not require the vast calculating ability of the world's most advanced chips. Instead, it is the desire to produce ever more accurately rendered fictional worlds—in game and movie form alike—that provides a nontrivial portion of the economic incentive to keep that element of the current technological revolution alive and thriving.[35] We use our most advanced machines to warn us—while entertaining us—of the danger of those self-same advanced machines. That, perhaps, is another evil joke.

All of this, fact and fiction alike, is making itself manifest once again—as it has so continually in the past—in the unholy and all too-real-world alliance in still-appallingly-communist China between the ideologically possessed tyrants who rule that dismal wasteland and the engineers who labor there, striving "naively" toward ever-greater heights of presumption and misguided prowess—all in delight of their own intellect; all instead of true devotion to what is properly highest. These are the orcs who inhabit the tower raising the all-seeing eye of Sauron[36] to the sky—who are according to their own idiot-savant testimony building the Skynet[37] that in its original fictional formulation waged war against the whole human race.[38] That Skynet system, consisting now of some 700 million closed-circuit TV cameras, is apparently fast enough to scan every citizen of the People's Republic of China in less than a second and has an accuracy rate with regard to individual identification of more than 99 percent.[39] The Chinese have also developed gait recognition systems that can identify individuals even when their faces are hidden or otherwise unavailable for view.[40]

Such overlap of name with the destructive cyborgs of Terminator fame is at minimum an evil joke—one reminiscent of the sign at the entrance of the death camp at Auschwitz featuring the slogan *Arbeit macht frei* (work will make you free), or the acronym MAD (for mutual assured destruction), which referred to a military strategy originating during the Cold War. MAD theorists touted the doctrine of rational deterrence—the belief that the certainty of mutual annihilation would produce a terror sufficient to maintain the peace among too-heavily-armed opponents[41] (in this case, the Soviet Union and the United States and its nuclear-armed allies). Who would dare make such a joke? Only the most evil of clowns.

That dark, parodying figure, closely allied with the Cain-like or Luciferian character, also features commonly and meaningfully in fiction, fantasy, and reality itself. Take for example, the science fiction writer Ray Bradbury's Mr. Dark, in *Something Wicked This Way Comes* (1962). The head of a carnival traveling from town to town, he offers sinister delights to the naive and unsuspecting. Then there is the Joker character in the *Batman* series: someone sufficiently frightening even to set Mafia dons back on their heels, which is also a theme particularly well developed in *The Dark Knight* (2008) (see also *Batman* (1989), *Suicide Squad* (2016), and *Joker* (2019)). Stephen King's *It* (1986) features Pennywise, an evil, immortal clown. He is somehow a cosmic entity or even a god, whose chosen dwelling place—the underworld, mythically speaking—is nonetheless the labyrinthine sewer system underlying the small town of Derry, Maine (TV version (parts 1 and 2, 1990); movie version (part I [2017]; part II [2019]). The mocking master of ceremonies of the Weimar Republic, extending an invitation of satanic hospitality to hedonist and Nazi alike, is the head clown of the piercingly accurate musical *Cabaret*,[42] perhaps the most comprehensive reflection of the evil dance of our times offered in the last half a century.

On the more ridiculous side, there are two characters from *The Simpsons*, Matt Groening's brilliant animated satire. Jeffrey Albertson, the Comic Book Guy character, is best known for his caustic and demeaning "intellectual" manner; his complete and utter personal and social failure; his endless supply of pointless knowledge; and, most tellingly, his absolute willingness to criticize and dispose casually with everything of value: *Worst. Comic. Book. Ever!*[43] *Worst. Movie. Ever!*[44] *Worst. Episode. Ever!*[45] *Worst. Sequel. Ever!*[46] *Worst. Crossover. Ever!*[47] and, most famously, *Worst. Sunset. Ever!*[48] The aptly named Sideshow Bob fleshes out the archetype. The pretentious Bob, like Cain, plays an eternally secondary role, despite his narcissistic confidence and showy erudition, and turns bitterly to the contemplation of grandiose plots, all of which fail dismally as well as comically when tried out in the real world. A broadly similar role is played, surprisingly, by the figure of the Georgian/Russian tyrant, as well as each of his henchmen and hangers-on, in their various ways, in Armando Iannucci's great black-comedy film *The Death of Stalin* (2017), which is easy to imagine as a close approximation of the dark circus that the Soviet Union most truly constituted. The adversary of God is well understood as a parody of the divine. This is perhaps because there is no shortage of the truly ridiculous in the lies that people tilting toward totalitarianism so readily and self-destructively adopt.

5.2. Pride and the fall, reprise: Descent into hell itself

Some brief consideration of the Greek myth of Daedalus and his son, Icarus, can aid us in further seeing the connection between overweening pride (particularly in the intellect), technology, and a fall—a descent from the heights; a collapse into chaos and confusion; a headlong plunge into the abyss; a dissolution into death. Daedalus, a skilled craftsman, was the architect of the labyrinth of Crete. King Minos, ruler of Crete, imprisoned Daedalus and his son within the architect's own creation. While trapped within the maze, Daedalus used wax and feathers to construct wings for himself and Icarus, so they could take to the skies and escape. As they soared above Crete, Icarus, enthralled by the exhilaration of flight, disregarded his father's warning not to raise himself too high in the heavens. But Icarus flew ever upward—ever closer to the sun, and to his fate. The heat melts the wax the held his wings together, so that he plummets into the sea and drowns.[49] It is tempting to employ technological solutions to the labyrinthine problems of life, and to rise in the world as a result, but hubris and the imprudent celebration of technology can make of those solutions an even worse problem. A warning to the engineers: do not presume to fly so high that God himself feels the necessity to intervene.

The stories of the biblical corpus repeatedly insist, likewise, that "Pride goeth before destruction, and an haughty spirit before a fall" (Proverbs 16:18). They also detail the inevitable allyship between arrogance and the proclivity to use force and compel. The expansive, poetic portrayals of the causal relationship between the Luciferian spirit and Babylon's rise and fall reflect many aspects of that ultimately doomed alliance, as intimated by Isaiah 14:12: "How art thou fallen from heaven." The eighteenth-century biblical scholar John Gill comments, with regard to such disintegrations and descents:

> This is not to be understood of the fall of Satan, and the apostate angels, from their first estate, when they were cast down from heaven to

hell, though there may be an allusion to it,[50] but the words are a continuation of the speech of the dead to the king of Babylon, wondering at it, as a thing almost incredible, that he who seemed to be so established on, the throne of his kingdom, which was his heaven, that he should be deposed or fall from it. So the destruction of the Roman Pagan emperors is signified by the casting out of the dragon and his angels from heaven (Revelation 12:7) and in like manner Rome Papal, or the Romish antichrist, will fall from his heaven of outward splendour and happiness, of honour and authority, now, possessed by him:

O Lucifer, son of the morning! alluding to the star Venus, which is the phosphorus or morning star, which ushers in the light of the morning, and shows that day is at hand; by which is meant, not Satan, who is never in Scripture called Lucifer, though he was once an angel of light, and sometimes transforms himself into one, and the good angels are called morning stars, (Job 38:7) and such he and his angels once were; but the king of Babylon is intended, whose royal glory and majesty, as outshining all the rest of the kings of the earth, is expressed by those names; and which perhaps were such as he took himself, or were given him by his courtiers.[51]

Violent demise is all too often and predictably the natural end of the tyrant; the ultimately personal consequence of the collapse of the Tower of Babel state. This is so fundamentally and basically true that it even appears to apply in the case of chimpanzees, who are our closest natural relatives.[52] Chimpanzees are characterized by the rule of something approximating a true patriarchy: although females can and do occupy positions of substantive authority, all chimp troupes have a male at the absolute head.

In his book *Chimpanzee Politics*, the influential and intellectually wide-ranging Dutch primatologist Frans de Waal describes how chimp leaders who rely on aggression and intimidation to maintain their power inevitably face dangerous challenge from subordinates who come to resent their tactics. He illustrates this principle with the story of the violent overthrow of a dominant male chimp named Yeroen, several years' ruler of the troupe at the Royal Burgers Zoo in Arnhem, Netherlands. When Yeroen became increasingly aggressive and unstable, his subordinates began to join together against him: "Yeroen was attacked by his coalition partners, who clearly intended to kill him. The struggle that ensued was intense and brutal, with blood and hair flying, until finally Yeroen lay motionless on the ground. He had suffered a fatal wound to the neck and never regained consciousness."[53] In another case: "a former alpha male called Luit was caught by the new alpha, Amos, and his coalition. Luit was completely overpowered and never recovered from his wounds. He died shortly afterward. In other cases, deposed males are castrated or chased away."[54]

De Waal notes that chimp leaders who by contrast rely on strategies of mutually beneficial reciprocation have longer reigns and more stable, pacific, and productive social groups: "The most successful individuals are not necessarily the strongest or most aggressive, but rather those who are best at managing relationships."[55] He states, elsewhere, that the "human capacity for empathy and cooperation may well have evolved from the cooperative tendencies of our primate ancestors, chimpanzees and bonobos."[56] That is a remarkable statement of biological fact, given the contemporary prevalence of the belief that even human social structures are at all levels best understood as manifestations of, first, nothing but social conditioning and, second, nothing but the will and ability to use power, force, and compulsion.[57] Consideration of the terrible fate awaiting chimp dictators might well give pause to those who lay claim to the desirability and utility of power as a unifying force; but if it fails to convince, there are also the salutary examples of once mighty rulers such as Benito Mussolini and Nicolas Ceauşescu.

In the closing days of WWII in Europe, Mussolini and his mistress, Claretta Petacci, fled Milan, where they had been based, and headed toward the Swiss border. They were captured in the small village of Giulino di Mezzegra in northern Italy on April 27, 1945, and shot by Italian partisans the next afternoon, two days before Adolf Hitler's suicide in Berlin. Their bodies were returned to Milan and left in the Piazzale Loreto, a suburban square, for a large, angry crowd to insult and desecrate. They were then hung, upside down, from a metal girder above a service station on the square.[58] A similar fate befell Nicolae Ceaușescu, the communist dictator of Romania, who had become increasingly repressive during the almost twenty-five years of his rule, imposing strict economic controls that led to widespread shortages of food and other goods, and cracking down on dissent, imprisoning or killing thousands of his opponents. In December 1989, protests against his regime erupted in the city of Timișoara, spreading quickly to other parts of Romania. Ceaușescu, forced to flee Bucharest, the capital, was captured a few days later, put on trial by a hastily convened military tribunal, and found guilty of genocide and other crimes against humanity. He and his wife, Elena, were executed in a military base outside Bucharest on Christmas Day. The execution was broadcast live on television, and it was watched by millions of people worldwide.[59] The moral of such stories? The fall from totalitarian heights is likely to be as total as the initial presumptions of the failed state. Furthermore, the collapse of the Tower of Babel is something personal and psychological as much as social.

There are echoes of the conflict between the more peaceful and therefore more successful and more truly "alpha" male and his power-obsessed and therefore genuinely although not obviously weaker opponent contained within the biblical corpus. In the story of David and Goliath, for example, it is David, the young shepherd, who defeats the giant Philistine warrior Goliath with a single stone from his sling. The Philistine army is set against its Israelite equivalent, in the broader context of the story. Single, man-to-man combat is proposed—the Philistine champion against the champion of the ancient Hebrews—as a means of concluding the conflict, with the defeated party's countrymen to serve as the slaves of the victor. Goliath was a terrifying physical specimen:

> And there went out a champion out of the camp of the Philistines, named Goliath, of Gath, whose height was six cubits and a span.
>
> And he had an helmet of brass upon his head, and he was armed with a coat of mail; and the weight of the coat was five thousand shekels of brass.
>
> And he had greaves of brass upon his legs, and a target of brass between his shoulders.

And the staff of his spear was like a weaver's beam; and his spear's head weighed six hundred shekels of iron: and one bearing a shield went before him.

1 Samuel 17:5–17

No Israelite was willing to engage this giant in battle, until David— laughably less impressive than his erstwhile opponent—makes his appearance:

And the Philistine came on and drew near unto David; and the man that bare the shield went before him.

And when the Philistine looked about, and saw David, he disdained him: for he was but a youth, and ruddy, and of a fair countenance.

And the Philistine said unto David, Am I a dog, that thou comest to me with staves? And the Philistine cursed David by his gods.

1 Samuel 17:41–44

But David—in his job as caretaker of the vulnerable—had become thoroughly accustomed to dealing with ferocious predators, as he informs Saul, the king, who nonetheless doubts his champion's ability:

And Saul said to David, Thou art not able to go against this Philistine to fight with him: for thou art but a youth, and he a man of war from his youth.

And David said unto Saul, Thy servant kept his father's sheep, and there came a lion, and a bear, and took a lamb out of the flock:

And I went out after him, and smote him, and delivered it out of his mouth: and when he arose against me, I caught him by his beard, and smote him, and slew him.

Thy servant slew both the lion and the bear: and this uncircumcised Philistine shall be as one of them, seeing he hath defied the armies of the living God.

1 Samuel 17:33–36

The famous story closes with the defeat of the arrogant giant, the subjugation of the Philistines, and the victory of the forces of Israel:

> And it came to pass, when the Philistine arose, and came and drew
> nigh to meet David, that David hasted, and ran toward the army to
> meet the Philistine.
>
> And David put his hand in his bag, and took thence a stone, and
> slang it, and smote the Philistine in his forehead, that the stone sunk
> into his forehead; and he fell upon his face to the earth.
>
> So David prevailed over the Philistine with a sling and with a
> stone, and smote the Philistine, and slew him; but there was no
> sword in the hand of David.
>
> Therefore David ran, and stood upon the Philistine, and took his
> sword, and drew it out of the sheath thereof, and slew him, and cut
> off his head therewith. And when the Philistines saw their cham-
> pion was dead, they fled.
>
> *1 Samuel 17:48–51*

The moral of the story? The true hero is he who defeats the giant tyrant of
the state. Similar tales of heroes and tyrants are universally present in the
folklore of mankind. In the *Epic of Gilgamesh*, for example, the hero Gilgamesh and his friend Enkidu defeat Humbaba, a giant guardian of the Cedar Forest. After slaying Humbaba, Gilgamesh uses his body to build the
gates of the city of Uruk.[60] The Norse god Thor similarly battles a number of
giants, including Jotunheim's king, Thrym, who steals Thor's hammer. Thor
kills him, in consequence, and retrieves his magic tool.[61] In the classic Chinese
novel *Journey to the West*, Sun Wukong, the Monkey King, battles the demon
bull king who is causing chaos in the underworld. Sun Wukong kills the
demon and saves the day.[62] This story parallels the classic Greek myth of Theseus and the Minotaur: Theseus, the legendary founder-king of Athens, defeats
the monstrous Minotaur, a half-man half-bull creature, and then uses a ball of
string to find his way out of the labyrinth where the creature was imprisoned.[63]
These narratives portray the battle between two spirits: the spirit char-

acterized as upward-aiming, dedicated to all good things, and striving forward on the side of the truth; and the spirit of Luciferian intellect and pride, prone to worship technology, willing to use compulsion, force, and power, liable to degenerate into hedonistic promiscuity, manifesting itself, inevitably, in the form of dark parody and the blackest comedy imaginable. The latter spirit serves chaos; is the precursor to or agent of chaos; wishes, in some fundamental sense, to rule over chaos. It can be understood both as the tyrannical state—the state where everyone lies—or as the pattern of resentful and deceitful worship, attention, and action that brings about the tyrannical state. That state—that kingdom turned to stone—is the evil brother of the once-great king, whose willful blindness enables the eternal usurper. The personality of Cain is the force animating that evil brother, just as the descendants of Cain are those who erect the doomed tower. The giant overthrown by the hero is the degenerate state. That pattern of overthrowing is a variant of the battle between order and chaos that constitutes creation itself, not least in that the rise of the evil state is precursor to the return of that pre-cosmogonic potentiality. God portrays Himself as precisely this victorious force in his presentation to the long-suffering Job:

> Behold now behemoth, which I made with thee; he eateth grass as an ox.
>
> Lo now, his strength is in his loins, and his force is in the navel of his belly.
>
> He moveth his tail like a cedar: the sinews of his stones are wrapped together.
>
> His bones are as strong pieces of brass; his bones are like bars of iron.
>
> He is the chief of the ways of God: he that made him can make his sword to approach unto him.
>
> *Job 40:15–19*

Speaking the truth that redeems to the authoritarian; and wrestling with possibility so that the order that is good or even very good can be established, or reestablished: these are the work—the sacrifice—of God, and the responsibility, obligation, and adventure of all those made in His image.

God, in the story of the Tower of Babel, is the transcendent being who is the absolute antithesis of presumptuous authority (just as He was when warning Adam and Eve against eating the fruit of the tree of knowledge of good and evil). He is the Being who eternally warns: "Do not replace Me with the worship of your own pride and power—because all hell is bound to break loose if you do." God is therefore reliably portrayed as what must be placed properly atop both the psychological and social hierarchy; what is signified properly by the gold cap at the pinnacle of the pyramid; what serves as the proper all-seeing eye or sage on the mountaintop, lest everything disintegrate—including, not least, the ability to see and speak. This is the God who manifests himself in the human willingness to engage in the productive upward-aiming dialogue, negotiation, and communication that provisions and stabilizes the psyche and the community alike. In this manner we reflect the image of our maker, bringing order to the world, or reestablishing that order, when it has been violated and corrupted.

What is the alternative? The rise of arrogant pride and presumption; the erection of grandiose monuments to the falsest of Gods; the invocation to the whore; the disappearance of the shared assumptions on which understanding itself rests; and the collapse of everything into a state indistinguishable from hell. So speaks wisdom from time immemorial.

5.3. Inability to understand one another

Our capacity to communicate is mysterious. Why can we understand one another at all, even in principle, given that we are separate, autonomous, and independent creatures? It is partly because we are very similar in our material natures, biologically and developmentally speaking. Our fundamental or basic psychophysiological structures are nearly identical, on a person-to-person basis. That similarity extends far down the phylogenetic, or evolutionary, hierarchy. We also share much in common with the nonhuman creatures with whom we share the garden. The fact of the very axioms that God does not allow human beings to question when he warns against incorporation of the final "knowledge" of good and evil, represented by the forbidden fruit, is a consequence not least of this shared psychophysiological identity.

It is such commonality that enables our understanding not only of other human beings but also of animals, and most truly to the degree that any animal is genetically and therefore psychologically and physically similar to us. Shared culture (and that means shared procedure, imagination, and explicit, semantically mediated knowledge, both fiction and fact) of course increases that similarity, so it is easier for us to understand other people who share the same tradition, who dream similar dreams, and who speak the same language. All these similarities allow us to start our conversational or communicative efforts with the same assumptions—to ground the words we exchange in the same background of imagination and the same practice of attention and action. This gives us ground to stand on while we speak. If we had to talk about everything, that ground would rapidly turn into sand. We would fall otherwise into the frustrating infinite regress where everything has to be explained—and endlessly. This is state (or lack thereof) portrayed in the "multiplication of languages" that emerges in parallel with the collapse of the Tower of Babel. Our words make sense only insofar as they refer to experiences that are self-evident in the absence of words—experiences that are grounded in the realms of matter, behavior, and imagination.

When you are arguing with someone, and you say, "I am angry with you," they typically ask, "Why are you angry?" and not, "What do you mean, 'angry?'" The interlocutor already knows what "angry" means, and not just semantically—not just as a word embedded in a web of words but also at an embodied, emotional, motivational, and experiential level. We do not have to ask another human being what it means to be angry and can even understand anger when manifested by a nonhuman animal, because we have been angry ourselves—because we share a biological platform with the person we are communicating with; can experience for ourselves the state of anger; can infer and assume a non-semantic similarity of rage-like experience. That shared embodiment, and not the abstract understanding, provides the foundation allowing for communication itself. This does not mean that everything human is translatable to the animal or vice versa. "If a lion could speak, we could not understand him"—so the philosopher Ludwig Wittgenstein claimed, in paraphrased essence.[64] It is more accurately stated: "If a lion could speak, we would still struggle to understand his point."

This is partly because to "understand" actually means to translate from the semantic to the imaginative and then to the embodied:[65] to change the way we perceive, conceptualize, and act as a consequence of communicating. This indicates profoundly that full "understanding" requires shared embodiment: similar emotion, motivation, and possibility for perception and action. Otherwise there would be no limit to the necessity of translation. We need a shared rock of certainty under our feet so that we can all stand upon it while we talk. This is the center that necessarily anchors even the marginal, and that gives even the later its possibility of existence, subdued place, and purpose. Prideful rejection of that underlying commonality makes all communication impossible. This is obvious once the preconditions for understanding itself are properly understood.

Some basics have to be assumed as axiomatic before inquiry into other ideas can even begin. Something, at least, has to be taken as a given; something has to serve as a maypole of orientation, a flag in the ground, around which everything else can unquestioningly rotate.[66] That is the one miracle that creation has to be granted even to exist. That is the reason not only for the necessity of faith but for its veritable inevitability. The question of faith itself is thus best conceptualized not as "is faith necessary?" but "in what form is the faith that is necessary best realized?" Without that shared center, the domain of disagreement rapidly becomes so large that either chaos itself reigns or conflict becomes inevitable. It is difficult enough to disagree civilly about one thing at a time. When everything is up in the air, there is nothing that can be jointly referred to even as a starting point for negotiation or potentially shared mutual aim.

The pathway to peace is therefore always initiated by something approximating "what, if anything, do we agree upon (hold constant; regard as sacred;

consider mutually indisputable) even in the midst of our disagreement? Can we therefore expand the domain of shared territory that we already jointly inhabit?" Married people, when arguing, better at least agree that the marriage should continue, and that the love that they at least once had could however hypothetically make itself known again—or at least that such rebirth and regeneration of continued and desirable relationship should be the aim. It is also the case that the flagpole, staff of tradition, or rod of patriarchal certainty had better be planted in the right place, or the ground so demarcated cannot be inhabited and the game cannot be played. The common narrative trope of the magician, wizard, or even god slamming his magic wand or hammer down into the ground with waves of invisible power that radiate outward from it reflects or indicates some like such a truth. What does this all mean in the context of the Tower of Babel story? *If the technological enterprise aims itself at something deviating too far from the necessary psychological and social ideal, the central uniting axis, even the possibility of communication vanishes.* Then, we become confounded in our language.

We find ourselves presently at war over the most basic of issues: that of sex. What is driving our confusion? It is certainly possible that the basic conceptual or even perceptual axiom—the most basic category of reality itself, whatever reality might be (and it is certainly more than the merely "objective" world)—is "male" and "female," as intimated in Genesis 1:27. ("So God created man in his own image, in the image of God created he him; male and female created he them.") Failure to differentiate on the basis of sex means failure to propagate, and failure to propagate means more than mere death: it means true extinction. Thus, the ability to differentiate man from woman is equivalent to the ability and willingness to circumvent nonbeing itself. Perhaps there might be an ability to categorize that is more fundamental: the capacity to distinguish edible from inedible, up from down, day from night, or even life from death. Nonetheless, the sexual distinction is so basic that life itself ceases in its absence. How could the same demise not await mere communication when the most basic of definitions is blurred?

Sexual differentiation itself occurred somewhere between 1.2 and 1.5 billion years ago. Nervous systems did not develop until something approximating a billion years later. This means that sexual differentiation was a brute fact of life for a thousand million years (!) before even the rudiments of conscious perception were possible. It is for this reason, among many others, *that sexual differentiation itself is employed with utter universality as a metaphor for the binary relationship between many other phenomena*, or even between the most basic classes of phenomena themselves.[67] So, for example, the Taoists divide the world of experience itself into yin and yang and presume that reality as such is comprised of the eternal interplay between these two permanent categories (each of which is associated with a sex: Yin is the feminine, associated with chaos, night, darkness, possibility, and change. Yang is the masculine, associated with order, day, light, actuality, and permanence).[68]

Why are we questioning that axiom now? How is that confusion associated with the pride, resentment, corruption, worship of the technological and hedonism of the Tower of Babel? Because we have decided to usurp the right to absolute self-definition instead of leaving that as an element of the transcendent, or the axiomatic—as an element of the faith that is necessary and inevitable. The person who insists on the unquestionable primacy of self-definition is, after all, stating, "I am that I am," or "I am who I am"— attempting thereby to elevate the self to the level of ultimate axiom—precisely as the God of the Old Testament does when he speaks to Moses of his Being. (And God said unto Moses, I AM THAT I AM: and he said, Thus shalt thou say unto the children of Israel, I AM hath sent me unto you" Exodus 3:14.) This means a denial not only of the transcendent on the spiritual side but also of the material, biological, and the social side. It is not for naught that the Narcissus who fell in love with his own reflection drowned, in consequence— and nothing more narcissistic than the absolute claim to self-identity can be posited or even imagined. And precisely what "self" is being thereby identified? It is far from obvious what the self actually constitutes, in the final analysis. The whim of the moment (particularly on the solely sexual front) seems like a poor candidate for elevation to that exalted and central position. Such subjugation to the grip and immediacy of instinct is nothing but the impulse of a toddler or, in the case of an adult, of a very immature and counterproductively self-centered man or woman indeed.

And why, therefore, is the "self" being announced as the master of the domain of so-called subjective identification axiomatically assumed to be identical to the latest whim celebrated in the popular culture? It is a perilously short distance from "I am whatever I desire sexually" to "I have the right to whatever I want, now" in relationship to any short-term consummatory desire. Thus, I can demand that all my economic needs be met by others, I can insist that no ideas that cause me anxiety ever arise, and I can reject all standards of beauty, merit, or value (whose existence might cause me to question my transcendent value and absolute right to immediate gratification). There is simply no compelling a priori reason—other than a staggeringly narcissistic desire for everything I want here and now and to hell with everything and everyone else—to identify the totality of the self with any element of that ever-shifting array of desires. And yet we are increasingly compelled to act, speak, and believe as if there is. That compulsion is identical to the worship of confusion, disunity, and the idiot immediacy of the moment.

This of course means that the so-called "true or genuine self," that unquestionable voice of "lived experience," is not only to take precedence over the needs and wants of other people but over the medium- to long-term stability, hope, and productive function of the individual in question. However, that self is little or even nothing more than the desire that currently dominates. The gratification of its desire is equivalent to the sacrifice of the other to the "self" and the future, even of the person concerned, to the present, to say nothing of the other to the "self." A lower and more counterproductive form of self-definition can hardly be imagined. No community whatsoever and certainly no civilization can be founded on that endlessly shifting sand. Obviously. That is why we do not see united tribes of two-year olds striking out successfully on their own.

This insistence on the primacy of subjective self-definition is therefore not only the subjugation of everyone and everything to the tyrannical demands of the present—a move providing no basis whatsoever for a stable, productive society—but the elimination of anything approximating a higher-order self, capable of acting in relationship to the broader social context and the future. This is most evident, perhaps, in the well-documented tendency of those characterized by Dark Tetrad personality traits (narcissism, Machiavellianism, psychopathy, and sadism) to prefer so-called "short-term mating strategies"—that is, pursuit of personal sexual pleasure in the absence of any commitment, practical or emotional (and that means without any relationship of any genuine kind).[69] The narcissists have an enhanced sense of self-importance, a desire for admiration, and a lack of empathy for others, expressed in their refusal to reciprocate. They pursue short-term sexual encounters as a means to gain validation, boost their comparative social standing (their "ego"), and fulfill their narrow desires. The Machiavellians, manipulative, exploitative, and skilled in strategic social maneuvering, deploy deceptive tactics to achieve their goals—including those involving sexual satisfaction. They use others for personal gain, engaging in casual sexual encounters or outright infidelity without emotional attachment. The psychopaths are characterized by an absence of empathy and remorse, disregard or even hold contempt for social norms, a comprehensive impulsivity, and inability to delay gratification (precisely that attitude of "I want what I want right now and to hell with you and the future"), and limited or no capacity to learn from experience.

They are, as well—unsurprisingly, since they don't care even for themselves— entirely exploitative on the sexual front, willing to dispense with such niceties as true consent, employing emotional manipulation and turning to more coercive tactics if mere manipulation fails. Sadistic individuals, finally, derive positive delight from humiliating and inflicting pain and suffering on others. Short-term mating strategies enable them to exert control, dominance, or power over their sexual partners.[70] This proclivity appears to be part of a broader pattern of valuation: short-term mating preference exists with the wish for power and the willingness or even eagerness to use it and a marked and conspicuous consumerism and associated materialism.[71] Shades of the orgiastic celebration of the golden calf.

The claim that the immediate demand of the short-term self takes priority over all other considerations, social and future, is the consequence of a stunningly counterproductive and personally and socially dangerous immaturity.

Bad as that is, it is not all: accompanying that immaturity is an associated rejection of the burden and responsibility of genuine adventure in life, and the resultant attraction of false and hypothetically easy-to-attain variants of meaning, worth, excitement, and identity. This is the Pleasure Island that the delinquent Lampwick (a name that clearly refers to Lucifer) entices Disney's Pinocchio to visit, after the false physicians convince the puppet that he is a sick victim, in need of holiday relaxation and amusement, as well as the Neverland that Peter Pan chooses as his domain to inhabit and rule (with its accompanying imaginary female companion, Tinkerbell, the porn fairy). Such false adventure might and often does include the immediate pleasures of drug and alcohol misuse (practices also integrally associated with both Dark Tetrad and antisocial personality attributes),[72] as well as acceptance and promotion of the moralizing and self-serving justifications of a purposefully thoughtless resentment and, if convenient, associated ideology.[73]

Why else might we currently find ourselves confused, Luciferian, and prone to erecting endless Towers of Babel? Perhaps because our very selves have become disoriented by the extension of our identity into the virtual world. We can be whomever we want to be in our online forms—or so we think. The more time we spend there, the more uncertain we become of who we are; the more time we can also break free—in some ways, many of which are ultimately destructive—of the limitations that bind us in the non-virtual "real" world. The lines between fiction, fantasy, and fact blur in the online world, and purposefully so: it is a place suited to experimentation. But it is absolutely one thing to toy with alternate selves so that a more effective mode of being or becoming can be realized, and another to maintain immaturity or adopt a delusional self for the purposes of immediate gratification and avoidance of responsibility. Abstraction allows for the thought that can die instead of us; it also gives rise to the possibility of possession by delusion when what is improper grows, cancer-like, instead of being pruned by judgment. This is another danger of the prideful and unwise presumption of the technologists.

Perhaps it is also because we have interfered with the pretend play that children must engage in to establish their adult identities, sexual and otherwise, replacing it with time spent engaged with screens.[74] Perhaps it is because we have become enticed to dream all-too-imprudently, even "transhumanly," of escape from the limitations of this mortal coil, lacking proper gratitude for the opportunities, challenges, and adventures that those very limitations provide. Perhaps it is, finally, because we have abandoned the respect for tradition, ancestry, and the paternal/maternal authority on which the desire to mature, as well as maturation itself, necessarily depends. This is a complex whose upshot is that we continually violate another fundamental commandment—the very one on which optimized childhood experience and parenting, as well as dignified aging—intergenerational cooperation itself, in a phrase—depends: Honor thy father and thy mother (Exodus 20:12). Without such honor, all the necessary constraints of tradition vanish; worse, if possible, the future itself degenerates—as absence of respect for father and mother simultaneously means absence of respect for the future self. We gaze without a commensurate shame[75] on the nakedness of our parents. How can that be anything but indicative of inevitable degeneration? Why not face that eventuality with nothing but anxiety and a nihilistic and destructive outlook?

All of those attitudes are variants of the spirit that built the Tower of Babel—a tower we currently inhabit and are building ever higher, while we simultaneously abandon the principles on which civility, peace, and generous productivity depend. In consequence, our psychological integrity degenerates[76] in tandem with our capacity to communicate with one another in peace, or even at all:

And the whole earth was of one language, and of one speech:

> And it came to pass, as they journeyed from the east that they found a plain in the land of Shinar; and they dwelt there,
>
> And they said to one another, Go to, let us make brick, and burn them thoroughly. And they had brick for stone, and slime they had for mortar.

And they said, Go to, let us build us a city and a tower, whose top may reach unto heaven; and let us make us a name, lest we be scattered abroad upon the face of the whole earth.

And the Lord came down to see the city and the tower, which the children of men builded.

And the Lord said, Behold, the people is one, and they have all one language; and this they begin to do: and now nothing will be restrained from them, which they have imagined to do.

Go to, let us go down, and there confound their language, that they may not understand one another's speech.

So the Lord scattered them abroad from thence upon the face of all the earth: and they left off to build the city.

Therefore is the name of it called Babel; because the Lord did there confound the language of all the earth: and from thence did the Lord scatter them abroad upon the face of all the earth.

Genesis 11:1–10

Men determine to raise their works upward, toward an ideal, to "make us a name," to establish a prideful notoriety and status and to unite under that falsehood ("lest we be scattered abroad upon the face of the whole earth"— that is, be divided and disunited). There is a truly admirable aspect of all of that, aim, ambition, and community, but not when narrowly self-serving; not when serving self or local potentate. Understanding this also clarifies what happens next—an occurrence, or happening, that could otherwise be attributed to an apparent jealousy on the part of God. ("And now nothing will be restrained from them, which they have imagined to do.") Is it that God is objecting to anything that might encroach on his territory, revealing a reprehensible jealousy on his part? Or is it instead that the human imagination is such that no form of hell is too low to be created by those with sufficient pretension, and that God rightfully objects to that eventuality and providentially attempts to interfere? The National Socialists were, after all, both imaginative and capable, even though they stretched their tower to the

Morning Star and not to God himself. Would a good God then not precisely be the force that sowed confusion and discord in the midst of a false unity? Is this then not divine envy but rather the attempt to foil the Luciferian spirit? Is this then not another revealed aspect of the unified Good? By definition? That is the insistence of the author of the story of the Tower of Babel.

5.4. God—or else

In the opening verses of Genesis, God is portrayed as the spirit, oriented by love and truth, who eternally generates from the primordial chaos of potential the habitable order that is good. That same spirit is soon said to govern the relationship between the opposites, darkness and light: "And God saw the light, that it was good: and God divided the light from the darkness. And God called the light Day, and the darkness he called Night. And the evening and the morning were the first day" (Genesis 1:4–5). That is the spirit characterizing men and women alike in their deepest essence and provides to human beings the consequential responsibility and opportunity of earthly governance (Genesis 1:26–27). This creative, transcendent, unifying spirit is also deemed to be radically pro-life and pro-child in its orientation (as in Genesis 1:28: "And God blessed them, and God said unto them, Be fruitful, and multiply, and replenish the earth"). It sets before men and women the initial Paradise of being, with all its manifest possibilities: "And God said, Behold, I have given you every herb bearing seed, which is upon the face of all the earth, and every tree, in the which is the fruit of a tree yielding seed; to you it shall be for meat. And to every beast of the earth, and to every fowl of the air, and to every thing that creepeth upon the earth, wherein there is life, I have given every green herb for meat: and it was so" (Genesis 1:30–31). The unifying spirit insists that this divine characterization of men and women and provision of commensurate responsibility and opportunity is maximally desirable and morally appropriate (hence the "very," which is only applied to the doings of the sixth day, which closes with this proclamation: "And God saw every thing that he had made, and, behold, it was very good" [Genesis 1:31]). It also establishes the limits on action and presumptions or axiomatic preconditions that make paradisal being possible:

> And the Lord God took the man, and put him into the garden of Eden to dress it and to keep it.
>
> And the Lord God commanded the man, saying, Of every tree of the garden thou mayest freely eat:
>
> But of the tree of the knowledge of good and evil, thou shalt not eat of it: for in the day that thou eatest thereof thou shalt surely die.
>
> *Genesis 2:15–17*

It is the same transcendent, unified, monotheistic spirit that assigns to Adam the as-of-yet incomplete (because unpaired with woman) ability and obligation to categorize and order the world (the crucial and responsible aspect of "subdue"):

> And the Lord God said, It is not good that the man should be alone; I will make him an help meet for him.
>
> And out of the ground the Lord God formed every beast of the field, and every fowl of the air; and brought them unto Adam to see what he would call them: and whatsoever Adam called every living creature, that was the name thereof.
>
> And Adam gave names to all cattle, and to the fowl of the air, and to every beast of the field; but for Adam there was not found an help meet for him.
>
> *Genesis 2:18–20*

That spirit also divides the original (symbolically hermaphroditic) man into the paired and contentious opposition that is nonetheless called on to become a harmonious unity:

And the Lord God caused a deep sleep to fall upon Adam, and he slept: and he took one of his ribs, and closed up the flesh instead thereof;

And the rib, which the Lord God had taken from man, made he a woman, and brought her unto the man.

And Adam said, This is now bone of my bones, and flesh of my flesh: she shall be called Woman, because she was taken out of Man.

Therefore shall a man leave his father and his mother, and shall cleave unto his wife: and they shall be one flesh.

And they were both naked, the man and his wife, and were not ashamed.

Genesis 2:21–25

More aspects of the same superordinate or "heavenly" spirit make themselves known as the next stories unfold, while the fundamental importance of certain aspects, already revealed, is reiterated, stressed, and characterized more thoroughly. This is all part of the process by which all that is good comes to be integrated. This means conflicts between moral duties can be minimized, and everything is put in its proper place, in relationship to one another. It is the process by which the sum of all good comes to be defined and understood.

Genesis 2:15–17, for example, establishes the injunction against presuming for oneself the right to question or establish the most basic of moral truths. That most basic truth is something like the axiomatic definition of good and evil themselves, or even the proclamation or assumption that such a distinction exists, which is in turn a fundamental and defining presumption about the nature of reality itself. Genesis 3 (the account of the serpent of the garden) is a deep exploration of that theme, which has as its conclusion, however implicit, that the fundamental enemy of stable, harmonious being and productive becoming is precisely that which tempts us to presume this right, by appealing to the most prideful desire of all: the wish to replace or become God Himself. Cataclysmic consequences ensue, as we have seen.[77]

The moral of the story, once again? Do not ascribe to yourself the right to question the minimal necessary preconditions for harmonious being established by what is truly transcendent—or all is lost. Certain axioms must be held as sacred for the game itself to proceed without degenerating into a fallen, self-conscious, prideful hell. Hence, our eternal enmity with the serpent; our conception in sorrow; the involuntary subjugation of woman to man; the cursed conditions of fallen toil; the expulsion from Paradise; and the barring of the pathway forward to heaven. Alternatively, perhaps: do not arrogate to yourself the right to become God, without engaging in the proper sacrifices—precisely those that because they are aimed at the highest possible pinnacle must be of the most complete, comprehensive, and dramatic nature. Such offerings are even by logical necessity those associated with the ultimately difficult process, say, of accepting responsibility for the sins of the world, and paying the price for exactly that. What is that price? To become God, in the absence of pride—or perhaps more subtly but accurately one with God—is to give up everything that is not God: happiness, security, wealth, love, friendship, national identity, as none of those are or should be God. This of course requires nothing less than the sacrifice that is ultimate.

And what presumptuous questions, exactly, should not be asked—or what voices not listened to? What places should not be regarded as acceptable to dwell? What, if anything—or who—is off limits? Is there any difference between such questions and the idea that there is some counsel that should not be followed, or some outsiders who cannot be brought into the fold, or some identities that cannot be adopted—or some foods that, because of their sheer and irremediable poisonousness, cannot be eaten? Are there no truly deadly and therefore properly forbidden ideas? Is all of this not the same as asking whether anything is truly evil—and, therefore, anything that is good; and, therefore, whether there is any distinction between good and evil? Was what transpired in Auschwitz, for example, in Nazi Germany, wrong or not? Were the actions of those who ran Unit 731[78] in China under Japanese occupation merely following orders; merely and righteously adhering to their own time-and-situation-specific relativistic ethic? Is there any real difference between man and woman, up and down, Abel and Cain, or Christ and Satan?

There is a price to be paid, no matter the answer. If morality is relative, then Auschwitz was not evil but only unfortunate—and the latter only from the far-from-universal perspective of the victims. For the absolute sadists of Unit 731, likewise, the victims were merely the justifiable means to the most desirable of purely narcissistic ends. Who is to say and why that the Nazi or Japanese self-definition of appropriate purpose was wrong? Particularly when done in the name of and even published under the guise of "scientific experimentation"? If morality is relative, then medical experiments of unimaginable horror (from the arbitrary perspective of the modern viewer) can be conducted without hesitation on those powerless enough to be made subject to them. If morality is relative, then no true distinction can be drawn between Stalin and Churchill; between Mao and Lincoln; between the mass murderer and sadist Carl Panzram[79] and the rescuing hero Oskar Schindler; between Simon Legree from *Uncle Tom's Cabin* and Alyosha Karamazov, from *The Brothers' Karamazov*—and, if no true distinction can be drawn; between the rationalists of the French Revolution and the subjective delights of the Marquis de Sade. If no true (that is, transcendentally and eternal true) judgment of relative worth is possible, even in principle—why follow the difficult, straight and narrow path that leads up, rather than the wide, easy, and immediately, even intensely pleasurable, road down?

It should be noted, in this regard, not least for the sake of a sufficiently thorough investigation, that it is not only a rational skepticism, which can be admirable in certain situations, that drives the relativistic endeavor. Everything has its shadow side. Just as religious belief, in its naive forms, can in fact serve those in power as the "opiate of the masses"[80]; can provide, as per the Freudian view, an immature and unsophisticated defense against death anxiety;[81] can more generally serve and maintain and justify a childish dependency—so, too, can the skepticism of an "enlightened" moral relativism enable, camouflage, and even justify delight in the rejection of all responsibility, and far worse. This is particularly true when the skeptic is simultaneously insisting that, in the final analysis, nothing really matters. This is the all-too-convenient shrugging off of all moral obligation; the rejection of all transcendent existential burden; the elimination of everything of crucial import—and the maintenance of an increasingly toxic immaturity and self-centeredness. That is the wish for the complete absence of any obligation whatsoever. This also means, in a manner darker still, the presumption at least of equality (with hints of an underlying, skeptical, superiority) to anything great, past or present, as nothing can be deemed truly great, in the absence of a nonrelative ethic. So there is no qualitative distinction between the childish dauber of mud on a canvas and the work of Rembrandt—a conclusion of great and unearned benefit to the former, if a little rough on the latter (and even that roughness might well be desirable, if the real game being played is vengeance by the usurper). If the cost of such overwhelming benefit to the prideful, impulsive, unreliable, and hedonistic is the absence of any deep purpose and meaning, so be it. Or so the devil who waits eternally at the crossroads of choice forever insists.

But if we accept the proposition that there is no real down, no real hell, no real and final moral transgression, then we also must accept the proposition that there is no real up, no real heaven, no real goal, and no hope—and in that acceptance itself there is no shortage of confusion, disorientation, abandonment in the desert, faithlessness, and despair. The affects that fill life with enthusiasm, curiosity, excitement, engagement, entertainment, and interest only make themselves manifest in relationship to a goal.[82] No goal? No hope—and worse. Life does not merely become meaningless, in the absence of such positive emotion, because meaning is not merely positive. Life is also suffering, and suffering is a form of meaning. Thus, in the place where there is no up, down remains unchanged in its essentially reality, being something far more than mere conception and, therefore, something much more inescapable, regardless of reigning delusion. Suffering continues unabated, in the realm of the nihilist; continues ameliorated by mere skepticism. And that means that an untrammeled relativism—the insistence that all things are open for question—destroys both faith and hope but leaves terror and pain absolutely untouched. There is little difference between that horrible leaving and the most precipitous fall into the deepest abyss. What is life without hope but hell? And that is the end result of moral relativism, not some neutral "rationality."

But, if we reject the blandishments of a careless relativism, what do we celebrate, worship, and leave unquestioned? What is it that is truly sacred? What is the Ark of the Covenant itself? What is touched, even accidentally, at the greatest of peril?

> Again, David gathered together all the chosen men of Israel, thirty thousand.
>
> And David arose, and went with all the people that were with him from Baale of Judah, to bring up from thence the ark of God, whose name is called by the name of the Lord of hosts that dwelleth between the cherubims.
>
> And they set the ark of God upon a new cart, and brought it out of the house of Abinadab that was in Gibeah: and Uzzah and Ahio, the sons of Abinadab, drave the new cart.
>
> And they brought it out of the house of Abinadab which was at Gibeah, accompanying the ark of God: and Ahio went before the ark.
>
> David and all the house of Israel played before the Lord on all manner of instruments made of fir wood, even on harps, and on psalteries, and on timbrels, and on cornets, and on cymbals.
>
> And when they came to Nachon's threshingfloor, Uzzah put forth his hand to the ark of God, and took hold of it; for the oxen shook it.
>
> And the anger of the Lord was kindled against Uzzah; and God smote him there for his error; and there he died by the ark of God.
>
> *2 Samuel 1–8*

What, to say it another way—a variety of other ways—is the unshakeable vow, the immoveable object, the unquestionable axiom, the inviolable covenant, the rock of ages, the cornerstone (albeit rejected by the builder) (Luke 20:17; Matthew 21:42; Mark 12:10)? It is the establishment in the highest place or at the ultimate foundation of being and becoming of the spirit variously characterized in the stories of the biblical corpus. It is the determination to imitate or incarnate that spirit. It is the God with whom we are eternally wrestling. By definition.

As Genesis 3 continues, God is revealed as he who walks with men and women, in the absence of prideful and painful self-consciousness (3:8–13); he who attends to and punishes presumptuous and imprudent deviations from the straight and narrow path (3:16–24). In the story of Cain and Abel, God is, as well, the highest good to which sacrifice must be devoted (Genesis 4:3–4), and the spirit who admonishes when the best is not forthcoming (Genesis 4:4–7). In the account of the flood, God is the spirit who calls the wise to prepare when the storms are brewing (Genesis 6:13–18). In the story of the Tower of Babel, God is characterized as the spirit that must be ensconced at the very top—lest everything catastrophically disintegrate, even the capacity to utter and abide by the redeeming Word (Genesis 11:7–19). Those who doubt the veracity of such stories might ask themselves: What does history teach us? What happens, in the real world, when we emulate the wrong model; when worship a false God; when we undermine the foundation, or place the wrong spirit at the top? What happens, more specifically, to the Towers of Babel that we constantly create and re-create—when they become top-heavy and arrogant; when they take to themselves the attributes of omniscience, omnipresence, and omnipotence? Is that not the very definition of the totalitarian state?

The leaders of such societies elevate themselves (or what they purport to believe—generally something that supports their claim to the moral necessity of elevating themselves to the top). Was that proclivity not precisely characteristic of the worst monsters of the twentieth century: of Stalin, Hitler, and Mao? And what was the consequence? Complete misunderstanding; complete inability to communicate; absolute absence of the ability to engage in productive dialogue—not least because the principle of the Logos itself, on which dialogos obviously depends, had not only been abandoned but inverted; not least because every inhabitant of such a state lied about absolutely everything to themselves and everyone else all the time; not least because participation in that endless litany of lies meant that what was most self-evidently true had to be continually denied.

One of the most frightening themes in the terrifying account of Soviet tyranny put forth by Alexander Solzhenitsyn was precisely that: if a Soviet citizen in the time of Stalin dared complain even of his own pain, he was immediately and irrevocably deemed an enemy of the state and made liable to brutal punishment (along with his family and, perhaps, all those who knew and supported him). You know you are truly in hell when you cannot even admit to the reality of your own suffering. There is nihilism and moral relativism taken to their final extremes: even your terror and pain—and worse, that of those you love—must be denied. Does this mean that no one who is truly in hell admits to the existence of the very place in which they dwell? Such is very likely to be the case, and more the horror.

Here is Solzhenitsyn, once again—postprison, meditating on his youthful pride and arrogance: "In the intoxication of youthful successes I had felt myself to be infallible, and I was therefore cruel. In the surfeit of power I was a murderer and an oppressor. In my most evil moments I was convinced that I was doing good, and I was well supplied with systematic arguments. And it was only when I lay there on rotting prison straw that I sensed within myself the first stirrings of good."[83] And the same author, somewhat later, commenting on the willingness of prideful ideologues to lie about even their own misery while refusing to accept the evidence of the suffering of others:

My friend Panin and I are lying on the middle shelf of a Stolypin compartment and have set ourselves up comfortably, tucked our salt herring in our pockets so we don't need water and can go to sleep. But at some station or other they shove into our compartment . . . a Marxist scholar! We can even tell this from his goatee and spectacles. He doesn't hide the fact: he is a former Professor of the Communist Academy. We hang head down in the square cutout—and from his very first words we see that he is: impenetrable. But we have been serving time for a long while, and have a long time left to serve, and we value a merry joke. We must climb down to have a bit of fun! There is ample space left in the compartment, and so we exchange places with someone and crowd in:

"Hello."

"Hello."

"You're not too crowded?"

"No, it's all right."

"Have you been in the jug a long time?"

"Long enough."

"Are you past the halfway mark?"

"Just."

"Look over there: how poverty-stricken our villages are—straw thatch, crooked huts."

"An inheritance from the Tsarist regime."

"Well, but we've already had thirty Soviet years."

"That's an insignificant period historically."

"It's terrible that the collective farmers are starving."

"But have you looked in all their ovens?"

"Just ask any collective farmer in our compartment."

"Everyone in jail is embittered and prejudiced."

"But I've seen collective farms myself."

"That means they were uncharacteristic."

(The goatee had never been in any of them—that way it was simpler.)

"Just ask the old folks: under the Tsar they were well fed, well clothed, and they used to have so many holidays."

"I'm not even going to ask. It's a subjective trait of human memory to praise everything in the past. The cow that died is the one that gave twice the milk. [Sometimes he even cited proverbs!] And our people don't like holidays. They like to work."

"But why is there a shortage of bread in many cities?"

"When?"

"Right before the war, for example."

"Not true! Before the war, in fact, everything had been worked out."

"Listen, at that time in all the cities on the Volga there were queues of thousands of people . . ."

THE TOWER OF BABEL: GOD VERSUS TYRANNY AND PRIDE

"Some local failure in supply. But more likely your memory is failing you."

"But there's a shortage now!"

"'Old wives' tales. We have from seven to eight billion poods of grain."

"And the grain itself is rotten."

"Not at all. We have been successful in developing new varieties of grain."[...]

And so forth. He is imperturbable. He speaks in a language which requires no effort of the mind. And arguing with him is like walking through a desert.

It's about people like that that they say: "He made the rounds of all the smithies and came home unshod."[84]

Why are Cain's descendants tempted to worship technological mastery? Not least because they are marked, and excluded from the presence of God. In his absence, something else inevitably attempts to manifest itself as a unity, else the terrors of an excessive plurality or legion make themselves known. Thus, something else, attempting to dominate, will both lurk and tempt. Cain has already set himself up as the absolute judge of being, as evidenced by the temerity he manifests when he calls out God for the shortcomings of creation, and simultaneously assumes, however implicitly, that he could do better. This is the heart of his resentment, leading to his welcoming the dominion of the spirit pride or arrogance. Hence the pathway from Cain through his descendants to the Tower of Babel, and their unstoppable proclivity toward and admiration for the spirit that totalizes. There is no difference between that progression and tendency and worship of the Luciferian intellect. The temptation to turn to purely technological solutions to eternal existential problems is in itself eternal, and the workings of men, intellectual and mechanical, do in fact have their pronounced and necessary place, at least when properly subdued. They nonetheless present a double-edged sword, as much danger, in potential, as benefit. Bigger cities and more material abundance also mean heavier weaponry and a more luxurious and increasingly dangerous complacence and arrogance. This is particularly true in the absence of a true covenant or ethic, which is the fundamental driver and source of peace, abundance, and opportunity.

Here is something to consider, when tempted to possession by the spirit that enticed and seduced Cain: if you do not perish in the flood, you may still die in the ruins of the Tower of Babel. The evil and prideful eternally drown in a plethora of chaos or find themselves crushed by the forces of tyranny.

Abraham: God as Spirited Call to Adventure

6.1. Go forth

By the time we encounter Abraham (first, Abram), we have met God in various ways. All those ways are, as we have intimated, the multiple and diverse characterizations of a unitary transcendent spirit. God is, variously, the creator of the order that is good from the chaos of possibility; the spirit of unselfconscious existence in the heavenly garden; the proper target of sacrifice; the voice compelling the wise to prepare in the face of the storm; and the foe of prideful and presumptuous tyrants. Genesis 12 shifts the focus. God Supreme now makes himself known as the voice of inspired adventure:

> Now the Lord had said unto Abram, Get thee out of thy country, and from thy kindred, and from thy father's house, unto a land that I will shew thee:
>
> And I will make of thee a great nation, and I will bless thee, and make thy name great; and thou shalt be a blessing:

And I will bless them that bless thee, and curse him that curseth
thee: and in thee shall all families of the earth be blessed.

Genesis 12:1–3

Much is condensed into these few lines. First is the idea that the divine
unity also includes the voice that calls even the comfortable, infantile, and
unwilling to the task and challenge of their life. This is same spirit that im-
pels the toddler to become the child, the child the adolescent, and the adolescent the self-determining adult. This is the same spirit making itself present
in the soul of the son or daughter who is granted ever more responsibility
and opportunity with each voluntary step toward maturity. Second in these
brief verses is an overwhelmingly optimistic promise: God tells those who
hearken toward true adventure in the service of what is highest that their
pursuit will fulfill not only the deepest longing of the forward-moving soul
but also constitute the most effective possible strategy for success.

That success takes many forms: the opportunity to found something of
lasting worth (Abram's dynastic or national line); to do so in a manner that
is profoundly meaningful and satisfying at the personal level (the promised
blessing to self); and to earn, simultaneously, a stellar and well-deserved reputation (valid greatness of name). The covenant offers more yet. Abram will
establish his dynasty, serve as a blessing to himself, and make his name while
doing so as a source of inspiration, encouragement, and genuine provision to
others. ("Thou shalt be a blessing.") Further, those who ally themselves with
his adventurous endeavors will also succeed, while those who oppose it will
fail. It is difficult indeed to imagine a better offer. But what does it mean
about the expanding characterization of the divine? That the source of the
impetus to develop, personally, is to be regarded as identical to the monotheistic Hebrew God, and that the manifestation of that divine spirit is what
inspires us to admire and imitate true and genuine success. It is the spirit
that establishes the legacy that endures; the same spirit that brings true benefit, simultaneously, to self and community; and which will be most resilient
in the face of enmity. This is the divine inspiration that realizes itself in the
calling to wrestle with self, world, nature, and God. What could be more

wonderful than the existence of a true harmony between the instinct to integrate, share, master, and mature, and the operation of the process that establishes productive, generous, stable, and sheltering social order?

This is the spirit that is simultaneously God, as the encouraging voice that calls to Abram and what Abram could be and later is: the father to nations. What does this mean? It means that the essence of fatherhood itself, whether conceived of as something divine or human, is precisely the encouraging voice that rewards the impulse or possibly instinct within a child, adolescent, and even adult to take on challenge, voluntarily; to develop further; to mature; to extend the self upward and grow, toward the light—to handle serpents and to confront dragons rather than to seek security, hedonic self-gratification, or power.

Thus, the Word of God in the story of Abram is deemed identical with the innate proclivity (although not the deterministic necessity) of a baby to take his or her first steps; to extend the hand of friendship and play courageously and hospitably with strangers, in a playground; to reject the false friendship of those who will take their ball and go home if they do not get their way in the schoolyard; to stand up against the bullies of the hallway and the alley, in favor of those who are younger or weaker and more vulnerable; and to desire and risk establishing a relationship with a member of the opposite sex and become reliable, loving husbands and wives and truly adult fathers and mothers themselves. This is what every true father is most deeply gratified to see when it realizes itself in the thoughts and deeds of his children; what most profoundly satisfies the man who has taken it on himself to care for his family. This speaks of the ultimate unity of father, child, and developmental trajectory both forward and up. Is this an instinct—the instinct of striving child and attentive father alike—or the voice or call of the divine? If there is an ultimate unity behind all things, and toward which all life strives, there can be no true difference between the two.

There is possibly nothing more optimistic than the idea that the path indicated by the spirit of adventure in childhood and adulthood alike is the same path whose walking is most pleasing to and, simultaneously, encouraged by the good father. That is something particularly true, in conjunction with the accompanying and parallel claim that constitutes the soul of the covenant offered to Abram by God—the insistence and assurance that walking that very path will mean life becomes a subjective blessing, in a manner that simultaneously ensures well-deserved social prestige and authority, establishes something of permanent value (even a worldwide dynasty), and that does all that in a form that brings nothing but benefit to everyone else, at the same time. And who would dare put forth the contrary claim of disbelief in such an offering, which would necessarily be that the very impulse moving us forward toward true maturity and responsibility in our lives somehow makes itself manifest in opposition to personal thriving, communal respectability, profound accomplishment, and the well-being of others? This would mean that the very essence of our striving for life exists in a manner antithetical to our own good or even the good itself, whether conceived of in the realm of the individual, the social, or the future. It is much simpler to presume—much more in keeping with the use of Occam's razor, scientifically, even evolutionarily, speaking—that our natural or implicit way of being and becoming is one that unites us with our environment, social and natural, in the most harmonious and productive manner possible, all things considered. And that such calling emerges within us as the deepest instinct of forward development (including the adult emergence of the spirit of encouraging fatherhood).

We have already encountered God as the Word of truth, aiming upward, that establishes and reestablishes the order that is good. That portrayal is part of the monotheistic insistence that the adventure beckoning to Abram is another characterization of the spirit of truth. This implies nothing less, as well—and nothing less magnificent and, once again, optimistic, in the highest possible sense—than that the truth is the ultimate adventure. Let us first consider the nature of the lie, which is the opposite of the truth, in our attempts to understand this identity. The liar lies either to gain something he does not deserve (would that these stones turn to bread; see Matthew 4:1–4), or to evade some responsibility or consequence that belongs rightfully to him (would that the dire fate I brought about myself would be lifted from me; see Matthew 4:5–7). In doing so, he forgoes the changes that would have come to him, had he told the truth: consciousness of the insufficiency that is underlying his desire for gain; exposure to the opportunities that might have opened themselves to him had he shouldered his obligation while making the necessary changes in his life and personality to bear that weight. He substitutes for all that the false adventure of the lie—false, because whatever happens in consequence of a lie is neither real, by definition, nor genuinely his, as it is not a manifestation of his true character but of the lie. Thus, the man who lives by the lie lives not his own life but the life of the lie and the life of the liar—and even the life of the spirit of the lie, which is a Luciferian and a dreadful life indeed. For it is true adventure, not the falseness of the lie, that constitutes the truly and necessarily sustaining meaning in life.

In establishing a covenant with the One True God, Abram swears, in essence, to live by the truth. He is by no means perfectly capable of doing so, at the beginning. He is, at best, an ordinary man. This is very good news for the rest of us, striving to put aim up and put our lives together, insofar as we are also ordinary men. In spite of this ordinariness, Abram decides to take a risk. He swears to alter his aim, and to accept, even welcome, whatever comes his way, along the pathway of the truth. It must be understood: that is the acceptance of adventure itself. Why? Because living in truth—acting truthfully; seeing truthfully; speaking truthfully—means accepting whatever happens in consequence, instead of aiming at the target of delusion motivated by the spirit of the lie. That ultimately unpredictable happening (what in the world will come next?) attendant upon the truth is exactly the adventure of life. It is in light of this connection between truth and adventure that Christ says, "The wind bloweth where it listeth, and thou hearest the sound thereof, but canst not tell whence it cometh, and whither it goeth: so is every one that is born of the Spirit" (John 3:8). Letting everything go—of the narrowly self-centered conniving and manipulating—means a radical opening up to the possibilities of life, but only those that emerge from the operation of what is true: "And you shall know the truth, and the truth shall make you free" (John 8:32). To accept the call, Abram must give up his own narrow, self-centered desires; must cease all his machinations, whether for security or unearned gain and privilege, and let the wind take him where it will.

Like most of us, Abram is an unlikely prophet; an unlikely candidate for this truthful, adventurous sojourn. He is privileged, in the modern parlance. We learn at the very onset of his story that he has lived in unearned comfort under the wing of his parents for more than seven decades. Abram has a rather serious case of failure to launch. There is more than an intimation in the story that this state of security is insufficient, even infantile. It is certainly unacceptable to God. Otherwise his call to Abram would have never been issued. Apparently, the proper relationship with God is not easily established while we are comfortably ensconced in the lap of luxury. How, then, might the good life be more truly constituted? Dostoevsky had some very wise things to say in this regard:

> Now I ask you: what can be expected of man since he is a being endowed with strange qualities? Shower upon him every earthly blessing, drown him in a sea of happiness, so that nothing but bubbles of bliss can be seen on the surface; give him economic prosperity, such that he should have nothing else to do but sleep, eat cakes and busy himself with the continuation of his species, and even then out of sheer ingratitude, sheer spite, man would play you some nasty trick. He would even risk his cakes and would deliberately desire the most fatal rubbish, the most uneconomical absurdity, simply to introduce into all this positive good sense his fatal fantastic element.[1]

We believe, and are constantly promised—seduced to believe, particularly on the political front—that the true paradise would be upon us if only our needs were reliably met; if our wishes were easily gratified. In all seriousness, however: When all of its desires are satisfied, does an infant not merely sleep? What then is consciousness for—even, what does it most truly want— over and above or even instead of mere physical gratification? Maybe it longs, however paradoxically, for trouble: hence the first sin in the Garden of Eden. Or maybe, more positively, it wishes to put everything behind the wheel and to push forward as strenuously as possible. Maybe it wishes to be put in a place of maximal responsibility and voluntarily accepted sacrifice and toil, even of the extreme sort. Is that not what is portrayed in every drama of romantic adventure—every movie of secret agent or superhero, when everything is put on the line for the highest possible return, by the man who every man wishes he could be? Are we infants, depending on others to quell our distress and provide us the necessities of life while we lie as passive recipients, or are we the men and women who can and should take on the world, and wrestle it into heavenly order? Christ says:

> Whosoever will come after me, let him deny himself, and take up his cross, and follow me.
>
> For whosoever will save his life shall lose it; but whosoever shall lose his life for my sake and the gospel's, the same shall save it.
>
> For what shall it profit a man, if he shall gain the whole world, and lose his own soul?
>
> Or what shall a man give in exchange for his soul?
>
> *Mark 8:34–37*

To "deny himself"—that means to forgo the blandishments of immediate self-serving instinctual gratification. To "pick up the cross"—that means to voluntarily face the reality of mortality and malevolence and to struggle uphill nonetheless. To "gain the whole world, and lose his own soul"? That is the substitution of the lie and what it offers for genuine participation in the creative process—the Logos—that engenders everything truly desirable in the best possible manner. This denying and bearing of maximal burden—this is the pathway of the most desirable responsibility and ultimate meaning. It is also the pathway to the Kingdom of Heaven. Truly—and the pathway that is as meaningful as journey as it is as destination.

Who could have possibly guessed that willingly accepted responsibility to bear the heaviest of loads is precisely what gives to life its sustaining purpose, creates the world, and sets it straight when it has deviated in its orbit? This is why the Christ who redeems is also the spirit that takes the sins of the world upon itself (John 1:29; 2 Corinthians 5:21). The essence of man and God is the will to take on the heaviest possible burden of life. How could it be any other way? How could any difficult problems otherwise ever be solved—even admitted to? And is it not the case that those who take it upon themselves to admit to and then solve such difficult problems—aiming upward, allied with the spirit of love and truth—appear as a blessing to themselves as the founder of dynasties, as a blessing to others, and as confounders of their enemies? Are they not the people who live the lives that we wish in our most courageous moments to live? Are they not the people that wise men and women strive to imitate, attracted as we are to those who properly make order out of chaos? Are they not therefore emissaries or avatars of the spirit that moves eternally over the waters and determines to attend and to speak productive words and to act?

All this seems obvious, once explicitly considered—and the conclusions thereby inevitably reached can be buttressed in their foundational certainty by the consequence of weighing the alternative and opposing hypothesis: that success in the world comes to those who shrink away, hide, waffle, prevaricate, and avoid. No one believes that, even when they do such things. No one offers that as the most desirable strategy of life to anyone they truly love and wish, therefore, to encourage. No one believes or even claims to believe that running away and lying is equivalent to what is admirable and good.

What is characterized as God in the Abrahamic account is the spirit that eternally says, in essence, even to the unwilling, "You must leave the comforts of your tent—your home and family—and journey into the terrible world." God is that which compels us outward. Is that a spirit to *believe in*? That depends entirely on what is meant by *believe*. The pragmatic choice is stark: when the voice of adventure makes its appearance, it can either be listened to and followed (which is what *believed in* truly means in such a context) or it can be ignored. It is instructive to note that in such a situation, either choice is a matter of faith, as the consequences are equally unspecified in both cases. Furthermore (and this is a true indication of what *believe* truly means), faith in one or the other is not indicated so much by declarative statement ("I believe in . . . ") as by action. The man who believes in the spirit of adventure is the one who hits the road. Belief is in this sense best revealed by commitment—all-in commitment; determination to trod the path of maximal encounter and comprehensive maturation. The man who fails to do so merely indicates by his inaction or avoidance his equally faith-based belief, but in the spirit diametrically opposed to progress; in the one that calls to continued infantile dependence. There is no nonfaith choice in the decision to move forward or not. The former is the sacrificial pathway of ever-expanding horizon. The latter is a deadening and stagnating stasis of spirit. This was Abram's life, before the call of God, the beckoning of great opportunity—even the appeal of conscience.

And what happens when the promised adventure commences? Abram is first called to go to the land of the Canaanites. The nineteenth-century biblical commentator J. Benson describes Canaan as "a country given up to the most gross, cruel, and barbarous idolatry, even the sacrificing of their own children."[2] The Canaanites are, by tradition, the children of Cain. The land they inhabit is a false dominion, because the habitation is established and continued in the wrong spirit—the spirit of false sacrifice, resentment, and the desire to deceive and usurp. What does it mean that God calls Abram to journey there? It means that every sojourner called forth by the spirit of adventure will suffer exposure to the full gamut of human sin and cruelty, and that such exposure must somehow be managed—even turned into part of the adventure. This point is repeated when the hero of our current story journeys into the absolute depths of depravity characterizing the doomed cities of Sodom and Gomorrah. Why is this all necessary? Because the world is fallen. Because the world is real. Because man has something genuine to do. Where there is no challenge and no limits there is no impetus upward, no growth, no development—even nothing real. The meaninglessness of such situations signifies exactly that. Obstacles make things real. Limits, constraints, and dangers make things real. Maybe death itself is necessary to make things real. Then the question arises: If the cost of reality is death, how might reality manifest itself, to justify that price? That is the ultimate question, with the paradisal dream providing the impossible answer. God provides an intimation, with the initial call. If the requirement to strive forward in the world is accepted, the reward is limitless: a life well-lived, the establishment of a genuine and stellar reputation, the founding of a nation, and a blessing on the entire world. Is that sufficient to pay for death? There is no a priori answer. That is the curse of the true existential dilemma. Is it worth it? You are fated to find out along the way.

What way?

That is the eternal question.

Abram does not sojourn alone. He is accompanied not only by his loyal and loving wife, Sarai, and his brother's son, Lot, but by God himself. Every time the prophet stops, furthermore, he consecrates his dwelling place to what is highest. He does this to sharpen and maintain his aim, buttress the spirit of adventure, to remind himself of his commitment, and to fortify his faith. God inevitably responds with an insistence on the integrity of and reality of his covenant:

> And the Lord appeared unto Abram, and said, Unto thy seed will I give this land: and there builded he an altar unto the Lord, who appeared unto him. And he removed from thence unto a mountain on the east of Bethel, and pitched his tent, having Bethel on the west, and Hai on the east: and there he builded an altar unto the Lord, and called upon the name of the Lord.
>
> *Genesis 12:7–8*

This is the calling forth of the God within, so to speak, to aid Abram in his struggles with the manifestations of God without. Something unfolds inside the courageous sojourner that makes him the equal of his challenges as he strives forward in faith, with the determination to face his fate honestly and completely. This continual sacrifice, marking the onset of a new chapter in the continuing story of adventure, is also something akin to the "consecrating the firstborn to God," as discussed previously.[3] Whenever a novel undertaking is conceived—whenever something new is beginning—it is necessary to reconsider both aim and intent. In what spirit is the next opportunity to be undertaken? Is it not necessary to reestablish the upward aim and swear to make the appropriate sacrifices, to ensure that everything is in proper alignment; that no bitterness, resentment, falsity, or spirit of pride is replacing the highest possible purpose? A similar tack is taken by all the true prophets and holy men: all of their actions and utterances are consecrated to God. This is the same thing as a reminder of the truth that is true adventure. Do we perform any similar rituals today? Do we regularly consult the highest spirit within us? Do we try to direct every glance and every action to the ends we have determined should reign supreme? And is the alternative not a dreadful weakness, anxious confusion, indecisiveness, a cowardly lack of hope, and an encroaching vengeful cynicism?

This is a detail of critical import. The risk of the adventure is absolute, given the undeniable and ever-present reality of death and evil. Such a risk cries out for the accompaniment of an infinite ally. Does such an ally exist? The question is ill-posed. The proper question is as follows: "What spirit of endeavor can be relied on in the time of greatest crisis?" "None," is an utterly unacceptable answer. In that case, there would be no aim or motivation, which is not a desirable state of affairs when catastrophe looms. Further, the absence of conscious alignment with the spirit that integrates the psyche and brings harmony to the social world leaves us without defense against the spirits of temptation that will instead strive to dominate. When attention must be prioritized and action undertaken, no atheism is possible. Something must be elevated and all other things sacrificed.

Abram, building his altars to God, is striving to best ensure that he maintains his alignment with the divine calling that brought him out of his hiding and guides him properly forward. Is this merely another variant of the superstitious search for illusory security that is hypothetically key to the religious endeavor—the "opiate of the masses"? Not in the least: it is precisely the faithful willingness to sojourn forward that catalyzes the process of internal development and, by voluntarily taking on the new challenge, makes the adventurous hero more than he would have otherwise been. What is the upper limit to that? That is the limit only defined by the ever-receding and ineffable unity occupying the highest rung on Jacob's infinitely upward-reaching ladder. Subjection to this demanding, strengthening, and ennobling developmental process is neither false superstition nor infantile comfort. Quite the contrary. It is instead the certain consequence of the bravest possible life;

the result of the radical acceptance—the veritable open-armed welcoming—of the entire panoply of even the most dire fate.

What happens as Abram continues to open himself to the call? He encounters a never-ending vista of expanding opportunities—one challenging escapade after another. Each of those new ventures, however, requires a sacrifice: of previous comfort, of previous commitment or aim, of previous identity. This is the pattern of individual development. Each opportunity requires a corresponding increment in maturity—a sacrifice of something that is now insufficient to the challenge at hand. Each sacrifice, in its turn, makes way for a new and ever-improved identity. This is a process of succession that is identical to the ongoing maturation and expansion of competence, psyche, and community. Each of those new and expanded identities must reaffirm their commitment to the spirit that is properly put in the highest place. Hence the repetitive acts of altar-building and offering engaged in by the burgeoning prophet and father of mankind. Abram is striving to do the right thing, at the right time, in the right place, so that heaven and earth fall into the kind of alignment that we all experience, albeit rarely and with difficulty, when life proceeds in a manner that is musical, even dance-like, in its unfolding.

Abram's life is therefore portrayed a sequence of sacrifices, each more exacting than the last, in keeping with the existential fact that each vista of increased opportunity and responsibility requires a sojourner whose aim is ever more precise, culminating in a transformation so complete that it requires a new name for its proper signification. This is how the life of every individual could unfold, if it unfolded completely. As our domains of mastery grow, we must increasingly let go of who we were so that we can become who we could more completely be. The apostle Paul writes, "When I was a child, I spake as a child, I understood as a child, I thought as a child: but when I became a man, I put away childish things" (1 Corinthians 13).

Even though it is God who calls Abram forward, the results are, in a sense, catastrophic, at least by the standards of the original personality. Abram's travails find their mere beginning with the degeneracy and enmity of Canaan, which is soon overcome, unsurprisingly, by famine. Why *unsurprisingly*? Because the descendants of Cain cannot make the land fertile or establish the means of distribution properly. Why? Because the polity they established is founded not on the divine Logos or in covenant with God but on resentment, pride, deceit, and the desire to usurp. The most fruitful plain or garden imaginable will soon become a desert inhabited by the starving if the highest conceivable ethos does not govern those who inhabit it. Abram is forced by the terrible circumstances characterizing the failed state of Canaan to journey once again—this time to Egypt, where the beauty of his wife poses a new and deadly threat—and, perhaps, an opportunity, however perverse.

> And it came to pass, when he was come near to enter into Egypt, that he said unto Sarai his wife, Behold now, I know that thou art a fair woman to look upon:
>
> Therefore it shall come to pass, when the Egyptians shall see thee, that they shall say, This is his wife: and they will kill me, but they will save thee alive.
>
> Say, I pray thee, thou art my sister: that it may be well with me for thy sake; and my soul shall live because of thee. And it came to pass, that, when Abram was come into Egypt, the Egyptians beheld the woman that she was very fair.
>
> *Genesis 12:10–14*

We are only several paragraphs into the story, and Abram and his family have already encountered a daunting range of life's horrors: corruption, starvation, authoritarian tyranny, and the covetous demands of a narcissistic aristocracy: "The princes also of Pharaoh saw her, and commended her before Pharaoh: and the woman was taken into Pharaoh's house" (Genesis 12:15). What troubles might befall any man with a beautiful wife, particularly when journeying with her through a strange land? The interest taken in her by the rich and powerful. Who are those princes? What havoc are they capable of wreaking? What might they have to offer? What kind of interest are they in fact manifesting? Perhaps the pharaoh of the time to whom Sarai was delivered was a chaste man, despite the fact of his harem. There is no getting around certain facts, however: First, that the pharaoh had an interest that was essentially carnal, although he apparently planned to marry Sarai, insofar as incorporation into a harem constitutes a marriage; second, that even if Abram did not offer his wife for the gain that was in any case pressed on him, he did so equally reprehensibly from fear; third, that he later re- peated that sin, betrayal of his wife, and sequence of deceit almost identi- cally. The entirety of the later Genesis 20 contains an account of a very similar sequence of events surrounding one King Abimelech who, like the pharaoh, is warned by God not to sin in consequence of Abram's lies.[4] It is clear in the second case that Sarai escapes the clutches of the king who de- sires her, but it is not at all obvious in the first case, and it was certainly at least a risk.

The pharaoh takes Sarai and rewards Abram materially: "And he en- treated Abram well for her sake: and he had sheep, and oxen, and he asses, and menservants, and maidservants, and she asses, and camels." Abram's lies apparently work. He does survive, although he might have anyway, and he does benefit economically. But they only work temporarily, and they carry risks of their own, which is the case with all lies, no matter who tells them and no matter who becomes tangled up in them.

> And the Lord plagued Pharaoh and his house with great plagues because of Sarai Abram's wife.
>
> And Pharaoh called Abram, and said, What is this that thou hast done unto me? why didst thou not tell me that she was thy wife?
>
> Why saidst thou, She is my sister? so I might have taken her to me to wife: now therefore behold thy wife, take her, and go thy way.
>
> Genesis 12:17–19

The visitation of plagues described in these short verses of course fore- shadows the visitation of ten calamities in Egypt during the time of Moses, and the meaning is the same: there is a divine pattern that stabilizes and encourages individual and community alike. Deviations from that pattern have deadly consequences. No one is exempt from that iron law, least of all stiff-necked tyrants. And all tyrants are stiff-necked. That is key to the nature of tyranny. Abram is thus now compelled to leave Egypt: "And Pharaoh commanded his men concerning him: and they sent him away, and his wife, and all that he had" (Genesis 12:20). It is somewhat surprising that the pharaoh whom Abram so feared does not kill him on account of his lies and the danger they posed to the ruler of Egypt and his house. Perhaps the apparently somewhat prudent head of state decides that neither Abram nor Sarai are worth any further trouble.

Abram does not come across particularly well in this episode. What are we to make of this? The simplest explanation is that he is not a thoroughly and perhaps even not a particularly good man at the beginning of his story. Does that make his story less or more believable? Who is wise enough to be good when they first embark on their adventure? Abraham is an everyman, in a profound sense: he has all the faults of someone real, with all the opportunity of someone who could yet become more than he is. What would have happened if Abram had dared to tell the truth—the whole truth, moreover, and nothing but the truth? He certainly had reason to believe that he would have been killed. When you are asked to give up your "sister" by the absolute monarch, "No, thank you, sir" is not an answer that is within your range of easy choices. The greatest prophets of all time do indeed later dare to tell their kings what they do not wish to hear—and, sometimes, to save and redeem those very kings, along with all their people. But the risk that such monarchs present is real, and so is the potential benefit of lying to them, in consequence—and people have betrayed those they love for lesser reasons than those of wealth and life.

This is not to excuse Abram's acting in fear, or worse, but to indicate his all-too-human nature and the realism of its portrayal in the biblical account. At this point in his journey, Abram simply lacks the sophistication to negotiate his way forward without relying on deceit when he finds himself in over his head. This does not make what he does moral, but it does make it understandable: Who dares proclaim the virtue to stand against tyranny on pain of death? That is a rare ability indeed—certainly not something characteristic of the common man. Such a complex blend of strength and weakness on the part of the biblical protagonists is part of what makes these ancient stories both sophisticated and great; makes them true literature, rather than propagandistic entreaty and delusion. Can a man capable of great things also be capable of great faults? No man at all would be great otherwise.

There is also something deeper happening here, which we can be blinded to when apprehending the apparent faults of the somewhat deceitful, craven, and opportunistic Abram. Although there is a substantive threat posed to him by the fact of the Pharaoh's interest in Abram's wife (who is in fact also his half sister, strangely enough, as indicated in Genesis 20:12), the end consequence of exposure to this danger is a palpable increase in Abram's wealth. What could this possibly mean? First, most broadly, the eternal truth: where dragons lurk, treasure is always to be found. What this means in the realm of concrete practicality is that the man who swears to aim upward and is diligent in that pursuit is in the best position to turn challenge, even of the dangerous kind, into positive opportunity. This is a helpful thing to know when adversity comes knocking, as it inevitably will. A question, then, should usefully spring to mind and potentially alter the entire framing of the event and modify all the attendant emotions: "What possible advantage might there be in this difficulty, which has emerged so suddenly and unexpectedly—even, unjustly?" Job manages something like this, and experiences a dramatic reversal of (mis)fortune, near the end of the account of his travail (Job 42:10–17). Such transformation is presented in its archetypally ultimate form in the passion of Christ. The reward granted to Jesus for His embrace of betrayal, pain, mortality, and hell is the Kingdom of Heaven and the triumph over death and evil. It is God Himself (and this, take note, is another description or characterization), as Milton states, who can take even what is ultimately aiming at evil and turn it into a positive good, while Satan strives to do the reverse:

> To do aught good never will be our task,
> But ever to do ill our sole delight,

As being contrary to his high will
Whom we resist. If then his Providence
Out of our evil seek to bring forth good,
Our labour must be to pervert that end,
And out of good still to find means of evil.[5]

God is the voice that calls us out into the terrible world and guides our way forward, if we maintain our covenant with it: such is the hypothesis presented here. Would Abram not have revealed himself as an even weaker man than he is with his half-deceptions—perhaps even fatally weaker—had he rejected the call to move out into the world entirely, at the outset of the story? He is indeed a bit fainthearted and greedy at the beginning, when he encounters the desirous Egyptian prince, but he is just getting his legs beneath him. Can he be forgiven for not being all he might be before accruing exactly the experience that would help him become so? Who among us is not both lacking courage and immaturely materialistic at the beginning of our sojourn? And, once again, let us consider the call to leave security and pursue adventure, identified with the very spirit of God, at the beginning of the story. Do we not reward exactly the proclivity to heed that call among our children, at least insofar as we truly love them? Do we not encourage their independence, their willingness to take risks, even though we understand that they will make mistakes because of fear and avariciousness along the way? Why not just keep them safe? We are doing plenty of that now,[6] and it is not evident that the consequences are any increase in true safety or even felt security.[7]

We admire households in which the spirit that governs is that which calls parent and child alike into the world with a dauntless and ambitious confidence. That admiration is a kind of celebration; a form of worship. Admiration compels imitation, and there is no higher form of *belief in* than imitation. Encouragement of forthright sojourning forward is in keeping with this fact, as much as doing so personally. Both are higher-order moral virtues: higher order because they rule over safety, security, dependence, and hedonistic gratification; higher order because they subordinates what is demanded in the present (the wish for safety, for example) to the longer-term strategy of functional independence and an accompanying generous productivity. Is it not better to make someone self-sufficient than to endlessly provide them with what they need? If adventure is the point of life, endless provision is not compassionate good, and it does not bring about the promised utopia. It is instead the unconscionable theft of destiny and the unconscious invitation of that comprehensive tyranny that is inevitable when the responsibility is abdicated.

Now and then you encounter someone, if you are fortunate, who has had a true adventure—and you find yourself thinking, "Oh, my God, I wish I could have had that." And if you heeded the call, perhaps you could have. My only sister, Bonnie Keller, is an interesting case in point. She is the only person I know who has had physical altercations with representatives of four of the major primate groups: human (that would be with the author of this work), bonobo, gorilla, and baboon. Bonnie packed herself away from home when she was eighteen years old. She left Fairview, our small northern Alberta place of origin, and went a thousand kilometers away, alone, to university in Saskatchewan, the Canadian province immediately to the east. Everyone, including her, believed that she was ready, that she was mature enough for the task. She had certainly been a lot less trouble than her older brother when she was a teenager, in any case, and appeared grown up as a result.

But Bonnie was not as thoroughly prepared to leave home as everyone assumed. She left for her adventure and could not handle it. Alone, distant from home and its sheltering familiarity, she became anxious, unsure, and depressed, and returned to her parents. This did not please my father, who was first very surprised (as he did not see this coming, something also true of my mother), second concerned that she was giving up prematurely, and finally more than willing to make his displeasure known. The enabling of dependency, it should be noted, is not admirable mercy. Quite the contrary: it is betrayal of the true spirit of the benevolent patriarchy itself. Perhaps my father was harsher than necessary, in response, and perhaps not. One thing is certain: Bonnie did come to fortify herself, once again, and leave for good, and my father had something to do with that. Now so did my mother, who let her daughter know when she returned home that although she was always both welcomed and loved her sooner rather than later mature departure was nonetheless the best conceivable outcome. There is obviously some laudable security in such welcoming, and sometimes of precisely the sort that can provide the foundation for a second effort—so good for Mom, particularly given her simultaneous wish for a successful second launch. Bonnie indeed left again, after making some real efforts to right herself while at home, where she found a job and enrolled in some distance education classes, despite the real misery she was suffering. Soon thereafter, returned to the university, this time in central Alberta itself—somewhat closer, but far away enough—rather than Saskatchewan. During a foreign language class she took there, another and more dramatic opportunity presented itself: the possibility of a summer job in Norway, on a strawberry farm. Our family happens to be of Norwegian extraction on my father's side, so that country had some particular personal attraction. My father primarily spoke Norwegian at home when very young, in his log cabin on the frigid expanses of the Saskatchewan plains, where his grandfather had homesteaded, broke the land, and established a family; in the same farming community where my paternal grandmother was known for the thoroughly Scandinavian *lefse* potato bread she baked and the *uff das* she frequently uttered.

My father wagered Bonnie $200—a fair bit of money in the early 1980s—that she could or would not go through with her summer plans. Was this a cruel bet, or an act of encouragement? It was certainly a challenge—and it made her angry. Anger, by the way, inhibits fear.[8] She thought something akin to "up yours, old man," and took him up on his wager. Then away she went, as promised, and she did not move home again. She broke the shackles of dependency this time, in one fell swoop. Bonnie returned to Fairview for a visit, months later, much more experienced, harder, and wiser—much more mature and adult. She then trained successfully as a nurse. The pursuit of that career enabled her to find employment anywhere—something her newfound and hard-earned confidence made it easy for her to do. Bonnie got every single job she ever applied for, after that, not least because she would tell her potential employers, and truthfully, that she knew what she was doing and that they would never regret hiring her. That is music to a potential employer's ears, part of the results of hearkening to the spirit of adventure, and God's honest truth, in Bonnie's case.

Nursing is a hard job, and a real one, and my sister learned a lot doing it. After receiving her certification, she traveled to Africa, and began working with a British ex-army officer, whom she eventually married. They ran safaris on the savannah for almost five years, taking care of often naive and sometimes spoiled North American and European tourists, dealing with the unexpected exigencies of animal and human alike as they made their way through the back trails and the bush. It was during that time that she tangled with a baboon that had made its way into her ramshackle hotel room, chasing it out, if I recall correctly, with a blow from her fist on its muzzle. After the safari ventures came to an end, she and her husband bought Mercedes trucks in France and smuggled them in convoys across the Sahara desert to Niger to sell them, until the Tuareg tribesmen who lived in the intervening territory made the trek too dangerous. Then she applied for a job serving as nurse to orphaned baby gorillas in the Congo. It was there she had the two remaining battles with top primates. The first was with an ill-tempered bonobo that had been placed under her care in a clinic. The second, more serious, occurred in the wild when Bonnie found herself under attack, along with a coworker, after trying to return three adult gorillas to their native habitat. While returning to camp, they re-encountered the animals, and one determined to attack. It is best to respond to such an attack by sitting down and remaining passive. The two girls did exactly that but were still subject to an onslaught by one angry and ungrateful male. For what it's worth, it had some justification, having been released one time previously, when younger, and undergoing a serious human assault itself shortly thereafter. In any case, it charged them both and attacked, biting my sister rather severely as she fought it off her partner.

That altercation with the gorilla did leave my sister Bonnie with a touch of post-traumatic stress disorder. However, she resolved that quite immediately, and returned to her adventures, moving back to London when civil war descended on the Congo. There, she bought a sequence of houses with her husband, renovating each of them and selling them profitably in turn. In her late thirties, however, she finally admitted or discovered that she deeply wanted children. Her husband did not. This was a point of irreconcilable difference, and they divorced, although they stayed on good terms and are still friends. She left and found another husband in due but efficient time thereafter—a man who is a brilliant adventurer in his own right. They soon started a family. Bonnie then transformed from comparatively hard and masculine in her essence, although still charming and attractive, to almost completely motherly and domestic, and just in the nick of time.

She told me once of returning to Fairview and relating her adventures to the friends she had left behind. "You are so lucky," they said, one after another. They were correct, in a sense. Terrible things do happen to people, unexpectedly and unfortunately, knocking them off what might otherwise be an exciting and fulfilling path. Bonnie could have fallen prey to some terrible disease, for example, in a manner that would have made any subsequent adventures impossible. She did in fact have a serious bout of stomach trouble in the midst of her early efforts, with some attendant surgery. That could well have taken her out. Such things happens to people, and often through no evident fault of their own. There is a random element in life, and providence is in some sense operating at every moment when absolute catastrophe is not rampaging forward. So luck was, as her envious friends insisted, indeed on her side.

But in another and perhaps more fundamental way, what was on Bonnie's side was not luck at all—or, perhaps, luck is more likely to come the way of the prepared and daring. Her adventures were certainly a consequence of her willingness to say "yes," to throw herself on the pyre, and to let what was not meet, good and proper in her burn away. That was her courageous heeding of conscience and the call. She sacrificed both her childhood and her parents when she left home the second time, as she later realized, with some real pain—as all who leave must—and my parents were wise enough to be thrilled that she did so. That means they were willing, like Abram (by then, Abraham) in the matter of Isaac, which we will soon discuss, to consecrate their child to God. Like Abraham, however, my parents' willingness to sacrifice their child also meant that she was returned to them. After Bonnie left home, she maintained excellent relations with my mom and dad, and took them on many adventures, to Africa and elsewhere, in their later years. All of that was to the good.

God, in the story of Abram, is the spirit that calls to the privileged and sheltered to leave the comforts of their home and to undertake the adventure of their life. Do you abide by that spirit? You were privileged and sheltered, at least to some degree, as a child—as my sisters—as well all had to be, lest we curl up and die.[9] Nonetheless, or even because of that, something called you out, however minimally, into the world. You abide by some set of principles, regardless of what you do. That abiding is your belief. You are an imitative animal. You have emulated something. You might not know what it is. It might well have been a confused mishmash of somethings. You might not have consciously chosen it, or them—not at the highest level of conceptualization. But none of that means you were not emulating. And that was your life. Was it enough? Were you a credit to yourself or your parents? Were you a blessing or a curse to the world? Did you father nations? Or did you instead hide your light under a bushel? What chasm in the structure of reality did your failure to bring everything you had into the world produce? And is it true that you will be held to eternal account for that refusal?

These are the truly hard questions of consciousness.

6.2. The devil at the crossroads

After he leaves Egypt, Abram and his nephew Lot, who has been traveling with him, find it necessary to part ways. They are both thriving but can no longer manage their affairs jointly. What does this mean? That people accompany us as we make our way through our lives, and they become close to us, but our parting with them is inevitable and must be managed, hopefully with good will, whether they are friends, entrepreneurial and creative partners, or family members. We are therefore called on to prepare ourselves and our children for that eventuality, accustoming us and them both to loss, developing the ability to derive out of that loss the next steps forward, buttressing and strengthening what remains, reaching out for new connections, maintaining our equilibrium or even improving our situations.

Abram travels west; Lot east. The latter's decision turned him east, toward Sodom and, therefore in an unholy direction:

> And Lot lifted up his eyes, and beheld all the plain of Jordan, that it was well watered every where, before the Lord destroyed Sodom and Gomorrah, even as the garden of the Lord, like the land of Egypt, as thou comest unto Zoar.
>
> Then Lot chose him all the plain of Jordan; and Lot journeyed east: and they separated themselves the one from the other.
>
> Abram dwelled in the land of Canaan, and Lot dwelled in the cities of the plain, and pitched his tent toward Sodom.
>
> But the men of Sodom were wicked and sinners before the Lord exceedingly.
>
> *Genesis 13:10–13*

Abram stays in the vicinity of Bethel, yet again renewing his covenant with God, who repeats and extends his previous promise. Why is that promise extended? It is something in keeping with the so-called Pareto or power distribution; in keeping with the so-called Matthew principle, well understood by economists—the principle that governs the inevitably and radically unequal distribution that characterizes much of the provisioning of the world, social, natural, and divine:[10] "For unto every one that hath shall be given, and he shall have abundance: but from him that hath not shall be taken away even that which he hath" (Matthew 25:29). Success breeds success, as it does so often, and Abram's faith is rewarded.

> And the Lord said unto Abram, after that Lot was separated from him, Lift up now thine eyes, and look from the place where thou art northward, and southward, and eastward, and westward:

For all the land which thou seest, to thee will I give it, and to thy
seed for ever.

And I will make thy seed as the dust of the earth: so that if a man
can number the dust of the earth, then shall thy seed also be numbered.

Arise, walk through the land in the length of it and in the breadth
of it; for I will give it unto thee.

Then Abram removed his tent, and came and dwelt in the plain of
Mamre, which is in Hebron, and built there an altar unto the Lord.

Genesis 13:14–18

Abundance is dependent on truly courageous moral action; on genuine
faith and forthrightness. This is forever the deepest of truths. The opposite is
also true: Satan himself eternally stands at every crossroads, as noted previously, as a crossroads is a decision point as is a parting of ways. Those who genuinely choose *up* at such moments head up, God willing, while those who
choose *down*—however inadvertently—head down. In doing so, they choose
the desert, or the tyranny, over the land of plenty—and that, as we shall see,
regardless of the intrinsic fruitfulness of the land, as we shall later see.

The great kings of the vicinity fall to war—the first in the biblical
narrative—and Lot is taken captive, along with all his possessions and people. This is held to be, traditionally, precisely because he turned ("pitched his
tent") toward Sodom, held to be an evil, materialistic, worldly, and corrupt
city.[11] This means, first, that Lot deviated from the true path of adventure,
when tempted toward what was immediately and foolishly attractive. Second, it means that those who turn from God (which is what Lot does when
he breaks with Abram) immediately fall prey to the war of the great kings—
the battle between principalities, many of which are dark—that inevitably
arises in the absence of what should be properly highest.

And the vale of Siddim was full of slimepits; and the kings of Sodom
and Gomorrah fled, and fell there; and they that remained fled to
the mountain.

And they took all the goods of Sodom and Gomorrah, and all
their victuals, and went their way. And they took Lot, Abram's
brother's son, who dwelt in Sodom, and his goods, and departed.

Genesis 14:10–12

Such kings can be well regarded as lesser uniting forces (power and hedonistic pleasure foremost among them; resentment, hatred, jealousy, and
other vices also vying for primacy). War breaks out when the superordinate
structure that holds things together in peace, or in a piece, collapses, or is
abandoned or betrayed. This is equivalent to the death of God. The factions
that tear at a culture's heart are kingships. This factional war always rages,
and people are always falling prey to it. Abram faces it forthrightly, transforming himself into a warrior when that becomes necessary. When Lot
becomes the slave of these lesser forces—a fate he sets himself up for by
wandering off the golden path, his uncle rises to the occasion, transforming
himself radically once again. Abram arms his trained servants, some three
hundred in number, and sets out to rescue his brother. Is the willingness and
ability to engage in such conflict validly part of heeding God's call?

Peace may well be the proper goal of those who are truly upward-aiming
and wise—the productive peace of a well-tended garden—but submission to
tyranny or participation in hedonistic chaos is not thereby to be abided.
Sometimes trusting in God means preparing for and engaging in battle. Are
we not morally obliged in some circumstances to rescue our lost brothers,
for example, when the tyrants have come for them? Even if that is the result
of some error, on the part of our kin? If such responsibility is not upheld, is it
not true that the same tyrants eventually threaten everyone? And this can
happen far faster than might comfortably be imagined. There is no difference in such situations, therefore, between rescuing our brothers and coming to the aid of our future selves, or between such rescue and the stabilization
of society itself. That is the iron law of iterative reciprocity—a significant
component of friendship and community itself.

Abram "retrieved all the goods, as well as his relative Lot and his possessions, together with the women and the rest of the people" (Genesis 14:16).

Afterward, he meets with the very king of Sodom, the leader of a dark principality indeed, who offers him the opportunity to profit from the spoils of war:

> But Abram replied to the king of Sodom, "I have raised my hand to the Lord God Most High, Creator of heaven and earth,
>
> that I will not accept even a thread, or a strap of a sandal, or anything that belongs to you, lest you should say, 'I have made Abram rich.'
>
> I will accept nothing but what my men have eaten and the share for the men who went with me—Aner, Eshcol, and Mamre. They may take their portion.
>
> *Genesis 14:22–24*

Abram wants nothing whatsoever to do with gains that might be ill-gotten. He is no war profiteer. Furthermore, he has no interest whatsoever in being beholden in reality or in reputation to the king of the corrupt state. Accepting even a hypothetically *no strings attached* donation from someone brings with it the liability of, if not outright ownership by that donor, subsequent self-serving rationalization of the act, and a strong tilt thereafter in the direction of the corrupt leader: *He must be a good man if I took money from him.* That is a great moral danger. *I could put the dirty money to good use* poses even greater peril: once you convince yourself that you had good reasons for doing something morally unjustifiable, you have fallen prey to the temptation to use God's name in vain (Exodus 20:7) or to pray self-righteously and narcissistically in public (Matthew 6:5–6). There is little worse than a sin justified with the claim of moral virtue (an apropos warning for our dismal and wayward times.) This is the reason, to say it again,[12] that God places cherubs and a terrible burning and twisting sword at the gate of paradise to guard the way to the tree of life. Nothing less than Edenic can, by definition, be allowed in the truly heavenly realm. If it were, then heaven itself would be lesser for the admission.

6.3. Life as sacrificial secession

God amplifies his promised reward yet again, as a consequence of Abram's latest triumph over temptation and the requisite sacrifice he has voluntarily made (Genesis 15:1–17). Throughout the text, there is a progression in sacrificial quality (and reward thereof). The choices laid before Abram improve as his adventure proceeds. His judgment improves in lockstep as his experience accumulates. This makes him ever more proficient at discrimination, judgment, and evaluation—at separating the wheat from the chaff (Matthew 13:24–30) or the sheep from the goats (Matthew 25:31–32). This means that he becomes a forever-polished reflection of the Logos as he develops. That might be well understood as a definition of upward development itself; as a representation of its essence, which is no different in principle from union with or possession by God himself; as one of the prime reasons for the reality of the recently mentioned Matthew principle.[13]

This is indicated, ritualized, and solemnized in the events that occur in the immediate aftermath of the war from which Abram refused to profit. God first says, "Fear not, Abram: I am thy shield, and thy exceeding great reward" (Genesis 15:1). These are very specific words, indicating something equally specific: that walking the proper path is both the best possible strategy of defense, keeping the terrors of life and the negative emotion associated with catastrophe most effectively at bay, but also the golden road itself, leading to the eternal land of milk and honey.

And he said, Lord God, whereby shall I know that I shall inherit it?

And he said unto him, Take me an heifer of three years old, and a she goat of three years old, and a ram of three years old, and a turtledove, and a young pigeon.

And he took unto him all these, and divided them in the midst, and laid each piece one against another: but the birds divided he not.

And when the fowls came down upon the carcasses, Abram drove them away.

And when the sun was going down, a deep sleep fell upon Abram; and, lo, an horror of great darkness fell upon him.

And he said unto Abram, Know of a surety that thy seed shall be a stranger in a land that is not theirs, and shall serve them; and they shall afflict them four hundred years;

And also that nation, whom they shall serve, will I judge: and afterward shall they come out with great substance.

And thou shalt go to thy fathers in peace; thou shalt be buried in a good old age.

But in the fourth generation they shall come hither again: for the iniquity of the Amorites is not yet full.

And it came to pass, that, when the sun went down, and it was dark, behold a smoking furnace, and a burning lamp that passed between those pieces.

In the same day the Lord made a covenant with Abram, saying, Unto thy seed have I given this land, from the river of Egypt unto the great river, the river Euphrates:

The Kenites, and the Kenizzites, and the Kadmonites,

And the Hittites, and the Perizzites, and the Rephaims,

And the Amorites, and the Canaanites, and the Girgashites, and the Jebusites.

Genesis 15:8–21

The sacrifice is ritualized and solemnized in this case by the offering of three animals and two birds, on which the spirit of God descends in the form of flame and smoke, passing through the divided carcasses, indicating divine approval of the covenant. What precisely is a covenant? A contract between two parties who agree to undertake or refrain from undertaking certain acts: a contract, compact, deal, or bargain. Why is the relationship with the source of Being itself conceptualized as contractual? The answer is found in the nature of work itself, as intimated previously:[14] actions in the present (sacrificial actions) will pay off in the future. Work is therefore a bargain with the future—a promissory note offered by God: "If thou doest well, shalt thou not be accepted? and if thou doest not well, sin lieth at the door" (Genesis 4:7). It is also in the nature of relationship: the conscience that speaks from within does not compel or force. Instead, it speaks as counsel, but it must be listened to.

The story of Cain and Abel relates God's rejection of Cain's second-rate sacrifices—an occurrence that leaves Cain with a choice: he can change, pull on his boots, and set forward to do things right, or he can turn toward Sodom, so to speak, drift downward into resentment and bitterness, shake his fist at God and his injustice, and set the stage for bloody mayhem. Abel's wayward, tyrannical and jealous brother determines to continue offering the wrong sacrifices, as we have seen, refusing to offer the best he has in the present, compromising not only his own future but that of his descendants and the broader community. In doing so, Cain does worse than abandon God. He establishes a relationship of enmity with him. Implicit in the story of the original hostile brothers is the insistence that a relationship with the divine is inevitable; the only question is its nature. This is at least in part because the human being is a personality, and personalities by their nature exist in relationship—contract, agreement, negotiation, or covenant—to what they encounter.

Is the fact that each of us is a personality not an indication that "personality" is what in fact faces the world, and in relationship with it? And if that is true (and what part of it is not?), then specifying and clarifying the nature of that relationship must be the primary goal of all our deepest endeavors to understand and to adapt. Cain could treat the eternal spirit of Being and Becoming as a father, ally, and guiding spirit, offering to it, as to an admired leader, his very best. He could accept full responsibility for his problems, no matter how large or even how evidently unfair, pick up his bloody cross, and stumble however badly and erroneously uphill. Alternatively, he could step forward in distrust, keeping his best for his narrow present self and treating the God eternally unimpressed by such reserve as an enemy. Cain is he who then and forever chooses the latter route, inviting in the devil himself, and embodying the very pattern of the eternal adversary. Everyone faces the same choice, every time a choice is made. The world lays itself out as the direct consequence of such choice.

Abram, the descendant of Seth, and not of Cain, makes the correct sacrifices, establishes a productive relationship with the still, small voice within, and has the redemptive adventure of his life. It is not by chance that his story is the first after the catastrophes of the flood of chaos and rise of the totalitarian state. He is the individual whose mode of being and becoming eternally sets things right. This setting right includes ensuring the success—a success that is both radical and lasting—of his progeny. Why the insistence in the text on the fate of his descendants? That is strange question, indeed, in a time so heavily influenced Darwin and Freud (to say nothing of the French postmodernist Michel Foucault, by some measures the world's most cited (shudder) scholar[15]); in a time when the primacy of the sexual impulse, the drive to reproduce, is held to be paramount in the realm of private motivation as well as the determining purpose of life as such. Even the biologists, who should know better, are mainly on board with this: the famous "selfish gene" cares for nothing, for example, but replication at any cost—or so goes the story.[16] Could it not be possible, however and instead, that the interests of the individual, truly pursuing his or her great adventure, do and must align perfectly with the demands of procreation, all things considered and wisely understood? This would mean a harmony from instinct to heaven, so to speak, instead of any inevitable and necessary opposition between biological impulse, motivation or drive (all inadequate conceptualizations) and the social order—no chaotic Hobbesian war of all against all or Rousseauian antithesis of society and noble savage.

The path that God has offered to Abram is that which leads him down the path most likely to make him a father, even under exceptionally difficult conditions, signified by the birth of Isaac even to his elderly wife and, second, the progenitor of a literal nation, albeit with some intermediating delay. How is that destiny to be understood most broadly—and how does it manifest itself in the particulars of Abram's life? Understanding all this requires a discussion of sex, but in the broadest possible sense; a discussion of sex and the place it plays in life—in blessing and dynasty, privately, immediately, and throughout the span of generations.

6.4. Sex and parasitism

Women choose men who are adventurous and able. They are attracted, first and foremost, by competence and confidence.[17] Competence is best marked by or consists of two traits:[18] first, the intelligence that is generative and sacrificial in that it produces variant possibly adaptive selves and then culls them; second, by the willingness to abide by contractual obligation or covenant, establish a relationship with tradition, and delay gratification—all features associated with the sacrifice of the narrow self to the future, to the community, and to the ideal. This is something that might well be regarded as the capacity for successful apprenticeship. Confidence, for its part, appears primarily marked by the trait markers most tightly associated with masculinity, cross-culturally:[19] at least, low neuroticism or negative emotionality (freedom from anxiety and pain) and perhaps the low agreeableness comprising the ability to disagree with social convention and to stand one's own ground. The proximal attractiveness of personality to women on the part of men is obviously the minimum precondition for the successful bringing forth of children. That means that even in the most immediate manner the capacity for relationship is the precondition for reproduction (and, therefore, for adaptation, in the sense that the evolutionary biologists typically mean when they use that word).

But survival itself in the multigenerational manner most relevant, say, to the Darwinists, is by no means merely a matter of proximate sexual attractiveness or prowess. If that were the case, then so-called short-term mating strategies would be the human norm and ideal, and that is clearly not the case.[20] They are, however, markedly more effective than no strategy at all. That can make those who employ them—typically, the quasi-psychopathic Dark Tetrad personality types—charismatically attractive to those too timid, immature, or dependent to try at all, not least because in their immaturity such individuals cannot discriminate between the false confidence of the narcissist or the psychopath and the true confidence of the genuinely competent and able. This is no indication, however, that manipulative, predatory, or parasitic approaches to the problems and opportunities of mating or that those who employ them can or should be regarded as optimal in any fundamental manner, whether considered at the individual, social, or natural levels of analysis. Long-term monogamous strategies are therefore not only the human norm, cross-culturally speaking,[21] but also the correct ideal.

The sacrificial and expansive adventure of Abram is thus best understood not only the conduct that makes him an attractive mate but the pattern that he embodies and passes on to his children in the form of the continuing mimetic tradition rendering his progeny successful across the generations to follow. This is the pattern of the wise father, not the pattern of the manipulative psychopath who manages to delude women and himself into sequential trysts. No less a figure than God himself points this out, insisting to Abram that the two of them are playing the long game. God even indicates that Abram's descendants will struggle for four generations before emerging triumphant: "And he said unto Abram, Know of a surety that thy seed shall be a stranger in a land that is not theirs, and shall serve them; and they shall afflict them four hundred years; And also that nation, whom they shall serve, will I judge: and afterward shall they come out with great substance" (Genesis 15:13–14).

There is an overwhelming relationship between male attractiveness to women, particularly as a long-term partner, and genuine ability (that is, the ability to pathfind in the world to acquire the necessary "resources," which can be both material and "spiritual," and to share them judiciously and effectively with others).[22] Good men engage in long- rather than short-term mating strategies; the best men, following Abram's example, employ the longest-term and most comprehensive strategies possible. What does all this mean? Nothing less than that the pathway to ultimate reproductive success among men is the same faithful pathway trod by those who remain loyal, all in, to the dictates of the animating spirit that establishes the order that is good, calls to adventure, and unites and fortifies psychologically and socially. It is all the same thing. That is of course the monotheistic insistence, however implicitly. Although sex is obviously a precondition for reproduction, sex and reproduction are by no means identical—particularly and especially not among human beings, who are long-lived, multigenerationally caretaking, high-investment maters and caretakers.[23] Thus, the most effective reproductive strategy is hardly that of "the selfish gene."[24]

What, then, of women? Sarai, Abram's wife, is famously barren until old age, and then she somewhat miraculously conceives, as we shall see (Genesis 17:15–17). What does this mean? First of all, conception is always somewhat miraculous, and is experienced as such, at least when it is desired and appropriate. Second: it is also the case for women that the divine pathway is the best strategy, all things considered, for successful partnership and reproductive success. Nothing is certain in life, not least the desired outcome regarding children; but women who retain their virtue (to use the old-fashioned terminology) and orient themselves in the direction of so-called "long-term mating strategies" are much more likely to be chosen as partners by men aiming at the same thing. Men genuinely seeking for classically virtuous women (which is what "genuinely seeking" actually means, as opposed to "preying upon") are also typically those who want the particular woman they are pursuing to find and adopt her desired role as genuine mate and conscious, voluntary mother. And those men are inclined to accept the responsibility that best guarantees the happiness, security, thriving, and even survival of all those they father.[25]

The tremendous and constant upheaval in our current culture (the fractiousness around consent; the outrage of women directed at the men by whom they feel exploited) is a consequence of our foolish demands for two simultaneously impossible outcomes: full sexual "freedom" and complete predictability and security in the course of short-term sexual endeavors. These are impossible goals to jointly fulfill, because women who make themselves easily available for short-term sexual access will inevitably fall prey to the worst sort of men.[26] There is no escape from this conundrum: the "better men" who would behave in whatever manner might be deemed proper in such situations are not going to be the men who are attracted to sequential opportunistic one-night stands. There is every reason to assume that increasing the ease of sequential access to women trains men who might otherwise be good to adopt the habits of psychopathic and exploitative manipulators—particularly since we tend very strongly to become what we practice. Women who desire a libertine allowance, however hypothetically, also face another terrible conundrum: they may well find themselves attracted to precisely the sort of men who will take advantage at every turn, because the predatory parasites who adopt that strategy are adept at mimicking the charisma of the genuinely able and confident. Ironically, this tactic makes them particularly attractive to younger women, who, because of inexperience, tend to be less able to distinguish between what is false and what is real in the masculine world.[27]

The importance of this realization and the magnitude of the danger that it poses can hardly be overstated. *Sex itself literally evolved to protect life against parasites.*[28] A more compelling testimony to the depth of the peril can barely be imagined. Parasites generally reproduce faster than their hosts and can therefore evolve with more rapidity. Over time, this ability can pose a deadly threat to those whose resources are being consumed. Locked in an evolutionary arms race, the parasite continually attempts to modify its assault so that it becomes more efficient at overcoming the defensive mechanisms produced to forestall its advance. Because it can reproduce faster, however, it can generally win the battle in the medium to long run. Organisms that merely produce exact genetic clones of themselves therefore risk permanent eventual defeat on the biological battlefront. Sexual reproduction is a strategy that allows for a continual mixing of genes, however, and a consequently unpredictable and ever-transforming biological environment for the parasite to inhabit. The cost is sacrifice of the progression forward in time of the fifty percent of genetic material that is not replicated in any single act of sexual reproduction. Consider for a moment how massive the threat being avoided must be, if almost all organisms (those that reproduce sexually) are willing to pay such a cost.

To repeat, therefore: parasitism is such a severe problem that sex itself evolved in no small part to solve it—and sexual exploitation of women on the part of psychopathic, narcissistic, Machiavellian, and sadistic men[29] is the human equivalent of parasitism. This is true with regard to reproduction itself, which is no small thing, but that is not all, as "parasitical lifestyle" is one of the clinically recognized diagnostic markers of the psychopathy[30] firmly associated with multiple partners and reliance on short-term mating strategies.[31] "Short-term" means no investment in sexual partner or subsequent children, and no desire whatsoever for such investment, no matter how delightfully the strategy is presented, marketed, or spun. Make no mistake about it: the promised land of the sexual revolution is not occupied so much by the delightfully carefree turn-on, tune-in, peaceful hippie dropout flower children of the juvenile 1960s progressive imagination as by the outright monsters who care for nothing but the gratification of their own whims (no matter how that might be obtained).

The long-promised "sexual marketplace" is, therefore—instead of the promised utopia—far too often a place of threat to women and children (often mortal in the latter case), as well a great impediment to the security and happiness of both.[32] In addition it is something that works against the interest of truly good men. Why? For starters: the relatively commonplace nature of sexual assault,[33] the widespread prevalence of abortion (by no means "safe, legal and rare," as so widely advertised, prior to its liberalization,[34] with close to a million conducted per year in the US alone),[35] and the increase of tension between single men and women. It is not by chance that university campuses are both hotbeds of sexual libertinism,[36] often alcohol-fueled,[37] and the very places that increasingly insist that every interaction between a young man and woman take explicitly contractual form.[38] The establishment of such a secure covenant was, by the way, the eternal purpose of marriage. The employment, idiot-enabling, and even celebration of what can so bloodlessly and easily be described as "short-term mating strategies" works across generations to destroy the trust that is vital between the sexes.[39] Women once severely burned—as they are certain to be, as the landscape becomes increasingly libertine—will tend strongly to adopt forever afterward a hypothetically protective skepticism, suspicion, and even hatred of men. The parasitic predators and the narrowly self-serving idiot-hedonist strategies they both adopt and tout pose a mortal threat to the integrity of culture and community itself. The truly parasitic predators will burn everything to the ground to gain the opportunity to fornicate in the ashes.

We are presently in great danger of enabling such players and their devious, camouflaged strategies. This is partly because of the naive or even willfully blind compassion that makes a victim even of the purposeful and committed criminal (a manifestation or even pathologically extended variant of the aforementioned juvenile inexperience or outright immaturity that makes young women the prime targets of antisocial, manipulative, and exploitative men). It is also because our new Tower of Babel communication methods do not allow us to implement our age-old mechanisms of defense against the psychopathic narcissists—or, worse, positively promote and enable the machinations of the psychopaths.[40] As the heavyweight fighter Mike Tyson—a man perfectly capable of dispensing with the real monsters—famously put it: "Social media made you all way too comfortable with disrespecting people and not getting punched for it."[41]

What is the truly functional alternative? To adopt, promote and celebrate the long-term monogamous mating "strategies" that are in the true best interest of children, women, men, and the social order alike; to oppose the celebration and the spread of the ethos of the hedonists, especially of the sexual variety; to aim up, tell the truth, and thereby find the redemptive romantic adventure of your life—in short, to walk and to indicate the straight and narrow pathway. Why? Not least because if you conduct yourself in this manner, the story of your life will not only be adventure but romantic adventure, as you are likely as such a practitioner to attract the best possible partner. This will also vastly increase the probability that you will have children, God willing, and that the high-investment relationship you have with them, along with your wife or husband, will be the most profound good that has come your way.

It is also fortunate in this regard that God appears to approve of sex, if only in the context of consecrated, covenantal relationships—but, of course, why would it be otherwise? How could it possibly be the case that the very continuation of the species could be properly pursued in a manner that was not in concordance with or was even opposed to the wishes of the most high (or, speaking biologically, in accord with the harmony of individual development, future stability, and the needs of the family and community)? In keeping with this is the theoretically unlikely (from the perspective of the utopian hedonists) fact that it is not the members of the wildly deviant fringe minority who are on average most successfully pursuing the pleasures to be found in the most private and intimate of physical moments. It is instead religious married couples who appear to have the most active sex lives.[42] A more ironically comical psychological or sociological empirical observation is hardly imaginable, this far into the 1960s-inspired sexual revolution.

It also turns out that the pursuit of sexual gratification in the absence of commitment and relationship is an endeavor that quite rapidly defeats even its own purposes—while simultaneously putting everything stable about psyche and society at risk. The widespread acceptance of sexual licentiousness in our culture—more accurately, its avid promotion, often commercial—has turned young men into online sex addicts, pathetically mating with Tinkerbell, the porn fairy, often unable to perform with real women.[43] The provision of a veritable plenitude of pornography in its increasingly diverse, inclusive, and equitable forms appears to be one of the major factors responsible for the radical decrease in actual sexual contact among young men and women.[44] Its production and distribution, in concert with the rise of the ethos making such things possible, has destabilized the traditional family, increasingly leaving responsibility for children on the shoulders of women who take the path of single or unmarried motherhood, or who fall into it by motivated accident.[45] One consequence of that? The radically increased distrust between men and women described as inevitable earlier.[46] Another? The demoralization, devastation, and, all too frequently, criminalization of a generation of fatherless children.[47] Finally, although this is not an exhaustive analysis of consequences, it has enabled the rise of pride (and in sexual identity!) as the prime publicly displayed virtue instead of the absolutely deadly and eternal sin that it is most truly.

And why would anyone with any sense not want their sexual relationship consecrated? Why would you not most devoutly desire to elevate the act of physical intimacy with a loving, willing, and playful partner to the highest of all possible standards? Why would you remain unwilling to proclaim your intention to do so in front of your family, community, and state, so that your seriousness of intent is indicated and noted, society therefore informed and onboard, and everyone on the same page? And why, if you truly loved the man or woman you chose for your partner and were simultaneously looking to for the long-term future (including your own old age), would you choose anything other than the path of the parent and, eventually, grandfather or grandmother? What the heck else are you going to do, for example, in the two decades between the ages of seventy and ninety? The idiot hedonism that so emphatically characterizes our age is something that can only work, even in principle, for those fortunate enough to be desirable (young, healthy, able, willing, physically attractive—wealthy enough even to afford the spare time that such pursuits absolutely and finally demand).

The alternative of participation in the mature order of relationship and sex does not necessitate a prim and proper Victorian-terrified-of-pregnancy-and-syphilis-or-sex-itself frigidity masquerading as moral virtue, as so often parodied by the hedonists (and sometimes true), but the proper placement of the sexual element of life into a thoroughly developed and sophisticated hierarchy of attentional priority. This means attending to your partner in imagination and deed. This means growing up, and the consequent making of a generous and honest sacrificial reciprocity the true basis of your most fundamental relationship. If sex is devoted to God, then all shame and fear thereof vanishes, and the spirit of true play can emerge with full and enthusiastic enjoyment. This can truly be, truly an approximation of Paradise, as the attraction of romantic adventure as the prime dramatic and literary genre clearly indicates. This is also the pathway that best ensures the continuation of the generations; the pathway that best unites the demands of individual desire with the wants and needs that characterize not only individual life in its totality but also the balance between those who live now and those who are yet to come in the future. God promises that Abram's descendants will spread everywhere and defeat all challengers. Why? Because those who walk the golden road win everything in the course of the endless game, as

God promises, as previously indicated, after His prophet's most thorough sacrifice (Genesis 15:17–21).

We still find Sarai struggling at this point with her inability to conceive. After many years of disappointment, she encourages Abraham to take her maid, Hagar, as another wife. This is an accurate representation of a conundrum faced by many couples—and one that often afflicts women most profoundly. In the majority of cases, particularly in later life, it is the woman who experiences infertility.[48] As the brunt of the immediate and even later reproductive burden (and all the remarkable transformations attendant during pregnancy, lactation, and dependent infant care) falls on females, there is something particularly tragic about such an outcome.[49] It is important to understand in this regard, as well, that women are accorded substantive status in accord with their apparent reproductive capacity—their apparent fertility—as indexed by the markers typically associated with female beauty.[50] Preference for women with features indicating such capacity also appears cross-culturally and temporally stable, the "beauty myth"[51] notwithstanding. Sarai's barrenness should thus be understood as a terrible cross for her to bear, as such a fate still can be and often is in the modern world.[52] The male equivalent might be the pain experienced by those men who appear doomed by fate to an inescapable destiny of low comparative status (as that is the prime marker for attractiveness on the mating front for men).[53]

Hagar, once pregnant, decides to lord it over Sarai, her erstwhile mistress, on the basis of her pridefully paraded hypothetical female superiority: "And Sarai said unto Abram, My wrong be upon thee: I have given my maid into thy bosom; and when she saw that she had conceived, I was despised in her eyes: the Lord judge between me and thee" (Genesis 16:6). It is a man or woman blind indeed who does not see this play in out in the modern world in patterns of female power-based jockeying for dominance, reputation-savaging, and outright bullying.[54] It must have been a series of pills bitter indeed for Sarai to swallow: first, to contend with the disappointment of failure to conceive; second, to have this happen despite her apparent compliance with all of God's wishes; third, to hand her husband over to a woman subservient in status to her; and, finally, to suffer the insults of that very woman when the latter provides the desired outcome. The fact that Sarai is sentenced to barrenness despite her proper sacrifices must have been particularly galling, rivaled only in intensity by her subjugation to actual insult. This also reflects a particularly female existential tragedy. Involuntary childlessness despite desire, opportunity, and appropriate moral effort is a rejected sacrifice very likely to cause a profound faith- and hopelessness—even a Cain-like bitterness on the part of women—and understandably although not helpfully so.

6.5. Sacrifice and transformation of identity: Abram, Sarai, and Jacob

It is at this point in the story that Abram becomes the much more well-known Abraham. The covenant he has established with God is renewed and extended once again—this time, it is implied, in a form so revolutionary that a change of identity occurs.

> And when Abram was ninety years old and nine, the Lord appeared to Abram, and said unto him, I am the Almighty God; walk before me, and be thou perfect.
>
> And I will make my covenant between me and thee, and will multiply thee exceedingly.
>
> And Abram fell on his face: and God talked with him, saying,
>
> As for me, behold, my covenant is with thee, and thou shalt be a father of many nations.
>
> Neither shall thy name any more be called Abram, but thy name shall be Abraham; for a father of many nations have I made thee.
>
> And I will make thee exceeding fruitful, and I will make nations of thee, and kings shall come out of thee.
>
> *Genesis 17:1–6*

With time and effort we change in small ways and in great. Small changes do not make us different people, but changes of sufficient magnitude can burst upon us like a rebirth (indeed, the symbolic motif of rebirth—baptism, ritualistically—portrays or is designed to catalyze exactly that, as is the common practice of adolescent initiation[55]). If our moral effort has been sufficiently diligent, we may find ourselves shaken to the very core, rearranged in entirety—attending now to different priorities, sequencing our actions in strikingly new ways. This happens when the most fundamental presumptions of value that guide our perceptions shift and change. This is apparently what happens to Abram, who is now walking before God and striving to be perfect (Genesis 17:1). The fact that he falls "on his face" (Genesis 17:3) while receiving the revelation from on high emphasizes this point: that utter prostration in the face of what is eternally right means comprehensive voluntary subordination of what is narrowly self-serving and instrumental—impulsive, hedonistic, and deceptive—to what is properly highest; to what unifies, gives direction, quells anxiety, and provides the eternal wellspring of hope. This change is so complete (analogous to the case of Jacob, later in Israel) that it requires signification with a new name.

This is all part of (now) Abraham's continual renewal through adventure. His sojourn is not so much Sisyphean as progressive: not the same damned boulder up the same brutal mountain, but a continual traversing up and down, toward higher and higher peaks—still an ordeal, perhaps, but with direction. This is the very archetype of the successfully upward-aiming individual—the man who reestablishes the proper pattern of personal being after the catastrophe of chaos that is the flood and of order that is the doomed Tower of Babel. Nietzsche's arguably most famous aphorism is relevant in this context: "He who has a why to live for can bear any how."[56] Abram's original name means *high father*; his new and transformed identity, *father of a multitude*. The perfection he is called to pursue, as his sacrifices mount and his identity thereby transforms, is in the most extreme case what Christ much later calls on his followers to emulate, echoing the idea implicit in the barring of the gates of Paradise: the flaming sword that turns every which way refuses entry to the eternal garden or destroys anything that is not perfect before entry is allowed: "Be ye therefore perfect, even as your Father which is in heaven is perfect" (Matthew 5:48). Insofar as Abraham is aiming up—at the good, or very good (or even the perfect)—he brings Heaven to Earth and shapes himself into a new Adam.

This is the idea driven home in the following sequence of strange events. Abraham's descendants must now mark their covenant or contract with God with—what? The sacrifice of all that which is extraneous? Perhaps:

> This is my covenant, which ye shall keep, between me and you and thy seed after thee; Every man child among you shall be circumcised.
>
> And ye shall circumcise the flesh of your foreskin; and it shall be a token of the covenant betwixt me and you.
>
> And he that is eight days old shall be circumcised among you, every man child in your generations, he that is born in the house, or bought with money of any stranger, which is not of thy seed.
>
> He that is born in thy house, and he that is bought with thy money, must needs be circumcised: and my covenant shall be in your flesh for an everlasting covenant.
>
> And the uncircumcised man child whose flesh of his foreskin is not circumcised, that soul shall be cut off from his people; he hath broken my covenant.
>
> *Genesis 17:10–14*

The designated and apparently requisite operation takes place on the most vulnerable part of the body—leaving it, if anything, even more vulnerable. This is then perhaps not only a gesture of casting away that which is superfluous, even a body part—"And if thy right eye offend thee, pluck it out, and cast it from thee: for it is profitable for thee that one of thy members should perish, and not that thy whole body should be cast into hell. And if thy right hand offend thee, cut it off, and cast it from thee: for it is profitable for thee that one of thy members should perish, and not that thy whole body should be cast into hell" (Matthew 5:29–30)—but also perhaps an allusion to a fully exposed nakedness and acceptance of mortal fragility, a desire to walk once again unselfconsciously and bravely without cover (without clothing; without deception) with God in the garden. These are dreamlike mysteries, still procedural; still embodied, rather than abstracted and explicitly understood. Their meaning transcends even the domain of imagination, remaining something that must be acted out (and, perhaps, within a community) to be "understood." There is also an element of the blood sacrifice of Abel, here, rather than the bloodless offering of Cain.

The extension of this requirement to everyone who is kin, or partnered or subordinate to the true devotees of God, indicates the hierarchical organization of the entire social structure under a single, monotheistic animating spirit. The fact that the practice is instituted at all indicates the necessity for harmonious relationships with true alignment of aim, interest, and most fundamental identity as the precondition for the productive, generous, stable, and inspirational psyche and polity. Without that transcendent unity, there is directionlessness (no set path forward), chaos (too much possibility and choice), hopelessness (no beckoning ideal), disunity, and consequent strife (as all pull in different directions). The danger of such disunity should not be underestimated: diversity may under some conditions be strength, but can also, more primordially, result in confusion, disorientation, and the war of all against all. Does that all mean that circumcision is an existential necessity? It certainly means that some important sacrifice is necessary— and one that is collective in some vital sense—in order for any community to establish itself, coalesce, and thrive.

Sarai (*my princess*) gains a new identity, as well, becoming Sarah— *princess, as such.*[57] Her progeny are also promised to be numerous beyond count. That transformation of essential personhood is marked by God's promise to bless her, despite her advanced years, with a son, as reward for her moral effort and upward striving, equal in its intensity and faithfulness to that of her husband. She is thus no longer mere partner of Abram, *high father*, honor though that was, but the very mother of kings and nation. Her status is no longer head of one family, but of multitudes: she is now therefore mother, *as such*, just as Abraham is now father in the same manner. An analogous transformation of identity occurs in the case of Abram's (now Abraham's) grandson Jacob. The mother of Jacob, Rebecca, was barren, like Sarai (now Sarah). She prayed for children and conceived twins, Jacob and Esau. Their relationship has a Cain and Abel quality to it—the struggle between hostile brothers—right from the beginning. They fight in the womb, and Jacob comes out literally clutching at Esau's heel (Genesis 25:26)—an event that is simultaneously the source of his name, as Ya'akov in Hebrew is connected to the verb *Akev*, which means, as well as heel, to take hold of, outwit, or supplant.[58] Thus, the one who lays hold of the heel can be well construed as a deceiver, or usurper, as in Lucifer tempting Eve, Adam, and Cain. This designation beautifully suits Jacob, who conspires with his mother to deprive Esau of the firstborn rights that are his due.

Esau is a wild man, stereotypically masculine, hirsute, continually outdoors— a hunter and the favorite of his father, Isaac (Abraham's son). Jacob, by contrast, is a tent dweller, more bookish, more devious in the intellectual manner; more civilized, with all the accompanying virtues and vices, and the favorite of his mother: a veritable mamma's boy. The first act of duplicity has Jacob taking advantage of Esau's impulsive nature and wild heedlessness of the future:

> And Jacob sod pottage: and Esau came from the field, and he was faint:
>
>   And Esau said to Jacob, Feed me, I pray thee, with that same red pottage; for I am faint: therefore was his name called Edom.
>
>   And Jacob said, Sell me this day thy birthright.
>
>   And Esau said, Behold, I am at the point to die: and what profit shall this birthright do to me?
>
>   And Jacob said, Swear to me this day; and he sware unto him: and he sold his birthright unto Jacob.
>
>   Then Jacob gave Esau bread and pottage of lentiles; and he did eat and drink, and rose up, and went his way: thus Esau despised his birthright.
>
> *Genesis 25:29–34*

This episode begins with Jacob preparing food. Esau is ravenous and requests something to eat. Jacob provides the food, but at great cost: he convinces his elder brother to give up his rights as firstborn. In ancient Hebrew culture the birthright was a special honor given to the firstborn son. The birthright holder, designated the principal heir, was entitled to receive twice as much of the inheritance as any other heirs. The firstborn also had the responsibility of carrying on the family name and could exercise considerable authority over younger siblings. It is all this that Esau trades so carelessly for his bowl of porridge. The elder brother, however, cannot be given all the blame: this offer to "trade" is a very conniving act on the part of Jacob and a setup, the text implies, that has been long thought through. It's as if the vices of the two brothers meet on this occasion and establish this appalling mutual covenant.

Something of this sort, although worse, happens again later. Isaac, old, blind, and near death, desires a potentially final meal to be prepared by his favorite son, the hunter Esau: "Now therefore take, I pray thee, thy weapons, thy quiver and thy bow, and go out to the field, and take me some venison; And make me savory meat, such as I love, and bring it to me, that I may eat; that my soul may bless thee before I die" (Genesis 27:3–4). Isaac makes this request in preparation to once again lay upon Esau the blessing that is rightfully his, in spite of Jacob's earlier attempts to usurp those rights for himself. However, Rebecca orchestrates a plan for Jacob to pose as Esau so that the great gift might be unjustly his. Jacob, dressed in Esau's clothes and goat skins to mimic Esau's hairiness, brings Isaac a meal and successfully convinces his father that he is Esau:

> And he came near, and kissed him: and he smelled the smell of his raiment, and blessed him, and said, See, the smell of my son is as the smell of a field which the Lord hath blessed:
>
> Therefore God give thee of the dew of heaven, and the fatness of the earth, and plenty of corn and wine:
>
> Let people serve thee, and nations bow down to thee: be lord over thy brethren, and let thy mother's sons bow down to thee: cursed be every one that curseth thee, and blessed be he that blesseth thee.
>
> *Genesis 27:27–29*

When Esau returns and realizes Jacob has taken his blessing, he cries out to Isaac, "Hast thou not reserved a blessing for me?" (Genesis 27:36, KJV). We can well imagine the father of the antagonistic sons both distressed and infuriated by the second deception. He is morally obligated by the standards of his time, however, to stand by the words he has uttered. Thus the great blessing for Jacob is maintained and the lesser granted to Esau. Jacob nonetheless pays a great price for his deception. Esau, furious at this turn of events, plots to kill his conniving brother after Isaac's death. Jacob therefore finds it immediately necessary to flee from his family—thus and fortunately separating himself from his mother—and to apprentice himself to his uncle Laban. This is where his adventure as a man of truth instead of falsehood begins. This is when he starts to transform himself into the likeness of his grandfather, Abraham, and to become a man who incarnates the Logos.

Arriving in Haran, the home of Laban, Jacob encounters Rachel, Laban's younger daughter, at a well and is struck by her beauty (Genesis 29:10–11). Haran, it should be noted, is a place of crossroads, or choice. Haran is also the place where Abraham tarried for a time and where Lot turned away from his uncle toward Sodom (Genesis 11:31). The first events that transpire at or near Haram in relationship to Jacob are in precise keeping with this theme of choice:

> And Jacob went out from Beersheba, and went toward Haran.
>
> And he lighted upon a certain place, and tarried there all night, because the sun was set; and he took of the stones of that place, and put them for his pillows, and lay down in that place to sleep.
>
> And he dreamed, and behold a ladder set up on the earth, and the top of it reached to heaven: and behold the angels of God ascending and descending on it.
>
> And, behold, the Lord stood above it, and said, I am the Lord God of Abraham thy father, and the God of Isaac: the land whereon thou liest, to thee will I give it, and to thy seed;
>
> And thy seed shall be as the dust of the earth, and thou shalt spread abroad to the west, and to the east, and to the north, and to

the south: and in thee and in thy seed shall all the families of the earth be blessed.

And, behold, I am with thee, and will keep thee in all places whither thou goest, and will bring thee again into this land; for I will not leave thee, until I have done that which I have spoken to thee of.

Genesis 28:10–15

Jacob dreams of the upward-spiraliing aim that connects earth with the divine at Haran: at the place of fundamental decision. The idea of expanding opportunity and sacrificial progression is thereby revealed to him in the form of his heavenly vision, which presents an archetypal image of the succession of upward choice. Instead of living a life of deceit and treachery, conniving with his mother, he could aim up, striving toward the good that at its pinnacle is identical with God, the spirit of his prophetic ancestors.

This is the decision that everyone who decides to change and improve makes, regardless of how minimal a step they first take when they decide to ascend, and no matter how unclear their vision of the ultimate up. This is partly because every decision to move truly forward increases the ability to see where up lies; and partly because every upward decision makes the next such decision more likely. Thus the starting point is eternally less important than the intent. This is good news indeed for the man who, like Jacob, has many flaws—good news for everyone, flawed as we all are, particularly when we beginning our adventurous strivings upward. After his realization that is indeed possible to aim heavenward—that is, after his dream—Jacob swears to make the attempt. He determines to sacrifice his previous mode of being, and to establish a new covenant with God. This is marked by the following acts, which duplicate the pattern of Abram's altar-building and offering:

And Jacob rose up early in the morning, and took the stone that he had put for his pillows, and set it up for a pillar, and poured oil upon the top of it.

And he called the name of that place Bethel: but the name of that
city was called Luz at the first. And Jacob vowed a vow, saying, If
God will be with me, and will keep me in this way that I go, and will
give me bread to eat, and raiment to put on,

So that I come again to my father's house in peace; then shall the
Lord be my God.

Genesis 28:18–21

Hard choices do further confront Jacob after leaving home, although he
has now determined to aim up. He contracts with his uncle to work for seven
years, for example, to earn Rachel's hand in marriage—and he makes this
sacrifice happily: "And Jacob served seven years for Rachel; and they seemed
unto him but a few days, for the love he had" (Genesis 29:20). This is the first
endeavor of true service that Jacob embarks on in good faith, in service to a
higher goal. It indicates some genuine maturation; some movement toward
integrity; some upward-aiming transformation of character.

After Jacob offers seven years of reliable labor, he celebrates his wedding
day with Rachel, as promised. Laban, however, conspires to slip Leah, his
eldest daughter, into Jacob's tent on the night of the marriage in place of Rachel, and the matrimonial union is consecrated with the substitute daughter.
He has his reasons: As a father, Laban has a responsibility to see his oldest
daughter settled first. That does not fully or perhaps even at all excuse his
actions. He could have stuck with his deal. Alternatively, he could have attempted to negotiate the situation honestly with Jacob, explaining his fatherly predicament (and that of his eldest daughter) instead of relying on
deception. Perhaps more surprising is that Jacob falls for the substitution.
The text is not entirely clear why. Situational factors unique to the culture in
question clearly played a role. Brides at that time would have been heavily
veiled during both the daytime celebration and when they were brought to
their groom's tent at night. The particulars notwithstanding, Laban manages his duplicitous act, which is realized only by Jacob at the dawn of the
next day: "And it came to pass in the morning, behold, it was Leah" (Genesis
29:25). Given the tricks he played on his brother, Esau, with his mother's

help, Jacob might not be regarded by a perspicacious reader as deserving of any real sympathy. What befalls Laban's nephew seems more in the vein of poetic justice, or karma, although Rachel seems truly and undeservedly to be given the wrong end of the stick.

The moral of this part of the story might be regarded as twofold, in biblical terms: first, that no sin goes unrecognized or unpunished ("For there is nothing covered, that shall not be revealed; and hid, that shall not be known" [Matthew 10:26].); second, that those who live by the sword are likely to die by the sword (a colloquial variant of Matthew 26:52). Perhaps if Jacob had not lived by the lie himself for so long and thereby clouded his vision he might have been wise enough to either discover Laban's manipulations— and perhaps very early—or even to have conducted himself in a manner that would have made his targeting by such treachery unlikely. "Oh what a tangled web we weave, when we first practice to deceive," as the Scottish poet Sir Walter Scott laments.[59] To what degree do people open themselves up to betrayal by broadcasting, however unconsciously, their suitability for exactly that fate? It is a rare man indeed who does not long, at least in the deepest recesses of his soul, for the punishment that resets the moral order in the aftermath of committing a crime.[60] Why? Because a world that appears to lack any true up or down is a place both terrifying and hopeless.

In any case, Jacob accepts Leah as his wife. In doing so, he repeats the faithful pattern of his father, Isaac, who stuck to his words after delivering Jacob the blessing that should have been Esau's. The deed is done, however crookedly, and Laban's now-moral nephew accepts responsibility for the outcome. In consequence, perhaps, Laban offers Jacob a new deal. He can work for another seven years and, at the end of that, truly obtain Rachel's hand: "And Jacob did so, and fulfilled her week: and he gave him Rachel his daughter to wife also." (Genesis 29:28). We can imagine Jacob much wiser by the end of that second apprentice and sacrifice. He has labored for fourteen years. In the process, he has accumulated a large family and substantial wealth, proving himself in the interim a good father and productive steward. He has undergone a series of transformations reminiscent of those that characterized Abram. Further, it is perhaps reasonable for God and fate to have demanded of Jacob some fourteen years of sacrifice so he could redeem himself after his misadventures with Esau.

The parallels between Jacob and Abram continue. Rachel is barren, like Sarai, and requests that Jacob take her handmaiden Bilhah so that children might be forthcoming, just as Sarai did with her maid and husband. This endeavor is successful, and Rachel appears grateful for it. This is the first intimation in this story of the great difficulties of negotiating with fate. After a second son is born to Bilhah, Rachel proclaims, "With great wrestlings have I wrestled with my sister, and I have prevailed" (Genesis 30:8). She has to take the long route to children through the means of another woman, but she considers herself blessed by the outcome, and appears to accept the children as her own. This is not a situation without its complexities, obviously—particularly given the comparative fecundity of Leah—but it is a solution much better than some, and in managing to reconcile herself with fate, With her gratitude, Rachel indicates the strength of character that is perhaps part of Jacob's attraction to her. Things turn around, too, for her, just as they did for her grandmother: "And God remembered Rachel, and God harkened to her, and opened her womb. And she conceived, and bore a son; and said, God hath taken away my reproach: And she called his name Joseph; and said, The Lord shall add to me another son" (Genesis 30:22–24). Perhaps she did everything that it was in her power to do to ensure that outcome. In any case, Rachel is truly blessed—a truly archetypal positive mother. It is appropriate, then, that her son Joseph becomes a type of Christ Himself, and does great things.

At this point Jacob begins to long for home. There are several reasons for this. First, he manages his uncle's flocks and affairs with great success, arranging to take a portion for himself, with which he does even better. This transforms him into something of a competitor in Laban's eyes, and tension grows between them. Second, it is intimated in the text that Jacob's conscience is calling on him to return to the place of his youthful treachery, rejoin his family and, above all, reconcile with his brother. The act of parting with Laban, who seems to be somewhat of a complicated character, has its troubles, but it is something finally managed in peace (Genesis 31). The hero of the story, accompanied by his wives and concubines, and now substantial possessions, is now able to make his way toward the land of his birth. He sends messengers forward to Esau, announcing his approach and indicating his hope that his older brother can show him grace. When the messengers return, however, they indicate that Esau has set out to meet him in the company of no less than four hundred men. This worries Jacob greatly, as he now anticipates an armed force. He reaffirms his relationship with God, in prayer, and sets forward despite the news, determining as he does so to offer a gift to his estranged brother. This is obviously another penitential sacrifice—this time, in the service of both apology and peace. He divides a very substantial number of his goats, camels, cows, and donkeys into multiple separate herds, sending them ahead with their tenders, telling them to let Esau know that each is a separate offering from his brother and that Jacob himself will be following at the end of the procession. Jacob then sends his wives across the river that borders his brother's territory, staying alone for one more night before making that crossing himself. It is there, on the very edge of his potential reconciliation, or his death at the hands of his brother, that he has another transformative experience:

> And Jacob was left alone; and there wrestled a man with him until the breaking of the day.
>
> And when he saw that he prevailed not against him, he touched the hollow of his thigh; and the hollow of Jacob's thigh was out of joint, as he wrestled with him.
>
> And he said, Let me go, for the day breaketh. And he said, I will not let thee go, except thou bless me.
>
> And he said unto him, What is thy name? And he said, Jacob.
>
> And he said, Thy name shall be called no more Jacob, but Israel: for as a prince hast thou power with God and with men, and hast prevailed.
>
> And Jacob asked him, and said, Tell me, I pray thee, thy name. And he said, Wherefore is it that thou dost ask after my name? And he blessed him there.

And Jacob called the name of the place Peniel: for I have seen
God face to face, and my life is preserved.

Genesis 32:24–30

On the edge of his homeland—on the very border between who he is now
and who he was; on the verge of facing all the remaining consequences of
who he was—Jacob of course wrestles with God, as we all do when we face
the most difficult of decisions. What path will we choose? What will we allow, or call upon, to guide us? What spirit will possess us in our decision?
The wrestling partner contending with Jacob is first presented as a man, but
later revealed as God—the very God we wrestle with when attempting to
make our difficult way forward. And who are the truly chosen people, according to this account? All those who wrestle with God honestly and forthright and prevail. Jacob sustains some genuine damage in the contest, as we
are all likely to do when the most difficult decisions of our life present themselves, but he comes out of the battle firm in his conviction to do right. He
fords the river, faces his estranged brother, atones for his past, and makes a
productive and united peace—establishing, like the God he now worships,
the order that is good. This agonizing decision transforms him so completely
that, like Abram, he now has a new identity, a new name: he is now *Israel*, he
who wrestles with God. The fact of that transformation is reiterated, later in
the account, when God furthers his covenant with Jacob, promising him a
destiny very much like that of his equally transformed grandfather:

> And God said unto him, Thy name is Jacob: thy name shall not be
> called any more Jacob, but Israel shall be thy name: and he called his
> name Israel.
>
> And God said unto him, I am God Almighty: be fruitful and
> multiply; a nation and a company of nations shall be of thee, and
> kings shall come out of thy loins;
>
> And the land which I gave Abraham and Isaac, to thee I will give
> it, and to thy seed after thee will I give the land.

Genesis 35:10–12

Jacob, like Abram, began his adventure on the wrong foot. Both men both determined to set themselves straight, despite their substantial flaws, and make a covenant with God to do exactly that. That is a decision; a moral decision, and it is the decision to begin the journey up—to mount the spiral of Jacob's Ladder toward the highest good. They then face a horizon of expanding opportunities, each of which demand, in sequence, a sacrifice of increasing magnitude—a maturation and transformation of character. In the case of both protagonists, this transformation proceeds to a point so revolutionary that the men who undergo are in some sense reborn, and become new people. Hence their new names, Abraham, "father of nations," and Israel, "he who wrestles with God." If that wrestling is done in the proper spirit, there is no difference whatsoever between those two newly bestowed, fully integrated, and properly sacrificial identities.

6.6. With the angels into the abyss

When we left Abram and Sarai, they had just been transformed into Abraham and Sarah; the former, after forgoing great gain to do the right thing in the eventually successful role of a warrior; the latter after enduring her barrenness forthrightly, maintaining her faith unshaken despite her somewhat bitter fate, even in the face of the presumption of her maid, Hagar, now the mother of her husband's first child. The couple is visited at this time by strangers, three of them, to whom they extend a courteous and inviting welcome:

> Let a little water, I pray you, be fetched, and wash your feet, and rest yourselves under the tree:
>
> And I will fetch a morsel of bread, and comfort ye your hearts; after that ye shall pass on: for therefore are ye come to your servant. And they said, So do, as thou hast said.
>
> And Abraham hastened into the tent unto Sarah, and said, Make ready quickly three measures of fine meal, knead it, and make cakes upon the hearth.

And Abraham ran unto the herd, and fetcht a calf tender and good, and gave it unto a young man; and he hasted to dress it.

And he took butter, and milk, and the calf which he had dressed, and set it before them; and he stood by them under the tree, and they did eat.

Genesis 18:4–8

Those who are striving to be perfect welcome each encounter as a divine opportunity and further call to adventure. This turns out to be extremely fortunate in the case before us, as the visiting trio are soon revealed to be emissaries of the divine itself, if not angels or even God himself.

What might this mean? At one level, that each encountered person is made in the image of God and is therefore a lurking angel—an avatar of the transcendent animating unity. This makes each meeting even between strangers an opportunity and a call; an opportunity for whatever might result from reciprocal exchange (and that can be plenty); a reminder to do right by each person and not to take advantage, particularly of people who, like these strangers, are vulnerable in consequence of their current dislocation and homelessness. It is very easy to underestimate or, worse, lord it over new acquaintances, particularly if they are however temporarily in straitened circumstances. God only knows what opportunities are lost for productive joint work and development of character in consequence of such pride. The proper response to that opportunity and call is instead precisely what is expressed by Abraham and his wife: gratitude for the encounter, humility in its receipt (and therefore open to the possibilities of exchange), and hospitality—generous sharing, with no holding back or resentment. Both members of the couple appear to consider the visit a veritable privilege, despite its unexpected nature. Imagine what it would mean for the state of the world if everyone treated every encounter in that way? It is instructive to contemplate the contrary as well. People who are faithless, narrowly selfish, begrudging, suspicious, and resentful in their offerings (and that certainly includes their hospitality or lack thereof) will find themselves rejected by others, by themselves, and by God. Pauline epistle 2 Corinthians 9:6–8 puts it this way:

But this I say, He which soweth sparingly shall reap also sparingly; and he which soweth bountifully shall reap also bountifully.

Every man according as he purposeth in his heart, so let him give; not grudgingly, or of necessity: for God loveth a cheerful giver.

And God is able to make all grace abound toward you; that ye, always having all sufficiency in all things, may abound to every good work.

It is of course Jesus who sets the ultimate standard for his followers, in keeping with such notions—the aforementioned call to perfection, in the name of the Father (Matthew 5:48).[61]

The strangers reassure Sarah that God's promise of fruitfulness will be fulfilled. Note here the strange conjunction of hospitality with fertility. It is the warm and proper welcome that Sarah offers, in keeping with or as a reflection of her faithful character, that inspires God to smile upon her—even to grant her more impossible wishes. It is important to establish this understanding now, so that the later events that unfold in Sodom itself—the epitome of the inhospitable city—can be understood, in all the details of their complexity. Abraham's still-barren wife has entered menopause, however, believes a child to be impossible, in consequence and laughs, no doubt somewhat ruefully, "within herself" (Genesis 18:12). Her husband, inspired by God, upbraids her for her momentary faithlessness, saying, "Is anything too hard for the Lord?" (Genesis 18:13).

It is easy for the modern mind to side with Sarah at a moment like this, but it is Abraham whose apparently unreasonable faith proves eventually justified. Perhaps God forgives her for her skepticism, as false hope in such regard is a particularly heavy cross to bear. In any case, the couple lay the matter aside, at least temporarily, turning their toward the now-threatened Sodom, while despairing of its faithlessness and sin. They lay out their intentions to investigate the city's situation further but, suspecting the worst, note that the city is indeed in grave danger or destruction: "And the Lord said, Because the cry of Sodom and Gomorrah is great, and because their sin is very grievous; I will go down now, and see whether they have done altogether according to the cry of it, which is come unto me; and if not, I will know" (Genesis 18:20–21). "Have done altogether" means "carried their iniquity to perfection, to the highest pitch of wickedness."[62] Presumably, had they not done so, there would still be room for mercy.

Abraham intercedes, objecting to the potential injustice of destroying the worthy in these cities along with the sinful. It is here that he bargains, or wrestles, with God quite directly, suggesting first that the city be spared if fifty righteous men can be found there, negotiating in a daring manner, pushing the limit of the details of the covenant, getting God to agree to spare the city if even forty-five, then thirty, then twenty, then ten can be found, determining to travel to the dangerous metropolis to find those good men (Genesis 18:22–33). What does this mean? If a community steps off the path, journeying toward a totalitarian madness, a collective impulsive hedonism, a Luciferian pride, or a compact of lies and conspiratorial silence, it might still be salvageable if the moral catastrophe has not engulfed everyone who could yet think and speak. The truth, perhaps, is so powerful that even a few unstilled voices can redeem the rest—perhaps even one "crying in the wilderness" (John 1:23). It is therefore incumbent on each of us, reflecting the image of God respectfully, to be among the ten—or even to be the one. This is precisely what is demanded of the unwilling Jonah, as we shall eventually see.

Two of the angels accompany Abraham to Sodom, joining Lot there. He extends the hospitality that typified his uncle and aunt to the visitors, although they first insist on staying in the street. He prevails upon them, nonetheless, to accept his invitation. They do so, entering his house, and dining there on unleavened bread. Why the latter? Because in that corrupt and licentious town, it is necessary to take nourishment and fortification only from what is truly unadulterated. Then the story takes a terrible and perverse twist: "But before they lay down, the men of the city, even the men of Sodom, compassed the house round, both old and young, all the people from every quarter: And they called unto Lot and said unto him, Where are the men which came in to thee this night? bring them out unto us, that we may know them" (Genesis 19:4–5).

"Know" here is the biblical *know*. It is the proper word for intimate congress, as the exploration that makes that act possible and properly done is a very deep form of knowledge indeed. But in this context it means "violently gang-rape," and in the most inhospitable and unproductive manner possible—precisely that manner which has come to be identified with the city's name. The Sodomites "welcome" their guests in the worst possible way, violating their integrity, and doing so such that nothing creative or productive could possibly emerge, in consequence of their actions. This barrenness of intercourse is contrasted at least implicitly with the warm and proper embrace of Sarah, in consort with Abraham, that eventually guarantees her fertility. The actions of the men of Sodom are both hostile and sterile, and that conjunction is emblematic of the dangerous fallenness of the city.[63]

In the face of this threat, Lot then does something that runs absolutely contrary to the mores of the modern world. His response is detailed in one of those biblical passages those with just enough knowledge to be dangerous frequently point to when trying mightily to throw the baby out with the bathwater. Abraham's nephew offers his two virginal daughters to the mob, insisting that his duty to hospitality (which they theoretically share as a sacred obligation) means that he must above all protect his guests. This does nothing, however, but further tempt and enrage the mob:

> And Lot went out at the door unto them, and shut the door after him,
>
> And said, I pray you, brethren, do not so wickedly.
>
> Behold now, I have two daughters which have not known man; let me, I pray you, bring them out unto you, and do ye to them as is good in your eyes: only unto these men do nothing; for therefore came they under the shadow of my roof.
>
> And they said, Stand back. And they said again, This one fellow came in to sojourn, and he will needs be a judge: now will we deal worse with thee, than with them.
>
> And they pressed sore upon the man, even Lot, and came near to break the door.
>
> *Genesis 19:6–9*

When the Sodomites gathered so threateningly at the door are reminded that they, like Lot, bear an intrinsic moral responsibility—not least to maintain hospitality; not least to serve whatever gods hypothetically guide them— they forgo the self-examination that should occur, rejecting the realization and confession of their wrongdoing, and doubling down, in the manner typical of power-mad and hedonistic tyrants. They even express a resentful outrage—not over their own actions, but over Lot's pretension in daring to serve as judge, particularly given his status as a foreigner, indicating their true status as children of Cain, in so doing. In consequence—instead of listening, and in the further celebration of their now self-righteous rage— they threaten Lot with worse even than they wish to press on his guests. Everything about the description of that response is correct psychologically. It is forever the case that those called to account in the midst of their iniquity will turn their full fury on the messenger, rather than attending to their own willful blindness, idiot hedonism (that is a phrase too weak to indicate the true magnitude of such error), and malevolence. It is also the case that such fury is likely to be amplified if it is someone foreign who presumes to point out sin.

It is necessary to understand exactly why hospitality was considered sacred, at the time of the account of Sodom and Gomorrah, to fully comprehend the meaning of this section of the story (in addition to due and necessary consideration of the sexual element). In the days before reliable policing, a sojourner in a hostile land was dependent for his security and his life on the honesty and reliability of his hosts. This may have been particularly true in the Middle East, with its arid climate and vast stretches of desert, intervening between cities. The trade routes that flourished and caravans that traveled there would not have been possible without the certainty that travelers could rely on their foreign hosts. The very architecture of houses and courtyards in the ancient cities of that area were was designed with the intent to offer accommodation to strangers. This was true even of the infrastructure, water systems, plentiful churches for visitors passing through, and general layout—all designed with hospitality in mind.[64]

This ideal of hospitality was also an early expression of the doctrine that the foreigner is also of intrinsic value and best treated with kindness. There is no one who has made himself more vulnerable, after all, than the person who is under the roof of another man—particularly in a strange place. The moral requirement to extend a kindness, consideration, and care is made explicit by the time of Leviticus: "And if a stranger sojourn with thee in your land, ye shall not vex him. But the stranger that dwelleth with you shall be unto you as one born among you, and thou shalt love him as thyself; for ye were strangers in the land of Egypt: I am the Lord your God" (Leviticus 19:33–34). The ensuing destruction of Sodom and Gomorrah occurs because God's inquiry into the conduct of people in that city reveals their extreme inhospitality, a sure sign of their complete moral collapse. They violate the principle of the gracious and secure provision of strangers, as well and in combination with their inhospitable and barren approach to sexuality itself.

Now, one of the clear advantages of dealing with new people is that they may know how to do things you do not know how to do, and to possess knowledge you have not yet acquired. It is for such reasons that we are an inherently trading species:[65] intrinsically interested in the mutually beneficial exchange of goods and services, as well as deeply communicative—prone to offer to the world, in other words, the fruit of our thoughts. This means that establishing a trusting and reciprocal relationship with an erstwhile stranger can bring all the resources of a foreign people to hand, and provide the immense mutual enrichment that such contact can engender. There is, however, an associated danger: the unknown and apparently isolated, and helpless man in your midst may well be very important to the other unknown people who value and love him, and only Gods know how many of them there might be, or how powerful their forces. Thus, if he is put at risk while discussing a trade deal (or for any other reason whatsoever), a very angry horde, or even an army, is likely to descend on the transgressor and everyone he loves—a fate that befell the marauding kings who purloined Lot and his people and provoked Abram to organize his forces, rescue them, and defeat the kidnappers.

In 2023, I organized a seventeen-part seminar on the Book of Exodus.[66] I invited about ten people to participate directly, although another ten to twenty were also involved on the filming, hosting, and production side. We set up a well-equipped local Airbnb in Miami to host everyone involved, held a dinner party with plenty of food and drink every night, and rented two Jet Skis for some daytime fun. This meant that we could all get to know one another, enjoy ourselves, analyze our temperaments and behaviors in a variety of situations (each conversational topic is another situation), test each other for humor, provoke, tease, share, commiserate, and speak freely together. Consequently, we came to trust one another much more; to discover a genuine pleasure in our mutual company; and to be much more likely to continue such discussion, even formally, if the opportunity to do so arose again in the future (as it did in the form of our soon-to-be-released seminar on the gospels).[67] This relationship-building turned out to be something key to the project's success.

We had to unexpectedly double its planned length because of the depth of the conversation, but this necessity was accepted, even welcomed, by everyone involved, in no small part because of the hospitality that had been both extended and welcomed. Because our socializing also deepened our trust, it also made us more willing to push the boundaries in our more formal and recorded conversations; more able to listen deeply and to risk both challenging others and saying things in a manner that would have been far more unlikely in the absence of the accompanying social exchange. True hospitality enables the fundamental and basic sharing that truly unites us. We must all eat, drink and talk, however casually, lightly, and entertainingly. If we can manage in a spirit of good will, fellowship, and play, maybe we could risk more difficult ventures together.

I have also witnessed what happens in the absence of that hospitality. This is particularly and dangerously true of the current situation in the political circles of Washington, DC, where I have spent some very pointed time. For a variety of reasons, the elected officials who serve there are less and less likely to also live there. Four out of ten congressmen sleep in their offices. Let that sink in. This has radically decreased the probability that the familiarity and collegiality necessary for peaceful governance will make itself manifest. In addition, the introduction of cameras into the cardinal institutions of governance have turned places where discussion once took place into public theaters, instead of forums for mutual understanding and negotiation. Finally, the party brass on both sides discourage cross-party collaboration and interaction, because of their belief that their people will become more difficult to predict and to control if they are consorting with the enemy. Now, because the congressmen and senators do not attend dinner or go for a drink together; because their children do not attend school or play baseball together; because they do not face the same local community together—the distrust across party lines has no chance to be ameliorated and every chance to grow (particularly when fanned by those who have decided to use fear, alienation, contempt, and force as their weapons of choice).

Several years ago, I arranged a lunch for junior congressmen, Democrat and Republican alike, in an attempt to address the growing cross-party hostility. To get the ball rolling, every participant (there were about twenty) introduced themselves and provided a three-minute summary of their motivation for coming to DC. It was an interesting anthropological venture. As a Canadian, I have always been impressed by the sheer theatricality and patriotism, both implicit and explicit, of Americans. This lunch was a jaunt through a sequence of micro movies: various versions of *Mr. Smith Goes to Washington*— and it was impossible to tell the touchingly patriotic compatriots of one party from the other. Each, in turn, described the decision taken by themselves and their families to offer their service to their country, in gratitude for all it had provided to them. Without exception, this was indicative of a genuine willingness to sacrifice. Everyone at that lunch after such mutual disclosure walked away feeling that they were now, if not among friends (because that takes more than one positive social interaction), at least among fellow Americans with whom much, if not almost everything, of import was truly shared. Without that operating at the superordinate level—which is the higher unity of national identity—all that is likely to manifest itself is political difference, and the apprehension of nothing but difference is dangerously similar to a state of genuine enmity. Thus, lack of opportunity for social interaction—lack of forum for hospitality—may pose a threat to the very sustainability of the state. This is no small problem, and nowhere near enough attention has been paid to it.

In any case, it is because of the sacred importance of hospitality to the inhabitants of the Middle East that Lot acts in the manner that appears so strange to the modern sensibility, and offers his daughters to the mob. Even that offer, by the way, indicates the relationship between the hospitality that is fertile versus the inhospitability (or, worse, perverse hospitality) that is barren. The men of Sodom are so thoroughly committed to mayhem and destruction, however, that they reject even this offer and attempt to storm the house. This is when they learn exactly what or who they are dealing with. The angels that Lot has unwittingly sheltered prove anything but defenseless: "But the men put forth their hand, and pulled Lot into the house to them, and shut to the door. And they smote the men with blindness, great and small, so that they wearied themselves to find the door" (Genesis 19:10–11). Why blindness, precisely? "For every one that asketh," it is said, "receiveth; and he that seeketh findeth; and to him that knocketh it shall be opened" (Matthew 7:8). What then of those who demand, instead of asking; insist, instead of seeking; and batter down the door, instead of knocking? They will soon find themselves unable to find the way forward, and unable to quell even their own self-defeating narrow desires.

Those who have rejected the true and humility-predicated asking, seeking, and knocking, and are blinded instead by narrow lust and rage, will find themselves unable even to find the way forward to fulfill their own self-defeating desires. What does this all mean? People can only sojourn along the path that is neither straight nor narrow for so long before they encounter the obstacle that cannot be circumvented, the pitfall that is truly deadly, or the dragon that cannot be defeated. There is an intrinsic moral order, as the biblical stories so continually insist, and its violation will result in punishment, no matter however avoided or delayed—and in precise proportion to the magnitude of sin involved. This stark fact, if fact it is, should give everyone who is tempted to stray in service of their own immediate desires pause of the most serious sort. Can we instead get away with absolutely everything? No one in their right mind believes that.

The attempts of the men to wreak havoc on Lot's guests indicate that Sodom has deteriorated to the point where redemption is impossible and destruction certain. The angels therefore warn Lot to flee with his kin. His sons and sons-in-law fail to heed his warning and are later consumed by the fires. Lot is, by contrast, wise enough to listen. He escapes with his wife and his two daughters, who are famously warned neither to tarry as they journey forward, nor to look back. What does it mean, to look back? When a tyrannical state collapses, a false nostalgia for the hypothetical certainties of the former totalitarian condition will invariably arise. Even now, a significant proportion of the Russian population still holds positive views, for example, of Stalin. According to the pollsters at Pew Research Center, almost 60 percent of adults in that country regard the man whose policies led to the death of some tens of millions of their countrymen more favorably than they do Mikhail Gorbachev, who presided over the USSR's final years and led the miraculously peaceful transition out of the communist catastrophe.[68] This is particularly true of the elderly, who no doubt found the demands of adaptation more disruptive and demanding, although that is no excuse, given the extremity and pervasiveness of Stalin's barbarism. The same holds true in China, with regard to the even more vicious Mao Zedong. Mao's image and legacy have been managed very carefully by the Chinese Communist Party, which presents that dread murderer as a national hero and architect of the forever glorious Chinese revolution.[69]

Something very similar to the emergence of this counterproductive and blind nostalgia is portrayed in the story of Moses, initiated in the Book of Exodus and continuing with Leviticus and Numbers. The Israelites, freed from the tyranny of Egypt, find it difficult, at first, to gain their feet. This reflected in the fact of their famed and otherwise mysterious wandering in the desert, and is a problem engendered in no small part by their own ungrateful, resentful, victimhood-claiming slavishness. Why does it take the Israelites three generations to traverse the small parcel of territory separating them from the promised land? Because those who are sufficiently confused and aimless can take forever to get nowhere at all. While moving forward to the promised land, the slavish escapees from Egypt whine and carp more or less continuously. One element of this is their constantly expressed longing for the comforts, much magnified in perverse memory, of their submission to the pharaoh and his taskmasters. False nostalgia as an escape from the realities and responsibilities of the present is an eternally present temptation.

C. G. Jung warned of a similar danger on the psychological front. He described the phenomenon of "regressive restoration of the persona" in this regard. That false recovery is the attempt of a person once burned and hypothetically twice shy to ignore the learning of painful experience, and to return to the blissful state of ignorance that previously prevailed. Christ warned, as well, in the Gospel accounts, of the danger of such self-defeating foolishness, particularly among people who through bitter experience should and even do know better: "he that knew not, and did commit things worthy of stripes, shall be beaten with few stripes" (Luke 12:48). In comparison, "that servant, which knew his lord's will, and prepared not himself, neither did according to his will, shall be beaten with many stripes" (12:47). The passage concludes with this dire warning: "For unto whomsoever much is given, of him shall be much required: and to whom men have committed much, of him they will ask the more" (also Luke 12:48). Jung states, in this regard:

> Take as an example a businessman who takes too great a risk and consequently goes bankrupt. If he does not allow himself to be discouraged by this depressing experience, but, undismayed, keeps his former daring, perhaps with a little salutary caution added, his wound will be healed without permanent injury. But if, on the other hand, he goes to pieces, abjures all further risks, and laboriously tries to patch up his social reputation within the confines of a much more limited personality, doing inferior work with the mentality of a scared child, in a post far below him, then, technically speaking, he will have restored his persona in a regressive way. . . . Formerly perhaps he wanted more than he could accomplish; now he does not even dare to attempt what he has it in him to do.[70]

The moral of the story? Do not look back at what you have left behind once you have learned to look forward in a better direction. Do not return to a road you have once trod when you have learned that it leads in a downward direction. Do not long for what you now recognize as evil. Or pay the price:

> Then the Lord rained upon Sodom and upon Gomorrah brimstone and fire from the Lord out of heaven;
>
> And he overthrew those cities, and all the plain, and all the inhabitants of the cities, and that which grew upon the ground.
>
> But his wife looked back from behind him, and she became a pillar of salt.
>
> And Abraham gat up early in the morning to the place where he stood before the Lord:
>
> And he looked toward Sodom and Gomorrah, and toward all the land of the plain, and beheld, and, lo, the smoke of the country went up as the smoke of a furnace.
>
> And it came to pass, when God destroyed the cities of the plain, that God remembered Abraham, and sent Lot out of the midst of the overthrow, when he overthrew the cities in the which Lot dwelt.
>
> *Exodus 19:24–29*

There is in fact a pillar of fossil salt known as "Lot's Wife" in the vicinity of the Dead Sea at Mount Sodom in Israel.[71] Perhaps it was the intermingling of the knowledge of the fact of that geographical feature with the creative imagination that gave rise to the story. That possibility does not in the least change its meaning.

Two stories of sexual misconduct quickly follow. Lot's daughters first get their own father drunk and "lay" with him one night after the other, one daughter at a time. This story, in conjunction with the description of the fate of Lot's wife, indicates that the iniquity of Sodom was such that its repercussions continue to echo, despite the destruction of the city itself, even among the wife and children of a hypothetically good man (although we must remember that Lot had been tempted earlier in his life to "pitch his tent" [Genesis 13:12] toward Sodom). It is apparently very difficult for people to learn even a painfully object lesson, even when they have taken concrete steps to do so. Is it telling, as well, that the daughters of Lot offer yet another form of false hospitality?

The story of lasting sin, or contamination thereby, does not end there. When Abraham journeys to Gerar, he once again pretends that Sarah is his sister, and she is once again taken by the king of the region, Abimelech by name. This duplication of deceptive act indicates something like a regression on Abraham's part—and to the very pattern of behavior characterizing him at the beginning of his adventure. Was this also a consequence of his proximity to the evils of Sodom and Gomorrah? The sequence of events appears to suggest such a thing. God nonetheless objects to the purloining of Abraham's wife, appears to Abimelech in a dream, and warns him of the dire consequences to come. The now-cautious king, who has fortunately not touched Sarah, claims innocence, upbraids Abraham, and restores Sarah to him, along with generous gifts of livestock and servants. Good relationships between the prophet, God, and the almost-erring earthly ruler in question are re-established. Furthermore, the fertility of the women of Abimelech's kingdom is restored, something that had been taken away because Sarah had been purloined.

This all appears to mean at least two things. First, even the new Abraham apparently still finds himself haunted by the ghosts of his previous self; the temptations of his habitual misbehavior; his proclivity to lie when he is threatened, particularly through his wife. Each man has his typical and particularized weaknesses—often those that are the shadow side of his strengths. We will see something very similar when we come to the case of Moses, the archetypal leader (as Abram/Abraham is an example of the archetypal individual). Moses is constantly tempted by power; it is his true Achilles' heel, a warning to would-be leaders everywhere, and the cause of the eventual insufficiency of his quasi-Messianic mission. The loss of the fecundity of the women of Abimelech's polity and then its restoration—the second meaning— reflects the fact that the example posed by the community head will be duplicated by the common people. Thus, if the king goes astray, in his sexual behavior, then so will everyone—and if the error is sufficiently egregious, reproduction will cease, until the order that is truly reflective of divine will, so to speak, is reestablished.

We might as well also inquire into why it is that even Abimelech, a great king, is threatened with punishment—first, if he breaks a rule (given his status as undisputed ruler) and second if it is a rule that he does not even know he is breaking (just as the earlier Egyptian pharaoh who tried the same was threatened)? Remember the fate that befell Uzzah, who was destroyed when he put out a well-meaning hand to steady the Ark of the Covenant?[72] The same principle applies here. Some rules are so fundamental that even the hypothetically powerful transgress against them at their great peril. Perhaps this is particularly true with regard to sexual conduct, given its grounding in the deepest of motivations and the vital importance of its regulation to the integrity of psyche and society alike. Transgression against the proper rules of physical intimacy, even when accidental or done in ignorance, are capable of destabilizing and destroying everything within a given person or polity. Paramount among these, according to the biblical tradition, are rules against fornication (sex out of wedlock), adultery, prostitution, incest, bestiality, and intra-sexual congress. There is no reason to assume that such warning is arbitrary, let alone a matter of implicit or explicit prejudice.

There are no relationships between people that are more delicate, more prone to cause conflict, and more necessary to maintenance and furthering of the intergenerational contract than those that are sexual. Thus, it stands to reason that sex must be regulated through custom and contract so that everyone knows where he or she stands and why. Everyone must come to understand in no uncertain terms how the most intense desire for immediate gratification must be bounded, so that medium- to long-term psychological health might be maintained and peaceful, productive, generous, social interaction at the level of both couple and community is best ensured—but not only that: so that sex itself might thrive, fertility make itself manifest, individuals find love, and society stabilizes and flourishes.

6.7. The pinnacle of sacrifice

Sarah miraculously conceives at this point in the story, as God has promised. God then tells Abraham that the new son, Isaac, will be the father of his named descendants, although Hagar's child will also sire multitudes. It is immediately after this that the story takes its most infamous turn. God follows this happy news with an unimaginable announcement, telling Abraham that he must take this late and long-desired son, the consolation of the couple's old age—the very son delivered by God himself as reward for Abraham and Sarah's continual faithfulness—put him on the altar, and immolate him in the most terrible possible sacrifice to God: "And it came to pass after these things, that God did tempt Abraham, and said unto him, Abraham: and he said, Behold, here I am. And he said, Take now thy son, thine only son Isaac, whom thou lovest, and get thee into the land of Moriah; and offer him there for a burnt offering upon one of the mountains which I will tell thee of" (Genesis 22:1–2).

How can a God who purports to stand for what is highest—to *be*, more accurately, that which is highest—demand such an apparently unholy thing? It is for this reason, and it makes perfect sense, once properly explicated: *all things, no matter how valuable, must be offered up to God.* Christ reiterates and expands upon this principle much later, when he says both this, "If any man come to me, and hate not his father, and mother, and wife, and children, and brethren, and sisters, yea, and his own life also, he cannot be my disciple. And whosoever doth not bear his cross, and come after me, cannot be my disciple" (Luke 14:26–27), and this, "And every one that hath forsaken houses, or brethren, or sisters, or father, or mother, or wife, or children, or lands, for my name's sake, shall receive an hundredfold, and shall inherit everlasting life" (Matthew 19:29).

Michelangelo's famous *Pieta* dramatizes this idea in the visual form of what might well be regarded as the female equivalent of the crucifix. The sculptor carved this masterpiece, which now occupies a place of honor in St. Peter's Basilica in Rome, from a single block of marble when he was twenty-three years of age. It represents Mary, eternal Mother of the Savior, contemplating in peace and humility the broken body of her crucified adult son. What is the meaning of this unforgettable work? It is this: *the good mother offers up her child to be broken by the terrible world.* It is the role of the properly sacrificial parent to encourage the child to act out his or her destiny, regardless of cost—and the cost is always suffering and death, remediated though it may be, at least in potential, by the true adventure of life. Is it not just as painful for a mother to give up her child to the world as it is to offer herself to fate and destiny—or perhaps more so? Is there any love greater than the love willing to offer a child in sacrifice to what is truly highest? This is of course as true for father as it is for mother. And with that question and its answer, we can also see in the story of Abraham and Isaac the foreshadowing of the idea of the death of the Son of God. We are all sons and daughters of God, or so insist the stories constituting the biblical corpus. And if those stories are not about us (and this is a serious question for atheists as well as believers), then who or what could they possibly be about? And how could it not be that the willingness to sacrifice even what is most dear to that which is yet better serves as the antithesis of the resentment that embitters and corrupts—given that there is necessarily no more extreme possible expression of gratitude?

It is a psychoanalytic truism, attributed to Austrian-born British psychoanalyst Melanie Klein,[73] that "the good mother necessarily fails." This "failure" is the polar opposite of the attitude of the devouring mother, whose perverse "success" at doing everything for her beloved child can easily become his or her most dangerous and destructive foe. The good mother is willing to sacrifice her child to God, partly because her service to what is highest must necessarily take priority, precisely because the lower should never be superordinate to the higher, and partly because it is also in following God (by definition) that her child can find his or her redemption. God himself does the same with his son, a sacrifice played out as the Passion of Christ—an offering and transformation that brings about the end of the dominion of death, harrows hell, and reconciles the sinful progeny of Adam to their heavenly Father. It should be remembered, too, that Abraham gets his son back, in consequence of offering him to God. What does this mean? The best way to truly obtain and to keep the beloved child, long promised by God, is to offer him or her up to the spirit that calls to the adventure of life; that is eternal counsel to the wise; that is the Logos that eternally broods over the potential that is endlessly deep.

The gospel lines pertaining to the necessity of forgoing even family for God follow closely on the heels of a story with a similar moral—the parable of the rich man, who has everything earthly he needs but still feels an unrequited longing in his soul: "And every one that hath forsaken houses, or brethren, or sisters, or father, or mother, or wife, or children, or lands, for my name's sake, shall receive an hundredfold, and shall inherit everlasting life" (Matthew 19:29). This is not a diatribe against wealth, as commonly presumed. It is for this reason that those who follow the commandments of Abraham, from Abel forward, are typically blessed with material prosperity and abundance, in keeping with the idea that the proper habitation of man and woman is a fruitful garden. It is the love of money, not money itself, that constitutes an impediment to the climbing of Jacob's Ladder: "Make sure that your character is free from the love of money, being content with what you have; for he himself has said, 'I will never desert you, nor will I ever abandon you'" (Hebrews 13:5, New American Standard Bible).

Money itself is only a token of exchange and promise and, when used honestly, a positive good. Raising the desire for material wealth to the position of the highest good (precisely what the Israelites do in the story of Exodus when they determine to worship the golden calf) is another thing altogether. Intellect in its proper place, sex in its proper place, and wealth and material prosperity in its proper place. When out of order, however—particularly when falsely elevated to the highest place—something that *could* be good can become a terrible master. This occurs in precise but inverse proportion to its potential for that good, when it has been properly subdued and named.

There is also a fundamental promise in such lines: that the eventual reward is directly proportional to the sacrifice. If it was otherwise, of course, no exceptional sacrifice would every be advisable. If every painful and upward-aiming offering was rejected, there would be no point in conscientious laboring or striving forward. I have watched such reward make itself manifest in the lives of many people I have had the privilege to observe. I saw, for example—and firsthand—what happened to people who said what they believed to be true and put their reputations and careers on the line to do so. The mob came for them, sure enough, and they paid precisely the nontrivial short-term cost that those who remain silent or lie outright scheme to avoid. But those who maintained faith in the truth invariably succeeded—not immediately, and there's the rub, but eventually. Sometimes reward came in the provision of opportunities from people who were impressed to the point of action by the very real sacrifices they observed. Sometimes it was a consequence of a profound psychological reorientation, attendant on living through and withstanding the firestorm of controversy that followed their disavowal of security in the name of truth. Sometimes it was both. This is akin to the material abundance enjoyed by Abraham and Sarah, and to the renewal of their identity, represented by their renaming—the beneficial fate shared by the Jacob who became Israel. There is literally nothing more practical than the proper sacrifices to what is highest, and there is simultaneously no limit to the demand for the sacrifice. Hence the offering of Isaac and, later, Jesus of Nazareth.

This pragmatic assertion can be regarded as a simple matter of priority: what is first must come first, no matter what and no matter who. This is in no small part because there will be situations in life, often of great tragedy and import, when the presence of material wealth will prove of no utility. In such cases, it is only the proper upward orientation, away from despair and bitterness, that can play a necessary salvific role. Divorces are common among the rich (as well as the poor, as poverty adds stress to the complex problem of maintaining a proper marital relationship), and wealth offers only limited protection against both aging and illness. Money can directly abet sin, too. I had many clients in my clinical practice who, on receiving their monthly unemployment or disability benefit, were swarmed by their ne'er-do-well parasitical friends, happy to spend precisely that windfall, leaving said clients all too often face down in a ditch, or its equivalent, after a three-day binge.

It is for such reasons that Christ therefore so directly insists: "Do not lay up for yourselves treasures on earth, where moth and rust destroy and where thieves break in and steal; But lay up for yourselves treasures in heaven, where neither moth nor rust doth corrupt, and where thieves do not break through nor steal" (Matthew 6:19–20). Earthly treasures are palpably material, including even such necessities as food and water. But Christ contrasts the heavenly bread with its insufficient material equivalent, describing the pattern of attentional prioritization and action he represents as the source of eternal food: "I am the living bread which came down from Heaven; if any man eat of this bread, he shall live for ever; and the bread that I give is my flesh, which I will give for the life of the world" (John 6:51).

How best to store resources? The proper answer to that question is "in genuine reputation"—because then everyone springs to your aid when the storms come, including you. ("For where your treasure is, there will your heart be also" [Matthew 6:20].) This is the reiteration of the second promise that the spirit of adventure that God makes to Abram, when the initial covenant that binds the two is formulated—when Abram decides to stop being a dependent, whiny coward and aim up: "I will bless thee, and make thy name great" (Genesis 12:2). This heavenly storehouse of value is something more abstracted and intangible than material wealth, per se; something more a consequence of higher-order spiritual striving (though even money is essentially nothing but a signifier of this heavenly reality, as its value is nothing, in the final analysis, but mutual promise). If you endeavor above all to treat your neighbor as yourself, for example (Matthew 22:29), or even to love your enemies (Matthew 5:44), that commitment will manifest itself in what you attend to and how you act, and other people will observe that and respond in kind. It is the garnering of this abstract, transcendent, or "heavenly," form of treasure that is of course the aim of the great prophets—and all those who live by the highest standards—and the truly imperishable and incorruptible gold.

The story of Abraham and Isaac carries within it a paradoxical promise: if a parent is willing to sacrifice his or her child to God, acting out that willingness in every micro glance and action, then the child *will not* be sacrificed or otherwise destroyed by the very hand of that parent (who might otherwise be tempted to do so, if doing so redounds in some pathological manner to their moral credit). It is not such a rare occurrence for parents to cripple their children so that they can make a public show of their martyrdom and compassionate virtue: *Sure, I am cursed with a monster, but look how well I am bearing up under the burden; look how much love I am still able and willing to pour out.* This is the terrible aim of the witch in the forest, much too good to be true, in her gingerbread house, who conspires to devour Hansel and Gretel when they are abandoned by their father. Fatten them up; then eat them: the full Oedipal nightmare in all its terrible reality. This is the catastrophe of the maternal instinct gone dreadfully wrong; the horror of compassion, when it is inappropriately put in the highest place; the full manifestation of the prideful sin of Eve.

Both sides of this story can hardly be dramatized emphatically enough: it is a terrible thing to offer son or daughter to God, but it is a positively hellish thing, an offering to the darkest abyss, to fail to do so. The parent who, for example, protects his or her child at all costs—thereby maintaining past its due date an increasingly corrupt and counterproductive infantilism—is simultaneously and often purposefully compromising that child's soul, dooming him or her to an everlasting insecurity, anxiety, hopelessness, and most bitter resentment and self-hatred.[74] If you as a parent are willing instead to offer your son or daughter to God—to the destiny that is both true and terrible—then you may be fortunate enough not to be complicit in his or her death, bodily or spiritual: "And the angel of the Lord called unto him out of heaven, and said, Abraham, Abraham: and he said, Here am I. And he said, Lay not thine hand upon the lad, neither do thou any thing unto him: for now I know that thou fearest God, seeing thou hast not withheld thy son, thine only son from me" (Genesis 22:11–12).

The spirit that is God in the Abrahamic story is not only the still, small voice that calls to adventure. It is also the same unitary spirit requiring those who welcome its presence to go all in, to risk everything. Optimal adaptation requires that no light is left languishing under a bushel; that nothing within is held in abeyance; that all potential strength is mustered for the fight; that all resources are brought to bear on the problems at hand. Is that surprising, given the ultimate seriousness and difficulty of life? When life itself is on the line, everything must be given. What stone can possibly be left unturned when the task that faces us is the dragon of chaos—the burden of death; the eternal reality of evil? It is therefore by necessity that God is the Father who will even and eternally sacrifice his own son to that which is truly holy. And, paradoxically, it is by means of that ultimate sacrifice, stalwartly undertaken by that very Son, that salvation and redemption is always and forever brought about. The son is set right by the father willing to do the right thing no matter what—even at the cost of everything else he loves. The son is set right (and sets everyone else right, not least by example) by his willingness to abide by the dictates of the father who loves him—and who is thereby willing to face even that which will destroy him and drag him to hell. Thus the God of Action and Adventure is also he who requires the ultimate sacrifice but, paradoxically, is least likely to demand it if it is truly offered.

Abraham and Sarah are elderly and rich. Isaac is their only son, promised by God and delivered after many pitfalls and very late in life. So they have every reason to dote counterproductively on the scion they have labored so long to produce and, in doing so, to devour him. They could very easily have justified to themselves the necessity of the very excess of "care" (really, narrowly self-centered desire) that would have made of their privileged and fortunate son a truly narcissistic piece of work—a true spiritual descendant of Cain and Luciferian spirit. Instead, Abraham and Sarah continue to act forthrightly and subordinate all that is lesser to that which is greater. They live their lives in the comprehensive and complete manner that grants them the adventure that perhaps justifies their suffering—that maybe atones for the great crime of their existence. They each live to a great age:

> And Sarah was an hundred and seven and twenty years old: these were the years of the life of Sarah.
>
> And Sarah died in Kirjatharba; the same is Hebron in the land of Canaan: and Abraham came to mourn for Sarah, and to weep for her.
>
> *Genesis 23:1–2*

And these are the days of the years of Abraham's life which he lived, an hundred threescore and fifteen years.

Then Abraham gave up the ghost, and died in a good old age, an old man, and full of years; and was gathered to his people.

Genesis 25:7–8

Did their lives justify the terrible limitations of mortal being? That is the promise of abiding by the true unitary animating spirit whose character is delineated in the great biblical corpus of dramatic stories. Their adventure is not the mere dwelling in the Paradise of infantile satiation. Nor is it the pointless, repetitive toil of the same damned thing over and over. It is instead a very sophisticated promised land—a sequence of journeys to better and better places, with each journey a more and more compelling adventure, resulting in the fullest of all possible lives and the echoing of that fullness and completion across the generations and into the distant future. It is the life that all of us could and should live, if we had the courage, and the adventure that would perhaps justify the fact of our fragility and mortal limitation.

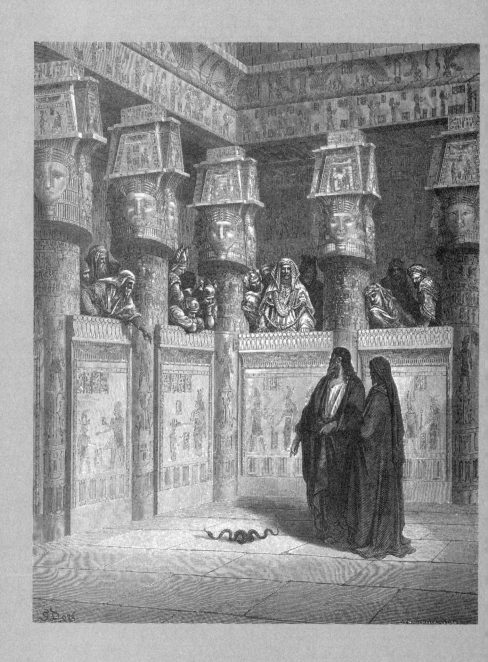

7

◆

Moses I: God as Dreadful
Spirit of Freedom

7.1. The Jews as unwelcome
sojourners and slaves

We encounter the Israelites in the Book of Exodus when they are in Egypt, but no longer under the protection established for them by Joseph, the son of Rachel and Jacob, who had saved the whole country from starvation. In the aftermath of that triumph and the goodwill that it produced, the kinsmen of Joseph had thrived: "And the children of Israel were fruitful, and increased abundantly, and multiplied, and waxed exceeding mighty; and the land was filled with them" (Exodus 1:7). Instead of being properly grateful for this aid and the provision of the labor of the Israelites, the pharaoh who succeeds Joseph's sovereign ally begins to view the Israelites as a threat: "Behold, let us deal wisely with them, lest they multiply, and it come to pass, when there falleth out any war, they join also our enemies, and fight against us, and so get them up out of the land" (Exodus 1:10). What might we note here? First, the ancient Jews have the temerity to be successful, even though they are strangers in a strange land; second, those who agitate against the Israelites foster hatred against them as a potential fifth column and justify this aggression as preemptive self-protection.

Some things truly never change. The Jews have existed as the prototypical successful minority for millennia. Why? Perhaps, a culture of literacy, schooling, and ambitious, disciplined striving, conjoined with true admiration for such endeavor;[1] perhaps, something approximating intragroup sexual and cultural selection for high intelligence.[2] Such ideas are perennially unpopular. What is the alternative explanation? The accusations that comparative success is due to perfidy, or conspiracy, in the form of prejudicial intragroup favoritism and unfair manipulation? This has been the age-old accusation, as evidenced, not least, in the opening of Exodus. The Egyptians enviously reduce their once-benefactors—the successful minority—to slavery. This is another manifestation of the spirit of Cain: "And the Egyptians made the children of Israel to serve with rigor; and they made their lives bitter with hard bondage, in mortar, and in brick, and in all manner of service in the field" (Exodus 1:13-14). When such oppression proves insufficient to break their spirit, the pharaoh commands the Hebrew midwives to kill all the boys they are charged with delivering at their birth.

A thematically similar threat is echoed much later in the time of Christ: "Then Herod, when he saw that he was mocked of the wise men, was exceeding wroth, and sent forth, and slew all the children that were in Bethlehem, and in all the coasts thereof, from two years old and under, according to the time which he had diligently inquired of the wise men" (Matthew 2:16). Herod had been warned that a king would be born to the Jews and threaten his reign, and took this action to forestall that threat. Something analogous is portrayed in the story of King Arthur.[3] King Vortigern, Arthur's uncle, is the evil brother to the latter's father—Cain to his Abel. That king was warned, as was Herod, that a recently born child would one day rise to overthrow him. All three of these stories rely on the plot device of "the hero endangered at birth," a common narrative trope.[4]

Why would the redeeming hero be portrayed as vulnerable at birth and the tyrant represented as infanticidal? Not least because all human beings, even those who grow up to triumph, are comparatively helpless as infants and young children, exposed as they must be to the depredations of nature and society. The preindustrial infant mortality rate was one in four; the child mortality rate, 50 percent.[5] Further, direct infanticide was far from uncommon, cross-culturally or in absolute numbers. Anthropologist Joseph Birdsell estimates that between one sixth and half of children in prehistoric times met their end in that manner.[6] And what is the risk of danger now to those who would be born, if it were not for the abortion, touted so deceptively when first made accessible as "safe, legal, and rare"?[7] Those were—and are—the direct threats. More indirectly and perhaps even more pervasively: all journeys begin with the first and often tentative steps, and all great men start small. And who else would the tyrant kill but the world-redeeming hero whose intrinsic mission is in some part the overthrow of the power-mad? And all such heroes make their beginning as the divine child.

Moses is born to a Hebrew mother during the period of danger decreed by the Egyptian pharaoh. She hides him from the murderous authorities for three months. Then, unable to continue the deception, she makes a little raft for him of bulrushes and places him on the river (Exodus 2:1–10). This is the first of many episodes associating the eventual leader of the Israelites with water in both its life-giving and destructive manifestations (contrasted with the unyielding and unmalleable stone signifying Egypt). The very name of Moses signifies his affinity with the liquid that gives life (Exodus 1:10). Like God himself, the eventual prophet is a master of chaos, of possibility, of the *tohu va bohu*, the primordial water over which the Word of God broods at the beginning of time and always; the water that finds its course, inevitably, as it wends its way downhill; the water whose persistence can wear away even the hardest stone. This motif of stone versus water is extended to the later desert sojourn as well, where Moses displays his ability to transform even the rocks of the wasteland into life-giving springs (Exodus 17:6; Numbers 20:7–12). This represents the fact that leadership in the right spirit can make even the desert bloom.

The pharaoh's daughter sees Moses on the water, identifies him as one of the threatened children, but decides to rescue and raise him as her own son (Exodus 2:1–10). She calls on a nursemaid to provide him with sustenance and care. Unbeknownst to her, Moses's true mother steps forward to do so. This is another mythological trope: the hero with dual ancestry. One set of the divine or semidivine protagonist's parents is common, or earthly; the other, kingly, magical, or divine. J. K. Rowling's Harry Potter has the Dursleys, for example, and his actual mother and father, a witch and wizard of renown.[8] Superman, the hero of DC Comics has the earthly Kents, but also his true parents on the alien planet of his birth (and thus "in heaven"). Disney's Sleeping Beauty is raised in a forest, away from her rightful kingdom,[9] just like the young King Arthur, who spends his childhood tutored by Merlin among the common people.[10] A common fantasy of unhappy children is, similarly, that they are orphans, abandoned by a mother and father who will someday reappear and rescue them.[11] The use of such motifs is staggeringly common in the literary domain.[12]

What do these literary themes imply? That every human being is a child of Nature and Culture, or of Nature and God, even more so than of his or her own parents; that every child grows up alienated from his or her rightful kingdom, ensconced for some time among those too common to realize their true destiny or ancestry; that every child will be enticed by fear to hide his or her light under a bushel to disguise what is best about them, to avoid the attention of the tyrants who might otherwise be jealously provoked; and that the One True King must realize his transcendent parentage and grow in consequence to take his proper place of ultimate responsibility and destiny (as Simba does, for example, in Disney's *The Lion King*[13]). The dual parentage motif also dramatizes the fact that with maturity we must cease laying responsibility for the existential conditions of life at the feet of our parents, and assign instead to the broader forces of biology and society.

This realization better enables individuals to lift the burden of blame for the inequities of life from their parents, insofar as that is possible, given a just apportioning of causal attribution. This means to transfer both dependency on and allegiance to away from the earthly father, so to speak, to the heavenly father, and to do the same with regard to mother and nature. The advantage, in terms of maturity? Once a man is responsible to God, he will no longer feel compelled to labor under the thumb (or, indeed, the sins) of his father, or to take shelter under the wing of his mother. The same is of course true of women.

When Moses reaches maturity, he encounters an Egyptian beating an enslaved Hebrew (Exodus 2:11–14). He takes great offense to this act, regarding it as unjust and unwarranted, and kills the perpetrator. This decision to stand on the side of the oppressed is a manifestation of a particular vision of leadership, the full significance of which is revealed only in the New Testament: that what is truly sovereign serves mercy and justice, supports those in peril, and forswears the advantages of arbitrary and undeserved power and lineage, particularly when that has become tyrannical. This is a true transformation of understanding: it is much simpler to assume that both position and might make for justifiable privilege and true right. This nonetheless murderous act is something that both foreshadows and directly indicates Moses's fatal flaw: the tendency to employ force, when it is not strictly necessary, and to do so somewhat impulsively. What does this mean? No less than that temptation of power inevitably accompanies the responsibility of leadership, even among the greatest of men. It proves, in the final analysis, to be the great prophet's Achilles' heel (Numbers 20:7–12).

In consequence of this act, Moses finds it necessary to flee from Egypt, learning that knowledge of what he has done has spread, fearing (and rightfully so) the pharaoh's vengeance (Exodus 2:15). He journeys to a foreign land, Midian, resting when he arrives by the side of a well. This is another example of his relationship with the water that transforms, renews, and replenishes. There he meets the daughters of a local priest, who are being harassed and interfered with in their attempts to draw water by a group of shepherds. Moses chases the ruffians away and then draws water for the young women and their flock (Exodus 2:16–17). Moses therefore does for Midian's daughters in miniature what he eventually does for his entire people. This is brilliant and subtle foreshadowing. The daughters of Midian return home and tell their father what transpired at the well. He encourages them to find Moses and offer him a seat at the family table. This hospitality works out well for Moses, who cannot yet return to Egypt. He stays with Jethro, the Midian priest, and marries Zipporah, one of his daughters. Jethro later plays a key role in Moses's work, and in a manner emphasizing his wise and caring nature. It is often the case in the biblical corpus and in literature more generally that the foreigner can stand for the wisdom that remains in the world when the home state has become corrupt.

7.2. The fiery tree as revelation of being and becoming

Back in Egypt, the pharaoh dies, although the Israelites remain in bondage, crying to God in their misery. God hears these cries and remembers the covenant he made with Abraham, Isaac, and Jacob, noting in doing so that the Israelites have not lost faith. Meanwhile, Moses remains in exile, minding his own business. We might consider the erstwhile prophet content, at least for the moment. He is away from Egypt and its tyranny and slavery. He has slipped from the constraints of his own past, from the complexity of his dual heritage and juvenile misadventures. He is free from any danger of pursuit or revenge, happy in love, and surrounded by people who admire his courage and have determined to share their lives with his. He has, in short, established himself successfully as an adult, with all the attendant responsibilities and advantages. More specifically and tellingly, Moses has become a shepherd, taking care of Jethro's flocks. The biblical shepherd is a type of hero, as we have seen in chapter 3: he must face trying circumstances, alone with his flock, establish the way forward, keep the wolves and lions at bay and, more generally, provide the care for "the least of these" (see Matthew 25:31–46) that is the hallmark of truly legitimate authority. Moses has become a man, in the typical manner, successfully negotiating the transition from impulsive youth to responsible, although still somewhat ordinary, adult. That is indeed a step forward and a true accomplishment, but it is insufficient.

One day Moses is leading his sheep through the desert, when he comes near "the mountain of God, even to Horeb" (Exodus 3:1). This Horeb is also Mount Sinai,[14] which is the eternal place of Jacob's Ladder, the place where heaven reaches down and earth extends upward to meet it; the

place where the narrative and the material worlds touch; the place of significant coincidence, or synchronicity, where events fall into a meaningful pattern;[15] the place where the magical, miraculous, or transcendent reveals itself
within the imminent in the manner insisted upon in Matthew 7:7–8 (King
James Version):

> Ask, and it shall be given you; seek, and ye shall find; knock, and it
> shall be opened unto you:
>   For every one that asketh receiveth; and he that seeketh findeth;
> and to him that knocketh it shall be opened.

Also:

> Behold, I stand at the door, and knock: if any man hear my voice,
> and open the door, I will come in to him, and will sup with him, and
> he with me.
>
> *Revelation 3:20; Christ speaking*

The connection between Jacob's Ladder and Mount Sinai was made explicit in certain medieval midrashim (the traditional Jewish commentaries
on the Torah) in two ways: first, conceptually, as the ladder is in fact the
structure that connects the spiritual world, or heaven, to the material world,
or earth (and is in that manner the equivalent of the liana or the tree that
unites the two realms in the much more archaic and ancient Neolithic shamanic understanding[16]); second, from the perspective of numerology, as the
number of the letters of the word *ladder* are equivalent to those of *Sinai* (or the
Hebrew equivalents) and were therefore deemed equivalent in meaning.[17]

We can picture Moses alone in contemplation, taking note of something
anomalous; something that appeals to his curiosity, to his adventurous spirit.
It beckons to him at the edges of his attention. He decides to investigate—
to walk off the beaten path and to see what lies beyond the day-to-day
and predictable—what still remains, outside the mere normal goodness of
his now well-established life. What does this indicate? No less than that

Moses—and therefore the leader, as Moses is the archetypal leader—*is he who attends voluntarily to his calling.* A calling is perhaps best understood as a manifestation, both proximal and tangible, of the eternal covenant between God and his people. Why phrase it like that? Not least because that is how the phenomenon (from the Greek *phainesthai:* to shine forth) manifests itself. We all have problems that beset us, obsess us, will not leave us alone, will not leave us in peace, call to us to attend to and investigate. Insoluble mysteries and impassable obstacles litter the landscape. Why are we possessed by certain concerns and not others? Is it because some problems happen to be *our* problems—our responsibilities—and we are called by ineluctable instinct either to address them or to be plagued by them without end? Who is to say? It is certainly as accurate, existentially or phenomenologically, to note that our problems choose us as much as the reverse. Not only do they choose us but they often literally will not leave us alone.

> Now Moses kept the flock of Jethro his father in law, the priest of Midian: and he led the flock to the backside of the desert, and came to the mountain of God, even to Horeb.
>
> And the angel of the Lord appeared unto him in a flame of fire out of the midst of a bush: and he looked, and, behold, the bush burned with fire, and the bush was not consumed.
>
> And Moses said, I will now turn aside, and see this great sight, why the bush is not burnt.
>
> And when the Lord saw that he turned aside to see, God called unto him out of the midst of the bush, and said, Moses, Moses. And he said, Here am I.
>
> *Exodus 3:1-4*

The branching form of a bush or tree is a standard symbol of life[18] (hence, most famously, the tree of life).[19] Fire, for its part (as the bush is burning) is a manifestation of transformation. It is also something permanently numinous[20] and intrinsically attractive, dancing as it does constantly on the edge of predictability in its musical manner, compelling attention both conscious and unconscious, and inviting the interaction that has made human beings masters of fire instead of victims to its power. A burning bush is therefore an amalgam of three things: being, particularly the being that is living; the becoming associated with transformation; and the phenomenon which can be ignored only at great peril and with great effort. Everything alive burns. That is metabolism itself. The burning bush is, therefore, life, with the spirit within it—the spirit of being and becoming; the stability and transforming into authentic ultimate form that characterizes everything living; the spirit that lurks behind or makes itself partly known in virtually every encounter with what sparks our interest and compels us forward. The burning bush is the same thing as the living staff of Moses, that transforms itself into the serpent of possibility and chaos, when called upon to do so (Exodus 4:2–4 and 7:10–12), and that of Aaron, which bursts into life when the moment is right (Numbers 17:8).

Moses turns and approaches. He walks away from predictability—away from his current concerns and aims, and into the domain of possibility, or potential, itself. As he does so, the deeper levels of reality begin to make themselves manifest to him. This is always what happens, to a greater or lesser extent, to those who sincerely and seriously heed what beckons to them. This is the act of coming to consciousness itself. Take, for example, the genuinely committed scientist. Such an individual frequently finds himself irresistibly fascinated by some domain of inquiry, some set of phenomena that calls him forward—and often early in life. The pursuit begins, inquiry by inquiry, conversation by conversation, book by book. That interest typically converges on a single point, a specialization, as the now-entranced investigator begins legitimately training in the scientific enterprise. The doctoral degree signifying expertise in a given field of sufficient quality to be regarded as both valid and original is the conventional marker of such study, successfully undertaken, and the beginning of the narrow but deep pursuit that will characterize the life of the persistent seeker.

I wrote my PhD thesis and its associated papers about the problem of male alcoholism—and, more specifically, about the response to an acute and intoxicating dose of alcohol. Even more particularly: my research team investigated the effect of such a dose on emotional response, both negative and positive, both baseline (elevation of resting mood) and provoked (reduced anxiety in the face of minor threat). This was very focused research: a tremendous amount of attention pinpointed on a very specific problem. The research team I was associated with (led by my graduate adviser, Dr. Robert O. Pihl) studied males only between the ages of eighteen and twenty-four. These subjects had to be social drinkers rather than teetotalers or alcoholics. Their mothers had to be nonalcoholic (heavy-drinking mothers often have children with fetal alcohol syndrome, subtle or fully manifest, and this poses a complication for the causal analysis of the mechanisms of familial transmission.) Our all-male subjects also had to have biological fathers, grandfathers, and at least one other first-degree alcoholic relative on the paternal side. What is the old joke? The specialist studies less and less until he ends up knowing absolutely everything about nothing at all. There is some cynical truth to such a criticism, but the opposite is more genuinely true, if the restriction of focus is something done in genuine pursuit of the truth.

In keeping with this, I soon found that my knowledge broadened tremendously, as I made my concern more precise and specific. This speaks to the relationship among aim, attention, and the growth of wisdom. To study alcoholism, I had to study the much more general proclivity to drug abuse and dependence. This meant familiarizing myself, in addition, with the realm of emotion and motivation, including their neurobiological underpinnings, as it is the primary emotional and motivational systems that are affected by drugs typical of abuse. This investigation eventually extended to an analysis of the mechanisms of perception itself. As I approached the target of my inquiry, therefore—"what is it about the response to alcohol of someone with a paternal lineage characterized by extensive and severe alcoholism that might differ from the norm and motivate the development of the disorder?":—my knowledge widened, until the one thing I was attending to in great detail began to make its connections with the entire world known.

What had I learned about learning itself, in addition to the specific knowledge I obtained during my quest? That those who attend assiduously to their focal "narrow" concerns will first journey deeper and deeper into the narrowly defined unknown at hand, learning first the details directly relevant to those concerns, but soon after coming to understand the broader webs of associations and causal pathways that are inevitably part of the phenomenon in question. Nothing exists in isolation. Anything studied with sufficient depth thus eventually comes to speak of everything. It is precisely this deepening and broadening that Moses experiences from his encounter with the burning bush. He continues his investigation in all due humility, attending diligently to what is so mysteriously being revealed. Tellingly, he removes his footwear. And God said, "Draw not nigh hither: put off thy shoes from off thy feet, for the place whereon thou standest is holy ground" (Exodus 3:5). What does it mean to approach and then stand upon holy ground—and to do so, moreover, unshod? It means, first, to get close to the bottom of things; to begin to apprehend or understand the foundation of things; to approach the depths (or the heights). It means, second, to do so allowing all the while for transformation of purpose and identity.

Shoes signify class, occupation, purpose, role, and destiny. Consider, for example, Cinderella's glass slippers,[21] or the role Dorothy's ruby shoes play in the Wizard of Oz,[22] or the "seven-league boots" of the European folk tradition, which enable the wearer to travel great distances with a single step.[23] To remove the current shoes is to abandon the present role, to make contact once again with the ground of being, and to prepare for the next step. To pursue what calls most deeply away from the present and toward that next step is to transform with the calling. The sequential transformation attendant on such calling is the adventure of life, as we saw in the cases of Abram, Sarai, and Jacob. The calling is also the invitation to leadership, as a man so transformed becomes charismatic in his commitment and depth; becomes the man whose actions will be attended to and whose words will be heeded. Moses takes seriously, even devoutly, that which glimmers and glistens and captures his attention. This puts him in touch with the deepest manifestations of the spirit on whose operation the world indeed depends.

The spirit of God calls to Moses from the depths. What does that notion of "depth" used in such a manner signify? The existence of an intrinsic hierarchy of import. Some things mean more than others. Some things are of a deeper import than others. We understand this intrinsically in the conversational, relational, and literary domains. We can engage with someone else in a shallow or a profound manner. We can have a conversation that is trivial or one that is memorable and moving. Someone with whom we habitually have moving conversations, or other deep communicative interactions, is someone with whom we have a deep relationship. We see the same thing reflected in the notion of literary depth. Some stories (novels, movies, biographical accounts) are light and trivial, the sort of mere entertainment that requires no effort, is satisfying in the short term, and has no lasting effect. Some works, by contrast, strike to the heart and change their readers or watchers on some permanent, even revolutionary, basis. There is a hierarchy of dependency in presumption of belief, as we indicated in our analysis of the story of the Tower of Babel.[24] Some ideas are shallow. They can be moved, displaced, or even ignored with very little consequence. Others (often those "taken for granted") are very deep, which means that very many other ideas depend on them for their continued validity.

Consider the issue of depth in a prosaic situation. Imagine a married couple addressing the issue of who does the dishes and who sets the table on a given Saturday evening with dinner guests. It might be hoped that such a negotiation is relatively trivial. Why? Because not much depends on its outcome; because variance in such outcome (whether it is husband or wife who undertakes one task or the other) is likely to have little effect on the marriage as a whole, past, present, and future. Consider, by contrast, the decision by one party to take one of the dinner guests aside for a wild and sudden sexual encounter—or, even more profoundly, to initiate a continuing affair, consisting of a sequence of such encounters. When discovered, such a move is virtually certain to rock the relationship to the foundation; to put all the meaning of the past into question ("Who exactly am I married to?"), to destabilize the present ("What exactly is going on here?!"), and to make of the future a threatening indeterminate chaos ("What in the world do we do with each other now?).

The integrity of the marriage contract, with all its anxiety-reducing and hope-producing or -maintaining functions, is not typically called into question by a brief conflict over who takes responsibility for what particular domestic task. Partner fidelity, by contrast, is an axiom of "we take these truths as self-evident"[25] depth: a marriage and all it entails is defined by certain contractual absolutes, and lack of extramarital sexual and emotional involvement is almost inevitably one of them. It is in fact in many ways the defining, or central, feature of the permanent intimate pairing that makes up marriage as such—or at least one of a mere handful of such central features. It is the core value on which all other values characterizing marriage depend. If fidelity vanishes, everything shakes. That is precisely what defines depth in the psychological and practical sense: the deeper an idea, the more other ideas depend on it. The deeper an axiom of contract or understanding, in other words, the more memories of the past, perceptions of the present, and plans for the future are shaped by it. Thus, the more profound the element of contract, the more anxiety is disinhibited and hope eliminated when betrayal occurs.[26] This is the return of the entropy of the psychophysiological theorists,[27] and the great dragon of chaos of the mythological universe.[28]

We therefore all approach sacred territory when we descend deeply (or ascend profoundly) into what calls to us. The sacred is that which moves us when we encounter it: that which produces awe in its apprehension; that which enlightens, cuts and burns away, and transforms. The transforming power of the depths is identical to the Logos that broods upon the deep, separates wheat from chaff and sheep from goats, and turns every which way as gatekeeper to Eden. Moses is instructed to further humble himself as he moves closer to the truth; as he moves closer to contact with the ground of being and becoming itself—and he does so. The place toward which Moses is advancing, as he continues in pursuit of what beckons to him, becomes increasingly holy, as it deepens—by definition. Eventually, in the culmination of this part of his adventure, he discovers the same unified spirit that had previously called to his ancestors: "Moreover he said, I am the God of thy father, the God of Abraham, the God of Isaac, and the God of Jacob. And Moses hid his face; for he was afraid to look upon God" (Exodus 3:6). That continued humility in pursuit of the depths is also the hallmark of the true investigator and adventurer: the willingness to drop all pretensions to knowledge and moral wisdom in pursuit of the truth is the precondition for further enlightenment. This is the equivalent in abstraction of the removal of the shoes that signifies acceptance of transformation of identity. Moses has immolated his previous self on the altar of renewal. The divine itself speaks to him out of the ashes. This is the phoenix, reborn, whose tears are the medication against the gaze of the paralyzing basilisk.[29]

It is precisely those who have honestly pursued what calls to them who get to the bottom of things. It is those who come to understand ever more deeply what lays itself out in front of them. It is such people who are apt to become genuine leaders—to become those to whom others will voluntarily turn, particularly in times of crisis. This is because they have discovered in their truthful pursuit what is necessary to know, but that others refuse to or simply do not yet know. It is the ability to give word to the vagaries of now and to lay out a compelling direction into the future that constitutes leadership— and the genuine article, not the counterfeit that uses fear and compulsion. Those who have looked deeply into things become those who speak with the strange and marked authority attributed so frequently to Christ himself, as in the following passage, which follows the Sermon on the Mount: "And it came to pass, when Jesus had ended these sayings, the people were astonished at his doctrine: For he taught them as one having authority, and not as the scribes" (Matthew 7:28–29). This sentiment is echoed elsewhere: "And they went into Capernaum; and straightway on the sabbath day he entered into the synagogue, and taught. And they were astonished at his doctrine: for he taught them as one that had authority, and not as the scribes" (Mark 1:21–22). Jesus wields the authority of one who has done the work and truly knows. He therefore speaks with the unshakeable and undecorated confidence that deadly serious inquiry and complete consequent transformation of idea and character confers: "But let your communication be, Yea, yea; Nay, nay: for whatsoever is more than these cometh of evil" (Matthew 5:37). It is for such reasons that Moses's destiny as a leader becomes ever more inexorably manifest as his encounter with the burning bush continues:

And the Lord said, I have surely seen the affliction of my people which are in Egypt, and have heard their cry by reason of their task-masters; for I know their sorrows;

And I am come down to deliver them out of the hand of the Egyptians, and to bring them up out of that land unto a good land and a large, unto a land flowing with milk and honey; unto the place of the Canaanites, and the Hittites, and the Amorites, and the Per-izzites, and the Hivites, and the Jebusites.

Now therefore, behold, the cry of the children of Israel is come unto me: and I have also seen the oppression wherewith the Egyp-tians oppress them.

Come now therefore, and I will send thee unto Pharaoh, that thou mayest bring forth my people the children of Israel out of Egypt.

Exodus 3:7–10

The leader is eternally the individual with the fortitude to stand against the tyrant, to speak the words that cannot be resisted—to lead the enslaved through the desert of uncertainty to the promised land. Moses, who has some real humility, does not believe that he is the man for the job. It is fre-quently the case those dramatically unsuited for "power" will pursue it for little more than narrowly serving and self-aggrandizing reasons. It is a dif-ferent matter when someone's leadership is requested by those who feel they would be well served by it; and it is a different matter entirely when the transformation attendant on intent seeking produces a character so compel-ling that leadership now seems destined or preordained. In the final analy-sis, however, the insufficiencies of ability and defects of character that typify even those who are chosen as spokesmen for the divine are not accepted by God as an excuse for failure to act. What are we to make of this? No more than this: We must all do the best we can with the talents that have been granted to us, and in spite of our multitude of faults, real and imaginary. Moses is therefore enjoined by God to claim his lineage; to proclaim kinship with Abraham, Isaac, and Jacob; and to take his place in the continuum of great prophets:

> And God said unto Moses, I AM THAT I AM: and he said, Thus shalt thou say unto the children of Israel, I AM hath sent me unto you.
>
> And God said moreover unto Moses, Thus shalt thou say unto the children of Israel, The Lord God of your fathers, the God of Abraham, the God of Isaac, and the God of Jacob, hath sent me unto you: this is my name for ever, and this is my memorial unto all generations.
>
> Go, and gather the elders of Israel together, and say unto them, The Lord God of your fathers, the God of Abraham, of Isaac, and of Jacob, appeared unto me, saying, I have surely visited you, and seen that which is done to you in Egypt.
>
> *Exodus 3:14–16*

The true leader must ally himself with the leading spirits of the past. He must come to embody—to stand for and speak for—the same principles that guided those who made the world, in the beginning, whether God or man. Otherwise he becomes the idiot puppet of his own desires or weakness, or, as happens to Aaron, brother of Moses, of the careless whims of the people (Exodus 32: 1–35). This is standing with the past is the motif of "rescuing the father from the belly of the beast"; the equivalent portrayed in recent times in Disney's film *Pinocchio*, when the marionette frees the good Geppetto from the belly of the whale—from the depths;[30] in *The Lion King*, as well, where the metaphor of what is properly put at the pinnacle is employed, instead of what is foundational.[31] The hero of that movie, Simba, has a vision of his father in the sky, assimilated by the sun. The resurrected Mufasa then tells his son of his identity, and his destiny: to abandon his present state of slavish subjection to his carelessly present-focused adolescent whims and adopt the responsibility to face the usurping tyrant, Scar, the resentful evil brother of the king. This vision and voice comes to him at the deepest point of his initial journey downward—something that was in turn both begun and guided by the shaman Rafiki, who uses his living rod of authority to rap Simba on the head to get his attention.

It is in this manner that the young lion comes to embody the spirit of the father, as such, which is the benevolent source of all that is good in the particulars of any given father. Simba determines not to invite in the spirit of bitter murderous resentment who conspires with Cain, as his uncle Scar clearly does. Instead, he determines to open himself up to the indwelling of the Holy Spirit. By definition. In consequence, he lets go of the past, sets his aim upward, gets his house in order, and heads voluntarily for the land of the tyrant for the ultimate confrontation. This is exactly what befalls Moses—or that he invites and enables—in the course of his off-the-beaten-track encounter with the burning bush. Such stories indicate and insist, as well, that the true leader is also not a revolutionary. He is instead someone who reestablishes the genuine covenant, or contract, that has always guided mankind. He is instead someone who brings his spirit into alignment with what has always been great. He is, therefore, someone who renews, rather than someone who shatters and then too radically and hubristically reshapes; someone who can identify and reserve what is truly nourishing and offer it once again for mass consumption. Such a figure only has as a revolutionary mien when the society against which he is standing has forgotten so much and become so corrupt that the good now makes itself manifest as a shocking revelation.

It is in all these manners that the genuine leader comes to speaks with the eternal voice of the Great Father, and to offer the bread and water that satisfies all hunger and slakes all thirst. He is also the man who leads his people from tyranny and slavery—albeit through the desert—to the promised land. Such tyranny and slavery can and does exist at every level of the psychological and social hierarchy: we tyrannize ourselves and are the craven servants of our own desires; we kowtow to or tyrannize over our wives, husbands, children, siblings, and friends. We set up our enterprises so that we can exercise power over the slaves we hire and exploit; we seek political office so that the influence we crave can be brought to serve the narrow self-interests that

possess us. True leadership—true character, more deeply—always and everywhere means opposition to the tyrant and the slave and, more deeply, to
the spirits that animate both. Such movement away from the enticements of
power and subjection is, eternally, the journey to the promised land: "And I
have said, I will bring you up out of the affliction of Egypt unto the land of
the Canaanites, and the Hittites, and the Amorites, and the Perizzites, and
the Hivites, and the Jebusites, unto a land flowing with milk and honey"
(Exodus 3:17).

God defines himself in his pronouncement to Moses as the principle of
being and becoming itself. There is substantive disagreement about the meaning of the Hebrew phrase contained within the story, in part because of its in-
determinacy regarding time. However, all of its various potentially valid
interpretations serve to flesh out the character in question—the One who
says, "I am who I am," "I will become what I choose to become," I am the
One Who Exists," "I am the Being," "I will become whatever I please," "I
create whatever I create," or "I will be what I will be." Even "who" is more
complex than a single translation might indicate: the meaning of the Hebrew
word *ăšer* is context dependent and can be read as *that, which,* and, *where.*[32]
All this variation is perhaps accurately understood as an appropriately
multidimensional characterization of the ultimate bedrock of reality. That
bedrock cannot be mere being, as *what is* constantly changes and transmutes.
Neither can it be mere random becoming, as the future is constrained by
the past enough so that a certain degree of predictability inevitably and
blessedly reigns (sometimes and with some things more than others).

God presents Himself, arguably, as the spirit behind both being and becoming; as the spirit of divine creativity itself; as the ultimate ground of reality; as that which is behind mere appearance (whether of past, present, or
future); as that which is immutable across the flow of time. Along with this
description or revelation comes the insistence that those who do not bow
down to this ultimate principle will suffer or be destroyed (or worse), regardless of their earthly status, and that the proper state is the one ruled by respect for and fidelity to what is most real. Thomas Aquinas conceived of the
universe, in keeping with this formulation, as a series of stepping stones ar-

ranged in ascending order from lowest to highest—shades of Jacob's Ladder—
at once crowned and created by God. Matter manifests itself in form;
existence—that is, human experience—plays out the possibility of essence.
God, by definition (and by self-definition in the Book of Exodus), is the underlying union of the two. God, the *Actus Purus*,[33] is the pattern of action
that is necessarily reflected by any given act (that makes that act an act); the
perfection that makes all things that reflect perfection possible (not least, all
things beautiful); the being and becoming that is in common to all things
that exist and emerge.

Perhaps a musical analogy might be helpful. Every piece of music shares
something in common, which might be regarded as the principle, or spirit,
of music. Every manifestation of this spirit makes itself known in a given
musical work that when played has a certain predictability and constancy as
well as a certain element of surprise. Each composition is thus a manifestation of the balance between being or order and becoming and chaos and, simultaneously, a manifestation of the deeper principle that eternally allows
those two domains to play. Each musical piece also fleshes out, or gives form
to, one element of the universe of potential musical forms. That universe is
also a kind of reality; a kind of "heavenly" or implicit reality; the reality of
possible forms, reflecting the full range of variation that defines music itself.
The cosmos, likewise, unfolds according to a set of principles that, if finally
noncontradictory, mutually commensurate and supporting, reflect an Ultimate Principle. The intuition of this idea drives the continual scientific
striving for a grand unified theory, free of internal contradictions. Such aim
also defines the cultural endeavor, broadly speaking: the "bringing together"
that is a necessary precondition to any social organization, at any level; family, community, city, state. This something very much akin to the drive toward
pathologically integrating ideology (in the worst case), metanarrative, or an
increasingly valid and productive unifying monotheism.

How could the world be any other way? How could reality be a plurality
without dissolving continually into an impossible warring chaos? How could
any pathway be forged forward in the presence of a fundamental disintegration? Furthermore and equally: How could adaptation to reality require

anything other than the deepest alignment or even embodiment of the deepest unifying principle of reality? If what is eternal and unchanging and therefore most reliable is the proper bedrock—and it is, by definition—then what transmutes in time or place cannot be properly regarded as what is most real. Thus, it will also be necessary in times of trouble to return to the foundation. Granted, it is no simple matter to determine what remains constant across the endless transformations of life, but it is clearly the case that a certain central constancy allows both for the maintenance of direction (toward that constancy) and the constraint of anxiety, which is a condition that manifests itself as a consequence of unforeseen change. We want constancy in what is crucial from our wives or husbands, our children, our friends—and from the world itself. We cannot be oriented without that central constancy. It is in keeping with this that the first of three responses given by God to Moses also implies a statement of incomparability ("I am without equal") and a covenant ("I will be with you").[34]

7.3. Return to the tyrannical kingdom

God warns Moses that the pharaoh will not easily accede to the demand for freedom. He will instead double down, as is the wont of tyrants. God also tells Moses that the reward of passing through the evil king's trials will be magnified, even by the fact of the latter's inevitable intransigence. There is more than a hint here that forthright resistance in the face of severe opposition may well turn the tide. It is even possible to imagine that the fact of the pharaoh's resistance is a great benefit to Moses, and that the opposition faced by the prophet does nothing in the final analysis—or all things considered—but redound to his benefit, and that of his people.

> And I will give this people favor in the sight of the Egyptians: and it shall come to pass, that, when ye go, ye shall not go empty:
> But every woman shall borrow of her neighbor, and of her that sojourneth in her house, jewels of silver, and jewels of gold, and rai-

ment: and ye shall put them upon your sons, and upon your daughters; and ye shall spoil the Egyptians.

Exodus 3:21–22

It is of course the most ancient idea that the treasure eternally sought by
the hero is guarded by a terrible dragon. Sometimes, perhaps, the treasure is
obvious, and the dragon lurking. The reverse should be equally true: when a
dragon appears, there is treasure to be found somewhere, if enough care is
taken to look, and enough faith manifested to make the search possible. This
is a very good thing to understand in times of trouble.

The text describing the despoiling of the Egyptians makes an analogous
point: When a society becomes tyrannical and turns to evil, it will leave all
of its true treasures on the table, available for those who determine no longer
to be slaves to take to themselves. Thus when the tyrannical state turns away
from the highest and proper aim, those that inhabit it can no longer distinguish truth from falsehood, justice from betrayal, the beautiful from the
hideous, or the valuable from the utterly worthless. When the state has given
itself over entirely to the lie, what is left for the faithful is self-evidently all
that is true and good. This means that the great value constituted by those
virtues can be gathered by those who desire to move forward and to be
free—free, that is, in the manner that true freedom must necessarily be conceptualized. This is not the hedonistic anarchy of immaturity, but the ordered freedom of the properly sacrificing and mature—the celebration, or
worship, of God in the desert that Moses offers to the captive Israelites as the
alternative to the tyranny of Egypt—and to slavery itself.

God warns his nascent prophet that the pharaoh will prove a tough nut to
crack, given his arrogance and power. He therefore grants to Moses the ability to perform magic, most notably with the crook, rod, or pointer his servant has heretofore used to guide his flocks. He instructs Moses to cast that
trusty walking stick to the ground, where "it became a serpent; and Moses
fled from before it. And the Lord said unto Moses, Put forth thine hand, and
take it by the tail. And he put forth his hand, and caught it, and it became a
rod in his hand" (Exodus 4:3–4). This act places Moses in the role of arbiter

of order, signified by the staff, which is something to rest or rely on—something that guides proper following or conduct (as when used to correct the actions of a wayward lamb). His staff is, as well, transformed into the agent of transformation and renewal. Thus, he can take what can be leaned on, what is solid—what can be used for guidance and support—and turn it into what is chaotic, subtle, hidden, dangerous, fluid, and transmutes. This makes him the master of the serpent/tree dynamic that is equivalent to the burning bush (transformation in the midst of living order) and the essence of the trees that stand in the midst of the eternal garden. Tellingly, God instructs Moses to engender the process of transformation in the manner that is most dangerous and that therefore requires the highest degree of faith: he is commanded to seize the serpent not by the head, which is clearly the safe thing to do (insofar as there is any safe way to grab a potentially poisonous snake), but by the tail. This is part of the insistence throughout Exodus that redemption is found through continual voluntary exposure to that which is threatening.

This staff, or rod, of Moses represents a continuation of the extremely ancient and foundational idea of the cosmic center. Mircea Eliade comments on the importance of the pole that signifies the center to a tribal group of the original inhabitants of Australia:

> According to the traditions of an Arunta tribe, the Achilpa, in mythical times the divine being Numbakula cosmicized their future territory, created their Ancestor, and established their institutions. From the trunk of a gum tree Numbakula fashioned the sacred pole (*kauwa-auwa*) and, after anointing it with blood, climbed it and disappeared into the sky. This pole represents a cosmic axis, for it is around the sacred pole that territory becomes habitable, hence is transformed into a world. The sacred pole consequently plays an important role ritually. During their wanderings the Achilpa always carry it with them and choose the direction they are to take by the direction toward which it bends. This allows them, while being continually on the move, to be always in "their world" and, at the same

time, in communication with the sky into which Numbakula vanished. For the pole to be broken denotes catastrophe; it is like "the end of the world," reversion to chaos. Spencer and Gillen report that once, when the pole was broken, the entire clan were in consternation; they wandered about aimlessly for a time, and finally lay down on the ground together and waited for death to overtake them.[35]

This staff, or rod, that defines the center is another representation of Jacob's Ladder or the holy mountain that unites heaven and earth. It is the tree that the ancient shamans climbed in their ritual attempts to attain the wisdom of the gods. It is the cosmic axis that stretches upward to the North Star, around which the entire visible cosmos rotates and that has been used since time immemorial as a means of orientation and navigation. Is it the beanstalk of *Jack and the Beanstalk*, a pillar that reaches up to the land of the giant where the greatest of all possible treasures is held. It is the ideal around which all perception of all things is organized; on which even the margin depends for its existence, protected as it is by that center—that ideal—however invisibly, from the chaos that sweeps everything away.[36] It is the midst of the city, the point of a ziggurat or pyramid, the dome of a cathedral, the spire of a church. It is the stabilizing effect of the spirit of the ancients on what could all too-rapidly become the demented consensus of the present. Its importance cannot be overstated: it is the traditional indicator and representative of the cosmic order itself.[37]

Until their conversion to Christianity, the Celts and Germans still maintained their worship of such sacred pillars. . . . The same cosmological image is found not only among the Romans and in ancient India, where we hear of the skambha, the cosmic pillar, but also among the Canary Islanders and in such distant cultures as those of the Kwakiutl and of the Nad'a of Flores Island.

The Kwakiutl believe that a copper pole passes through the three cosmic levels; the point at which it enters the sky is the "door to the world above." The . . . work of the gods, the universe, is repeated and imitated by men on their own scale. The axis mundi, seen in the sky the form of the Milky Way, appears in the ceremonial house in the form of a sacred pole. It is the trunk of a Cedar tree, thirty to thirty-five feet high, over half of which projects through the roof. This pillar plays a primary part in the ceremonies; it confers a cosmic structure on the house. In the ritual songs the house is called "our world" and the candidates for initiation, who live in it, proclaim: "I am at the Center of the World; I am at the Post of the World," and so on. The same assimilation of the cosmic pillar to the sacred pole and of the ceremonial house to the universe is found among the Nad'a of Flores Island. The sacrificial pole is called the "Pole of Heaven" and is believed to support the sky.[38]

In keeping with this provision of word and artful play, God gives Moses with the ability to perform other miracles: "And the Lord said furthermore unto him, Put now thine hand into thy bosom. And he put his hand into his bosom: and when he took it out, behold, his hand was leprous as snow. And he said, Put thine hand into thy bosom again. And he put his hand into his bosom again; and plucked it out of his bosom, and, behold, it was turned again as his other flesh" (Exodus 4:6–7). Moses is granted the ability to play at the interface between sickness and health. This is in keeping with the rod/snake symbolism. The staff, or rod, of Asclepius (a Greek example) is the al-most universal symbol of the medical profession. The physician Galen, one of the most accomplished medical researchers of antiquity, specifically asso-ciated the Asclepian rod with the staff/serpent of Moses:

> The serpent is placed on the staff because it is a creature that is very long-lived and very healthy, and because it is said to have the power to renew its youth by casting its skin. The staff represents the sup-port that Asclepius gives to those who are sick, and the serpent rep-resents the power of healing that he possesses. . . .
>
> The staff of Aesculapius is derived from the brazen serpent that Moses made, and which was placed on a pole in the desert. The Isra-

elites who looked at the brazen serpent were cured of the bites of the serpents that God had sent to punish them.[39]

We will return to the serpent/staff motif later.[40] Suffice it to say for now that, finally, Moses is granted the ability to transform water into blood, the very stuff of life: "And it shall come to pass, if they will not believe also these two signs, neither hearken unto thy voice, that thou shalt take of the water of the river, and pour it upon the dry land: and the water which thou takest out of the river shall become blood upon the dry land" (Exodus 4:9). This third miracle establishes the pattern: one is a fluke, two is suggestive, and three is rhetorically convincing—memorable—perhaps because three repetitions takes the observer out of the realm of ignorable randomness and chance.[41] This means that Moses has been given compelling proof of the magic he might wield if he chooses the path of the leader. Nonetheless—despite his direct experience of the depth and the magic at hand, he remains uncertain, beset by doubt. This is another response that should arouse sympathy rather than the judgment that castigates in the imagination of the astute and careful reader. We would all like to think that if faced directly with a miracle or two or three, we would immediately become resolute and implacable in all things; would become upward-aiming and devout followers of God. We are simply not that faithful however, being instead just as stubborn and hard of heart as the pharaoh; just as likely to stick to our tyranny in whatever domain of power we have managed to establish, however trivial and small-scale it might be. If in all our corrupt striving we have not managed to ensnare some inno- cent others, we can at least tyrannize our petty subjective selves, rejecting information that would be inconvenient to assimilate, however necessary it might be to save the sanity of those around us and to protect our equally vulnerable future selves. It should therefore be easy to have some sympathy for Moses and his doubt.

The would-be prophet is still concerned that neither the Egyptians nor the Israelites will find anything he says remotely credible, much less com- pelling enough to produce a social transformation. He expresses his doubt, starting, in all humility (or perhaps in fear) with his reservations about him-

WE WHO WRESTLE WITH GOD

self: "And Moses said unto the Lord, O my Lord, I am not eloquent, neither heretofore, nor since thou hast spoken unto thy servant: but I am slow of speech, and of a slow tongue" (Exodus 4:10). It is unsurprising that a man of limited rhetorical gifts harbors misgivings about his prospects as a leader. How can you lead when your capacity to communicate is questionable? It might well be objected, however (as God almost immediately does), that the chosen prophet is overestimating the necessity in leadership for glib fluency and underestimating the impact of the divine truth, however haltingly uttered. This is in addition to the aforementioned fact[42] that there is no valid excuse for failing to move forward, when we are called to, regardless of our personal shortcomings or faults. God therefore reprimands Moses for his lack of faith—or encourages him, depending on your point of view: "And the Lord said unto him, Who hath made man's mouth? or who maketh the dumb, or deaf, or the seeing, or the blind? have I not the Lord? Now therefore go, and I will be with thy mouth, and teach thee what thou shalt say" (Exodus 4:11–12). What does it mean to speak with the words of God? Have we not all met people who perhaps do not say too much but whose gravitas, depth, and sincerity are such that all who hear listen and consider?

The divine reveals to Moses another truth: no one could or should do what the now-specified leader of the Israelites will be attempting—the undertaking of the grand adventure of his life—alone. Even though he has been chosen by God to lead, there is plenty left for everyone else to do, just as there was, for example, for Lot, Sarai, and the other allies and compatriots of Abram. God therefore tells Moses to ally himself with his brother, Aaron, who has the gift of a golden tongue:

Is not Aaron the Levite thy brother? I know that he can speak well. And also, behold, he cometh forth to meet thee: and when he seeth thee, he will be glad in his heart.

And thou shalt speak unto him, and put words in his mouth: and I will be with thy mouth, and with his mouth, and will teach you what ye shall do.

And he shall be thy spokesman unto the people: and he shall be,
even he shall be to thee instead of a mouth, and thou shalt be to him
instead of God.

Exodus 4:14–16

Aaron, who becomes the political arm of Moses and his mission, has his
place, as much as his more divinely connected brother—and a place which if
occupied to the utmost would become as important as the role played by Moses
himself. The world is apparently constituted such that each participant in it
could and should play a central role. Thus, all would-be saviors (including those
who are genuine) must realize that every other person also has a cross to bear
and world to redeem. We are all charged with the necessity to do the best we can,
no matter what, with all the talents granted to us, in spite of our multitude of
faults, whether real or imaginary. We must as well ally ourselves with people we
can trust and who bring to the table what we know we lack, so that we can properly shoulder our full responsibility in concert with all upward-aiming others.

There is thus more than enough for everyone to do while journeying together toward the promised land. To put in another way: the great adventure
of any one person does not interfere with the equally great potential adventure of all others. Instead, exemplary action on the part of one does nothing
but increase the opportunity of others. The world we inhabit is no mere
zero-sum game. The *tohu va bohu* that surrounds us and out of which order
constantly emerges is instead vast enough so that there is plenty to go
around, and more than enough room for all, "In my Father's house are many
mansions," Christ tells his disciples (John 14:2), indicating with deadly pre-
cision the inexhaustible quality of the properly established heavenly order.
Moses is therefore commanded by God to take up his mantle; enjoined to
claim his lineage—to accept his kinship with Abraham, Isaac, and Jacob;
and to take his place in the continuum of great prophets:

And God said unto Moses, I AM THAT I AM: and he said, Thus
shalt thou say unto the children of Israel, I AM hath sent me
unto you.

And God said moreover unto Moses, Thus shalt thou say unto the children of Israel, The Lord God of your fathers, the God of Abraham, the God of Isaac, and the God of Jacob, hath sent me unto you: this is my name for ever, and this is my memorial unto all generations.

Go, and gather the elders of Israel together, and say unto them, The Lord God of your fathers, the God of Abraham, of Isaac, and of Jacob, appeared unto me, saying, I have surely visited you, and seen that which is done to you in Egypt.

Exodus 3:14–16

This sharing by Aaron of the burden of Moses is our first indication of the principle of subsidiarity. That is the distribution of responsibility down the social hierarchy to every level of community—married couple, family, town, state, and nation—that is the only genuinely viable alternative to the stony prison of tyranny, or crimson chaos, and desert; the only true replacement for the king constantly clamored for by the irresponsible people of Israel (Samuel 1:8) but who also poses the most serious of dangers to their true psychological and social maturity and integrity.

7.4. Back to the land of doubling down

With the details now arranged, and his support staff in hand (both in the form of magic rod and Aaron), Moses agrees to return to Egypt. God warns him of the difficulty awaiting: "And the Lord said unto Moses, When thou goest to return into Egypt, see that thou do all those wonders before Pharaoh, which I have put in thine hand: but I will harden his heart, that he shall not let the people go" (Exodus 4:21). Further, this kingly resistance will be severe: "And thou shalt say unto Pharaoh, Thus saith the Lord, Israel is my son, even my firstborn: And I say unto thee, Let my son go, that he may serve me: and if thou refuse to let him go, behold, I will slay thy son, even thy firstborn" (Exodus 4:23). It is of course paradoxical that the very God who is commanding Moses to confront the pharaoh and lead his enslaved people to freedom is the same force that is simultaneously hardening the heart of the tyrant. The authors of this account refused to shy away from the complex oppositions inherent in life: a monotheistic and all-powerful God is behind everything that happens. The mere fact that this omnipresence is not always comprehensible to human beings, given their limited scope of apprehension, does not eliminate the necessity of attributing to God all authority, including that which seems to run counter to his character, as currently understood.

The tendency of the tyrant's heart to harden when challenged appears to be part of the intrinsic nature of being (and, therefore, something attributable in the final analysis to God) given the high probability of that occurrence, and the persistence of the trait across time. Why that might be is an important question to answer; but admitting that it is the case is equally important (and might even be the precursor to answering the question of why). We might speculate, poetically or metaphorically: Does eternal justice dictate that the punishment must fit the crime? If so, those who have persisted in their malfeasance (and have therefore set themselves up to deserve harsher recrimination) are also of their own accord more prone to stick stubbornly to their misbehavior when challenged, or even to further instantiate that very stubbornness in the face of challenge, rather than to admit to error and change. Is it not in the very nature of tyranny to respond to correction with ever more insistent refusal? It is for this reason that the tyrant doubles down; for this reason that he is symbolically allied with the kingdom of stone—and the savior who redeems and transforms associated, by contrast, with the living water. From the *Tao Te Ching*:

There is nothing more yielding than water,
yet when acting on the solid and strong,
its gentleness and fluidity
have no equal in any thing.
The weak can overcome the strong,
and the supple overcome the hard.

Although this is known far and wide,
few put it into practice in their lives.
Although seemingly paradoxical,
the person who takes upon himself,
the people's humiliation,
is fit to rule;
and he is fit to lead,
who takes the country's disasters upon himself.[43]

After his encounter with the burning bush—after receiving the revelations thus imparted—Moses informs his father-in-law, Jethro, of his intention to return to Egypt with his wife and sons, and departs with his blessing. They all sojourn, along with Moses's brother, back to the kingdom of the pharaoh, where Aaron relates what has transpired to the Israelites. The strength of his words, the accompanying signs performed by Moses, and the oppressed Israelites' fundamental desire for salvation work together to convince the people that the time for their freedom has come. Moses meets with the pharaoh and utters, for the first time, the famous line, "Let my people go." (Exodus 5:1). But that is not all he says. The remainder is not only equally relevant—the very meaning of the first section depends upon it. Moses says, more completely, "Thus saith the Lord God of Israel, Let my people go, that they may hold a feast unto me in the wilderness" (Exodus 5:1). This means first, that this is not a request from Moses, which can be easily ignored (given that it derives from one relatively powerless man), but from the source of being and becoming itself; second, that freedom and the cessation of tyranny is intrinsically desired, at least by those who wrestle with God; and third (and most easily and conveniently overlooked), that such freedom is to be given not even for the virtues of freedom in and of itself but so that the people so freed can "hold a feast" unto God "in the wilderness."

Alternative versions put it this way: "Let my people go, so that they may hold a festival in my honor in the wilderness" (New Living Translations); "Let my people go, so that they may celebrate a feast to Me in the wilderness" (New American Standard Bible); "Let my people go into the desert, so they can honor me with a celebration there" (Contemporary English Version);

"Let my people go, that they may hold a feast to me in the wilderness" (Douay-Rheims Bible); "Let my people go so they may make a pilgrimage for me in the desert" (International Standard Version). It is worthwhile attending to the similarities and the differences across these interpretations to get the story straight, and that story is this: God is calling on the pharaoh, through Moses, to free the Israelites—and on the Israelites to claim the right to and responsibility for that freedom—not so they can be free in some absolute sense, but so that they can sojourn from tyranny into the wilderness and organize themselves there in a celebratory pilgrimage dedicated to God.

This is a freedom organized under the rubric of the highest possible good—a continual pilgrimage to the highest possible place—a celebration of sacrifice, truth, adventure, wise caution, courage: all the virtues that have already been deemed characteristic of God himself and demanded of his true followers. The command, or injunction, is repeated no fewer than seven times in the text—a repetition obviously designed to ensure that the full point is not missed (Exodus 5:1, 7:16, 8:1, 8:20, 9:1, 9:13, 10:3). This is no different than the upward sacrifice of Abraham that accompanies movement along the pathway of adventure, or the offering that is required of Jacob, then Israel, as he climbs the ladder toward the divine. This is the same thing, in the broadest sense, as the maturation that turns all those who would otherwise remain Peter Pans or worse into true men of God.

It is forever tempting to assume that the demise of an arbitrary tyranny will immediately be followed by the establishment of a paradise of unrestricted freedom, and it is a great convenience to ignore the accompanying insistence by God that the sojourn into freedom is to be a celebration of that which is properly put in the highest place. But that is nonetheless the command—and Moses repeats it in the many subsequent meetings he has with the increasingly intractable king of Egypt, to ensure there is no misunderstanding. The clarion call of Moses to freedom—eternally away from tyranny and slavery—is most decidedly not a call to anarchy or hedonism, but an invitation to the voluntary disciplined striving upward that was most truly echoed by the writers of the US Declaration of Independence when they insisted that the sovereign individuals who make up a free state have the right to pursue happiness. For a mature and well-constituted people, this is not a call to self-gratification and to hell with the future and everyone else. It is the pursuit of a higher harmony of self and other, now and later, that constitutes the proper celebration in what would otherwise be a wasteland. The inspired repetition of Moses with regard to that point is an indication of the difficulty of the lesson, and the depth of the immature wish for the untrammeled false freedom or the anarchy of immediate gratification of equally immediate desire.

The calling on the people of Israel to organize themselves maturely in proper celebration is another early hint toward the idea of subsidiarity, which allows the ordered freedom that exists when individual psyche and society alike are organized in a harmonious hierarchy (with everything and everyone in the proper place, up and down the ranks). That is, first, a hierarchy of responsibility—and voluntarily undertaken responsibility, at that, and second a structure with something at its pinnacle to unite it (otherwise there is no harmony). That uniting ultimate pinnacle, is by definition, the spirit of God. The very name of Yahweh is derived from the description of the principle of being itself, *hayah*, and has as its core the same ambivalence or comprehensiveness as the description that emerges from the midst of the burning bush: *I am what I am,* or *I will be what I will be.* Subsidiarity works when each individual, married couple, family, local community, state, and nation bears the duties, or has the meaningful adventure, appropriate to their position.

If that responsibility is properly distributed and voluntarily and effectively borne, the bearers free themselves from the shackles of their slavish habits and keep for themselves the authority and freedom of choice that the tyrant will otherwise appropriate. A self-governing people do not require a king. Alternatively: all abdicated responsibility will be taken up by the power-mad and used against those slavish enough to reject their calling and conscience. It might be noted, as well, with regard to the notions both of ultimate and ineffable that are intrinsically associated with the divine pinnacle: just as the pillars of light and dark that later guide the Israelites keeps its leading distance as the chosen people move forward, what is at the top of the striving forward of those aiming at God recedes as it is approached. This means not least that the goodness of God is inexhaustible, and that new vistas of promise and perfection still beckon, even as the promised land nears— even after it is established, at least insofar as that is possible, on Earth.

The pharaoh rejects Moses's entreaty, voicing his disbelief in the existence of the Lord, noting his countrymen's dependence on the labor of the Israelites and, to top it off (just because he can), spitefully heaping an additional set of arduous tasks upon them:

> And Pharaoh commanded the same day the taskmasters of the people, and their officers, saying,
>
> Ye shall no more give the people straw to make brick, as heretofore: let them go and gather straw for themselves.
>
> And the tale of the bricks, which they did make heretofore, ye shall lay upon them; ye shall not diminish ought thereof: for they be idle; therefore they cry, saying, Let us go and sacrifice to our God.
>
> Let there more work be laid upon the men, that they may labor therein; and let them not regard vain words.
>
> *Exodus 5:6–9*

This response demoralizes Moses. He takes up the case with God, pointing out that his efforts in delivering the call for freedom from on high has done nothing but increase the burden borne by his fellow Israelites. This is an allusion to the cost of the truth: just as people lie so that comfort, however false, remains intact in the present, or so that they positively gain something undeserved, the revelation of the truth often makes things worse, however temporarily, as what is not right but has previously escaped attention is perceived, and as the powers that be, psychological or social, refuse to budge, punish the messenger, and double down. God reassures his prophet, telling him that things will work out even better because of the pharaoh's stubborn resistance, and instructs him to organize his people into ancestral groups as a prerequisite to their new organization as a free state.

If ethical action and honest speech always produced immediate benefit, no one would be tempted to shirk responsibility or lie. People are tempted to wander off the righteous path, so to speak, precisely because doing so often produces the immediate consequences desired. Just because something works well now does not mean that it will suffice for the longer term. Similarly, just because something works once, or for one person (now), does not mean that it iterates well or that it will prove of communal benefit. It is in fact the sacrifice of what is best for the medium- to long-term and the peace of the community to the immediate benefits of the individual (and, generally, to the whim of that individual) that constitutes the motivation for deceit and the rejection of responsibility, and that is the very definition of immaturity. In stark contrast with this pathologically maintained childishness is the adult sacrifice that is productive work toward the highest conceivable end. Always, the forgoing of immediate gratification—the offering of now to tomorrow, narrow self to future self, and individual to community—is the sacrifice on which the stable psyche and state depend. The alternative—stubborn adherence to a counterproductive highest principle (the pharaoh's insistence on his absolute sovereignty, for example—reflecting any individual's prideful insistence that his or her subjectivity reign supreme)—will inevitably produce a cascade of always-dire consequences.

The pharaoh wants his own way. He elevates his narrowly defined self-interest to the highest place. Consequently, he comes to worship not just himself but his most immature and impulsive self—a proclivity which all too easily shifts into the demand that everyone else bow down and follow suit. It is this dance that constitutes the eternal dynamic of the hedonist and the tyrant. The hedonist wants nothing but the gratification of desire and must turn to power if he can gain the means to enable that, as no one else remotely sane wants to be reduced to the means of gratifying his desire. The reasons for the dance run deeper yet. Rule of psyche or society by whim means running riot in the present and abandoning responsibility for the future self, for others, and for the future itself. When the partying mounts and becomes unsustainably riotous, either the outside force that represses and restrains will manifest itself, or the flood will rise. Any reality that attempts to orient itself around such the narrow, unreliable, and transient axis of whim, whether of citizen or ruler, cannot survive let alone thrive. Why would the world shift to present what immediate selfish desire requires? What is to be done with the competing demands of every other animate being? What is to become of the future, sacrificed as it will be to the vagaries of the present? Even the sovereign must humble himself in the face of what is truly ultimate: the proper first and last principle, or spirit. Authentic power is that which flows from the ultimate source of being and becoming, and woe betide anyone, regardless of earthly prowess, who refuses to recognize that primal fact—which is exactly what the pharaoh proceeds to do, an increasingly dire ten times.

The second time Moses appears before the pharaoh, he casts down the staff of his authority. It transforms again into the serpent. The magicians of Egypt duplicate (more concisely, *mimic;* more truly, *parody*) the demonstration, but the serpent of Moses's staff devours their lesser snakes. This intimates that the principle of being and becoming on whose behalf Moses speaks is the true superordinate principle, even of sovereignty itself. The fakers, psychopaths, and narcissists can imitate the authority of God—in fact, as usurpers, that is their specialty. But in the final analysis that is nothing but a show at court, the narcissistic attempt to gain false reputation, an empty show signifying nothing. The victory of Moses's staff is part of the process by which the true source of the productive harmony that should be the foundation of the state makes itself known: God is that to which even the magicians of the most magnificent court must bow—that to which even the commander of those magicians must bow. By definition.

It is not at all that the Israelites are insisting, with the fervor of authoritarian believers, that the God they worship must be the One True God; it is that the true followers of Yahweh—those who wrestle with God—are always those seeking to discover what constitutes the genuine highest and uniting principle and then to live in accordance with that revelation. This is very different than the power-mad insistence that a given ideology or principle of power must rule; it is instead submission to the divine order, accompanied by willingness to make the painful, genuine, and personally costly sacrifices that are the eternally valid marker of true belief. This sacrificial behavior is the voluntary subjection of the Israelites to the divine order; their refusal to take to themselves the fruit of the tree of the knowledge of good and evil; their refusal to consort with or bow down to Luciferian presumption and the temptation to usurp. The legitimate followers of the God of Abraham do not create their own values, as the philosopher Nietzsche insisted so wrongly that we must do, in the aftermath of the hypothetical demise of the divine.[44] Quite the contrary. They seek to discover the implicit moral order, signified not least by their tradition, and then to align themselves in harmony with that order. This duty and invitation is their subjugation to God, and what frees them from the tyranny and enslavement of even their own selfish desires.

Pharaoh maintains his opposition to the requests of Moses, and to God himself, speaking through the prophet. The rivers of Egypt therefore turn to blood, in keeping with the power granted to the Israelite leader (this is the first of the plagues detailed in Exodus 7–12). The main source of the Egyptians' water, the Nile, was central or even sacred to the Egyptians; its transmutation or pollution is thus a blow struck at the foundation of Egyptian culture. It is also an intimation of worse to come: it is hard to read the appearance of literal rivers of blood as anything other than a dire warning. This occurrence is also a foreshadowing of the utter destruction that takes place later in the Red Sea—another flood of blood. The second plague is one of frogs. The frog is a border-dweller, living on the edge of the depths. Symbolically, the frog is a psychopomp: a mediator between the divine that harbors itself in the depths and the upper or airy world. In the Brothers Grimm story *The Frog Prince*, it is that green amphibian who rescues the golden ball (the sun, the image of perfection, that which rules consciousness, the hero who slays the dragon at night) that disappears when the princess inadvertently drops it into the depths. This is an indication of the alienation of the daughter of the king from that which is most life-giving, necessary, and rejuvenating. It is the frog, as psychopomp, existing on the border between realms who rescues and restores the divine order. A plague of such frogs indicates nothing less than that the God who is the terrible and eternal judge is about to make himself manifest. Woe betide those who under such conditions have wandered far from the strait and narrow path.

The next plagues are of lice and flies. This is the inevitable subjugation of the tyrants to the parasites; the endlessly predictable susceptibility of those who arbitrarily deem themselves highest to invasion by the lowest of the low. When insistence on improper order rules—when true merit is no longer valued—heaven turns to iron (Leviticus 26: 19) and the world flips upside down. The ensuing usurpers are also forever precisely those who lead the charge to criticize and question genuine accomplishment and ability—merit, in a word—always in the name of the hypothetically oppressed, but truly so that their claims to unearned status and privilege may be guised in the cloak of moral purity. If the tyrant did not continually insist, falsely, that what is of genuine primacy be devalued, his dominance would not remain unquestioned. This forceful insistence increasingly comes to destabilize the judgment and discrimination of individual and state alike, until what is productive and good is deemed usury and deceit; until success is defined as theft; until those who claim victimization at the hands of the meritorious can put forward, without resistance, their psychopathic predatory and parasitical claims. The tyrants tyrannize for their own narrow purposes; but they lay themselves open to waste by the parasites. As this process of invasion unfolds, the unrighteous autocrats become increasingly paranoid—and rightly so. Why rightly? Because those willing to strive under such inverted conditions multiply uncontrollably beyond control, in the parasitical manner, as they continue their mad rampage through whatever is decent and true.

Despite all this mounting calamity, the pharaoh is stubbornly unwilling to change. This inflexibility is the hallmark of the totalitarian, with his certainty that everything that needs to be known is already known. This is particularly true of the committed ideologues; of those who so self-righteously make the doctrines of men their infallible dogmas (Matthew 15:8–9; Mark 7:6–9). A true tyrant resists the correction of error in precise proportion to his prideful certainty. This means that the individuals or the societies that have journeyed the farthest down the path to perdition have to suffer the most torment before they abandon their false worship, forgo their pride, and bend a knee in recognition of the insuperable obstacles reality itself is arraying before them.

Next the livestock disappear. That is a partial intimation of the destruction not only of the present but also of the future, as such animals are literally food not just for now but for later, and indefinitely later if they are managed properly. After the demise of the livestock comes the onset of disease, in the form of a plague of boils. This is an illness simultaneously painful, disgusting, and shameful, thereby combining the worst of the revenge of the natural and social worlds alike. Devastated, the pharaoh's magicians find themselves no longer able to duplicate Moses's actions. This is the point when the magic of the false state ceases to operate; when the cracks in the foundation truly begin to show. This is also the transition point between the plagues indicating the collapse of the earthly or material domain, symbolically speaking, and the rebellion of the skies or heavens (first, ashes and dust in the air, bringing with them a disease of the skin; then a plague of lightning, thunder, and hail; then locusts, winging their rapacious way forward until everything green vanishes from the earth; then darkness, which means the disappearance of the sun itself, the veritable king of the sky).

Disorder now reigns. The earth protests first, then the heavens—until chaos is everywhere. The pharaoh is compelled to bend a bit: "And Pharaoh called unto Moses, and said, Go ye, serve the Lord; only let your flocks and your herds be stayed: let your little ones also go with you" (Exodus 10:24). Moses, who seems more than a little impatient at this point, refuses, telling the king that even the cattle must be allowed to participate in the divine desert sacrifice. This is, by the way, an indication of the extension of divine grace even to the beasts of the field—an indication of the proper stewardship of the garden and the subduing of the natural order. The pharaoh rejects the demand and tells Moses that he will be put to death if he ever dare show his face at court again.

A final and most terrible plague remains. God tells Moses first to ask the Egyptians for their treasure and second that all the firstborn of the land of Egypt shall be put to death—the progeny of beast and king alike. The Egyptians, sufficiently plagued, appear positively happy to comply with the first request. God also tells the Israelites to mark the entryway to their houses, side posts, and lintels with the blood of a perfect lamb, so that the angel of death of God will pass over those dwelling places and leave the children residing there intact. God simultaneously informs Moses that the month in which the Passover sacrifice occurs is to be deemed the first month of the year. How is this to be understood? There is a necessary and tight association between the end of one event, time, or epoch and the beginning of something else—in this case, the movement of the enslaved Israelites to their eventual freedom. It is for such reasons that the sacrificial lamb is roasted and then eaten (accompanied by what is bitter) by people dressed for action. The Israelites eat unleavened bread because there is no time for it to rise. They eat with loins girded, shoes on feet, staff in hand—and in haste. With the dawn of something new it is always time to act. They are preparing to respond to the call—a requirement that is echoed in Christ's much later warning that he will come like a thief in the night:

> Watch therefore: for ye know not what hour your Lord doth come.
>
> But know this, that if the goodman of the house had known in what watch the thief would come, he would have watched, and would not have suffered his house to be broken up.
>
> Therefore be ye also ready: for in such an hour as ye think not the Son of man cometh.
>
> *Matthew 24:42–44*

When the call comes—when conscience speaks—it is high time to go. No matter what or when. The wise prepare themselves so they are always ready (Matthew 25:1–13).

The present has already been destroyed by the nine previous plagues. The death of the firstborn means the eradication of the future, or at least of the best of the future, for the Egyptians. The true tyrant will not quit until both what is and what is yet to be have been destroyed. The sacrifice that eternally protects—the blood of the lamb, in this case—is the willingness to offer up everything, so that the tyrant can be defeated. It is exactly this requirement that those who claim kingship falsely reject. A healthily dynamic relationship—the kind that constitutes a solid marriage, for example—is the consequence of the myriad of small sacrifices of the narrow wants and wishes of the individual husband and wife to the higher and more inclusive good of the couple and the family. Each small sacrifice keeps the relationship on track, guided by the spirit of meaningful and honest communication. Each bit of honest communication requires at least the small death of some previous commitment or belief, however innocent (or guilty). Each bit of honest communication must begin with an attitude of humility ("I have something to learn"), the willingness to aim at a higher goal ("I am committed body and soul to the integrity of this marriage") and, most importantly, the willingness to give something up ("I am willing to sacrifice whatever reveals itself as an impediment to the furtherance of the relationship").

Here are the eternal questions, facing each member of a couple, aiming at permanent union: Would you rather establish a productive and generous peace, or prove yourself right? Would you forgo the delights of victory, in other words, to free your wife or husband from the burden of defeat? This is a particularly relevant question to consider when contemplating the fact that many disputes are likely to arise in the course of a marriage. If you always win, what does that leave for the person with whom you share a household? What are you willing to offer on the narrowly personal side, so that the marriage or the family can be strengthened? This may well be a further question, in disguise: What would be better for you, all things considered, than even the good thing that you want or value right now? The same principle of wise and mature negotiation applies to the family and the broader community: continual incremental self-sacrifice both facilitates opportunity and staves off disaster. The tyrant, by contrast, sticks to his guns regardless of evidence to the contrary. He or she never solves problems when they are small. The snakes inevitably aggregate, in consequence of such avoidance—such stubborn refusal—until they lurk underneath everything, and they grow, too. When there are enough of them, and when they are large enough, they merge together. Then the dragon of chaos reemerges, ready and willing to devour everything. This is literally the oldest of stories.[45]

The death of the firstborn is enough to convince even the pharaoh that he is powerless before God. The Egyptians load the Israelites with jewels, gold, silver, and clothing and send them packing. Those who abide by the proper faith will end up with everything, even that which the tyrants have attempted to sequester. Moses tells his departing people, segregated into their familial tribes, that the promised land of milk and honey beckons. This can be profitably read as the better future, *as such*: every individual and every society is motivated in the positive sense by the vision of improved condition. We are always sojourning from a place that is not yet good enough to a place that is better. That is the very structure of the human journey; the very basis of positive emotion itself. We can flee from what terrifies us, and that is also motivation; but we are eternally attracted by—divinely inspired or made enthusiastic ("from French *enthousiasme* (16c.) and directly from Late Latin *enthusiasmus*, from Greek *enthousiasmos* 'divine inspiration, enthusiasm (produced by certain kinds of music, etc.),' from *enthousiazein* 'be inspired or possessed by a god, be rapt, be in ecstasy,' from *entheos* 'divinely inspired, possessed by a god,' from *en* 'in' + *theos* 'god'").[46] The true leader is precisely the person who offers a destination so attractive that his people are motivated to sojourn forward voluntarily, made enthusiastic—that is, God-inspired—by the visionary revelation of possibility and promise.

7.5. The inevitable interregnum of chaos and the guiding spirit

Why is it out of tyranny and into the desert instead of out of tyranny and into the promised land? The narrative frame outlined in Exodus reflects the archetypal manner in which human frames of perception, attention, and action are transformed.[47] There is, first, the insufficient current state (the tyranny of the present); then, the chaos that makes itself manifest when that state is disrupted; and, finally, the aim of the sojourn—the desired future. Between disruption of tyranny and arrival in the promised land we inevitably traverse the desert. Imagine that you (or your family or your community) have been existing within a landscape of sterile and outdated preconceptions. Imagine as well that you and yours have been making yourselves smaller and less consequential as a result, so that you can all continue to fit however uncomfortably within that increasingly restricted dwelling place. People do this to each other all the time, and then perish of the consequential predictability, dullness, and boredom. Imagine then that you decide to let go of all that—to abandon what you believed; or instead, as in the case of the pharaoh, that you have been forced to do so, because everything has collapsed. This does not mean that all the problems you avoided while refusing to confront and change have disappeared. Quite the contrary. They will have instead multiplied in force and number, in keeping with the ineluctable iron law of entropy. [48]

This means that what replaces the tyranny is chaos—uncertainty and directionlessness—and that is the desert. Anxiety and hopelessness rule in that place.[49] A great leader, a true visionary, can inspire with possibility and bring hope to the journey. Absent that, there is only confusion and strife. Someone under the thumb of a tyrant—even if that tyrant is him- or herself—has direction and order, no matter how false and pathological. As soon as that disappears, every direction (or none) beckons simultaneously, and that is too much. That emergent absence of aim and structure is anxiety, because it is too much, and hopelessness, because nothing now beckons to be pursued, asks to be accomplished, or can be productively moved toward. This is not a situation materially better than tyranny. It is merely its dance partner, as intimated previously.[50] It is merely the chaos that is the equally terrible opposite of tyranny. If you have tyrannized and enfeebled yourself, and you decide to let that go, your life is unlikely to immediately improve. It may well get worse, however temporarily. The habits that made you a slave have not yet been changed. The consequences of such abdication of responsibility are still likely to remain. This is all in addition to the lack of direction that paralyzes and destroys hope. Why do people refuse so stubbornly to change, even in the presence of overwhelming evidence; even in response to their own pain and suffering? Because a sojourn in the desert inevitably follows a period of subjugation to the tyrant. Because something vital—something that has been worshipped, however falsely; something loved, however pathologically—must be sacrificed, with the attendant cost, before true freedom can be attained. The eternal clarion call of the man who doubles down on his own misery? "Better the tyrant than the desert."

The Israelites muster up the faith and courage to depart for the barren wilderness. But they bring with them the habits of dependents, and have no idea what to do once on their own. Why? The tyrant exercises power, to be sure, but it does not manifest itself in one dire blow. The would-be authoritarian pushes forward, inch by inch, chipping away. The would-be enslaved retreat in the same manner, in unconscionable silence, rendering themselves willfully blind to the evidence of their own cowardice; abdicating the responsibility that would if properly borne make them noble, instead of voluntarily voiceless beasts of burden. This is exactly what happens to Disney's Pinocchio, for example, when he lets the false diagnosis of neurotic victimhood open him up to the blandishments of the delinquents on Pleasure Island. Soon he is reduced to the status of a braying donkey—all in preparation for his service in the salt mines of the tyrants. Generations of such retreat and rejection of responsibility leave their mark. The habits of free men disappear, and the ways of the slave emerge.

Moses has offered the promised land itself to his Israelite compatriots and would-be citizens. The destination itself may be clear in the purely practical sense. Moses and his people are set to occupy the land of Canaan, which is not far away, geographically. It is very far away, however, spiritually. First, there is nothing paradisal about even the most verdant and productive land if the people who occupy it insist on being self-centered, aimless, and fractious. Those who are careless enough can starve and die in the midst of plenty. Second, the truly slavish and directionless can take forever to get nowhere. Aimless wandering can make any voyage interminable, no matter

how brief it might be, if undertaken practically. Hence the otherwise mysterious three generations it takes the Israelites to make a journey that is short,
in absolute terms.

What should guide those who are lost after misadventure? God presents
himself to the Israelites as what should properly lead those who are adrift,
right on the brink of the wilderness; who are standing on the line between
the order that has rigidified into tyranny and the chaos of the wasteland;
who are trapped between the murderous armies of the totalitarian state and
the bloody uncertainty of the Red Sea. How does the divine make itself
known in such a circumstance? As a pillar of light in the blackness of the
night and a pillar of darkness (cloud) in the light of day. This is a manner
that echoes the eternal interplay between opposites from which the world
itself emerges, in the Genesis account;[51] a mode of representation with its
analog everywhere and in every time.[52] This is the divine that is not least the
interplay between calling and conscience—the dance between what beckons
to us and leads us forward when things are darkest and what warns us of the
danger and darkness that still threaten when we are in the light and on the
straight and narrow path. This is the orienting function of emotion itself,
that guides us as we make our way into the future—the invitation that is
positive emotion itself (hope, longing, excitement, curiosity, the aforementioned enthusiasm) and the caution that is its negative counterpart and independent opposite (terror, grief, and pain). Those who are lost and who cannot
find the God who guides have therefore forgotten where to look—at what
eternally beckons forward and wisely cautions. This is a fundamental, even
instinctual, manner of conceptualizing the source of the meaning that
guides us. It is a view remarkably duplicated by the Taoist traditionalists of
the Far East, struggling with the same extensional problems—remarkably
because the pattern of characterization appears identical, despite its independent manifestation. This must be regarded at minimum as a profound
and telling case of parallel evolution, natural as well as cultural.

The spirit of reality itself, for the Taoists, is composed of the eternal interplay of chaos and order, each opposed to the other and each embedded
deeply within the other—and this is the reality of experience, as such, and

not the reductive reality of the material world. The cosmic image of the Taoists is that of two serpents, head to tail, one black, signifying chaos, darkness, confusion, possibility, and the night; the other white, signifying order, light, clarity, actuality, and the day. Embedded into the head of each serpent, however, is a signifier of its opposite: the white serpent has a black eye and vice versa. This is the eternal interplay between light and darkness—and, more subtly, the eternal emergence of light even in the darkness, and vice versa; an indication or representation of the emergence of the real and meaningful from the realm of potential, or possibility, in creative consort with the principle, process, or spirit that wrestles with that *tohu va bohu* and establishes the order that is good. It is in precisely this interplay and emergence that God makes himself manifest to the Israelites at the height of their trouble, when they are most in need of the guidance of the divine. A certain degree of conceptual sophistication is required to understand and represent this dynamic—unsurprisingly, given that it is a representation of reality itself. Order is best comprehended not only as order itself, already established (as in the staff of Moses), but as the principle that gives rise to and establishes that order. Chaos, for its part (the serpent in the staff) must likewise be considered in its dual element: as potential or possibility itself, as well as the spirit that challenges, nurtures, renews—or usurps.

What else might be understood about the eternal play of yin and yang? That the rug can be pulled out at any time; that beneficial and stable order can transform itself suddenly, accidentally—or as a consequence of willful blindness—into utter chaos and catastrophe. There is a certain arbitrariness and randomness about existence, of course, which is simply a fact of potential and possibility, but the role of the conscious choice of men and women in the emergence of chaos should never be underestimated or downplayed. Such a collapse is often precipitated directly or indirectly by the "sins of men," as we have seen,[53]—whether those are the prideful presumptions of Adam and Eve, the failure to offer properly and descent into bitterness characteristic of Cain and his descendants, the disloyalty of Ham, or the false celebrations and aim of the engineers of Babel. On the positive side, however, it is the case that a new order can realize itself in the midst of even extreme confusion and uncertainty, such that everything previously established is restored and something additional added. This is the nature of the progress that occurs as a result of the interplay of yin and yang, the continued upward spiral around the trunk of the tree of life, up Jacob's Ladder, toward the ever-receding heights of heaven itself.

It is the eternal dynamic of order and chaos that makes the world. This is the interplay between what you have come to understand, and what you do not yet and may never understand. This is the incomprehensible union of the territory you have mastered and the territory you have still to encounter and explore, or what you have presently conceptualized and what remains beyond understanding for now—and even what you have mastered and conceptualized can and does dissolve into the unknown when things fall apart around you. This is the Taoist and the Biblical world, simultaneously, and it is an accurate representation of the reality that has in truth shaped our adaptation—even when considered in the purely biological and evolutionary sense. The fact of a reality structured in this manner is reflected neurologically, not least, which is an indication as profound as any of its truth. Delving into this fact helps establish the validity of the symbolic representations under consideration, providing them with a physical analog or foundation (as opposed to their descent from on high, so to speak).

The brain's left hemisphere is not specialized for the linguistic and the right for the nonverbal, as is commonly held, but for operation in the known and unknown, respectively (with the linguistic/nonlinguistic division of labor a subset of that more fundamental distinction).[54] This implies very strongly, even from the bottom-up materialist perspective (insofar as that is reflected in the consequences of natural selection), that the cosmos is in fact as well as metaphor the unknown and foreign, as such, in a musical dance with the known and familiar. This in turn implies something even more fundamental—that meaning is not a mere epiphenomenon, a transient and mutable subjective overlay on an intrinsically senseless material substrate, but a manifestation of what is most real, instinctively and actually (insofar as what is real and actual is reflected in the organization of the highest reaches of our nervous systems). Our very physiology bears the implicit and indwelling image of the world, as well as our psyches or souls. We are veritable microcosms, reflecting not only the deepest order of things but also the order of the spirit of things itself.

The atheist evolutionary biologist Richard Dawkins himself has made precisely this case, stating explicitly not only that "a living organism is a model of the world in which it lives"[55] but is also all of the following:

> But I began by saying, not that an animal's brain contains a simulated model of its world . . . but that an animal is a model of its world. What is the sense of such a statement? One way to approach it is to realize that a good zoologist, presented with an animal and allowed to examine and dissect its body in sufficient detail, should be able to reconstruct almost everything about the world in which the animal lived. To be more precise, she would be reconstructing the worlds in which the animal's ancestors lived. That claim, of course, rests upon the Darwinian assumption that animal bodies are largely shaped by natural selection.[56]
>
> The zoology of the future . . . will perfect techniques of combining sources of information and analysing their interactions, resulting in inferences of enormous power. The computer, incorporating everything that is known about the body of the strange animal, will construct a model of the animal's world, to rival any model of the Earth's weather. This, it seems to me, is tantamount to saying that the animal, any animal, is a model of its own world, or the world of its ancestors.[57]

If all that is true, how can the instinct that compels and guides development— the intuition of meaningful structure and of meaningful advance—be anything other than a true reflection of the structure of being and becoming itself; be anything less than the image of God in man and woman alike? In the world of existential apprehension—in the world of experience itself (and how even in principle can there be a more fundamental reality)—it is eternally meaning first and matter later. And that is the very world of perception, all protestations of the empiricists to the contrary. There are a vast multitude of facts, a chaotic plethora of facts, an incomprehensible plenitude of facts. Consciousness lends value to that chaos, subdues it, puts everything in its proper place, and forever establishes the order that is good.

In keeping with such a conceptualization, Dawkins also notes the following: "We could say that the nervous system uses short, economical words for messages that occur frequently and are expected; long, less economical words for messages that occur rarely and are not expected."[58] That efficiency is a crucial part of the ordering process: part of the manner in which our linguistic ability establishes the fundamental traditions and assumptions of its patterns of representation. What makes itself manifest as self-evident across time becomes coded ever more deeply, efficiently, and immutably. This is the very staff of tradition—the staff which springs to life, when planted in the ground; the staff around which the serpent that changes and varies eternally twines itself. The same thing appears true of the genetic code itself, which may mutate randomly, but which conserves what is fundamental and vital in spite of that randomness, repairing what is crucial with one hundred percent accuracy when it is damaged by the process that drive mutation, while allowing necessary experimentation on the fringe.[59] The importance of this relatively recent discovery can hardly be overstated, as it changes the very way we understand the development of life, the conservation of what is crucial, and the variation that allows for vital change—and is something whose discussion we will therefore return to.[60]

Dawkins additionally—and in the same vein—points out that we can simulate the future, abstracting from past regularities, and that we do this in stories, using imagination.[61] Thus the structure of reality is, according to the evolutionary biologist and atheist, mirrored in imagination and presented in narrative form. Why would this dictum somehow not apply to the very stories on which the entirety of Western civilization is predicated? More from the same source: "Natural selection built in the capacity to simulate the world as it is, because this was necessary to perceive the world."[62] His closing remarks?

And once natural selection had built brains capable of simulating slight departures from reality into the imagined future, a further emergent capacity automatically flowered. Now it was but another short step to the wilder reaches of imagination revealed in dreams and in art, an escape from mundane reality that has no obvious limits.[63]

Perhaps not an escape, Dr. Dawkins, as adaptation itself is what is being portrayed and described. Perhaps instead a voyage precisely paralleling that of Abraham, following the call of the spirit of adventure, or of Jacob, climbing the ladder heavenward, or of Moses, peering into the ultimate depths of reality? Not an escape, at all (except when immature or pathological). Instead, a use of the power of imagination—use of drama; use of abstraction into the transcendent realities of "fiction"—allowing a simulation superseding anything mere so-called and impossible in any case "direct perception" might be capable of managing. Are abstractions more or less real than the data from which they are abstracted? What about mathematics, sir, or the eternal world of the Platonic forms, or the vital, necessary, and irreplaceable fact of the functional[64] ideal[65] that is a necessary prerequisite or precondition for all perception of "empirical sense data"?

By the same logic: the fact that the psychological and underlying physiological structure of a human being is that of a personality (essentially, a hierarchy of attentional and action prioritization, each bearing a particular character) implies that the "environment" to which that personality is adapted—more accurately, of which it is a "model"—is in some real sense also a personality. It might be objected: this cannot possibly be true of the purely material world, even if it is true of the aggregate social world to which each person is necessarily adapted and after which each is modeled (this would be *adaptation to society as if it were a person with whom a relationship must be established*). This may be true, which would mean that the spirit of the biblical corpus and, more broadly, of the mythological realm is "nothing but" the reflection of the realm of human interaction, past and present. However, given that the social realm is itself necessarily an adaptation to and therefore a model of the underlying material world, that is not much of a reduction—and definitely not one that fundamentally dispenses with the deeper issue at hand.

Why would we presume that the spirit giving rise to being and becoming itself is something dead, unconscious, pointless, and lacking identity when adaptation to that reality has required consciousness, teleology and purpose, and personality? Is it merely chance, or even the arbitrary requirements of human society, that has organized the world, such that some patterns of moral striving further life, individual and communal, and others do not; or is that instead not and inevitably a reflection of the deepest of underlying realities? If the concept of God as Personality works, so to speak, in the time-tested manner—in the pragmatic manner[66]—why is that model not aptly regarded as most accurate? This is all keeping in mind the fact that the God of the biblical corpus is, as is constantly insisted on in the text and the tradition, ineffable and, finally, incomprehensible—outside even of nature; even of time and space (Exodus 3:14; Job 38–41; Isaiah 55:8–9). This is why even the greatest of prophets, Moses himself, can see no more of God than his back, in passing (Exodus 33:17–23). This fundamental mystery of the divine does not mitigate comprehensively against the possibility of characterization—else adaptation itself, as well as comprehension, would be impossible. Instead what seems to be true is something very much akin to or even identical with the axiomatic Judeo-Christian assumption and the subsequent and derivative scientific insistence that the cosmic order is characterized by its Logos—its intelligibility—and that the human mind and soul can and should investigate, comprehend, and ally itself with that intrinsic order.

It is also the case that the future can be negotiated with (through sacrifice), and that the proper sacrifices (generally of the narrow to the broad and the present to the future) can ensure abundance, security, and opportunity in that very future. Reality is best conceptualized as something that human beings exist in relationship with or to, and it can and should be conceptualized akin to or like a personality. We are characterized in the biblical texts as "images" of God. This implies or indicates that whatever God is greater than a mere human personality, but something that is at least sufficiently similar so that the idea that we are reflections of the divine nature is valid. Thus, the "personality" of God.

The fact of such representation or conceptualization can, once again, be attributed to the human attempt to characterize the meta-spirit of humanity itself (the necessity to represent the existential requirement to negotiate honestly and productively with other people; the necessity to represent the consequences of such negotiation, when successful or failed). Such attribution, to say it again, does not solve the problem. The very humanity in question emerged out of the dust of the world, so to speak. It therefore seems reasonable to assume that this very dust had in its implicit structure and organization the pattern reflected in the social world. Why is there such great insistence on the fact that reality itself is dead and blind, in some final sense, when the organisms that inhabit it live and see? Is this not more likely a consequence of our ignorance, with regard to the final nature of the material, rather than a limitation placed on the nature of being by that material? It is not as if we understand what the world is made of, materially, in any "scientific" and simple reductionistic sense. The dust out of which we all emerge is unimaginable in its central aspect. The mysteries of the quantum world have assured of that: whatever is at the bottom of things appears no less incomprehensible than any spirit, hypothetical or otherwise, that might characterize the cosmos. And, perhaps, our reductive materialism is a reflection of something worse than mere ignorance: maybe we insist on the deadness and intrinsic meaningless of the world to rationalize our unwillingness to accept the immense burden of opportunity and obligation that a true understanding of our place in a truly meaningful world would necessitate. Perhaps it is not religion that is the opiate of the masses. Perhaps it is instead that a rationalist, materialist atheism is the camouflage of the irresponsible.

Let us return to the immediacies of the story at hand. We left the Israelites just as they had made off with the treasures abandoned by the morally inverted and careless Egyptians, on the knife-edge of their next adventure, suspended between the rigid stone tyranny of the pharaoh and their disoriented but upward-aiming desert sojourn. They had determined to risk the adventure of journey to the promised land under the guidance of Moses, proximally, and God, distally—and with all their belongings, livestock, and families intact (despite the pharaoh's initial forbidding of exactly that departure). Perhaps they feel that the worst is behind them. But the reality of yesterday and habit is a tricky thing to contend with, as the American novelist William Faulkner so famously indicated: "The past is never dead. It's not even past."[67] The desperate king of Egypt, humiliated by his sequential defeats, angry at the loss of his indentured servants, and grief-stricken by the death of his son vows to pursue "the children of Israel" (Exodus 14:8) and arranges the full might of his army—"all the horses and chariots of Pharaoh"—to do so. The Israelites catch word of this. Terrified, they begin to doubt the wisdom of their movement forward:

> And when Pharaoh drew nigh, the children of Israel lifted up their eyes, and, behold, the Egyptians marched after them; and they were sore afraid: and the children of Israel cried out unto the Lord.
>
> And they said unto Moses, Because there were no graves in Egypt, hast thou taken us away to die in the wilderness? wherefore hast thou dealt thus with us, to carry us forth out of Egypt?
>
> Is not this the word that we did tell thee in Egypt, saying, Let us alone, that we may serve the Egyptians? For it had been better for us to serve the Egyptians, than that we should die in the wilderness.
>
> *Exodus 14:10–12*

Moses upbraids his timorous followers, calling on them to have faith in the spirit that drove them out of the hands of their oppressors. The pillar of light and darkness leading the chosen people shifts position, so that it is now an obstacle to the approaching Egyptians. It is at this point that Moses expands his mastery of the water:

> And the Lord said unto Moses, Stretch out thine hand over the sea, that the waters may come again upon the Egyptians, upon their chariots, and upon their horsemen.

And Moses stretched forth his hand over the sea, and the sea returned to his strength when the morning appeared; and the Egyptians fled against it; and the Lord overthrew the Egyptians in the
midst of the sea.

And the waters returned, and covered the chariots, and the
horsemen, and all the host of Pharaoh that came into the sea after
them; there remained not so much as one of them.

But the children of Israel walked upon dry land in the midst of
the sea; and the waters were a wall unto them on their right hand,
and on their left.

Exodus 14:26–29

The Israelites find themselves between the proverbial rock and hard place.
The Red Sea that confronts them—and, equally, the Egyptians—is the eternal flood of blood, confusion, and bedlam engendered by the worst of the
tyrannical states. There is no going back, however: the very armies of the
Egyptian state have arrayed themselves in a manner that precludes retreat.
There is only the decision to wayfind through the blood, uncertainty, and
possibility that is the crimson chaos itself; the dreadful and potentially
deadly intermediary between stone and desert. Moses is he who finds firm
ground, step by careful step, guided as he is (as all the Israelites are at this
time) by the very instinct that orients us in the face of life's uncertainties. His
discovery of a pathway through is what we all seek whenever we encounter
the unknown after leaving the zone of comfort, familiarity, and security—
however false and tyrannical that may have been.

We perceive not the dead and meaningless material objects of the world
in their endless multiplicity, but the way forward.[68] If our aim is true, the
pathway is cleared for us precisely by the spirit of the highest, as our perceptions, patterns of attention, and actions are specified by our aims. The spirit
we most truly call upon is inevitably the spirit that emerges to guide us. This
is true technically as well as metaphysically. Perception itself is motivated.
The true leader calls on the eternal spirit of being and becoming to specify
the destination. The pathway through the waters that would otherwise de-

stroy us thereby makes itself known. Firm ground appears magically beneath our feet as we walk forward courageously and in good faith—eyes heavenward—toward the promised and proper destination. Those who are by contrast possessed by the spirit of their own machinations will find themselves flooded, drowned and destroyed.

Afterward Moses demonstrates yet again his mastery of the chaotic element (as well as his ability to rule over tyranny). The Israelites stop next at a well in Marah, after three days without water, but the well proves to be bitter. God shows his prophet a tree, which he casts into the water, removing the bitterness. What does this mean? That the succor offered by the leader whom God provides the water that is forever sweet. The Gospel of John (4:10) similarly recounts the tale of Christ meeting a Samaritan (or foreign) woman by a well. She asks him to procure for her a drink. "Jesus answered and said unto her, If thou knewest the gift of God, and who it is that saith to thee, Give me to drink; thou wouldest have asked of him, and he would have given thee living water." Likewise, but more extensively, Revelation 21:5–6 (King James Version), announcing a new heaven and a new earth (that is, the re-creation of the cosmic order):

> And the One seated on the throne said, "Behold, I make all things new." Then He said, "Write this down, for these words are faithful and true."
> And He told me, "It is done! I am the Alpha and the Omega, the Beginning and the End. To the thirsty I will give freely from the spring of the water of life."

The water provided by those who abide by the dictates of the God of Abraham and Isaac is the water that is eternally granted to and fulfills those who "thirst after righteousness" (Matthew 5:6). The voluntarily self-sacrificing individual on whose offering the community—the stability of the present and the promise of the future—is most truly based, is also the source of the water that does not end and that flows even in the desert. This is a meta-water, a reflection of the ethical process or mode of being by which the liquid that nourishes both concretely and spiritually is forever wrested from the intransigent material matrix. It is better to dig a well than to drink. It is better to know how to cooperate and compete productively and generously than to dig a well. It is even better yet to aim up and tell the truth than it is to plan to cooperate and compete productively and generously—not least because planning requires for its success a concrete and defined outcome rather than the higher faith that love and honest conduct will bring about what is best, regardless of evident consequence.

Two and a half months into the desert the Israelites once again lose faith and carp, protest, and grumble in a manner both derisive and resentful:

> And the whole congregation of the children of Israel murmured against Moses and Aaron in the wilderness:
>
> And the children of Israel said unto them, Would to God we had died by the hand of the Lord in the land of Egypt, when we sat by the flesh pots, and when we did eat bread to the full; for ye have brought us forth into this wilderness, to kill this whole assembly with hunger.
>
> *Exodus 16:2–3*

Sad: but they did have the habits of slaves. The sloughing off of responsibility is part of voluntary slavishness, a veritable prerequisite to domination by tyranny. This means to abandon the duty to reflect the image of God, to confront chaos and pathological order, and to forgo the adventure and the meaning that sustains through crisis. The cost of failure to shoulder the cross, so to speak, is sacrifice of the relationship with what is truly highest and consequent weakness in the face of the crises of life.

God tells Moses that he will provide manna from heaven and flesh from the earth. Thus the Israelites are provided with both spiritual nourishment (the bread from above) and material (in the form of the quails that gather around the camp in the evening). This is an indication in imaginative terms of the fact that provision in the wasteland is dependent both on what matters (that is the heavenly pattern of meaning) and on matter itself (that is the abundance of the Earth in the most concrete sense). The Israelites are instructed not to gather more sustenance than is necessary for the day but to trust entirely in God as they make their way through the desert. This is a precursor or variant of the later Gospel injunction: "Therefore do not worry about tomorrow; for the morrow shall take thought about its own things. Sufficient for the day is its own trouble." (Matthew 6:34). God tells the Israelites at the same time to make a container and to place some of the manna within it so that it can be retained for the observation and consideration of later generations (Exodus 16:32). This is a poetic indication that society itself is required for its maintenance to remember the "spiritual food" that nourished it; to gather it up, to preserve it and pass it down; to place it in a treasure box so that everyone knows and is reminded of its existence—so that tradition itself becomes the storehouse of the eternally nourishing value that descends from heaven.

It is at this point that we are informed that the Israelites are destined to wander for forty years—for three generations—feeding on manna and quail before they enter the promised land (Exodus 16:35). Does it take that long to shed the habits of slaves? A transformation that comprehensive could easily be a multigenerational venture. And another mystery: the land itself—Canaan—is inhabited. This raises the question: Would a just and merciful God offer a land already occupied to a new people? The answer, perhaps, is this: those who organize themselves, psychologically and communally, into a hierarchy of properly divine order will inevitably and finally triumph over those who do not. The Canaanites, it should be remembered, are the descendants of Cain, the resentful people, bitter worshippers of false idols, hedonistic and mad for power. The delivery of Canaan to those who truly wrestle with God is the inevitable and promised triumph of those who adopt the adventurous path and make the proper sacrifices that constitute genuine maturity, orientation to the future, and productive social being.

When the Israelites run short of water, they look back, yet again—toward Sodom, as it were—pining for the niceties of the Egyptian tyranny and adding to that hypocrisy another litany of complaints. God tells Moses to strike the rock of Horeb with his staff, which he does, and water flows from it. This is a callback, and in a few dimensions: Moses previously overcame the rigid stone kingdom of Egypt with his staff of transformation, both tree of life and serpent. Now, in the desert, he does the same under different conditions, calling forth what is necessary for life from the barren and lifeless elements. This narrative note also serves to bolster his identity and status as master of eternal water. Horeb is also Sinai, as indicated previously—the holy mountain connecting earth to heaven; the *axis mundi* around which all conceptions and the whole world rotates; the staff of tradition that anchors and establishes; the center of all the order that is good or very good. It is always where heaven reaches down to kiss the earth that the water that quenches all thirst springs forth. This is exactly what happens when calling makes itself known, when a new revelation is realized, and when something truly meaningful occurs. That is all a manifestation, materially speaking, of the instinct calling us all to transform upward and develop in the manner that is the genuine redeeming adventure of life.

Shortly thereafter, the Israelites face a major threat. The Amalekites, a passing nomadic tribe, attack. Moses climbs a nearby hill and brandishes the magic staff of his divine authority—the magic wand of Gandalf and Dumbledore, the shepherd's crook of David, the light saber of Obi-wan Kenobi, the spear of Odin that never misses the center of the target, the flag that rallies the troops, the branch that makes the bitter water sweet, the tree of life itself. As long as the prophet holds the staff aloft, the Israelites prevail. This reflects the necessity of the center as uniting and motivating standard, particularly to those in crisis. This is the Platonic ideal that gives necessary and heavenly form even in the midst of the crimson chaos. When Moses tires and involuntarily lowers his staff, the marauding Amalekites gain ground.

Fortunately, the prophet had listened to God and allied himself with strong and reliable compatriots. When he is incapable of holding his own arms and magic wand overhead, his brother and political arm, Aaron, and a new ally, Hur, help him to maintain his encouraging and faithful stance. Hur appears as a representative of the reliable everyman—the good citizen who upholds his responsibility in the ordinary but absolutely necessary way that the vast majority of people who do their jobs well so miraculously manage, despite the difficulties of their lives. His grandson, Bezalel, carrying on his admirable lineage, is later celebrated for his skill and divine inspiration when the Tabernacle is constructed (Exodus 31:1–5, Exodus 35:30–35). This motif of aid to the leader is another indication of the principle of subsidiarity: even the most capable leader cannot support the tradition and practices that protect and guide by himself. The three keep the banner waving high, so to speak, from sunrise to sundown, and the Israelites prevail.

7.6. The subsidiary state as alternative to tyranny and slavery

It is shortly after the Amalekite battle that Jethro, Moses's father-in-law, re-enters the story (Exodus 18). First, the two meet and happily reunite, Jethro perceiving and noting all the positive progress made by the former slaves of the Egyptians and his son-in-law, their leader. Then they join together in worship—a transformation for Jethro, who was a Midianite priest. It seems that seeing all the miraculous changes wrought in the destiny of Moses and his people unites his aim with that of the family and the people he is visiting. Jethro then observes Moses in his newly acquired role as judge of the Israelites. This is something they themselves have demanded of him—in principle, because of his prophetic capacity. Moses's people remain a dis-united, self-centered, faithless, and fractious bunch, unable and, more significantly, unwilling to mediate their own disputes—that is, unwilling to take on themselves the responsibility to be self-governing. In their immaturity, they have forgone the obligation to delve deeply into the structure of morality and squandered the opportunity to learn for themselves what constitutes appropriate conduct.

When two people have a dispute, each could take the occasion to divine what future option—what balance between justice and mercy—might be regarded by both parties as a satisfactory solution. A dispute emerges when the structure of meaning that one person is using to orient him- or herself and to move forward conflicts with the dictates of the structure used by another.

This produces a clash between two hierarchies of values or principles. From that clash can emerge a deeper, uniting principle or value, but only if the conflict is faced forthrightly and then judged fairly. Existence in accordance with that emergent uniting principle is the sacrifice of narrow self-interest that makes community possible, as well as from the work that integrates the present with the future when undertaken optimally.

The justice of a given judgment, rendered in consequence of a conflict, can be determined by the acceptability of the solution to the parties involved. The judgment will supplant the conflict if it is regarded as just—as preferable to the complexities and troubles of the current conundrum. In consequence, peace and the possibility of cooperation will be reestablished. Poor judgment— including that imposed by force or fiat—merely ensures that the conflict will continue, even (and often) in a different guise. The true judge must come to deeply understand the nature of the morality that brings peace, harmony, and productivity to his people. The Israelites give up the authority to address their own troubles to Moses, who groans under the weight of the task. All that deferred responsibility is simply too much. Jethro observers this from his stance as benevolent foreigner and objects:

> And it came to pass on the morrow, that Moses sat to judge the people: and the people stood by Moses from the morning unto the evening.
>
> And when Moses' father in law saw all that he did to the people, he said, What is this thing that thou doest to the people? why sittest thou thyself alone, and all the people stand by thee from morning unto even?
>
> And Moses said unto his father in law, Because the people come unto me to inquire of God:
>
> When they have a matter, they come unto me; and I judge between one and another, and I do make them know the statutes of God, and his laws.
>
> And Moses' father in law said unto him, The thing that thou doest is not good.

Thou wilt surely wear away, both thou, and this people that is
with thee: for this thing is too heavy for thee; thou art not able to
perform it thyself alone.

Exodus 18:13–19

Three sets of dangers lurk within this situation, each realized at a different level of the psychological and social hierarchy. First is the danger posed
to the Israelites, both culturally and individually, in the decision to abandon
responsibility for ordering their own personal affairs. They hope to shed that
hypothetical burden (which is in actuality opportunity itself), but in so doing, doom themselves to a contemptible and counterproductive dependency
and forgo the benefits of true maturity. They flirt with refusing their destiny,
preferring to pass that obligation up the social hierarchy, and remain immature, childish, narrowly self-centered, resentful, derisive, incoherent, lost and
divided instead. The second danger is that of the reestablishment of tyranny.
The elevation of their prophet to the status of judge is one step away from his
crowning as king, the replacement of the Pharaoh, and the exposure of the
Israelites to all the dangers from which they so recently escaped.

A king can all too easily become an absolute monarch, and an absolute
monarch the head of a degenerating dynastic authoritarian regime. It is in
this manner that the irresponsible and slavish call forth the power-hungry
tyrants. Third is the allied psychological threat to Moses; the temptation of
egotism and pride. Elevated above his fellow citizens by their very unwillingness to take responsibility, Moses could all too easily think proudly and
highly of himself, and be tempted to wield his authority in the form of compulsion and power. This is in fact his biggest temptation, as is dramatized
time and time again. Moses has the proclivity of the leader to employ force
in excess of its necessity when invitation and persuasion would suffice. This
occurs when he slays the Egyptian who beats a Hebrew slave (Exodus 2:11–
12); when he enables the death of the three thousand after the excesses of the
golden calf (Exodus 32:27–28); and following Korah's rebellion, when the
earth opens up and swallows the usurpers (Numbers 16). This tendency is so
marked that it becomes evident even when God indicates precisely the con-

trary, as indicated in Numbers 20:1–13, the incident at the waters of Meribah, where Moses uses the force of his authority to compel the rocks to bring
forth water when he has been called on to employ his words of magic.

The invitation to become judge of the Israelites therefore poses the risk of
a dangerous inflation of ego or narrow self[69] to Moses—the threat to the integrity of his soul attendant on his taking to himself as his own accomplishment or talent the authority that has been delegated to him as a prophet of
God. This is the terrible path of the religious hypocrites, those who use
God's name in vain (Exodus 20:7) and who pray in public (Matthew 6: 5–6),
for the social benefit of being seen to do so—the mode of being of the Pharisees who much later conspire in such a deadly fashion against Christ himself. There is little doubt that this offer of elevation to tyrant would be
tempting, in the main, to the fractious and irresponsible rabble who Moses is
attempting to guide to the promised land. The Israelites, after all, repeatedly
stress their nostalgia for the good old days of the iron rod of the pharaoh
while bemoaning the fact of their terrible freedom (Exodus 16: 2–3; Numbers 11: 4–6). They would make Moses a new tyrant in a heartbeat, if that
would only alleviate them of the burden of their independent destiny. It is
also the rare man indeed who can and will refuse the freely offered plaudits
of the masses—"Who am I to object when everyone clamors to make me the
savior?"—even when that offer is made as a bribe by those who wish to reject
their own personal sovereignty and responsibility.

Jethro objects, in no uncertain terms—and in a manner that echoes down
the centuries. He tells Moses to hand back the responsibility, to teach his
people how to solve their own problems, mediate their own disputes, and
govern themselves:

> Hearken now unto my voice, I will give thee counsel, and God shall
> be with thee: Be thou for the people to God-ward, that thou mayest
> bring the causes unto God: And thou shalt teach them ordinances
> and laws, and shalt shew them the way wherein they must walk, and
> the work that they must do.
>
> *Exodus 18:19–20*

This is salutary advice, on the psychological front, for the Israelites themselves, as well as something that alleviates the strain on Moses, and reduces the temptation of power that is being dangled in front of him. Jethro calls on his son-in-law instead, to instruct his people so that they can become bearers of their own destiny and authors of their own fate. His words are highly practical and immediately implementable:

> Moreover thou shalt provide out of all the people able men, such as fear God, men of truth, hating covetousness; and place such over them, to be rulers of thousands, and rulers of hundreds, rulers of fifties, and rulers of tens:
>
> And let them judge the people at all seasons: and it shall be, that every great matter they shall bring unto thee, but every small matter they shall judge: so shall it be easier for thyself, and they shall bear the burden with thee.
>
> If thou shalt do this thing, and God command thee so, then thou shalt be able to endure, and all this people shall also go to their place in peace.
>
> *Exodus 18:21–23*

This idea of a necessary hierarchy of ordering and responsibility both inspired and is evident in the most highly functional of the communal institutions of the present day. We have in the West, for example, a subsidiary structure of court justice, with the lower courts rendering judgment on matters of rather local and specific importance, and higher courts at the ready when more fundamental disputes make their appearance—or when the decision of a lower authority is regarded by the protagonists, complainants, victims, or perpetrators as insufficiently just. Moses's subsequent actions constitute the prototype for such arrangements.

> So Moses hearkened to the voice of his father in law, and did all that he had said.

And Moses chose able men out of all Israel, and made them heads over the people, rulers of thousands, rulers of hundreds, rulers of fifties, and rulers of tens.

And they judged the people at all seasons: the hard causes they brought unto Moses, but every small matter they judged themselves.

Exodus 18:24–26

Task accomplished, Jethro returns home: "And Moses let his father in law depart; and he went his way into his own land" (Exodus 18:27).

The importance of these two micro-narratives can hardly be overstated. The first concentrates on matters more psychological and is predicated on the twin presumptions that a people capable of self-governance must be sufficiently educated to manage the task, and that it is the duty of the just and sovereign leader to ensure the provision of such education. The second focuses on the social and describes the erection of a hierarchy of distributed responsibility. This new organization is the eternal alternative both to the anarchic wasteland inhabited by slaves in the desert and the heavy-handed, arbitrary, and whim-governed tyranny of fear, force, compulsion, and power. An authentically responsible people require—and will brook—no autocrat. A truly responsible people will take it on themselves to become their own leaders, and protect themselves in that manner from slavish subservience and the despair and hopeless nihilism of the desert chaos. An educated, responsible citizenry dispenses with slavish habits, adopts the mindset of true maturity, looks to the best of the past to guide the future, and forges its own fate.

It is a paradoxical truth, as well, that the voluntary shouldering of precisely the responsibility of self-governance lends to life the meaning that keeps hope alive and despair at bay, even during times of trouble, when simple happiness is far out of reach. This shouldering is, yet again, the transforming adventure of Abraham (of Jacob—of the Israelites themselves, of the eventual followers of Christ). There is nothing "morally relative" about any of this: the adoption of the responsibility for self and communal governance

is identical to adulthood—identical even to the neurophysiological integration or maturity that at the highest level comprises the individuality that
is farseeing, sacrificial, autonomous, hospitable, productive, generous, and
properly communal.

The two innovations suggested by Jethro and carried out by Moses are
mutually reinforcing, as well as alternative to tyranny and slavery. Educated
and responsible people make much more able judges, while the establishment of a hierarchy of judgment enables those willing to educate themselves
ever more deeply and take on more responsibility as they climb upward, incrementally, toward the pinnacle of Moses; toward God himself, above that.
This is a hierarchy of competence and ability, rather than one of power and
force—that competence, in the case of judgment, adjudicated by the peers of
the would-be judges, who choose from their lower ranks those who should
rise, as well as by the beneficiaries of the judges' decisions. The decisions of a
competent authority will be accepted voluntarily—even with relief—by those
directly affected, who will in turn not so much submit to the authors of such
decision but actively work to support and honor them. It is this competent
authority that makes tyranny unnecessary; it is this competent authority
whose defining characteristics and principles are criticized derisively and
forcefully during times of cultural uncertainty (the "death of God") by precisely those who would rule tyrannically if they could but seize the occasion.
It is also this competent authority that eliminates slavery itself, by requiring
the development of the attitudes and habits of the self-governing at every
level of the inevitable social hierarchy.

The principle of subsidiarity elaborated in this story—that of decentral-
ized and distributed hierarchical responsibility as the alternative to the
pathological order of tyranny or chaos of the desert—states that as much
freedom and responsibility as possible should be devolved down the chain of
command from highest to lowest, so that the former does not presume or
take too much and the latter abdicate the responsibility that generates sustaining meaning and sacrificial maturity. The higher levels of a given hierarchy should be making decisions or even providing guidance only when it is
impossible for individuals and the more local groups they belong to (couples,

families, business enterprises, towns and cities, even more localized states) to do that in their more local, particularized, and generally more specifically informed environs. When individuals genuinely consult their own conscience and formulate their own goals, they are bringing what might otherwise be a fractious and disjointed intrapsychic multiplicity into a unity. In so doing, they open themselves up to receive a revelation of motivation. They also become determined in what they are willing to prioritize or celebrate or worship and what they are willing to give up in that pursuit. This united determination is the very basis of a desirable emotional stability (freedom from pain, guilt, grief, and anxiety) and a consequent and an accompanying resilience.[70]

Truly motivated individuals allowed the opportunity to organize their own destinies—or better yet encouraged to do so—can then negotiate in good faith with those they deal with most directly (their marital partners, children, business associates, and neighbors) to produce the increasingly higher-order covenants or contractual arrangements that most effectively arrange a productive, generous, secure, and meaningful society. Individuals who have taken responsibility for their own lives can then bargain effectively and honestly to produce agreements that unify them in vision and purpose. This renders those who have done so both predictable and comprehensible to one another, as well as engendering the functional and positive relationships that are defined by a mutual aim. People who truly share a vision, motivated to shoulder the responsibility necessary for its realization, can then cooperate and compete peacefully, within the zone of proximal development[71] established by that vision, in a manner that can facilitate the mutual gain made possible by voluntary division of labor (better conceptualized as the exchange of specialized skill) and, equally, voluntary trade. This means that there will be as little as possible left over to do for those playing at higher-order and more abstract levels of governance. Referees are hardly necessary in a game where no one is motivated to cheat.

It is for such reasons that those who abide by the principle of subsidiarity in political matters insist that governments should refrain from usurping psychological or social functions that could be managed by individuals, couples, families, businesses, or other local institutions. Another reason is that the information necessary to act effectively becomes attenuated as the distance between problem and problem solver increases. Firsthand reports are more reliable than second, and second more reliable than third. As information propagates up a hierarchy of responsibility, the amount of noise to signal almost inevitably increases, and the ability of the upper levels to ensure the desired form of attention or action at the lower decreases. The executives of Tower-of-Babel corporations lose sight of what the engineers who build their products and the salesmen and marketing personnel know about their customers. If there are too many intervening levels of communication, each of which introduce their own bias into the information-propagation process, then the head can completely lose track of what the hands and feet are actually doing. This is one of the fundamental problems of gigantism. Power (no—*authority*) should therefore be devolved to the lowest and most local possible players in a complex game.

Paradoxically, this devolution and distribution of responsibility is precisely what enables those who are truly capable of generating a unifying collective vision, abstracting and strategizing over the long term, to do so: if the leaders of a given enterprise assign requisite and challenging responsibility to those who serve them, they are in turn then freed up to operate at the highest levels of abstraction and development they can personally manage. This is a good deal for everyone involved, when done properly; when done in a state of play.[72] The more explicitly political formulations of subsidiarity (drawing on what is still implicit or acted out or dramatically portrayed in the Exodus narrative) were developed by the Catholic theologian Thomas Aquinas, who insisted that the proper function of any superior power was to aid the inferior, not to supplant it.[73]

The development of the idea of subsidiarity as a tenet of Catholic social thought was inspired by the work of Wilhelm Emmanuel von Ketteler, the Bishop of Mainze in the mid-to-late nineteenth century. The notion was further elaborated upon by other thinkers in the Catholic tradition, such as Luigi Taparelli d'Azeglio, who coined the term *subsidiarity* in the nineteenth century.[74] The Catholic church formally adopted the subsidiarity principle under the rule of Pope Leo XIII, in the encyclical *Rerum Novarum* (1891), widely disseminating and further developing it with Pope Pius XI's encyclical Quadragesimo anno, thus formulated: "Just as it is gravely wrong to take from individuals what they can accomplish by their own initiative and industry and give it to the community, so also it is an injustice and at the same time a grave evil and disturbance of right order to assign to a greater and higher association what lesser and subordinate organizations can do."[75] The principle of subsidiarity serves as one of the three cornerstones of Catholic social teaching, in concert with an emphasis on human dignity and solidarity.[76]

Later more secular and purely political thinkers such as the German economist Wilhelm Röpke argued that the same principle could and should be used to conceptualize and shape governmental and economic structures.[77] The principle was also advocated for strongly by the Austrian-British economist Friedrich Hayek.[78] The founders of the American state likewise viewed authority as residing most properly first in the individual, then the family, town, county, state, and then—and only then—federal government. This ethos is reflected in the Tenth Amendment to the American Bill of Rights, which states explicitly, "The powers not delegated to the United States by the Constitution, nor prohibited by it to the States, are reserved to the States respectively, or to the people."[79] The idea of subsidiary responsibility and organization was also incorporated into the European Union's founding treaties,[80] although a skeptic might argue that the centralizing tendency in that organization has now become so strong that breach occurs with more frequency than honor. Such concepts have exerted and continue to exert a powerful influence on political thinkers, primarily in the conservative camp.[81]

It is immediately after the establishment of this structure of subsidiarity that the Israelites travel to the base of Mount Sinai, the eternal place where earth reaches up to heaven and the heavenly makes contact with the earthly and material. God instructs Moses to tell the children of Israel the following:

> Ye have seen what I did unto the Egyptians, and how I bare you on eagles' wings, and brought you unto myself.
>
> Now therefore, if ye will obey my voice indeed, and keep my covenant, then ye shall be a peculiar treasure unto me above all people: for all the earth is mine:
>
> And ye shall be unto me a kingdom of priests, and an holy nation.
>
> *Exodus 19:4–6*

The Israelites have now followed the proper leader, manifested the appropriate faith in the highest of principles, and organized themselves into a responsible hierarchy. They are thus prepared for something deeper: the revelation of the explicit principles of sustainable order themselves. It is appropriate that Moses is the one to receive the revelation. He has faithfully followed the path of the burning bush, attended to what resists tyranny and sustains in the desert wastelands, and meditated deeply on the nature of justice and its interplay with mercy. The great prophet of God has therefore readied himself to acquire knowledge of the Law itself.

7.7. The Commandments as explicit revelation of custom

God tells Moses to have his people to wash their clothes and sanctify themselves, in preparation for an appearance of the divine at the uppermost reaches of the holy mountain:

> And Moses brought forth the people out of the camp to meet with God; and they stood at the nether part of the mount.
>
> And mount Sinai was altogether on a smoke, because the Lord descended upon it in fire: and the smoke thereof ascended as the smoke of a furnace, and the whole mount quaked greatly.
>
> And when the voice of the trumpet sounded long, and waxed louder and louder, Moses spake, and God answered him by a voice.

And the Lord came down upon mount Sinai, on the top of the mount: and the Lord called Moses up to the top of the mount; and Moses went up. And the Lord said unto Moses, Go down, charge the people, lest they break through unto the Lord to gaze, and many of them perish.

Exodus 19:17–21

Why would a full encounter with God be fatal? Biblically speaking, this might be understood by reference, for example, to the cherubim with flaming swords, which, as we have seen and understood, turn "every which way" (Genesis 3:24) so they can cut and burn away everything that is not acceptable in the Kingdom of Heaven.[82] Nothing imperfect can exist at the highest reaches of the strait and narrow path. This is a dictum that is very challenging to sinful and wayward people. If the sad creatures desiring to approach what is highest have practiced to deceive, and consequently embodied much of what is not right and good, there might not be much left of them or her once the swords have done their work. Are the fires of hell proportionate in their intensity to the distance that has been voluntarily established between the sinner and God? Is the terrible swift sword of the divine something experienced as the flames of perdition themselves by those who have consigned themselves to gnashing their teeth in the outer darkness? Something of this sort seems to be implied by both Dante and Milton, from who we have derived much of our modern conception of hell a place about which virtually nothing is said in the biblical texts.

How might this damage attendant on contact with what is corrective be understood concretely—materially; psychologically and biologically? We have already established that there is little if any difference between what is deep—between that on which much depends—and what is sacred, or holy.[83] In many ways, this is a matter of mere definition: there is a category that applies to the most fundamental presuppositions of the hierarchy of presuppositions that prioritizes our attention and sequences and arranges our actions. There is proportionate emotion associated with shift and movement and change in those depths—ranging from unbearable exhilaration to the worst of terror. Some things make very little difference to us one way or another, while others strike us deeply. If we are hit hard enough in the heart—if what is profoundly important and fundamental makes itself manifest to us, it is unclear that we can withstand the upset. The most serious forms of stress can produce permanent psychophysiological damage,[84] even death. In the short term, the stress response induced by exposure to what is anomalous, corrective, unexpected, and undesired is salutary and helpful, preparing us to muster our resources in the event of an emergency. By contrast, chronic activation of the stress response systems—that is, their constant operation in the medium- to long-term—brings with it a host of detrimental effects, consequent to what has become known as "allostatic load":[85]

> The primary hormonal mediators of the stress response, glucocorticoids and catecholamines, have both protective and damaging effects on the body. In the short run, they are essential for adaptation, maintenance of homeostasis, and survival (allostasis). Yet, over longer time intervals, they exact a cost (allostatic load) that can accelerate disease processes. The concepts of allostasis and allostatic load center around the brain as interpreter and responder to environmental challenges and as a target of those challenges. In anxiety disorders, depressive illness, hostile and aggressive states, substance abuse, and post-traumatic stress disorder (PTSD), allostatic load takes the form of chemical imbalances as well as perturbations in the diurnal rhythm, and, in some cases, atrophy of brain structures. In addition, growing evidence indicates that depressive illness and hostility are both associated with cardiovascular disease (CVD) and other systemic disorders.[86]

Those who have been exposed to violation of their assumptions sufficient to produce severe suffering in the aftermath[87]—those who experience post-traumatic stress disorder—experience post-event growth of the amygdala, a brain area specialized in the production of negative emotion, as well as shrinkage of the hippocampus,[88] a brain area that inhibits negative emotion by placing otherwise incomprehensible occurrences into a comprehensible and familiar context. Other changes also occur when things move too rapidly in the depths. For example, the thalamus—a structure key to the intensity of consciousness—becomes increasingly sensitive to sensory stimuli, a transformation that increases the general apprehension associated with virtually every experience.[89] Once bitten; twice shy—and that applies particularly if the wound went deep. Generally speaking—with treatment or natural recovery, often through voluntary exposure[90]—such damage can be rectified. The hippocampus can, for example, regrow and its inhibition is restored.[91] When what is experienced, in consequence of voluntary approach, is predictably and orderly—when what is experienced can be perceived, conceptualized, and contextualized as familiar, harmless, or useful, at least when approached with requisite ability or skill—then anxiety becomes unnecessary and is constrained.[92]

The rites of purification and sanctification that the Israelites undergo are practices to protect themselves against a too-intense encounter with the divine. We can and do undertake actions and erect structures of interpretation to filter the world. This idea could be broadened to cover knowledge itself: the representations we develop as a consequence of repeated experience with a given phenomenon contextualize that phenomenon,[93] and either strip it completely of its significance or narrow it to the particulars of function specific to the skill we have developed while previously interacting, mastering or, for that matter, ritualizing the phenomenon. With this, memory inhibits the intensity of the miraculous.[94] C. G. Jung said as much when he intimated that organized religion provides a defense against religious experience, pointing out as well that a counterproductive narrowing can easily accompany that defensive process, strategy, or tradition:[95]

What is ordinarily called "religion" is a substitute to such an amazing degree that I ask myself seriously whether this kind of "religion," which I prefer to call a creed, may not after all have an important function in human society. The substitute has the obvious purpose of replacing immediate experience by a choice of suitable symbols tricked out with an organized dogma and ritual. The Catholic Church maintains them by her indisputable authority, the Protestant "church" (if this term is still applicable) by insistence on belief in the evangelical message. So long as these two principles work, people are effectively protected against immediate religious experience. Even if something of the sort should happen to them, they can refer to the Church, for she would know whether the experience came from God or from the devil, and whether it is to be accepted or rejected.[96]

And so we replace the eternal burning bush with merely generic perception, draining it of what might otherwise be overwhelming eternal significance:

> But there's a Tree, of many, one,
> A single field which I have looked upon,
> Both of them speak of something that is gone;
> The Pansy at my feet
> Doth the same tale repeat:
> Whither is fled the visionary gleam?
> Where is it now, the glory and the dream?[97]

It is not obvious at all that our mortal frames can withstand a direct confrontation with the Absolute—and the degree to which such an encounter could harm us may also be affected by the volume of spiritual deadwood we have accumulated. The purifying fire of God's burning sword could easily look like hell to those most fundamentally characterized by the accretion of sin.

At the peak of the mountain—that is, at the top of the hierarchy; at the pinnacle of the system of values—Moses, receives the explicit revelation of the rules that guide society from God himself. Psychologically speaking, he experiences a profound, even revolutionary moment of insight,[98] which might be regarded as an instance of translation of one form of knowing to another. Imagine for a moment a wolf pack or troupe of chimpanzees. Their constant competitive and cooperative interactions eventually settle into a predictable—even multigenerationally stable[99]—pattern.[100] That pattern is the hierarchical structure of the society in question: the relatively permanent status of each individual, compared and contrasted with every other. Each member of the pack or troupe "knows" his or her status. It as if the small society is organized according to a set of social rules—but it is not, because "rules" are statable. The hierarchical arrangement is instead a pattern that characterizes and stabilizes the interactions of the group members.

Suppose next that the pack or troupe members now develop the ability not only to govern their attention and actions in keeping with that pattern but to represent that same pattern in image—to *imagine* the pattern of habit and custom. This is development of the ability to translate purely procedural knowledge—embodied skill—into pictorial abstraction; into something dream-like, that can be present in the absence of the actors in question; even manipulated and experimented with when the ability develops further. This now means that the world can be transformed in imagination without direct practical consequence. This constitutes a great leap forward in the capacity to abstract; a major milestone in the development—a veritably qualitative transformation—of thought. Once the image of the action has been established—or, more generally, an image of the pattern of the action—a further possibility opens up for creatures that have established the ability to communicate and apprehend semantically or linguistically: *the subsequent or consequent translation of the image into the word*. It is in this manner that the habits that come to govern the interactions of a society can first be portrayed, dramatically; and then from that dramatic portrayal, represented explicitly in language. This is the emergence of the law, but a law that is simultaneously mirrored in the underlying dream or image and in the behavioral practices that make up group tradition, expectation, norm, ideal, and taboo. This translation of form—this flash of intuition—strikes Moses with the force of a divine revelation, and well it should. The explicit understanding of the structure of psychological integration and social unity alike is a profoundly revolutionary development; a genuine and qualitatively transformative milestone in the development of higher, conscious culture—something on the order of a fundamental biological mutation.

The coding of behavioral patterns in image gives the image the depth of the behavioral pattern, which is in turn something that emerged in an interactive, iterative, and, ultimately evolutionary manner. The behavioral pattern, as such, is both embodied and distributed, rather than being explicitly understood, or something characteristic of a particular individual. It is the consequence of all the interactions of all the individuals in question, past and present, who established the "traditions" (the hierarchical structure of interactions, in large part) of the group. The nuances of that structure are clearly more complex than can be acted out completely, let alone fully understood, by any given member of the group. This means that the pattern of interactions characterizing the group contains more information than any of the individual members realize, regardless of how completely they have adapted to that pattern behaviorally or mapped it imaginatively or linguistically. This pool of implicit information comes to serve as the storehouse of behavior and imagination enabling further revelation. How? The behavioral pattern of the group is a model of the environment in which the group emerged, including the environment constituted by the group, as indicated previously.[101] Since that behavioral pattern supersedes in its complexity and subtlety the understanding of any individual within the group, society is therefore complex in its totality beyond comprehension, leaving us all to be anthropologists even within our own tribe. The structures and processes of imagination that depict that pattern in drama and dream re-represent that information, but in a manner more complete than any explicit emergent semantic coding can manage. The dream is thus the birthplace of what comes to be coded verbally, as well as the container within which it rests and the intermediary between the explicit and behavior itself (the behavior that encompasses both the pattern of attention and the pattern of action). This is why a dream can present to a dreamer information that the dreamer himself does not yet know. The dream encodes the depth of the culture in a manner transcending that which is merely statable.

This is why Shakespeare and Dostoevsky could see beyond even the ken of a thinker with the genius of Nietzsche, to take particular examples from the parallel worlds of the writers of fiction and the philosophers. This is why the world of the great literary masters are both inexhaustible and unerring in a manner that even the most stellar and brilliant operators in the more purely verbal and explicit domain cannot manage. This is why literary criticism, as well as its twin, the analysis of dreams, are not only both possible and necessary but of a rather stunning crucial importance. This is how philosophy is necessarily embedded in the narrative, and the narrative in ritual and cultural tradition. This is how the rules, once made explicit, retain their connection with the underlying imagination, practices, and even environment (or cosmos) of people now aware in a communicable manner of the rules that govern their individual and collective existence. It is no wonder that all this is represented as an encounter with God on Mount Sinai by the imaginative authors of the great Book of Exodus.

The mountain itself is arranged such that God is at its pinnacle. Moses, prophet of God, is next. The priests are third in line ("And let the priest also, which come near to the Lord, sanctify themselves, lest the Lord break forth upon them" [Exodus 19:22]), and the common people at the base. This is another representation of Jacob's Ladder, as well as an analog of the structure of subsidiarity:

> And all the people saw the thunderings, and the lightnings, and the noise of the trumpet, and the mountain smoking: and when the people saw it, they removed, and stood afar off.
>
> And they said unto Moses, Speak thou with us, and we will hear: but let not God speak with us, lest we die.
>
> And Moses said unto the people, Fear not: for God is come to prove you, and that his fear may be before your faces, that ye sin not.
>
> And the people stood afar off, and Moses drew near unto the thick darkness where God was.
>
> *Exodus 20:18–21*

Why all the smoke and fire? Because it is no small matter for a people to become explicitly conscious, no matter how shallowly, of the divine order that governs them. This is, after all, nothing less than the beginning of the law. Should something that revolutionary—that epoch-making—not be signified by something of dramatic portent?

The rules are both much more detailed in their connotations and deeper in their essence than casual familiarity with the Ten Commandments themselves might indicate. They exist to some degree as the so-called "self-evident"[102] axioms of assumption that all more-differentiated moral claims rely on for their apparent validity, with the ten familiar to most making up the core. That sense of self-evidence is in itself a reflection of the concordance of the commandments with long-established behavioral practice and cultural custom, and the structures of imagination that secondarily come to represent and contain that practice and custom. It is the fact of such concordance that belies any claim of moral equivalence or relativism: there is a very limited number of complex, sustainable, productive, generous, voluntary social games; a clear pattern of their portrayal in the dramas of imagination; and a clearly identifiable and stable set of rules, or principles, that can be derived from that underlying pattern and representation. The Ten Commandments reflect the patterns of attention and action on which many other patterns rest—or are, in other words, the rules on which many other rules rest. They are deep or fundamental because of that—by definition.

Under those ten, according to later revelation, lurks something even deeper, the so-called Great Commandment, which has two separate elements that are in turn united, in their essence: "Thou shalt love the Lord thy God with all thy heart, and with all thy soul, and with all thy mind" (Matthew 22:37) and "Thou shalt love they neighbor as thyself" (Matthew 22:39). Why united? Because there is no difference (and this, once again, is the monotheistic insistence) between the spirit of God and the spirit that calls to each of us to treat all the members of our community as if they were extensions of the ultimate self. The Great Commandment is a meta-rule, describing as it does the founding principle, or pinnacle aspiration, of the ten separate explicit rules.

The Great Commandment also characterizes the nature of the spirit and relationship that gives rise to those rules or that emerges in consequence of their devout following. Christ states, in conclusion, with regard to his uniting, an unexpected and brilliant utterance: "On these two commandments hang all the law and the prophets" (Matthew 22:40). What does this all mean? Set your sights, first, on the highest possible goal. Then understand that there is no real difference between regard for the self, at least as conceptualized in the most sophisticated manner, and the treatment of others (not least because of the inevitable reciprocal consequences of iterated social interactions). Realize as well that there is no difference between that regard and treatment and belief in or even embodiment or incarnation of the spirit of God. In consequence of that underlying unity, the two elements of the Great Commandment emerge; in consequence of those two, the Ten Commandments, which are the panoply of differentiated rules that make up the explicit semantic representation of the traditional stabilizing, regulating, and enabling practices of the culture.

It is a corollary of this hierarchical structure that the more peripheral laws are liable to be more culture-specific and the deeper principles more universal. This realization allows for a certain relativism in some moral matters (some rules are going to be very specific to the vagaries of particular time and place) but a necessary absolutism in others (some rules are so fundamental that no human game can be played in their absence). This can be seen in the relationship between the first stated canonical Ten Commandments and the many more specific and situation-dependent rules that follow.

I. Thou shalt have no other gods before me. (Exodus 20:3)

II. Thou shalt not make unto thee any graven image, or any likeness of any thing that is in heaven above, or that is in the earth beneath, or that is in the water under the earth. (Exodus 20:4)

III. Thou shalt not take the name of the Lord thy God in vain; for the Lord will not hold him guiltless that taketh his name in vain. (Exodus 20:7)

IV. Remember the sabbath day, to keep it holy. (Exodus 20:8)

V. Honor thy father and thy mother: that thy days may be long upon the land which the Lord thy God giveth thee. (Exodus 20:12)

VI. Thou shalt not kill. (Exodus 20:13)

VII. Thou shalt not commit adultery. (Exodus 20:14)

VIII. Thou shalt not steal. (Exodus 20:15)

IX. Thou shalt not bear false witness against thy neighbor. (Exodus 20:16)

X. Thou shalt not covet thy neighbor's house, thou shalt not covet thy neighbor's wife, nor his manservant, nor his maidservant, nor his ox, nor his ass, nor any thing that is thy neighbor's. (Exodus 20:17)

Contrast those with the rules listed in the following chapters—mainly dealing with the specific dispensation of property, elements of social responsibility, and the details of the administration of justice tempered by mercy (Exodus 21–23):

If a man opens or digs a pit and fails to cover it, and an ox or a donkey falls into it, the owner of the pit shall make restitution; he must pay its owner, and the dead animal will be his. (Exodus 21:33–34)

If a fire breaks out and spreads to thornbushes so that it consumes stacked or standing grain, or the whole field, the one who started the fire must make full restitution. (Exodus 22:6)

You must not exploit or oppress a foreign resident, for you yourselves were foreigners in the land of Egypt. (Exodus 22:21)

You must not mistreat any widow or orphan. (Exodus 22:22)

If you take your neighbor's cloak as collateral, return it to him by sunset, because his cloak is the only covering he has for his body. (Exodus 22:26)

You shall not follow the crowd in wrongdoing. When you testify in a law-suit, do not pervert justice by siding with the crowd. (Exodus 23:2)

And do not show favoritism to a poor man in his lawsuit. (Exodus 23:3)

The precise placement of each rule in the hierarchy of desirable practice is subject to constant debate, which is intrinsic to the constant theological, narrative, and philosophical enterprise of mankind; which is part of the building of the eternal pyramid stretching to heaven and its tempering by heat and pressure; which is part of the process of naming and subduing the world that God gave Adam as endless mission. The existence of this justly debatable variability does not imply that nothing is central; that everything is equally and nihilistically, anarchically or hedonistically, peripheral.

The Golden Rule—"And as ye would that men should do to you, do ye also to them likewise" (Luke 6:31)—is a variant of the second part of the Great Commandment (indicated more clearly in Matthew 7:12 [King James Version]): "Therefore all things whatsoever ye would that men should do to you, do ye even so to them: for this is the law and the prophets." That Rule is an example of the explicit statement of an evolved indirect reciprocity: "I help you and somebody else helps me."[103] The same pattern has been modeled or observed emerging by game theorists, formally modeling iterative interactions, and has been summarized by such researchers as follows:

> Firstly, individuals tend to adopt cooperative strategies in the long-term process of building interpersonal networks. Secondly, stronger trust foundations between individuals lead to greater cohesiveness under cooperation strategies. Finally, to maintain interpersonal networks under the betrayal strategy, it is essential to continuously add new nodes to the network.[104]

The latter comment indicates what is necessary for the betrayers (the psy-chopaths; the predatory parasites) to continue successfully implementing their nonreciprocal or narrowly self-serving strategy: a continual stream of new and naive, willfully blind or otherwise unknowing victims. This tactic is, by the way, identical to the necessary, inevitable and unconscious wandering of Cain. Why? Because all those who depend on a pattern of second-rate sacrifice, embittered by their rejection, aiming at revenge, find themselves compelled to move from place to place, seeking out new victims. Those they betray once, twice or even thrice remember, and subsequently refuse to continue in their role as pawns, patsies, lackeys, or worse. The cross-cultural prevalence of a conception or principle of moral conduct similar to that of the Golden Rule has been noted by many authors, and is something held as central by the practitioners and formulators of many of the world's religions.[105] This is as much evolved adaptation as divine injunction.

God then reiterates to the Israelites his promise of eventual universal victory if they abide by the delivered dictates:

> So you shall serve the Lord your God, and He will blesse your bread and your water. And I will take away sickness from among you.
>
> No woman in your land will miscarry or be barren; I will fulfill the number of your days.
>
> I will send My terror ahead of you and throw into confusion every nation you encounter. I will make all your enemies turn and run.
>
> I will send the hornet before you to drive the Hivites and Canaanites and Hittites out of your way.
>
> *Exodus 23:25–28*

Those who follow the angel of the Lord will triumph. This is a reiteration of the continual insistence in the Old Testament (and the New) that those who align themselves with the implicit moral order will triumph.

Moses convenes with God on the peak of Mount Sinai for forty days and nights in what appears as a "consuming fire in the eyes of the Israelites" (Exodus 24:17), and receives, in consequence, the stone tablets with the Ten Commandments inscribed upon them. Inscribed stone signifies (as in the case of a grave marker) permanence, memory, reverence, and attention—as it takes time and care to carve stone. After his receipt of the rules, the prophet

is given detailed instructions for the construction of the Ark of the Covenant, designed to contain the stone tablets as well as the mobile tabernacle,
or church, that will surround and house that Ark. Moses is given the law,
and the means of transmitting it across time: the church or temple that came
over the ensuing millennia to occupy central, or prime, position in the increasingly permanent settlements established everywhere. The law is therefore
established in the explicit form of the commandments and their accompanying rules at the same time as the ineffably divine at the center of the community. That allows for both a place for and reminder of the proper upward
sacrifice on which both psychological stability and social being are necessarily predicated.

God is therefore placed in the central position of the community, accompanied by the central rules he established, hemmed in by the successive veils
of the tabernacle (another indication of hierarchy and subsidiarity), surrounded in turn by the community. The pattern is established not only for
all social arrangement but also for the psyche that is unified, and for both
perception and conception—even in their individual or particular elements.
Everything consciously apprehensible is a divine or heavenly idea, surrounded
by a periphery of increasing distance and multiplicity. This is as true for the
"objects" of our perception as it is for our ideas about those objects. The
community within which the ideal is thereby situated is enjoined to offer
something of value (gold, silver, brass, dye and skins, oil and incense, and
precious stones) so that this holy sanctuary can all be made possible. This is
one of the aforementioned sacrificial acts allowing for the very existence of
the productive social world.

Obviously, something must be given up by each individual so that the
benefits of community can be obtained. A world of all against all, which is
the alternative, is a world of endless war and privation—and not the paradise
of anarchic hedonism imagined by the Canaanites, the occupants of Sodom
and Gomorrah, and the worshippers of the golden calf. This practice of offering to establish a place of divine beauty is simultaneously both the founding and explicit sanctification of the practice of patronage for the arts, which
are the manifestation in imagination and play of the spirit that exists at the

center and unites. Beauty and deep story are avenues to the divine—alternative and accompanying forms of worship, however implicit that worship might yet be.

The Ark's cover—the mercy seat—was held to be the place or symbol of atonement (at-one-ment); the place of reconciliation between fragmented, anxious, and hopeless sinner and God—and in keeping with that central role, constructed of pure gold, the noblest of metal, unwilling even as an empirical fate to "mate promiscuously" with other metals, and able to keep its purity forever.[106] This throne was bracketed by two cherubim, reminiscent of the angels guarding the gates of Paradise. Is this combination of the idea of atonement and the harshest of discrimination and judgment a reflection of the idea of the gathering of the wheat and the shedding of the chaff (Matthew 3:12)? Is the repentance of sins equivalent to the shedding of deadwood and the cutting away of what would be inappropriate in heaven itself? Is this all something attained as a consequence of the highest conceivable or ultimate form of sacrifice?

The mercy seat was located within the tabernacle in the central place, the Holy of Holies—a room that could be entered only once a year, on the Day of Atonement, and then only by the high priest. On that day, he would sprinkle upon it the blood of a sacrificial lamb. This is voluntary celebratory giving up of everything lower to that which higher and, ultimately, highest. That is also atonement, the production of the one from the many, because everything comes together under what is highest in precise proportion to the degree of sacrifice. This is something external, perfect, and innocent; the offering of some property or other item of genuine value. But that is insufficient just as the externalization of evil is insufficient: there are, indeed, predators—literal serpents and beasts of prey. However, there are also snakes in the heart of your enemies, metaphorically speaking, and they can present an even greater danger. Such realization and representation is the first stage in the transformation of the idea of predatory evil into something deeper, more profound and psychological. But that that is not yet sufficient abstraction. There is also all too often evil lurking in the hearts even of family members and friends. Betrayal is common. The closer the relationship within which it makes itself present, the closer it cuts to the bone. But the worst snake of all is the one that dwells within: we are never betrayed more seriously than when we betray ourselves.

The same inexorably psychologizing logic applies in the case of good: It is difficult for a rich man to enter the kingdom of heaven (Matthew 19:23–26) because he may well choose what is comfortable or proximate or status-enhancing over what strikes a balance or produces a harmony between now and later and individual and community. We are all constantly tempted, therefore, to perform reverse sacrifices; to invert the proper cosmic order. We do so when we place the gratification of our immediate needs and wants or the desire to deceitfully escape from the consequences of erring before what is good for us, *all things considered*; to prioritize the narrowest of our desires and avoidance of responsibility over the more encompassing good of the community in which we and all others are sustained.

Something is inevitably imitated, celebrated, and even worshipped, no matter which way we turn; no matter whether we engage in an ultimately counterproductive selfishness or a productive reciprocal generosity. One thing or another is being elevated to the highest place, which is an act always necessary before attentional resources can be allocated and forward movement initiated. To attend to one thing, or to do one thing, is to sacrifice everything else that could have instead been noticed or done. To prioritize is to sacrifice, and to sacrifice properly is to atone. By definition, therefore, there is no difference between atonement and the assiduous devotion of everything lower to what is higher. This is the eternal alternative to the Luciferian Tower of Babel, the liana that unites earth with heaven. This is Jacob's Ladder, Mount Sinai, and the subsidiary pyramid.

The necessity of sacrifice—and bloody sacrifice, at that—should really be self-evident. The relationship between giving up something of value in the attempt to establish a covenant with friend, neighbor, and future self alike no different from the honest, productive, and generous work that obviously redeems. In the same vein, the sacrifices we make in life are no different from the maintenance and continuation of life. This is true at all levels of experience, simultaneously. The community has to sacrifice its desire for unrestricted gain to the current limits of the natural environment. Failure to do so results in the tragedy of the commons and the collapse of what might otherwise be a sustainable relationship ("resource"). The individual has to sacrifice his or her desire for immediate narrow gratification to the further-ance and maintenance of his or her future self—to the hierarchical commu-nity of marriage, family, community, and environment. There is no difference between the harmony that is established when such sacrifice is undertaken in the highest degree and the construction of a subsidiary structure of fealty, rights, and responsibility: One nation, under God.

8

◆

Moses II: Hedonism and Infantile Temptation

8.1. Materialism and orgiastic celebration

While Moses is on the mountaintop communing with God—a terrible but enlightening enterprise—and establishing the explicit rules and rituals by which the people of Israel are to live, the people themselves turn with appalling immediacy to the worship of false idols (Exodus 32:1–6). Moses is apparently a bit delayed in returning. Impatient, his slavish and fractious people demand that Aaron make them a golden calf, to which end they offer all the golden earrings worn by the Israelite women. This is another example of the sacrifice on which community is based; this time, however, it is an offering to the gods of immediate gratification and worship of the narrow self. This is not freedom; the Israelites have regressed to the paganism of possession by instinct:

> And he received them at their hand, and fashioned it with a graving tool, after he had made it a molten calf: and they said, These be thy gods, O Israel, which brought thee up out of the land of Egypt.

WE WHO WRESTLE WITH GOD

And when Aaron saw it, he built an altar before it; and Aaron made proclamation, and said, To morrow is a feast to the Lord.

And they rose up early on the morrow, and offered burnt offerings, and brought peace offerings; and the people sat down to eat and to drink, and rose up to play.

Exodus 32:4–6

Where is the materialism, *per se*? A calf is a storehouse of value, for a herder; a golden calf is the intermediary stage between a concrete possession—and something directly either edible, or capable of producing what is edible in time—and money itself, which is an entirely abstract standard or bank of value. To worship the golden calf is to succumb to something approximating the love of money, much later deemed the root of all evil (1 Timothy 6:10). There is very little difference between worship of materialistic gratification and the possession by impulsive and destructive whim.[1]

Aaron as political leader falls prey to the temptation and accedes to the impulsive demands of his people as soon as the voice of the divine Himself (in the form of Moses) falls silent. God nonetheless lets the absent Moses know what is going on (Exodus 32:7), directly; lets him know that he is sufficiently unhappy enough about this betrayal to contemplate destroying the Israelites. He then offers Moses the possibility of being the sole progenitor, like Noah or Abraham, of the future chosen people of God. Moses rejects this offer, choosing instead to set his brother straight and upbraid his people. The prophet returns to the camp in angry haste, dashing the tablets he has just received against the ground and breaking them. He then incinerates the golden calf, grinding the remains to powder, casting that upon the water— back to the chaos from which it emerged. He then requires the children of Israel to drink that very mixture of powder and water; to swallow and digest what they had done (Exodus 32:19–22).

Aaron's politic willingness to bow to even the evil impulses of his people has rendered them weak, vulnerable, and even contemptible to their enemies: "Moses saw that the people were running wild and that Aaron had let them get out of control and so become a laughingstock to their enemies"

(Exodus 32:25 New International Version); "Moses saw that Aaron had let the people get completely out of control, much to the amusement of their enemies" (Exodus 32:25 New Living Translation); "And when Moses saw that the people had broken loose (for Aaron had let them break loose, to the derision of their enemies)" (Exodus 32:25 English Standard Version); "Now when Moses saw that the people were out of control—for Aaron had let them get out of control to the point of being an object of ridicule among their enemies" (Exodus 32:25 New American Standard Bible); "And when Moses saw that the people were naked; for Aaron had made them naked unto their shame among their enemies" (Exodus 32:25).

The narrative here, describing the rise of a corrosive populism, indicates the fundamental problem of truth or even social agreement arising from mere consensus, in the absence of any true correspondence with an intrinsically structured overarching reality[2] or a priori cosmic order. The staff of tradition, planted in the ground, around which everything necessarily rotates, has been uprooted from its necessarily central position—replaced by the immature hell of hedonistic anarchism:

> Turning and turning in the widening gyre
> The falcon cannot hear the falconer;
> Things fall apart; the centre cannot hold;
> Mere anarchy is loosed upon the world,
> The blood-dimmed tide is loosed, and everywhere
> The ceremony of innocence is drowned;
> The best lack all conviction, while the worst
> Are full of passionate intensity.[3]

In the absence of Moses's words and uniting staff of living tradition, the Israelites decide to prioritize the celebration and worship of something that leads them almost immediately to behave irresponsibly and weakly enough to become objects of mockery to their potentially deadly foes. There is also a clear indication of hedonistic celebration—irreverent, drunken partying— in the Israelite's worshipping of the golden calf: "It is not the voice of them that shout for mastery, neither is it the voice of those who cry for being over-come: but the noise of them that sing do I hear" (Exodus 32:18). This passage in the Book of Exodus is alternatively translated as follows:

> And Moses says, It is not the voice of them that begin the battle, nor the voice of them that begin the cry of defeat, but the voice of them that begin the banquet of wine do I hear." (Brenton Septuagint Translation)

> But Moses replied, "It doesn't sound like they are shouting because they have won or lost a battle. It sounds more like a wild party!" (Contemporary English Version)

> Moses replied, "It's not the sound of winners shouting. It's not the sound of losers crying. It's the sound of a wild celebration that I hear." (God's Word Translation)

> But he said, "It is not the sound made by victors, or the sound made by losers; it is the sound of revelers that I hear." (New Revised Standard Version)

This sudden decadent descent of the Israelites is presented as a danger to their very survival. The purely political divorced from the traditional is not only susceptible to domination by the careless momentary whim of the people but also, as it turns out, by the careless momentary whim of the worst within a small minority of people. This strongly implies that in the absence of the voice of truly upward and difficult aim, the most immature and dys-regulate will clamor, successfully, for control. And why would it be otherwise? Regression is easier and more likely than progression, precisely as movement toward entropy is easier than movement away—even though the latter defines life itself.[4]

Moses calls on those the remaining faithful to God to join him near the gate of the camp (Exodus 32:26). The Levites do so under the guidance of Phinehas, a son of Aaron, and their leader. The gathered force then determine to slay about three thousand of the unfaithful Israelites (Exodus 32:28). What proportion that was of the total population is unclear. When Jethro counsels Moses to divide his people into a hierarchy of responsibility, they are grouped in tens, fifties, hundreds, and thousands, so there are clearly enough Israelites to form multiple groups of thousands. Exodus 12:37 indicates six hundred thousand men—and therefore perhaps something approximating two million as a total population, and this number is essentially reiterated in Numbers 1:46 and 11:21. There are those who think that this is a substantive overestimate, suggesting instead a number closer to thirty thousand.[5] Even if the latter estimate is accepted, however, the three thousand slain still represents a small percentage of the population.

The indication that the political realm can be rapidly corrupted by a dedicated minority, bent on gratifying its narrowly self-interested desires, when separated from its association with or proper subsidiary nesting within the prophetic or traditional realm, is therefore further emphasized. This is a very rough ending to this part of the journey. It indicates two things: First, the danger of the descent of a wayward people into the collective immaturity of the hedonistic and self-absorbed mob; and second—and equally dangerously—the calling forth of the tyrannical spirit by that mob, in this case in the form of the deadly reprisal of Moses, whose cardinal sin is his tendency to use compulsion and force (power, in a word) when invitation and discussion might suffice. Neither of these tendencies is separable from the other. A people who abandon all responsibility and maturity in pursuit of what is carnally and hedonistically desirable, now, are the same people who cannot make the sacrifice necessary to best ensure future survival or peaceful communal life—and the same people whose every attitude calls for the presence of the heavy-handed authoritarian. What does this mean for understanding what constitutes necessary action in the face of crisis and degeneracy? Does the text highlight both the dangers of an idiot tolerance (in that the Israelites are overwhelmed by a small number of bad actors) and the repressive state (in the form of the turn by the more traditional state to deadly force)? Remember: in the Book of Revelation, at the archetypal end time, the crimson beast kills the pleasure-serving mother of all prostitutes. This is a vision about how people and societies can so terribly meet their end.[6]

After the purging, Moses intercedes yet again on behalf of the wayward people of Israel, telling God that he wants no part in determining the future if they are not forgiven. In verse 32:10, God threatens to consume them completely. After Moses's intercession (Exodus 32:35), this sentence is replaced with a somewhat unspecified but lesser punishment (as "plagued" can be read as "struck" as well as visited with illness[7]). Immediately thereafter, God reiterates his desire for the Israelites to sojourn to the promised land, but withdraws his direct leadership, substituting instead the much lesser form of an angel:

> And the Lord said unto Moses, Depart, and go up hence, thou and the people which thou hast brought up out of the land of Egypt, unto the land which I sware unto Abraham, to Isaac, and to Jacob, saying, Unto thy seed will I give it:
>
> And I will send an angel before thee; and I will drive out the Canaanite, the Amorite, and the Hittite, and the Perizzite, the Hivite, and the Jebusite:
>
> Unto a land flowing with milk and honey: for I will not go up in the midst of thee; for thou art a stiff-necked people: lest I consume thee in the way.
>
> *Exodus 33:1–3*

What does this at least partial departure of God indicate? That people who turn faithlessly from what should be held in the highest place risk permanently damaging the relationship with conscience and calling that would otherwise orient them in times of trouble and good alike. This is a sentiment echoed in Jeremiah 5:21: "Hear now this, O foolish people, and without understanding; which have eyes, and see not; which have ears, and hear not"; and Isaiah 42:20, "Seeing many things, but thou observest not; opening the ears, but he heareth not"; and emphasized in Matthew 13:14, "And in them the prophecy of Isaiah is fulfilled, which says: 'Hearing you will hear and shall not understand, And seeing you will see and not perceive.'" People become what they practice. Our very perceptions are shaped by our intentions and our aims, which when habitual can screen from consciousness all that is not pertinent to the ruling ethos. When sin is practiced, the good recedes. Vision is obscured. At the individual level, that is alienation from conscience and rejection of calling; at the collective, the very Death of God. In the case of sufficient sin, the divine itself disappears into obscurity and chaos. Is even repentance then only able to bring forth a shadow of what could have otherwise been present?

8.2. Desperate reestablishment of the covenant

The Israelites, dreadfully and appropriately unhappy about this turn of events, strip themselves of their ornaments and mourn. Moses pitches a temporary tabernacle outside the camp so that everyone who desires can worship there. This means that the holy center has now become marginalized—a restatement of the idea that God has been replaced by a lesser angel. The Israelites are fortunate indeed that the divine has not absconded completely, which is the state, for example, that earlier characterized Sodom and Gomorrah. The prophet uses the opportunity to speak directly to God (hidden within the pillar of cloud)—wrestling once again with the divine[8]—while his people safely stay put near their tents. He expresses doubt concerning his leadership in the journey to come, not least because God has indicated that he is going to withdraw his favor, at least to some degree.

Moses therefore asks God to clarify the situation, to show him the way and buttress his belief that Israel is still God's favored nation: "For wherein shall it be known here that I and thy people have found grace in thy sight? is it not in that thou goest with us? so shall we be separated, I and thy people, from all the people that are upon the face of the earth" (Exodus 33:16); alternatively translated, for example, as "For how then can it be known that Your people and I have found favor in Your sight? Is it not by Your going with us, so that we are distinguished, Your people and I, from all the [other] people on the face of the earth?" (Amplified Bible). When God withdraws from the people, it is only the prophets on the margin who can still see and hear the truth. These are precisely the voices "crying in the wilderness," such as the gospel's John the Baptist, saying both "Repent, for the king for the kingdom of heaven is at hand!" and "Prepare the way of the Lord; Make his paths straight" (Matthew 3:1–3).

God agrees, in consequence, to show himself to Moses. This is both a reward for his faithful servant, and an indication that Moses has remained close to God, despite his marginalization. Thus, at least one Israelite is still in sufficient and direct contact with the divine—and one might be enough, as it was in the case of the Elijah with whom Moses is so famously later paired.[9] God hides his faithful servant in the cleft of a rock and passes by, shielding his face from Moses but allowing him to see his back (Exodus 33:12–23). Moses can see, therefore, where God has been—can see the back of him; the consequences of his presence—and that is more than sufficient to buttress his faith. As the Pulpit Commentary has it: "The anthropomorphisms of the passage are numerous and strong—they must, of course, be regarded as accommodations to human ideas. After the Divine Presence had passed by, Moses was to be permitted to look out, and would see so much of the Divine glory as he would be able to bear."[10]

Even for someone of Moses's moral stature and standing with God, the full experience of divinity is too much, but a partial glimpse appears sufficient to reconnect him with what is in the depths, quell his doubts, and rekindle his hope. Such conceptions of God make mockery of any strawman attempts to reduce the divinity characterized in the biblical account to anything finally comprehensible, let alone material ("Is God real?") or simply personal, as the much-derided but more sophisticated than it might appear metaphor of old man in the sky might have it. Why *more sophisticated*? Because there is nothing more complex in all of existence than the human psyche, as far as can be determined; because a human being is a microcosm or model of the cosmic order. So as far as metaphors or characterizations go "sky-father" is better than most. But there is absolutely no indication in the ancient accounts we are considering that such a representation is to be regarded in any manner as complete or final. Dawkins, again:

It is often said that there is a God-shaped gap in the brain which needs to be filled: we have a psychological need for God—imaginary friend, father, big brother, confessor, confidant—and the need has to be satisfied whether God really exists or not. But could it be that God clutters up a gap that we'd be better off filling with something else? Science, perhaps? Art? Human friendship? Humanism? Love of this life in the real world, giving no credence to other lives beyond the grave? A love of nature, or what the great entomologist E. O. Wilson has called Biophilia?[11]

How naively optimistic, in the face of the eternal tendency toward the golden calf. How about the worship of power, to fill the God-shaped gap? The envious blandishments of the great Communist delusion? The rabid celebration of racial identity that characterized the National Socialists? How about a vicious and demoralizing turn toward the blandishments of nihilism? Or the immediate pleasures of hedonism—even the outright self-congratulatory sadism of the Marquis de Sade, shadow twin of the French Revolution and the Enlightenment? Shades of Michel Foucault.[12]

How about the so thoroughly, carefully, and rationally justified murderousness of *Crime and Punishment*'s Raskolnikov? The demented incoherencies and witchcraft of the so-called New Age? Are those not manifestations of a foundationless rationalism as well? Everything logically flows, but the underlying axioms are flawed. That is the situation of someone seriously paranoid but still rational, except in their very perceptions. There's the rub, for the rationalist: What is to be placed at the bottom of things or at the pinnacle of aspiration? And, with regard to "biophilia": let us not forget that love of the planet all too often means hatred for those who inhabit it. The worship of Baal, god of nature, was typically associated with the sacrifice of children (Jeremiah 19:5). And if you do not think we are capable of that in the modern world, think again: How much of the profoundly anti-child sentiment that pervades our culture is an inevitable consequence of the elevation of the terrible goddess Gaia to the highest place? In concert, of course, with the irresponsible, narrowly self-serving and terminally naive pleasure-seeking of the so-called sexual revolution, enticing toward perdition those who might otherwise with care become mature and responsible mothers and fathers?[13] It takes someone blind indeed not to see the stunning anti-humanism that immediately emerges when the hypothetically laudable nature worship so thoughtlessly promoted by Dr. Dawkins takes central place. *The planet has too many people on it!*[14] Has there ever been a more intrinsically murderous, or even genocidal, slogan? Who is exactly to go then? Who decides? Is it only the poor, so carelessly multiplying, or perhaps their unwanted children?[15] Particularly those in the developing world, who can by no means be allowed to use the fossil fuels that have lifted those in the West out of poverty?[16]

After the destruction of the original Commandment inscriptions, God instructs Moses to hew two new tablets of stone and to incise the laws once again upon them. These appear to be somewhat lesser artifacts, as the original tablets and the writing alike were the "direct work of God" (Exodus 32:16). Necessitated by the faithlessness of the Israelites and Moses's consequent demolition of the original contract, the new covenant appears to be a comparatively degenerate variant, indicating once again some permanent deterioration of the relationship between the divine and the chosen people, as the notable biblical interpreter suggests: "Something is always lost by sin, even when it is forgiven."[17] To receive the renewed divine word, Moses dutifully repeats his ascent up Mount Sinai once again, new and blank tablets in hand. This is a re-presentation of his Abraham-like adventure, in microcosm; another ascent up Jacob's Ladder.

Along the way, God reminds his prophet yet again of the cost of iniquity, describing himself as "Keeping mercy for thousands, forgiving iniquity and transgression and sin, and that will by no means clear the guilty; visiting the iniquity of the fathers upon the children, and upon the children's children, unto the third and to the fourth generation" (Exodus 34:7). No warp put into the structure of reality by misaligned aim disappears of its own accord. The error must be corrected, if not by the sinner himself, then by those who follow in his wake. This is a terrible truth. But it can hardly be otherwise, if human beings themselves have something important to do, and if the reality we inhabit is truly real. This is why Christ so much later utters these terrible words: "Think not that I am come to destroy the law, or the prophets: I am not come to destroy, but to fulfill. For verily I say unto you, Till heaven and earth pass, one jot or one tittle shall in no wise pass from the law, till all be fulfilled" (Matthew 5:17–18). A "jot" is a transliteration of the smallest letter in the Hebrew alphabet (yod). A "tittle" is a term used to describe the smallest distinguishing features in the Hebrew script. Jesus indicated with these words that not the tiniest detail of the Mosaic Law will be left unfulfilled or unenforced. Alternatively stated: nothing done for ill vanishes of its own accord. This is also why the sins of men eternally call forth the revenge of the mother of all dragons—as the *enuma Elish* so starkly indicates[18] and the Mesopotamians so painfully learned. We pay—or our children pay—for every sin.

Moses is so affected by his encounter with God that when he descends from the mountain and rejoins his people, his face, suffused with reflected glory, is intolerable in its sheer intensity of gaze. He must veil himself to lessen his people's holy terror. This is a reflection of two facts: first, the genuine closeness to the divine of the prophet, remaining in faithful communion with God; second, the opposing state of the Israelites, steeped as they remain in sin. The more distance from God, or from his prophet, the more terrifying and unbearable the act of beholding the face of divinity. Someone pure has little to fear from what is perfect; but someone impure, confronted with the ideal, must also confront the brute fact of his or her impurity. If that impurity is a consequence of willful blindness—if it was due to step-by-step refusal to atone and improve when conscience indicated that necessity—how would it be possible for the person (or people) thus compromised to possibly withstand direct exposure to the judgment implicit in the Ideal itself? Something similar is intimated elsewhere in the biblical corpus, when Christ is transfigured on the mount in front of his disciples, in the miraculous company of Moses and the prophet Elijah (Matthew 17:1–9), in the visions of Ezekiel (Ezekiel 1), and in the revelation of Saint John:

And I turned to see the voice that spake with me. And being turned,
I saw seven golden candlesticks;

And in the midst of the seven candlesticks one like unto the Son
of man, clothed with a garment down to the foot, and girt about the
paps with a golden girdle.

His head and his hairs were white like wool, as white as snow;
and his eyes were as a flame of fire;

And his feet like unto fine brass, as if they burned in a furnace;
and his voice as the sound of many waters.

And he had in his right hand seven stars: and out of his mouth
went a sharp two-edged sword: and his countenance was as the sun
shineth in his strength.

And when I saw him, I fell at his feet as dead. And he laid his
right hand upon me, saying unto me, Fear not; I am the first and
the last:

I am he that liveth, and was dead; and, behold, I am alive for ev-
ermore, Amen; and have the keys of hell and of death.

Revelation 1:12–18

The meaning of this text is twofold. First, every ideal is also inescapably a
judge; second, every deviation from the ideal makes the inevitable judgment
harsher. This is the pattern of the plagues that visit the Egyptians, called
forth by Moses, acting on behalf of God. The increasing difficulty of atonement is the inevitable consequence of repeated sin. This is also a callback, in
a sense, to the experiences of Moses when he encounters God in the form of
the burning bush and while ensconced in rock and protected by the hand of
the divine and to the terrible cleansing and burning blade of Genesis 3:23–
34,[19] also referred to in Isaiah 34:5–6: "For my sword has drunk its fill in the
heavens; behold, it descends for judgment upon Edom, upon the people I
have devoted to destruction." Why does the face of Moses shine, when he is
filled with the glory of the divine? Because whatever God might be is so
much that even those who merely reflect his majesty become intimidating,
even unbearable in their enlightenment and illumination; become terribly
and deeply threatening to those steeped in sin.

A reminder to keep the Sabbath and to fabricate the Tabernacle follows.

To their credit, the Israelites pitch in with great enthusiasm, having perhaps at least for a time learned their lesson. They are so enthusiastic in their offerings for the construction of the holy sanctuary that they have to be restrained— but they complete the project successfully (Exodus 36–40). In consequence of their sacrifice, "a cloud covered the tent of the congregation, and the glory of the Lord filled the tabernacle" (Exodus 40:34). This is the cloud by day, as previously, and the pillar of fire by night, which either rests immobile on the new structure (in which case the Israelites remain encamped), or travels ahead (in which case they follow). This seems like a better deal than the replacement of God with a mere angel, as was threatened. It seems that the intercession of Moses, the successful negotiation of the second covenant, and the willingness of the Israelites to sacrifice for the Tabernacle have convinced God to reestablish his direct leadership.

Thus ends the Book of Exodus and a crucial step in the development of something approximating settled civilization: The Tabernacle of the Israelites is precursor to the synagogue, the cathedral, and the church. It is what becomes the center of town and city, the place of gathering for the sacrificial offering of the united community, the establishment within which the confession, repentance, and atonement that stabilizes and recalibrates the misaligned psyche can occur, so that it once again aims in the upward direction that harmonizes individual with the hierarchy of society and the present with the future. This central edifice and its later variants are replications of the holy mount, Sinai or Horeb, architectural representations of the transforming or living rod of Moses, the center of the Platonic ideal around which all perceptual forms necessarily arrange themselves. They are the place of the sacrifice on which community itself must be founded, as the individual always offers or gives up something to take his or her place in the social world. That can be done without the necessity of compulsion, or force, when the divine invitation is gracefully accepted. Alternatively, it can be managed with kicking and screaming when immaturity is prolonged, conscience ignored, and the call to adventure and truth rejected.

The journey of the Israelites continues with Leviticus, Numbers, and Deuteronomy. The first of these opens with instructions to the Israelites about proper use of the Tabernacle and details further explicit rules, dividing what is clean and meet from what is unclean and taboo and establishing the Holiness Code (Leviticus 17–26). God takes the opportunity in Leviticus 26 to remind the Israelites of the two paths that eternally lay in front of them. The first is the consequence of putting what is properly holy in the highest place:

> If ye walk in my statutes, and keep my commandments, and do them;
> Then I will give you rain in due season, and the land shall yield her increase, and the trees of the field shall yield their fruit.
> And your threshing shall reach unto the vintage, and the vintage shall reach unto the sowing time: and ye shall eat your bread to the full, and dwell in your land safely.
> And I will give peace in the land, and ye shall lie down, and none shall make you afraid: and I will rid evil beasts out of the land, neither shall the sword go through your land.
> And ye shall chase your enemies, and they shall fall before you by the sword.
> And five of you shall chase an hundred, and an hundred of you shall put ten thousand to flight: and your enemies shall fall before you by the sword.
> For I will have respect unto you, and make you fruitful, and multiply you, and establish my covenant with you.
>
> *Leviticus 23:3–9*

What is taboo and unclean is what is forbidden by conscience, what contaminates, what poses a threat to the harmonious integrity of individual and community. There is a certain arbitrariness to or variation in what is forbidden, society to society, in keeping with the theme of allowance for exploration at the margins.[20] The vegans, vegetarians, carnivores, and omnivores of the modern world disagree, for example, about what is to be consumed ethically and for reasons of health. What they do not disagree on, however, is the fact that there are borders surrounding the domain of acceptable conduct in such matters—that there is some dividing line between what is acceptable and what is forbidden. It is precisely in the communal acceptance of such strictures that much of social stability depends.

Thus, there is always what is sacred and what is taboo whenever there is society, because agreement about what can and cannot e done is the very essence of communal being. This is the very division between chaos and order that constitutes the living creation itself. Willingness to abide by those somewhat arbitrary commandments or traditions (which is a form of sacrifice of mere self-interest) is not least an important indication of ability to delay gratification, take others into account, play by the rules, and put shoulder voluntarily and cooperatively to wheel. The acceptance of such "arbitrary" constraints by the members of a community is an indication of the mutual willingness of all involved to attend to the same upward uniting aim, and to pay the requisite individual and communal price. Thus, the attendance to the niceties of taboo is at least a signal of individual acceptance of the sacrifice upon which society is necessarily predicated—and, therefore, of who can and cannot be trusted.

God's promises of victory for those of the lineage of Moses are reminiscent of the offering made to Abraham when he is called to adventure.[21] This is another indication of the conjunction of the divine path and the deepest instincts of mankind. Even the most atheistic of evolutionary biologists admits to the motivating power of the reproductive impulse, whether it be as narrow as sexual desire or as broad as the proclivity to pair-bond permanently and act as father and mother. However, the offer made to Abraham and Moses is much broader, deeper and more significant than the mere immediately sexual: it is instead the assurance that aiming upward, maturing and transforming in the necessarily sacrificial manner, is also the mode of being that best assures long-term dynastic success. This is the harmonious integration of the instincts for survival and reproduction that are part and parcel even of the Darwinian definition of life's purpose.

God has just offered a description of the consequences of following his invitation, or call. He adds to that a warning of ultimate conscience, the hellish consequence of wandering off the path, whether wittingly or otherwise:

> But if ye will not hearken unto me, and will not do all these com-
> mandments;
>
> And if ye shall despise my statutes, or if your soul abhor my judg-
> ments, so that ye will not do all my commandments, but that ye
> break my covenant:
>
> I also will do this unto you; I will even appoint over you terror,
> consumption, and the burning ague, that shall consume the eyes,
> and cause sorrow of heart: and ye shall sow your seed in vain, for
> your enemies shall eat it.
>
> *Leviticus 26:14–16*

And that is not all: God promises domination by enemies and wild beasts, endless hunger (even in the midst of plenty), failure of crop and livestock, death of children, destruction of all habitation and places of worship, eternal diaspora, and worse:

> And upon them that are left alive of you I will send a faintness into
> their hearts in the lands of their enemies; and the sound of a shaken
> leaf shall chase them; and they shall flee, as fleeing from a sword;
> and they shall fall when none pursueth.
>
> And they shall fall one upon another, as it were before a sword,
> when none pursueth: and ye shall have no power to stand before
> your enemies.
>
> *Leviticus 26:36–37*

Here the eternal question of the skeptical atheist might well make its presence once again known: How is possible to have faith or believe in a God such as this, with all his apparent jealousy, anger, rage, and cruelty? These passages present a very stark choice, with regard to the divine, although one that must be regarded as all-too-terribly realistic. If what is highest is not imitated and worshipped, things either fall apart, as everything vies for predominance and confusion reigns, or something that is not meet is elevated to the status of God. Either way, all hell is liable to break loose. Anyone even vaguely familiar with the literature of the horrors of the twentieth century and who understands the catastrophic price paid by subjection to the tyrannies of fascism and communism (or even the nihilism that might beckon as a hopeless alternative) knows full well that the punishments prophesied in the latter part of Leviticus 26 are, if anything, less severe than they might be. Conscience, in the divine sense, is what truly warns against the dominion of hell.

How could that be other than a warning most dire? And if such warning reflects reality, in that there are indeed the harshest of consequences for the sins of pride, resentment, rebellion, usurpation, and deceit, why should warning against them be regarded as cruel? Truly cruel to those facing a fate worse than death would be the absence of strict guidance. No feelings are hurt when no barriers are erected—when "no" is never said—but the impulsive anarchy and power-mad competition that soon rises in consequence is devastating, and all the pain forgone by the absence of necessary discipline returns manifold and with a vengeance. That is the fate of those suffering the flood of Noah, the fire and brimstone of Sodom and Gomorrah, and the utter devastating chaos of the Red Sea. There is nothing compassionate about the failure to act that brings about such catastrophe. It is mere abdication of the most essential patriarchal responsibility.

When the social order that is true degenerates—when the faith in God that is most truly commitment to the sacrificial upward aim vanishes—the terrible tarantella of the slave and tyrant inevitably begins. Subsidiary responsibility is abandoned, replaced by concentration on the pleasures of the moment. The heavy hand of the authoritarian must then be invited in to replace the order of genuinely productive cooperation, competition, and future orientation with the strictures of compulsion and force. The absolute ruler—the pharaoh himself—is elevated to the highest place, where inevitably he becomes tempted by power (and in precise proportion to the waywardness of the people). Hedonistic anarchy requires regulation by the terrible father. Those who are enslaved in the grip of a true tyranny experience no fraternity, no cooperation, no playful competition, and no love. Productive generosity ceases and is replaced by jealous and resentful guarding and hoarding of the ever-diminishing resources at hand. That is a state that might as well be hell itself, and even if it does not last for eternity, it will certainly feel like it does. In the grip of sufficient hopelessness, death itself may well come to be preferred to life. Under such dismal conditions, the past is a pit of misery, the present an endless wasteland, and the future, more of the same and worse. Every step forward is involuntary and forced, and all directions appear equally pointless. This sterility of, and slavery to, authoritarian compulsion breeds a littleness, resentment, and sadism that knows absolutely no bounds.

A single example: when the Japanese invaded the city of Nanking in China in 1937, they began a program of systematic brutality and execution that led to the deaths of more than three hundred thousand civilians in six weeks:

> The Japanese not only disemboweled, decapitated, and dismembered victims but performed more excruciating varieties of torture. Throughout the city they nailed prisoners to wooden boards and ran over them with tanks, crucified them to trees and electrical posts, carved long strips of flesh from them, and used them for bayonet practice. At least one hundred men reportedly had their eyes gouged out and their noses and ears hacked off before being set on fire. Another group of two hundred Chinese soldiers and civilians were stripped naked, tied to columns and doors of a school, and then stabbed by *zhuizi*—special needles with handles on them—in hundreds of points along their bodies, including their mouths, throats, and eyes.[22]
>
> The soldiers then stripped the girls and took turns raping them: the sixteen-year-old by two or three men, the fourteen-year-old by three. The Japanese not only stabbed the older girl to death after raping her but rammed a bamboo cane into her vagina. The younger one was simply bayoneted and "spared the horrible treatment meted out to her sister and mother," a foreigner later wrote of the scene. The soldiers also bayoneted another sister, aged eight, when she hid

MOSES II: HEDONISM AND INFANTILE TEMPTATION 421

with her four-year-old sister under the blankets of a bed. The four-year-old remained under the blankets so long she nearly suffocated. She was to endure brain damage for the rest of her life from the lack of oxygen.[23]

Everyone choosing a path forward has a devil sitting on one shoulder and an angel on another—or so goes the comic trope. But that is an idea—a representation of a deep reality—that is far from childishly amusing. The road to hell begins with a single step, and then another, and each step downward can too easily be rationalized, even celebrated as moral.[24] But the speed and angle of descent increases with persistence, and down can be a terribly long way down. This is why hell is a bottomless pit, archetypally speaking. This means that God is acting in mercy, when He warns the Israelites in no uncertain terms not to deviate. Thus, the "cruelty" of God is much better understood as the inevitable consequence of sin, voluntarily undertaken. This is also an attitude that is the polar attitude of Cain's endlessly destructive adoption of the stance of resentful victimization.

The Book of Numbers details the travails and sojourning of the Israelites after they have received the law and renewed the covenant, however compromised, at Mount Sinai. They are called on to take possession of the promised land. The people and the details of the state are counted (hence, "Numbers"), accounted for, and laid out geographically and hierarchically in a comprehensible and agreed upon manner. It is easy to overlook the significance of this text, light on plot and characterization as it is, and concentrate instead on technical matters. It does no more and no less, however, than establish the statistics on which the modern state depends—the accounting of and for sophisticated social groups, and the technical arrangement and analysis of society itself.

These are all major steps forward in the process enabling the emergence of a highly organized large-scale civilization, allowing as they do the process of numerical abstraction and calculation to be applied to the problem of organizing and understanding the details of communal life. Even the groundwork for the empirical attitude, as such, is thereby laid, particularly in

relationship to the social sciences—establishing the deep notion that count-
ing and formal quantitative categorization and division are both necessary
and useful in our attempts to comprehend the world and deal with its practical necessities. In this manner, the Book of Numbers continues the transformational journey of what was once a ramshackle band of freed slaves into
a structured and functioning society—a progression elevated and facilitated
by numerical abstractions and the resulting societal order.

Numbers also subtly portrays the division of labor that is an additional
vital precondition for the communal provision of abundance. Various sons
of the tribes are assigned, for example, to the army (Numbers 1:20–42); the
Levites, spared that particular duty, are charged with the care of the Tabernacle (Numbers 1:47)—and in a detailed and particular manner in keeping
with the spirit of Numbers. The various subclans of the Levites are given
very specific roles and duties. The Gershonites, for example, are held responsible for "the tabernacle, and the tent, the covering thereof, and the hanging
for the door of the tabernacle of the congregation, And the hangings of the
court, and the curtain for the door of the court, which is by the tabernacle,
and by the altar round about, and the cords of it for all the service thereof"
(Numbers 3:25–26), while the Merarites must take care of "the boards of the
tabernacle, and the bars thereof, and the pillars thereof, and the sockets
thereof, and all the vessels thereof, and all that serveth thereto, And the pillars of the court round about, and their sockets, and their pins, and their
cords" (Numbers 3:36–37). Every man, family, and clan is given its properly
subdued place within the overarching organization of the emerging state
(Numbers 2:34). This painstaking attention to what is essentially administrative detail is a necessary precondition to the subsidiary organization of
responsibility within an increasingly large, productive, and cooperate polity.
It is in such a manner that the Kingdom of God, aimed at by the Israelites, is
brought down to earth.

All this organization makes the renewed march forward possible. On the
continued sojourn, however, the faithless once again begin to "complain
about their hardship" (Numbers 11:1, Berean Study Bible). This is, once again,
an indication of the tendency of the erstwhile chosen people to adopt the role

of victims, just as Cain did. They regard themselves as oppressed by God and Moses; by the natural world and their fellow men; even by their own tendency to regress. The danger of adopting this attitude can hardly be overstated. The tendency to claim victimization is a pronounced tendency of the worst of people—the very Machiavellians, manipulators, narcissists, psychopaths, parasites, and sadists studied by modern analysts of deepest and most destructive of psychopathologies. Once they have defined themselves as unjustly situated and cursed, nothing is forbidden to them—and this is the true motivation for the claims of oppression. As they degenerate, the Israelites gossip, grumble, and backbite. They employ speech in the spirit of the enemy; in the hidden, underground, and cowardly manner later described so well by the shepherd-king David: "For there is no faithfulness in their mouth; their inward part is very wickedness; their throat is an open sepulchre; they flatter with their tongue" (Psalms 5:9). They "imagine mischiefs in their heart" (Psalms 140:2); have "sharpened their tongues like a serpent" (Psalms 140:3) and he places "Adders poison" "under their lips." (Psalms 140:4). They lay snares, and "spread a net by the wayside" (Psalms 140:5). This is the strategy by those who invert the Logos, using words not to communicate but to subvert and destroy; by those who:

> whet their tongue like a sword, and bend their bows to shoo their arrows, even bitter words;
>
> That they may shoot in secret at the perfect: suddenly do they shoot at him, and fear not.
>
> They encourage themselves in an evil manner: they commune of laying snares privility; they say, Who shall see them
>
> They search out iniquities; they accomplish a diligent search: both the inward thought of every one of them, and the heart, is deep.
>
> *Psalms 64:3–5*

In their turn to self-pity, the Israelites display the traits of the faithless and cowardly. They regress, prevaricate, deceive, and turn to resentment. They wax sentimental, yet again, about Egypt, pining hypocritically for the good old days. Instead of adopting an attitude of humility, asking for revelation, thinking critically, exploring, clarifying, and negotiating, they subvert, camouflage, and sow dissent. They plot revenge, jockey for unearned virtue, exclude, shun, inform upon, dismiss, and deride. Then they get worse: "And the mixt multitude that was among them fell a lusting; and the children of Israel also wept again and said, Who shall give us flesh to eat?" (Numbers 11:4). Not only lust, let it be noted—"lusted exceedingly" (Benton Septuagint Translation). What does this mean? That the Israelites, in their new state of relative predictability, stability, calm, and peace unnecessarily and unwisely cultivate their desires, instead of being grateful for what they have been given and have done.

The chosen people at this time are hardly in a state of privation, having been granted manna in plentiful supply; having established, in their diaspora, a productive and functional state. But they voluntarily and thanklessly nurse and brood upon a state of resentful desire, longing for the days in Egypt when (at least in memory) there was an endless supply of fish, cucumbers, melons, leeks, onions, and garlic and rejecting the perfect heaven-provided food bequeathed to them: "But now our soul is dried away: there is nothing at all, beside this manna, before our eyes" (Numbers 11:6). They make such a clamor in their discontent that Moses again reproaches God for his decision to appoint him as the Israelite leader: "Have I conceived all this people? have I begotten them, that thou shouldest say unto me, Carry them in thy bosom, as a nursing father beareth the sucking child, unto the land which thou swarest unto their fathers?" (Numbers 11:12). The constant clamoring and wailing makes him sick to the point of wishing for death: "And if thou deal thus with me, kill me, I pray thee, out of hand, if I have found favor in thy sight; and let me not see my wretchedness" (Numbers 11:15).

God lightens Moses's burden—once again in the subsidiary manner—by distributing some of the responsibility and authority to a group of seventy elders. He then commands his prophet to issue a warning: "And say thou unto the people, Sanctify yourselves against to morrow, and ye shall eat flesh: for ye have wept in the ears of the Lord, saying, Who shall give us flesh to eat? for it was well with us in Egypt: therefore the Lord will give you flesh, and ye shall eat" (Numbers 11:18). God says, in essence, "You have made your bed; now you are going to lie in it."

> Ye shall not eat one day, nor two days, nor five days, neither ten days, nor twenty days;
>
> But even for a whole month, until it come out at your nostrils and it be loathsome unto you; because that ye have despised the Lord which is among you, and have wept before him, saying, Why came we forth from Egypt.
>
> *Numbers 11:19–20*

The displeased divinity sends hordes of quail to the Israelites, until the foul are piled a yard high a day's walk in every direction. About to slake their contemptible appetite, the Israelites are then struck with plague. Those who die and are buried there are "the people that lusted" (Numbers 11:34). This is all a dire warning against ingratitude—and, more specifically, against the unnecessary provocation of the impulsive hedonism that desires nothing but immediate gratification.

As the Israelites approach Canaan, the promised land itself, God tells Moses to send a man from each tribe to "spy out the land" (Numbers 13:17). It is a matter of fact, geographically speaking, that the Israelites are now near their devoutly desired destination. Metaphysically, however, they are so placed because of their continual sacrifice, disciplined obedience, faith, courage, and willingness to abide in the truth (despite the lapses so frequently noted). What are the apparent preconditions for life more abundant? Not the effortless provision of the past, the natural world or even of God Himself, except in covenant. Instead, the moral orientation that provides direction, leading away from tyranny and through the desert; the upward aim that unites the individual within him or herself and all individuals with all others. This is the establishment of a productive hierarchy, predicated upon mutual sacrifice, establishing mutual trust. There is no difference whatso-ever in the biblical narrative between moral conduct and success, all things considered, and over the longest span of time imaginable.

How is this success, or even success itself, to be understood at the deepest level of existential significance? How is this success, predicated upon the es-tablishment of a mature morality, to be conceptualized and appreciated, given the suffering that still appears attendant on even the most fortunate of lives? How are we to reconcile ourselves to the dread and pain of life, bounded as it is by the dire reality of our own truncated existence; our own mortality? It is a strange and mysterious axiom of Judeo-Christian belief (and others) that "the wages of sin is death" (Romans 6:23)—a notion inti-mated in the early paragraphs of Genesis (3:1–7; 3:14–19), detailing the pride-induced fall of man and woman out of Paradise and into mortality; and stated explicitly in Romans 5:12 (King James Version): "Wherefore, as by one man sin entered the world, and death by sin; and so death passed upon all men, for that all have sinned." This idea presents a true conundrum for the faithful—given that all living things die, including animals, who do not in any obvious manner "sin"—and can easily become an object of ridicule. All living things die, and man is in this regard a living thing among all others. The tension produced by this realization—this reality—was if anything heightened by the attribution of the existence of man to the same evolution-ary biological processes and limitations that characterize every other living thing. It seems beyond dispute that death is something built into the very structure of being, and not a consequence of moral error, no matter how ex-treme.

Perhaps, however, the case is not so clear-cut. Is death a preprogrammed biologically inevitability, part of the natural order of things, or a conse-quence of the result of multiple cumulative system failures—the accumula-tion of damage at the molecular and cellular level, the eventual failure of organs, and the inability of the body to repair itself? Death is by no means obviously one thing. Equally obvious is the fact that death comes to some early and some late—and that clearly stupid or wise paths of action can bring about a relatively early demise or reliably lengthen not only life itself but healthy, productive, desirable life. Since the dawn of the industrial revolution, we have radically increased the average span of life, not least through a radical reduction in child mortality. This improvement is often attributed solely to technological progress, an accounting that fails to take into account the improvement in moral conduct that made that very technological progress possible.[25] There would have been no technological miracle without prior development of the true humility and spirit of genuine inquiry that made possible the scientific discovery upon which that technology depended. That in turn depended on faith: first, that the world was comprehensible; second, that men of good will and courage could turn their comprehension to positive advantage; and third, that free and generous exchange of such comprehension would prove of sustained, mutual benefit.

Nor would there have been any generation or accumulation of the wealth that eventually made everyone comparatively rich without a radical and somewhat miraculous widespread acceptance and even appreciation of the inequality of distribution of resources and talent that was a precondition for the initial wealth creation and subsequent dissemination. This meant trust: trust that those who had were benefitting not from their misuse of others but because of their productive labor. This meant admiration for success, rather than resentment and envy—and also meant, in the main, that those who were striving for and attaining success had been acting in good faith. This outlook is something that arguably characterizes the attitude of the individual citizen of the United States, first and foremost, although it can also be seen to a greater or lesser degree across the economically successful countries of the world. Thus, our collective partial defeat of death is a consequence most fundamentally of a sustained and successful moral endeavor—a secondary result of the technological miracles that such reorientation (or proper orientation) makes possible.

This begs a question: If we all acted in a manner that would best enable us to optimize our exploration, our exchange of information; best enable us to rely on one another and therefore to cooperate without doubt; without unnecessary obstacle or stumbling block—what if any problems would remain beyond our capacity to solve? Thus, the questions remain: How much is mortal suffering and even death itself a consequence of the inexorable effects of entropy and disorder, say, intrinsic to the existential situation of man as a material organism; and how much is it due to the moral failings that destabilize and corrupt our collective enterprises and make each of us much less than we could otherwise be? And if none of that fundamentally changes the fact of death itself, is it not till the case, as noted earlier,[26] that full commitment to the upward aim that is adventure takes the sting out of painful limitation and mortality? This, too, is a form of triumph over death and hell. What all this means is that the terrors and boundaries of life can be overcome, to a finally indeterminate degree: practically, in that suffering, physical degeneration, and even death itself can be limited and life-abundant promoted and extended; psychologically, in that the responsible and meaningful pursuit of genuine adventure can sustain and motivate even in the midst of the worst conceivable privations.[27]

The promised land should therefore not so much be conceptualized as a place journeyed to geographically (although is also that) as a place established through sustained moral striving, individual and collectively. After the Israelites have organized themselves psychologically—shedding, at least in part, their unwillingness to adopt responsibility, their fractious squabbling, their faithlessness and false nostalgia for the days of tyranny; after they have as well organized themselves socially in accordance with the principle of subsidiarity—they are now advanced enough to see the promised land itself on the horizon. They therefore send scouts to provide a detailed survey of the territory: "And the Lord spake unto Moses, saying, Send thou men, that they may search the land of Canaan, which I give unto the children of Israel: of every tribe of their fathers shall ye send a man, every one a ruler among them" (Numbers 13:1). The true leaders of men are visionaries. It is inevitable that they will be the surveyors of new territory, as that is the role of the prophet who can see the proper path forward with untrammeled vision and moral clarity. The scouts return with a report of the great potential that is waiting there, warning simultaneously that the problems that remain to be solved (including the fact of the current inhabitants) still loom large:

And they returned from searching of the land after forty days.

And they went and came to Moses, and to Aaron, and to all the congregation of the children of Israel, unto the wilderness of Paran, to Kadesh; and brought back word unto them, and unto all the congregation, and shewed them the fruit of the land.

And they told him, and said, We came unto the land whither thou sentest us, and surely it floweth with milk and honey; and this is the fruit of it.

Nevertheless the people be strong that dwell in the land, and the cities are walled, and very great.

Numbers 13:25–28

As we move into the future, we encounter the endless spirits of opposition that dwell there. These are, all too often, the descendants of Cain: the prideful and resentful presumptions and habits of self and other that will make of that future nothing but the repetition of the sins and errors of the past. Those are the inhabitants that have to be overcome. Whatever proves counterproductive or insufficiently upward-aiming there must therefore be cleared out or converted for the promise to be truly realized. This is another example of the separation of wheat from chaff or the operation of the swift sword that cuts and burns that comprises the eternal battle between evil and good, or even between good and better. Movement forward into the better future is a daunting task. Many such potential promised lands are already occupied by the Canaanites who failed at the task—something both indicative of the difficulty, and part of it. It is for such reasons that the majority of the scouts prove faithless and pessimistic in the face of the challenges that remain:

And Caleb stilled the people before Moses, and said, Let us go up at once, and possess it; for we are well able to overcome it.

But the men that went up with him said, We be not able to go up against the people; for they are stronger than we.

And they brought up an evil report of the land which they had searched unto the children of Israel, saying, The land, through

which we have gone to search it, is a land that eateth up the inhabitants thereof; and all the people that we saw in it are men of a great
stature.

And there we saw the giants, the sons of Anak, which come of the
giants: and we were in our own sight as grasshoppers, and so we
were in their sight.

Numbers 13:30–33

This caution is best read as a failure of leadership rather than as an honest
accounting of the trials and tribulations that still confront the Israelites.
God's chosen people have been continually enjoined to manifest faith in the
fact that what is truly moral will prevail. God has made it clear that his people, if they maintain the true covenant, will prevail even against apparently
insuperable odds. The more timorous leaders nonetheless exaggerate the
danger still to come, falsely and manipulatively portraying their remaining
opponents as giants, contrasting them with their comparatively insect-like
selves. These are hardly the actions of men capable of taking the next steps
forward or of motivating others to do so. They are instead the actions of
those who have renounced the responsibility and burden (and forgone the
attendant redemptive meaning) of authentic pathfinding. They deliver the
words that terrify and demoralize, instead of fortifying and renewing. It is
hard not to nurture the suspicion, as well, that this is done for underground
reasons. People can be frightened into precisely the submission that both
keeps them slaves and enables the up and coming would-be tyrants—the
very scouts who doomsay.

What might we distill from this account, in our modern time; in the face
of the continually dire and dangerously authoritarian cautions about the future that flood both the airwaves and our consciousness? The planet has too
many people on it; the apocalypse is nigh. Perhaps we should beware the
faithlessness of those constantly crying that the sky is about to fall while we
attempt in good faith to make our way forward. It is a truism that the eternal
usurper sows doubt and terror to aid his attempts to demoralize, seduce, and
obtain power. Why *demoralize*? Because doubt about the future produces

anxiety and destroys hope. Why *seduce*—a strategy that works so well with demoralization? Not least because terror and its consequent anxiety and hopeless is, simultaneously, an invitation to abandon responsibility and regress to the infantile pleasures of immediate gratification. "What's the point?" is a question that logically precedes a certain self-serving conclusion: "Everything is hopeless; it is time to live like there's no tomorrow": Shades of the faithless and orgiastic worship of the golden calf. That enticement to slavish hedonism is part and parcel of the degeneration of the voluntarily subsidiary society into the authoritarian polarity of slave and tyrant.

The demoralizing rumors spread like wildfire. The people, yet again, cry piteously, murmuring "against Moses and against Aaron" (Numbers 14:1), moaning even the fact that they are still alive; lamenting that they have come so far only to face defeat: "Would God that we had died in the land of Egypt! or would God we had died in this wilderness! And wherefore hath the Lord brought us into this land, to fall by the sword, that our wives and children should be a prey? were it not better for us to return unto Egypt?" (Numbers 14:2–3). Caleb and a few others attempt to restore their spirits, but the Israelites have embraced panic so thoroughly that they turn against the faithful and forthright optimists—the deniers of the impending apocalypse—and stone them. When a people have fallen into the grip of the lie that produces terror, those who tell the truth—the optimistic truth—become regarded as veritable enemies. This is a state that makes hope itself a crime. That is a state very close to hell.

It may come as no surprise by this point that none of this pleases God. He tells Moses that he really has had enough, and is tired of being called on to demonstrate his redemptive power. He determines, therefore, to disinherit the Israelites; to smite them with a good batch of pestilence and to begin again with Moses as he had threatened to do before, and as he actually did in the case of Noah. Moses, who is nothing if not long-suffering, bargains with God, pleading for him to once again forgive his sinful followers and to continue providing for them what has been promised, in spite of their faithlessness, noting that failure to do so will damage his holy reputation (Numbers 14:15), reminding him, perhaps, that he had famously agreed to permanently forgo such extreme measures (with the placement of the rainbow, for example, in Genesis 9:8–17). God agrees to be good, so to speak—but not to completely forgo his vengeance. All those who have decided to look away, turn tail, and run are barred from entry into the promised land. Those who maintained faith, even in the face of the doubt so thoroughly sowed by the schemers and the cowards, are by contrast invited forward:

> And the Lord said, I have pardoned according to thy word:
> But as truly as I live, all the earth shall be filled with the glory of the Lord.
> Because all those men which have seen my glory, and my miracles, which I did in Egypt and in the wilderness, and have tempted me now these ten times, and have not hearkened to my voice;
> Surely they shall not see the land which I sware unto their fathers, neither shall any of them that provoked me see it:
> But my servant Caleb, because he had another spirit with him, and hath followed me fully, him will I bring into the land whereinto he went; and his seed shall possess it.
>
> *Numbers 14:20–24*

Furthermore, the faithless scouts of the future are struck by a devastating plague (Numbers 14: 36–37), leaving live among them only Caleb and Joshua, who maintained their optimism as they explored and reported.

This is yet another example of the action of the Logos, of the separation of wheat from chaff and sheep from goats; of the work of the terrible swift and burning sword. The hypothetical giants of Canaan are tantamount to the monstrous cherubim who wields such a blade. The fact of the presence of those formidable foes, even if imaginary, serves to differentiate the wheat from the tares, or chaff, and the lambs from the goats. In this manner, the obstacles and enemies in the path—the thistles and the thorns of the fallen world (Genesis 3:18)—do the work of separating that which is worthy from that which is not. Only what is truly faithful and courageous will enter the promised land, as indicated previously.[28] How could it be otherwise and still be that perfect land? "Your carcases shall fall in this wilderness; and all that were numbered of you, according to your whole number, from twenty years old and upward, which have murmured against me, Doubtless ye shall not come into the land, concerning which I sware to make you dwell therein, save Caleb the son of Jephunneh, and Joshua the son of Nun" (Numbers 14:29–30). The degradation to carcass begins with the faithless leaders and spreaders of demoralizing rumors themselves: "Even those men that did bring up the evil report upon the land, died by the plague before the Lord" (Numbers 14:37). Hopelessness and terror can become exactly that plague.

This forbidding of movement forward and delivery of death is followed immediately by a terrible military defeat, suffered at the hands of the very Amalekites the Israelites imagined to be giants. Moses warns them explicitly that they are in no shape to battle: "For the Amalekites and the Canaanites are there before you, and ye shall fall by the sword: because you are turned away from the Lord, therefore the Lord will not be with you" (Numbers 14:43). Insisting that forward movement into the future is impossible— insisting that the promised land is uninhabitable and poisoned, regardless of all moral effort; demoralizing with the dissemination of such a negative vision; punishing those who dare say anything heartening, optimistic, and requiring responsible and courageous conduct—none of this is acceptable to the spirit inhabiting the great stories of the Old Testament. God's punishment for such betrayal is harsh but realistic: there is no possible way for a people who have lost faith to reach their proper destination. Before the plague, the barring of the pathway forward, and the defeat in battle, a mere four men remained faithful in all the multitude of Israel—Moses, Aaron, Caleb, and Joshua. Those four were, furthermore, the very men upon whom the wrath of the mob turned (shades of Sodom, prior to God's destruction of that city [Genesis 19]). It is an eternal truth that those who practice genuine faith in the presence of the cowardice and derisive fatalism of the mob will be persecuted for their temerity rather than merely ignored. This is part of the pattern of destruction of the ideal characteristic of the descendants of Cain. None of this excuses failure to stand up and be counted when the time comes.

In the aftermath of this mass rejection of the covenant, as well as God's warning and punishment and Moses's successful intercession, the laws are once again reviewed—particularly those pertaining to sacrifice and the keeping of the Sabbath (Numbers 15). This is not the only manner in which the pathetic dissatisfaction and murmuring of the Israelites is dealt with. God also hands down at the same time a seemingly minor instruction: "And the Lord spake unto Moses, saying, Speak unto the children of Israel, and bid them that they make them fringes in the borders of their garments throughout their generations, and that they put upon the fringe of the borders a ribband of blue" (Numbers 15:37–38). Like so many of the (apparently) arbitrary rules put forward in the biblical narrative, God's order follows a broader pattern of injunction—which in turn reflects something very deep about the structure of reality itself, at least insofar as reality is *perceived* or *experienced* reality. This commandment with regard to clothing is a further proclamation[29] about the necessary dynamic and stabilizing relationship of the center or ideal to the marginal or experimental. The pattern of injunction—there is to be a center and a fringe, and both are to be recognized and marked—is also evident in the commands for land ownership and harvesting:

> And when ye reap the harvest of your land, thou shalt not wholly reap the corners of thy field, neither shalt thou gather the gleanings of thy harvest.
>
> And thou shalt not glean thy vineyard, neither shalt thou gather every grape of thy vineyard; thou shalt leave them for the poor and stranger: I am the Lord your God.
>
> *Leviticus 19:9–10*

The law immediately preceding this one deals with the nature of proper sacrifice; the one immediately following forbids theft, false dealing, and deception. Thus it is implied that allowance for the margin, or fringe, is akin to the appropriate sacrificial offering and something antithetical in its spirit to thievery. If you own something, which means that you have it and others do not, it is perhaps necessary (to salve your own conscience properly; to propitiate the potential anger of the community; to practice a generous productivity) to be liberal at the margins. That is, to not be too exacting and mean where the boundaries are not clear to better allow for what has not yet been integrated into the social order and cannot easily thrive in its place. If that generosity is provided, the marginal can exist without undue suffering and, perhaps, without generating a counterproductive resentment against what is inevitably and even sometimes necessarily central. That means that success might be possible without it being equated (however rightly or falsely) with theft; it means that an individual can both rise and be acclaimed in that rise, instead of being regarded as the one who exploited or climbed uphill on the backs of others. This protects both the striving individual and society from descent into the pathological victim/victimizer dynamic represented archetypally in the account of Cain and Abel. Finally, the provision of some generous but wise allowance to the excluded or marginalized might aid in their valid incorporation or movement upward into the center. This means more of the competence characterizing every individual could be used productively, and it means that the community expands and stabilizes.

The necessity for this balance between ideal and fringe is further illustrated in the Book of Ruth. Ruth is a Moabite woman—and therefore an outsider—who initially marries an Israelite man named Mahlon. Her husband dies, as does his brother, leaving Ruth widowed and alone. Naomi, her mother-in-law, suggests that Ruth return to her own people to start her life again. Instead, she proclaims her loyalty and willingness to serve, and sojourns with Naomi to initiate and accept a life of poverty in Bethlehem: "And Ruth said, Intreat me not to leave thee, or to return from following after thee: for whither thou goest, I will go; and where thou lodgest, I will lodge: thy people shall be my people, and thy God my God: Where thou diest, will I die, and there will I be buried: the Lord do so to me, and more also, if ought but death part thee and me" (Ruth 1:16–17). While there, she gleans in the fields of Boaz, a well-to-do landowner. Impressed by her loyalty and kindness, he marries her. The couple has a son, Obed, who becomes the grandfather of King David. It is in this manner that Ruth, gathered from the fringe to the middle or even ideal, then comes to play a crucial role in the unfolding destiny of the Israelites.

The margin has value, just like the center. Without a center, nothing can hold. Without the margins, however, there is no possibility for experimentation. There is nowhere for the new ideas that might at some point prove central, or crucial to the maintenance of what is now central, to manifest themselves. The balance between these two—stability or ideal, the stake in the ground that establishes habitable territory and even conception; mutability or experiment, the variation that allows for exploration and necessary change—is evident even at the most profound and fundamental levels of biological existence, as intimated earlier.[30] It is a truism that mutation is random, and that the variation on which adaptive transformation depends (in tandem, of course, with selection both natural and sexual) is a consequence of this random mutation. This truism turns out to be much less than strictly true, however.

It is the case that the process of mutation is genuinely random in at least some of its aspects, depending as it does, for example, on the absolutely unpredictable effects of so-called cosmic rays on DNA itself. But DNA is very good at repairing itself. This turns out to be especially the case when the genes that have been subject to transformational damage are crucial to the production of forms and function that would compromise survival or reproductive fitness if damaged. In such cases the repair processes function with essentially perfect accuracy. Variation is allowed, by contrast, on the fringe, with regard to functions that are not crucial. So even in the molecular domain on which life depends there is conservation of the center, with allowable experimentation on the margin or the fringe.[31] This is a truly revolutionary finding, transforming as it does our understanding of the hypothetically random nature of evolution. If the center is conserved across mutational transformation, the progression forward is hardly random, even at the level of the mutation itself. That is particularly true given that selection itself is anything but random (especially when it is of the highly choosy sexual variety, which allows for the discriminating effect of conscious choice itself on evolutionary progress).

It is in the dynamism between center and fringe that true stability—the meta-stability that can adapt to change with the least possible disruption—is forever negotiated. That meta-stability is guaranteed by respect for the Logos that transforms (creative thought, free speech, exploration, and play) and its crystallization into the fatherly tradition that stabilizes (something akin to the law and the prophets). It may seem an odd paradox that the Israelites are asked specifically to look upon the outer edge to remember God:

> And it shall be unto you for a fringe, that ye may look upon it, and remember all the commandments of the Lord, and do them; and that ye seek not after your own heart and your own eyes, after which ye use to go a whoring:
>
> That ye may remember, and do all my commandments, and be holy unto your God.
>
> I am the Lord your God, which brought you out of the land of Egypt, to be your God: I am the Lord your God.
>
> *Numbers 15:39–41*

Is it too much of a stretch to assume that it is in the very act of considering the fringe that the wisdom of the center is remembered? When dealing with clinical clients unhappy in their marriage and tempted toward misbehavior such as an affair (perhaps with that opportunity immediately at hand), I always counseled them to think it through. What are you doing when you deviate from the vows of your marriage? Are you delivering to your mistress all the attention properly devoted to your wife, without requiring her to share any of the true responsibilities of your life (and, perhaps, hers)? Are you pretending that this will be all benefit and no cost? Are you discounting the terrible and tearful conversations to come, the betrayal, the effect on your children, the inevitable courtroom confrontations and costs? Are you assuming that this new paramour will somehow magically overlook all the faults you carry personally that have compromised your marriage? Are you, in other words, refusing to look at the fringe and thereby forgetting the vital importance of the center?

Could it not be then that it is precisely in the deepest consideration of the true nature of the fringe (including its genuine attractions and possibilities as well as its inescapable dangers) that what is important is most profoundly conceptualized, clarified, and remembered? The fool is there, in part, to remind us of the wise; the bearer of tragedy to highlight the comedy of the victor; the villain to clarify the role of the hero. The margin, in its proper place, signifies the necessity and value of the center. Out of place—attempting to usurp the center—it is an agent of chaos; and the very chaos that destroys the marginal itself first, due to its comparative instability and fragility. The monstrous and the misfits have their place, but it is not and cannot be the center. Their placement there—even when requested—poses more of a risk to them, to say it again, than to those who occupy the hypothetically challenged but fundamentally more stable ideal or tradition.

Moses soon thereafter addresses yet another challenge to his leadership (Numbers 16). This time, the rebellion appears in the form of an egalitarian populism. Korah, a member of the Levite priestly caste, emerges as a challenger, saying to Moses and Aaron: "Ye take too much upon you, seeing all the congregation are holy, every one of them: wherefore ye then lift ye up yourselves among the congregation of the Lord?" (Numbers 16:3). This objection is reiterated later, when Moses reproaches Korah, pointing out that God himself has assigned differentiated responsibility for leadership:

> Seemeth it but a small thing unto you, that the God of Israel hath separated you from the congregation of Israel, to bring you near to himself to do the service of the tabernacle of the Lord, and to stand before the congregation to minister unto them?
>
> And he hath brought thee near to him, and all thy brethren the sons of Levi with thee: and seek ye the priesthood also?
>
> For which cause both thou and all thy company are gathered together against the Lord: and what is Aaron, that ye murmur against him?

Numbers 16:9–11

This narrative sequence makes perfect sense, following as it does the presentation of the fringe-center dynamic. The revolutionary impulse of Korah is precisely the marginal attempting to usurp the center. The would-be rebels claim that the current structure of authority is nothing but the machinations of the will to power and self-gratification, claiming that all the work of Moses and Aaron was naked self-interest. This is also a variant of the victim/victimizer narrative, or a re-presentation of the story of the hostile brothers, with the claim of oppression being used by the complainants to justify their adoption of power.

Moses's genuine attempt to reconcile is rejected forthwith. Why? The rebels do not want peace. They want to invert the order they attribute to nothing but power and to take all the positions of hypothetical dominance and force for themselves. It is the rare revolutionary indeed who has any other motivation—all compassionate protestations to the contrary:

> We will not come up:
>
> Is it a small thing that thou hast brought us up out of a land that floweth with milk and honey, to kill us in the wilderness, except thou make thyself altogether a prince over us?
>
> Moreover thou hast not brought us into a land that floweth with milk and honey, or given us inheritance of fields and vineyards: wilt thou put out the eyes of these men? we will not come up.
>
> *Numbers 16:12-14*

Moses is facing foes who claim the moral upper hand, maintaining that they act on behalf of the people and are therefore justified in their attempts to usurp, doing what they are doing for the victimized others. Moses must therefore face down a series of accusations that are, on the face of it, potentially valid: How is it that he (or anyone he leads) can be sure that his leadership is not merely the result of his own grandiosity, narcissism, desire for power, privilege (he was a son of the pharaoh), and corruption? In large part, because his own conscience remains clear on the matter. Their attempts to manipulate him fall flat: "And Moses was very wroth, and said unto the Lord, Respect not thou their offering: I have not taken one ass from them, neither have I hurt one of them" (Numbers 16:15).

The true leader, who embodies the spirit of God, the law, and tradition, who nonetheless speaks with a prophetic voice, can remain sanguine in the face of even the most adversarial accusations as a direct result of that fidelity and humble openness to revelation. The good man has nothing to hide; has already genuinely sacrificed his narrow and hedonistic self-interest to the transcendent good. He has abided by the dictates of his conscience and faithfully followed the voice of his calling, and can trust himself, as anyone might trust another who acts honestly and consistently regardless of situation or temptation. In consequence, he is immune to the imputation of wrongdoing, not because he is blind to his own fault or sin. Indeed, as a genuine devotee of sacrificial conduct and transformational progress, he is constantly attending to his own shortcomings. This means that the man who like Noah is "wise in his generations" and who "walks with God" (Genesis 6:9) can stand, naked, upright, and without shame in the very face of the moralizing mob, and stare them down. It is also that capacity for unselfconscious and therefore unashamed attention, speech, and conduct that lends him credence and charisma as a leader.

Moses and those who stand with him separate themselves from Korah and the remainder of the rebels, expressing sorrow for what they believe now to be inevitable. The terrible consequences of Korah's deceptive rebellion immediately make themselves manifest:

> And it came to pass, as he had made an end of speaking all these words, that the ground clave asunder that was under them:
>
> And the earth opened her mouth, and swallowed them up, and their houses, and all the men that appertained unto Korah, and all their goods.
>
> They, and all that appertained to them, went down alive into the pit, and the earth closed upon them: and they perished from among the congregation.
>
> *Numbers 16:31–33*

When the marginal claims the right to be central, it is not the center that typically collapses into destruction but the unrighteous usurpers themselves. This is why the excess and usually false pity for those who inhabit the outer darkness of the world (that, remember, is the eternal sin of Eve[32]) is so inexcusable. The very targets of that indiscriminate and hypothetically merciful judgment will be the first to be destroyed by its consequences. The world is not destroyed in its totality when the toddler is encouraged by an excess of care to maintain his infancy (although the holy babe who is world-redeemer in disguise may well be threatened). The world is likewise very unlikely to rearrange itself to adapt to the whims of the now-misbehaving child, then adolescent or adult. It is instead the individual so pampered and falsely encouraged who is sorely threatened and damaged. It is instead the integrity, maturity of psyche, opportunity for true adventure and hope for upward development that would otherwise characterize that child that is put at risk by the devouring mother.

There is more yet to the story of Korah's revolution, failure, and destruction—and that is the indication that the proper subsidiary structure of responsibility established by God, through Moses, is not to be overthrown by a false egalitarianism. Moses and Aaron—and, to a lesser degree, the leaders of the specific tribes of Israel and the common people themselves—have done the genuine work and therefore acquired the authority and competence necessary to maintain order and specify the way forward. They have sufficiently maintained their covenant with what is highest and continued their upward-aiming striving away from tyranny and slavery, through the trials of the desert and toward the promised land. That is not a pattern to be casually undone by usurpers claiming righteous revolution in the name of the easily manipulated and resentful mob of the fringe.

Such things never change.

Even after all this punishment is meted out to the rebels (and even though it follows the plague, death, and military defeat that was not so long before visited on those who had the temerity to lose faith and to complain), the Israelites continue to proclaim their grievances against God, Moses, and Aaron. The sojourn of this once again unhappy people thus continues into

the desert of Zin (another desert following a bout of faithlessness and rebellion), where they run short of water and begin even more loudly to chide and
murmur. Their two leaders, prophet and political voice, nonetheless plead
the case of the desperate people before God. The divine voice, in turn, instructs Moses, very specifically, to speak in the presence of his people to the
hard stones of the desert land, and invite them to bring forth the life-giving
liquid. Moses and Aaron depart and gather the Israelites together, as instructed, "before the rock" (Numbers 20:10).

Moses does not employ his words in invitation, however, as he has been
explicitly told to do. Instead, the great and erstwhile devotee of God delivers
the rock two solid blows with his staff. This use of force and compulsion
(this unnecessary display of power) displeases God immensely—so much so
that it is easy to regard what comes next as incomprehensibly harsh. God
denies his disobedient prophet entrance into the promised land itself, despite the decades he has spent in the service of the people and the divine:
"And the Lord spake unto Moses and Aaron, Because ye believed me not, to
sanctify me in the eyes of the children of Israel, therefore ye shall not bring
this congregation into the land which I have given them" (Numbers 20:12).
Aaron is barred, as well, perhaps because he was there when the initial instructions were delivered and did not act to ensure they were undertaken in
the proper spirit. Did his conscience bother the brother of the prophet when
he was apprised (if he was) of Moses's intentions? Of did Aaron believe, so
conveniently, and in his political manner, that a little show of power might
have been just the thing to keep a fractious people in check?

Moses's staff is the rod of tradition and order. Misused, it easily becomes
the cudgel of compulsion and power. A stout stick can point in an inviting
direction, or beat a reluctant or involuntarily traveler into submission. It depends on the aim, will, and temptation of he who wields it. Moses brandishes
his staff with undue force, using stick when carrot is called for—when called
for by God Himself. He does so twice, as well, so there is no mistaking his
intent. Further, both he and Aaron indicate directly that it is the two of them
performing the redemptive act, instead of explicitly and in all due humility
laying the glory at the feet of God. Moses says, directly, "Listen, you rebels,

must we bring you water out of this rock?" (Numbers 20:10). Both men are very experienced at this point and stand at the very threshold of their ultimate goal. It is at such moments when the temptation to become arrogant arguably looms largest—and when it might well have the most damning and degrading consequences. At this crucial moment—right on the very cusp of his potentially highest success; right when he most truly has the opportunity to become the new man in the new world that he has been constantly called to be—Moses succumbs, as does his brother, to the spirit of the prideful usurper, taking to himself in the Luciferian manner the right to establish the moral order. The great leader has got too big for his britches, and Aaron stays in lockstep. This is a psychological and social catastrophe, given the height of the stakes currently in question.

It might still be objected: surely, Moses and his brother have earned the right to be forgiven a momentary lapse of faith and reason, if anyone has ever earned that right. Apparently not, at least in the judgment of what is truly and forever sovereign. Is it so unreasonable to assume that the privilege of leadership must necessarily be attended by the requirement for the utmost care in moral conduct, particularly in matters serious enough to provoke divine intercession? Is that not particularly true when the goal is to avoid establishing a new tyranny and establishing the eternal promised land? This is a high order of moral enterprise, which carries with it an equally high level of demand in relationship to conduct. It was apparently necessary for Moses to have completely sacrificed his temptation to wield force to manage the next step in his personal transformation and as leader of his people. Because he failed to do so, he cannot progress, and falls prey, so to speak, to the sword of judgment. It seems that disobedience in any matters involving the very water of life, conjoined with careless and haughty default to force and fear, is a conjoint sin of sufficient magnitude to bar even leaders who have otherwise been the best of men from the privilege of mounting the final foray into the reestablished Garden of Eden or the Heavenly Kingdom. The punishment for Aaron, the political arm, is the ultimate barring of the way forward. Aaron is stripped of his garments of authority—his very identity as earthly leader—and dies:

And the Lord spake unto Moses and Aaron in mount Hor, by the coast of the land of Edom, saying,

Aaron shall be gathered unto his people: for he shall not enter into the land which I have given unto the children of Israel, because ye rebelled against my word at the water of Meribah.

Take Aaron and Eleazar his son, and bring them up unto mount Hor:

And strip Aaron of his garments, and put them upon Eleazar his son: and Aaron shall be gathered unto his people, and shall die there.

And Moses did as the Lord commanded: and they went up into mount Hor in the sight of all the congregation.

And Moses stripped Aaron of his garments, and put them upon Eleazar his son; and Aaron died there in the top of the mount: and Moses and Eleazar came down from the mount.

And when all the congregation saw that Aaron was dead, they mourned for Aaron thirty days, even all the house of Israel.

Numbers 20:23–29

This is truly a cautionary tale: If men such as Moses and Aaron are unworthy to take that final step, who then can be saved?

It is only Joshua and Caleb who retain faith alongside Moses and Aaron, despite the danger of Canaan, real or imagined, and the cowardly and fearmongering reports of the scouts sent to the promised land (Numbers 13–14). Joshua shares a name very tightly associated with the Christian savior himself. Both appellations are variants of *Yeshua*, which means salvation; the longer variant, *Yehoshua*, means "Yahweh saves." It is this Joshua who takes the reins of leadership from Moses, guiding the Israelites along the final step of their journey. Christians have traditionally read this story at a higher level of abstraction, presuming that redemption itself is dependent on what Christ embodies, incarnates, or represents superseding the exemplary pattern of spirit even of the leadership of Moses (and presuming that this necessity is foreshadowed by the manner in which the Israelite sojourn concludes). Aaron dies, as God has indicated, outside the land "given unto the children of Israel" (Numbers 20:24). The political, corrupted by pride and power, can in no wise be the spirit that leads the way to paradise—and this regardless of its history of guidance and triumph.

Numbers continues with another round of faithlessness, rumormongering, and irresponsible rebellion on the part of the Israelites—a story that also foreshadows the story of Christ in a nigh-miraculously deep manner. It is impossible to imagine how the layers of concordance and cross-reference characteristic of this closing story could possibly have been crafted. The meaning of the story is almost self-evident once revealed, but so remarkably subtle, sophisticated, and implicit prior to that revelation. How could such a thing be possible—particularly given the millennia that transpire between the narrative setup, so to speak, and the denouement of the story. Who could possibly manage such a feat of storytelling genius?

The only credible secular explanation for the attainment of the profound characterization and representation we will soon lay bare is the operation of something equivalent to the collective unconscious of mankind, as formulated by C. G. Jung and the thinkers of his school:[33] The imagination of the race, *writ large*—first, puzzling out the central nature of adaptation in a process of trial and error; then, representing the results of that painful process in abstracted narrative; finally, the weaving together and editing of that narrative over centuries—the removal of internal contradiction; the crafting of the most compelling meta-story conceivable. Separating that process from divine revelation itself appears practically impossible. Either explanation appears equally implausible and unlikely. Both might best be regarded as variants of the same thing: one viewed, in the case of the unconscious, from the bottom up; the other, in the case of divine revelation, from the top down. In either case, the miracle remains.

After the events in the desert of Zin, the Israelites continue what by now must be feeling like their interminable journey forward. They travel "from Mount Hor by the way of the Red Sea, to compass the land of Edom" (Numbers 21:4). Once again, "the soul of the people was much discouraged because of the way" (Numbers 21:4). Petulant and peevish, as is so often the case, they rail against the privations they are experiencing, expressing dissatisfaction with the heavenly fare that makes up their provisioning: "And the people spake against God, and against Moses, Wherefore have ye brought us up out of Egypt to die in the wilderness? for there is no bread, neither is there any water; and our soul loatheth this light bread" (Numbers 21:5). It is perhaps understandable that the Israelites are frustrated with the lightness of their fare: for decades they have wandered with little more than faith and hope to guide them, and that is certainly the airiest of foods. Nonetheless, the return to aggrieved victimhood on the part of His people does not please God. This time, however, He takes a different tack in response to their inconstancy: "And the Lord sent fiery serpents among the people, and they bit the people; and much people of Israel died" (Numbers 21:6).

This seems heavy-handed—much as the punishment meted out to Moses and Aaron is, arguably, heavy-handed (to say nothing of the ongoing smiting of faithless Israelites as well as their enemies). The poor Israelites are clearly thinking, and with some reason, "tyranny and slavery, then decades of lost wandering, desert, and chaos—it is already all too much. And now we have to put up with poisonous snakes biting us, because—apparently—the desert wasteland was somehow not burdensome enough." It is easy to feel sympathy for their plight, and perhaps appropriately so. Out of tyranny, into the endless wasteland: this is no laughing matter. The poisonous snakes can be reasonably apprehended as a bridge too far. Is there another interpretation, more favorable to God? Certainly, and it is another unbearable truth: There is no pit of hell so deep that something more bottomless could not yet be revealed—brought about by some faithless, treacherous, and craven act or omission.

This is true for individual and society alike: the abyss is truly bottomless. If you are visited by misfortune, however just or unjust, and you maintain your faith, you at least have the consolation of your courage and faith to accompany the misery visited upon you. If you lose hope, turning instead to the path indicated by the spirit of resentment, arrogance, and deceit, the hell you have already suffered—no matter how bad it is—will be nothing compared to the hell you will bring about. Thus arrive the snakes, fiery and poisonous, even in the midst of the most desiccated, vast, and harsh of deserts.

It is not even so much a punishment as an inevitability: There is no situation so terrible that some stupid son of a bitch cannot make yet worse. And that means you—and me.

After suffering from sufficient biting to think again, or at least to wish the snakes away, the Israelites repent and come to Moses, saying, "We have spoken against the Lord, and against thee; pray unto the Lord, that he take away the serpents from us. And Moses prayed for the people" (Numbers 21:7). One of two very predictable and straightforward outcomes appears likely. God could refuse and strike down the wayward rebels. Alternatively, he could show some mercy and get rid of the snakes—which were, after all, his creation. That is not what happens. Instead, God instructs Moses: "Make thee a fiery serpent, and set it upon a pole" (Numbers 21:8). The interplay of pole (rod, staff) and serpent has been indicated on multiple occasions by this time, in various forms. There is the snake in the tree of the knowledge of good and evil (Genesis 3). There is the staff of Moses, which can transform itself into a serpent; and into the serpent that can devour all other rods and serpents. That fiery reptile is chaos itself, the unknown itself, in all its predatory manifestations; in all its dragon-like combination of cat, snake, bird, and fire (the ancient foes of man and other primates);[34] in all its capacity to shed its skin, and be reborn.

Perhaps it might be imagined that Paradise is the place where all the snakes have been vanquished; the place that is eternally secure and safe. But what of challenge? Or adventure? Or the promise of something new? Perhaps it is better to learn to handle snakes than to rid the world of snakes. Do those who love their children protect them from all danger, or encourage them to become contenders—veritable slayers of dragons? Whenever we approve of the steps that a diligent and focused child is taking toward competence and maturity, rather than continued infantile dependence, we take the latter path, rather than the former.

This is the quest that is of course represented in what might well be the most fundamental of all the stories of mankind—that of the dragon fight. First detailed in written form in the Mesopotamian epic *Enuma elish*,[35] the battle with the immortal serpent is re-represented constantly in literature, both ancient and modern.[36] Its basic hypothesis, so to speak—the moral that it conveys—is that voluntary confrontation with what is most frightening and repellent provides the riches than never cease (the gold hoarded by the dragon; the grateful and now-willing virgins freed from the dragon's lair and profoundly and rightly impressed by their rescuer). It is precisely to indicate and encourage this brave response that God does not banish the snakes. He decides, instead, to fortify and strengthen the Israelites themselves, as a good father would be wont to do. After the serpent is cast and set upon the rod, or staff, of tradition, he calls on his wayward people to gaze upon that conjoint presence of order and chaos, and to do so voluntarily, in good faith: "And the Lord said to Moses, Make thee a fiery serpent, and set it upon a pole: and it shall come to pass, that everyone that is bitten, when he looketh upon it, shall live. And Moses made a serpent of brass and put it upon a pole, and it came to pass that if a serpent had bitten any man when he beheld the serpent of brass, he lived" (Numbers 21:8-9).

When even neurotic, dependent, and avoidant individuals practice the countervailing strategy of approach and observe themselves doing so successfully, they master the thing or situation to which they have approached. In doing so, they also update and expand their self-conceptualizations, viewing themselves increasingly as people who *can* rather than people who *cannot*.[37] Reaching this generalized conclusion changes their behavior, and not just their behavior in the face of a particular stimulus, but to the entire class of stimuli they fear.[38] This means that their character transforms. There is little difference between such change and learning itself. The experience that transform us, even in their micro-manifestations, always occurs on the edge, in the face of the unknown, in the zone of proximal development—in the realm of the deep meaning that sustains and motivates that exists on the border between *yin* and *yang*.[39]

In consequence of practicing the voluntary approach and exploration that transforms, the once-timid become at least partial incarnations of the dragon slayer. This is a much more salutary and appropriate response, considering the further reaches of human nature, than cowering timorously and ashamed in the village cellar while the winged serpent spreads fire and destruction.

The practitioners of such approach become those who take active steps, alternatively conceptualized, to free themselves from the belly of the beast that devoured them when they ran and tried to hide—become those, in yet another narrative variant, who truly confront tyranny and escape from slavery. The Israelites gaze on the snake to regain their faith, to become braver, to become less afraid and more willing to continue into the desert, despite the snakes, because they now regard themselves as those who can look upon the poisonous and paralyzing and prevail. Thus emboldened by God, (paradoxical origin of both snakes and the courage that deprives them of their venom), the slavish and apprehensive move upward to their destiny.

What is the ultimate exemplar of this motif of exposure to serpent hung on tree? And where does the sheer genius of the ineffable author of the text make itself so clearly manifest? With this detail, which is anything but a detail: Millennia later, in the Gospel of John, Jesus draws a strange comparison between himself and this bronze snake: "And as Moses lifted up the serpent in the wilderness, even so must the Son of man be lifted up: That whosoever believeth in him should not perish, but have eternal life" (John 3:14–15). What is to be made of this most peculiar and unexpected comparison? In what wise could the benevolent Savior be akin to the most terrible and poisonous of serpents? Here is the first of the conceptual tools necessary to solve the mystery of that problem: The miraculous provision and flowing water that God provides to the Israelites and the loaves and fishes that Jesus later provides are meta-foods, as intimated previously.[40] They are emblematic of the heavenly ethos, spirit of psychological integrity and community aim that ensures the promised life more abundant, rather than concrete instantiations of food and water themselves. Christ similarly presents himself—the spectacle of his example, more particularly—as a meta-serpent; as the sum or more accurately essence, or spirit, of all the terrible things about human existence that must be looked upon voluntarily—even accepted gratefully and welcomed—for ultimate sacrificial offering most pleasing to God to be fully realized.

The spirit of divine calling and conscience, seeking to redeem the lost sheep of Israel, insists on them facing their fears, voluntarily confronting the venomous serpent their faithless and cowardice called into being. Are such snakes, however toxic they might be, the sum total or essence of all real and possible evil? Not in the least. The snake in the Garden of Eden is a mere proxy for Lucifer himself—and the terror engendered by the deadly reptiles of the desert wasteland is likewise a mere instantiation of the essence of what is terrifying and deadly. What is the worst possible of all tragic and malevolent outcomes? The most dismal and unfair fate visited on the least deserving individual imaginable. It is for this reason that the Passion of Christ constitutes the definitive redemptive catastrophe, the absolute terror lurking behind all proximal terrors; the pattern of confrontation with mortality and evil as such. It is the cross that is the ultimate dragon; the cross that is the union of the Leviathan of chaos and the Behemoth of pathological order that the Logos overcame at the very beginning and continues to defeat always and everywhere.

The danger starts right at Christ's birth; lowly as it is, threatened by the powers of the state, forcing the obedience of its subjects (Matthew 2:1; Luke 2:1-7) and then aiming death directly at the Hebrew infants of the time (Matthew 2:16). Jesus confronts Satan himself and his temptations in the wilderness (Matthew 4:1-11; Mark 1:12-13; Luke 4:1-13) and is rejected by his community at Nazareth (Matthew 13:53-58; Mark 6:1-6; Luke 4:16-30). He is made subject to the tender mercies of the religious, academic, and legal hypocrites—the Pharisees, scribes, and lawyers (Matthew 21-23; Mark 12; Luke 20). Jesus is betrayed by his closest compatriot, Judas (Matthew 26:14-16; Mark 14:10-11; Luke 22:3-6), and denied by Peter, the rock on which He founds His church (Matthew 26:69-75; Mark 14:66-72; Luke 22:54-62; John 18:15-27). All that horror, voluntarily accepted, proves insufficient, hard though the going is. He must further experience unjust trial and crucifixion, exposure to the vengeful mob, scourging and sentencing by the foreign tyrant (all of whom know of his fundamental innocence), selection for torture and death for instead of a known criminal, and then subjected to a death designed specifically for its humiliating quality and pain. All that while still young and unmarried and in the presence of the mother who loves Him, while He watches her anguish (Matthew 26:57-27:66; Mark 14:53-15:47;

Luke 22:54–23:56; John 18:12–19:42). Then to top it all off, He is called on to harrow hell itself, which means that he journeys to the very heart of malevolent darkness itself.

This is the existential catastrophe we have all been attempting to voluntarily face and contend with, like the poisoned Israelites in the desert, for the two thousand years of the dominion of Christianity in the West. There is simply no worse and then better fate than that of Christ. We have chosen to place the crucifix, the terrible symbol of all that, at the very center of the central place of our cathedrals and churches—the place where the Holy Sacrifice that unites psyche and community is eternally offered. We place those tabernacles likewise at the center of our towns, with that cross serving as the staff of tradition and transformation, put firmly in place to mark the ideal and establish the psychological and social order that is good or very good. In this manner we duplicate the redemptive ritual of exposure that God offered the Israelites in their misery, and lift up the Son of Man so that we do not perish of desperation while bearing the burdens of our lives. Who could have possibly imagined such a daring concordance of idea and characterization? And how can it be that this pattern of identity has remained essentially implicit during all the centuries that separate us from the desert people of ancient Israel and still have played such a central role? Whatever managed that feat of imaginative representation and characterization well deserves the place of honor due the transcendent and ineffable.

The adventures of the Israelites continue, ever more roughly, after their baptism by serpent and God, with their constant engagement in the battles chronicled in the last third of Numbers. Numbers 21 details the initial defeat of some Canaanite tribes. The original inhabitants of the promised land were, however, a widespread people, kin to the Amorites, Moabites, and Midianites, all of whom also clash with the invading Israelites, and all of whom suffer defeat (along with the Amalekites, Sihonites, and Ogites, whose relations to or derivation from the Canaanites remains unknown). These multiple military victories buttress the Israelites in their belief that they could obtain the final triumph over those who stood in their way and occupy the promised land. The events that transpire around Balak, king of Moab, also increase their confidence while demoralizing their foes. Balak asks whether a Mesopotamian prophet, Balaam, might curse the Israelites as they advance. It seems quite clear that Balaam is regarded as a true man of God by moral reputation, and he is called on by the king precisely for that reason. As might be expected of such a man, Balaam warns the king that he will tell the truth, no matter how much he is paid or who is paying for his services. He nonetheless agrees to voyage with the princes of Moab to assess the situation, and the king accepts his offer.

On the way, an angel appears to the Mesopotamian prophet, telling him that he can continue—reminding him once again that he is only to utter God's word, despite being in the employ of the king. Four times the prophet observes the Israelites. Four times he blesses them instead of cursing them, indicating as he does so the favor they have found with God, noting their numerous nature, their lack of iniquity and perverseness (Numbers 23:21), the plentifulness of their tabernacles (Numbers 24:5), and their future victoriousness:

> He hath said, which heard the words of God, and knew the knowledge of the most High, which saw the vision of the Almighty, falling into a trance, but having his eyes open:
>
> I shall see him, but not now: I shall behold him, but not nigh: there shall come a Star out of Jacob, and a Scepter shall rise out of Israel, and shall smite the corners of Moab, and destroy all the children of Sheth.
>
> And Edom shall be a possession, Seir also shall be a possession for his enemies; and Israel shall do valiantly.
>
> Out of Jacob shall come he that shall have dominion, and shall destroy him that remaineth of the city.
>
> *Numbers 24:16–19*

The blessing of the Israelites occurs despite Balak's attempts to tempt Balaam with increased pay and the seductive offerings of the king's own daughters. The Israelites continue their habit of straying along the way, stopping in Shittim, part of the Moabite kingdom of Balak, to "commit whoredom with the daughters of Moab" (Numbers 25:1), who tempt them into the worship of Baal. This disloyalty results in the predictable dissatisfaction of God and an accompanying plague, yet another punishment meted out by the divine forces opposed so carelessly by the chosen people.

Numbers 26 follows, portraying the second census of the book (the first is described in Numbers 1). The text continues and extends the sociology[41] and technical assessment of the state,[42] detailing the division of labor and social organization among the Israelites—describing their segregation, differentiation, and specialization into the slaves, farmers and shepherds, soldiers, merchants, craftsmen, musicians, judges, and priests that make up the state. This identifying and sifting is all part of a developing and advancing self-consciousness; the beginning of a formal typology and analysis of individual and society alike—the beginnings, as indicated previously,[43] of the formally analytic mode of observation, description, thought, and record that we now take for granted. It is also all part of the continued development of the subsidiary structure of the new nation, including its capacity to represent and monitor itself.

In Numbers 27, God provides Moses with a final reward for his faithful service, despite his being barred from the promised land. It appears to be granted in response to Moses's direct request, as recounted later in Deuteronomy 3:25: "I pray thee, let me go over, and see the good land that is beyond Jordan, that goodly mountain, and Lebanon." God tells the prophet to scale Mount Abarim, the last of the sequential pinnacles climbed in the course of Moses's storied life, so that he can "see the land which I have given the children of Israel" (Numbers 27:12). This adventure is tempered somewhat in its positive aspect, as God simultaneously lets his prophet know of his impending demise. Is it possible to imagine Moses satisfied with all that he has done? He has destroyed a tyrant; provided his people with a vision of freedom and responsibility; led them through the desert; chastised, protected, and interceded for them when they fell prey to temptation; and helped them to establish a truly functional and victorious state. Is this an example of the aforementioned possibility that a fully lived life justifies itself, rife with tragedy and error though it may be—ending in death though it inevitably does?[44]

Moses appoints the faithful and courageous Joshua as his successor, after God shows him the promised land, and does so before Eleazar the priest and all the congregation (Numbers 27). It is thus that the great prophet appoints and specifies his successor, ensuring a successful transfer of power. After this, as is appropriate, the details of the covenantal law are reviewed (Numbers 28–30). This specifies the proper continuity of tradition and contract that are to govern the tenure of the new ruler, as they did in the time of Moses. Immediately thereafter a terrible war, difficult to justify in its ruthlessness, is waged on the Midianites (Numbers 30). The Israelites bring home the spoils, which includes the Midianite women. Moses angrily chastises his soldiers: "Have ye saved all the women alive? Behold, these caused the children of Israel, through the counsel of Balaam, to commit trespass against the Lord in the matter of Peor, and there was a plague among the congregation of the Lord" (Numbers 31:15–16). He calls on them to put all the female captives, except the virgins, to the sword, and has the same done to all the Midianite boys. It is sections such as these, following hard on the heels of the death of the three thousand, the opening up of the earth under Korah, the plagues attendant upon those who consort with the whores of Moab, that give the modern reader convinced of his or her comparative moral virtue great pause. Is all this violence nothing but a clear indication of the vengefulness and jealousy of an archaic and blindly superstitious people's God? Dr. Richard Dawkins makes that case without hesitation:

> The God of the Old Testament is arguably the most unpleasant character in all fiction: jealous and proud of it; a petty, unjust, unforgiving control-freak; a vindictive, bloodthirsty ethnic cleanser; a misogynistic, homophobic, racist, infanticidal, genocidal, filicidal, pestilential, megalomaniacal, sadomasochistic, capriciously malevolent bully.[45]

This is clearly a motivated misreading on the part of the evolutionary biologist, at least insofar as the interpretations of the present text are both sympathetic and accurate (to say nothing of the entire history of Jewish and

Christian apologetics). However, the moral difficulties posed by the current text arguably remain.

Does it suffice to claim that the danger posed by the incorporation of many foreign women, whose capacity to entice, seduce, and convert the Israelites has already been demonstrated, was too great to bear, and that Moses could see this clearly? Can the same be said about the potential danger posed by the Midianite boys? Did these captives represent a possible future fifth column and source of destabilization? It is not clear under what conditions we can rightly apply our hypothetically higher moral standards to the societies of the past, laboring as they did under conditions of privation, threat, and difficulty almost (and fortunately) unimaginable to us. It is very easy for us to perceive ourselves as better than our forebears, to damn them for their vicious proclivities, and to assume that we would and should act better in the same situation. But is also too easy to rationalize away actions such as those undertaken in the war against the Midianites and to assume the events so described are not to be taken literally; to insist uncritically and merely as a matter of blind and self-justifying "faith" that God's word must be followed even if the commands seem cruel and unjust, and to therefore sidestep the eternal problem of trying the spirits, to determine—in the presence of many false prophets and prophecies—to see if they are of God (1 John 4:1). But we are trying to extract out a universal thread of moral gold by walking through these ancient stories, and the bitter parts of the biblical corpus must be swallowed along with the sweet.

Under what conditions is killing justifiable, necessary, or even morally obligatory? How do we deal with the fact that war, and everything brutal that inevitably accompanies it, is a universal feature of our past and present struggles forward? How can we conceptualize ourselves as essentially admirable moral agents—as intrinsically good beings—given our universal proclivity for intertribal conflict; given the existence of the powerful motivations that operate within us, sweeping us toward the gun and the sword when our borders, our axioms—our families; our tribes—are under threat, or are at least convincingly deemed so? Virtually everyone understands, accepts, and promotes the right to self-defense as well as the analogous and extended right and responsibility to protect kith and kin. Under what circumstances does obligation to the local, the familial, the tribal supersede that owed to a stranger—an enemy, a man or a people who were once an enemy? It is murder, *per se*, and not killing that is forbidden by the sixth commandment,[46] and murder has been held since time immemorial to be something different than war. These are all questions that are among the most difficult we face, in our wrestling with the divine.

The classic justifications for the slaying of the Midianites take two traditional forms. The first is that such actions were typical for the times,[47] when the utter destruction of a conquered enemy was regarded as necessary to protect against the influence they might otherwise retain and wield. Such actions (and their understanding or rationalization) is based on the presumption that the presence of foreigners and the ideas they bear can pose a threat to the integrity of the psyche and the state. Why? Because the conflict between their fundamental presuppositions and those of the conquerors is the very war of the gods that can undermine and bring down a state. It is therefore something very common and perhaps biologically hardwired to regard foreign ideas as pathogens that can invade, spread, and kill.[48] A stout conservatism is very likely to make itself manifest, for example, in locales that are typified by the heightened presence of transmissible disease[49]—a fact indicating the essential psychological identity between the strange idea and the predator and parasite.[50] The second justification is more subtle:[51] the Midianites are seen as being in league with the Moabites, who were presented in Numbers 25 as inviting the Israelite men to "indulge in sexual immorality with the daughters of Moab" (Numbers 25:1) and to "to the sacrifices for their gods," which included Baal—twin offerings that were positively responded to by the invitees. (Numbers 25:2) The consequences? The "anger of the lord burned against them" (Numbers 25:3).

There are reasons to be concerned with what is foreign that are so deep that we have adapted, biologically, to their presence. It is equally the case, however, that what is strange and new—as in the case of the beneficial foreigner, as outlined previously—can be a saving grace, both practically and metaphysically.[52] It is no small matter that Jethro—Moses's admired and beloved father-in-law, who saved him from becoming a tyrant and saved the Israelites from reestablishing their slavery—was also a Midianite and, therefore, from the same foreign tribe that is now presented as a deadly threat.[53] This is another case of the paradoxical ultimate reality of treasure, in concert with dragon. How then do we deal with the all too often repressed and unspoken fact that the presence of oft-foreign threats, real or imagined, can awaken within us a powerful longing for mayhem, a lust for battle, a self-righteous and murderous clamoring for blood, and the accompanying enthusiastic demonization of anyone who, under such circumstances, dares argue for peace?

How do we separate out our right to self-defense in its immediate and broader senses from our Cain-like desire to find a target upon who we can release all our pent-up existential frustration, resentment, bitterness, arrogance, and cruel vengefulness? How do we understand and atone for the atrocities of history, the territorial expansions that are part of the historical record of virtually every people, and the participation of our ancestors and ourselves in the wars that have both marred and made our present what it is today? How do we atone for the privilege bestowed upon us, not least as a result, however partial, by the blood spilled—by guilty and innocent alike—in the past? How do we sacrifice properly, singly and communally, for the sins of those who came before us and which are all too likely to manifest again with dreadful suddenness whenever the conditions are ripe? Striving to answer such questions is the dreadful necessity of wrestling with God.

There is an alternative view to the damning modern characterization of the ancient Old Testament, or Torah, God of the Judeo-Christian tradition. It is stark and simple in its portrayal of reality, although still undeniably bitter. Perhaps it is all the more believable because of that. Consider that there are a million paths of deviation, detour, and defection, and very few (perhaps one) that enable effective, efficient, productive, generous, and unified movement forward. Consider as well that the punishment (of "natural consequences,"[54] even) for such deviation can be and too often is catastrophic suffering and mass death. Speaking pragmatically and nontheologically: Why then must the capturing of this brutal truth in the characterization of God be interpreted as the will of something with malevolent intent? The path chosen by the National Socialists, the Soviets, and the Maoists was one that deviated seriously, to say the least, from the injunctions of the Judeo-Christian tradition. The fate that descended upon the people of those cultures as a direct result was as terrible as anything represented as the vengeance of the Old Testament's angry God. Non-playable games degenerate first into chaos and then into hell. This reflects something akin to the consequences of transgressing against the underlying moral order of the cosmos.

Is it so surprising and so morally unacceptable that the inevitable outcomes[55]—part of the pattern of the cause and effect that most truly characterizes the world, especially from the scientific perspective—might come to be understood and portrayed as the "jealousy" of God? Might it come to be represented, as well or alternatively, as His insistence that nothing and no one except Him is to be elevated to the status of highest place? If everything necessarily and inescapably tumbles into the abyss when certain strictures are violated, is it not an act of mercy, not of malevolence, to indicate precisely that beforehand? And how could it conceivably be any other way, in a world characterized by the existence of free will, genuine reality, and true and irreducible import of human action? If we have important things to do, and the unrestrained capacity to choose to do them, or not—and if such choices determine the manner in which reality unfolds and whether the order that is good or even very good makes itself manifest—then our poor choices will also have their consequences, as dire in error as they are good in faithful service.

Moses makes the dire decision that the Midianite captives cannot be incorporated into Israelite society without undue risk. They are therefore put to the sword, and the Israelites proceed to the conclusion of their long, trying, and momentous journey. Whether this is the fault of the desert sojourners, their Midianite enemies, sin, or God Himself is something that we remain confused about to this day. It is perhaps the case that the permanent solution to this conundrum of threat versus opportunity or protection versus oppression is the specification of and then practice of diligent upward aim. Whether a foreign agent is deemed a welcome and necessary deliverer or ultimate foe is going to forever remain a matter of judgment—a matter that would be best served by the counsel of wisdom. It is the eternal hope of the religious striver that those who formulate a covenant with what is highest and divine will also become precisely those who are wise—those who are best able to separate, once again, wheat from chaff, and sheep from goats. This might mean that the best we can hope for when called upon to determine what is appropriate in our relationship with what is foreign is that we have developed the sagacity and judgment of those who walk with God, and that, in consequence, the appropriate decision is made at the appropriate time.

And with that, essentially, Numbers ends. The book of Deuteronomy opens with a retelling of the Exodus/Numbers story. Moses, weary after all this strife, facing the end of the road, delivers a lengthy bout of thunderous declaiming to his people, a summation of his times and teaching (Deuteronomy 1–30). He closes that with an announcement of the end of his days: "I am an hundred and twenty years old this day; I can no more go out and come: also the Lord hath said unto me, Thou shalt not go over this Jordan" (Deuteronomy 31:2–3). He tells the Israelites they will continue to travel in God's company under the guidance of their new leader: "The Lord thy God, he will go over before thee, and he will destroy these nations from before thee, and thou shalt possess them: and Joshua, he shall go over before thee, as the Lord hath said" (31:3). Moses encourages them to maintain their faith despite this transition of leadership: "Be strong and of a good courage, fear not, nor be afraid of them: for the Lord thy God, he it is that doth go with thee; he will not fail thee, nor forsake thee" (31:6). He then directly addresses his successor, handing to him the reins of authority; encouraging him as well: "And Moses called unto Joshua, and said unto him in the sight of all Israel, Be strong and of a good courage: for thou must go with this people unto the land which the Lord hath sworn unto their fathers to give them; and thou shalt cause them to inherit it. And the Lord, he it is that doth go before thee; he will be with thee, he will not fail thee, neither forsake thee: fear not, neither be dismayed" (31:7–8). This is another marker of the excellence of the now-aged prophet's leadership: he takes pains to ensure that the man who takes his place is worthy, ready to do so, and blessed by his predecessor.

God tells Moses that the Israelites will again lose faith in the future, break the divine covenant, and suffer dreadfully in consequence. He tells his prophet to write a song to be sung in the future to remind the all too often wayward chosen people of their faith and the eternal existence of the promised land: "And it shall come to pass, when many evils and troubles are befallen them, that this song shall testify against them as a witness; for it shall not be forgotten out of the mouths of their seed: for I know their imagination which they go about, even now, before I have brought them into the land which I sware. Moses therefore wrote this song the same day and taught it the children of Israel" (31:21–22). This song contains the final words of Moses to the people he has led for so long. It opens with the following verses of remembrance:

> Give ear, O ye heavens, and I will speak; and hear, O earth, the words of my mouth.
>
> My doctrine shall drop as the rain, my speech shall distil as the dew, as the small rain upon the tender herb, and as the showers upon the grass:
>
> Because I will publish the name of the Lord: ascribe ye greatness unto our God.
>
> He is the Rock, his work is perfect: for all his ways are judgment: a God of truth and without iniquity, just and right is he.
>
> They have corrupted themselves, their spot is not the spot of his children: they are a perverse and crooked generation.
>
> Do ye thus requite the Lord, O foolish people and unwise? is not he thy father that hath bought thee? hath he not made thee, and established thee?

Remember the days of old, consider the years of many generations: ask thy father, and he will shew thee; thy elders, and they will
tell thee.

Deuteronomy 32:1–7

And with that the greatest of the Old Testament prophets reviews, once
again, the destination of his people, high above the plains of Moab, and goes
to meet his maker:

And Moses went up from the plains of Moab unto the mountain of
Nebo, to the top of Pisgah, that is over against Jericho. And the Lord
shewed him all the land of Gilead, unto Dan,

And all Naphtali, and the land of Ephraim, and Manasseh, and
all the land of Judah, unto the utmost sea,

And the south, and the plain of the valley of Jericho, the city of
palm trees, unto Zoar.

And the Lord said unto him, This is the land which I sware unto
Abraham, unto Isaac, and unto Jacob, saying, I will give it unto thy
seed: I have caused thee to see it with thine eyes, but thou shalt not
go over thither.

So Moses the servant of the Lord died there in the land of Moab,
according to the word of the Lord.

And he buried him in a valley in the land of Moab, over
against Bethpeor: but no man knoweth of his sepulchre unto
this day.

And Moses was an hundred and twenty years old when he died:
his eye was not dim, nor his natural force abated.

And the children of Israel wept for Moses in the plains of Moab
thirty days: so the days of weeping and mourning for Moses were
ended.

And Joshua the son of Nun was full of the spirit of wisdom;
for Moses had laid his hands upon him: and the children of Israel hearkened unto him, and did as the Lord commanded Moses.

And there arose not a prophet since in Israel like unto Moses, whom the Lord knew face to face,

In all the signs and the wonders, which the Lord sent him to do in the land of Egypt to Pharaoh, and to all his servants, and to all his land,

And in all that mighty hand, and in all the great terror which Moses shewed in the sight of all Israel.

Deuteronomy 34:1–12

9

✦

Jonah and the Eternal Abyss

We know nothing about Jonah when we're introduced to him. We might infer that there is nothing remarkable about him—that he is as ordinary and unknown as any other man—until he hears the voice of God: "Now the word of the Lord came unto Jonah the son of Amittai, saying, Arise, go to Nineveh, that great city, and cry against it; for their wickedness is come up before me" (Jonah 1:1–2). Why Jonah? This is a question echoed by everyone required by circumstance to undertake a singular duty or bear a rare existential burden: "Why me, God? What have I ever done, to deserve such a fate?" But our destinies call to each of us, not least in the form of what interests us or gets under our skin, despite our wishing it might be otherwise.

Why Nineveh? This is an equally complex question. It is a city obviously known to Jonah. Otherwise, it would not make much sense for God to direct His potential servant's attention to it. Nineveh is inhabited by the sworn enemies of Israel, and by no means a place that Jonah would be inclined to consider in a kindly fashion. The Kingdom of Israel was conquered by the Neo-Assyrian monarchs Tiglath-Pileser III and Shalmaneser V, and later by Sargon II and his son Sennacherib. The same Assyrians carried out a policy of forced resettlement (with those so moved coming to be known as the Ten Lost Tribes) (see 2 Kings 17:3–6). Nineveh was the capital of the Assyrian Empire. The unfolding story therefore makes it quite clear that the erstwhile prophet would be thoroughly pleased to see the people of Nineveh go to hell in precisely the handbasket of their own making. Thus, not only did God call upon Jonah to face down a whole city on his own—and a degenerate, terribly misbehaving city at that—He asked him to preach to his own people's sworn enemies, and hypothetically save them from the destruction that, in his prophet's opinion, they richly and justly deserved.

It is the same still, small voice that spoke to Elijah[1] that calls upon Jonah, suggesting that he journey alone, to a hated foreign city, to face down its tens of thousands of inhabitants, none of whom have any reason to bear anything but enmity toward him. In short, he is called by the divine to work at immense risk to save those he hates from punishment from Jonah's own God, which he thinks should be visited upon them sooner rather than later and with all the intensity that God can muster. Is it any wonder, then, that Jonah does what any sensible person might do, upon hearing God's apparently far from reasonable request, making tracks as rapidly as possible, in the precisely opposite direction? "But Jonah rose up to flee unto Tarshish from the presence of the Lord, and went down to Joppa; and he found a ship going to Tarshish: so he paid the fare thereof, and went down into it, to go with them unto Tarshish from the presence of the Lord" (Jonah 1:3). It was literally not possible to get any farther away from Nineveh than Tarshish at the time.

Jonah's dilemma is reminiscent of that confronted by a great man of an entirely different culture, the Greek philosopher Socrates, when he faces his final ordeal. Socrates has been diligently instructing the people of his city, Athens, to think. (Was he in fact the world's first genuinely expert thinker? Was that very capacity for thought the same as the emergence of the inner voice?) There were plenty of powerful people in Athens who were not happy about that enterprise, or its fruits. Those same people accused him of both failing to acknowledge the gods recognized by the city and corrupting the city's youth—crimes punishable by death. They threaten Socrates, in consequence, with a public trial. To his enemies' credit, they warn him of their plans. A sensible man would have regarded this as a clear message: get out of Dodge City, or else. The popular philosopher had clearly annoyed some powerful people. They were not inclined to murder him on the street or in his bed—not unless such action became necessary—but they were perfectly willing to let him know that bad things were coming his way if he failed to vanish. Socrates gives great consideration to his situation, conferring intensely with his *daimonion*, his muse or inner voice. He had heard and attended to this voice since childhood, according to his own testimony, and it guided him away from harm and toward the immense virtue he embodied and promoted. Terribly enough, when met with the threat of the trial, the *daimonion* tells Socrates not to run: it advises him instead to stay and enter the fray and, if necessary, to take his bitter medicine. He tells his friends and admirers about this decision. They are, as might be expected, none too pleased.[2]

The relevant text, Crito, details a conversation between the man of the dialogue's name and Socrates. The former has made arrangements to smuggle the old philosopher out of prison and into exile, where he will be safe. All things considered, that would be better for Socrates, as well as his sons and friends, who might otherwise look and feel like they did nothing to help him, and a set of actions leading to a more just outcome. Furthermore, arrangements have been made by those same friends to provide the great teacher with a comfortable retirement. Socrates rejects all these plans and pleas, indicating instead that a citizen owes allegiance to the laws of his state, however unjust a given application of those laws might be—a rationale in keeping with the statements of his inner voice. He remains, famously, in Athens, undergoes the trial promised by his foes, and makes a terrible hash of their reputation while on the stand. It is clear from the accounts of the hypothetical prosecution why the philosopher was unpopular with the elite. He turns the trial on its ear, telling those who are there to see him finished exactly what he thinks of them, and why, in the most public manner possible. Unlike Jonah, Socrates devoutly followed the dictates of his conscience, and says to his enemies what he has been called upon to say. He has been remembered ever since, at least in part because of that awful courage, whose expression cost him his life. Is it reasonable to do so? Is this the path that a good God would ask His followers to walk?

It is very easy, at the beginning of this story, to sympathize with Jonah, the reluctant prophet, unwilling as he was to make the choice of Socrates. It is no surprise that he is loathe to follow even a divine prompting, given the impossibility of his situation. How are we to make sense of this apparently ignorant command, particularly given God's omniscience, omnipotence, and omnipresence? What exactly does Jonah's problem signify? First, perhaps, this: we all, no matter how hypothetically ordinary, face challenges, obstacles, and calls to duty in our lives that seem too much to bear. Thus, the idea that God sometimes presents ridiculous demands upon us appears existentially sound (even if secularized; even if conceptualized as "sometimes life is simply too much"). Second, perhaps this: everyone knows, at least at a level appropriate for their current state of development, what is right and what is wrong. Everyone knows when it is their duty to set things right when they see them going wrong, and to risk themselves in that attempt (not least because it is a clear risk to let things deteriorate; not least because of their obligations to the future and to others). This "setting right"—this confronting of the crisis—can be a dangerous task, however, in the short term; can present a practical and psychological challenge; can set the would-be speaker against the rough and immediate judgment of the mob.

There is something of an eternal contest to shirk responsibility, however necessary it might be—to let someone else be the sacrificial voice in the wilderness; to hide unwanted things in the fog; to pretend that what is wrong is unimportant; to rationalize and prevaricate; to claim the moral virtue of false compassion; to turn a blind eye to growing viciousness; to hide from reality and destiny (even though such hiding also means the forgoing of adventure itself). This is part of the attractiveness of the lie, which can so often be silence rather than the sin of commission that is outright manipulation or deception. Keeping quiet when threat is near has the obvious short-term advantage of safety and security. But there's the rub: there is much that works well for now, and for the narrowly selfish, that compromises the future and the community. Perhaps the voice of conscience is part of the spirit that sees all; that can navigate past, present, and future simultaneously, and that unites the individual with the group. This at least is the insistence of text and tradition: "I am Alpha and Omega, the beginning and the ending, saith the Lord, which is, and which was, and which is to come, the Almighty."

Jonah has been told by God in no uncertain terms that the people of Nineveh have deviated from the proper path in a serious manner, and that they are threatened with divine apocalypse in direct consequence. The erstwhile prophet knows full well that this is true, that it has become his personal problem, and that it is his proper and ordained destiny to say what he has to say—and the devil takes the hindmost. But, as a sensible but insufficiently God-fearing person might, he rejects the call. And what happens when such responsibility is abdicated? The winds blow, and the waves rise up, and the eternal ship of soul and state itself is threatened:

> But the Lord sent out a great wind into the sea, and there was a mighty tempest in the sea, so that the ship was like to be broken.
>
> Then the mariners were afraid, and cried every man unto his god, and cast forth the wares that were in the ship into the sea, to lighten it of them. But Jonah was gone down into the sides of the ship; and he lay, and was fast asleep.
>
> So the shipmaster came to him, and said unto him, What meanest thou, O sleeper? arise, call upon thy God, if so be that God will think upon us, that we perish not.
>
> *Jonah 1:4–6*

Jonah's sleeping during this crisis is a re-representation of the theme of his fleeing—except this time he is retreating from the realities and demands of the current situation by escaping into unconsciousness (just as Cain did previously, when he is banished to the land of Nod in the aftermath of Abel's murder; just as Peter and the rest of the disciples do, much later, (Matthew 26: 36–46) when asked to stay awake and accompany Christ during His intense suffering in the Garden of Gethsemane). It is no wonder that the shipmaster is displeased, as is Jesus in the Garden: What dutiful man sleeps when there is a catastrophe unfolding? We are often called upon by our consciences—by our higher selves, in the psychologized but somehow secularly acceptable parlance—to speak or act when the most craven parts of us would rather remain silent; we are often called upon to maintain an alert wakefulness just when we might desperately crave the bliss of nonbeing, temporary or permanent.

The situation of storm, peril, and unconsciousness is paralleled elsewhere in Christ's life, with a very different immediate outcome:

> And when he was entered into a ship, his disciples followed him.
>
> And, behold, there arose a great tempest in the sea, insomuch that the ship was covered with the waves: but he was asleep.
>
> And his disciples came to him, and awoke him, saying, Lord, save us: we perish.
>
> And he saith unto them, Why are ye fearful, O ye of little faith? Then he arose, and rebuked the winds and the sea; and there was a great calm.
>
> But the men marvelled, saying, What manner of man is this, that even the winds and the sea obey him!
>
> *Matthew 8:23–27*

Instead of being cast into the sea as a consequence of the storm (and, more distally, as result of rejecting God's word) the man who is the Word itself has no need to be taken involuntarily into the depths. He speaks His Word of love and truth conjoined and the waters that threaten the (eternal) ship calm.

The sailors transporting Jonah have an intuition that they have taken on board someone not right with the divine. They throw dice, essentially, just to test their hypothesis, reasoning that the loser will be the one indicated as out of favor with the proper order of being itself. Jonah is the unlucky but deserving recipient of that honor. "And they said every one to his fellow, Come, and let us cast lots, that we may know for whose cause this evil is upon us. So they cast lots, and the lot fell upon Jonah" (Jonah 1:7). The fleeing captive then makes his situation worse, if possible, by stressing the power of the God he purports to worship, describing Him in the highest possible terms—as the ultimate creator of the cosmos itself. This further terrifies the already frightened seamen, not least because Jonah had previously let his dispute with that very God become public. Weighted down, perhaps by his conscience, he informs on himself, letting his oceangoing compatriots know that he was fleeing an order delivered from the highest possible place, implying as he did no doubt about the credibility of the source, and an unwillingness to shoulder the risk attendant upon complying with the command:

> Then said they unto him, Tell us, we pray thee, for whose cause this evil is upon us; What is thine occupation? and whence comest thou? what is thy country? and of what people art thou? And he said unto them, I am an Hebrew; and I fear the Lord, the God of heaven, which hath made the sea and the dry land.
>
> Then were the men exceedingly afraid, and said unto him, Why hast thou done this? For the men knew that he fled from the presence of the Lord, because he had told them.
>
> *Jonah 1:8-10*

To his credit, however, in this dire situation, honesty returns to Jonah, and he offers himself up as a sacrifice to save the ship and its sailors, entreating them to throw him overboard, so that he might drown and they survive:

> Then said they unto him, What shall we do unto thee, that the sea may be calm unto us? for the sea wrought, and was tempestuous.
>
> And he said unto them, Take me up, and cast me forth into the sea; so shall the sea be calm unto you: for I know that for my sake this great tempest is upon you.
>
> Nevertheless the men rowed hard to bring it to the land; but they could not: for the sea wrought, and was tempestuous against them.
>
> *Jonah 1:11-13*

We can infer from his truthfulness and emergent willingness to sacrifice himself in the throes of a genuine crisis that Jonah was a basically good man, despite his (understandable) situational cowardice. Maybe it was for this reason that the voice of conscience descended upon him in the first place.

Failing in their attempts to make for the safe haven of shore, the sailors relent, however reluctantly, and decide to go through with the necessary sacrifice: "Wherefore they cried unto the Lord, and said, We beseech thee, O Lord, we beseech thee, let us not perish for this man's life, and lay not upon us innocent blood: for thou, O Lord, hast done as it pleased thee." So they took up Jonah and cast him forth into the sea: "And the sea ceased from her raging" (Jonah 1:14–15). The sea immediately calms. Their ship is saved. This convinces the men of God's ultimate dominion, and they turn their worship toward him, promising to maintain that attitude on a permanent basis. "Then the men feared the Lord exceedingly, and offered a sacrifice up to the Lord, and made vows" (Jonah 1:16). Does the threat posed to the ship not signify that those who refuse their divine calling threaten the state itself? Does this not indicate that those who run and hide must be admonished, by themselves and the community—even that the domination of sin will become so complete and dire, as a consequence of such refusal, that even those initially unwilling to discriminate, judge, and reject will be driven by emergent necessity to do so, as everything shakes and creaks around them? What is the alternative? How can sanity prevail, stability maintain itself, and adaptation proceed if the individuals who make up the state reject the responsibility they know full well in their heart of hearts to be theirs? If they refuse to make what they know beyond a shadow of a doubt public knowledge? If they hold their tongue when something necessary and vital burns to be said?

What is the moral of the story of Jonah, so far? Speak truth to the mad urban mob at your great peril, but fear even more the God who tells you to speak when you have something to say. Maintain silence when called upon to testify, and pay the price. The tempest will rise, and the waves will tower ever higher, until the very ark that protects you from chaos itself will be imperiled. Then your compatriots in their desperation will abandon you to the tender mercies of the darkest and deepest waters, and you will swim or perish. And that is not yet enough: as you find yourself in peril of drowning, a terrible monster will arise from the abyss itself and haul you down to the very bottom of the world. It is no coincidence that the three days that Jonah spends in the belly of the whale are symbolically paralleled to the hell that Christ Himself harrows in the aftermath of his crucifixion. Degeneration, destruction, and death will threaten, in the aftermath of rejection of the divine call to voice, but that is not all. Such threat will be followed by a fate so terrible that death itself will be viewed as a most desirable alternative. Drowning is one thing, bad as it is; hell is a whole different kettle of fish. And what does this mean?

One who has lived truly rarely fails to understand that there are worse things than mere cessation of being. Compliance with the authorities in Auschwitz was worse than death. Life as a trustee in the Soviet Gulag was worse than death. Acting as an agent hell-bent on the destruction of the innocents is worse than death. Hell is much worse than death, and those who insist that hell does not exist know little of history and utterly lack informed imagination. The spirit that creates hell is that of malevolence itself, that bitter combination of envy, spite, arrogance, deceit, disdain, and resentment; that endless longing of the Luciferian intellect to usurp, replace, and sit on the highest seat. It is far easier to "believe in" the reality of that spirit than to profess the allegiance to God, which requires courage, despite suffering; humility, despite pride; gratitude, instead of resentment; discipline, instead of an immature narcissism, multiplied in its pathology by a blind and narrowly self-serving hedonism; and, of course, the self-sacrifice demanded, say, by the true followers of Christ.

Why does the terrible truth that Jonah is called upon to utter something place him in peril? Well, first of all, that is not what it is. It is something that temporarily places him in peril but that redeems him, and everyone else, in the "fullness of time" (Galatians 4:4). Why should we presume anything other than that the deepest instincts that orient us speak with what is in our best interest in mind, all things considered, and over the longest possible span of time and community, even if there is a price to be paid for that—a sacrifice to be made—in the present? Second, it is obvious that there is going

to be danger in confronting the accrued consequences of a misaligned aim—
of sin—given that there were at least micro-reasons for the acts of avoidance
(omission) and outright deception (commission) that aggregated the trouble
in the first place. If a building is not maintained, then the work required to
do so not only adds up but multiplies, as one damn thing leads not only to
another but to a teeming multitude of others:

> And they came over unto the other side of the sea, into the country
> of the Gadarenes.
>
> And when he was come out of the ship, immediately there met
> him out of the tombs a man with an unclean spirit,
>
> Who had his dwelling among the tombs; and no man could bind
> him, no, not with chains:
>
> Because that he had been often bound with fetters and chains,
> and the chains had been plucked asunder by him, and the fetters
> broken in pieces: neither could any man tame him.
>
> And always, night and day, he was in the mountains, and in the
> tombs, crying, and cutting himself with stones.
>
> But when he saw Jesus afar off, he ran and worshipped him,
>
> And cried with a loud voice, and said, What have I to do with
> thee, Jesus, thou Son of the most high God? I adjure thee by God,
> that thou torment me not.
>
> For he said unto him, Come out of the man, thou unclean spirit.
>
> And he asked him, What is thy name? And he answered, saying,
> My name is Legion: for we are many.
>
> *Mark 5:1–9*

This means that Jonah and all of those called to speak truth to power, to
employ a phrase mouthed to death by the Pharisees of the modern world, will
inevitably be required to face all the perils that have accrued through sin. Of
course this is dangerous and ineluctably so: it was from the minor dangers that
originally existed, to say it again, that all the sinners who aggregated that danger were originally attempting to flee. This cost them the opportunity to par-

ticipate in the great and true romantic adventure of their miserable lives, but—what is it? Better the devil you know than the God you know not?

This is malevolence itself, in each of the micro-actions or inactions that created the cumulative hell, in that hell itself, and in the form of the cowardly, resentful, and arrogant spirit that motivated each sinful act or failure to act—and it is something far easier to "believe in" than God, given the self-imposed terrors of human history. Those who insist that hell does not exist are either willfully blind, or so fortunate and protected by a benevolent fate that they have not visited that dread domain long enough to learn the terrible lessons that are learned there. Through the darkness however, and into the light. This is also what Jonah learns. It is not until he has descended into the hell that also characterizes both the situation of the Ninevites but also the spirit that led them there that he truly confronts the reality of God. What does this mean? That the stark reality of evil is perhaps the most compelling evidence for God? How could this be?

If it is true that evil exists, and if the reality of this truth becomes self-evident, once evil has been encountered and seen for what it is, then the opposite of evil is something equally real, even in the "mere" form of the contrary direction; even in the ineffable form of the alternative to the journey to hell. If there is a pathway to the abyss, our direction on that road can be reversed. Why should we assume that there is any difference between getting as far away from Satan as possible and climbing Jacob's Ladder? Or, are we somehow willing to admit that only hell truly exists—once again, say, in the form of the trustee in Auschwitz or the Soviet Gulag who enjoys the delights of his power; in the form of the veritable devil who takes pleasure in sticking the prongs of his pitchfork in others, even if it means submitting himself in turn to the even larger pitchforks of the even bigger devils who inevitably rule over him? Only hell, then, and some idiot neutrality, a land where neither good nor evil live, the equally damned land of the fence-sitter, is the final destination of those who turn without reservation away from the idiot blandishments of Satan in the desert.

We have been specifically warned against such an assumption by none other than Christ Himself, in the terrible form of the judge, at the end of times: "I know thy works, that thou art neither cold nor hot: I would thou wert cold or hot. So then because thou art lukewarm, and neither cold nor hot, I will spue thee out of my mouth" (Revelation 3:15–16). Or is instead the case, as was intimated to Tolstoy,[3] that the infinite expanse above us towers as high as the terrible abyss below us endlessly gapes? Is it not also the case that the reality of God, and the necessity of the strictest of obedience, is revealed to us in consequence of the hardness of our hearts not in what beckons to us in the form of calling or even warns us in the form of conscience but in the most dire moments of our life, made dire by the very consequences of our Jonah-like attempts to run away and hide?

There is more yet to the devouring monster of the rift, as well, than mere beast and underworld: something individual and social, in addition to natural and abysmal or hellish. That *more* is part of the strange juxtaposition of image and idea that is so characteristic of the dreamlike thought of thoroughly distilled story. The terrible Leviathan of the deep is the maw of Hades, but at the same time something alive and immensely valuable. A creature of that size is an intrinsically useful commodity. It is precisely for that reason that whales have been hunted by human beings for thousands of years. At its peak in the mid-nineteenth century, the whaling industry was the fifth largest commercial enterprise in the U.S.[4] and was a major contributor to the burgeoning industrial revolution, which relied on the fuel, bone, meat, and keratin products derived from the great denizens of the deep. The fact of this value of carcass is part of the complex of meaning that surrounds the idea of the whale. Herding people calculate their wealth by the size of their herds and flocks—by the weight of the bodies of the animals they care for and live off—and there is simply no body larger than that of a giant cetacean. Thus, a whale is also both a storehouse of immense value and one of the most potent symbols of such a storehouse.

This means, surprisingly enough (at least on first encounter) that there is an equivalence between the giant corpses of whales and the traditions and institutions bequeathed to us by our ancestors—as similarity highlighted by such turns of phrase as "body of law," "of knowledge," and "of wisdom." These are also treasure houses—place where accrued value is deposited and kept. The great bodies in question, whether of the living or institutional type, are also similar in that their stored value is a product of forces beyond the immediate control of those alive in the present. In the case of the institutional type (think "social capital"), those forces are the productive, cooperative activities of the people who left more behind them than they consumed, so their children—and others' children—could benefit. In the case of the living type (think "natural resource"), the bestowing agent is nature, rather than culture, although nature always lurks behind the cultural and the social, and can be properly regarded as the more distal source even of what is economic and communal. Regardless of source, the same endpoint is reached: something is left for the using, preserving, and enriching—or for the mere taking. Wise societies, composed of grateful and awake people, live in conscious appreciation for what has been given to them and attempt to pay the favor forward.

A carcass the size of a whale is indeed the most salient possible direct embodiment and representation of the accrued value that is in its most fundamental form a storehouse of food and energy. The man fortunate enough to stash a whale in his storehouse, if he can only preserve and keep it, is someone provisioned as well as possible against all but the most extreme of conceivable famines. And what if the whale has only washed up on shore, so to speak—that is, made itself available by the vagaries of fate, with no effort on the part of those who can now benefit—with no necessity to strive to bring about its benefits; with no understanding whatsoever of what miraculous mustering of inconceivable forces that must have occurred for such a creature to exist, and to present itself for use? The fact of that possibility—or, indeed, ultimate reality—is exactly what God Himself attempts to impress upon Job when the latter is tempted by what does in fact appear to be a rather dismal fate to question the propriety of the cosmic order:

Canst thou draw out leviathan with an hook? or his tongue with a cord which thou lettest down?
Canst thou put an hook into his nose? or bore his jaw through with a thorn?

Will he make many supplications unto thee? will he speak soft words unto thee?

Will he make a covenant with thee? wilt thou take him for a servant for ever?

Wilt thou play with him as with a bird? or wilt thou bind him for thy maidens?

Shall the companions make a banquet of him? shall they part him among the merchants?

Canst thou fill his skin with barbed irons? or his head with fish spears?

Lay thine hand upon him, remember the battle, do no more.

Behold, the hope of him is in vain: shall not one be cast down even at the sight of him?

None is so fierce that dare stir him up: who then is able to stand before me?

Job 41:1–10

Unwise societies (think Nineveh) take the fact of their traditions and accrued resources for granted. They live unconsciously on the wealth of the past, narcissistically and destructively consuming more than they earn; even irresponsibly destroying the very spirit whose activity gave rise to the wealth in question. We can regard the wealth offered to us by past and nature alike as our entitlement, even our earned due, and act far too casually and carelessly in consequence, despising our birthright and its source: privilege. This is exactly what is portrayed in the *Enuma elish*, the genesis tale of the ancient Mesopotamians: the careless inhabitants of the first creation kill their father, Apsu, and attempt to live upon or within his dead corpse.[5] Something in the same vein is portrayed in the Disney movie *Pinocchio*. Midway through the movie, Geppetto, the benevolent father of the movie's marionette/hero, finds himself trapped in the belly of a whale, with no real explanation for his predicament offered by the filmmakers—except, by implication, that the desperate patriarch is willing to search everywhere for his missing son. The carpenter/father's loss of the son is equivalent in meaning to Jonah's loss of his living voice, as the son is traditionally the active agent of the father—the eyes or voice of the father; the spirit of what otherwise might be stultified or static tradition. The carpenter/father's loss of the son, and his consequent grief, is a representation of the longing of God for a true covenant or relationship with man. Are we not in fact the cocreators of this realm—and, perhaps, of heaven itself? We can certainly create hell alone. What could we do if we were instead aligned with the highest we could imagine?

Does not the sojourn of the (voluntarily) unconscious in the belly of the whale signify that those bestowed the unearned benefits of culture and nature can exist, blindly and stupidly, in consequence of that unearned largesse, stripping the bodies so provided of their flesh, even living inside their protective and plentiful confines, so to speak—in their bellies? Is that not the same thing as a profound ignorance, ingratitude, arrogance, immaturity, and willful blindness? Is that not the same place as the paternal tent that Abraham dwelt within for so many dependent and infantile decades before embarking on the true adventure of his life? Does this not mean that in developed societies and even successful micro-societies (corporations and other subcultures) the acquisition of wealth over time is likely to enable a collapse of values—the veritable death of God—in consequence of the irresponsibility such wealth allows, however temporarily?

Does this all mean, in turn, that the corpses of whales, whether natural or institutional, inevitably become overwhelmed by the willfully blind, painfully unconscious, terminally ungrateful, devouring scavengers that produce nothing but can and will strip everything to its bones—even burning what remains, in increasing desperation, to ashes? Is it the case, then—to say it slightly differently—that the storage of wealth well represented by the idea of the body of a giant cetacean is an enticement both to the unconsciousness of undeserved privilege and the proliferation of the scavengers motivated by their own narcissism and psychopathy to do nothing but strip that carcass of its stored value? The moral danger of wealth and privilege: an enticement to immature hedonistic narcissism. This implies that the strictures of brute natural necessity can also be viewed as regulatory and salutary, however terrible and even potentially deadly they might be. The wealthy have every-

thing they need, excepting deprivation. Worse: the same is true of their children. God only knows what that threat finally entails on the existential and
social front.

There is a deeper meaning here, too: when the wisdom of the past is forgotten or betrayed (that is, an occurrence equivalent to the death of God) the
lost value then lurks, unconsciously, in the remnant institutions and traditions of that past. This is the reversion to the implicit of what was once explicit, or at least more explicit. This is a transformation aptly represented in
narrative as the descent of the father into the belly of the whale. This has
implications for the hero, as well, as we also see in the story of *Pinocchio*. The
lost, even prodigal son of the now-missing father may well find himself
called or impelled by conscience to journey into the abyss, into the entrails
even of the most terrifying denizen of the deep, to find and rescue the now
implicit or unconscious spirit of the patriarch. This is an analog of Christ's
harrowing of hell:

> But unto every one of us is given grace according to the measure of
> the gift of Christ.
>
> Wherefore he saith, When he ascended up on high, he led captiv-
> ity captive, and gave gifts unto men.
>
> (Now that he ascended, what is it but that he also descended first
> into the lower parts of the earth? He that descended is the same also
> that ascended up far above all heavens, that he might fill all things.)
>
> *Ephesians 4:7–10*

This is, by tradition, the rescue of Adam and Eve from the abyss,[6] as well
as a variant of the primordial and fundamental dragon/treasure motif. Remember, with regard to this equivalence, that *Pinocchio's* Monstro literally
transforms into a fire-breathing dragon when he manifests himself in his
most dangerous guise. This is no easy trick for an aquatic animal, by the
way, but it still makes sense to the viewer of the story. Does all this not mean
that the God who dies is by necessity entombed, symbolically speaking, in
the corpse of a whale? Does that not mean that the hero who now searches

risks his own entrapment, until he revivifies his father, thereby freeing both God and man? All this is also part of finding what most desperately needs to be found in the most dangerous and unlikely of places. *In sterquiilinis invenitur,*[7] as the ancient alchemists had it: *in filth it will be found.*

"Now the Lord had prepared a great fish to swallow up Jonah. And Jonah was in the belly of the fish three days and three nights" (Jonah 1:17). This provides precisely the kind of narrative detail that reductive rationalists cite when trying to demonstrate the lack of veracity characterizing the biblical accounts. Although it is technically possible for a large enough whale to engulf a grown man in its mouth, and even to swallow him, there is no space within such creatures (a la Monstro in *Pinocchio*) that could be inhabited, however temporarily, let alone for a three-day period. Furthermore, the idea that someone on the outs with God could be identified by the casting of lots is indicative of the kind of superstitious mindset we moderns have thankfully outgrown (or so we arrogantly think, in the time of the New Age). Thus, it is foolish to believe such things when the clarity and objective truth of rationality and science beckons as alternative, or so goes the argument—of Marx; of Freud; of Darwin, at least by implication; of Dawkins, by intent. It is said, the entire archaic library should be, if not thrown out altogether, relegated to the domain reserved for children, naive adults, and students of anachronistic mythology (preferable those with plenty of time on their hands) and replaced. With what? There's the rub. By the insistence that sex (Freud, Darwin, Dawkins; far worse, the Marquis de Sade) or power (Nietzsche, Foucault) rules instead? By the terrible, devouring nihilism that Nietzsche, for all his faults, so accurately foretold? By the idiot immaturity fostered by the devouring Oedipal mother? By the blandishments of the hedonists, who worship the very sex postulated as both fundament and pinnacle by those who confuse the momentary although highly valuable pleasure of the bed and boudoir with the continuance of the species?

The existence of tropes such as the devouring cetacean of the story of Jonah does make it hard going for scientists too daft and self-satisfied to learn anything about literature and, equally, for those believers who insist upon a naive literalism. That is not a problem, however, that should preoccupy or

concern anyone conducting a serious investigation into narrative significance, not least because those who make such claims generally do not understand what they mean when they use a term such as "literal." They mean
"true," and identify "true" with "literal," but that indicates little besides philosophical naiveté of the most profound sort. Jonah's story is a warning: pick
up your damn cross and bear it or face the consequences. And what is worse,
yet, than the cross? Hell: hell for you, for those you love, and for everyone
else—and a hell that is on you, of your doing for remaining silent when you
have something to say; for running away or escaping into unconsciousness
when the voice of God, as the ineluctable call of conscience, makes itself
known. Pick up the hell of human making and hoist that, too. When you are
required to speak truth into possibility to make, maintain, or reconstitute
the order that is good and you reject the call, you invite the devil himself into
the game. Really. Truly. Or did we learn anything from the great moral catastrophes of the twentieth century? The answer? Very little.

And bloody well beware of presuming that in the situation facing Jonah,
you would have acted differently. Jonah is everyman—even better than most.
When push comes to shove, after all, that reluctant prophet at least had the
decency to admit to his error, to save those he was traveling with. What
makes you so sure you would do the same? What makes you so sure that the
silence you are almost inevitably maintaining right now in your life about things
of absolutely cardinal import—of import to you, by your own standards—is not
dooming you and those you love to absolute perdition? How do you think
totalitarian states establish themselves? It is not the obedience of the glorious
would-be free to the solely dominating tyrant that creates the totalitarian
state. It is instead the allegiance of every damned soul to the dominion of the
lie—and silence, when there is truth to be told, is the most subtle and perhaps even the most inexcusable lie. As we learned from Solzhenitsyn,[8] everyone in a tyranny lies about absolutely everything to themselves and to
everyone they purport to love all the time. It is the classic Soviet joke: "We
pretend to work and they pretend to pay us." And it is worth thinking about
just who would formulate and tell such a joke for the rest of your life. *Arbeit
macht frei.* Mutual Assured Destruction (MAD). Satan himself is an evil

clown, ruler over the bitter parody of God's creation that inevitably emerges when those who could know better bite their tongue—or give it over entirely to the Great Deceiver himself.

It is the rare person indeed who when push comes to shove will not put his or her head in the sand. Are you everything you could be? Or have you instead hidden your candle under a bushel and thereby refused to light the world (Matthew 14–15)? Is the world not therefore markedly lesser for your reticence and rejection? How much of a hole has your failure to realize the best within you left in the world? How much is that hole—that wound, even; that gaping wound, even (because that is certainly how you and those around you experience the consequences, even if that experience has remained unconscious)—a portal to hell itself? The one willing to give expression to conscience—the Old Testament prophet—is the exception, not the norm. He is the one willing to say "come what may" and "God's terrible will be done;" the one who knows that, terrible though that will may be (and this is a deadly seriously caution), the alternative can be and has been almost unimaginably worse; the one who in small numbers says the words that could have saved even Sodom and Gomorrah (Genesis 18–19).

What do you know about the way things should be, that gives your prediction a certainty above the consequences of the truth? Why are you so convinced that your wish, will, and whim should take precedence over what merely lays itself out, with ultimately irresistible force, when the truth is spoken? There are, too, soul-deadening as well as practically deadly consequences for hiding your light from yourself and your fellow man; for rejecting the call of destiny, however minor it may initially appear; for pretending that you are less good (or less evil) than you truly are. How did the Nazis gain the upper hand? Because of the silence of the "good." How did the Soviets maintain the rule of evil for seven decades? Because of the silence of the "good." How did the brutal monsters of Maoist China murder tens of millions with gleeful impunity? Because of the silence of the "good." Butter would not melt in their mouths.

Ignore your conscience at the peril of hell. Really. Truly.

As it is said: "If you bring forth what is within you, what you bring forth will save you. If you do not bring forth what is within you, what you do not bring forth will destroy you."[9] Is this not how God balances the cosmos, morally? As it is also said: "For unto whomsoever much is given, of him shall be much required" (Luke 12:48). There is, as well, a terrible warning at the beginning of that passage from Luke: "But he that knew not, and did commit things worthy of stripes, shall be beaten with few stripes." "Stripes" means "lashes with the whip"—most often, the whip of fate. The statement means: if you erred, but truly did not know better, you will be punished comparatively lightly for the mistake. It is in such a manner that the providence of God protects the innocent—even the naive. But no such mercy is reserved for those who know better and sin, whether by commission or omission. If you err, in spite of your own true knowledge, you will be punished not only by the consequences of that error but also for the much greater crime of betraying yourself—and, worse, betraying that which eternally serves as the True Guide. And how can you ever be found, if you turn voluntarily from that, and have therefore become lost?

Cast into hell, Jonah repents, lifting his eyes once again above the horizon, orienting himself along the axis of Jacob's Ladder, placing his head in the stars, gathering his faith in the very abyss itself. Faith is the courage to be, instead of to not be, despite the catastrophe of existence. Faith is the courage to determine to maintain stalwart and upward aim at the good, even in the midst of hell—"yet I will look again toward thy holy temple":

> Then Jonah prayed unto the Lord his God out of the fish's belly,
>
> And said, I cried by reason of mine affliction unto the Lord, and he heard me; out of the belly of hell cried I, and thou heardest my voice.
>
> For thou hadst cast me into the deep, in the midst of the seas; and the floods compassed me about: all thy billows and thy waves passed over me.
>
> Then I said, I am cast out of thy sight; yet I will look again toward thy holy temple.

The waters compassed me about, even to the soul: the depth closed me round about, the weeds were wrapped about my head.

I went down to the bottoms of the mountains; the earth with her bars was about me for ever: yet hast thou brought up my life from corruption, O Lord my God.

When my soul fainted within me I remembered the Lord: and my prayer came in unto thee, into thine holy temple.

They that observe lying vanities forsake their own mercy.

Jonah 2:1–8

"They that observe lying vanities forsake their own mercy," indeed. Did the whale really swallow Jonah? Is it not only the terminally naive who believe such things? Perhaps, insofar as "belief" can be the childish faith in the genuine rather than metaphorical existence of Santa Claus—but even then the desire to maintain this belief is understandable, and even admirable, insofar as it is part of a genuine attempt to maintain the foundational or aspirational belief that characterizes nothing less than Judeo-Christian civilization itself.

Furthermore, those with the temerity to presume that their attitude of hypothetically enlightened doubt is the proper and admirable response to these deepest of all fairytales manifest a naiveté of equal depth—naiveté, conjoined with a moral superiority and worship of untrammeled intellect that makes of that naiveté something prideful and perverse. That combination of lack of discernment on the literary front and intellectual arrogance is something more than capable of gathering the forces of the abyss around itself, as all those that have the eyes to see and the ears to hear (Matthew 11:15) should now be able to perceive. It is the falsely wise who confuse their inability and unwillingness to separate wheat from chaff in relationship to these ancient stories with genuine, even scientific, enlightenment. Moral dwarfs, equipped with hydrogen bombs. The whale always and inevitably closes its jaws over the Jonahs who have determined to be silent, and drags them to the most dreadful of underworlds. And most stay there, in the belly of the beast, after having dragged those they love down with them. And that is the lesson of the twentieth century. Have we learned it, or does a deeper hell yet await us?

Jonah manages the impossible. In the abysmal depths, he expresses his gratitude. Job, much later, does the same. That is also not naiveté. It is instead the bloody but unbowed courage of faith itself, despite the horrors of the world. Because of this—in combination with God's grace—the cursed prophet returns from the grip of death and the underworld:

> But I will sacrifice unto thee with the voice of thanksgiving; I will pay that that I have vowed. Salvation is of the Lord.
> And the Lord spake unto the fish, and it vomited out Jonah upon the dry land.
>
> *Jonah 2:1-10*

In the aftermath of his descent, and his resurrection, Jonah puts the devil behind him, just as Christ does after forty nights and days in the desert, and advances toward Nineveh, with the truth welling up inside him and spilling over. He has become the man who sought out and found the light in the darkness. He has become the man who has deeply learned what to fear and what not to fear: the deep blue sea, hell, and God Himself, not his own ease and comfort, and not his fellow man. He has learned not to seek the security of his own body, and the quelling of his desires, but the salvation of his very soul. He has become the man whose depth of suffering has made his word irresistible, even to those who are sinning deeply themselves:

> And the word of the Lord came unto Jonah the second time, saying,
> Arise, go unto Nineveh, that great city, and preach unto it the preaching that I bid thee.
> So Jonah arose, and went unto Nineveh, according to the word of the Lord. Now Nineveh was an exceeding great city of three days' journey.
> And Jonah began to enter into the city a day's journey, and he cried, and said, Yet forty days, and Nineveh shall be overthrown

JONAH AND THE ETERNAL ABYSS

So the people of Nineveh believed God, and proclaimed a fast, and put on sackcloth, from the greatest of them even to the least of them.

For word came unto the king of Nineveh, and he arose from his throne, and he laid his robe from him, and covered him with sackcloth, and sat in ashes.

And he caused it to be proclaimed and published through Nineveh by the decree of the king and his nobles, saying, Let neither man nor beast, herd nor flock, taste any thing: let them not feed, nor drink water:

But let man and beast be covered with sackcloth, and cry mightily unto God: yea, let them turn every one from his evil way, and from the violence that is in their hands.

Who can tell if God will turn and repent, and turn away from his fierce anger, that we perish not?

And God saw their works, that they turned from their evil way; and God repented of the evil, that he had said that he would do unto them; and he did it not.

Jonah 3:1–10

The Word of the One eternally redeems the many. The truth that reveals itself in the soul of man must find its expression in the world for Paradise to reveal itself; or, at least, for hell and its ruler to be kept at bay. God is eternally willing to show His mercy to those who repent, despite their past sins—despite even their enmity with God's chosen people themselves, the Jews. God forgives, and sheathes His sword, but man does not. Thus, Jonah finds himself outraged by the escape of his foes from the divine wrath he believes should be justly visited upon them. He tells God that he ran from Tarshish in the first place, when called upon to speak, not least because he suspected that if he did so, those upon whom he wished the utmost harm would be presented with the opportunity to repent and survive. Thus, the story tells us that those who remain silent may also do so because their revelation of truth might free even their enemies from suffering—an unacceptable outcome to those who have not yet learned to love their foes or to drop their desire for vengeance.

9.1. Jonah repents of his virtue

Jonah has thereby done a very good deed. He does not so easily forgive himself, however, for the dreadful crime of redeeming his enemies, and he acts and speaks in a manner that indicates that he is none too happy with God for requiring him to do so. In fact, he is so upset by the success of his venture that he calls upon God to end his existence: "Therefore now, O Lord, take, I beseech thee, my life from me; for it is better for me to die than to live" (Jonah 4:3). We should once again beware of imagining ourselves better than the now-miserable prophet. Who would willingly forgo the delights of feeling morally superior to his enemies? Maybe it is even worth the trouble of being hated so that such a pleasure can be sustained. It is very difficult to make the sacrifices necessary to be a good person—to allow all the deadwood and detritus to burn off—whereas it is very easy to regard others, particularly if foreign, with contempt, an emotion that has as one of its advantages the clear implication that the object of derision and target of disgust is lesser or even subhuman. Is it easier to lower others or to strive genuinely upward? The answer is obvious, at least in the short term.

It is genuinely likely that Jonah feels himself to be a traitor, as the people of Nineveh were the true foes of the Israelites; of the worshippers of Jehovah. There is also more than a hint in the text that the man God calls upon to save the lost city is more than a bit of a misanthrope. Adam refuses to walk with God in the garden after the fall because he recognizes that he is naked; because he comes to self-consciously believe that he is defined by insufficiency, weakness, and vulnerability. How can a creature so afflicted retain any respect for himself? He extends his self-contempt, as well, to Eve, cursing God for having made her. A man who has little use for himself and even less for women is certainly not going to be any friend to mankind, as such—and the pride that drove Adam to eat the fruit Eve offered to him is the same tempter that places him in the position of the judge who finds man himself, as such, wanting. This is the same attitude that drives Cain to call God out for the imperfection of the moral order, the putative cause of his suffering; the same attitude that Job rejects, deciding instead to maintain faith in creation and creator, despite the apparent unjust suffering meted out to him.

Jonah does not believe, in keeping with this attitude of contempt for the human (particularly when erring) that the Ninevites are worth saving, and the exceedingly strange and mysterious story appended to the end of his tale makes the fact that this attitude is associated with a counterproductive contempt and faulty moral ordering quite clear. God remonstrates with his prophet: "Then saith the Lord, Doest thou well to be angry?" (Jonah 4:4), but the target of the question does not take the hint and drop his resentment and desire for revenge. The Lord Himself is pleased that the people of the otherwise doomed city have turned from their evil ways, unlike the stiff-necked and eventually self-destructive inhabitants of Sodom, Gomorrah, and Egypt. He appears to be striving diligently to separate nothing but true chaff from wheat so that everything of genuine value (however small) can be gathered to him.

Jonah, however—less patient and forgiving than the God who has called upon him—leaves the city in a huff, and sets himself up in a small shack of interlaced sticks on the outskirts, hoping that some catastrophe might still strike down those he still hated and waiting to see that glorious day arrive. God prepares a gourd-bearing tree to shade him from the hot sun—an *elkeroa*, common in the sandy regions of Palestine, and which grows to a "considerable height" in only a few days[10]—although it suffices to say that it was lush and leafy enough to provide those taking shelter under its boughs with some respite. Jonah was "exceedingly glad" of the shade (Jonah 4:6)— thus, grateful for the fact of the plant and its shelter. But God has another trick up His sleeve, hoping to lead His still wayward and aggrieved follower further toward a generous wisdom:

But God prepared a worm when the morning rose the next day, and it smote the gourd that it withered.

And it came to pass, when the sun did arise, that God prepared a vehement east wind, and the sun beat upon the head of Jonah, that he fainted, and wished in himself to die, and said, It is better for me to die than to live.

And God said to Jonah, Doest thou well to be angry for the gourd? And he said, I do well to be angry, even unto death.

Jonah 4:7–9

Jonah is rightfully grateful for the benefits offered to him by the shady tree that grows so suddenly and so fortunately, but he has not yet by any means put his values into the proper order. He is glad of the provision of nature, celebrates nature—even worshipping it, for all intents and purposes, as he mourns its destruction with near-suicidal intensity. He is glad of the respite offered to him by nature, grateful for that mercy and care, but he remains angry at God above for the much greater respite, mercy, and care offered to the Ninevites. Jonah therefore reveals that he appreciates nature much more than man—and the men he has enmity toward are still men, despite their transgressions, and should be valued by a properly oriented moral agent much more than the mere manifestations of the natural world. Jonah thus replaces the true morality that would make him love even his enemies with the false aim and presumption that makes him a self-serving ally to forest and tree.

Thus, there is another serious warning embedded in this story of conscience and its call—one against a self-serving veneration of nature, disguising a deep hatred of mankind. This is a reversion to the very idolatry that Elijah warned and warred against. Jonah is very grateful for the tree that grows to provide him with shade, and is upset at its demise, regarding that as a moral transgression. God upbraids him, and rightfully so, for so valuing something that he had neither endeavored to produce, and had no rights over, and which was in addition transient and essentially insignificant: "Then said the Lord, Thou hast had pity on the gourd, for the which thou hast not laboured, neither madest it grow; which came up in a night, and perished in a night" (Jonah 4:10). There are no "natural resources"—no "environment," no matter how much vaunted; no intrinsic interest of "the planet"—whose value exceeds the value of mankind—or, perhaps, of any individual man or woman.

Instead, therefore–when nature is elevated above man—the true reason is the pride of the person engaging in that elevation, elevating himself to the position of the eternal judge of mankind, and eternally finding it wanting. That is not true celebration of the natural world, but a corrupt and stunningly self-serving denigration of what is purported to be God's highest creation: "I abrogate to myself the right to be the judge of all mankind—and, along with them, the spirit who gave them life." The judge, therefore, of God himself. Along with that prideful, usurping self-elevation comes an inevitable and sure-to-be-moralized cruelty and sadism: if nature is more than man, after all, then any aspect of nature can quickly be deemed of more value than any given man. If any man is then no more than a rat, or an insect, then anything that might be visited upon a rat or an insect—or even upon a tree, a shrub, or a weed—can with even more justification be visited upon man in general, or upon any man, in particular.

This is an attitude that can only end in disaster, as well as one that is aimed at that very disaster, all protestations to the contrary, from the beginning. To put the natural world above mankind in the hierarchy of ultimate value is to regress to the worship of Baal, to use the archaic conceptualization, and to risk the terrible consequences thereof. To elevate nature in this manner is simultaneously to denigrate both the God Who stands outside nature, and humanity itself. How could hell not appear, and prevail, when the cart is thus put before the horse? God therefore rightfully objects. His valuation of the people of Nineveh, despite their sins, is of much greater moral worth than Jonah's self-serving commitment to the gourd-tree; to the natural world and its capacity to shelter and provide: "And should not I spare Nineveh, that great city, wherein are more than sixscore thousand persons that cannot discern between their right hand and their left hand; and also much cattle?" (Jonah 4:7–11).

Thus ends the great story of the reluctant and flawed prophet, Jonah, so mysteriously swallowed by the whale. What then are we to conclude, in closing, from this, the final tale we will consider in our sampling of the ancient stories that serve as the bedrock for our culture; that enable us to see truth itself? That, as in the case of Elijah, God is well-characterized as conscience, although not only as conscience; that the individual who refuses to speak when the divine itself comes knocking—whether conceived of in the materialist sense as instinct or the religious as the direction of heaven itself—dooms himself and his culture to a fate worse than death; that even in the aftermath of such cowardly silence, and in the pit of hell itself, redemption can still be gained and integrity reestablished, if the will to do so is there; that there is no difference between the silence of the good and the victory of the authoritarian and evil; that even the city of enemies can be saved by the individual willing to utter the plain truths whose lack engenders the apocalypse itself; that the prophet who redeems can fall prey to his wish for vengeful retribution, even after he has been successful as that redeemer; and that love for man even in his fallen condition is a moral virtue higher than worship of the generous, necessary, and bountiful provisions of the natural world.

There is, in short, no real difference between the silence of the good and the victory of evil. That is a lot to learn, from a single story; a lot packed into a very little space; a lot to digest in a very short time—but all the books we have walked through and considered have that nature, that intense distilling, those continual punches of redeeming wisdom, those profound and vital dramatizations of God, man, and woman. Creation itself, Adam and Eve, Noah and the Tower of Babel, the adventure of Abraham and Moses, the descent and ascent of the reluctant prophet, Jonah: these are the accounts that structure our perception itself, that give the proper weight to our apprehensions, that provide the place to put our experience, that allow us to balance the wisdom of tradition that is the true stake in the ground around which everything rotates with the living experience of the present. The story of man, woman, and God is not one of power, or pleasure, but of the sacrificial sequence of transformation that lifts us upward, reconciles now and then and reconciles individual and community—the very story that unfolds in its profoundly multifaceted manner as the biblical library proceeds. That is the story we must be told, to be sane; that we must now come to understand, explicitly, to proceed as the pace of the world increases so exponentially; that we are called upon and directed by conscience to embody and incarnate, so that we can once again become the inhabitants of the Garden of Eden and play forever in the Kingdom of God.

CONCLUSION

The world, as we have seen, is far more than a mere collection of facts. In keeping with that is the observation that there is no simply and directly self-evident pathway from *what is* to *what ought to be*—from the fact to the act. Finally, the world is also not a straightforwardly deterministic place either; not a place where atoms, marble-like in their essence, bump up against one another, producing the predictable chain of events that drives or even constitutes our destinies. Instead, at every moment, what we experience, confront, and wrestle with is a domain of vast possibility. We do that in our capacity as veritable images of God, akin to the Logos, the creative spirit whose actions give rise to the cosmos itself, with its goodness of order. We do that as we hover with the divine over the primordial waters, speaking reality into being. That spirit of voluntary creative engagement is the first characterization of what is properly put in the highest place in the biblical corpus. This sets the stage for everything that follows—for our understanding of the spirit and story that renders the innumerable facts of reality into something limited and makes them the focus of attention and action in the manner that makes the world habitable, welcoming, stable, opportune, and productive.

Our kinship with the Logos comes with a set of responsibilities: to properly name and subdue; to act as foil or partner to that process, to steward the
walled garden that is the eternal environment of man and woman alike, and
to engage in the process of upward-striving sacrificial transformation that
reconciles the human and the divine. This means, as well, to hoist the world,
voluntarily, on our shoulders—to attend to the threat of chaos, when it
emerges; to keep our technological presumption under control; to brave the
romantic adventure of our lives; to become the leader of slaves, away from
the tyrant; and to speak the words that redeem, even to our enemies. We are
to do all that in keeping with the intrinsic moral order, the spirit of which is
God's, the results of which are written in the great book of the heavenly order, captured in the biblical text and inscribed on the human soul.

Adam and Eve find themselves tempted, however, wishing to become as
gods, taking to themselves the right to eat the forbidden fruit, inviting in the
influence of the great usurper—the serpent that is both the snake in the
grass and the prideful spirit of Lucifer, the highest angel in God's heavenly
kingdom gone most dreadfully wrong. Eve presumes the right and ability
to clasp even what is truly venomous to her breast. This is the pathology
of compassion, extended pridefully beyond its purview—the devouring
mother, warned of by myth and psychoanalysts alike, the witch in the gingerbread house that is the place of delicious security too good to be true and
the real home of the enemy of the spirit of the Son of Man. "There is no limit
to my love (look at me, look at me)." Adam's companion, tempted by her
pathological upward aim, calls upon her partner to incorporate the inedible
and welcome the betrayer and usurper, reshaping the cosmic order in the
process.

Adam, forever willing to strive falsely to impress his mate, agrees, however cravenly, to do so. What are his eternal rationalizations? Of course I can
do it; there is no limit to my competence; anything for you, dear; (nothing is
beyond me); (it is easier to go along than to oppose or negotiate); (I am truly
your harmless little friend)—agrees to do so. Both man and woman fall, in
consequence of their pride—both in the way that characterizes the temptation specific to each sex; both manifesting the inversion of their own unique

and fundamental strength. In the case of woman, this is the capacity to care and nurture; her great calling to people. In the case of man, it is the passion to understand and master the things of the world.[1]

Both descend, therefore, into a bitter self-consciousness, nakedness, and estrangement from the God they are now too cowardly to walk with. The world becomes a fallen place, furthermore, after the aim of the archetypal mother and father of mankind goes astray. Condemned to bitter toil, the first couple find themselves outside the heavenly garden, facing the dreadful cherubim who guard the gate, accompanied by the flaming sword that turns every which way and burns. What does this signify? That nothing imperfect can make its way into paradise, and that to sinners the discriminating process—the Logos—that bars the road may well look like hell.

This is when profane history begins. Cain and Abel, first two sons of the primordial parents, are also the first two naturally born inhabitants of the world we all now live in. As such, they embody and represent two archetypal and fundamentally opposed modes of being and becoming, which set or constitute the pattern for all human work; which define all the modes of sacrifice of present to future and individual whim to communal harmony and productivity (or the reverse) that define the well-constituted person and state. Abel offers what is of the highest quality, keeping nothing in reserve. He accepts the responsibility that is also adventure and meaning, and it transforms him as he matures and grows. Cain, by contrast, holds back. He offers what is second-best, burying his talents, and hiding his light under a bushel. He thereby comes under the sway of the spirit of manipulation and deceit. Everyone who takes the easy road ends up lying to themselves about who they are, what they are doing, and why they are doing it, attempting as they do so to distract and mislead God Himself. But life is a difficult game. The price of entry is death and the possibility of hell, and any player who does not bring his best to the table will not succeed. The life that could be paradisal is a reward given only to those who willingly, voluntarily and even gratefully bear the heaviest of all possible burdens; who take even the sins of the world onto themselves. Abel wrestles with the potential that could be Eden if his aim is sufficiently upward, his attention properly directed, and his sacrifices of the utmost quality. In consequence, God has respect unto his offering.

Cain, by contrast, chooses the wide and easy road, scheming as he does so for false benefit and escape from the inevitable consequences of his sacramental failures. While walking there, he encounters the same tempter whose blandishments caused the fall of his parents and initiated the dawn of the fallen world. Nothing but misery ensues. Instead of noting his failure, confessing his sins, repenting and atoning, Cain decides to call out God Himself for the inequity of the world, resentfully indicating the unbearable success of his brother, insinuating and accusing, proclaiming to himself and God that the cosmic order is flawed and the spirit that gave rise to it unjust. The evidence? His own failure. God is having none of this. He informs his wayward grandson in no uncertain terms that he has opened the door to sin, in the throes of his self-induced suffering and isolation, and invited the dread spirit who sat at the threshold in to have its way with him. Cain's bitter brooding on his fate is nothing less than the consummated marriage of man and the hateful and envious spirit who rules over hell.

Incensed, the brother who refuses to admit to his own error conspires to and then murders Abel, who is also his own ideal—not least to spite the God who rejected his second-rate offerings and then dared to upbraid him. This leads to the punishment that is more than Cain can bear, and his sentencing to wander endlessly in the lonely desert of unconsciousness and obscurity. The trouble does not end there. The spirit of Cain reappears in his descendants, doomed not only to become careless worshippers of technology instead of avatars of the ethos that properly orients the world, but increasingly genocidal agents of vengeance whose actions threaten the order that is benevolent itself. Hard on the heels of this degeneration of the generations follow the cataclysm of the flood, and the rise of the Tower of Babel. This is the return of the dominion of Leviathan and Behemoth; the emergence first of confusion and chaos and then of pathological, presumptuous and misaligned order. Lucifer himself could not have done worse, and that is exactly the point.

God makes himself manifest to Noah, the master of the flood, as a character yet fully unrevealed—but at least as the impulse, voice or spirit that comes to those who have kept their eyes open and prepared themselves properly for the calling. Being a good man—subject of course to the limitations of his time and place—Noah can trust himself and God, and therefore has the faith in his intuitions that stems from trustworthy conduct and that guides and motivates forthright action. Sensing that all hell is going to break loose, understanding that God is displeased and cannot be mocked, the prophet and savior builds the Ark. This is the vessel that represents the psyche fortified by integrity, the marriage that is committed, the family that abides together, the community built on an unshakeable foundation, and the state that is one under God above. Noah pilots his ship through crisis and catastrophe, shepherding his family, nascent community, and the entire natural order—whose survival does in fact depend on the uprightness and reliability of the human soul. In so doing, he saves and reestablishes the world. The failure of gratitude emerges again soon after, however, in the actions of his son Ham, who laughs when the flaws of his great father are revealed. Ham's descendants are the Canaanites, the eternally resentful failures, sentenced to always be the servants of slaves; doomed to be continually subjugated by and delivered over to the devout followers of the one true God.

The presumptuous engineers who are Cain's grandchildren then take it upon themselves to build the Tower of Babel, monument to the pride and self-aggrandizement of the tyrant who wishes to take the place of what is transcendently sovereign. But the inhabitants of the monstrous state soon find themselves unable to communicate with each other. Why? When the proper foundation is carelessly destroyed; when the transcendent spirit of upward striving and truth is forgotten—everyone becomes inarticulate, and everything undefined. Everyone scatters, unable to cooperate or compete in peace and harmony; unable to unite, in a single direction. Language—the very words of thought and mutual fruitful offering—loses all meaning. Everyone speaks a different tongue. When the central skewer of the world is loosed, attention is fatally divided and fractured, the city disintegrates, and the precosmogonic chaos returns.

God reveals yet a different aspect of His character to Abram, later Abraham, the archetypal individual adventurer. Abram is a late starter, who decides finally to embark on the journey of his life, in consequence of the call to conscience that constitutes the divine voice. He decides, when that voice hearkens, to build his initial altar, to consecrate his life to the upward path and to sacrifice whatever is necessary in that pursuit. This is what we all still do whenever we swear to straighten up, fly right and set our houses in order; when we determine and decide to improve instead of destroy our lives and the lives of everyone around us. Aim up, insofar as up can be conceived; abandon everything that gets in the way of that to the fires of perdition that constitute the flaming sword: that is the belief in God to which the discriminating spirit of the divine shows the respect due a proper and acceptable sacrifice. That is the path Abram chooses, as he becomes, first, deceitful scoundrel, then warrior and ally of kings, then sojourner and traveler with the angels of God—or even with God himself. This true follower of the divine calling even shows himself willing, as his character develops, to offer his beloved and long-promised and awaited son to the God to whom he has sworn unshakeable fealty. What could such an offering possibly signify? *That nothing whatsoever, no matter its value, is to be held in reserve. That everything, particularly that which is most loved, is to be sacrificed to what is yet higher—and, in consequence, and so remarkably, that everything so offered will be retained.*

Abram changes so completely in the course of his adventure so completely that he earns a new name. The Abraham that he becomes is the very spirit of the good father himself—and, therefore, the spitting image of divine encouragement and chastisement; the very embodiment calling and conscience. This is the Abrahamic pattern that makes of the art of reproduction not mere sexual congress but the establishment of the ethos that both spans generations and most truly ensures the survival of the family, and the race— that makes the true man the father of nations. And that is not all: Abraham accomplishes all this while acting in the productive, hospitable, generous and sacrificial manner that makes his mode of conduct in the world a blessing for himself, a means to a stellar reputation, and a benefit to everyone else. He does this as well with the companionship of his wife, Sarai (then Sarah), who simultaneously experiences the revolution of romantic adventure, and becomes the true wife and mother of the world. This successful covenant with God, undertaken by man and woman alike, indicates nothing less than the absolute and final alignment of the instinct that invites every child outward into the world with the implicit order of society, nature and the divine. Why would we expect anything less—anything other than this fundamental harmony of human soul and desire with the cosmos itself? Are we strangers in a strange land, or the rightful inhabitants of the Edenic garden? Even the most reductive and materialist of atheistic biologists understands that man is by necessity a microcosm, a mirror of the ultimate and absolute.

God is yet a different character, again, for Moses and the Israelites. He is the calling upward from the very foundation of the world—the calling that beckons to the worthy to leave the beaten path, pursue their dangerous destiny and to become, like Abraham and Sarah, who they truly are. The God of Exodus, Numbers, and Deuteronomy is the blazing and intensively alive phenomenon whose investigation produces the deepest transformation of character; the divine impulse and voice impelling man to become the leader who eternally invites himself and his people away from the tyrant into the chaotic desert and on to the promised land. That is the archetypal pattern of our striving, of motivation itself—of the story of our life[2]—in its unified and mature form. Moses faces his adversary, too; just like Adam and Eve; just like Abel. In part, that is the Pharaoh, but it is also more abstractly and fundamentally the temptation of power, with the Pharaoh a mere avatar of that alluring spirit. Moses employs force and compulsion when persuasion and invitation would serve. As a result, he finds himself barred by the intractable hand of God from entering the promised land, despite his decades of faithful service. This characterization of the divine makes a mockery of any claim that the Biblical God is a tyrant. Complex, yes; multifaceted, yes; beyond human comprehension, in the final analysis—but no friend whatsoever to the tyrant or the would-be slave.

Our investigation ended with Jonah, the man who holds his tongue when commanded by God himself to do otherwise. This is a very subtle accounting, and there are few if any with more resonance in the modern world.

What is the moral of the story of Jonah? That each man is called upon to say his piece, lest the world suffer in the absence of that singular and unique truth. That every man who fails to offer his best and who hides his light and his talent leaves a hole in the world that the offering of his best could have filled—a failure that is on him. That every person bears the responsibility to keep the ship of state afloat, to repent even in the depths of hell, and to journey to the very place where destiny is trying to make itself manifest. We all know, in the aftermath of the horrors of the twentieth century, that there is no difference between the lying silence of the cowardly good (but not nearly good enough) and the victory of the forces of the abyss. We all know that there are some sins that corrupt not only the soul but the world—those very crimes against humanity whose transcendent reality was insisted upon by the judges of Nuremberg, in the aftermath of the horrors of the Holocaust.

There is simply nothing more real than such evil and the good that eternally opposes it—and, therefore, nothing more real than the rulers of those respective domains. We know this. We aim our entire literary effort at its representation. We need to know the story. We need to get it straight. We need to live it out. It is no mere matter of mouthing the holy words and making a show of such practice. It is the willingness to bare all in the confident nakedness that is assured by a voluntary covenant with God. That courage to speak is, simultaneously, the willingness to become an avatar of the divine Logos, the Word that spoke and continues to speak the benevolently ordered cosmos into being, the spirit of the conqueror of chaos and tyrannical state, the voice of wise counsel in times of crisis, the dynamic process that leads the lost across the desert wasteland. This the reflection of God and the foundation of the rights and responsibility of man and woman, as well as the presence on the receding pinnacle of the entire sequence of challenging peaks and valleys that make up the opportunities and crises—the treasure and the dragons—of our venturing forth into the world.

All these great, profound and unalterably memorable stories are characterizations of God—and, inevitably, of the men and women who live inevitably in some form of relationship with or to that God. They are, of course, not the only characterizations of the divine that exist. Neither are they the only portrayals or dramatizations of those who abide by its dictates, spirit or principles—or who fail in that regard. We touched upon some of the alternatives of import, historical and current, in the course of our investigation, discussing the *enuma Elish* of the Mesopotamians, which was a precursor to, variant upon or a parallel of the most archaic accounts of God in Genesis and elsewhere, particularly in relationship to His role as victor over the great dragon of chaos; considering the great story of Osiris, Seth, Isis, and Horus, whose characterizations shaped the Egypt in which the ancient Hebrews sojourned, first as guests, later as slaves, and from which they escaped; and analyzing the sophisticated Taoist conceptions of the moral landscape as the dynamic of yin and yang, feminine and masculine or, equally profoundly and more generally, chaos and order. This is to say nothing of the many other traditions so well investigated and interpreted by the school of Jung, Neumann and Eliade or, indeed, presented and examined in and by the many other stories of the Old and New Testament. Another book on the latter, with some additional forays into the former will follow the present volume.

Those gospel accounts and their accompanying texts of course continue the characterization of God well begun in the more ancient works, describing His full descent into the suffering world of man; describing the Abraham-like offering of God's Son, who was also Himself, to ensure redemption, salvation, and the victory over death and hell; to bring the will of God and the Kingdom of Heaven to earth. The life and words of Jesus dramatize and describe precisely the pattern of upward-striving abandonment of all that is insufficient in the pursuit of the perfect harmony that characterizes the heaven that could be spread upon the earth, if only men and women kept their covenant with the divine, realized their true nature, and adopted the responsibility of walking with God. This is the upward-striving spirit exemplified by all the various characters of God, reflecting in the deepest possible manner the ultimate united monotheism—the coming together of everything at the foundation or in the highest place that appears central to the motivation of man, woman and cosmos alike.

In all these stories, all these dramas, all these descriptions of aim—all these characterizations—God is presented as the unity that exists at the foundation or stands at the pinnacle. In the absence of that unity, there is either nothing that brings together and harmonizes, in which case there is a deterioration into anarchy and chaos, or there are the various replacements that immediately swoop in, in their foul way, to usurp and dominate: the spirit of power that characterizes the Luciferian realm and produces the scarlet beast of the degenerate state. Does that make the divine real? This is a matter of definition, in the final analysis—and, therefore, or faith. It is real insofar as its pursuit makes pain bearable, keeps anxiety at bay, and inspires the hope that springs eternal in the human breast. It is real insofar as it establishes the benevolent and intelligible cosmic order, that infinite place of sinful toil or faithful play. It is as real as the force that opposes pride and calls those who sacrifice improperly to their knees. It is as real as the further reaches of the human imagination, striving fully upward.

It is more real than the hell it opposes. It is more real than all that totalitarian certainty and its pathological offer of a life free of burden and duty and, therefore, of adventure and meaning. It is more real than power; more real than impulse, desire, wish or whim. It is as real as the consciousness that contends with the possibilities of life; as real as the burden of decision comprising every glance, utterance and step forward. It is the offer of redemption and atonement to those who are lost, the foundation of the rights that make free countries both free and desirable, and the spirit of all voluntary and productive relationship—with self, with husband or wife, with child, parent and sibling, with friend and fellow citizen. It is as real as the wrestling with destiny that necessarily characterizes our lives, regardless of how they unfold. There is no perception, absent belief; no framing that protects and inspires, absent belief; no resilience and moving forward; no unity of psyche or society—no faith, hope, or courage, absent belief.

We are therefore by necessity those who wrestle with God. If we do that while gazing heavenward, we can align ourselves with the reality that is eternal and walk with that God while we keep and dress the paradisal garden. If we tread the properly sacrificial path, offering upward what is best, keeping to the strait and narrow, maintaining nothing in reserve for ourselves, in the narrow sense; if we heed the call of conscience and calling—we can have the redemptive romantic adventure of our life, transforming ourselves as we do so into the giants who once walked the earth; transmuting into the true Sons and Daughters of God, called upon to do greater things than did the single Son who has already and so famously made His appearance and revealed Himself. And so, in response to the brilliant Nietzsche, who insisted that man must become he who creates his own values, replicating thereby the call of the serpent in the garden; in response to the nihilists and hedonists who worship the Whore of Babylon and thereby risk the elimination of pleasure itself; in response to the reductionistic materialist atheists who deny even the logical conclusion of their own investigations into the guiding role of the deepest of involved instincts, I say this:

It is high time to rescue the highest from its unconscious existence in the lowest; to become fully aware, in the face of the magical transformations that now so rapidly face us, and to reestablish our covenant with the God whose magic words structure our consciousness and our societies, insofar as they are functional and productive. It is time to take up the wrestling in earnest, to awaken, to return to our origin, and to know the place, as conscious adults, for the first time.

God is dead?

No.

Deus renatus est.

NOTES

Frontispiece

1. Hopkins, G. M., and Phillips, C. (2002). *Gerard Manley Hopkins: The Major Works.* Oxford University Press. See poetryfoundation.org/poems/44392/carrion-comfort. Thank you to Dr. Michael Hurley for bringing this to my attention during our travels in Samos and Patmos, Greece.
2. Eliade, M. (1959). *The Sacred and the Profane.* Translated by Willard R. Trask. New York: Harcourt, Brace and Company, 8.

Foreshadowing: The Still, Small Voice

1. Goldberg, E. (1981). Hemisphere differences in the acquisition and use of descriptive systems. *Brain and Language 14,* 144–75; McGilchrist, I. (2009). *The Master and His Emissary: The Divided Brain and the Making of the Western World.* New Haven: Yale University Press; Peterson, J. B. (1999). *Maps of Meaning: The Architecture of Belief.* New York: Routledge.
2. Newman, J. H. (1875). *A letter addressed to the Duke of Norfolk on occasion of Mr. Gladstone's recent expostulation: certain difficulties felt by Anglicans in Catholic Teaching (Volume 2):* newmanreader.org/works/anglicans/volume2/gladstone/section5.html; see also Hansen, C. (2011). Newman, conscience and authority. *New Blackfriars 92,* 209–23; Gage, L. P. (2020). Newman's argument from conscience: why he needs Paley and natural theology after all. *American Catholic Philosophical Quarterly 94,* 141–57.

3. Dennett, D. C. (1984). Cognitive Wheels: The Frame Problem of AI. In C. Hookway (Ed.), *Minds, Machines and Evolution: Philosophical Studies* (129–50). Cambridge University Press, 130; see also McCarthy, J., and Hayes, P. J. (1969). Some philosophical problems considered from the standpoint of artificial intelligence. In B. Meltzer and D. Michie (Eds.), *Machine Intelligence* (Vol. 4, 463–502). New York: Elsevier; Dennett, D. C. (1984). Medin, D. L. and Aguilar, C. M. (1999). *Categorization*. In Wilson R. A. and Keil, F. (Eds.). MIT Encyclopedia of Cognitive Sciences (104–105). Cambridge, MA: MIT Press; Miller, G. A. (1956). The magical number seven, plus or minus two: Some limits on our capacity for processing information. *Psychological Review 63*, 81–97; Nørretranders, T. (1998). *The User Illusion: Cutting Consciousness Down to Size*. Penguin Books.

1. In the Beginning

1. Hirsh, J. B., Mar, R. A., and Peterson, J. B. (2012). Psychological entropy: a framework for understanding uncertainty-related anxiety. *Psychological Review 119*, 304–20.
2. White, L. (1967). The historical roots of our ecological crisis. *Science 155*, 1203–7.
3. as detailed in Peterson, J. B. (1999). *Maps of Meaning: the Architecture of Belief*. New York: Routledge.
4. Chomsky, N. and Halle, M. (1968). *The Sound Pattern of English*. Cambridge, MA: MIT Press.
5. Blevins, J. (2004). *Evolutionary Phonology: The Emergence of Sound Patterns*. Cambridge University Press.
6. Blevins, J. *Evolutionary Phonology*.
7. All these associations were generated by X's *Grok* in response to the prompt "What ten words or concepts are most likely to exist in close proximity to the word? Do not provide any duplicate words."
8. Rowling, J. K. (2000). *Harry Potter and the Chamber of Secrets*. London: Bloomsbury.
9. Disney, W. (Producer), Luske, H., Hee, T., Jackson, W., Kinney, J., Roberts, B., and Sharpsteen, B. (Directors). (1940). *Pinocchio* [Film]. USA: Walt Disney Productions.
10. Nolan, C. (Director), Thomas, E., and Nolan, C. (Producers). (2008). *The Dark Knight* [Film]. USA: Warner Bros. Pictures.
11. Derrida, J. (1976). Of grammatology (G. C. Spivak, Trans.). Baltimore, MD: Johns Hopkins University Press; Foucault, M. (1972). The archaeology of knowledge and the discourse on language (A.M.S. Smith, Trans.). New York: Pantheon Books; Lyotard, J. F. (1984). The postmodern condition: a report on knowledge (G. Bennington and B. Massumi, Trans.). Minneapolis, MN: University of Minnesota Press.
12. The most well-known current examples being Open AI's *ChatGPT* and X's *Grok*.
13. see *GPT4*, Wikipedia: en.wikipedia.org/wiki/GPT-4.
14. The February/March 2024 debacle caused by the release of Google's appalling artificial intelligence/large language model Gemini (gemini.google.com/app) offered ample illustration of that, particularly with regard to image generation(nytimes.com/2024/02/24/opinion/google-gemini-artificial-intelligence.html); see also Rozado, D. (2024, February 2).

The Political Preferences of LLMs. davidrozado.substack.com/p/the-political-preferences
-of-llms.

15. for a quick overview, see *Zeitgeist*, in Wikipedia: en.wikipedia.org/wiki/Zeitgeist.

16. Marx, K. (1875/1970). *Critique of the Gotha program.* In Marx/Engels Selected Works, Volume 3. Moscow: Progress Publishers: marxists.org/archive/marx/works/1875/gotha /ch01.htm.

17. Freud, S. and Breuer, J. (1955). *Studies in hysteria.* (J. Strachey, Trans.). New York: Basic Books; Freud, S. (1955). *The interpretation of dreams.* (J. Strachey, Trans.). New York: Basic Books.

18. Jung, C. G. (1976). *Letters of C. G. Jung*, Volume 2, 1951–61 (G. Adler, Ed.). Princeton University Press, 610–11.

19. Peterson, J. B. *Maps of Meaning.*

20. Nietzsche, F. (2005). *Thus Spake Zarathustra: A Book for Everyone and No One.* (T. Common, Trans.). New York: Penguin Classics, 125.

21. Peterson, J. B. *Maps of Meaning.*

22. Jung, C. G. (1953). *Two Essays on Analytical Psychology.* Princeton University Press, para 384.

23. Jung, C. G. The structure and dynamics of the psyche. In *Collected Works of C. G. Jung* (Vol. X). Princeton University Press, paragraphs 924–40; Dawkins, R. (1976). Worlds in Microcosm. In R. Dawkins (Ed.). *Inside the Survival Machine.* New York: Oxford University Press, 115–30.

24. See analysis and discussion by C. G. Jung, who opposed this reduction: Jung, C. G. (1952). *Symbols of Transformation: An Analysis of the Prelude to a Case of Schizophrenia* (2nd ed.). New York: Harper & Brothers. (Original work published 1912); Jung, C. G. (1913/1950). The theory of psychoanalysis. In *Collected Works of C. G. Jung* (Vol. 4). Princeton University Press.

25. Dawkins, R. (1976). *The Selfish Gene.* Oxford University Press.

26. Derrida, J. (1976). *Of Grammatology.* (G. C. Spivak, Trans.). Johns Hopkins University Press. (Original work published 1967); Foucault, M. (1991). *Discipline and Punish: The Birth of a Prison.* London: Penguin; Foucault, Michel (1998). *The History of Sexuality: The Will to Knowledge,* London: Penguin.

27. Pageau, J. and Peterson, J. B. (2023). *Identity: Individual and the State versus the Subsidiary Hierarchy of Heaven.* London: Alliance for Responsible Citizenship Publications (arc-research.org/s/The-Subsidiary-Hierarchy-Jonathan-Pageau-and-Jordan-Peterson -ARC-Research-Paper).

28. Peterson, J. B. *Maps of Meaning*; Jung, C. G. (1967). *The Collected Works of C. G. Jung: Vol. 5. Symbols of Transformation* (2nd ed.). (In H. Read, et al., Eds.). (R. F. C. Hull, Trans.). Princeton University Press; Campbell, J. (2012). *The Hero with a Thousand Faces* (3rd ed.). New World Library; Neumann, E. (2014). *The Origins and History of Consciousness.* Princeton University Press; Neumann, E. (2015). *The Great Mother.* Princeton University Press Platform.

29. Neumann, E. *The Great Mother.*

30. For a quick overview, see *Daniel Defoe*. Wikipedia: en.wikipedia.org/wiki/Daniel_Defoe.

31. Defoe, D. (1726). *The History of the Devil*. London: Thomas Warner, 106.

32. Peterson, J. B. *Maps of Meaning*; see also Jung *Collected Works: Vol. 5*; Campbell, *Hero with a Thousand Faces*; Neumann, *Origins and History of Consciousness*; Neumann, *The Great Mother*.

33. Freedman, R. D. (1983). Woman, a power equal to man. *Biblical Archaeology Review 9*, 56–58.

34. Vygotsky, L. S. (1978). *Mind in Society: The Development of Higher Psychological Processes*. Cambridge, MA: Harvard University Press, 86.

35. Costa, P. T., Jr., Terracciano, A., and McCrae, R. R. (2001). Gender differences in personality traits across cultures: Robust and surprising findings. *Journal of Personality and Social Psychology 81*, 322–31; Feingold, A. (1994). Gender differences in personality: A meta-analysis. *Psychological Bulletin 116*, 429–56; Schmitt, D. P., Realo, A., and Voracek, M. (2008). The big five factor model of personality across cultures: Robust and generalizable across 55 cultures. *Journal of Personality and Social Psychology 94*, 26–40; Weisberg, Y. J., Deyoung, C. G., and Hirsh, J. B. (2011). Gender differences in personality across the ten aspects of the Big Five. *Frontiers in Psychology 2*, 178–89.

36. Lippa, R. A. (2010). Gender differences in personality and interests: When, where, and why? *Social and Personality Psychology Compass 4*, 1098–110.

37. Weisberg, Y. J., Deyoung, C. G., and Hirsh, J. B. (2011). Gender differences in personality across the ten aspects of the Big Five. *Frontiers in Psychology 2*, 178; Benenson, J. F., Webb, C. E., and Wrangham, R. W. (2022). Self-protection as an adaptive female strategy. *Behavioral and Brain Science 45*, e128.

38. Trousdale, G. and Wise, K. (Directors), and Woolverton, L. (Writer). (1991). *Beauty and the Beast* [Film]. Walt Disney Pictures.

39. Jonason, P. K., Webster, G. D., Schmitt, D. P., and Li, N. P. (2009). The dark tetrad of personality: Narcissism, Machiavellianism, psychopathy, and sadism. *Journal of Personality and Social Psychology 97*, 1295–1308; Buss, D. (2021). *When Men Behave Badly*. New York: Little and Brown; Brazil, K. J., Forth, A. E. (2020). Psychopathy and the Induction of desire: formulating and testing an evolutionary hypothesis. *Evolutionary Psychological Science 6*, 64–81; Carter, G. L., Campbell, A. C. and Muncer, S. (2014). The dark triad personality: attractiveness to women. *Personality and Individual Differences 56*, 57–61.

40. See section 1.3.

41. Peterson, J. B. (1999). *Maps of Meaning*.

42. Bak, P., Tang, C., and Wiesenfeld, K. (1987). Self-organized criticality: An explanation of the 1/f noise. *Physical Review Letters 59*, 381; Peterson, J. B. *Maps of Meaning*; Stephen, D. G. and Dixon, J. A. (2009). The self-organization of insight: entropy and power laws in problem solving. *The Journal of Problem Solving, 2*, 72–101. Vervaeke, J. and Ferraro, L. (2013). Relevance, meaning and the cognitive science of wisdom. In M. Ferrari and Weststrate, N. M. (Eds.). *The Scientific Study of Personal Wisdom* (21–51). New York: Springer; Vervaeke, J. (2013). Relevance realization and the neurodynamics and neuroconnectivity of general intelligence. In I. Harvey, Cavoukian, A., Tomko, G., Borrett, D., Kwan, H., and

Hatzinakos, D. (Eds.). *SmartData: Privacy Meets Evolutionary Robotics* (57–68). New York: Springer Science; see also Andersen, B. Order, chaos, relevance realization and mythology: brettandersen.substack.com/p/order-chaos-complexity-and-mythology.

43. For an extended discussion, see Peterson, J. B., *Maps of Meaning*.

44. Heidel, A. (1951). *The Babylonian Genesis: The Story of the Creation*. University of Chicago Press.

45. Eliade, M. (1954). *The Myth of the Eternal Return: Cosmos and History*. Princeton University Press.

46. see Foreshadowing: The Still, Small Voice

47. Shakespeare. W. (1606). *King Lear*. Act 4, Scene 1: shakespeare.mit.edu/lear/lear.4.1.html.

48. classics.mit.edu/Homer/iliad.html.

49. Peterson, J. B. (1999). *Maps of Meaning*, 105.

50. Taleb, N. N. (2007). *The Black Swan: The Impact of the Highly Improbable*. New York: Random House.

51. Walleczek, J. (2019.) Agent inaccessibility as a fundamental principle in quantum mechanics: objective unpredictability and formal uncomputability. *Entropy 21*, 4.

52. Simons, D. J. and Ambinder, M. S. (2005). Change blindness: theory and consequences. *Current Directions in Psychological Science 14*, 44–48.

53. The German philosopher Martin Heidegger made the idea of care central to his thought, conceptualizing it as the existential mechanism through which Being revealed itself; defining it as something deeper and more fundamental than mere emotion: Heidegger, M. (2008). *Being and Time*. New York: HarperCollins.

54. reviewed in Peterson, J. B. *Maps of Meaning*.

55. Tomkins, S. (2007). *William Wilberforce: A Biography*. London: Lion Books.

56. See, for example, in the case of slavery: Metaxas, E. (2009). *Amazing Grace: William Wilberforce and the Heroic Campaign to End Slavery*. New York: HarperCollins.

2. Adam, Eve, Pride, Self-Consciousness, and the Fall

1. From kenosis, the "act of emptying" (en.wikipedia.org/wiki/Kenosis), as in Philippians 2:5–9 NRSV): "Let the same mind be in you that was in Christ Jesus, who, though he was in the form of God, did not regard equality with God as something to be exploited, but emptied himself (*ekenōsen heauton*), taking the form of a slave, being born in human likeness."

2. From the Sanskrit *avatāra*, which means "descent" or "incarnation": dictionary.com /browse/avatar; in addition: "The manifestation of a god in bodily form on earth; the period of such a manifestation. Also (now more usually): a particular bodily form in which a god is manifested": oed.com/dictionary/avatar_n?tl=true.

3. "The word 'paradise' entered English from the French paradis, inherited from the Latin paradisus, from Greek parádeisos (παράδεισος), from an Old Iranian form, from Proto-Iranian*parādaiĵah- 'walled enclosure', whence Old Persian p-r-d-y-d-a-m /paridaidam/, Avestan pairi-daêza-. The literal meaning of this Eastern Old Iranian language word is

'walled (enclosure)', from pairi- 'around' (cognate with Greek περί, English peri- of identical meaning) and -diz 'to make, form (a wall), build' (cognate with Greek τεῖχος 'wall'). The word's etymology is ultimately derived from a PIE root *dheigʷ 'to stick and set up (a wall)', and *per 'around.'" en.wikipedia.org/wiki/Paradise.

4. "The name derives from the Akkadian edinnu, from a Sumerian word meaning 'plain' or 'steppe', closely related to an Aramaic root word meaning 'fruitful, well-watered'. Another interpretation associates the name with a Hebrew word for 'pleasure'; thus the Vulgate reads 'paradisum voluptatis' in Genesis 2:8, and the Douay-Rheims Bible, following, has the wording 'And the Lord God had planted a paradise of pleasure'." en.wikipedia .org/wiki/Garden_of_Eden.

5. I also cited this in Peterson, J. B. (1999). Maps of Meaning, 124.

6. Stevenson, M. S. (1920). The Rites of the Twice-Born. London: Oxford University Press, 354.

7. Eliade, M. (1991). The Myth of the Eternal Return, or, Cosmos and History. Princeton University Press, 19.

8. Jung, C. G. (2014). Concerning Mandala symbolism. In Collected Works of C.G. Jung, Volume 9 (Part 1): Archetypes and the Collective Unconscious (355–84). De Gruyter.

9. There is a particularly apropos example—given the representation of hierarchical nesting— here: en.wikipedia.org/wiki/Mandala#/media/File:Manjuvajramandala_con_43_divinit %C3%A0_-_Unknown_-_Google_Cultural_Institute.jpg; for an image more specifically related to Paradise itself, see here: metmuseum.org/art/collection/search/228991.

10. see section 1.2. The spirit of man in the highest place.

11. Pater, W. (1912). The Renaissance: Studies in Art and Poetry. London: Macmillan: gutenberg.org/files/2398/2398-h/2398-h.htm. Thank you to Mr. Rex Murphy, journalist extraordinaire, for bringing this to my attention.

12. Extraordinary claims require extraordinary evidence, Wikipeidia: en.wikipedia.org/wiki /Extraordinary_claims_require_extraordinary_evidence.

13. Tolstoy, L. (1983). Confessions (D. Patterson, Trans.). W. W. Norton & Company.

14. see section 1.4. Eve from Adam.

15. Shiner, R. L. (2019). Negative emotionality and neuroticism from childhood through adulthood: A lifespan perspective. In D. P. McAdams, R. L. Shiner, and J. L. Tackett (Eds.), Handbook of Personality Development (137–152). Guilford Press; Salk, R. H., Hyde, J. S., and Abramson, L. Y. (2017). Gender differences in depression in representative national samples: Meta-analyses of diagnoses and symptoms. Psychological Bulletin 143, 783–822; Chaplin T. M. (2015). Gender and emotion expression: a developmental contextual perspective. Journal of the International Society for Research on Emotion, 7, 14–21.

16. Ben Mansour, G., Kacem, A., Ishak, M. et al. (2021). The effect of body composition on strength and power in male and female students. BMC Sports Science Medicine and Rehabilitation 13, 1–11.

17. Vanhouten, J. N., and Wysolmerski, J. J. (2013). The calcium-sensing receptor in the breast. Best practice and research. Clinical endocrinology and metabolism 27, 403–414; Mamillapalli, R., VanHouten, J., Dann, P., Bikle, D., Chang, W., Brown, E., and Wysolmerski, J. (2013). Mammary-specific ablation of the calcium-sensing receptor during lacta-

tion alters maternal calcium metabolism, milk calcium transport, and neonatal calcium accrual. *Endocrinology 154*, 3031–42.

18. Buss, D. M. (1989). Sex differences in human mate preferences: Evolutionary hypotheses tested in 37 cultures. *Behavioral and Brain Science 12*, 1–49.

19. Buss, D. M., and Barnes, M. (1986). Preferences in human mate selection. *Journal of Personality and Social Psychology 50*, 559–70; Buss, D. M. (1989). Sex differences in human mate preferences: Evolutionary hypotheses tested in 37 cultures. *Behavioral and Brain Science 12*, 1–14; Buss, D. M., Shackelford, T. K., Kirkpatrick, L. A., and Larsen, R. J. (2001). A half century of mate preferences: The cultural evolution of values. *Journal of Marriage and Family 63*, 491–503.

20. Jauk, E., Neubauer, A. C., Mairunteregger, T., Pemp, S., Sieber, K. P., and Rauthmann, J. F. (2016). How alluring are dark personalities? The dark triad and attractiveness in speed dating. *European Journal of Personality 30*, 125–138.

21. Clark, R. D. and Hatfield, E. (1989). Gender differences in receptivity to sexual offers. *Journal of Psychology and Human Sexuality 2*, 39–55.

22. Rosenfeld, M. J. (2018). Who wants the breakup? Gender and breakup in heterosexual couples. D. F. Alwin, F. Felmlee, and D. Kreager. (Eds.), *Social Networks and the Life Course.* New York: Springer, 221–43.

23. Reynolds, T., Baumeister, R. F., and Maner, J. K. (2018). Competitive reputation manipulation: women strategically transmit social information about romantic rivals. *Journal of Experimental Social Psychology 78*, 195–209; Björkqvist, K., Lagerspetz, K., and Kaukiainen A. (1992). Do girls manipulate and boys fight? Developmental trends in regard to direct and indirect aggression. *Aggressive Behavior 18*, 117–122; Lagerspetz K., Bjorkqvist, K., and Peltonen, T. (1988). Is indirect aggression typical of females? Gender differences in aggressiveness in 11- to 12-year-old children. *Aggressive Behavior 14*, 403–14; Werner, N. E. and Crick, N. R. (1999). Relational aggression and social-psychological adjustment in a college sample. *Journal of Abnormal Psychology 108*, 615–23.

24. Congreve, W. (1697). *The mourning bride.* London: Jacob Tonson.

25. It is such differences that most truly make up so-called "gender," which is the reflection of sex in temperament, insofar as it can be validly and reliably measured, and which does vary in relationship to the underlying true binary of functional reproductive capability (as there are men with more feminine temperaments; just as there are women who are more masculine).

26. Jung, C. G. (1969). Archetypes and the collective unconscious. *Collected Works of C.G. Jung, Volume 9 (Part 1):* (G. Adler and R.F.C. Hull, Eds.). Princeton University Press, para. 292–94. See also DeVun, L. (2008). The Jesus hermaphrodite: science and sex difference in premodern Europe. *Journal of the History of Ideas 69*, 193–218.

27. Isbell, L. A. (2011). *The Fruit, the Tree and the Serpent: Why We See So Well.* Cambridge: Harvard University Press.

28. In that vein: the so-called Dark Tetrad personality traits (narcissism, manipulativeness, psychopathy and sadism) mimic competence in an attractive and cross-generationally tempting manner—and are particularly to naïve and inexperienced young women. Buss, D.

(2021). *When Men Behave Badly*. New York: Little, Brown and Company; Brazil, K. J. and Forth, A. E. (2020). Psychopathy and the Induction of desire: formulating and testing an evolutionary hypothesis. *Evolutionary Psychological Science 6*, 64–81; Carter, G. L., Campbell, A. C. and Muncer, S. (2014). The Dark Triad personality: attractiveness to women. *Personality and Individual Differences 56*, 57–61. "Wilfully blind" might well be added to that triumvirate of vulnerabilities, although I know of no experimentally-validated demonstration of that hypothesis.

29. Milton, J. (1674). *Paradise Lost: Book 1*: poetryfoundation.org/poems/45718/paradise-lost -book-1-1674-version.

30. Nietzsche, F. W. and Kaufmann, W. (1989). *Beyond Good and Evil: Prelude to a Philosophy of the Future*. New York, Vintage Books.

31. Milton, J. (1674). *Paradise Lost: Book 1*: poetryfoundation.org/poems/45718/paradise-lost -book-1-1674-version.

32. Goethe, J. W. (2008). *Faust: Part One*. (B. Taylor, Trans.). Project Gutenberg. Retrieved from gutenberg.org/files/14591/14591-h/14591-h.htm.

33. Goethe, *Faust: Part One*.

34. Goethe, *Faust: Part One*.

35. Augustine, S. (1961). *Confessions* (R. S. Pine-Coffin, Trans.). London: Penguin Classics. (Original work written 397); Augustine, S. (2003). *The City of God* (H. Bettenson, Trans.). London: Penguin Classics. (Original work written 426).

36. See Vygotsky, L. S. (1962). *Thought and Language*. Cambridge, MA: MIT Press.

37. Vygotsky, *Thought and Language*; Carhart-Harris, R. and Peterson, J. B. (2023). Consciousness, chaos and order. *The Jordan B Peterson Podcast, 314* (youtube.com/watch?v=4NtK disg0GA&ab_channel=JordanBPeterson); Anderson, B. (2022). Consciousness emerges at the border between order and chaos. *Intimations of a New Worldview* (brettandersen .substack.com/p/consciousness-emerges-at-the-border); Carhart-Harris, R. L. (2018). The entropic brain—revisited. *Neuropharmacology 142*, 167–78.

38. Hakkarainen, P. and Bredikyte, M. (2019). The zone of proximal development in play and learning. *Cultural-Historical Psychology 4*, 2–11.

39. Jonason, P. K., Webster, G. D., Schmitt, D. P., and Li, N. P. (2009). The Dark Tetrad of personality: Narcissism, Machiavellianism, psychopathy, and sadism. *Journal of Personality and Social Psychology 97*, 1295–1308.

40. Reynolds, T., Baumeister, R. F. and Maner, J. K. (2018). Competitive reputation manipulation: women strategically transmit social information about romantic rivals. *Journal of Experimental Social Psychology 78*, 195–209; Björkqvist, K., Lagerspetz, K. and Kaukiainen A. (1992). Do girls manipulate and boys fight? Developmental trends in regard to direct and indirect aggression. *Aggressive Behavior 18*, 117–122; Lagerspetz K., Bjorkqvist, K., and Peltonen, T. (1988). Is indirect aggression typical of females? Gender differences in aggressiveness in 11- to 12-year-old children. *Aggressive Behavior 14*, 403–14; Werner, N. E. and Crick, N. R. (1999). Relational aggression and social-psychological adjustment in a college sample. *Journal of Abnormal Psychology 108*, 615–23.

41. Brewer, G., De Griffa, D., and Uzun, E. (2019). Dark triad traits and women's use of sexual

deception. *Personality and Individual Differences 142*, 42–44; Lauder, C. and March, E. (2023). Catching the catfish: Exploring gender and the Dark Tetrad of personality as predictors of catfishing perpetration. *Computers in Human Behavior 140*, 107599.

42. Peterson, J. B. (1999). *Maps of Meaning*, 240–43.

43. DeYoung, C. G., Quilty, L. C., and Peterson, J. B. (2007). Between facets and domains: 10 aspects of the Big Five. *Journal of Personality and Social Psychology 93*, 880–96.

44. Church A. T. (1994). Relating the Tellegen and five-factor models of personality structure. *Journal of Personality and Social Psychology 67*, 898–909.

45. Self-consciousness is literally a facet of the well-established NEO-PI Big Five Personality model (see the 240-item Neuroticism Extraversion Openness Personality Inventory Revised: Costa, P. T., Jr., and McCrae, R. R. (1992). *Revised NEO Personality Inventory (NEO-PI-R) and NEO Five-Factor Inventory (NEO-FFI): Professional manual*. Odessa, FL: Psychological Assessment Resources); see also ". . . neuroticism is associated with heightened self-awareness, which in turn leads to increased self-consciousness in social situations" in Watson, D., and Hubbard, B. (1996). Adaptational style and dispositional structure: Coping in the context of the five-factor model. *Journal of Personality 64*, 737–74, 753; "High self-consciousness is likely to be associated with high levels of neuroticism, given that both constructs involve a focus on one's internal experience" in Tangney, J. P. and Dearing, R. L. (2002). *Shame and guilt*. New York: Guilford Press, 375.

46. Leary, M. R., Tambor, E. S., Terdal, S. K., and Downs, D. L. (1995). Self-presentational concerns in social interaction. *Journal of Personality and Social Psychology 68*, 517–25.

47. Bruch, M. A., and Heimberg, R. G. (1994). Self-consciousness and social anxiety: A review of the literature. *Clinical Psychology Review 14*, 77–95.

48. Hong, K., Nenkova, A., March, M. E., Parker, A. P., Verma, R. and Kohler, C.G. (2015). Lexical use in emotional autobiographical narratives of persons with schizophrenia and healthy controls. *Psychiatry Research 225*, 40–49; Fineberg, S. K., Leavitt, J., Deutsch-Link, S., Dealy, S., Landry, C. D., Pirruccio, K., Shea, S., Trent, S., Cecchi, G., and Corlett, P. R. (2016). Self-reference in psychosis and depression: a language marker of illness. *Psychological Medicine 46*, 2605–15.

49. Rudolph, K. D. and Conley, C. S. (2005). Self-consciousness, social anxiety, and maladjustment during adolescence: A longitudinal investigation. *Journal of Personality and Social Psychology 88*, 1074–86.

50. Leary, M. R., and Kowalski, R. M. (1990). Social anxiety and cognitive interference: A mediational analysis. *Journal of Personality and Social Psychology 58*, 636–45.

51. Beilock, S. L., and Carr, T. H. (2001). On the fragility of skilled performance: What makes experts susceptible to choking under pressure? *Journal of Experimental Psychology 130*, 701–24.

52. Barrick, M. R., Stewart, G. L., and Piotrowski, M. (2002). Personality and job performance: A meta-analysis. *Personnel Psychology 55*, 529–52.

53. see section 2.5.

54. Freedman, R. D. (1983). Woman, a power equal to man. *Biblical Archaeology Review 9*, 56–58.

55. according to such luminaries as Associate Professor of Old Testament Phyllis Trible, "it is superfluous to document patriarchy in Scripture," in Trible, P. (1973). Depatriarchalizing in biblical interpretation. *Journal of the American Academy of Religion 41*, 30–48, 30; for another particularly egregious additional example, see Williams, J. (2011, January 18). The book of Genesis, part 6: Patriarchs and others. *The Guardian*: theguardian.com/com mentisfree/belief/2011/jan/18/book-genesis-patriarchs-women; alternatively, Schwark, M. (2021, March 2). Avenging Eve: the death of Eden and the birth of patriarchy. *Bitchmedia*: bitchmedia.org/article/avenging-eve-the-death-of-eden-and-the-birth-of-patriarchy.

56. Gruss, L. T. and Schmitt, D. (2015). The evolution of the human pelvis: changing adaptations to bipedalism, obstetrics and thermoregulation. *Philosophical Transactions of the Royal Society of London. Series B, Biological Science 370* (1663); Fischer, B. and Mitteroecker, P. (2015). Covariation between human pelvis shape, stature, and head size alleviates the obstetric dilemma. *Proceedings of the National Academy of Sciences of the United States of America 112*, 5655–60. Rosenberg, K. R. (1992). The evolution of modern human childbirth, *Yearbook of Physical Anthropology 35*, 89–124.

57. This general truth (Hyde, J. S. (2005). The gender similarities hypothesis. *American Psychologist 60*, 581–92) is somewhat complicated by the apparent fact of more variability in intelligence among men (Johnson, W., Carothers, A., and Deary, I. J. [2008]. Sex differences in variability in general intelligence. *Perspectives on Psychological Science 3*, 518–31)—a fact which might account to some degree for the differential dominance of men in many areas of cognition-dependent endeavor.

58. Weisberg, Y. J., Deyoung, C. G., and Hirsh, J. B. (2011). Gender differences in personality across the ten aspects of the Big Five. *Frontiers in Psychology 2*, 178.

59. Barrick, M. R. and Mount, M. K. (1991). The Big 5 personality dimensions and job-performance: A meta-analysis. *Personnel Psychology 44*, 1–26.

60. Johnson, R. W., Smith, K. E., and Butrica, B. *Lifetime employment-related costs to somen of providing family care.* Washington DC: Urban Institute: Program on Retirement Policy. US Department of Labor's Women's Bureau: dol.gov/sites/dolgov/files/WB/Mothers -Families-Work/Lifetime-caregiving-costs_508.pdf.

61. Buss, D. (1989). Sex differences in human mate preferences: Evolutionary hypotheses tested in 37 cultures. *Behavioral and Brain Science 12*, 1–14; Buss, D. M., and Schmitt, D. P. (1993). Sexual strategies theory: an evolutionary perspective on human mating. *Psychological Review 100*, 204–32; Buss, D. (2021). *When Men Behave Badly*. New York: Little and Brown.

62. Jackson, J. J., Wood, D., Bogg, T., Walton, K. E., Harms, P. D., and Roberts, B. W. (2010). What do conscientious people do? Development and validation of the Behavioral Indicators of Conscientiousness (BIC). *Journal of Research in Personalit 44*, 501–11; Barrick, M. R. and Mount, M. K. (1991). The Big 5 personality dimensions and job-performance: A meta-analysis. *Personnel Psychology 44*, 1–26.

63. DeYoung, C. G., Flanders, J. L., and Peterson, J. B. (2008). Cognitive abilities involved in insight problem solving: an individual differences model. *Creativity Research Journal 20*, 278–90.

64. Gibson, J. J. (1979). *The Ecological Approach to Visual Perception.* New York: Houghton Mifflin.

65. Jung, C. G. (1977). *Mysterium Coniunctionis: An Inquiry into the Separation and Synthesis of Psychic Opposites in Alchemy* (2d ed.). Princeton University Press, paragraph 750.

66. Tversky, A. and Kahneman, D. (1973). Availability: A heuristic for judging frequency and probability. *Cognitive Psychology 5*, 207–32.

67. Vygotsky, L. S. (1986). *Thought and Language.* Cambridge, MA: MIT Press.

68. en.wikipedia.org/wiki/Socratic_dialogue.

69. This is discussed in detail in Peterson, J. B. (1999). *Maps of Meaning: The Architecture of Belief.* New York: Routledge; previously in Jung, C. G. (1970). Mysterium coniunctionis (R. F. C. Hull, Trans.) In *The Collected Works of C.G. Jung* (Volume 14). (H. Read et al., Eds.). Princeton University Press. (Original work published 1955–56).

70. Lambdin, T. O. (Trans.). (n.d.). *The Gospel of Thomas.* The Gnostic Society Library. Retrieved from gnosis.org/naghamm/gthlamb.html.

71. Kabat, P., Fresco, L., Stive, M., Veerman, C., Alphen, J., Parmet, B., Hazeleger, W., and Katsman, C. (2009). Dutch coasts in transition. *Nature GeoScience 2*, 2. 10.1038/ngeo572.

72. Roth, L. H. (2005 ca). *The New Orleans levees: the worst engineering catastrophe in US History—what went wrong and why.* American Society of Civil Engineers: powerpoint presentation, slide 23: biotech.law.lsu.edu/climate/ocean-rise/against-the-deluge/01-new_orleans_levees.pdf.

3. Cain, Abel, and Sacrifice

1. Popper, K. (1963). *Conjectures and Refutations: The Growth of Scientific Knowledge.* New York: Routledge, 29.

2. Gray, J. A. and McNaughton, N. (2000). *The neuropsychology of anxiety: an enquiry into the functions of the septo-hippocampal system.* New York: Oxford University Press; Gray, J. A., and McNaughton, N. (2003). *The neuropsychology of anxiety: an enquiry into the functions of the septo-hippocampal system.* New York: Oxford University Press; Peterson, J. B. *Maps of Meaning*; Panksepp, J. (2004). *Affective neuroscience: the foundations of human and animal emotions.* New York: Oxford University Press.

3. Friston, K. (2009). The free-energy principle: a rough guide to the brain? *Trends in Cognitive Sciences 13*, 293–301; Hirsh, J. B., Mar, R. A., and Peterson, J. B. (2012). Psychological entropy: a framework for understanding uncertainty-related anxiety. *Psychological Review 119*, 304–20.

4. Swanson, L. W. (2000). Cerebral hemisphere regulation of motivated behavior. *Brain Research 886*, 113–64 for a brilliant summary of this unifying process, developmentally speaking.

5. Feyerabend, P. K. (1967). Epistemology without a knowing subject. In P. K. Feyerabend, and G. Maxwell (Eds.), *Mind, Matter, and Method: Essays in Philosophy of Science in Honor of Herbert Feigl* (233–48). University of Minnesota Press, 245.

6. en.wikipedia.org/wiki/Entertainment.

7. Van Gogh, V. (1898). *Still life: vase with five sunflowers*. From Martin, B. (2013). The sunflowers are mine: the story of van Gogh's masterpiece. London: Frances Lincoln Ltd. 54; van Gogh, V. (1890). *Still life with irises against a yellow background*. Van Gogh Museum, Amsterdam.

8. Huxley, A. (1954). *The Doors of Perception*. New York: Harper & Brothers.

9. Peterson, J. B. (2018). Q & A 2018, 03 March. *The Jordan B. Peterson Podcast* (youtube .com/live/c-kWEDr6VS0?feature=share).

10. The true winners chase the revelations of the divine, no matter what other game they might be playing. The name "golden snitch" itself reveals the relationship between calling and conscience: an ordinary snitch calls out misconduct to authority. A golden snitch, by contrast, indicates deviation from the heavenly pathway. The original snitch, according to Potter lore, was a bird called a snidget (see Rowling, J. K. [2001]). *Fantastic beasts and where to find them*. London: Bloomsbury. It does not take much imagination to realize the association between such ideas and the dove that is held traditionally to represent the Third Person of the Trinity.

11. Rowling, J. K. (1997). *Harry Potter and the Philosopher's Stone*. London: Bloomsbury.

12. Jung, C. G. (1967). The spirit Mercurius. In H. Read et al. (Eds.), *The Collected Works of C. G. Jung*: Vol. 13. Alchemical studies (R. F. C. Hull, Trans., 2nd ed., 169–201). Princeton University Press.

13. The phrase "Jiminy Cricket" has long been used as a minced oath since at least 1803 (en.wikipedia.org/wiki/Jiminy_Cricket).

14. Solzhenitsyn, A. (1974). *The Gulag Archipelago, 1918–1956: An Experiment in Literary Investigation*. (Volume 1; T. P. Whitney, Trans.). New York: Harper & Row, 168.

15. White, L. K. and Klein, D. M. (2008). *Family Theories: An Introduction*. New York: Sage Publications.

16. Conger, K. J. and Conger, R. D. (1994). Differential parenting and change in sibling differences in delinquency. *Journal of Family Psychology* 8, 287–302.

17. Conger, K. J. and Conger, R. D. (1994). Differential parenting and change in sibling differences in delinquency. *Journal of Family Psychology* 8, 287–302.

18. Gilligan, T. D., Sansone, R. A., and Hervey, G. R. (2010). Sibling rivalry as a predictor of borderline personality. *Personality and Mental Health* 4, 159–64.

19. Kernberg, O. (2014). Sibling relationships and narcissistic pathology. *Psychoanalytic Inquiry* 34, 46–61.

20. Cousineau, K. M., Domene, J. F., and McGregor, L. N. (2018). Dark personality and sibling relationships. *Journal of Research in Personality* 73, 157–63.

21. Langergraber, K. E., et al. (2012). Generation times in wild chimpanzees and gorillas suggest earlier divergence times in great ape and human evolution. *Proceedings of the National Academy of Science 109*, 15716–21; Bjorklund, D. F. (2011). *Children's Thinking: Cognitive Development and Individual Differences*. Los Angeles: SAGE; Kuzawa, C. W. and Thayer, Z. M. (2011). Timescales of human adaptation: The role of epigenetic processes. *Epigenomics 3*, 221–34; Hrdy, S. B. (2009). *Mothers and Others: The Evolutionary Origins of Mutual Understanding*. Cambridge, MA: Harvard University Press; Konner,

M. (2010). *The Evolution of Childhood: Relationships, Emotion, Mind.* Cambridge, MA: Harvard University Press.

22. Rosenberg, K. R., Trevathan, W. R., and Fuentes, A. (2009). Revising the human evolutionary paradigm: The need for a broader view of diversification within Hominidae. In W. R. Leonard, M. F. Oxner, and M. T. Baca (Eds.), *Human Biology: An Evolutionary and Biocultural Perspective* (3–17). New York: John Wiley & Sons.

23. Hewlett, B. S. and Lamb, M. E. (2005). *Hunter-Gatherer Childhoods: Evolutionary, Developmental, and Cultural Perspectives.* Piscataway NJ: Aldine Transaction; Kaplan, H., Hill, K., Lancaster, J., and Hurtado, A. M. (2000). A theory of human life history evolution: Diet, intelligence, and longevity. *Evolutionary Anthropology: Issues, News, and Reviews 9,* 156–185.

24. Buhrmester, D. and Furman, W. (1987). The development of companionship and intimacy. *Child Development 58,* 1101-13; Brody, G. H. and Stoneman, Z. (1994). Sibling relationships in middle childhood and adolescence: A developmental perspective. In P. Salovey (Ed.), *The Psychology of Jealousy and Envy* (331–50). Guilford Press; McHale, S. M., Updegraff, K. A., and Whiteman, S. D. (2012). Sibling relationships and influences in childhood and adolescence. *Journal of Marriage and Family 74,* 913-30.

25. Perreault, T. and Wittman, H. (2010). Anthropology, food policy, and food security. In J. G. Carrier and James, D. (Eds.), *The Routledge Handbook of Anthropology of Policy* (403–20). Routledge; Batterbury, S. P. J. (2001). Landscapes of diversity: A local political ecology of livelihood diversification in southwestern Niger. *Cultural Geographies 8,* 437–64; Durrenberger, E. P. (2012). Agriculture and the rural environment: Conflict and change. *Annual Review of Anthropology 41,* 45–62; Garcia, E. (2018). The contested ecology of cattle ranching and agricultural expansion in Brazil. *Journal of Peasant Studies 45,* 1442–62.

26. from Davidson, A. B. (Ed.). (1899). *Cambridge Bible for schools and colleges.* Cambridge, UK: Cambridge University Press; taken directly from biblehub.com/commentaries /genesis/25-26.htm.

27. Trousdale, G., and Wise, K. (Directors), and Woolverton, L. (Writer). (1991). *Beauty and the Beast* [Film]. Walt Disney Pictures.

28. Rowling, J. K. (2005). *Harry Potter and the Half-Blood Prince.* New York: Arthur A. Levine Books.

29. Nolan, C. (Director), and Thomas, E., and Nolan, C. (Producers). (2008). *The Dark Knight* [Film]. USA: Warner Bros. Pictures.

30. Tolkien, J. R. R. (1993). *The Lord of the Rings* (2nd ed.). Boston: Houghton Mifflin Co.

31. Milton, J. (1674). *Paradise Lost*: poetryfoundation.org/poems/45718/paradise-lost-book -1-1674-version.

32. Goethe, J. W. (2008). *Faust* (B. Taylor, Trans.): Project Gutenberg. Retrieved from gutenberg .org/files/14591/14591-h/14591-h.htm.

33. Allers, R. and Minkoff, R. (Directors). (1994). *The Lion King* [Film]. Walt Disney Pictures.

34. Coffin, P. and Renaud, C. (Directors). (2010). *Despicable Me* [Film]. Universal Pictures.

35. Clements, R. and Musker, J. (Directors). (1992). *Aladdin* [Film]. Walt Disney Pictures.

36. Bird, B. (Director). (2004). *The Incredibles* [Film]. Buena Vista Pictures.

37. Chase, D. (Creator). (1999–2007). *The Sopranos* [TV series]. Chase Films; Brad Grey Television; HBO Entertainment.

38. Gilligan, V. (Creator). (2008–2013). *Breaking BAD* [TV series]. High Bridge Productions; Gran Via Productions; Sony Pictures Television.

39. Dostoevsky, F. (1992). *Crime and Punishment* (R. Pevear and L. Volokhonsky, Trans.). New York: Vintage Books.

40. Dostoevsky, F. (2002). *The Brothers Karamazov* (R. Pevear and L. Volokhonsky, Trans.). New York: Farrar, Straus and Giroux.

41. Dostoevsky, F. (1994). *The Possessed (or the Demons)* (R. Pevear and L. Volokhonsky, Trans.). Vintage Books.

42. Jung, C. G. (1959). *Archetypes of the COLLECTIVE UNCONSCIOUS.* New York: Routledge.

43. Wooldridge, A. (2021). *The Aristocracy of Talent: How Meritocracy made the Modern World.* New York: Skyhorse.

44. Rowling, J. K. (2003). *Harry Potter and the Order of the Phoenix.* New York: Scholastic Press.

45. Ogas, O. and Gaddam, S. (2011). *A Billion Wicked Thoughts: What the World's Largest Experiment Reveals about Human Desire.* New York: Dutton/Penguin Books.

46. Buss, D. (2021). *When Men Behave Badly.* New York: Little and Brown; Brazil, K. J., Forth, A. E. (2020). Psychopathy and the Induction of desire: formulating and testing an evolutionary hypothesis. *Evolutionary Psychological Science 6,* 64–81; Carter, G. L., Campbell, A. C., and Muncer, S. (2014). The Dark Triad personality: attractiveness to women. *Personality and Individual Differences 56,* 57–61; Diller, S. J., et al. (2021).The positive connection between dark triad traits and leadership levels in self- and other-ratings. *Leadership, Education, Personality: An Interdisciplinary Journal 3,* 117–31.

47. See Peterson, J. B. and Willink, J. (2019, July). Be dangerous but disciplined. *Jocko Podcast* (youtu.be/a4PS_DhzyDg?si=NnrKidwZ3Y1pNtgS).

48. for a very nicely elaborated and comprehensive examination, Ogas, O. and Gaddam, S. (2011). *A billion wicked thoughts: What the world's largest experiment reveals about human desire.* New York: Dutton/Penguin Books; for recent representations in popular culture, see Disney's *Beauty and the Beast (2017);* James, E. L. (2012). *Fifty Shades of Grey.* New York: Random House.

49. see section 3.4. The good shepherd as archetypal leader.

50. see, for example, Exodus 13:1–2: And the Lord spake unto Moses, saying, Sanctify unto me all the firstborn, whatsoever openeth the womb among the children of Israel, both of man and of beast: it is mine.

51. as pointed out by Giszczak, M. (2013, June 26). Nine biblical metaphors for sin. In *Catholic Bible Student*: catholicbiblestudent.com/2013/06/biblical-metaphors-sin.html.

52. Peterson, J. B. *Maps of Meaning.*

53. see the MacLaren commentary at biblehub.com/commentaries/genesis/4-7.htm; taken from MacLaren, A. (1891). *Expositions of Holy Scripture—Genesis, Exodus, Leviticus and Numbers.* London: Hodder and Stoughton.

54. Story taken from the Chester Beatty Papyri, a collection of early Greek papyrus manuscripts, housed primarily at the Chester Beatty Library in Dublin, Ireland and at the University of Michigan; see Schrire, T. (1972). *The Chester Beatty Biblical Papyri: Descriptions and Texts of Twelve Manuscripts on Papyrus of the Greek Bible*. Dublin: Hodges, Figgis.

55. Peterson, J. B. *Maps of Meaning*.

56. Peterson, J. B. *Maps of Meaning*.

57. Lichtheim, M. (1976). *Ancient Egyptian Literature: A Book of Readings (Vol. 2)*. University of California Press.

58. Rowling, J. K. (2005). *Harry Potter and the Half-Blood Prince*. London: Bloomsbury.

59. This theme is exceptionally well-developed in Terry Zwigoff's brilliant documentary *Crumb*, Zwigoff, T. (Director). (1995). *Crumb* [Film]. Sony Pictures Classics), which portrays the relationship between the three brothers of the Crumb household. One of them, Robert, manages his exodus out into the world, where he becomes a very successful and famous author and illustrator of underground comics, although he still has his problems, to say the least. He parlays even his resentment and desire for vengeance into a genuine and even admirable career. His brothers, however—equally or even more brilliant and talent—disappear, instead, into the abyss. A more comprehensive study of psychological and familial dysfunction, with all its murderousness and sadistic torture, has seldom been offered. There is no shortage of angry, bitter, resentful, fallen and sardonic countenance on display in *Crumb*—including the Cain-like fratricidal murderousness.

60. The first statutory reference to this concept: Pardon of Offences Act 1389, 13 Rich. II St. 2 c. 1.

61. Bonanno, G. A. (2004). Loss, trauma, and human resilience: have we underestimated the human capacity to thrive after extremely aversive events? *The American Psychologist 59*, 20–28.

62. Piaget, J. (1962). *Play, Dreams, and Imitation in Childhood*. New York: Norton; Piaget, J. (1965). *The Moral Judgment of the Child*. New York: Free Press.

63. Lakoff, G. (1987). *Women, Fire, and Dangerous Things: What Categories Reveal about the Mind*. University of Chicago Press, 108.

64. He that descended is the same also that ascended up far above all heavens, that he might fill all things.

65. Eliade, M. (1981). *A History of Religious Ideas* (Vol. 2). University of Chicago Press, 18.

66. Eliade, M. (2004). *Shamanism: Archaic Techniques of Ecstasy*. Princeton University Press, 61.

67. Eliade, *Shamanism*, 18.

68. Pagels, E. (1979). *The Gnostic Gospels*. New York: Random House, xv.

69. see, for example, the bitter comments about God's cruelty by atheist and student of mythology Stephen Fry, in Fry, S. and Peterson, J. B. (2021, May). An atheist in the realm of myth. *The Jordan B. Peterson Podcast, 169* (youtu.be/fFFSKedy9f4?si=GLj__Y1z9rd1NHOO).

70. Jung, C. G. (1958). *Answer to Job*. New York: Routledge and Kegan Paul.

71. Why *son*? ". . . there was a day when the sons of God came to present themselves before the Lord, and Satan came also among them" (Job 1:6).

72. Keathley, J. H. (n.d.). *Biblical Typology: A Brief Overview*. Bible.org. Retrieved from bible .org/article/biblical-typology-brief-overview.

73. Stevenson, R. L. (1913). The land of Nod. In *A Child's Garden of Verses*. New York: Charles Scribner's Sons.

74. Robinson, H. W. (1913). *Genesis*. Cambridge, UK: Cambridge University Press, 98–99. See biblehub.com/commentaries/genesis/4-24.htm.

75. citation within the quoted text: Gordon, C. H. (1907). *Early Traditions of Genesis*. University of Chicago Press, 204.

76. Josephus. (n.d.). *Antiquities of the Jews* (W. Whiston, Trans.). Retrieved from gutenberg. org /files/2848/2848-h/2848-h.htm.

77. commentary on Genesis 4:15; biblehub.com/commentaries/pulpit/genesis/4.htm, drawn from Spence-Jones (1890), H. D. M. (Ed.). Genesis. In *The Pulpit Commentaries* (Vol. 1, 82). Funk & Wagnalls Company.

78. Chagnon, N. A. (1988). Life histories, blood revenge, and warfare in a tribal population. *Science 239*, 985–92.

79. Stringer, C. (2016). The origin and evolution of *Homo sapiens*. Philosophical Transactions of the Royal Society B. *Biological Science 371*, 1698–1702.

80. Kelly, R. L. (2005). The evolution of lethal intergroup violence. *Proceedings of the National Academy of Science 102*, 15294–98.

81. Wikan, U. (2008). *In honor of Fadime: murder and shame*. University of Chicago Press.

82. Hobbes, T. (1651). *Leviathan, Part I, Chapter XIII*. Retrieved from gutenberg.org/files /3207/3207-h/3207-h.htm#link2HCH0013.

83. Milton, J. (1674). *Paradise Lost: Book 1*: poetryfoundation.org/poems/45718/paradise-lost -book-1-1674-version.

84. specifically derived from biblehub.com/genesis/4-16.htm#commentary; drawn from Spence-Jones, H. D. M. (Ed.). (1890). *The Pulpit commentary*. London: Funk & Wagnalls.

85. Jung, C. G. (1958). Answer to Job. In H. Read, M. Fordham, G. Adler, and W. McGuire (Eds.), *The Collected Works of C. G. Jung* (Vol. 11, 355–470). Princeton University Press.

86. Kiehl, K. A. and Hoffman, M. B. (2011). The criminal psychopath: history, neuroscience, treatment and economics. *Jurimetrics 51*, 355–397; Patrick, C. J., and Drislane, L. E. (2015). *Psychopathy: An Introduction to Clinical and Forensic Aspects*. New York: Guilford Press; Jonason, P. K., Kaźmierczak, I., Campos, A. C., and Davis, M. D. (2021). Leaving without a word: Ghosting and the Dark Triad traits. *Acta Psychologica 220*, 103425; Jonason, P. K., Luevano, V. X., and Adams, H. M. (2012). How the Dark Triad traits predict relationship choices. *Personality and Individual Differences 53*, 180–84; see as well, for a more anachronistic characterization, en.wikipedia.org/wiki/Haltlose_personality_disorder.

87. Farrington, D. P., Ullrich, S., and Salekin, R.T. (2010). Environmental influences on child and adolescent psychopathy. In R. T. Salekin and D. R. Lynam (Eds.). *Handbook of child and adolescent psychopathy* (Chapter 9). New York: Guilford.

88. see section 2.7 Loss of Paradise and the flaming sword.

89. see 2.4. The eternal sins of Eve and Adam.

90. Dostoevsky, F. (1880). *The Brothers Karamazov*. Chapter 7: The Old Buffoon (Trans. Constance Garnett (1912): online-literature.com/dostoevsky/brothers_karamazov/7.

91. see section 3.6. Creatively possessed by the spirit of resentment.

4. Noah: God as the Call to Prepare

1. Rashi (1040–1105). *The Complete Jewish Bible with Rashi Commentary.* Genesis 4:25. chabad.org/library/bible_cdo/aid/8165/showrashi/true.

2. Ibn Ezra (1089–1167). *The Complete Jewish Bible with Ibn Ezra's Commentary.* Genesis 4:25. chabad.org/library/bible_cdo/aid/8173/showrashi/true.

3. Ramban (1194–1270). *The Complete Jewish Bible with Ramban's Commentary.* Genesis 4:25. chabad.org/library/bible_cdo/aid/8200/showrashi/true.

4. Ellicott, C. J. (1878). *Ellicott's Commentary for English Readers.* London: Cassell, Petter, and Galpin; Spence-Jones, H. D. M. (Ed.). (1890). *The Pulpit Commentary.* London: Funk & Wagnalls; Perowne, J. J. S. and Howson, J. S. (Eds.). (1885). *The Cambridge Bible for Schools and Colleges.* Cambridge University Press (biblehub.com/genesis/6-4.htm#commentary).

5. Eliade, M. (1958). *Patterns in Comparative Religion.* New York: Sheed and Ward, 258.

6. Eliade, M. (1954). *The Myth of the Eternal Return: Cosmos and History.* Princeton, NJ: Bollingen Foundation Press, 215.

7. Milton, J. (1674). *Paradise Lost: Book 1:* poetryfoundation.org/poems/45718/paradise-lost -book-1-1674-version.

8. Heidel, A. (1965). *The Babylonian Genesis.* Chicago University Press (Phoenix Books). Tablet 1:133–38, 23.

9. as detailed extensively in Peterson, J. B. *Maps of Meaning;* see also Jung, C. G. (1967). *The Collected Works of C. G. Jung: Vol. 5. Symbols of Transformation* (2nd ed.). In H. Read, et al., Eds. (R. F. C. Hull, Trans.). Princeton University Press; Campbell, J. (2012). *The Hero with a Thousand Faces* (3rd ed.). New World Library; Neumann, E. (2014). *The origins and history of consciousness.* Princeton University Press; Neumann, E. (2015). *The Great Mother.* Princeton University Press.

10. Nietzsche, F. (2005). *Thus Spake Zarathustra: A Book for Everyone and No One.* (T. Common, Trans.). New York: Penguin Classics, 125.

11. Allers, R. and Minkoff, R. (Directors). (1994). *The Lion King* [Film]. Walt Disney Pictures.

12. Kaufmann, W. (Ed. and Trans.). (1954). *The Portable Nietzsche.* New York: Viking Press, 211–12.

13. Nietzsche, F. (1969). *Thus Spoke Zarathustra: A Book for Everyone and Nobody.* (W. Kaufmann, Trans.). (Original work published 1883–1885). Harmondsworth, UK: Penguin Books, 70.

14. Nietzsche, F. (1967). *On the Genealogy of Morals and Ecce Homo.* (W. Kaufmann, Trans.). Vintage Books. (Original works published in 1887 and 1908), First Essay, Section 10, 30.

15. Kaufmann, W. (1974). *Nietzsche: Philosopher, Psychologist Antichrist.* Princeton University Press. 98.

16. Pevear, R. (1995). *Foreword to Demons* (Pevear and Volokhonsky, Trans.). In F. Dostoevsky, *Demons.* New York: Vintage, xvii.

17. Solzhenitsyn, A. (1974). *The Gulag Archipelago, 1918–1956: An Experiment in Literary Investigation* (T. P. Whitney, Trans.). New York: Harper and Row.

18. Peterson, J. B. (2018). Foreword. In A. Solzhenitsyn, *The Gulag Archipelago: Abridged Edition* (J. Whitney, Trans.). Vintage Classics, xii.

19. see section 2.6. Naked suffering as the fruit of sin.

20. Shakespeare, W. (2008). As you like it. In S. Greenblatt, W. Cohen, J. Howard and K. Eisaman Maus (Eds.), *The Norton Shakespeare: Based on the Oxford Edition* (2nd ed., 1611–63). New York: W. W. Norton & Company.

21. Solzhenitsyn, A. (1972). Nobel lecture in literature. In M. Slonim (Ed.), *Alexander Solzhenitsyn: A Documentary Record*. Hardmondsworth, UK: Penguin Books, 284.

22. Solzhenitsyn, Aleksandr Isaevich. (1974). *The Gulag Archipelago, 1918–1956: An Experiment in Literary Investigation*. New York: Harper and Row; Dreher, R. (2020). *Live Not By Lies: A Manual for Christian Dissidents*. New York: Sentinel; Orwell, G. (1949/2021). *1984*. New York: Penguin Classics.

23. Dostoevsky, F. (1880). *The Brothers Karamazov*. Chapter 25: Father Ferapont (1912). (Constance Garnett, Trans.) online-literature.com/dostoevsky/brothers_karamazov/25.

24. Dostoevsky, *Brothers Karamazov*. Chapter 41: Conversation and Exhortations of Father Zossima.

25. As in, "we hold these truths to be self-evident"—part of the famous opening lines of the second paragraph of the American Declaration of Independence.

26. Eliade, M. (1978). *A History of Religious Ideas: Volume 1: From the Stone Age to the Eleusinian Mysteries*. Chicago University Press, 62–63.

27. see section 1.1. God as creative spirit.

28. Goebel, T., Waters, M. R., and O'Rourke, D. H. (2008). The late Pleistocene dispersal of modern humans in the Americas. *Science 319*, 1497–1502.

29. Martin, P. S. (1967). *Prehistoric Overkill*. New York: Wiley; Steadman, D. W. and Martin, P. S. (2003). The late Quaternary extinction and future resurrection of birds on Pacific islands. *Earth's Insights 6*, 49–60; Fariña, R. A., Vizcaíno, S. F., and De Iuliis, G. (2013). *Megafauna: Giant Beasts of Pleistocene South America*. Indiana University Press; Barnett; Shapiro, R. et al. (2009). Phylogeography of lions (*Panthera leo ssp.*) reveals three distinct taxa and a late Pleistocene reduction in genetic diversity. *Molecular Ecology 18*, 1668–77; Meachen, J. A. and Janowicz, A. C. (2015). Morphological convergence of the prey-killing arsenal of sabertooth predators. *Paleobiology 41*, 280–312.

30. Martin, P. S. (1967). *Prehistoric overkill*. New York: Wiley; Johnson, C. N. and Miller, W. E. (2002). Australasia's own 'Lost World': The late Pleistocene fossil mammal deposits of the Naracoorte Caves, South Australia. *Transactions of the Royal Society of South Australia 126*, 1–12.

31. Huffman, T. N. (2019). *Handbook to the Iron Age: The Archaeology of Pre-Colonial Farming Societies in Southern Africa*. New York: Springer.

32. Steadman, D. W. and Franz, R. (2017). Prehistoric extinctions of Pacific island birds: Biodiversity meets zooarchaeology. *Science 358*, 911–14; Pregill, G. K. and Steadman, D. W. (2019). Extinctions and declines of terrestrial vertebrates in the Hawaiian Islands. *Journal of Mammalogy 100*, 1907–24; Burney, D. A., James, H. F., Grady, F. V., Raferty, J. P., and Talbot, S. L. (1997). Ecology, extinction and conservation of island birds: La Parguera, Puerto Rico. *Bird Conservation International 7*, 209–42.

33. Worm, B. et al. (2006). Impacts of biodiversity loss on ocean ecosystem services. *Science* *314*, 787–90; Myers, R. A., and Worm, B. (2003). Rapid worldwide depletion of predatory fish communities. *Nature 423*, 280–83.

34. It is now 1 in 20 Americans who consider themselves vegetarians and 1 in 33 as the more extreme vegans: Saad, L. (2020, August 3). *In U.S., 5% Consider Themselves Vegetarian*. Gallup. Retrieved from news.gallup.com/poll/317077/five-consider-themselves-vegetarian.aspx.

35. specifically derived from biblehub.com/genesis/9-4.htm#commentary; drawn from Ellicott, C. J. (1905). *Ellicott's commentary for English readers*. London: Cassell and Company, Ltd.

36. Luther, M. (1966). *Luther's Works, Volume 42: Devotional Writings I* (P. D. W. Krey, Ed.). London: Fortress Press. 91.

37. specifically derived from biblehub.com/genesis/9-22.htm#commentary; drawn from Spence-Jones, H. D. M. (Ed.). (1890). *The Pulpit Commentary*. London: Funk & Wagnalls.

38. This modernist (post-modernist) moralizing can be seen reflected even in the behavior of modern AI large-language model systems, which have apparently either learned from imbibing literary material biased in its content by the arbitrary dominance of modern writing over classic (given the ease of producing sharing printed material that now exists for technological reasons) or programmed post-hoc by politically-motivated would-be censors to produce the appropriately cautious and mealy-mouthed answers that cowards think are both moral and socially-acceptable. This is how Chat GPT (chat.openAI.com), for example, concluded its response when asked "tell me about the biblical role and characterization of the Canaanites": "It is worth noting that the biblical depiction of the Canaanites has been subject to criticism and revision, with some scholars arguing that the portrayal is biased and reflects the political and theological concerns of the Israelite writers. Additionally, archaeological and historical evidence suggests that the Canaanites were a diverse and complex society with their own distinct culture and traditions, and that their interaction with the Israelites was more nuanced than the biblical narrative implies" (retrieved May 1, 2023). It is impossible for anyone sensible to read such self-serving, self-aggrandizing, pathetic nonsense (machine-generated or otherwise) without feeling great shame for the crime of merely being human.

39. see section 1.5. In God's image.

40. see, for example, Monuments and Memorials Removed in Canada 2020–2022, Wikipedia: en.wikipedia.org/wiki/Monuments_and_memorials_in_Canada_removed_in_2020-2022.

41. for a take that is both particularly reprehensible and telling, see Nayeri, F. (2023, May 2). The conflict over vandalizing art as a way to protest. *The New York Times*, nytimes.com /2023/05/02/arts/design/vandalizing-art-protests.html.

42. specifically derived from biblehub.com/genesis/10-6.htm#commentary; drawn from Spence-Jones, H. D. M. (Ed.). (1890). *The Pulpit Commentary*. London: Funk & Wagnalls.

5. The Tower of Babel: God versus Tyranny and Pride

1. en.wikipedia.org/wiki/Ziggurat: retrieved June 18, 2024.

2. en.wikipedia.org/wiki/Mesoamerican_pyramids: retrieved June 18, 2024.

3. Maslow, A. H. (1943). One famous example is the "hierarchy of needs" developed by the psychologist Abraham Maslow, one of the founders of the humanist school of psychotherapy. A theory of human motivation. *Psychological Review 50*, 370–96). Although Maslow did not employ such an image himself (Ballard, J.A. [August 2006]. *The diffusion of Maslow's motivation theory in management and other disciplines.* Paper presented at the 66th Academy of Management Annual Meeting, Knowledge, Action and the Public Concern: Atlanta GA, USA) his ideas are generally and commonly presented with images derived from ziggurats (nietzscheselfhelp.com/single-post/2017/12/31/maslow-s-ziggurat) or even more frequently pyramids (en.wikipedia.org/wiki/Maslow%27s_hierarchy_of _needs; simplypsychology.org/maslow.html.).

4. Eliade, M. (1959). *The Sacred and the Profane.* Translated by Willard R. Trask. New York: Harcourt, Brace and Company, 40–41.

5. Lipiński, E. (2000). *The Aramaeans: Their Ancient History, Culture, Religion.* Leuven, Belgium: Peeters Publishers, 87.

6. Lipiński, E. (1992). *Dictionnaire de la Civilisation Phénicienne et Punique.* Turnhout, Belgium: Brepols.

7. George, A. (2007) The tower of Babel: archaeology, history and cuneiform texts. *Archiv für Orientforschung 51*, 75–95.

8. Walton, J. H. (2006). *Ancient Near Eastern Thought and the Old Testament: Introducing the Conceptual World of the Hebrew Bible.* Grand Rapids, MI: Baker Academic, 179.

9. Black, J. A., Cunningham, G., Robson, E., and Zólyomi, G. (2006). *The Epic of Gilgamesh: A New Translation, Analogues, Criticism.* Oxford University Press.

10. Van der Toorn, K. (2007). *Scribal Culture and the Making of the Hebrew Bible.* Cambridge: Harvard University Press, 133.

11. The seven-headed scarlet beast of the state featured in the terrible imagery of Revelation 17 is traditionally regarded as a reference to Rome, founded as it was on seven hills.

12. Hess, R. S. (1994). Babel, Tower of. In D. N. Freedman (Ed.), *The Anchor Yale Bible Dictionary* (Vol. 1, 522–26). New York: Doubleday.

13. Menner, Robert J. (1938). Nimrod and the Wolf in the Old English "Solomon and Saturn," *Journal of English and Germanic Philology 37*, 332–84.

14. This is a happening reminiscent of the re-emergence of the monstrous chaos of Tiamat after the elder Mesopotamian guards so casually slay Apsu and attempt to use his corpse as a foundation.

15. Coogan, M. D. (2009). *A Brief Introduction to the Old Testament: The Hebrew Bible in Its Context.* Oxford University Press.

16. for a recent illustration of this, see Folk, J. (Director). (2022). *What Is a Woman?* [Film]. Nashville: Daily Wire Plus.

17. Wittgenstein, L. (1953). *Philosophical Investigations.* London: Blackwell Publishing, section 31.

18. Milton, J. (1674). *Paradise Lost: Book 7*: poetryfoundation.org/poems/45743/paradise-lost -book-7-1674-version.

19. see section 1.4. Eve from Adam.

20. Marelich, W. D., Lundquist, J., Painter, K., and Mechanic, M. B. (2008). Sexual deception as a social-exchange process: Development of a behavior-based sexual deception scale.

Journal of Sex Research 45, 27–35; see also Brewer, G., De Griffa, D., and Uzun, E. (2019). Dark triad traits and women's use of sexual deception. *Personality and Individual Differences 142*, 42–44.

21. Milton, J. (1634). *Comus: A Mask Presented at Ludlow Castle.* Retrieved from Project Gutenberg: gutenberg.org/files/24353/24353-h/24353-h.htm#link2H_4_0003; specifically derived from biblehub.com/revelation/17-4.htm#commentary; drawn from Ellicott, C. J. (1905). *Ellicott's Commentary for English Readers.* London: Cassell and Company, Ltd.

22. Ogas, S. and Gaddam, S. (2011). *A Billion Wicked Thoughts: What the Internet Tells Us about Sexual Behavior.* New York: Plume.

23. for a how-to guide (how utterly inexcusable) see Episode 113: how porn drives tech innovation. *Tech for Non-Techies:* techfornontechies.co/blog/how-porn-drives-tech-innovation; Waddell, K. (2016, June). How porn leads people to upgrade their tech. *The Atlantic:* theatlantic.com/technology/archive/2016/05/how-porn-leads-people-to-upgrade-their-tech/484132/; Arlidge, J. (2002, Mar). The dirty secret that drives new technology: it's porn. *The Guardian:* theguardian.com/technology/2002/mar/03/internetnews.observerfocus.

24. Freud, S. (1905). Three Essays on the Theory of Sexuality. In J. Strachey (Ed. and Trans.), *The Standard Edition of the Complete Psychological Works of Sigmund Freud* (Vol. 7). London: Hogarth Press.

25. specifically derived from biblehub.com/revelation/18-24.htm#commentary; drawn from Ellicott, C. J. (1896). *A New Testament Commentary for English Readers.* London: Cassell and Company, Ltd.

26. See section 1.4. Eve from Adam.

27. McManus, L. (2023, November 3). AI sex robot technician jokes 'women are becoming extinct' as doll sales sky-rocket. *Daily Star:* dailystar.co.uk/news/weird-news/ai-sex-robot-technician-jokes-31356090.

28. "Now there was a day when the sons of God came to present themselves before the LORD, and Satan came also among them" (Job 1:6; see also Job 2:1).

29. See section 2.5. The eternal serpent.

30. Milton, J. (1674). *Paradise Lost: Book 1:* poetryfoundation.org/poems/45718/paradise-lost-book-1-1674-version.

31. Milton, *Paradise Lost: Book 1.*

32. Milton, *Paradise Lost: Book 1.*

33. Milton, *Paradise Lost: Book 1.*

34. Milton, *Paradise Lost: Book 1.*

35. Personal communication from famed engineer James (Jim) Keller, inventor of many of the computer chips that keep the world's technology operative: for background, see en.wikipedia.org/wiki/Jim_Keller_(engineer).

36. Tolkien, J. R. R. (1993). *The Lord of the Rings* (2nd ed.). Boston: Houghton Mifflin Co.

37. see, for example (there are many) Shen, X. (2018, October 4). "Skynet," China's massive video surveillance network. *South China Morning Post:* scmp.com/abacus/who-what/what/article/3028246/skynet-chinas-massive-video-surveillance-network.

38. Cameron, J. (Director). (1984). *The Terminator* [Film]. Orion Pictures; (1991).*Terminator 2: Judgment Day* [Film]. TriStar Pictures; Mostow, J. (Director). (2003). *Terminator 3: Rise*

of the Machines [Film]. Warner Bros. Pictures; McG (Director). (2009). *Terminator Salvation* [Film]. Warner Bros. Pictures; Taylor, A. (Director). (2015). *Terminator Genisys* [Film]. Paramount Pictures; Miller, T. (Director). (2019). *Terminator: Dark Fate* [Film]. Paramount Pictures.

39. Peterson, D. (2021). *China's "sharp eyes" program aims to surveil 100% of public space.* Center for Security and Emerging Technology, cset.georgetown.edu/article/chinas-sharp-eyes-program-aims-to-surveil-100-of-public-space, retrieved May 15, 2023.

40. Kang, D. (2018). *Chinese "gait recognition" tech IDs people by how they walk.* Associated Press, apnews.com/article/china-technology-beijing-business-international-news-bf75dd1c26c94 7b7826d270a16e2658a, retrieved May 15, 2023.

41. George, A. L. and Smoke, R. (1974). *Deterrence in American Foreign Policy: Theory and Practice.* New York: Columbia University Press.

42. Movie version: Fosse, B. (Director). (1972). *Cabaret* [Film]. Hollywood, CA: Allied Artists Pictures.

43. *The Simpsons.* Season 4, Episode 21: "Marge in Chains" (1993).

44. Season 11, Episode 14: "Alone Again, Natura-Diddily" (2000).

45. Season 12, Episode 11: "Worst Episode Ever" (2001).

46. Season 18, Episode 14: "Yokel Chords" (2007).

47. Season 23, Episode 5: "The Food Wife" (2011).

48. Season 2, Episode 13: "Homer vs. Lisa and the 8th Commandment" (1991).

49. Ovid. (2004). *The Metamorphoses* (D. Raeburn, Trans.). London: Penguin Classics. (Original work published circa 8 CE.)

50. "And he said unto them, I beheld Satan as lightning fall from heaven" (Luke 10:18).

51. specifically derived from biblehub.com/commentaries/isaiah/14-12.htm; taken from Gill, J. (1748). *A commentary on the whole Bible: Explaining and defending the sacred text.* London: J. and J. Knapton.

52. as detailed in Wrangham, R. and Peterson, D. (1996). *Demonic Males: Apes and the Origins of Human Violence.* New York: Houghton Mifflin.

53. De Waal, F. (1982). *Chimpanzee Politics: Power and Sex among Apes.* Baltimore MD: Johns Hopkins University Press, 138.

54. De Waal, F. (2001). *The Ape and the Sushi Master: Cultural Reflections by a Primatologist.* New York: Basic Books, 46.

55. De Waal, *Chimpanzee Politics*, 223.

56. De Waal, F. B. M. (2013). *The Bonobo and the Atheist: In Search of Humanism among the Primates.* New York: W. W. Norton & Company, 11.

57. as outlined so pathologically by Foucault, M. (1991). *Discipline and Punish: The Birth of a Prison.* London: Penguin; Foucault, M. (1998) *The History of Sexuality: The Will to Knowledge.* London: Penguin.

58. en.wikipedia.org/wiki/Death_of_Benito_Mussolini: retrieved May 15, 2023.

59. en.wikipedia.org/wiki/Nicolae_Ceau%C8%99escuL: retrieved May 15, 2023.

60. George, A. R. (2003). *The Epic of Gilgamesh.* New York: Penguin Classics.

61. Sturluson, S. (2011). *The Prose Edda.* London: Penguin Classics.

62. Wu, C. (1977). *The Journey to the West.* University of Chicago Press.

63. Graves, R. (1955). *The Greek Myths*. London: Penguin Books.

64. see Wittgenstein, L. (1953). *Philosophical Investigations*. (G. E. M. Anscombe, Trans.). Oxford, UK: Basil Blackwell.

65. This is exceptionally well explained in Nørretranders, T. (1991). *The User Illusion: Cutting Consciousness Down to Size*. New York: Viking.

66. This appears to be something approximating a variant of the theorem formulated by Gödel and outlined previously.

67. see Neumann, E. (2014). *The Origins and History of Consciousness*. Princeton University Press; Neumann, E. (2015). *The Great Mother*. Princeton University Press; Jung, C. G. (1967). *The Collected Works of C. G. Jung: Vol. 5. Symbols of Transformation* (2nd ed.). (In H. Read, et al., Eds.). (R. F. C. Hull, Trans.). Princeton University Press; Peterson, J. B. *Maps of Meaning*.

68. The axiomatic nature of such a supposition, or its equivalent, was in part the theme of my 1999 book *Maps of Meaning: The Architecture of Belief*, as well as the works upon which it was in part based. See further in section 7.4.

69. Jones, D. N. and Paulhus, D. L. (2021). The explanatory power of the Dark Tetrad of personality in the prediction of risk-taking behaviors. *Australian Journal of Psychology 73*, 253–61; Watts, A. L., Lilienfeld, S. O., Smith, S. F., Miller, J. D., and Campbell, W. K. (2021). Deception and the Dark Tetrad of personality: The roles of psychopathy and Machiavellianism. *Personality and Individual Differences 185*, 111243; Movahedi, S., Kajbaf, M. B., and Rasekh, A. (2021). Dark Tetrad personality traits and different beliefs: Exploring the links. *The Journal of Social Psychology 161*, 433–51.

70. Cale, E. M. and Lilienfeld, S. O. (2002). Sex differences in psychopathy and antisocial personality disorder: a review and integration. *Clinical Psychology Review 22*, 1179–1207; Jonason, P. K. and Li, N. P. Relationship between number of sexual partners and involvement in an antisocial lifestyle among young adults. *Journal of Social Psychology 149*, 222–25.

71. Lee, K., Ashton, M. C., Wiltshire, J., Bourdage, J. S., Visser, B. A., and Gallucci, A. (2013). Sex, power, and money: Prediction from the Dark Triad and Honesty–Humility. *European Journal of Personality 27*, 169–84.

72. Łowicki, P., Zajenkowski, M., Golec de Zavala, A., and Piotrowski, J. (2019). Dark Triad of personality and its association with addictive behaviors, both substance-related and non-substance-related: A systematic review. *Frontiers in Psychology 10*, 1–18; Van Schie, C. C. and Van Roekel, E. (2021). The relationship between Dark Triad personality trait levels and addiction tendencies to "substances" and "processes." *Addiction Research and Theory 30*, 184–193; Lewis, C. E. and Bucholz, K. K. (1991). Alcoholism, antisocial behavior and family history. *British Journal of Addiction 86*, 177–94; Pihl, R. O. and Peterson, J. B. (1991). Attention-deficit hyperactivity disorder, childhood conduct disorder, and alcoholism: Is there an association? *Alcohol Health and Research World 15*, 25–31.

73. Moss, J. and O'Connor, P. J. (2020). The Dark Triad traits predict authoritarian political correctness and alt-right attitudes. *Heliyon 6*, e04453.

74. Concerns were already emerging on that front when the screens of concerned were those of the mere television: Hill, D. J. et al. (2016). Media and young minds. *Pediatrics 138*: e20162591.

75. See section 4.4. The faithless son doomed to enslavement.

76. Haidt, J. (2024). *The Anxious Generation: How the Great Rewiring of Childhood Is Causing an Epidemic of Mental Illness* New York: Penguin Press.

77. see section 2.6. Naked suffering as the fruit of sin.

78. a sufficiently informative although hardly exhaustive account can be found at Unit 731. *Wikipedia*: en.wikipedia.org/wiki/Unit_731.

79. Panzram, C. (2002). *Panzram: a journal of murder*. T. E. Gaddis and Long, J. (Eds.). Gardena, CA: Amok Books.

80. Marx, K. (1843). A contribution to the critique of Hegel's philosophy of right: marxists .org/archive/marx/works/1843/critique-hpr/intro.htm.

81. Freud, S. (1927). *The Future of An Illusion*. London: Hogarth Press.

82. This is technically true. See Gray, J. (1982). *The Neuropsychology of Anxiety*. Oxford University Press.

83. Solzhenitsyn, A. (1973). *The Gulag Archipelago, 1918–1956: An Experiment in Literary Investigation, Volume III*. New York: Harper and Row, 615.

84. Solzhenitsyn, *Gulag Archipelago*, 338–39.

6. Abraham: God as Spirited Call to Adventure

1. Dostoevsky, F. (1918). *Notes from the Underground* (C. Garnett, Trans.). gutenberg.org /files/600/600-h/600-h.htm

2. specifically derived from biblehub.com/commentaries/genesis/12-1.htm; drawn from Benson, J. (1857). *Benson Commentary*. New York: T. Carlton and J. Porter.

3. see section 3.5. The sacrifice pleasing to God.

4. see section 6.6. With the angels into the abyss.

5. Milton, *Paradise Lost: Book 1*.

6. Lukianoff, G. and Haidt, J. (2018). *The Coddling of the American Mind: How Good Intentions and Bad Ideas Are Setting Up a Generation for Failure*. New York: Penguin Press.

7. Haidt, J. (2024). *The Anxious Generation: How the Great Rewiring of Childhood Is Causing an Epidemic of Mental Illness*. New York: Penguin Press.

8. Gray, J. (1982). *The Neuropsychology of Anxiety*. Oxford University Press.

9. see the work by Jaak Panksepp and Tiffany Field on the necessity of touch, for example, to even the life of children.

10. as reviewed in my last book: Peterson, J. B. (2022). *Beyond Order: 12 More Rules for Life*. London: Allen Lane.

11. see the MacLaren commentary at biblehub.com/commentaries/genesis/13-1.htm, taken from MacLaren, A. (1891). *Expositions of Holy Scripture—Genesis, Exodus, Leviticus and Numbers*. London: Hodder and Stoughton.

12. see section 2.7. Loss of Paradise and the flaming sword.

13. see section 6.2. The devil at the crossroads.

14. see section 3.1. The identity of sacrifice and work.

15. the most cited thinker in the humanities. Van Noorden, R. (2010). The top 100 papers. *Nature 463*, 569–571. See Foucault, M. (1991). *Discipline and Punish: The Birth of a*

Prison. London: Penguin; Foucault, M. (1998). *The History of Sexuality: The Will to Knowledge.* London: Penguin Books.

16. Dawkins, R. (2006). *The Selfish Gene.* Oxford University Press.

17. Buss, D. (1989). Sex differences in human mate preferences: Evolutionary hypotheses tested in 37 cultures. *Behavioral and Brain Science 12,* 1–14; Buss, D. M. and Schmitt, D. P. (1993). Sexual strategies theory: an evolutionary perspective on human mating. *Psychological Review 100,* 204–32; Tucaković, L., Bojić, L., and Nikolić, N. (2022). The battle between light and dark side of personality: how light and dark personality traits predict mating strategies in the online context. *Interpersona: An International Journal on Personal Relationships 16,* 295–312.

18. Barrick, M. R. and Mount, M. K. (1991). The Big Five personality dimensions and job performance: A meta-analysis. *Personnel Psychology 44,* 1–26; Hogan, R. and Ones, D. S. (1997). Conscientiousness and integrity at work. In R. Hogan, J. Johnson, and S. Briggs (Eds.), *Handbook of personality psychology.* San Francisco: Academic Press, 85–110; Higgins, D. M., Peterson, J. B., Pihl, R. O., and Lee, A. G. M. (2007). Prefrontal cognitive ability, intelligence, Big Five personality, and the prediction of advanced academic and workplace performance. *Journal of Personality and Social Psychology 93,* 298–319.

19. Costa, P. T., Jr., Terracciano, A., and McCrae, R. R. (2001). Gender differences in personality traits across cultures: Robust and surprising findings. *Journal of Personality and Social Psychology 81,* 322–31; Feingold, A. (1994). Gender differences in personality: A meta-analysis. *Psychological Bulletin 116,* 429–56; Schmitt, D. P., Realo, A., and Voracek, M. (2008). The big five factor model of personality across cultures: Robust and generalizable across 55 cultures. *Journal of Personality and Social Psychology 94,* 26–40; Weisberg, Y. J., Deyoung, C. G., and Hirsh, J. B. (2011). Gender differences in personality across the ten aspects of the Big Five. *Frontiers in Psychology 2,* 178.

20. Brown, D. (1991). *Human Universals.* Philadelphia, PA: Temple University Press.

21. Brown, D. *Human Universals.*

22. Buss, D. (1989). Sex differences in human mate preferences: Evolutionary hypotheses tested in 37 cultures. *Behavioral and Brain Science 12,* 1–14.

23. as reviewed in Scheiber, I. B. R., Weiß, B. M., Kingma, S. A., and Komdeur, J. (2017). The importance of the altricial/precocial spectrum for social complexity in mammals and birds—a review. *Frontiers in Zoology 14,* 3–13.

24. Dawkins, R. (1976). *The Selfish Gene.* Oxford University Press.

25. Farrell, W. and Gray, J. (2018). *The Boy Crisis.* Dallas, TX: BenBella Books.

26. Jonason, P. K., Luevano, V. X., and Adams, H. M. (2012). How the Dark Triad traits predict relationship choices. *Personality and Individual Differences 53,* 180–84.

27. Carter, G. L., Campbell, A. C., and Muncer, S. (2014). The dark triad personality: Attractiveness to women. *Personality and Individual Differences 56,* 57–61; Qureshi, C., Harris, E., and Atkinson, B. E. (2016). Relationships between age of females and attraction to the Dark Triad personality. *Personality and Individual Differences 95,* 200–203.

28. briefly reviewed here (new.nsf.gov/news/benefits-sexual-reproduction-lie-defense-against#); see Jaenike J. (1978). An hypothesis to account for the maintenance of sex within populations. Evolutionary Theory, 3, 191–94; Hamilton, W. (1980). Sex versus non-sex versus parasite. *Oi-*

kos 35, 282–90; Bell, G. (1982). *The Masterpiece of Nature: The Evolution and Genetics of Asexuality*. Berkeley: University of California Press; King, K. C., Delph, L. F., Jokela, J., and Lively, C. M. (2009). The geographic mosaic of sex and the Red Queen. *Current Biology 19*, 1438–41.

29.   see section 1.4. Eve from Adam.

30.   Thompson, D. F., Ramos, C. L., and Willett, J. K. (2014). Psychopathy: clinical features, developmental basis and therapeutic challenges. *Journal of Clinical Pharmacy and Therapeutics 39*, 485–495.

31.   Jonasaon, P. K., Li, N. P., Webster, G. D. and Schmitt, D. P. (2009). The Dark Triad: Facilitating a Short-Term Mating Strategy in Men. *European Journal of Personality 23*, 5–18; Brewer, G. et al. (2018). Dark triad traits and romantic relationship attachment, accommodation, and control. Personality and Individual Differences, 120, 202–208; Figueredo, A. J., Gladden, P. R., Sisco, M. M., Patch, E. A., and Jones, D. N. (2015). The unholy trinity: The Dark Triad, coercion, and Brunswik-Symmetry. *Evolutionary Psychology 13*, 435–454; Jonason, P. K., and Burtăverde, V. (2023). The dark triad traits and mating psychology. In D. M. Buss (Ed.), *The Oxford Handbook of Human Mating*. Oxford University Press, 590–605.

32.   Frankl, G. (2003). *The Failure of the Sexual Revolution*. Free Association Books; Perry, L. (2022). *The Case Against the Sexual Revolution*. New York: Polity Press.

33.   Dworkin, E. R., Krahé, B., and Zinzow, H. (2021). The global prevalence of sexual assault: a systematic review of international research since 2010. *Psychology of Violence 11*, 497–508.

34.   Flanagan, C. (2019). Losing the *Rare* in "Safe, Legal and Rare." *The Atlantic*, theatlantic.com/ideas/archive/2019/12/the-brilliance-of-safe-legal-and-rare/603151.

35.   Diamant, J., Mohamed, B., and Leppert, R. (2024). What the data says about abortion in the US. Pew Research Center: pewresearch.org/short-reads/2024/03/25/what-the-data-says-about-abortion-in-the-us.

36.   Garcia, J. R., Reiber, C., Massey, S. G., and Merriwether, A. M. (2012). Sexual hookup culture: a review. *Review of General Psychology 16*, 161–176.

37.   Abbey, A., Zawacki, T., Buck, P. O., Clinton, A. M., and McAuslan, P. (2001). Alcohol and sexual assault. *Alcohol Research and Health 25*, 43–51; see also (if you must) Miodus, S., Tan, S., Med, Evangelista, N. D., Fioriti, C., and Harris, M. (2023). Campus sexual assault: Fact sheet from an intersectional lens. *American Psychological Association of Graduate Students Resourcs for Students*: apa.org/apags/resources/campus-sexual-assault-fact-sheet.pdf.

38.   Young, C. (2014). Want to have sex? Sign this contract. *Minding the Campus: Reforming our Universities*:, mindingthecampus.org/2014/02/20/want_to_have_sex_sign_this_con.

39.   Eberstadt, M. (2013). *Adam and Eve After the Pill: Paradoxes of the Sexual Revolution*. San Francisco: Ignatius Press; Perry, L. (2022). *The Case Against the Sexual Revolution*. New York: Polity Press; Harrington, M. (2023). *Feminism Against Progress*. Washington, DC: Regnery Publishing.

40.   Pineda, D., Galán, M., Martínez-Martínez, A., Campagne, D. M., and Piqueras, J. A. (2022). Same personality, new ways to abuse: How Dark Tetrad personalities are connected with cyber intimate partner violence. *Journal of Interpersonal Violence 37*, 13–14; Pineda, D., Martínez-Martínez, A., Manuel Galán, M., Pilar Rico-Border, P., and Piqueras, J. A.

(2023). The Dark Tetrad and online sexual victimization: Enjoying in the distance. *Computers in Human Behavior 142*, 107659; Costa, R., Fávero, M., Moreira, D., Del Campo, A., and Sousa-Gomes, V. (2024). Is the link between the Dark Tetrad and the acceptance of sexual violence mediated by sexual machismo? *Aggressive Behavior 50*, 1, e22116.

41. snopes.com/fact-check/mike-tyson-social-media.

42. Institute for Family Studies and Wheatley Institute. (2018). *Global Family and Gender Survey:* ifstudies.org/ifs-admin/resources/global-family-and-gender-survey-2018-gfg -1.pdf.

43. Park, B. Y. et al. (2016). Is internet pornography causing sexual dysfunction? A review with clinical reports. *Behavioral Sciences (Basel, Switzerland), 6*, 17–24; Foubert, J. D. (2017). The public health harms of pornography: the brain, erectile dysfunction, and sexual violence. *Dignity: A Journal of Analysis of Exploitation and Violence 2*, Article 6; Fog-Poulsen, K., Jacobs, T., Høyer, S., Rohde, C., Vermande, A., De Wachter, S., and De Win, G. (2020). Can time to ejaculation be affected by pornography? *The Journal of Urology 203 (Supplement 4)*, e615; Sharpe, M. and Mead, D. (2021). Problematic pornography use: legal and health policy considerations. *Current Addiction Reports 8*, 556–67. There are contrary or lesser findings, not least because the causes of erectile dysfunction and sexual violence are manifold: Landripet, I. and Štulhofer, A. (2015). Is pornography use associated with sexual difficulties and dysfunctions among younger heterosexual men? *The Journal of Sexual Medicine 12*, 1136–39.

44. This appears particularly although not uniquely true of Japan, with other western or westernized countries following: Ghaznavi, C., Sakamoto, H., Yoneoka, D. et al. (2019). Trends in heterosexual inexperience among young adults in Japan: analysis of national surveys, 1987–2015. *BMC Public Health 19*, 355–63.

45. reasonably reviewed at Single parents in the United States, *Wikipedia*: en.wikipedia.org /wiki/Single_parents_in_the_United_States.

46. Perry, L. (2022). *The Case against the Sexual Revolution.* New York: Polity; see also Perry, L. and Peterson, J. B. (2023). Against the sexual revolution. *The Jordan B. Peterson Podcast, 331* (youtu.be/rGsZ_HI_q1M?si=jvCcDwRT_PeJKSyR).

47. Farrell, W. and Gray, J. (2018). *The Boy Crisis.* Dallas, TX: BenBella Books.

48. Harris, I. D., Fronczak, C., Roth, L., and Meacham, R. B. (2011). Fertility and the Aging Male. *Reviews in Urology 13*, e184–90.

49. Monga, M., Alexandrescu, B., Katz, S. E., Stein, M., and Ganiats, T. (2003). Impact of infertility on quality of life, marital adjustment, and sexuafunction. *Urology 63*, 126–30; Peterson, B. D., Newton, C. R., Rosen, K. H., and Skaggs, G. E. (2006). Gender differences in how men and women who are referred for IVF cope with infertility stress. *Human Reproduction 21*, 2443–449; Ying, L.Y., Wu, L.H., and Loke, A.Y. (2015). Gender differences in experiences with and adjustments to infertility: a literature review. *International Journal of Nursing Studies 52*, 1640–52.

50. Lassek, W. D. and Gaulin, S. J. C. (2008). Waist-hip ratio and cognitive ability: Is gluteofemoral fat a privileged store of neurodevelopmental resources? *Evolution and Human Behavior 29*, 26–34; Buss, D. (1989). Sex differences in human mate preferences: Evolutionary hypotheses tested in 37 cultures. *Behavioral and Brain Science 12*, 1–14; Cloud, J. M. and Perilloux, C. (2014). Bodily attractiveness as a window to women's fertility and

reproductive value. In V. A. Weekes-Shackelford and T. K. Shackelford (Eds.), *Evolutionary Perspectives on Human Sexual Psychology and Behavior*. New York: Springer, 135–48.

51. Wolf, N. (2015). *The Beauty Myth*. New York: Vintage Classics.

52. Shaw, S. J. and Peterson, J. B. (2023). The epidemic that dare not speak its name. *The Jordan B. Peterson Podcast, 338* (youtu.be/Qrg8t34yXRs?si=gYoS9S9rXlkAzE7R).

53. This is a well-established finding in the field of evolutionary psychology: Buss, D. M. and Barnes, M. (1986). Preferences in human mate selection. *Journal of Personality and Social Psychology 50*, 559–570; Buss, D. M. (1989). Sex differences in human mate preferences: Evolutionary hypotheses tested in 37 cultures. *Behavioral and Brain Science 12*, 1–14; Buss, D. M., Shackelford, T. K., Kirkpatrick, L. A., and Larsen, R. J. (2001). A half century of mate preferences: The cultural evolution of values. *Journal of Marriage and Family 63*, 491–503.

54. Crick, N. R. and Grotpeter, J. K. (1995). Relational aggression, gender, and social-psychological adjustment. *Child Development 66*, 710–22.

55. Eliade, M. (1959). *The Sacred and the Profane*. Translated by Willard R. Trask. New York: Harcourt, Brace and Company.

56. Nietzsche, F. (1990). *Twilight of the Idols and The Anti-Christ*. (R. J. Hollingsdale, Trans.). New York: Penguin Classics.

57. specifically derived from biblehub.com/commentaries/genesis/17-15.htm; drawn from Benson, J. (1857). *Benson Commentary*. New York: T. Carlton and J. Porter.

58. specifically derived from biblehub.com/hebrew/6117.htm; drawn from Strong, J. (1996). *Strong's Exhaustive Concordance of the Bible*. Nashville, TN: Abingdon Press.

59. Scott, W. (1808). *Marmion: A Tale of Flodden Field*. Edinburgh, Scotland: John Ballantyne and Co.

60. that is precisely the theme of the aforementioned Dostoevsky masterpiece, *Crime and Punishment*. Raskolnikov, the dark hero of the story, gets away with murder—but cannot withstand the psychological aftermath and exposes himself as the man responsible for the crime.

61. see section 6.5 Sacrifice and transformation of identity: Abram, Sarai, and Jacob.

62. specifically derived from biblehub.com/genesis/18-21.htm; drawn from Spence-Jones, H. D. M. (Ed.). (1890). *The Pulpit Commentary*. London: Funk and Wagnalls.

63. I am endebted to Jonathan Pageau of Symbolic World fame (thesymbolicworld.com) for this interpretation (personal communication).

64. Al-Shorman, A., Ababneh, A., Rawashdih, A., Makhadmih, A., Alsaad, S., and Jamhawi, M. (2017). Travel and hospitality in late antiquity. *Near Eastern Archaeology 80*, 22–28.

65. Brown, D. (1991). *Human Universals*. Philadelphia, PA: Temple University Press.

66. Peterson, J. B. et al. (2023). Biblical series: Exodus. *The Jordan B. Peterson Podcast (Exodus Episodes 1–17)*. First episode at youtu.be/GEASnFvLxhU?si=YKbupJppve1iSDbO.

67. Peterson, J. B. et al. (2024). Biblical series: The Gospels. *The Daily Wire Productions* (forthcoming).

68. Masci, D. (2017, June 29). In Russia, nostalgia for Soviet Union and positive feelings about Stalin. Pew Research Center: pewresearch.org/short-reads/2017/06/29/in-russia-nostalgia-for-soviet-union-and-positive-feelings-about-stalin/; Dadabaev, T. (2020). Manipulating post-Soviet nostalgia: contrasting political narratives and public recollections in Central Asia. *International Journal of Asian Studies 18*, 61–81; Nemtsova, A. (2019, December 7).

Russia's twin nostalgias. *The Atlantic*: theatlantic.com/international/archive/2019/12/vladi
mir-putin-russia-nostalgia-soviet-union/603079.

69. Ding, I. and Javed, J. (1092, May 29). Why Maoism still resonates in China today. *Washington Post*: washingtonpost.com/politics/2019/05/29/why-maoism-still-resonates-china
-today; Yue-Jones, T. (2011, September 8). Witness: nostalgia for Mao era lives on 35 years
after his death. *Reuters*: reuters.com/article/us-china-mao-idUSTRE7872EY20110908.

70. Jung, C. G. (1921). *The Relations between the Ego and the Unconscious*. Princeton University Press, paragraph 254.

71. Lefond, S. J. (2012). *Handbook of World Salt Resources*. New York: Springer, 337.

72. See section 5.4.

73. Klein, M. (1957). *Envy and Gratitude*. London: Tavistock, 190.

74. see Neumann, E. (2014). *The Origins and History of Consciousness*. Princeton University
Press; Neumann, E. (2015). *The Great Mother*. Princeton University Press; Jung, C. G.
(1967). *The Collected Works of C. G. Jung: Vol. 5. Symbols of Transformation* (2nd ed.). In
H. Read, et al. (Eds.). (R. F. C. Hull, Trans.). Princeton University Press; see as well *Crumb*
Zwigoff, T. (Director). *Crumb* [Film] (1995). Sony Pictures Classics.

7. Moses I: God as Dreadful Spirit of Freedom

1. Sarna, J. D. (2004). *American Judaism: A History*. New Haven, CT: Yale University Press.

2. Cochran, G. and Harpending, H. (2009). *The 10,000 Year Explosion: How Civilization Accelerated Human Evolution*. New York: Basic Books.

3. Malory, T. (1485). *Le Morte d'Arthur* [The Death of Arthur]. Middle English. (Eugène Vinaver, Ed.). London: J. M. Dent & Sons Ltd.

4. Eliade, M. (1954). *The Myth of the Eternal Return: Cosmos and History*. Princeton University Press.

5. Roser, M. (2023, April 11). Mortality in the past: every second child died. *Our World in Data*: ourworldindata.org/child-mortality-in-the-past#.

6. Birdsell, J. B. (1986). Some predictions for the Pleistocene based on equilibrium systems among recent hunter gatherers. In R. Lee and Devore, I. (Eds.). *Man the Hunter*. London: Aldine Publishing Company.

7. see Flanagan, C. (2019). Losing the *Rare* in "Safe, Legal and Rare." *The Atlantic*, theatlantic.com/ideas/archive/2019/12/the-brilliance-of-safe-legal-and-rare/603151.

8. Rowling, J. K. (1997). *Harry Potter and the Philosopher's Stone*. London: Bloomsbury.

9. Disney. (1959). *Sleeping Beauty* [Film]. USA: Walt Disney Productions.

10. Malory, T. (1485). *Le Morte d'Arthur* [The Death of Arthur]. Middle English. (Eugène Vinaver, Ed.). London: J. M. Dent & Sons Ltd.

11. Jung, C. G. (2014). The psychology of the child archetype. In *Collected Works of C. G. Jung*, Volume 9 (Part 1); Archetypes and the Collective Unconscious (151–81). De Gruyter.

12. see Orphan characters in literature, *Wikipedia*: en.wikipedia.org/wiki/Category:Orphan
_characters_in_literature.

13. Disney, W. and Allers, R. (Directors). (1994). *The Lion King* [Film]. USA: Walt Disney Pictures.

14. see Mount Horeb, *Wikipedia*: en.wikipedia.org/wiki/Mount_Horeb.

15. Jung, C. G. (1952). *Synchronicity: An Acausal Connecting Principle*. New York: Routledge and Kegan Paul.

16. Peterson, J. B. (1999). *Maps of Meaning: The Architecture of Belief*. New York: Routledge.

17. Liser, P. (date unknown). *Understanding Jacob's Ladder: Commentary on Parashat Vayetzei, Genesis 28:10–32:3*: myjewishlearning.com/article/on-dreams-and-reality/; derived from Genesis Rabbah, a religious text from the Jewish Classical period, written between 300 and 500 AD (see Genesis Rabah, *Wikipedia*: en.wikipedia.org/wiki/Genesis_Rabbah).

18. see, for example, Jung, C. G. (1967). The philosophical tree. In R.F.C. Hull (Trans.), *Alchemical Studies* (333–44). New York: Routledge and Kegan Paul.

19. This motif is well-reviewed in Tree of Life, *Wikipedia*: en.wikipedia.org/wiki/Tree_of_life; see also Eliade, M. (1959). *The sacred and the profane*. Translated by Willard R. Trask. New York: Harcourt, Brace and Company.

20. Otto, R. (1923). *The Idea of the Holy*. Oxford University Press.

21. Disney, W. (Producer), and Geronimi, C. Luske, and Jackson, W. (Directors). (1959). *Sleeping Beauty* [Film]. USA: Walt Disney Productions.

22. LeRoy, M. (Producer) and Fleming, V. (Director). (1939). *The Wizard of Oz* [Film]. USA: Metro-Goldwyn-Mayer.

23. see Seven League Books, *Wikipedia*: en.wikipedia.org/wiki/Seven-league_boots.

24. see chapter 5, The Tower of Babel: God versus Tyranny and Pride.

25. These are of course the words that open the US Declaration of Independence, after the preamble: archives.gov/founding-docs/declaration-transcript.

26. Hirsh, J. B., Mar, R. A., and Peterson, J. B. (2012). Psychological entropy: a framework for understanding uncertainty-related anxiety. *Psychological Review 119*, 304–20; Friston, K., Kilner, J., and Harrison, L. (2006). A free energy principle for the brain. *Journal of Physiology 100*, 70–87; Janoff-Bulman, R. (1992). *Shattered Assumptions: Towards a New Psychology Of Trauma*. New York: The Free Press.

27. Janoff-Bulman, R., *Shattered Assumptions*.

28. Peterson, J. B. *Maps of Meaning*.

29. As portrayed, for example, in Rowling, J. K. (1999). *Harry Potter and the Chamber of Secrets*. New York: Scholastic.

30. Disney, W. (Producer), and Luske, H., Hee, T., Jackson, W., Kinney, J., Roberts, B., and Sharpsteen, B. (Directors). (1940). *Pinocchio* [Film]. USA: Walt Disney Productions.

31. Allers and Minkoff, *The Lion King*.

32. This is well summarized at I Am that I Am, *Wikipedia*: en.wikipedia.org/wiki/I_Am_that_I_Am.

33. Reviewed in Common being and Being as pure Act, *Wikipedia*: en.wikipedia.org/wiki/Actus_purus#Common_being_and_Being_as_pure_Act.

34. Van der Toorn, K. (1999). Yahweh. In K. van der Toorn, B. Becking, and P. W. van der Horst (Eds.), *Dictionary of Deities and Demons in the Bible* (952–60). Grand Rapids, MI: Eerdmans.

35. Eliade, M. (1959). *The Sacred and the Profane*. Translated by Willard R. Trask. New York: Harcourt, Brace and Company, 33.

36. See section 8.2. Desperate reestablishment of the covenant.

37. All reviewed in Eliade, *Sacred and the Profane.*

38. Eliade, *Sacred and the Profane*, 34–36.

39. Galen (1968). *On the Usefulness of the Parts of the Body.* Translated by M. T. May. Ithaca, NY: Cornell University Press.

40. See section 8.2. Desperate reestablishment of the covenant.

41. See Rule of Three (writing), *Wikipedia*: en.wikipedia.org/wiki/Rule_of_three_(writing).

42. see section 7.2. The fiery tree as revelation of being and becoming.

43. This is a translation I happened along about two decades ago, and which became my favorite: Rosenthal, S. (1984). *Tao Teh Ching: The Way and Its Power* (verse 78): http://enlight.lib.ntu.edu.tw/FULLTEXT/JR-AN/an142304.pdf.

44. Nietzsche, F. (1969). *Thus Spoke Zarathustra: A Book for Everyone and Nobody.* Translated by W. Kaufmann. (Original work published 1883–1885.) Harmondsworth, UK: Penguin Books, 70. Part 1: On the Gift Giving Virtue.

45. In the form, for example, of the aforementioned *enuma Elish.*

46. *Online Etymology Dictionary.* Enthusiasm (n): etymonline.com/word/enthusiasm.

47. Outlined in great detail in Peterson, J. B. (1999). *Maps of Meaning: The Architecture of Belief.* New York: Routledge.

48. This is true technically: the collapse of a system of belief—a map—produces an increase in entropy, signified by anxiety, as well as a decrease in positive emotion, in consequence of confusion and increasing distance from a valued goal: see Hirsh, J. B., Mar, R. A. and Peterson, J. B. (2012). Psychological entropy: a framework for understanding uncertainty-related anxiety. *Psychological Review*, 119, 304–20; Friston, K., Kilner, J., and Harrison, L. (2006). A free energy principle for the brain. *Journal of Physiology, Paris 100*, 70–87; Janoff-Bulman, R. *Shattered Assumptions*; Gray, J. A. and McNaughton, N. (2004). *The Neuropsychology of Anxiety.* Oxford University Press.

49. Gray and McNaughton. *The Neuropsychology of Anxiety.*

50. see section 7.3. Return to the tyrannical kingdom.

51. see chapter 1, In the Beginning.

52. Peterson, J. B. *Maps of Meaning*; see also Jung, C. G. (1967). *The Collected Works of C. G. Jung: Vol. 5. Symbols of Transformation* (2nd ed.). In H. Read, et al., Eds. Translated by R. F. C. Hull. Princeton University Press; Campbell, J. (2012). *The Hero with a Thousand Faces* (3rd ed.). New World Library; Neumann, E. (2014). *The Origins and History of Consciousness.* Princeton University Press; Neumann, E. (2015). *The Great Mother.* Princeton University Press Platform; Eliade, M. (1978). *A History of Religious Ideas (Volumes I–III):* Chicago University Press; Eliade, *Sacred and the Profane.*

53. see section 4.3. Salvation by the wise and the reestablishment of the world.

54. reviewed in Peterson, J. B. *Maps of Meaning*; see also Goldberg, E. and Costa, L.D. (1981). Hemisphere differences in the acquisition and use of descriptive systems. *Brain and Language 14*, 144–73.

55. Dawkins, R. (1976). Worlds in Microcosm. In R. Dawkins (Ed.). *Inside the Survival Machine* (115–30). New York: Oxford University Press, 202.

56. Dawkins, Worlds in Microcosm. In *Survival Machine.*

57. Dawkins, Worlds in Microcosm. In *Survival Machine*, 203.

58. Dawkins, Worlds in Microcosm. In *Survival Machine*, 210.

59. Donehower, L. A., et al. (2019). Defining a mutational hierarchy of cancer drivers based on the distribution of somatic mutations. *Nature Genetics 51*, 27888, 1.

60. see section 8.2. Desperate reestablishment of the covenant.

61. Dawkins, R. (1976). Worlds in Microcosm. In *Survival Machine*, 217.

62. Dawkins, Worlds in Microcosm. In *Survival Machine*, 219.

63. Dawkins, Worlds in Microcosm. In *Survival Machine*, 220.

64. Gibson, J. J. (1979). *The Ecological Approach to Visual Perception*. New York: Houghton Mifflin.

65. Katsikopoulos, K. V., Şimşek, Ö., Buckmann, M., and Gigerenzer, G. (2020). *Classification in the Wild: The Science and Art of Transparent Decision Making*. Cambridge, MA: MIT Press.

66. Menand, L. (2001). *The Metaphysical Club: A Story of Ideas in America*. New York: Farrar, Straus and Giroux.

67. Faulkner, W. (1951). *Requiem for a Nun*. New York: Random House, Act I, scene III: see fadedpage.com/books/20190243/html.php.

68. see Foreshadowing: the Still, Small Voice.

69. for a brilliant discussion of such danger, and how to avoid it, see Jung, C. G. (1921). *The Relations between the Ego and the Unconscious*. CW 7. Princeton University Press.

70. A short review of the extensive literature on the salutary effects of voluntary goal setting can be found at Peterson, J. B. and Mar, R. (2014). The Benefits of Writing: selfauthoring .blob.core.windows.net/media/Default/Pdf/WritingBenefits.pdf; see, as well, Morisano, D., Hirsh, J. B., Peterson, J. B., Shore, B., and Pihl, R. O. (2010). Personal goal setting, reflection, and elaboration improves academic performance in university students. *Journal of Applied Psychology 95*, 255–64; Pennebaker, J. W. and Seagal, J. D. (1999). Forming a story: The health benefits of narrative. *Journal of Clinical Psychology 55*, 1243–54.

71. Vygotsky, L. S. (1986). *Thought and Language*. Cambridge, MA: MIT Press.

72. Peterson, J. B. and Flanders, J. L. (2005). Play and the regulation of aggression. In R. E. Tremblay, W. W. Hartup, and J. Archer (Eds.), *Developmental Origins of Aggression*. New York: Guilford, 133–157; Flanders, J. L., Leo, V., Paquette, D. Pihl, R. O., and Séguin, J. R. (2009). Rough-and-tumble play and the regulation of aggression: an observational study of father-child play dyads. *Aggressive Behavior 35*, 285–95.

73. Zimmerman, A. (2019). Subsidiarity and a free society: the subsidiary role of the state in Catholic social teaching. *Solidarity: the Journal of Catholic Social Thought and Secular Ethics 8*, 1–19.

74. Behr, T. (2019). *Social Justice and Subsidiarity: Luigi Taparelli and the Origins of Modern Catholic Social Thought*. Washington DC: The Catholic University of America Press.

75. Zimmermann, A. (2017). Reforming the democratic state: subsidiarity and a vision of limited government. *Revista de la Facultad de Jurisprudencia 1*, 1–15.

76. Shields-Wright, K. (2017). The principles of Catholic social teaching: a guide for decision making from daily clinical encounters to national policy-making. *Linacre Quarterly 84*, 10–22.

77. Röpke, W. (Author), Hugger, D. J. (Ed.), and Kolev, S. (Intro.). (2019). *The Humane Econo-mist: A Wilhelm Röpke Reader.* Grand Rapids, MI: Acton Institute.

78. Hayek, F. A. (1944). *The Road to Serfdom.* University of Chicago Press.

79. Kieffer, J. W. (2017). Subsidiarity: restoring a sacred harmony. *Linacre Quarterly 84,* 1–9.

80. The principle of subsidiarity. *Fact Sheets on the European Union.* European Parlia-ment. (n.d.). Retrieved July 31, 2023, from europarl.europa.eu/factsheets/en/sheet/7/the-principle-of-subsidiarity; Cygan, A. (202). Participation by national parliaments in the EU legislative process. *ERA Forum 22,* 421–35.

81. Vischer, R. K. (2001). Subsidiarity as a principle of governance: beyond devolution. *Indi-ana Law Review 34,* 103–32.

82. see section 2.7. Loss of Paradise and the flaming sword.

83. see Foreshadowing: The Still, Small Voice.

84. van der Kolk, B. (2014). *The Body Keeps the Score.* New York: Viking. The recent work, previously cited, on the relationship between perception, conceptualization, entropy and emotional regulation is also relevant when considering such things: see Friston K. (2009). The free-energy principle: a rough guide to the brain? *Trends in Cognitive Sciences, 13,* 293–301; Hirsh, J. B., Mar, R.A., and Peterson, J. B. (2012). Psychological entropy: a frame-work for understanding uncertainty-related anxiety. *Psychological Review 119,* 304–20.

85. McEwen, B. S. (1998): Protective and damaging effects of stress mediators. *New England Journal of Medicine 338,* 171–79.

86. McEwen, B. S. (2000). Allostasis and allostatic load: implications for neuropsychophar-macology. *Neuropsychopharmacology 22,* 108–24, 108.

87. Janoff-Bulman, R. *Shattered Assumptions*; Edmondson, D., Chaudoir, S. R., Mills, M. A., Park, C. L., Holub, J., and Bartkowiak, J. M. (2011). From shattered assumptions to weak-ened worldviews: trauma symptoms signal anxiety buffer disruption. *Journal of Loss & Trauma 16,* 358–85.

88. Bremner, J. D. (2006). Traumatic stress: effects on the brain. *Dialogues in Clinical Neuro-Science 8.* 445–61.

89. Huffman, N., Shih, C. H., Cotton, A. S., Lewis, T. J., Grider, S., Wall, J. T., Wang, X., and Xie, H. (2023). Association of age of adverse childhood experiences with thalamic vol-umes and post-traumatic stress disorder in adulthood. *Frontiers in Behavioral NeuroSci-ence 17,* 1147686.

90. Foa, E. B. and McLean, C. P. (2016). The efficacy of exposure therapy for anxiety-related disorders and its underlying mechanisms: the case of OCD and PTSD. *Annual Review of Clinical Psychology, 12,* 1–28.

91. Lindauer, R. J., Vlieger, E. J., Jalink, M., Olff, M., Carlier, I. V., Majoie, C. B., Den Heeten, G. J., and Gersons, B. P. (2005). Effects of psychotherapy on hippocampal volume in out-patients with post-traumatic stress disorder: a MRI investigation. *Psychological Medicine 35,* 1421–31.

92. Gray, J. A. and McNaughton, N. (2004). *The Neuropsychology of Anxiety.* Oxford Univer-sity Press; see also Vinogradova O. S. (2001). Hippocampus as comparator: role of the two input and two output systems of the hippocampus in selection and registration of infor-mation. *Hippocampus 11,* 578–98.

93. Carhart-Harris, R. L. and Friston, K. J. (2019). REBUS and the anarchic brain: toward a unified model of the brain action of psychedelics. *Pharmacological Reviews 71*, 316–44; Friston K. (2009). The free-energy principle: a rough guide to the brain? *Trends in Cognitive Sciences 13*, 293–301; Hirsh, J. B., Mar, R.A., and Peterson, J. B. (2012). Psychological entropy: a framework for understanding uncertainty-related anxiety. *Psychological Review 119*, 304–20. Aldous Huxley was pointing in this direction with his inspired work in the middle of the twentieth century. Huxley, A. (1954). *The Doors of Perception*. London: Chatto & Windus.

94. This is often confused with defense against death anxiety, following Becker, E. (1973). *The Denial of Death*. New York: Free Press.

95. Jung, C. G. (1963). *Psychology and Religion*. New Haven: Yale University Press, paragraph 82.

96. Jung, *Psychology and Religion*, paragraph 75.

97. Wordsworth, W. (1807). Ode: Intimations of immortality from recollections of early childhood. In *Poems in Two Volumes* (285–96). London: Longman, Hurst, Rees, Orme, and Brown.

98. DeYoung, C. G., Flanders, J. L., and Peterson, J. B. (2008). Cognitive abilities involved in insight problem solving: an individual differences model. *Creativity Research Journal 20*, 278–90.

99. Pusey, J. M. and Packer, C. (1997). The evolution of social structure in female baboons. *Advances in the Study of Behavior 27*, 1–79; Gilby, M. L., Hill, R. A., and Barton, R. A. (2006). Social rank stability in male baboons: The role of kinship and social learning. *Animal Behavior 71*, 513–22.

100. de Waal, F. (1982). *Chimpanzee politics: Power and Sex among Apes*. New York: Harper & Row.

101. see section 7.5. The inevitable interregnum of chaos and the guiding spirit.

102. as in the statement "we hold these truths to be self-evident" which so famously opens the second paragraph of the American Declaration of Independence.

103. Axelrod, R. and Hamilton, W. D. (1981). The evolution of cooperation. *Science 211*, 1390–96; Nowak, M., Sigmund, K. (2005). Evolution of indirect reciprocity. *Nature 437*, 1291–98, 1291; see also Bicchieri, C. (2012). *The Grammar of Society: The Nature and Dynamics of Social Norms*. Cambridge, MA: MIT Press; Fehr, E. and Fischbacher, U. (2002). The nature of human altruism. *Nature 415*, 752–55; Hofstadter, D. R. (1983). The prisoner's dilemma: computer tournaments and the evolution of cooperation. In D. R. Hofstadter (Ed.). *Metamagical Themas: Questing for the Essence of Mind and Pattern* (715–34). New York: Basic Books.

104. Yan, J. Personal sustained cooperation based on networked evolutionary game theory. *Scientific Reports 13*, 9125–30.

105. Brief but instructive summaries can be found at newworldencyclopedia.org/entry/Golden_Rule; Golden Rule, *Wikipedia*: en.wikipedia.org/wiki/Golden_Rule.

106. Jung, C. G. (1967). Alchemical studies (R. F. C. Hull, Trans.). Princeton University Press; Jung, C. G. (1968). Psychology and alchemy (R. F. C. Hull, Trans.). Princeton University Press.

8. Moses II: Hedonism and Infantile Temptation

1. Kasser T. (2016). Materialistic values and goals. *Annual Review of Psychology 67*, 489–514; Dittmar, H., Bond, R., Hurst, M., and Kasser, T. (2014). The relationship between materialism and personal well-being: A meta-analysis. *Journal of Personality and Social Psychology 107*, 879–924.

2. as argued, for example, by Rorty, R. (1979). *Philosophy and the Mirror of Nature*. Princeton University Press and at least strongly implied by the works of Foucault, such as Foucault, M. (1991). *Discipline and Punish: The Birth of a Prison*. London: Penguin; Foucault, M. (1998). *The History of Sexuality: The Will to Knowledge*. London: Penguin.

3. Yeats, W. B. (1989). *The Collected poems of W.B. Yeats*. New York: Collier Books.

4. Schrödinger, Erwin (1951). *What is Life? The Physical Aspect of the Living Cell*. Cambridge University Press.

5. This issue is intelligently discussed at gotquestions.org/Israelites-exodus.html.

6. as described in 5.1. Lucifer and the engineers.

7. specifically derived from biblehub.com/exodus/32-35.htm#commentary; drawn from Spence-Jones, H. D. M. (Ed.). (1890). *The Pulpit Commentary*. London: Funk & Wagnalls.

8. see biblehub.com/exodus/33-12.htm#commentary; drawn from Spence-Jones, *Pulpit Commentary*.

9. see Foreshadowing: The Still, Small Voice.

10. see biblehub.com/exodus/33-23.htm#commentary; drawn from Spence-Jones, *Pulpit Commentary*.

11. Dawkins, R. (2006). *The God Delusion*. New York: Houghton Mifflin Harcourt, chapter 10.

12. "A fellow intellectual, Guy Sorman, has unleashed a storm among Parisian 'intellos' with his claim that Foucault, who died in 1984 aged 57, was a pedophile rapist who had sex with Arab children while living in Tunisia in the late 1960s": thetimes.co.uk/article/french -philosopher-michel-foucault-abused-boys-in-tunisia-6t5sj7jvw. This is to say nothing of his insistence on continuing his promiscuous and sadomasochistic sexual escapades after becoming a known carrier of AIDS: See Kimball, R. (1993, March). The perversions of M. Foucault. *New Criterion*: newcriterion.com/article/the-perversions-of-m-foucault.

13. Perry, L. (2022). *The Case against the Sexual Revolution: A New Guide to Sex in the 21st Century*. New York: Polity.

14. Ehrlich, P. R. (1968). *The Population Bomb*. New York: Ballantine Books; see also the equally reprehensible and unwarranted missive from the so-called Club of Rome: Meadows, D. H., Meadows, D. L., Randers, J., and Behrens III, W. W. (1972). *The Limits to Growth: A Report for the Club of Rome's Project on the Predicament of Mankind*. New York: Universe Books.

15. Conly, S. (2016). *One Child: Do We Have a Right to More?* New York: Oxford University Press.

16. For a review of and critique of such views, see Lomborg, B. (2020). Welfare in the 21st century: Increasing development, reducing inequality, the impact of climate change, and the cost of climate policies. *Technological Forecasting and Social Change 156*, 119981; see

also Epstein, A. (2022). *Fossil Future: Why Global Human Flourishing Requires More Oil, Coal, and Natural Gas—Not Less.* New York: Penguin.

17. specifically derived from biblehub.com/exodus/34-1.htm#commentary; drawn from Ellicott, C. J. (1905). *Ellicott's Commentary for English Readers.* London: Cassell and Company, Ltd.

18. see section 1.5. In God's image.

19. see section 2.7. Loss of Paradise and the flaming sword.

20. see section 2.2. Pride versus the sacred moral order.

21. see section 6.1. Go forth.

22. Chang, I. (1997). *The Rape of Nanking: The Forgotten Holocaust of World War II.* New York: Basic Books, 104.

23. Chang, *The Rape of Nanking,* 109–10.

24. Browning, C. R. (1992). *Ordinary Men: Reserve Police Battalion 101 and the Final Solution in Poland.* New York: HarperPerennial.

25. For a thorough and insightful review of such matters, see Landes, D. S. (1998). *The Wealth and Poverty of Nations: Why Some Are So Rich and Some So Poor.* New York: W. W. Norton.

26. see section 8.2. Desperate reestablishment of the covenant.

27. Frankl, V. E. (1963). *Man's Search for Meaning: An Introduction to Logotherapy.* New York: Washington Square Press.

28. see chapter 6. Abraham: God as Spirited Call to Adventure.

29. see section 2.2. Pride versus the sacred moral order.

30. see section 8.2. Desperate reestablishment of the covenant.

31. Donehower, L. A., et al. (2019). Defining a mutational hierarchy of cancer drivers based on the distribution of somatic mutations. *Nature Genetics 51,* 278–88.

32. see section 2.4. The eternal sins of Eve and Adam.

33. See, for example, Peterson, J. B. *Maps of Meaning;* see also Jung, C. G. (1967). *The Collected Works of C. G. Jung: Vol. 5. Symbols of Transformation* (2nd ed.). In H. Read, et al., Eds. Translated by R. F. C. Hull. Princeton University Press; Campbell, J. (2012). *The Hero with a Thousand Faces* (3rd ed.). New World Library; Neumann, E. (2014). *The Origins and History of Consciousness.* Princeton University Press; Neumann, E. (2015). *The Great Mother.* Princeton University Press Platform; Eliade, M. (1978). *A History of Religious Ideas (Volumes I–III):* Chicago University Press; Eliade, M. (1959). *The Sacred and the Profane.* Translated by Willard R. Trask. New York: Harcourt, Brace and Company.

34. Jones, D. E. (2002). *An Instinct for Dragons.* New York: Routledge.

35. see section 1.5. In God's image.

36. see section 1.5. In God's image.

37. Foa, E. B. and McLean, C. P. (2016). The efficacy of exposure therapy for anxiety-related disorders and its underlying mechanisms: the case of OCD and PTSD. *Annual Review of Clinical Psychology 12,* 1–28.

38. Vervliet, B., Vansteenwegen, D., and Eelen, P. (2004). Generalization of extinguished skin conductance responding in human fear conditioning. *Learning and Memory 11,* 555–58;

Preusser, F., Margraf, J., and Zlomuzica, A. (2017). Generalization of extinguished fear to untreated fear stimuli after exposure. *Neuropsychopharmacology 42*, 2545–52.

39. Piaget, J. (1962). *Play, Dreams, and Imitation in Childhood*. New York: Norton; Piaget, J. (1965). *The Moral Judgment of the Child*. New York: Free Press; Vygotsky, L. S. (1986). *Thought and Language*. Cambridge, MA: MIT Press; Peterson, J. B. *Maps of Meaning*.

40. see section 3.6. Creatively possessed by the spirit of resentment.

41. Douglas, M. (1970). *Numbers*. Pelican Books; Peterson, J. B. and Flanders, J. L. (2005). Play and the regulation of aggression. In R. E. Tremblay, W. W. Hartup, and J. Archer (Eds.), *Developmental Origins of Aggression*. New York: The Guilford Press, 133–57.

42. see section 8.2. Desperate reestablishment of the covenant.

43. see section 8.2. Desperate reestablishment of the covenant.

44. see section 6.7. The pinnacle of sacrifice.

45. Dawkins, R. (2006). *The God Delusion*. New York: Houghton Mifflin Harcourt, 295.

46. Prager, D. (2018). *The Rational Bible: Exodus*. Washington, DC: Regnery Faith; see also Prager, D. (2014, December). Do not murder. *Prager U.* youtu.be/0RENPaY043o?si=35PHj hPgVj8QfZSu.

47. Niditch, S. (1995). *War in the Hebrew Bible: A Study in the Ethics of Violence*. New York: Oxford University Press.

48. Peterson, J. B. and Thornhill, R. (2021). Death, disease and politics. *The Jordan B. Peterson Podcast, 184* (youtu.be/6DqJ1Wv6EtQ?si=sZJA5pvUchlNbsWN).

49. Fincher, C. L, Thornhill, R., Murray, D. R., and Schaller, M. (2008). Pathogen prevalence predicts human cross-cultural variability in individualism/collectivism. *Proceedings of the Royal Society: Biology 275*, 1279–85; Fincher, C. L. and Thornhill, R. (2012). Parasite-stress promotes in-group assortative sociality: The cases of strong family ties and heightened religiosity. *Behavioral and Brain Science 35*, 61–79; Murray, D. R., Schaller, M. and Suedfeld, P. (2013). Pathogens and politics: Further evidence that parasite prevalence predicts authoritarianism. *PLoS One 8*, e62275; Thornhill, R. and Fincher, C. L. (2014). *The Parasite-Stress Theory of Values and Sociality: Infectious Disease, History and Human Values Worldwide*. New York: Springer; Thornhill, R., Fincher, C. L., and Aran, D. (2009). Parasites, democratization, and the liberalization of values across contemporary countries. *Biological Reviews of the Cambridge Philosophical Society 84*, 113–31.

50. Further explanation for the psychological identity of the stranger, the strange idea and the strange itself can be found in Peterson, J. B. *Maps of Meaning*.

51. Blenkinsopp, J. (1981). *Gibeon and Israel: The Role of Gibeon and the Gibeonites in the Political and Religious History of Early Israel*. Cambridge University Press. 184.

52. see section 7.1. The Jews as unwelcome sojourners and slaves.

53. see section 7.1. The Jews as unwelcome sojourners and slaves.

54. Ingersoll, R. G. (1905). The punishment of natural consequences. In *The Works of Robert G. Ingersoll* (Vol. 10, 39–40). Joliet, IN: Freethought Press Association.

55. for an analysis of this causal relationship with regard to communism and its horrors, see Solzhenitsyn, A. (1974). *The Gulag Archipelago, 1918–1956: An Experiment in Literary Investigation*. Translated by T. P. Whitney. New York: Harper & Row.

9. Jonah and the Eternal Abyss

1. see Foreshadowing: The Still, Small Voice.
2. Plato. (1997). Apology. Translated by G.M.A. Grube. In J. M. Cooper (Ed.), *Plato: Complete Works*. Hackett Publishing Company, 17–38.
3. see section 2.2. Pride versus the sacred moral order.
4. Thompson, D. (2012, February). The spectacular rise and fall of US whaling: an innovation story. *The Atlantic*, theatlantic.com/business/archive/2012/02/the-spectacular-rise-and-fall-of-us-whaling-an-innovation-story/253355.
5. see section 4.2. Sin and the return of chaos.
6. see, for example, The Harrowing of Hell: fresco in the parecclesion (side chapel) of the Chora Church, Istanbul. In this image, Christ is depicted as pulling Adam and Eve from hell, and by their wrists, rather than their hands (indicating that the work is being done by the divine reaching down rather than in consequence of the efforts of man and woman).
7. Peterson, J. B. (1999). *Maps of Meaning: The Architecture of Belief.* New York: Routledge.
8. Solzhenitsyn, A. (1974). *The Gulag Archipelago, 1918–1956: An Experiment in Literary Investigation* (T. P. Whitney, Trans.). New York: Harper and Row.
9. From the Gospel of Thomas, cited in Pagels, E. (1979). *The Gnostic Gospels*. New York: Random House, p. xv.
10. specifically derived from biblehub.com/jonah/4-6.htm#commentary; drawn from Spence-Jones, H. D. M. (Ed.). (1890). *The Pulpit Commentary.* London: Funk & Wagnalls.

Conclusion

1. Blau, F. D. and Kahn, L. M. (2017). The gender wage gap: Extent, trends, and explanations. *Journal of Economic Literature 55*, 789–865; Charles, M. and Grusky, D. B. (2004). *Occupational Ghettos: The Worldwide Segregation of Women and Men.* Stanford University Press; Croson, R. and Gneezy, U. (2009). Gender differences in preferences. *Journal of Economic Literature 47*, 448–74; Del Giudice, M. (2022). Measuring sex differences and similarities. In D. P. VanderLaan and Wong, W. I. (Eds.), *Gender and Sexuality Development: Contemporary Theory and Research* (pp. 1–38). Cham, Switzerland: Springer Nature AG; Falk, A., Becker, A., Dohmen, T., Enke, B., Huffman, D., and Sunde. U. (2018). Global evidence on economic preferences. *Quarterly Journal of Economics 133*, 1645–92; Kahn, S. and Ginther, D. (2017). Women and STEM. *NBER Working Paper 23525*; Kuhn, A. and Wolter, S. C. (2022). Things versus people: Gender differences in vocational interests and in occupational preferences. *Journal of Economic Behavior & Organization 203*, 210–34; Weisberg, Y. G., DeYoung, C. G., and Hirsh, J. B. (2011). Gender differences in personality across the ten aspects of the big five. *Frontiers in Psychology 2*, 178.
2. Peterson, J. B. (1999). *Maps of Meaning: The Architecture of Belief.* New York: Routledge.